Lloyd's MIU Handbook
of Maritime Security

With the inescapable importance of maritime trade to the integrity of the global economy, maritime security remains of vital interest to commercial and governmental practitioners alike. Widespread criminal trafficking, piracy and terrorism compound the vulnerability of infrastructure, vessels and supply chains within this vast environment. As a consequence, navies and coast guards are adapting themselves to confront asymmetric and criminal threats in the maintenance of their pivotal role in helping to ensure maritime security. They regard an in-depth appreciation of the threats and vulnerabilities within this environment as the central prerequisite for conducting Maritime Security Operations.

In reflection of the above realities, the editors of the *Lloyd's MIU Handbook of Maritime Security* have drawn together a range of professionals, experts and academics from around the world. The handbook offers an important collection of thoroughly researched and impressive essays that examine a diverse range of maritime security concerns. These essays will be of interest to all, whether commercial, legal, military or governmental, in ensuring the security of the world's shipping, ports and sea lanes of communication.

Admiral Sir Mark Stanhope
Commander-in-Chief Fleet

This Handbook provides a broad overview of current issues in maritime security. It is crisply written, well organized and includes contributions by leading authorities in maritime security. The Handbook is strongly recommended to those involved in policy making on security issues, students of maritime affairs and industry professionals.

Ambassador Barry Desker, Dean
S. Rajaratnam School of International Studies
Nanyang Technological University, Singapore

Although maritime security has received a significant amount of attention in recent years, this has not been reflected in literature on the subject. This is rectified by this excellent collection that covers the subject thoroughly from A to Z. Edited and compiled by prominent experts in the area, the Handbook provides the first clear, substantive and practical analysis of this complex subject. It is bound to become required reading for all in the shipping industry, as well as those with an interest in international security.

Professor Edgar Gold
The Nautical Institute

Lloyd's MIU Handbook of Maritime Security

Edited by
Rupert Herbert-Burns
Sam Bateman
Peter Lehr

CRC Press
Taylor & Francis Group
Boca Raton   London   New York

CRC Press is an imprint of the
Taylor & Francis Group, an **Informa** business

The leader in global maritime information
www.lloydsmiu.com

Lloyd's MIU, is a trading name of Informa UK Limited. Registered in England under no. 1072954. Registered office: Mortimer House, 37 – 41 Mortimer Street, London, W1T 3JH. Lloyd's is the registered trademark of the Society incorporated by the Lloyd's Act 1871 by the name of Lloyd's.

Lloyd's MIU, is a trading name of Informa UK Limited. Registered in England under no. 1072954. Registered office: Mortimer House, 37 - 41 Mortimer Street, London. W1T 3JH. Lloyd's is the registered trademark of the Society incorporated by the Lloyd's Act 1871 by the name of Lloyd's.

Auerbach Publications
Taylor & Francis Group
6000 Broken Sound Parkway NW, Suite 300
Boca Raton, FL 33487-2742

© 2009 by Taylor & Francis Group, LLC
Auerbach is an imprint of Taylor & Francis Group, an Informa business

No claim to original U.S. Government works
Printed in the United States of America on acid-free paper
10 9 8 7 6 5 4 3 2

International Standard Book Number-13: 978-1-4200-5480-4 (Hardcover)

Library of Congress Cataloging-in-Publication Data

Herbert-Burns, Rupert.
   Lloyd's MIU handbook of maritime security / Rupert Herbert-Burns, Sam Bateman, Peter Lehr.
     p. cm.
   Includes bibliographical references and index.
   ISBN 978-1-4200-5480-4 (hbk. : alk. paper)
   1. Merchant marine--Security measures. 2. Shipping--Security measures. 3. Harbors--Security measures. 4. Maritime terrorism--Prevention. 5. Sea control. I. Bateman, W. S. G. (Walter Samuel Grono) II. Lehr, Peter. III. Lloyd's (Firm) IV. Title. V. Title: Handbook of maritime security.

VK203.H48 2008
363.12'3--dc22   2008023679

Visit the Taylor & Francis Web site at
http://www.taylorandfrancis.com

and the Auerbach Web site at
http://www.auerbach-publications.com

Contents

SECTION 1   The New Maritime Security Environment

SECTION 2   Industry Sectors: Threats and Responses

SECTION 3   Legal Frameworks for Maritime Security

SECTION 4   Regional Responses

SECTION 5 National Responses

List of Figures

List of Tables

Foreword

Maritime security has been of perennial concern to all involved in the business of maritime transport. Hence, owners and operators of ships as well as governments and relevant international organizations have, over the years, sought to develop legal and administrative mechanisms and procedures to ensure maximum security for ships, and for persons and cargoes onboard ships.

The measures undertaken to safeguard maritime transport have taken many forms, beginning with legal rules to combat old forms of piracy on the high seas to a wide-ranging regime designed to prevent "all incidents involving piracy, armed robbery, and other unlawful acts against or onboard ships" at sea and in ports. An even more comprehensive scheme has been introduced following the catastrophic incidents of September 11, 2001. The elements of this scheme are contained in the International Ship and Port Facility Security (ISPS) Code, the various amendments to the Safety of Life at Sea (SOLAS) Convention, the 2005 revised Convention for the Suppression of Unlawful Acts against the Safety of Maritime Navigation (SUA Convention), and related instruments such as those intended to establish secure and reliable identification for seafarers and tracking of ships. This new regime does not only prescribe measures to be taken by states to improve physical security for ships at sea and in ports but also places significant obligations on crews aboard ships, and even on persons in charge of companies that are engaged in various aspects of shipping.

As often happens with well-meaning attempts to resolve difficult problems, the new maritime security regime has brought in its train of new problems and has raised new questions. Thus new questions have arisen with regard to which measures are suitable for national or regional regulation as opposed to those that must necessarily be developed at the international level; how to coordinate the many and various agencies involved in different aspects of maritime security; how to harmonize international measures with the requirements of states with special needs; how to balance the benefits of increased security with the need to avoid unnecessary additional costs, especially for developing countries; the need to avoid security requirements becoming additional barriers to international trade and competition; and the appropriate criteria for apportioning the costs of increased security to the various beneficiaries of the new system.

These and other matters are the subject of the present publication—*Lloyd's MIU Handbook of Maritime Security*. The purpose of this book is to provide a "reality check" of the new mechanisms, measures, and procedures that have been introduced and developed since the events of September 11, 2001. By bringing together a wide range of different perspectives on the key maritime issues that face nations and organizations around the world, this book seeks to explore the operational, policy, and legal realities of the new global maritime security system.

A major focus of this book is the identification of problems that have been encountered, or may reasonably be expected, in developing and implementing the various measures as well as possible ways of overcoming these problems. The five sections of this book examine, among others, the new maritime security environment, including the different but complementary interests of the shipping industry, on the one hand, and of national regulatory agencies (including the military), on the other. There are analyses of the different threats to maritime security and how they are perceived by different actors in the maritime field. In addition, there is an evaluation of the international and national legal frameworks that have been developed for specific sectors, and the responses that different states have given to these initiatives.

By pooling together the knowledge and insights of a very broad range of learned contributors, the editors have provided an excellent opportunity for airing a large number of the difficult issues that need to be dealt with by both the authorities and bodies that devise and implement maritime security systems, and by entities and operators who are required to comply with the requirements of the respective systems. Although the chapters do not attempt to give definitive answers to the various questions, they all seek to assist our appreciation of the issues involved and the facts and considerations that should be taken into account in addressing them.

Maritime security has now become an issue of major concern to the international community. Unlawful and violent acts against shipping, whether they partake of the nature of the traditional forms of piracy or qualify as acts of terrorism, have impacts that are of relevance to governments and people all over the world. For apart from their undoubted adverse effects on the integrity of international maritime transport and, ultimately, on international trade, such acts are incompatible with the fundamental imperatives of the contemporary world. As noted by the General Assembly of the United Nations, they "endanger or take innocent human lives, jeopardize fundamental freedoms, and seriously impair the dignity of human beings." Above all, international and national measures of maritime security constitute an important part of the international community's tools for maintaining and enhancing safety and security for maritime transport without which world trade would be impossible.

Introducing effective but cost-effective maritime security is not an easy process. The issues to be resolved are complex. Particularly, there is a need for greater understanding of the special characteristics and demands of the maritime sector. This requires much better community appreciation of the nature and complexity of the operations of ships and ports and, more importantly, their economic significance and vulnerability. If this publication helps to promote and increase the necessary understanding and appreciation, it will fully justify the labor of those who contributed to it. Hopefully, it will also repay the time and attention of the readers.

Thomas A. Mensah
Inaugural President
International Tribunal for the Law of the Sea

Acknowledgments and Sponsoring Organizations

LLOYD'S MIU

Lloyd's MIU (formerly Lloyd's Marine Intelligence Unit) is the leader in global maritime information and a member of the publicly quoted Informa plc, which has a 300-year-old history in providing information to the maritime world. Lloyd's MIU data is published online (www.lloydsmiu.com), in hardback (publications include the market-leading *Lloyd's Maritime Directory*, *Lloyd's List Ports of the World*, and *Containerisation International Yearbook*), on CD (*The Lloyd's Shipping Information Database*), in bespoke reports (including in-depth consultancy, investigations, and credit reports), and in magazines (such as *Lloyd's Shipping Economist*). Sister companies within Informa publish the world-renowned *Lloyd's List* and a host of other titles. The Informa group is also a major events and training organizer in the maritime sector.

The Web site www.lloydsmiu.com is unlike any other online maritime information database and remains the only integrated Web site in the market today that provides detailed and up-to-date vessel data (movements, ownership, characteristics, and casualties), port information, and in-depth company information (credit reports). The site incorporates the world's largest Automatic Identification System (AIS) vessel tracking network (reports on millions of daily vessel movements are uniquely corroborated by visual reports from thousands of exclusive contacts around the globe). The site, which also hosts the world's biggest dedicated marine/energy credit report database, is underpinned by the shipping information database (SID), which contains details of over 120,000 vessels, 163,000 shipping companies, and comprehensive information on all of the world's commercially active ports.

Lloyd's MIU has a global presence—its principal offices are located in the United Kingdom (London, Colchester, and Oxford), United States (New York), and Singapore. In addition, Lloyd's MIU directly employs expert shipping analysts and researchers in Athens, Barcelona, Mumbai, and Vancouver. Information is sought from a multitude of sources, including the Lloyd's Agency Network of 700 agents and subagents for vessel movements data, the leading registries and classification societies for vessel characteristics, and the major company registries around the globe for corporate data. Lloyd's MIU also comprises a highly experienced team of consultants, investigators, analysts, researchers, marketers, and information technology (IT) specialists offering comprehensive bespoke commercial maritime intelligence services and effective business solutions.

In addition to providing the commercial and business investigative and analytical services discussed earlier, Lloyd's MIU has in-depth experience in gathering and collating shipping data to assist government and commercial-sector clients in enhancing Maritime Domain Awareness (MDA) as part of their national and international Maritime Security Operations (MSO) and initiatives. In addition to data provision for MDA, Lloyd's MIU also provides discrete consulting services and software packages to clients for the intelligence-related and risk-assessment aspects of MSO.

S. RAJARATNAM SCHOOL OF INTERNATIONAL STUDIES, NANYANG TECHNOLOGICAL UNIVERSITY

The Institute of Defence and Strategic Studies (IDSS) was established at the Nanyang Technological University (NTU) in Singapore in 1996. Over the following 10 years, IDSS acquired the reputation as a leading research and graduate teaching institution in strategic and international affairs in the Asia-Pacific region. A major development occurred on January 1, 2007 when IDSS was formally inaugurated to become the S. Rajaratnam School of International Studies (RSIS). The name of the school honors the contributions of the late S. Rajaratnam who held various cabinet appointments over his long years of service to Singapore. He was one of Singapore's founding fathers and well respected as a visionary diplomat and strategic thinker.

In this new school, IDSS remains a key component focusing on security research to serve national needs, while the school took over its teaching functions. RSIS brings IDSS and NTU to the next level of achievement while enhancing Singapore's standing as a regional and international hub for higher education and research. The flagship teaching programs at RSIS, the Master of Science (MSc) in strategic studies, international relations, and international political economy, have become widely popular with 151 students enrolled in the 2007/2008 academic year. New programs in Asian studies and business administration (international studies) will be introduced in 2008/2009.

As well as IDSS, RSIS includes the International Centre for Political Violence and Terrorism (ICPVTR), the Centre of Excellence for National Security (CENS), and the Centre for Non-Traditional Security Studies (CNTSS) in Asia. RSIS hosts many local and foreign scholars under its Visiting Research Fellow Program. With the growing international stature of RSIS, the school is able to attract world-class scholars to participate in its programs.

The Maritime Security Program was established at IDSS in 2004 as a reflection of growing concerns over the security of ports and sea-lanes in the region. Since then, the program has maintained a research focus on piracy, armed robbery, maritime terrorism, and the security of sea-lanes, in addition to a more general interest in regional maritime security, including naval developments and maritime regime-building. A key outcome in 2006 was the publication of the policy paper "Safety and Security in the Malacca and Singapore Straits." The paper proposed 21 recommendations to enhance safety, security, and environmental protection of these waterways, and attracted significant attention throughout the region.

Networking is an important aspect of the work of the Maritime Security Program. An edited volume on *Maritime Security in Southeast Asia* was published in 2007, as a result of a joint project between the school and the Norwegian Institute of International Affairs (NUPI), and two workshops, one in Oslo and the other in Singapore. The program has also recently developed links with the National Maritime Foundation, based in New Delhi, and the Shanghai Academy of Social Sciences in China. In January 2008, RSIS through the Maritime Security Program joined with the Center for Oceans Law and Policy, University of Virginia School of Law in organizing the 32nd Oceans Conference: Freedom of the Seas, Passage Rights, and the 1982 Law of the Sea Convention in Singapore. An edited work on *The South China Sea: Towards a Cooperative Management Regime* will be published in 2008 with papers from a conference on that topic held in 2007.

Members of the Maritime Security Program regularly give lectures and briefings on maritime security–related topics to staff colleges, visiting delegations, and industry conferences in Singapore and elsewhere. A subject on "Contemporary Maritime Security in Asia" is taught as an elective subject in the RSIS MSc program, and this has proven to be very popular, attracting 25 students in the 2007–2008 academic year.

THE AUSTRALIAN NATIONAL CENTRE FOR OCEAN RESOURCES AND SECURITY, UNIVERSITY OF WOLLONGONG

The Australian National Centre for Ocean Resources and Security (ANCORS), University of Wollongong, New South Wales, is a center of excellence in oceans governance and maritime security for Australia and the Asia-Pacific region. ANCORS provides multidisciplinary university-based research, education, and high-level advice on national and international oceans governance and law, maritime security, and ocean resource management to Australia and regional states, particularly in the western Pacific, Indian Ocean, and Southern Ocean regions.

ANCORS evolved from the Centre for Maritime Policy, which was originally established in 1994. ANCORS encompasses a significantly expanded role in recognition of the rapidly changing international environment and includes an increased priority on maritime security and ocean resource management. The center has forged a strong reputation for leading-edge research, education, training, and advisory services with the following core strengths:

- Oceans governance law and policy
- Maritime strategy and security
- Maritime regulation and enforcement
- International fisheries law and policy
- The delimitation of maritime boundaries

Capacity-building activities include education and training in the law of the sea, maritime security, international fisheries law and policy, maritime boundary delimitation, regulation of shipping, ecosystem-based management, and multiple-use management of marine resources.

The University of Wollongong offers the only multidisciplinary maritime postgraduate degree program in Australia, and is one of only a very small number of universities around the world to do so. It combines aspects of marine policy, law, science, economics, and security to offer a genuinely comprehensive and multidisciplinary approach to the study of maritime issues, and includes a large PhD program. ANCORS has a highly qualified staff, headed by Professor Martin Tsamenyi, and maintains a cadre of professorial fellows of international repute in marine affairs and maritime security; and the center is guided by an advisory board.

ANCORS has established a very strong track record in research and advisory services. Highly competitive and prestigious research grants have been won from the Australian Research Council and the Australian Centre for International Agricultural Research. Research has also been undertaken, for example, for the Asia-Pacific Economic Cooperation (APEC) forum, the Pacific Islands Forum Fisheries Agency (FFA), and many regional countries. ANCORS has developed strong and diverse partnerships in the maritime environment, which include, for example, active and productive links with the Royal Australian Navy—especially the Navy's Sea Power Centre, Australia—and Department of Defence, the Department of Environment and Water Resources, and the Department of Agriculture, Fisheries, and Forestry. For more information on ANCORS, see www.ancors.uow.edu.au.

THE CENTRE FOR THE STUDY OF TERRORISM AND POLITICAL VIOLENCE, UNIVERSITY OF ST. ANDREWS

The Centre for the Study of Terrorism and Political Violence (CSTPV) is an independent academic research center within the School of International Relations of the University of St. Andrews in Scotland. The center was established in 1994 and is Europe's oldest center for the study of political violence.

The CSTPV is dedicated to the study of the determinants, manifestations, and consequences of terrorism and other forms of political violence. In addition, the CSTPV investigates the responses of states, civil society, and international organizations to violent modes of waging conflict.

As a basis of its work, the CSTPV maintains databases, collects and analyzes documents of militant and terrorist groups, and engages in the systematic evaluation of responses to terrorism.

Furthermore, the center conducts contract research for foundations as well as national and international bodies and organizations. In doing so, it is committed to rigorous, evidence-based scientific analysis that is policy-relevant but not supporting any particular partisan policy.

The CSTPV seeks to provide, within its area of expertise, high-quality education to students at the University of St. Andrews and, beyond that, through its training sessions, conferences, and its new E-learning program to a wider public. In their teaching, the CSTPV staff seek to familiarize students with the latest research findings, ensure that they acquire a sound basis in scientific methodology, and foster critical thinking. The CSTPV's research and teaching are grounded in a belief in public service, global responsibility, and the desire to contribute to the enhancement of human security.

The CSTPV and the London offices of Informa plc currently offer an unparalleled professional education and training in global terrorism. This program covers theory and practice, as well as counterterrorism strategies and techniques. E-learning content is delivered in a collaborative learning environment, with tutor support for offline assignments. In today's complex security environment, the program enhances the skill and knowledge base so critical to countering the growing phenomenon of terrorism. Experienced professionals will enhance their knowledge and sharpen their skills with the latest information and thinking about terrorist organizations and their *modus operandi*. Similarly, heads of organizations stand to benefit, as with the CSTPV they now have an opportunity to help their staff become more educated in the causes of terrorism and methods for countering terrorism at the deepest levels.

A major component of the course, the Introduction to Maritime Terrorism and Security module provides participants with a solid foundation in the complex and often obscure world of maritime security. Starting with a brief overview of threats to the maritime domain—ranging from piracy and trafficking to terrorism—the module provides participants with tools to analyze emerging and future threats to maritime trade and security. Participants will gain a solid foundation in

- Current threats to the maritime domain
- The capabilities of groups involved in maritime-related terrorism and crime
- The major maritime security initiatives to date, including the International Ship and Port Facility Security Code, Container Security Initiative, Proliferation Security Initiative, and Customs-Trade Partnership Against Terrorism
- The role of private security firms in combating piracy

In September 2008, CSTPV will launch its E-learning masters degree (MLitt) in terrorism studies, which will build on the successes of the "certificate in terrorism studies" and deliver an advanced rigorous academic program in this vital area of study.

Introduction

Global maritime security has been through radical changes in recent years. Many changes were necessary and long overdue, but others seem to have created situations in which the only beneficiaries appear to be the providers of security services and equipment. Against this background, this book sets out to provide a reality check. It brings together a range of different perspectives of key maritime issues from around the world. It includes chapters that explore the operational, policy and legal realities of the new maritime security measures instigated post-9/11.

This book is aimed at those with an interest in any dimension of the new security measures. This interest might be a general one in maritime security, or it could be a more specific one, such as implementing the International Ship and Port Facility Security (ISPS) Code, devising and executing practical maritime security measures both at sea and in port, or in assessing security threats and risks inherent in the vast and often opaque realm of international shipping. Hopefully, everyone will find something of interest in this book.

THE NEW MARITIME SECURITY MEASURES

The new maritime security measures comprise those introduced at the global, regional, and national levels. At the global level, we have most notably the ISPS Code, other amendments to the International Safety of Life at Sea (SOLAS) Convention (1974), the 2005 Protocol to the Convention for the Suppression of Unlawful Acts (SUA) against the Safety of Maritime Navigation, the revised Seafarers' Identity Documents (SID) Convention 2003, and plans to introduce a global system for the long-range identification and tracking (LRIT) of ships. Then we have the various measures instigated directly by the United States, particularly the Container Security Initiative (CSI), Customs-Trade Partnership against Terrorism (C-TPAT), and "24-hour manifest rule." Regional measures include the Secure Trade in the Asia-Pacific Region (STAR) initiative developed by the Asia-Pacific Economic Cooperation (APEC) forum and North Atlantic Treaty Organization's (NATO) Operation Active Endeavor.

Most problems have been encountered at the national level. These relate to the provision of physical security for ships and ports as well as to security in the maritime surroundings and of inbound cargoes. The staffs of national maritime administrations have expanded to meet the demands of managing and implementing new strategies. More agencies are now involved in providing some type of maritime security than was the case previously. Regardless of the size of the country, there is a premium on the effectiveness of interagency coordination.

It was relatively easy for developed countries to implement the new global measures, particularly those such as the United States that already have an effective maritime or coast guard administration. However, developing countries, particularly those heavily involved in shipping as either flag states or seafarer-providing nations, faced greater problems. Some measures imposed at the national level, such as the U.S. requirement for 100 percent screening of sea containers bound for an American port, have global ramifications that "push out the borders" of national jurisdiction. Meanwhile, all countries have experienced difficulties in introducing measures to provide more secure and reliable identification for maritime workers both at sea and in ports.

Unfortunately, these new measures have led to additional barriers to international trade and competition. Few would deny that shipowners, port operators, and shippers all now face markedly increased costs, but whether these costs are outweighed by the benefits of additional security is yet to be conclusively tested. There is also a significant human cost. Seafarers have additional and onerous security tasks, but yet tend to be underappreciated and, in many ports around the world, they now have extra restrictions on shore leave and access to port facilities.

Seafaring has become less attractive as a career, and some seafarers of the Muslim faith have been laid off by shipping companies as a consequence of the additional constraints imposed on their ships when they visit American ports. Any possible manning shortage, as shipowners scrape around to find properly trained and experienced crews, could in the long run pose a greater threat to the safety and security of shipping than any threat from terrorism. Paradoxically, the shortage is occurring at a time when there are increased concerns about the human factor as a cause of maritime accidents and of the need for increased standards of competence among seafarers.

Despite all the activity to devise and implement the new maritime security measures, basic questions remain unanswered. Two of these are as follows: How much security is enough? Whose security are we talking about? Although it is beyond the scope of this book to provide definitive answers to these questions, at least the chapters should help in providing an appreciation of the issues that need to be considered.

HOW MUCH SECURITY IS ENOUGH?

This is a familiar question for defense planners who have the basic problem of determining how much defense is enough. Similarly, there is a challenge with providing maritime security against the threat of maritime terrorism in finding the right balance between assessments of risk on the one hand and realistic costs on the other. It is not just a matter of identifying threats and possible scenarios, but there is also the need to assess risk probabilities to guide policy and achieve a realistic allocation of resources.

It is a normal practice for government departments to bid for more resources than their government's budget can allow. In defense organizations, exhaustive analytical processes test new acquisition proposals. However, due to doubt about perceptions of an urgent need following 9/11 to make major improvements in maritime security, there seems to have been little testing, at least initially, of maritime security risk assessments and maritime counterterrorism measures. These were simply asserted by the government, and the private sector had to comply. This situation was not satisfactory, particularly for the longer term. As chapters of this book confirm, there is a need for greater transparency of the process to avoid excessive burdens being placed on industry.

WHOSE MARITIME SECURITY ARE WE TALKING ABOUT?

This is a question at the national level of sharing the burden between the public and the private sectors. At an international level, the situation becomes more complicated with issues of globalization and equity coming into play between the developed and the developing worlds. However, the same basic principle applies—the one who gets the benefit of enhanced maritime security should meet the costs of that additional security.

By expecting industry to bear the full costs of the new security measures, a government is treating these measures as though the benefits accrue only to the shipowner, shipper, or port or port facility operator. But it is the community at large that is ultimately being made more secure. At least in part, the new maritime security measures display many of the characteristics of a "public good" whose benefits are indivisible. If the measures are treated solely as "private goods" with benefits only for industry, then inevitably industry will tend to do the minimum possible to ensure compliance with regulations.

A distinction can be drawn between the costs of the physical measures to protect a ship (i.e., the costs of meeting the requirements of the ISPS Code) or a port or port facility (e.g., enhanced physical security with additional perimeter fencing, access controls, and closed-circuit television [CCTV]) and those of the operational measures associated with preventing (e.g., additional patrolling of harbors and their approaches) or responding to a maritime terrorist attack. The former involves the costs of doing business and should principally be borne by the owner or operator of the ship or facility. However, the latter display more of the attributes of a public good. Their aim is not to protect the ship or facility, but rather to protect the community from a massive disaster and its consequences. Governments should bear these costs.

At the global level, the situation is more difficult. It is still a matter of burden sharing, but arguably the greatest beneficiaries of the new security measures are the developed countries. Generally, developing countries have been less concerned about the terrorist threat, but they are also facing increased costs with upgrading port facilities to comply with the ISPS Code; in making their national flag ships compliant with the code; and in providing new government machinery to oversee the new arrangements, including those for oversight of the training and licensing of seafarers. Certainly, there are large costs for the developed countries as well, but they are also the major beneficiaries.

STRUCTURE OF THE BOOK

In outline, this book examines in detail the issues pertaining to assessing contemporary maritime security threats, vulnerability and risk; the nature and current status of the ISPS Code and other leading maritime security initiatives and regimes; security issues specific to vessel operations; and security concerns and measures at ports of different types and with different levels of resource. There is a particular focus on the identification of problems that have been encountered in developing and implementing relevant measures and possible ways and means of overcoming them. These experiences and perspectives come from around the world.

This book is divided into five sections:

- The New Maritime Security Environment
- Industry Sectors: Threats and Responses
- Legal Frameworks for Maritime Security
- Regional Responses
- National Responses

THE NEW MARITIME SECURITY ENVIRONMENT

This section starts with Chapter 1 in which Raymond and Morriën lead off with an overview of the vulnerability of the world's transport system to attack and new measures that have been introduced post-9/11. In a broad-ranging and candid piece, they critically analyze a number of these measures, especially the ISPS Code, as well as various other measures that have been implemented at the local or regional level. The analysis offers examination of the differing perspectives taken by various states' policymakers and practitioners in how they view maritime security, and how this has manifested itself in various situations, particularly since 9/11.

In Chapter 2, Murphy assesses the origins, purposes, and benefits of the Automatic Identification System (AIS) and Long-Range Identification and Tracking (LRIT) and how they contribute to the much-vaunted concept of maritime domain awareness (MDA). MDA is becoming a major focus of the U.S. maritime security initiatives. MDA provides early knowledge of what is happening in the maritime environment, including details of cargoes and people heading toward an American port. Murphy considers the purpose and limitations of MDA and the expectations about what can be achieved cost-effectively with these systems, particularly the AIS. In broadening the discussion beyond merely technological essentials, he cautions against the temptation to place too much emphasis on technical solutions—an overdependence on surveillance at the expense of intelligence—in pursuit of meaningful MDA, and suggests that with the debate concerning the endemic utilization of LRIT still ongoing, a truly holistic picture is still in progress.

Pegg addresses military support as an instrument in fortifying maritime security for commercial seafarers in Chapter 3, which examines NATO's naval coordination and guidance for shipping

(NCAGS), Operation Active Endeavor, and other coalition task forces in detail. He completes the picture by calling for the need of greater reciprocity among navies, merchant seafarers, and, where necessary, national law enforcement agencies in helping to further more robust security at sea and in ports. After all, seafarers are at the "coal face" of maritime security, and it is extremely important to have them onside.

In Chapter 4, Rahman focuses mainly on the American policy and strategy framework for security in the maritime domain and, in particular, how strategies formulated to improve the security of the American homeland have impacted maritime security considerations on a truly global scale. In doing so, special attention is given to the implications of the U.S. Navy's proposed Global Maritime Partnership Initiative (GMPI) or the 1000-ship navy concept. Despite its worthy aspirations, there will be doubts in many regions of the world about whether the GMPI is a genuinely inclusive global network working for the common good or an American-led coalition serving primarily American strategic objectives. Significantly, the term "1000-ship navy" is no longer used due to the recognition that it implied going well beyond the normal roles and expertise of navies.

In Chapter 5, Lehr argues that the flurry of activities in the wake of 9/11 resulted in the emergence of a new kind of maritime terrorism industry, in which an equally new variant of maritime "terrorologists" is busy conjuring up maritime versions of "megaterrorism," resulting in something called the "maritime terrorism nightmare charts." He concludes that, so far, acts of maritime terror have been few and far between, and that in all probability, the number of such attacks will not rise drastically in the foreseeable future.

In Chapter 6, Hansen argues that the identification and categorization of security threats in the maritime realm have become oversimplified and complicate the design of the most appropriate strategies to address distinct forms of threat. He suggests, for example, that the media, for the sake of argument simplification, tend to label these threats as being either "pirate" or "terrorist" in nature. However, deeper understanding of security threats in the maritime domain is much more complex, and careful analysis of the potential perpetrators is necessary. Chapter 6 sets out a more holistic perspective where the gray areas among piracy, terrorism, insurgency, and organized crime are identified as distinct phenomena and also demonstrates how, why, and where they converge within an incisive and nuanced framework.

INDUSTRY SECTORS: THREAT AND RESPONSES

This section addresses particular issues with the contemporary maritime security environment, specifically the new concepts and threat appreciations. Writing on the implications and effects of maritime security initiatives on the operation and management of merchant vessels, Jones in Chapter 7 starts by pointing out that currently "security" seems to be neither a popular word nor a terribly popular concept across certain areas of the maritime industry. He emphasizes that it is important to remember that anything that sees individual seafarers arriving home safe, sound, and in one piece cannot be all bad. After describing the new roles, responsibilities, and interactions within shipping companies and onboard ships in the wake of the ISPS Code, Jones concludes by defending these operational changes very convincingly, arguing that there are a whole host of benefits associated with the correct application of the ISPS Code.

In Chapter 8, Chalk discusses the threat posed by maritime terrorism to container ships, cruise liners, and passenger ferries; different attack contingencies; and their likely implications. He argues that it is reasonable to assume that the maritime environment will remain an interest to terrorist organizations because of its expanse, lack of regulation, and general importance for global trade. He also provides an assessment of some of the major international initiatives meant to enhance the safety of the global sea lines of communication (SLOC). He concludes by offering some tentative policy recommendations for guiding and enhancing future maritime security drives.

In Chapter 9, Herbert-Burns examines the operational-level security realities that challenge those involved in the export and conveyance of bulk oil and product cargoes by sea, specifically the coastal and offshore terminals and tankers in littoral waters that are typically more prone to security threats and risks. Chapter 9 begins by considering current and possible future axes of risks and threats, followed by searching commentary on the limitations of the ISPS Code as it pertains to the security of processing and trade of bulk petroleum cargoes. The remaining parts of Chapter 9 more specifically examine the factors that give rise to the vulnerability of tankers, floating production storage and offloading vessels (FPSOs), drill ships, and coastal and offshore terminals.

In Chapter 10, Martin explores the measures that have been put in place to improve safety in the maritime sector of the liquefied natural gas (LNG) industry. This is against the background of rapid growth in demand for LNG and the associated increase in LNG shipping traffic, which has led to some public anxiety, particularly in North America, about the potential for a terrorist attack on an LNG ship or facility. Chapter 10 uses the rejection of the proposed LNG facility at Cabrillo Port in California to demonstrate how the threat of terrorism can disproportionately affect community perceptions and energy choices.

Utilizing the Australian approach as a case study, Cordner in Chapter 11 analyzes security risk assessments in the context of possible terrorist threats to the offshore oil and gas industry. Risk management processes fundamentally underpin offshore oil and gas industry security processes. Chapter 11 describes these processes, as practiced in Australia, as well as the comprehensive set of legislation, regulations, guidelines, and mechanisms introduced by the Australian government to enhance maritime security in the offshore oil and gas industry against terrorism, within the broader national counterterrorism framework.

LEGAL FRAMEWORKS FOR MARITIME SECURITY

This section considers aspects of the new international law that have evolved to provide the legal framework for the new maritime security environment. This section starts with Chapter 12, in which Beckman leads off by tracing the development of modern international conventions for combating piracy and armed robbery against ships and maritime terrorism. It starts with the 1982 United Nations Convention on the Law of the Sea and then devotes more attention to the 1988 Suppression of Unlawful Acts (SUA) Convention and its 2005 protocol. The long and difficult negotiations on the boarding provisions of the 2005 protocol show that the international community is very reluctant to create new exceptions to the principle of flag-state jurisdiction.

In Chapter 13, Kaye examines both longer-standing protocols of the SUA convention and recent developments such as the Proliferation Security Initiative (PSI). He considers in detail the relevant international law that pertains to the interdiction and boarding of vessels at sea in the contemporary security environment. There will always be a need for governmental vessels to intercept, board, and if necessary bring ships at sea under control. This reality has garnered greater attention in recent times due to the added concentration on illicit activity by vessels at sea fueled by concern about the possible use of vessels, the maritime domain by terrorists for attacks, and the proliferation of weapons of mass destruction.

In Chapter 14, Tsamenyi and Palma provide analysis of the status of the LRIT system and the legal, administrative, and practical implications of its implementation. It also discusses concerns with respect to the draft technical standards for LRIT, and highlights the measures that the International Maritime Organization and its contracting governments need to take to advance its implementation. After intense negotiation, agreement was reached on access to LRIT information by various categories of states, including the distance from shores from which information may be received. Cost and confidentiality issues have been of major concern. In practice, developed countries will end up being the major beneficiaries of the LRIT system. Chapter 14 concludes that there is still much to be addressed before the system becomes functional.

In Chapter 15, Tsamenyi, Palma, and Schofield outline the pre-9/11 international regulatory framework for seafarers' identification before examining post-9/11 developments, notably the conclusion of the SID convention. It has a specific focus on the limitations of the regulatory framework from a maritime security perspective. The costs of issuing biometric identity cards and administering the national electronic database of thousands of seafarers place a large financial burden, particularly on the developing nations that provide most of the world's seafarers. Furthermore, tighter seafarers' identification arrangements and related port security measures impact on the basic rights of seafarers to access services and facilities in ports. Inconsistencies also remain evident not only among national practices, but also between national laws and the implementation of relevant conventions.

REGIONAL RESPONSES

Although the new maritime security measures are mainly devised at the global level, their effectiveness ultimately depends on how they are implemented at the regional and national levels. In Chapter 16, Banlaoi argues that although ASEAN members pursue a complex web of bilateral cooperation to secure the waters of Southeast Asia, their sensitivity on the issue of national sovereignty slows down any meaningful cooperation. He also alerts readers to the fact that national capacities to manage maritime security threats remain rather weak. Banlaoi concludes by emphasizing that any attempt to address maritime security threats in Southeast Asia must start by looking into the root causes of these threats.

In Chapter 17, Boutilier argues convincingly that we are witnessing the most dynamic maritime era in living memory. In recognizing the sheer pace and expansion of container flows, shipping schedules, shipbuilding tempos, port development, energy flows, naval construction, coast guard activity, submarine acquisition, maritime terrorism, and piratical attacks, Boutilier has carefully crafted a macropicture of all of the essential maritime phenomena in this enormous and dynamic maritime space. Chapter 17 examines how the forces of globalization, and more specifically, the economic vitality of nations such as China and India, have contributed directly to this dynamism.

In Chapter 18, Snoddon explores the continued evolution of maritime security operations (MSO) within NATO and explains what commercial maritime companies, merchant vessels, and others in the shipping industry can expect in terms of NATO's areas of responsibility, operational activity, and its limitations—specifically the legal parameters under which NATO warships must function when conducting MSO. Chapter 18 examines NATO's Operation Active Endeavor in the Mediterranean—specifically the identification of maritime security concerns such as possible terrorist use of the sea for conducting offensive operations and managing appropriate operational responses. It also addresses NATO's expanding roles in MSO in areas outside of its nominal areas of operational coverage, such as counternarcotic operations and counterpiracy patrols in the Gulf of Guinea and Horn of Africa.

NATIONAL RESPONSES

This section covers a range of responses at the national level. It begins with Chapter 19 in which Craig and Seher provide a comprehensive overview of the high-profile U.S. maritime transportation and port security measures that have been initiated since the terrorist attacks of 2001. The chapter's centerpiece is a candid case study of the controversial bid by DP World to complete its acquisition of P&O Ports' global operations with the takeover of the latter's U.S.-based terminals; a case that pitted the White House–backed DP World against a rarely unified Congress concerned about the possible implications for national security of foreign-owned terminals located within major U.S. ports.

Stubbs and Truver also address maritime security developments in the United States in Chapter 20. This chapter describes the risk-managed, layered, and cost-benefit approaches adopted by the Department of Homeland Security to triage and select those elements of port security and the container supply chain that are most vulnerable, while letting the vast majority of commerce go unimpeded. With the layered-security efforts already in place, and the efforts proposed for the future, port security will be substantially improved but questions remain—how much security "is" too much for the globalized U.S. economy, and at what point will there be unintended ripple effects throughout the U.S. international maritime supply chain lingering?

In Chapter 21, Ho describes contemporary maritime security arrangements in Singapore. Singapore is the world's busiest port, situated at the crossroad of maritime traffic between the Indian and the Pacific Oceans. It is also the third largest oil-refining center in the world. Security was a concern before 9/11, but since then extensive new arrangements have been introduced. These demonstrate a high level of coordination and close working partnerships among all stakeholders, be they government agencies or private organizations, which in many ways is a model of "best practice" for port and ship security elsewhere in the world.

In Chapter 22, Lavers describes the Canadian experience by introducing the ISPS Code. The Canadian maritime industry cautiously welcomed the new security measures, but not the forecasted costs that accompanied the new regulations associated with bringing the ISPS Code into law. Although there have been many positive outcomes of the new security measures, problems still remain, including apportioning costs, information sharing, and the need to maintain the momentum of enthusiasm and interest.

In Chapter 23, Grewal first describes the institutional arrangements and legislation that have been introduced in Australia to establish a new maritime security regime. The Office of Transport Security (OTS) in the Department of Transport and Regional Services (DOTARS) administers this regime, and the Maritime Transport and Offshore Facilities Security Act (MTOFSA) is a key piece of legislation. The second part of the chapter discusses some of the difficulties involved, including costs, the impact on seafarers, and a possible lack of understanding of the maritime industry in terms of expression and commercial needs.

In Chapter 24, Osnin discusses the current state of ISPS implementation in Malaysia. Against the backdrop of the gradual rise of both the Malaysian economy and its shipping services, he draws the reader's attention to the fact that for countries such as Malaysia, ISPS implementation does not come cheap—to comply with the ISPS Code, the 78 Malaysian port facilities will have to spend about U.S.$5.7 million, whereas Malaysian shipping companies have to spend more than U.S.$3 million for 341 ships.

In Chapter 25, Dodd examines how the U.K. military has been involved with operations "other than war" for many years. The chapter considers how the military is often specifically called on to support the civil authorities in fighting organized crime wherever it impacts the United Kingdom's interests and national security. He argues that this can only be effective if supported by military intelligence, not only for its operational- and tactical-level contribution to ships and commanders at sea and at regional component commands, but also because of its unique strategic-level collection and assessment capabilities.

SOME LAST THOUGHTS

The OECD has described international shipping as

> a sector characterised by an extremely diverse international labour force, transporting a vast range of goods whose provenance, description and ownership are often left remarkably vague. This is a system where international transport chains involved thousands of intermediaries, on vessels registered in dozens of countries that sometimes choose not to uphold their international responsibilities and where some vessel owners can and do easily hide their true identities using a complex web of international corporate registration practices.[*]

Introducing an effective maritime security regime for this sector has proven to be much more complex and difficult than many governments and international organizations may have anticipated.

---

[*] OECD, *Security in Maritime Transport: Risk Factors and Economic Impact*, July 2003, p. 5.

Chapters in this book address some of the difficulties that are encountered. Inevitably there has been some overreaction. Many threats and scenarios have been identified for attacks on ships and ports, or for the use of the maritime transportation system to convey terrorists or their material, in the worst case, a weapon of mass destruction. However, rather less attention appears to have been paid to the likelihood of such activities or of the relevant costs and benefits.

In some areas, maritime security was seen as much like aviation security. Obviously, the initial emphasis post-9/11 was on aviation security and it may not have been appreciated just how much more complex the maritime sector is. The security of ports and ships must consider all environments—land, air, sea surface, and subsurface. Airports have defined perimeters and usually some form of "buffer zone" between an airport and other activities. Access is fairly easily controlled. Airline passengers are screened with their baggage and airline and airport workers are closely monitored. In comparison, ports may not have a clearly defined perimeter, even on the landside, and most communities are accustomed to having free access to the waterfront.

Underpinning any misunderstanding of the maritime sector is the belief that there is relatively little community appreciation of the nature and complexity of the operation of ships and ports or of their economic significance and vulnerability. Hopefully, the chapters of this book will help to provide some of this understanding and introduce more rationality to the discussion of maritime security.

Rupert Herbert-Burns
Sam Bateman
Peter Lehr

Editors

Rupert Herbert-Burns is the lead maritime security consultant for the Lloyd's Marine Intelligence Unit (Lloyd's MIU) in London, and associate consultant for Risk Intelligence, Copenhagen. He specializes in security and geopolitical issues within the commercial shipping and petroleum sectors, and consults on asymmetric and criminal security concerns within the maritime realm. Since joining Lloyd's MIU in 2002, he has worked on projects for branches of the U.S. government, New York Police Department, Project SeaHawk at the Port of Charleston, the U.K. Metropolitan Police, Transport Canada, and NATO. He has also briefed international media on various aspects of maritime security, and authored several articles and chapters on issues pertaining to maritime security threat and risk assessment. Before his work in the commercial sector, Mr Herbert-Burns served as a warfare officer in the Royal Navy in operational theatres worldwide. Ensuing military service also included appointments as an infantry platoon commander and an intelligence officer within the British Army's Brigade of Gurkhas. Mr. Herbert-Burns has a BSc (Hons) in International Relations and Politics, and a masters degree (M.Litt) in International Security Studies from the University of St. Andrews, Scotland. He is currently a final year PhD candidate at the University of St. Andrews, completing a treatise on *Petroleum Geopolitics.*

Sam Bateman is a senior fellow and advisor to the Maritime Security Program at the RSIS, NTU, Singapore. He is a former seaman officer in the RAN, rising to the rank of commodore, and became the first director of the Centre for Maritime Policy (now the ANCORS) at the University of Wollongong. He remains an adjunct professorial research fellow of this center. He has written extensively on defense and maritime issues in Australia, Asia-Pacific, and Indian Ocean. He was awarded his PhD from The University of New South Wales in 2001 for a dissertation on "The Strategic and Political Aspects of the Law of the Sea in East Asian Seas."

Peter Lehr is a lecturer in terrorism studies at the CSTPV, School of International Relations, University of St. Andrews and visiting lecturer at the South Asia Institute, University of Heidelberg, Germany. Before taking up his current position in September 2007, Dr. Lehr was Informa Group's research fellow at the CSTPV; and before this, a lecturer at the Department of Political Science, South Asia Institute, University of Heidelberg and visiting fellow at the Institute for Strategic and International Studies (ISIS), Chulalongkorn University, Bangkok. He has considerable research and teaching experience in the subject areas of terrorism/political violence and Asian security relations. Being a regional specialist on the Indian Ocean, he currently specializes in research in the following areas: the Indian Ocean as a strategic arena; maritime security in the Indian Ocean/Asia-Pacific (including piracy and maritime terrorism), political violence and terrorism in south and Southeast Asia, organized crime in south and Southeast Asia, and critical infrastructure protection (focusing on air and seaport security). Dr. Lehr is also one of the tutors of the CSTPV/Informa Group distance-learning course on terrorism (http://terrorismstudies.com). For this certificate course he developed the module on maritime terrorism. Additionally, he is involved in developing a module for the new masters (MLitt) in terrorism studies E-learning course, which started in spring 2008.

Contributors

Rommel C. Banlaoi is the executive director of the Philippine Institute for Political Violence and Terrorism Research (PIPVTR). He was a professor of political science and international relations at the National Defense College of the Philippines (NDCP), where he served as the course director of the political dimension of national security from August 1998 to March 2007. He was an assistant professor of international studies at De La Salle University from 1996 to 1997 and instructor in political science at the University of the Philippines (Los Banos campus) from 1992 to 1995. Professor Banlaoi has published 7 books to date (1 edited, 3 single author, and 3 coauthor), 3 monographs, and at least 45 internationally refereed scholarly articles and book chapters on various issues related to Philippine electoral politics, Philippine foreign and security policy, international relations, bilateral diplomacy, international terrorism, and regional security. His latest books are *War on Terrorism in Southeast Asia* (2004) and *Security Aspects of Philippines–China Relations: Bilateral Issues and Concerns in the Age of Global Terrorism* (2007). He is currently the chairman of the Programs Oversight Committee of the League of Municipalities of the Philippines (LMP), member of the Board of Trustees of the Strategic and Integrative Studies Centre (SISC) while lecturing at the Command and General Staff College (CGSC) of the Armed Forces of the Philippines (AFP) and Intelligence Training Group (ITG) of the Philippine National Police (PNP).

Robert C. Beckman is an associate professor at the Faculty of Law, National University of Singapore (NUS), where he has taught since 1977. He is an international lawyer who specializes in law of the sea and the international regulation of shipping. During his sabbatical leave in academic year 2006–2007, he was a visiting senior fellow at the RSIS, NTU, Singapore. He is currently an adjunct senior fellow in the Maritime Security Program at the RSIS. Professor Beckman serves as an advisor to the legal committee of the Singapore Shipping Association (SSA) and has served as an advisor to the Maritime and Port Authority of Singapore (MPA). He has represented Singapore in the "track two" meetings of the Study Group on Maritime Security of the CSCAP. He has been actively involved in the issues relating to the Strait of Malacca and Singapore for many years, and has presented papers at numerous workshops and conferences on ocean law and policy in Asia.

James A. Boutilier is the special advisor (policy) at Canada's Maritime Forces Pacific Headquarters in Esquimalt, British Columbia. Dr. Boutilier attended Dalhousie University (BA in history, 1960), McMaster University (MA in history, 1962), and the University of London (PhD in history, 1969). Dr. Boutilier has held posts at various universities throughout his career, including The University of the South Pacific in Suva, Fiji; Royal Roads Military College in Victoria, British Columbia; and the University of Victoria, British Columbia. Dr. Boutilier's field of expertise is in Asia-Pacific defense and security. He published *RCN in Retrospect* in 1982 and has written extensively on maritime and security concerns. He lectures nationally and internationally on political, economic, and security developments in the Asia-Pacific region.

Peter Chalk is a senior policy analyst with the RAND Corporation, Santa Monica, California. He has worked on a range of projects, including studies examining unconventional security threats in Southeast and south Asia; new strategic challenges for the U.S. Air Force (USAF) in Latin America, Africa, and south Asia; evolving trends in national and international terrorism; Australian defense and foreign policy; international organized crime; the transnational spread of disease; U.S. military links in the Asia-Pacific region; and internal security reform in Pakistan. He is a specialist correspondent for *Jane's Intelligence Review* and associate editor of *Studies in Conflict Terrorism*—one of the foremost journals in the international security field. Dr. Chalk has regularly testified before the U.S. Senate on issues pertaining to national and international terrorism, and is the author of numerous books, book chapters, monographs, and journal articles dealing with various aspects of low-intensity conflict in the contemporary world. Dr. Chalk also serves as an adjunct professor at the Naval Postgraduate School in Monterey, California, and regularly works with both the Asia-Pacific Center for Security Studies (APCSS) in Honolulu and the United States Institute of Peace (USIP) in Washington, DC. Before joining RAND, Dr. Chalk was an assistant professor of politics at The University of Queensland, Brisbane, and a postdoctoral fellow in the Strategic and Defence Studies Centre of The Australian National University, Canberra. Apart from his academic posts, Dr. Chalk has acted as a research consultant in the United Kingdom, Canada, and Australia, and has experience with the U.K. Armed Forces.

Lee Cordner is a principal research fellow at the ANCORS, University of Wollongong, Australia. From 2001 to 2005, he was the managing director of Future Directions International (FDI), an independent strategic "think tank" based in Perth, Western Australia. In his capacity as the managing director, he conducted numerous strategic risk analyses for resource sector companies. Until 2001, he served for over 30 years in the RAN, retiring at the rank of commodore. He held a number of senior strategy and policy positions in Navy Headquarters, Canberra and commanded several warships. His research interests include strategic analysis and maritime strategy, security, and policy matters.

Ashley W. Craig focuses his practice on legislative, regulatory, and policy matters affecting cross-border interests. Particularly, Craig's experience includes transportation, homeland security, defense, and international trade (with an emphasis on international liner shipping, domestic and international multimodal transportation, and customs compliance). He is also actively involved in various matters before the U.S. Executive Branch, U.S. Congress, and federal agencies (such as the Departments of Homeland Security, Transportation, State, and Defense of the United States) and works closely with clients on transportation security, third-party logistics, and related commercial matters.

Peter Dodd joined the Royal Navy as a radio operator in 1978. After serving in a number of surface ships and shore establishments he was transferred to the Communications Technician branch in the late 1980s. Ensuing service was spent in ships and submarines, including a four and a half year posting to Gibraltar monitoring the shipping lanes in the Strait of Gibraltar. In 2001, following officer training at Britannia Royal Naval College, he obtained a commission and has since served in a number of intelligence-related posts including one as a part of the U.K. Ministry of Defence Central Staff where he was a subject matter expert on illicit activity in the global maritime domain, specifically narcotics, human and contraband trafficking, piracy, and organized crime. He is currently serving as a part of the intelligence staff at the NATO Maritime Component Command in Naples.

Devinder Grewal has been the head of the Department of Maritime and Logistics Management at the Australian Maritime College since 1998. He has nearly two decades of experience in the international shipping industry, is a master mariner class 1, obtained his PhD from the University of Wales, and is a visiting fellow at various universities in the Asia-Pacific region. In 2004, he was seconded to the OTS at the DOTARS to assist with the development and implementation of the maritime security regime in Australia. In addition to publishing widely on matters related to maritime management and policy, Devinder Grewal provides his expertise on multimodal transport networks, ports and shipping management, and security to various organizations and government agencies in the region. His areas of research include holistic approaches to safe management of operations in the industry, future skills requirements and policies needed to address them, and effective management of security initiatives.

Hans Tino Hansen is the founder and executive partner of Risk Intelligence (formerly Protocol), a private security intelligence company serving both private and governmental clients from 19 countries. Risk Intelligence specializes in security intelligence; threat and risk analysis; and assessment of terrorism, counterterrorism, insurgency, organized crime, and piracy. Risk Intelligence's main geographical areas are Southeast Asia, south Asia, the Middle East and the Persian Gulf, the Horn of Africa, west Africa, and South America. Hansen's specialty is piracy and maritime aspects of terrorism, insurgency organizations, and military conflicts as well as intelligence and the future of intelligence. He has a master's degree in economics from the University of Copenhagen. He has written articles for newspapers and journals, is employed as an expert commentator by BBC World, AFP, Reuters, Associated Press (AP), Radio France, Danish national television and radio stations, as well as all major newspapers and news services in Denmark. Hansen was president and CEO of East and Central European Advisors Ltd. (ECEA) from 1997 to 2001 working with political intelligence, networking, and business management consulting for international clients in east and central Europe.

Joshua Ho is a senior fellow at the RSIS, Singapore and coordinator of the Maritime Security Programme. He has an MA from Cambridge University, United Kingdom on an SAF (overseas) scholarship and also holds an MSc in management from the Naval Postgraduate School, California, where he was awarded the Graduate School of Business and Public Policy Faculty Award for excellence in management. Joshua is a serving naval officer with 20 years of service and currently holds the rank of lieutenant colonel. He is a coeditor for the volumes *Best of Times, Worst of Times: Maritime Security in the Asia-Pacific* and *The Evolving Maritime Balance of Power in the Asia-Pacific: Maritime Doctrines and Nuclear Weapons at Sea.* He has also published in local and overseas journals such as *Asian Survey, Contemporary Southeast Asia, Defence Studies, Security Challenges, Maritime Affairs, Maritime Studies, Military Technology, Australian Army Journal, Journal of the Australian Naval Institute,* and *Pointer.*

Steven M. Jones after having been attacked by pirates when serving as a deck officer in the merchant navy, has long had an interest and subsequent involvement in maritime security issues. This led to his attendance at the International Maritime Organization (IMO) during the sessions leading to the adoption of the ISPS Code; consequently, Jones has advised numerous shipping companies on their security planning. Having worked in marine fraud investigations and as a security specialist at a major protection and indemnity association, he then applied his years of research, professional involvement, and in-depth knowledge of the ISPS Code to produce a book titled *Maritime Security,* published by the Nautical Institute. Jones is currently the communications manager at The Nautical Institute and also provides security comment and assessment for a number of maritime publications. He is a member of the advisory panel for the diploma in maritime and supply chain security at the University of Leicester, England.

Stuart Kaye was appointed to a chair in law at the University of Melbourne in 2006. He was dean of law at the University of Wollongong between 2002 and 2006. Before this appointment, he was head of the School of Law at James Cook University and a senior lecturer in law at the University of Tasmania. He holds degrees in arts and law from The University of Sydney and a doctorate in law from Dalhousie University. He is admitted as a barrister of the supreme courts of New South Wales, Tasmania, and Queensland. He has an extensive research interest in the law of the sea and international law. He has written a number of books, including *Australia's Maritime Boundaries* (2001), *The Torres Strait* (1997), and *International Fisheries Management* (2001). He was appointed to the International Hydrographic Organization's panel of experts on maritime boundary delimitation and list of arbitrators under the Environmental Protocol to the Antarctic Treaty in 1995 and 2000, respectively. He has been chair of the Australian Red Cross National International Humanitarian

Law Committee since 2003. He has undertaken consultancy work for government and industry in Australia and overseas, including appearing as one of the counsel before the high court in *Grain Pool of WA* v *Commonwealth* in 1999. He is also a legal officer in the RAN Reserve and a fellow of the Royal Geographical Society.

John W. Lavers is an assistant director with the International Chamber of Commerce (ICC)—Commercial Crime Services (CCS), London. Previously, John served in a senior management capacity with the Government of Canada, which included tenures with the Department of Transport (Transport Canada) and Department of National Defense (DND). John led the operational team that implemented the ISPS Code on behalf of the Department of Transport—directorate of marine security as well as contributing to the implementation of Canada's first-ever national security policy dealing with the establishment of the Marine Security Operations Centre project. Holding a Canadian Forces Officers' Commission, John achieved an MA in police and criminal justice studies from Exeter University and is currently researching his PhD in maritime security.

Peter Martin completed a 23-year career as a seagoing officer in the RAN where he was a navigation specialist and principal warfare officer. After retiring from the RAN, he studied at the Australian Maritime College and is now a master mariner. He holds a masters of defense studies from the University of Malaya and The University of New South Wales and is now undertaking a PhD with ANCORS, University of Wollongong researching "the strategic implications of Australia's maritime (LNG) trade with China." Peter is an active member of the international Nautical Institute (NI), Company of Master Mariners Australia (COMMA), Australian Institute of Navigation (AIN), Australian Marine Pilots Association (AMPA), and RAN Maritime Trade Organisation (MTO). He is currently a pilot in the Australian Torres Strait and Great Barrier Reef.

Arthur Morriën joined Control Risks in 2004 and heads the firm's maritime security consulting practice. He is responsible for coordinating Control Risks' maritime-related assignments and advising clients within Europe, the Middle East, and Africa on maritime security in particular and supply chain security in general. Within the maritime security practice, his primary expertise areas are global supply chain (and maritime security) regulations, vessel and port facility security design, and piracy protection. After earning his master's degree (MSc in engineering—applied mathematics and risk management), he worked for over ten years as a risk management consultant, specializing in maritime safety and port operations. Working for a maritime simulation center in the Netherlands, he has been involved in improving vessel traffic management in ports, performing port development studies, and research on the safety of shipping in European coastal waters. Following this appointment, he has been an external advisor to the Dutch Aerospace Laboratory on improving air traffic control procedures and air safety. In the three years before joining Control Risks, he worked as a regional sales and account manager for an engineering and management consultancy firm.

Martin N. Murphy is an associate fellow at the Corbett Centre for Maritime Policy Studies, King's College, London, specializing in maritime irregular warfare. His book on modern piracy and maritime terrorism, *Small Boats, Weak States, Dirty Money*, will be published in 2008. He is the author of *Contemporary Piracy and Maritime Terrorism* (Adelphi Paper) published in 2007. His recent journal articles include "The Blue, Green and Brown: Insurgency and Counterinsurgency on the Water" in *Contemporary Security Policy* and "Suppression of Piracy and Maritime Terrorism: A Suitable Role for a Navy?" in *Naval War College Review*. He has written several book chapters, and articles for journals including *Armed Forces Journal, Jane's Intelligence Review* and *Maritime Studies*, on naval special forces, littoral warfare, maritime security including the maritime terrorist threat, and the marine insurance industry. He speaks regularly on maritime security and irregular warfare. He has acted as a research consultant for the U.K. Ministry of Defence. He holds a BA from The University of Wales and an MA and doctorate from the University of Reading.

Noor Apandi Osnin is an accredited maritime arbitrator (KLRCA/IKMAL) and research fellow and head of the Centre for Ocean Law and Policy, Maritime Institute of Malaysia (MIMA). He has an MSc in marine policy from Cardiff Business School, The University of Wales, United Kingdom (2004), and a certificate of competency as a master of foreign going ships from the Ministry of Transport, Malaysia (1995). He has served in various capacities for the maritime industry beginning as a deck cadet and achieving his master of foreign going ships ticket while working on various types of ships including general cargo vessels, container ships, bulk carriers, and LNG carriers. On leaving the sea as a master, he joined SGS as a marine surveyor and later moved on to become a nautical lecturer and maritime policy researcher with MIMA. Osnin is a Malaysian delegate to the IMO and a member of its working groups. He has been on a sabbatical from international maritime affairs since late 2007 to pursue commercial sports activities and recoup the basics of navigation through involvement with groups of boatmen, fisherman, and islanders in general.

Mary Ann Palma is a research fellow at ANCORS, University of Wollongong, Australia. Palma finished her PhD with the centre in 2006 and her dissertation analyzed the Philippine legal, policy, and institutional framework to address illegal, unreported, and unregulated fishing. Her previous research includes LRIT of vessels, maritime security in the Strait of Malacca and Singapore, Philippine–China conflict, and cooperation in the Kalayaan Island Group, and formulation of the *Magna Carta* for Filipino seafarers.

Russel Pegg, OBE, joined the Royal Navy in 1979. He qualified as a principal warfare officer in 1989 and after a number of operational positions was appointed to the staff of Director Naval Officers Appointments in 1993. In 1995 he saw his selection as the first Royal Navy representative to attend the South African Command and Staff Course. In 1996, he had a fulfilling and rewarding period that ended with selection for promotion to commander and a move to the staff of the British Embassy in Washington, DC. Further appointments to the Ministry of Defense and NATO followed. Before joining the Ministry of Defense in January 2008, Captain Pegg served as the head of operations at NATO's Maritime Component Command Headquarters, Naples, where he was responsible for Operation Active Endeavour and the development of maritime situational awareness.

Chris Rahman is a research fellow at ANCORS, University of Wollongong, Australia. His current research interests center around contemporary issues in maritime strategy and security, including U.S. maritime strategy, Australian maritime security, MDA, Chinese maritime power, and maritime security in both the Asia-Pacific region and Africa.

Catherine Zara Raymond is currently an associate at the Corbett Centre for Maritime Policy Studies, based at the Defence Studies Department, Joint Services Command and Staff College, Shrivenham. Raymond is also a PhD student at King's College, London, where she is writing her thesis on Islamic radicalization in the United Kingdom. Previously, Raymond worked as an analyst for the security consultancy, Control Risks, in Singapore and as an associate research fellow at the IDSS also in Singapore. She is a coeditor and contributing author of the volume *Best of Times, Worst of Times: Maritime Security in the Asia-Pacific* (World Scientific 2005), and the policy paper titled "Safety and Security in the Malacca and Singapore Straits" (IDSS 2006). Her articles have been published in the *Harvard Asia Quarterly*, the *Maritime Studies Journal, Jamestown Foundation's Terrorism Monitor*, the *Journal of the Australian Naval Institute, The Straits Times*, and a number of other publications. Her latest papers were published in the *Journal of Terrorism and Political Violence* and in an edited volume produced by Routledge titled *Maritime Security in Southeast Asia*. She is regularly consulted by the media. Recently she was interviewed by CNBC regarding security in the Strait of Malacca. Raymond holds an MA in international relations from St. Andrews University and an MSc in international and European politics from The University of Edinburgh.

Clive Schofield is a QEII research fellow based at ANCORS, University of Wollongong, Australia. Schofield is a political geographer specializing in the study of maritime boundaries, transboundary resource management, technical aspects of the law of the sea, and the political geography of Southeast Asia. Previously, he has served as a vice-chancellor's research fellow at the School of Surveying and Spatial Information Systems, The University of New South Wales and director of research, International Boundaries Research Unit, University of Durham, United Kingdom.

John F. Seher focuses on federal government affairs with a particular emphasis on Congress and the legislative process. He provides expertise on legislative strategy, issue management, coalition building, and political analysis. His background includes nearly ten years in Capitol Hill as a staff member in the office of Senator Joseph R. Biden, Jr (D-DE) and as a member of the finance division of the Democratic Congressional Campaign Committee. Seher was the legislative director at the law firm of O'Connor & Hannan and later established the Washington, DC office of U.S. Smokeless Tobacco (UST) Inc. as vice president of government affairs.

Robert Snoddon joined the Royal Navy in 1972 as a boy seaman and was commissioned in 1989. A specialist in electronic warfare, he has also held several naval intelligence posts, at sea as the intelligence officer of HMS *Invincible*, the defense intelligence staff of the MOD, and as the U.K. exchange officer at the Office of Naval Intelligence, Washington, DC. He left the navy in 2005 and worked as military consultant for a subsidiary of Lloyd's Maritime Intelligence Group as well as other commercial companies. After leaving the Royal Navy, he joined the naval reserves and is currently back in uniform on a full-time reserve service contract at the NATO headquarters at Northwood, Middlesex.

Bruce B. Stubbs is a former career U.S. Coast Guard officer who served on staff of the National Security Council, as a senior strategic and force planner at the Coast Guard Headquarters, on a combat tour in Vietnam with the U.S. Navy, as a professor of strategy and operations at the Naval War College, and in command of a major Coast Guard ship conducting maritime security missions throughout the Caribbean. After his Coast Guard service, he has worked as a national security consultant and served as the principal author of the *Coast Guard's Maritime Strategy for Homeland Security* and the Coast Guard's first white paper on MDA. Additionally, he is one of the five principal authors of the *National Strategy for Maritime Security*. He has authored numerous articles for the U.S. Naval Institute's journal, proceedings, as well as for *Armed Forces Journal International*, *Sea Power*, *Government Executive*, and *Joint Forces Quarterly*. He has also authored papers for the Heritage Foundation.

Scott C. Truver is the group vice president of National Security Programs and directs the Center for Security Strategies and Operations (CSSO) in Anteon's Systems Engineering Group. In addition to his management and business development responsibilities, he supervises and carries out research and analytical efforts relating to international relations and U.S. national security, defense, naval, and maritime issues and concerns. Dr. Truver holds a PhD degree in marine policy studies (1978)—the first PhD in this field ever awarded by an institution of higher education—and an MA in political science in international relations (1974) from the University of Delaware. Since 1972, he has participated in numerous studies for government and private industry in the United States and abroad; he has also written extensively for U.S. and foreign publications; and is the author, coauthor, or editor of numerous papers and reports, several hundred articles, and four books—*The Strait of Gibraltar and the Mediterranean Sea* (1980), *Weapons That Wait* (2nd edition, 1991), *America's Coast Guard: Safeguarding U.S. Maritime Safety and Security in the 21st Century* (2000), and *Riders of the Storm* (2000).

Martin Tsamenyi is a professor of law and director of the ANCORS, University of Wollongong, Australia. Professor Tsamenyi graduated with an LLB degree from the University of Ghana and master of international law and PhD from The Australian National University. Professor Tsamenyi has over 25 years of research and teaching experience on policymaking and legal framework development for the management of the oceans, marine living resources, and maritime enforcement and security. Professor Tsamenyi has published extensively in leading journals in the field; provided training to government officials, including diplomats; and supervised higher degree research students in international law, international fisheries law, maritime law, and maritime security law.

Section 1

The New Maritime
Security Environment

1 Security in the Maritime Domain and Its Evolution Since 9/11

Catherine Zara Raymond and Arthur Morriën

CONTENTS

The maritime domain, a majority of which is international waters, has traditionally been characterized by a lack of control bordering on the anarchic. It has therefore proved to be an ideal environment for those engaged in transnational crime such as piracy and terrorism, as well as those waging an insurgency against a greater power. The attacks on the USS *Cole* in 2000 and the *M/V Limburg* in 2002, executed through the use of explosive-laden speedboats, showed that the international terrorist network, Al-Qaeda, had developed the capability of carrying out attacks in the maritime domain. Meanwhile in 2002, the U.S. government announced that it had identified approximately 15 freighters around the world that they believed were controlled by Al-Qaeda and used both for generating profit and for aiding terrorist operations.

Recently, the maritime domain was exploited by insurgents in Iraq in their war against the United States. In April 2004, three American servicemen were killed during a maritime interdiction operation, which prevented attempted attacks on two offshore Iraqi oil terminals in the Persian Gulf. A traditional *dhow* and two speedboats were used to carry out the attacks; the *dhow* exploded in the vicinity of the Khor Al Amaya Oil Terminal as it was being boarded by U.S. military personnel, whereas the two speedboats exploded when security forces opened fire to prevent them from reaching the Al-Basrah Oil Terminal. Although the attacks failed, the attempted destruction of two U.S.-controlled oil facilities in Basra by Iraqi insurgents equipped with explosive-laden speedboats underlined the ease with which the marine environment can be utilized with only minimal operational capability in an attack against a significant target.

In addition, piracy has plagued the world's waters for centuries, with reported attacks reaching its peak in 2000 when 469 actual and attempted attacks were recorded.[1] Particularly in Southeast Asia, it has been a significant problem, with the waters around Indonesia being labeled the most piracy prone in the world for well over a decade.[2] In Southeast Asia too, the Jemaah Islamiah (JI) terrorist group is suspected of utilizing the maritime domain when transferring its personnel from

Malaysia to training camps in the Philippines, whereas the Abu Sayyaf Group continues to conduct terrorist attacks on Philippine ferries and other maritime targets.

However, it was the September 11 attacks, which highlighted the vulnerability of the world's transport system to attack, triggering the introduction of a raft of new laws and conventions— most of them implemented with the encouragement of the United States—which were designed to enhance maritime security in both a specific locale and in key components of the maritime industry that were deemed to suffer from inherent weaknesses, which could be exploited by criminals. This chapter critically analyzes a number of such measures including one of the most significant developments—the introduction of the International Ship and Port Facility Security (ISPS) Code, as well as various other measures that have been implemented at the local or regional level. This will be followed by an examination of the differing perspectives taken by the states' policy makers and practitioners in how they view maritime security, and how this has manifested itself in various situations throughout the years.

THE INTERNATIONAL SHIP AND PORT FACILITY SECURITY CODE

Under the auspices of the International Maritime Organization (IMO), a comprehensive security regime was formulated for international shipping to strengthen maritime security in general, and prevent and suppress acts of terrorism against the maritime realm more specifically. The series of measures, which were adopted in July 2004, included several amendments to the 1974 International Convention for the Safety of Life at Sea (SOLAS), which aimed at enhancing maritime security onboard ships and at ship–port interface areas.

Among other things, the amendments created a new SOLAS chapter XI-2 (Special measures to enhance maritime security) dealing specifically with maritime security, containing the mandatory requirement for the following SOLAS member states' ships and port facilities to comply with the ISPS Code:

- Passenger ships (including high-speed passenger craft)
- Cargo ships of 500 gross tonnage and above (including high-speed craft)
- Mobile offshore drilling units (MODUs)
- All port facilities serving ships engaged in international voyages

The ISPS Code came into force on July 1, 2004, and aimed at providing a standardized, consistent framework for evaluating risk, enabling governments to offset changes in threat levels with changes in vulnerability for ships and port facilities. This imposed wide-ranging obligations on governments, shipping companies, and port facilities.

THE IMPLEMENTATION PHASE

In its current setup, the implementation of ISPS Code involves a number of steps and efforts such as undertaking security assessments, developing security plans, designating security officers, and establishing training and drill programs. To prove compliance with the Code, maritime security operators have to put procedures in place for monitoring access, activities of personnel, and cargo operations, conduct regular security inspections of port facilities and ships, provide adequate training for security personnel, report to the relevant authorities, and ensure that security and communications equipment is properly operated, tested, and maintained.

In the period up to the July 2004 implementation deadline, various press reports drew attention to the challenging task facing the global maritime industry and raised doubts about its ability to implement the ISPS Code requirements in such a limited time frame.[3] However the ISPS Code, against all odds, had a "relatively smooth" start-up.[4] To ensure compliance before the deadline of July 1, 2004, a considerable amount of effort was put in by all the parties involved, including

Contracting Governments, their agencies and local administrations, and the shipping and port industry (including the Recognised Security Organizations [RSO] authorized by the Contracting Governments to act on their behalf). As a result of these efforts, by September 2004, 90 percent of above 9000 declared port facilities had approved port facility security plans (PFSPs), and 90 percent of the ships subject to the security regime had been issued with an International Ship Security Certificate (ISSC).[5]

At the same time, despite the overall optimism of the implementation success, there were geographical areas and countries that had not been as rapid in establishing compliance levels for their port facilities as hoped for. Africa lagged behind other continents, with barely half of its 30 SOLAS member states reporting for the approval of port security plans by September 2004. Countries in the former Soviet Union and Eastern Europe also appeared slower than average to implement the measures.

WHAT HAPPENED NEXT?

After the initial burst of activities, the rates of implementing the ISPS Code became a topic of less interest. Generally, it was suggested that global compliance was achieved with limited exceptions of a temporary nature. Studies performed to clarify matters relating to the implementation process and level of compliance performed in later years, for example, by the United Nations Conference on Trade and Development (UNCTAD),[6] confirmed this conclusion. This particular study showed almost 100 percent compliancy rates, although this number could only be based on the response of 800 ISPS-designated port facilities, or approximately 7 percent of the total number of the declared ISPS port facilities. The few that reported less than 100 percent compliance cited that the certification process for some facilities was still underway.

What did not change, however, was the worldwide focus on security in general and terrorism in particular. Besides the continuous efforts, maritime operators have to put into maintaining ISPS compliancy for their existing fleet or facilities, and into getting certificates of approval for new vessels and sites, both global and local regulatory authorities also continued to strive to secure homelands, supply chains, and trade. This has led to the introduction of amendments to, or new, maritime and supply-chain security regulations such as the Maritime Transportation Security Act of 2002 (MTSA), the Advance Manifest System (AMS/24 hour rule), the Container Security Initiative (CSI), the Technology Asset Protection Association (TAPA), the U.S. Customs-Trade Partnership Against Terrorism (C-TPAT), and the Smart and Secure Tradelane (SST) program, to name a few. Bilateral and regional initiatives such as Free and Secure Trade (FAST) between the United States and Canada, the EU Customs Security Programme (CSP) and Authorized Economic Operator (AEO) were adopted too.

Together with regulations and awareness of the importance of being able to protect, monitor, and control operations worldwide, came the introduction of all kinds of electronic tools into the maritime industry to "enhance" security. Examples of these tools are the Automatic Identification System (AIS), the Ship Security Alert System (SSAS),[7] electronic seals for containers, biometric identification systems, and radio-frequency identification (RFID) (as control devices for tracking of goods and activities around cargo). Other features and measures included high-voltage fences and long-range acoustic devices to mitigate waterborne attacks. Some of these techniques have found their way into the everyday life of sailors and ship operators, where others still have a long way to go to be accepted as a valuable resource in the fight against maritime terrorism and other waterborne criminal threats such as piracy.

THE REALITIES OF ISPS CODE IMPLEMENTATION

Despite the introduction of the ISPS Code, the increase of security awareness and all the various regulations and tools available to "support" maritime entrepreneurs in their efforts to maintain a safe and secure operation, it must be concluded that dealing with security in a controlled and organized way still has insufficient priority in the shipping industry. Although other industries, for example, have adopted security management as an integral part of their quality management structures, the majority of the shipping industry still treats security management as a regulatory nuisance. Most ship owners and operators have performed the "tick-in-the-box" ISPS compliance exercise, without following up the initial investments with recurring processes of performing checks and making meaningful improvements to the system. For many, the ISPS Code became nothing more than a checklist with temporary priority; part of a string of other compliance projects that also needed to be completed to stay in business.

So where did it go wrong? It is important to understand that the reason why the implementation of the ISPS Code went relatively smoothly and quickly in the initial phase is also why the ISPS Code has not been very effective in mitigating security threats to the maritime industry. The ISPS Code provides a framework of requirements without stipulating specific standards for satisfying those requirements. Ships and port facilities must have security plans, security officers, and certain security equipment; but the code leaves it up to each individual government to provide the specifics. For example, the ISPS Code does not provide minimum standards for access control, perimeter control, electronic surveillance, guards, and communications. There are no mandatory guidelines for what constitutes perimeter security or mandated requirements to govern facility access controls. The ISPS Code does not even establish minimum training standards for becoming a "qualified" security officer.

Another downside of the ISPS Code in its current definition is that its requirements are only for SOLAS-class ships. Therefore, the requirements do not apply to warships, government vessels, fishing vessels, and ships weighing less than 500 t. These vessels, however, are found everywhere in the maritime environment, and therefore, also in areas where maritime terrorism is perceived to be a threat, such as Southeast Asia and the Persian Gulf. This situation results in gaps in the maritime security system that, in almost any other industrial setting, would not be considered acceptable. In recognition of this, in 2006, the IMO started addressing issues related to the security aspects of the operation of ships that do not fall within the scope of SOLAS chapter XI-2 and the ISPS Code, agreeing that non-SOLAS vessels shared the same operational environment as ISPS compliant ships, and that the operations of the former affect the security of the latter.[8] Although the IMO recognized that it was necessary to address the security aspects of the operation of non-SOLAS ships in a systematic and analytical manner, it stepped away from taking responsibility to correct what went wrong when the ISPS Code was initiated by agreeing that any guidelines developed were nonmandatory and that their application should once again be under the purview of the individual Contracting Governments concerned.

The International Chamber of Commerce's International Maritime Bureau (IMB) Director, Pottengal Mukundan, acknowledged this flaw when he stated:

> The ISPS code is a necessary first step in establishing a global maritime security framework, but it has to be recognized as only a baseline standard. Improving maritime security requires the active support, in the spirit and in the letter, of ship's crews and, perhaps more importantly, port authorities and shore-based personnel. We should aim for an environment that motivates all parties to actively participate. The code alone cannot defeat the challenges facing maritime security.[9]

However, rather than being merely a baseline standard, the ISPS Code was sold on the generally misleading premise that it would fundamentally address the threat of terrorism to the shipping industry. However, this was neither achieved nor was the regime able to support the shipping industry with other challenges it faces such as piracy and armed robbery, and human and narcotics trafficking at sea. Consequently, the ISPS Code carries the burden of having been forced on the industry whereas arguably conceived and implemented in haste, without providing instant tangible results with regard to improving the security of shipping. As a result, most shipping operators and port authorities have been reluctant to make major new investments in security or to build their security management structure on the basis provided by the initial implementation of the ISPS Code.

EFFECTIVENESS OF ISPS CODE MEASURES ON OTHER (NONTERRORIST) MARITIME THREATS

Many in the shipping industry today are convinced that the ISPS Code was designed only to counter terrorism. This no doubt accounts for today's skepticism voiced by many shipping companies, especially those operating in areas not historically prone to terrorism or piracy threats. Theoretically, however, compliance with the ISPS Code, or any other global security regulation, should at least reduce the risk of piracy and armed robbery at sea. Statistical evidence, for example, provided by the IMB Piracy Reporting Centre in Kuala Lumpur, does not indicate that this has been the case. The reporting center's statistics indicate that there has not been a dramatic decline in the number of pirate attacks since the new regulatory regime was implemented. This may support the skeptics in their criticism of the effectiveness of the ISPS Code, but more realistically it proves that sufficient efforts have not been taken to implement security management as an integral part of the shipping industry.

The ISPS Code itself, as a security management structure, is in fact ideally suited to help protect the ship, cargo, and crew against any unlawful act. However, for it to be effective, security management has to be dealt with in a similar way as most companies deal with quality management today. Security as a management tool needs a cyclical approach of planning, implementation, checking, and adjusting. For the ISPS Code, this means that it is essential for companies to evaluate and update their Ship Security Assessments (SSAs) and Ship Security Plans (SSPs) frequently to ensure the most cost-efficient and response-effective security system.

LOCAL MARITIME SECURITY INITIATIVES

In addition to the ISPS code, many other maritime security initiatives have been implemented; although some of the measures with a more global reach have already been mentioned, such as CSI, TAPA, US C-TPAT, and MTSA; a number of region-specific measures have also been introduced. One such initiative is the Australian Maritime Identification System (AMIS), which requires, among other things, that ships proposing to enter Australian ports provide comprehensive information including ship identity, crew, cargo, location, and course at 1000 nm from Australia's coast. Another is Combined Task Force 150, a joint naval unit that includes forces from the United States, Germany, France, and sometimes Britain and Italy that patrols off the coast of Somalia with the aim of reducing maritime threats such as piracy. However, one locale that has received by far the most attention and perhaps generated the most debate in terms of maritime security regimes or initiatives is the Strait of Malacca, a waterway of significant strategic importance given that over 60,000 vessels pass through the channel annually.

The waterway has been at the center of the maritime security debate for a number of reasons. First, it has historically been exploited by a number of criminal elements, including what is perceived to be one of the main threats to the security of international shipping—piracy. At its peak in 2000, there were 75 actual and attempted pirate attacks in the Strait of Malacca.[10] The waterway and the vessels that transit it are also at potential risk of attack from several terrorist groups that operate in the region, including the ASG and the Moro Islamic Liberation Front (MILF)—both of which are based in the Philippines—and JI, which primarily operates from Indonesia. Before signing a peace agreement with the Indonesian government in 2005, the Free Aceh Movement (GAM) was yet another group operating in the region. The Al-Qaeda network is also believed to have established a presence in Southeast Asia following the destruction of its bases in Afghanistan. All of these groups are known to use the maritime environment for logistical purposes. These groups have developed a maritime capability or have made preliminary steps toward acquiring capability in this area.

In addition, either through statements or past activities, all of these groups have displayed an interest in attacking economic or maritime targets.

The second reason for the Strait of Malacca to attract so much attention in the debate on maritime security is that a host of different parties have an interest in or a claim over the waterway: from the three littoral states of Indonesia, Malaysia, and Singapore, whose territorial waters make up the majority of the strait, to the so-called "user states," whose trade is dependent on the safe and unimpeded passage of shipping through the strait, as well as international powers such as the United States, whose main concern is to eradicate international terrorism.

These two factors have given rise to a situation where on the one hand, there is a need for the implementation of maritime security measures to guard against the various threats that the vessels face while transiting the straits, and on the other hand, an unwillingness to agree on what exactly needs to be implemented and whose responsibility it is to implement it. The result is foot-dragging, political inertia, and the implementation of inadequate symbolic measures, which do little to address the problems at hand.

In this context, various initiatives have been introduced with the aim of enhancing the security of the Strait of Malacca. The first of these was the introduction of the Trilateral Coordinated Patrol in 2004, which involved the navies of Malaysia, Indonesia, and Singapore patrolling in a coordinated fashion in their respective territorial waters. Following the introduction of this new measure, there was, however, no significant reduction in the total number of incidents of piracy in the region in the second half of 2004. The main problem with this new measure is that there was lack of a provision for cross-border pursuit into each of the participating states' territorial waters; cross-border pursuit across territorial boundaries was not considered an option during the formulation of this measure because it would have been viewed by the participating states as an infringement of their sovereignty.

Another measure, introduced in September 2005, by the littoral states, with Thailand as an observer, was the program of joint air patrols over the strait. Each of the three states donated two planes for the patrols, which have been dubbed as the Eyes in the Sky plan. It was envisioned that the aerial patrols would provide a valuable supplement to the trilateral coordinated sea patrols because under this initiative, the aircraft are permitted to fly up to 3 Nmi inside the territorial waters of the participating states. In the trilateral coordinated sea patrols, the navies are limited to patrolling in their own territorial waters. In the political context, Eyes in the Sky was important for one particular reason, which was spelt out by the Malaysian Defense Minister Najib Razak at the launch of the initiative "Hopefully this will send a very strong message to the international community that we are serious about maintaining the security of the Malacca Strait."

Although the implementation of this measure was a significant achievement for the littoral states, in that it signaled a new willingness to overcome, at least partially, the sensitive issue of sovereignty, the Eyes in the Sky plan could be criticized as being superficial and perhaps, a reflection of the desire of the littoral states to be seen as doing something. It is estimated that 70 sorties per week need to be carried out by the aerial patrols to effectively monitor the strait 24/7. However, currently only eight take place. There is also a lack of sea-patrol vessels available to carry out investigation and interdiction if necessary, following the sighting of a suspect vessel by the aerial patrols.

Encompassing the region as a whole, the Regional Cooperation Agreement on Anti-Piracy (ReCAAP) came into force in 2006. The agreement, which was drafted in 2004, required the signatures and ratification of ten of the participating countries to enter into force (participating countries include all ASEAN nations and Japan, China, Korea, India, Bangladesh, and Sri Lanka); its aim being to foster multilateral cooperation to combat the threat of piracy and armed robbery against ships in the region. A total of 14 countries have now signed and ratified the agreement, and an Information Sharing Centre (ISC) has been set up in Singapore to facilitate communication and information exchanges between the member countries.

Despite having been ratified by 14 of the participating states, the agreement has not yet been signed or ratified by Malaysia and Indonesia; the two countries have signaled a willingness to cooperate with the ISC, but till date, no progress has been made toward securing their formal acceptance of the agreement. The lack of participation by Malaysia and Indonesia casts doubt on the effectiveness of the agreement, particularly given Indonesia's status as the most pirate-prone country in the world, and both countries' strategic position along the Strait of Malacca.

DIFFERING PERSPECTIVES ON MARITIME SECURITY

In the aftermath of the September 11 attacks on the United States, many global and local regulatory authorities responded to the worldwide focus on security by beginning a process of securing their homelands, supply chains, and trade. What became clear from this flurry of activity in the maritime domain is that there are a number of differing perspectives on the issues surrounding maritime security, and as discussed earlier, this has become particularly evident in the context of security in the Strait of Malacca. Using the Strait of Malacca as an example, it is possible to analyze these differing perspectives and although the focus will be on this particular waterway, it is likely that these divergent perspectives are also reflected in other parts of the world.

Broadly speaking, three issues appear to trigger notable disagreement among the interested parties. First, the prioritization of maritime security measures; this points to the more specific question of to what extent is terrorism and piracy a threat to shipping in the waterway? Second, whose responsibility is it to implement the measures, which relates to the debate on "burden sharing?" Third, exactly how these measures should be implemented and in particular, what level of cooperation is necessary? The different perspectives taken in this debate reflect the various priorities, values, and concerns of each of the interested parties.

The numerous perspectives on the prioritization of security in relation to other issues of significance in the maritime domain were evident at a meeting convened by the IMO on 18–20 September 2006, in Kuala Lumpur, Malaysia. The event was titled Meeting on the Straits of Malacca and Singapore: Enhancing Safety, Security and Environmental Protection, and sought to "further discussions on the recent developments relating to safety, security, and environmental protection of the Straits of Malacca and Singapore with the aim of developing mechanisms and programmes to facilitate co-operation in keeping the straits safe and open to navigation, including the possible options for burden sharing."[11] Before the meeting, the three littoral states were asked to outline a number of projects for which they wished to seek cooperation, for implementation, from interested stakeholders.

However, none of the projects outlined were related to reducing the threat of piracy or maritime terrorism, which has dominated the security agenda and strategy of the United States since 9/11. All of the projects rather focused on enhancing safety and environmental protection in the straits. For example, one proposal was for the replacement and maintenance of aids to navigation in the straits, whereas the other was the removal of wrecks in the Traffic Separation Scheme (TSS) in the straits.[12] This underlines the perception of the littoral states, namely, Indonesia and Malaysia, that is, addressing the threats of piracy and maritime terrorism is of less priority than improving navigational safety in the straits and the protection of its marine resources. It also reflects the view of these states that the problems of piracy and terrorism are domestic issues, best mitigated by internal efforts, and under some circumstances, limited regional cooperation.

One particular development, which highlighted the divergent views on maritime security in the straits, particularly in terms of whose responsibility it is to secure the waterway, was the proposal of a Regional Maritime Security Initiative (RMSI) by the United States. Thomas B. Fargo, former Commander of the U.S. Pacific Command, introduced the RMSI in a speech to the U.S. Congress on March 31, 2004. In his speech, he remarked that "we're looking at things like high-speed vessels, putting Special Operations Forces on high-speed vessels to conduct effective interdiction in, once again, these sea lines of communication where terrorists are known to move about …"[13]

The announcement prompted a strong reaction from Indonesia and Malaysia, which saw the initiative as an attempt by the United States to internationalize security in the waterway. In response, Malaysian Prime Minister, Abdullah Ahmed Badawi, remarked "I think we can look after our own area,"[14] whereas Malaysian Deputy Prime Minister, Najib Tun Razak, said that the use of forces in Southeast Asia to fight terrorism would only serve to fuel Islamic fundamentalism.[15] Additionally, the former director general for political affairs in the Indonesian Ministry of Foreign Affairs stated that the deployment of foreign forces in Indonesia's territorial waters would run counter to "one of the basic principles on Indonesian foreign policy, the policy of nonalignment."[16] This sentiment was also reflected in a statement by the Indonesian Foreign Ministry spokesman, Marty Natalegawa, who stated "It is the sovereign responsibility and right of the coastal states of Indonesia and Malaysia to maintain safety and security of navigation in the Malacca Strait."[17] Although the United States subsequently claimed that the RMSI had been misrepresented and that it had no plans to place its forces in the waterway, the incident underlines the sometimes opposing views on who should maintain security in the waterway and the high priority the littoral states place on guarding their sovereignty.

Although the littoral states wish to limit the "internationalization" of the straits and will continue to prevent any direct participation in its maintenance by external powers, they do not wish to entirely shoulder the burden of the costs associated with this responsibility, particularly as it now includes securing the waterway against the threats of piracy and maritime terrorism, in addition to providing maritime safety and environmental protection. However, recent calls by the littoral states for "burden sharing" in the straits again led to a situation in which it could be argued that the United States attempted to "internationalize" security in the waterway. At a meeting in Jakarta in September 2005, cosponsored by the IMO and the Indonesian government, it was agreed that "a mechanism be established by the three littoral states to meet on a regular basis with user states, the shipping industry and others with an interest in keeping the Straits of Malacca and Singapore open for navigation."[18]

Despite the agreement made in Jakarta (the Jakarta Statement), before consulting the littoral states, the United States held a meeting of the user states[19] in Alameda, California on February 15–17, 2006 to "focus littoral assistance requests and to coordinate potential donor contributions to enhance safety, security, and environmental protection in the Straits of Malacca and Singapore."[20] As Sam Bateman points out in his article Burden Sharing in the Straits: Not So Straight Forward,[21] this move by the United States appears to disregard the Jakarta Statement in that it preempts the identification of areas in need of assistance by the littoral states and "allocates a leading role to the user states."[22]

Divergent national concerns and priorities also dictate the implementation of maritime security measures at the regional level, particularly when it comes to the level of cooperation that is acceptable. For example, the sea patrols in the straits have been limited to being coordinated patrols only, and not what is arguably a more effective method: joint patrols with a provision for cross-border pursuit. Another such example is that of ReCAAP, and the fact that the agreement has not been signed and ratified by Malaysia and Indonesia, despite the fact that they were among the 16 nations that launched the pact in 2004. According to media reports, the Indonesian government is determined to postpone ratification of ReCAAP because it believes it impinges on the sovereignty of the three littoral states that secure the Strait of Malacca.[23] However, the Malaysian government is reportedly concerned that the ISC is located in Singapore—a strong supporter of the agreement—whereas the long-established International Maritime Bureau's Piracy Reporting Centre (PRC), which provides a similar service, is situated in Kuala Lumpur.

CONCLUSION

Post 9/11, the ISPS Code—and to some extent, maritime security in general—continues to suffer from an image and acceptance problem. It is a problem that can be rectified, but to do so requires a much greater collective willingness to move security up the chain of management priorities. As the old saying goes, you only get out what you put in. If we really want to reap the benefits that improved standards of security management can bring, now is the time to take maritime security beyond merely a matter of regulatory compliance and the superficial implementation of inadequate measures. However, issues such as differing priorities and interests, concerns over the erosion of sovereignty and resource constraints will need to be overcome if this is to be achieved. Whether these factors will ever be completely surmounted or not is doubtful given the continued failure of some of the interested parties, namely, the United States, to recognize the sensitivities involved when it comes to securing the maritime domain.

How easily and efficiently our endeavors can be assessed and reassessed to enable them to remain focused on the current pressing issues is another criterion for sucessfully securing the maritime domain. Despite concerns that it was only a matter of time before terrorists carried out an attack on international shipping on the scale of 9/11, this threat is yet to materialize. Meanwhile, piracy, the illegal trafficking of drugs, arms, and people continue to take place. This highlights a need for more accurate understanding of the problems we face today; only then will it be possible for maritime security measures to become completely comprehensive.

NOTES

1. IMB Piracy Report 2004.
2. Ibid.
3. Container Security: Major Initiatives and Related International Developments, UNCTAD/SDTE/TLB/2004/1, UNCTAD, February 26, 2004, pp. 33–34, at http://www.unctad.org/en/docs/sdtetlb20041_en.pdf.
4. Øivin Lorentzen, Classification news no.3—ISPS implementation close to 90 percent, but more needs to be done, at DNV website, September 1, 2004 at http://www.dnv.co.uk/publications/classification_news/class_news_3_2004/ISPSimplementationcloseto90percentbutmoreneedstobedone.asp.
5. IMB Statement on Cargo Security International website—September 23, 2004.
6. UNCTAD report UNCTAD/SDTE/TLB/2007/1—March 14, 2007.
7. The use of SSAS was enforced as an integral part of the ISPS Code implementation.
8. IMO Maritime Safety Committee (MSC), 82nd session, November 29 to December 8, 2006.
9. Statement issued by the IMB on September 22, 2004.
10. IMB Piracy Report 2000.
11. Kuala Lumpur Statement on Enhancement of Safety, Security and Environmental Protection in the Straits of Malacca and Singapore, September 20, 2006 at http://www.imo.org/includes/blastDataOnly.asp/data_id%3D15677/kualalumpurstatement.pdf.
12. IMO Press Briefing at http://www.imo.org/.
13. David Rosenberg, Dire Straits: Competing Security Priorities in the South China Sea, April 13, 2005 at http://www.zmag.org/content/showarticle.cfm?ItemID=7632.
14. Sudha Ramachandran, Divisions over terror threat in Malacca Straits, *Asia Times*, June 16, 2004 at http://www.atimes.com/atimes/Southeast_Asia/FF16Ae01.html.
15. Ibid.
16. Ibid.
17. Indonesia joins Malaysia in shunning U.S. help in Malacca Straits, *Associated Press Newswires*, April 12, 2004.
18. IMO Press release at www.imo.org, January 16, 2006.
19. Australia, Japan, Republic of Korea, United Kingdom, Germany, the Netherlands, India, Norway and the Philippines.
20. http://naha.usconsulate.gov/wwwh-20060417a.html.
21. Sam Bateman, Burden Sharing in the Straits: Not So Straight Forward, RSIS, March 20, 2006.
22. Ibid.
23. Indonesia determined to postpone ratification of Malacca Strait pact, *BBC Monitoring Asia Pacific*, September 27, 2006.

2 Lifeline or Pipedream? Origins, Purposes, and Benefits of Automatic Identification System, Long-Range Identification and Tracking, and Maritime Domain Awareness

Martin N. Murphy

CONTENTS

The sea is a restless realm. This restlessness is timeless—the action of wind and waves that can lead to shipwreck; ancient—the direct threat of pirates and more indirect threat from other maritime criminals ranging from smugglers to the perpetrators of hull frauds that put mariners' lives at risk; and very modern—the threat of terrorism that has been felt acutely since the events of September 11, 2001. President George W. Bush claimed that these events changed the world; they did not change the world but the reaction to them did.[1] This reaction has had a profound and continuing impact in the maritime domain.[2]

This chapter focuses on the Automatic Identification System (AIS) and Long-Range Identification and Tracking (LRIT) and explores how they contribute to the concept of "Maritime Domain Awareness (MDA)", which is an attempt by a limited number of states, the United States, Canada and Australia in particular, to gain a greater understanding of the threats (criminal and political), which exist in their coastal waters or might enter them from the vastness of the deep ocean. The scheme is complex and definitions of its purpose, and expectations about what can be achieved cost-effectively, change regularly. To succeed in its broad aim of building an intelligible picture of threats at sea that is clear and accurate enough for action to be taken demands that several substantial technical and procedural problems be overcome. The peculiar American temptation to place too much emphasis on technical solutions, which in this case would translate into an overdependence on surveillance at the expense of intelligence, needs to be checked.[3] However, the scale of the project and difficulties that it faces illustrate the immense challenges posed by the ever changing and multiple character of illicit maritime activity.[4]

AUTOMATIC IDENTIFICATION SYSTEM: WHAT IS IT?

In 2000, the International Maritime Organization (IMO) adopted a new Regulation 19 as part of a revised chapter V of the Safety of Life at Sea Convention (SOLAS).[5] This required all ships over 300 gross registered tons (GRT), or that carried 12 or more passengers on international voyages, to install an AIS to enhance ship safety.[6] Although it was envisaged initially as a Vessel Traffic Services (VTS) aid, the enhancement of safety and then security quickly became its main roles.[7] Traditional watch-keeping methods including visual observation; the use of audible warnings such as foghorns, bridge-to-bridge Very High Frequency (VHF) radio communications; and radar (including the Automatic Radar Plotting Aid [ARPA]) have all improved over the years but still suffer from three limitations: first, they are not always able to identify another vessel positively; second, even if the vessel is identified, problems often arise when attempts are made to contact the vessel quickly; and, third, radar suffers from time delays and other target discrimination problems. As narrow waters became more crowded, these issues, when taken together, meant that the chances of accidents when ships were maneuvering had increased.[8]

AUTOMATIC IDENTIFICATION SYSTEM: TECHNICAL FEATURES

The AIS signal is transmitted at intervals that vary according to a ship's maneuvering status within 2 seconds when it is exceeding 23 knots and changing course, to 3 minutes when it is at anchor.[9] Signals in this interval range transmit what is called "dynamic" information:

- Maritime Mobile Service Identity (MMSI) unique number
- Navigation status, for example, "at anchor"
- Rate of turn—port or starboard, 0–720°/ minute (where available)
- Speed over ground—0.1 knot resolution from 0 to 102 knots
- Position accuracy and integrity status
- Longitude and latitude to 1/10,000 minute
- Course over ground—relative to true north to 0.1°
- True heading—0–359°
- Time stamp—based on coordinated universal time (UTC), otherwise known as "Zulu" time, accurate to nearest second
- Optional—angle of heel, pitch, and roll (where available)

Additional (static) data is transmitted every 6 minutes (or on request):

- IMO number
- International radio call sign

- Vessel name
- Ship type
- Ship's dimensions to nearest meter
- Ship's draft from 0.1 to 25.5 m
- Location of positioning system's antenna on board the vessel
- Type of positioning system, for example, Global Positioning System (GPS), Differential Global Positioning System (DGPS), or long-range navigation (LORAN-C)
- Hazardous cargo (as required by the competent authority)
- Destination based on UTC time (at master's discretion)
- Optional—route plan (way points)[10]

Although every AIS unit includes a global navigation satellite system (GNSS) receiver, which is generally based on GPS, for synchronization and time-mapping purposes, positioning data is drawn from the ship's own GPS and other variable data from the ship's other equipment. Such data, including name and destination, is entered manually using a small keypad which is a Minimum Keypad Device or MKD. Information received from other stations, such as other vessel positions to aid maneuvering and names and radio call signs to expedite communication, can be displayed on a screen or chart plotter.

The signal is broadcast autonomously and continuously; any ship or a shore-based station with the appropriate equipment can pick it up: "everybody sees everybody". Coverage is similar to any other digital VHF signal and likewise affected by antenna height and signal propagation. The ranges at which the signal is usually regarded as effective between ships and from ship to shore are 20 miles (37 km) and 40 miles (74 km), respectively. If atmospheric conditions are favorable for the phenomenon known as 'atmospheric ducting' to occur, signals can be received at 50 miles (93 km) and in some cases considerably more.[11] Shore and ship-based equipment can also retransmit data received and therefore "daisy chains" can form whereby signals are propagated at even greater distances.

The AIS standard is divided into two classes: class A for use on SOLAS chapter V vessels and class B, a less expensive, less powerful version for non-SOLAS vessels and leisure craft.[12] Currently installation of AIS on non-SOLAS vessels is not mandatory; although in some jurisdictions, such as the United States, it is under active consideration. It is a matter of concern that when ships are close together in ports the AIS signals might merge and become hard to distinguish. As far as terrestrial receivers are concerned, these fears are largely but not completely unfounded. First, the system uses two radio channels to avoid interference. Second, it uses Self-Organized Time Division Multiple Access (SOTDMA) multiplexing technology, which drives the different transmission intervals; ships maneuvering at speed present a greater potential hazard than those at anchor and therefore transmit information on their position more frequently.[13] Third, there are 2250 time slots established on each frequency every 60 seconds.[14] Each AIS station synchronizes itself to other stations continuously to avoid transmission overlaps, such that when a station changes its randomized slot selection, it announces the change to other stations.[15] This means that as soon as a vessel comes within range, its signal will be received. Lastly, the IMO standard demands a minimum of 2000 time slots per minute, but the system provides 4500 time slots. By means of time sharing, the SOTDMA technology allows the system to be overloaded by up to 500 percent and still provides almost full functionality between ships up to 10 miles apart leaving only the ships further away, which are of less immediate interest from a safety perspective, to "drop out".[16] In practice, however, the number of drop outs or incidents "when the AIS signals from two or more ships cancel each other out" are unknown but might be numerous, possibly as a direct result of the technology's self-organizing nature. For example, "if two ships are out of range of each other but are entering the coverage of a third from opposite directions, it is possible for them to choose the same time slot. When this happens the signals from both ships are lost."[17] Moreover the class B system, which does not use SOTDMA and therefore has a significantly smaller capacity because it does not share transmission slots, might well become overwhelmed in locations where hundreds of leisure craft can be concentrated, such as the Solent in England and Long Island Sound in the United States.[18]

AUTOMATIC IDENTIFICATION SYSTEM: THE ADVANTAGES

AIS enhances maritime safety by providing all ship and shore stations with details of the position, course, and speed of all other AIS-equipped vessels within range. It facilitates more rapid and precise communication between stations in cases of emergency and can provide warning of rocks and shoals (although it generally does not do so currently). Information exchange is simplified because the need for voice communication is reduced through the use of short, safety-related messages in free text form and binary messages that follow a defined purpose and structure.[19] Furthermore, it has improved the ability of VTS centers to monitor and manage traffic flows.[20] It is anticipated that as mariners and port authorities become more experienced, and if confidence in the system's abilities grows, it will contribute to a wider range of tasks including search and rescue (SAR); real-time weather and oceanographic information provision; fisheries supervision; environmental response; piracy warnings; commercial fleet management; and the supply of port service such as pilotage, tugs, bunkering, and berth allocation.[21]

AUTOMATIC IDENTIFICATION SYSTEM: THE DISADVANTAGES

AIS has the following seven disadvantages:

1. It is a local signal, that is, unless it is repeated, it can only be received within a radius of 20 miles, although this can increase significantly when atmospheric conditions are favorable.
2. Not all vessels are equipped with AIS, therefore the system may not be able to identify all contacts.
3. The signal is broadcast and open to anyone with an appropriate receiver. These cost no more than a few hundred dollars and their wide availability has led to concerns that pirates or terrorists could monitor transmissions to select or track targets. It is undoubtedly a risk. However, although there has been some suspicion that this might have taken place off Nigeria, incidents have not been confirmed there or anywhere else. Nonetheless, the possibility has led a significant number of masters (including those working for major shipping lines) to exercise their right to turn off their AIS equipment when traveling through piracy-prone areas or anchored in ports where they feel threatened.[22] Over and above this specific concern, somewhat more widespread misgivings have arisen as a consequence of the maritime industry's traditional reticence and need for discretion. There are sound reasons why carriers of all types wish to maintain commercial confidentiality, particularly when ships are operating in "spot" markets, even though there is no evidence that the use of AIS has influenced prices.[23]
4. Because equipment may not be maintained as well as it should be, transmitted information can be inaccurate and, because some of the basic information provided by each ship is entered manually via the awkward MKD, errors and even deliberate misinformation can enter the system.[24] Poor equipment installation, including antenna shrouding, and poor training, have also led to problems.[25] Additional examples recorded by Lloyd's Maritime Intelligence Unit (Lloyd's MIU) include:
   • Various cases of AIS equipment on vessels configured either deliberately or accidentally with false MMSI and IMO numbers and vessel names
   • The "bound for" voyage data field left empty or completed using incorrect or false information such as "hell" or "home"
   • Two vessels from the same owner, each transmitting the same identity[26]

   AIS is not formally policed, but conscientious coast guards do monitor errors and carry out inspections if these are not corrected. Although there has been some improvement in input quality and discipline, IMO polls show that the problem is nevertheless continuing.[27] The system, in other words, can be "spoofed" and there is a growing recognition that AIS information cannot always be relied upon.[28]

5. Errors are transmitted to all ships; avoiding such errors demands close adherence to procedures.[29]
6. AIS may contribute to the information overload that affects bridge teams more generally.[30] Radar needs to remain the basis of collision avoidance. However, it suffers from a number of drawbacks: ARPA data and maneuver detection can be slow; accuracy can be limited and degraded further by sea clutter and weather conditions;[31] detection can be masked by shore features and proximity; the center of the radar reflection might not coincide with the center of the target; tracked targets can be lost due to clutter, maneuver speed, and "target swap".[32] ARPA and AIS should work together to compensate for their respective drawbacks.[33] The concern, however, is that if the radar plot is cluttered with additional AIS information, the watch keepers can become overly dependent on it or confused.[34] If the AIS system displays an incorrect heading, for example, as it can do when ships have had the wrong heading offset data set during installation or are using older equipment, then problems can arise that can have potentially serious consequences.[35] Errors in AIS data and incorrect use of the equipment have given rise to a new type of collision risk, the "way-point collision", which has already resulted in an accident.[36] Training is required in the use of AIS, and especially AIS and ARPA together, to ensure that the correct procedures are followed.[37]
7. Finally, outside the perimeters of ports, AIS coverage is limited to the coasts of Europe and parts of North America, but is patchy elsewhere and in some places frequencies are shared with nonmaritime users (a problem that exists in some parts of the United States where the same frequencies are used by taxi companies).

LONG-RANGE IDENTIFICATION AND TRACKING: WHY HAS IT COME ABOUT?

AIS is a local system with restricted range. The 9/11 attacks on the United States gave rise to concerns that ships could be sailed into ports and detonated or explosive devices (or components) could be imported hidden among innocent cargo. To guard against such eventualities, security and law enforcement agencies need to know in advance not only what ships are due to enter port and what they are carrying but also to observe their progress. To gain the maximum warning, and also identify possible suspect vessels, this surveillance would need to be global and effectively continuous. Although the AIS signal is detailed and transmitted effectively on a continuous basis, when stations are transiting in oceanic spaces, it cannot be picked up readily and utilized by shore-based security centers. Consequently, in the aftermath of 9/11, the United States passed the Maritime Transportation Security Act (MTSA) of 2002, which authorized the development and implementation of port security and vessel tracking measures. In the same year, the United States proposed that the IMO adopt similar measures. In response, the IMO proposed the International Ship and Port Facility Security (ISPS) code and LRIT initiatives, although there has been no link between the two since then (except that port facility and ship security officers are responsible to ensure that LRIT works correctly).

In May 2006, the IMO's Maritime Safety Committee (81st session) adopted the amendments to the SOLAS convention necessary to make LRIT a reality.[38] Reaching this point was, however, technically, legally, and politically very difficult and there is no guarantee that the remaining difficulties will be ultimately resolved.[39]

LONG-RANGE IDENTIFICATION AND TRACKING: WHAT IS IT?

LRIT is intended to provide reliable and persistent global surveillance of maritime traffic for the purposes of detecting, identifying, and classifying vessels.[40] It is not a modified version of AIS. There can be no connectivity between the two systems. AIS is an open system whereas LRIT is a closed system designed solely for security.

LONG-RANGE IDENTIFICATION AND TRACKING: TECHNICAL FEATURES

The IMO learnt from its experience with AIS that if LRIT was to work, it needed to be designed differently. In particular, the system had to be satellite–based, could not be an open broadcast network, information distribution needed to be restricted and existing equipment had to be used rather than new equipment to enable ship owners to forgo additional expense and staff training.

Since 1999, all SOLAS vessels have had to be fitted with a satellite terminal. The decision was taken to make LRIT functionally compatible with Inmarsat-C (a low data-rate device with an automatic location reporting facility included) because it is fitted to all SOLAS ships to satisfy the Global Maritime Distress Safety System (GMDSS) requirement. LRIT is also compatible with Inmarsat Mini-C and D+, but other, non-Inmarsat equipment can also be used provided it can transmit the four reports that are required every day and be remotely configurable.

LRIT equipment onboard ship transmits a very restricted range of information every six hours: the ship's identity, position, and date and time of position. It was decided originally to include the ship's course and speed but this requirement was eventually rejected as being of little value as both could change immediately before, during, or after transmissions. In 2008, consideration was given to increasing the reporting interval to 12 hours in the interests of economy. However, although the USCG has expressed the opinion that this reduction would have "little, if any, adverse impact on the maritime domain awareness benefits to be derived from LRIT," it could degrade significantly the ability of agencies to conduct effective "track analysis."[41] Additional information requirements can be added in the future.

The basic reporting interval of six hours can be increased to every 15 minutes using Inmarsat SOLAS equipment and up to every 2 minutes with Inmarsat non-SOLAS equipment. Increases may be called for if a security incident occurs in a specific area and a more detailed surveillance picture is required. The design requirement that all such reconfigurations had to be done remotely is therefore vital. The equipment, for example, can be "polled" to ascertain the ship's position instantly. This means that to eliminate the problems of human error that affects AIS, ships' crews cannot alter settings or input information. However, masters do have the right to silence LRIT transmissions in high-risk areas; although if a ship is in danger it is more likely that the data flow would be frozen at the data center ashore rather than by turning off the onboard device.[42]

Unlike AIS, LRIT is a point-to-point signal and is therefore secure from all but state-sponsored interception. The signal from the ship to the shore-based data center is not encrypted but as per the standard Inmarsat protocol it is transmitted in random packets. Although final decisions are yet to be taken, data-exchange ashore is likely to be based on public key (128 bit) encryption making it as secure as any other commercially encoded information.[43]

The relevant SOLAS regulation (chapter V/19-1) came into force on January 1, 2008. The system was usable and available from anywhere in the world from then on. However, not all SOLAS vessels will be required to transmit information immediately; different categories of vessels will be introduced at different stages starting on December 31, 2008. Inmarsat is a geosynchronous network providing surface coverage between 76° N and 76° S. As the polar ice cover shrinks, this lack of cover will become an issue; the Russian polar route is already open and the Northwest Passage looks as if it might open in the near future, although heavy commercial usage is not thought to be likely. If coverage is required in the polar regions, then Low-Earth Orbiting (LEO) satellites, with identity and position reporting systems such as ORBCOMM, or communications satellites that have been adapted for this purpose, such as Iridium, will be needed.[44]

Ship-tracking capabilities have been included in Inmarsat-C since its inception in 1991. Although several suppliers are now interested in becoming involved, LRIT has essentially been built on the basis of this capability. Looking into the future, there has been talk of increasing the number of ships providing LRIT reports, but this would require that the Inmarsat equipment be upgraded to Enhanced Pre-assigned Data Reporting (EPADR) standard. Inmarsat-C is currently a random-access system. To increase efficiency, transmission slots would need to be preassigned. If the Time Division Multiple Access (TDMA) system of EPADR were to be chosen, efficiency could theoretically increase to 100 percent.

LONG-RANGE IDENTIFICATION AND TRACKING: WHO BENEFITS?

Flag, port, and coastal states benefit from LRIT; the benefits to shipping, however, are not so apparent. Nonetheless, the commercial shipping sector realized that the 9/11 attacks changed perceptions of terrorism in the United States and, in particular, induced feelings of vulnerability that it had not felt earlier in its history. Aircraft and ships are no longer seen as benign tools for transportation, commerce, and leisure but also as potential weapons. The industry recognized that it was better to cooperate willingly with the new security measures that were introduced rather than incur the difficulties and costs of an imposed regime.

For its part, the IMO recognized that if LRIT was to be adopted quickly, the commercial sector could not be expected to pay for the equipment or the service; shipping companies would not be given access to LRIT data and would therefore derive no advantage from it. The information would be paid for by the countries' national maritime administrations as and when they used it. The original estimate was that each transmission would cost around 25 cents (excluding overheads such as the International Data Exchange [IDE] and LRIT coordinator), that is, $1 per ship per day at the minimum six hourly reporting schedule but by 2008 that estimate had risen to between 30 and 35 cents for each transmission resulting in a daily cost of between $1.20 and $1.40 per ship per day.[45] However, a number of countries have yet to accept this arrangement.

LONG-RANGE IDENTIFICATION AND TRACKING: INFORMATION FLOWS

All the obstacles that have delayed, and may ultimately circumscribe, the introduction of LRIT involve questions of sovereignty and the assertion of jurisdiction beyond the territorial seas. The original idea was that a single, global data center would handle all information sharing, billing, security, and administrative tasks. However, LRIT operates when ships are in international waters yet the United Nations Convention on the Law of the Sea (UNCLOS) guarantees the right of free navigation in all sea areas outside territorial waters. Therefore, there is a concern that coastal states could use LRIT to demand ships provide information that could undermine this right. Although the United States had reservations about the procedures proposed for the international coordination of the system, several countries, including China and Russia, were unwilling to allow data on their ships to be handled centrally or made accessible to other states without limitation. The system was therefore redesigned based on the idea of National Data Centers (NDC) that would release data to an International Data Exchange (IDE) on a strictly regulated basis. Some countries then balked at the cost of building their own national centers and instead moved to the idea of regional (RDC) or cooperative (CDC) data centers but this threw up the additional complication of countries that were unwilling to participate in these alternatives and would only work through an International Data Center (IDC). The intention is that an IDE will facilitate Web-based data flows among these various centers, although its precise remit and how it will work remains the subject of discussion.

The fundamental problem is who pays? Ships and ship owners do not pay for providing the data. Only those countries that request LRIT data will pay for it and so far only the United States and Australia have declared that they will. However, if very few countries want to use and pay for the data, then this will generate insufficient income to pay for the IDE, IDC (if it is ever established), and for International Maritime Satellite Organization (IMSO) to carry out its IMO-mandated coordination role.[46]

LONG-RANGE IDENTIFICATION AND TRACKING: INFORMATION MECHANISMS

Only states receive LRIT information:

- Flag states can receive information about ships on their registers wherever they are.
- Port states can receive information about a ship once it declares it will visit a port in that state.
- Coastal states can receive information about all ships within 1000 NM of their coastlines.[47]

Furthermore, all states are entitled to receive information when a SAR incident occurs (although this is a potential loophole that needs to be monitored and acceptable practice established).

Currently, LRIT is not generating data. A small number of national reporting systems exist such as the Russian Federation's "Victoria" vessel monitoring system, Australian "AUSREP", US Coast Guard (USCG)-sponsored "AMVER", and the Republic of Korea Ship Reporting System. In addition, commercial vessel-tracking systems used by shipping companies and some flag state authorities, such as Pole Star's "Purplefinder", have been operational for many years.[48] If LRIT is to function as intended, the national responses from the Contracting Governments (CGs) that are signatories to SOLAS will need to be coordinated to handle the estimated minimum 73 million ship reports that will be generated every year based on the coverage agreed currently. This will demand that the IDE be fully tested and declared ready by then. An initial system trial, based on the Marshall Islands' register, was conducted and the results, which were reported to the COMSAR 11 meeting in February 2007, showed an 83 percent success rate; although issues were experienced with older equipment, the most serious of which was system not responding (SNR) when stations could not be identified by an Inmarsat Land Earth Station Operator (LESO).[49]

Each flag state will decide to which national, regional, cooperative, or international data center their ships should report. Each ship will report through a communications service provider (CSP) that will forward the data to an Applications Service Provider (ASP). The data does not have to be routed through Inmarsat-C exclusively; ASPs are talking to ship owners about using other onboard terminals such as the Ship Security Alert System (SSAS), much of which is built around Inmarsat's Mini-C system. ASPs will generally be commercial suppliers; the assumption is that there will be around ten or so when the system is launched but this number will reduce over time. The ASPs will manage and add to the basic LRIT data received from ships and integrate it with ship-specific information, such as reconciling the terminal number with the ship's IMO or Lloyd's number, before forwarding it to the data center chosen by the ship's national administration. The data center will distribute clean and complete information on request to

- The flag state on a routine basis
- The port state that asks for information about a ship once it declares its intention to enter its control area
- The coastal state that is entitled to information on any ship passing within 1,000 nautical miles of its coast providing that ship is not within the territorial waters of another state.

If the data center does not have the information asked for, it will ask the IDE to obtain it from the data center or centers that have it. A data distribution plan will be set up and maintained by the IMO secretariat to regulate the data exchange process. The IDE will also act as an auditable cutout to ensure privacy. However, it is still unclear whether the final arrangement will be an integrated global system or one that operates as a series of linked regional systems.

Progress has been marked by public shows of confidence and behind the scenes disagreements about how LRIT should operate and be paid for. The IMO Maritime Security Committee meeting which took place in Copenhagen in October 2007 agreed that LRIT should proceed but in a modified form. No agreement was reached, however, on the establishment of the IDC, which meant that states that had planned to route their data through this center will have to conclude arrangements with alternative regional or national centers. Funding for the IDE was also not agreed; consequently the United States offered to fund, host, and run the IDE on a temporary and interim basis for two years until a permanent IDE could be established. In addition, no start-up funding for the IMSO to carry out its audit and review responsibilities was agreed, although a number of countries offered to provide some money. Therefore, although it remains likely that LRIT will be realized, the flow of data will be considerably more complicated than was envisaged originally and the volume that will be bought and exchanged between contracting governments, and thus the system's long-term financial viability, remains unclear.[50]

These uncertainties were carried over to the Maritime Security Committee meeting 84 held in London in May 2008 at which the reluctance of many of the Contracting Governments, influenced in some cases by commercial interests, to pay for a comprehensive system became so apparent that the viability of the project as a whole was brought into question. Even though the Contracting Governments continued to support the role of a coordinator in principle, several states branded the proposed costs as unaffordable and indicated that they may be prepared to opt out. This opposition was not counterbalanced by a demonstrable enthusiasm from other states such as the United States and Australia, and the EU, even though the United States has announced its intention to require all U.S. ships, and all ships entered U.S. ports, to report their position using LRIT from January 2009. However, if sufficient states continue to oppose the introduction of LRIT on the basis proposed currently, it is difficult to see how the United States (and the small number of other interested states) could enforce its implementation without causing massive disruption to the global maritime trading system. Any steps they took would, furthermore, fall outside the IMO environment and be driven solely by national legislation. The willingness of these states to force the issue is likely to be tempered by their ability to track ships of concern using existing "national-technical" means. Therefore, although it would be premature to write off LRIT, it is encountering difficulties that could undermine the supervisory aspects of its operational concept, which if not addressed might enable ships engaged in illicit activity to transfer their registrations to flag states that had refused to participate, thereby making surveillance of their movements more difficult.

LONG-RANGE IDENTIFICATION AND TRACKING: THE DISADVANTAGES

Reports will not include a ship's previous sailing history, an omission that is regarded as a serious disadvantage if a comprehensive risk assessment is the desired outcome. A state can refuse a request for information about its own flag vessels.[51] Although the assumption is that most administrations will cooperate when it comes to information requests, this is not guaranteed where states are at odds.[52] Once the information has been released, there is nothing that a state can do to prevent the recipient from sharing the information with its allies on an informal basis. More fundamentally, LRIT (and AIS Class A) only applies to SOLAS vessels. The vast majority of vessels are excluded, and so far it is the small vessels that have been maritime terrorists' weapons of choice.

LRIT is intended to fill in the huge gap between areas of AIS coverage. The information it will provide has been deliberately restricted. This information will cost money and may not, in the end, be available at all if the system proves economically unviable. To overcome these concerns, Transport Canada and the USCG have looked at capturing the more comprehensive and "free-to-air" AIS data on a larger scale. The first step the USCG has taken is to install a network of AIS receivers on National Oceanic and Atmospheric Administration (NOAA) weather buoys at sea, on its own cutters and aircraft, and on other vessels.[53] The second step involves, merchant vessels, which as discussed transmit and receive AIS data constantly. Consequently, the USCG has held discussions with Maersk Line about capturing this data via satellite link and streaming the signals to a data center such that a picture can be built up of shipping, on a worldwide basis if necessary, based on the signals collected its ships during the normal course of business.[54]

AIS signals are essentially VHF transmissions and as such also propagate vertically. Norway has published a number of papers on the subject and launched an experimental satellite to demonstrate the feasibility of satellite-based capture. The USCG has worked on a more ambitious program with the satellite operator ORBCOMM to develop what would be, in effect, a parallel LRIT system.[55] The intention is that it will use more than 30 LEO satellites to "grab" AIS transmissions from the approximately 60,000 ships fitted with the equipment currently. Even when ships are concentrated in ports, the Doppler effect would permit signal discrimination. Polarization effects can also provide a further check. A USCG test satellite is due to be launched during 2008.[56] If this proves successful, six ORBCOMM satellites fitted with the appropriate transponders will follow.[57] A potential limitation is that shipboard AIS equipment and antenna are not optimized for satellite transmission. The United States has applied to the International Telecommunications Union (ITU) for an additional frequency specifically for this purpose but this request has not yet been granted. If it is then all AIS equipment installed currently will need to be modified.

MARITIME DOMAIN AWARENESS

AIS and LRIT furnish states with surveillance data. They can help to deliver what has been called the "primary component" in vessel monitoring, a ship's geospatial track or position.[58] They can also identify them positively, which radar alone cannot do. Up to a point, analysts can use "anomalies resulting from comparison of vessel tracks to historical tracks of similar vessels" to help assess risks.[59] Track and pattern analysis are useful analytical tools; however, in reality, there are a multitude of legitimate reasons why merchant vessels deviate from planned tracks, speed up or slow down, or even make unscheduled port calls.[60] Navigational changes can be instigated for a number of reasons such as sheltering from adverse weather conditions, bunker replenishment, mechanical difficulties, medical emergencies, or changes in chartering particulars. What surveillance systems cannot do is to put the data they generate into context. They cannot, in other words, reveal purpose or intention. It is this recognition that has driven interest in the development of MDA.[61]

The term itself is not new. It was coined in the late 1990s by the USCG, well before the current security concerns came to the fore. MDA was a way of describing a concept that brought together SAR activity, law enforcement, and environmental response planning.[62] The aim from the outset was to construct what is called a "common operating picture" (sometimes described as a "user-defined operating picture"), that is, a real-time understanding of what is happening on the water. Shorn of its new name, MDA is something navies and coast guards have done for a long time. During the Cold War, navies focused on finding and tracking Soviet merchant and naval vessels, particularly submarines.[63] Coast guard and maritime police forces had a parallel focus on tracking criminal activity at sea, particularly drug smuggling. In both cases, MDA has had two elements: first, situational awareness; second, finding out what the "blips" on the screen were, what they were doing, and why they were there. Since 9/11, the concept has been expanded hugely to include potentially all ship and boat movements. This expansion has been driven by the fear that terrorists could use almost any ship to mount attacks or carry supplies necessary for an operation or attack ashore. It is also recognized that any illegal activity at sea has, or could have, security implications.[64] This expansion has been accompanied by the temptation to collect more and more data, in other words, to be aware rather than to be informed.

MDA that seeks to take account of all vessel movements in a given area, certainly one that aims to track vessel movements globally, depends largely on ships and flag states supplying the correct information and complying with their reporting obligations. True intentions, however, can be masked and the situational picture can be confused by deception achieved by spoofing or provision of inaccurate information. To take an actual example, a vessel, that left a port transmitting one AIS identity but after a short while changed its identity was found, on inspection, to have two AIS transmitters which the master was switching between. GPS equipment can also be manipulated to send out false signals. Basic information such as names of ships and other data can be changed and the precise ownership of ships (the "beneficial owner") can be veiled, a practice that is both common and perfectly legal under certain registries.[65] States may be able to enforce sanctions against noncompliance; however, in the case of AIS, this is complicated by the fact that the equipment is not tamperproof and both AIS and some types of LRIT equipment can be transferred to other ships.[66] There are reasons to believe that purposeful deceptions have been carried out by North Korean and Chinese ships, and by Vietnamese ships possibly under Chinese ownership.[67] More generally, masters can and do silence AIS if they believe the transmissions expose their ships to any danger. Even in congested shipping lanes, the Strait of Malacca in particular, many ships (including those owned or managed by major shipping lines) make the passage with their AIS turned off. Even then there is no absolute way a receiver can tell whether a master has turned the ship's equipment off deliberately or if the signal has suffered from a lack of range or some other transmission inconsistency.

Consequently, MDA needs to be layered if it is to be effective. As with port and cargo security measures, such as ISPS or the Container Security Initiative (CSI), the different elements need to overlap. Wherever possible, AIS should be supplemented by other technical means of monitoring and surveillance, the most common of which is radar. If a ship sailing with its AIS silenced is detected visually or by radar, this would obviously be grounds for suspicion. Where radar coverage is patchy or nonexistent, such suspicious activity is unlikely to be detected. In the face of evidence that criminal organizations and some intelligence services are actively involved in the development of "spoofing" techniques, some states, Canada in particular, are investing in geospatial imaging technology, which can provide them with surveillance that is independent of ship's transit data. As with all forms of satellite-based imagery, this is not an exact science and the necessary analysis is manpower intensive and time consuming.

Ships that are being used for illicit purposes can avoid detection by not entering jurisdictions that enforce reporting requirements. If uncovering illicit intentions depends on identifying anomalies, then it is possible that ships can remain undetected by abiding by the rules. Deception can only be overcome by the use of reliable intelligence. Surveillance can provide useful information but it is only truly effective once observers know what they are looking for. It may be possible to locate every ship on the ocean but it is impossible, using surveillance alone, to know which one might pose a security threat. The *Nisha* incident is a case in point.

The MV *Nisha* aroused suspicion because it made port calls in Djibouti and Eritrea. The U.K. authorities then tracked the ship from the Indian Ocean on the suspicion that it was being used to transport Weapons of Mass Destruction (WMD) materials. Once it reached U.K. territorial waters, it was boarded and searched. No suspicious material was found. Subsequent inquiries showed that the ship's movement pattern, which was one of the primary indicators that had aroused concern in the first place, was not, in fact, abnormal.[68] As the draft of the U.S. MDA technology roadmap made clear: "A robust, effective international HUMINT (human intelligence) network is a critical component for successful maritime domain awareness efforts, and cannot be overemphasized."[69] The scale of the task means that it is hard to see how it can be achieved successfully without the close involvement of the commercial sector, given the labryinthine nature of this industry.

Therefore, there is dual challenge for MDA: first, because the threat spectrum is more widespread, analysts need to look beyond the traditional information sources to the broad range of open source maritime information—reports from the Lloyd's Agents Network, information from flag states, customs administrations, and signal intercepts.[70] Second, to transform the "common operating picture" from the one that is specific to one agency, as it has been in the past, to one that can be shared at an unclassified level with allies, other agencies, and the commercial sector. This will require solutions for substantial interoperability, regulatory, and legal problems. It will also demand that the instinct to withhold rather than to share information, something that is ingrained deeply within the military and intelligence communities, is relaxed.

The hope is that by "fusing" various data sources, unknown contacts can be sorted from the known, which will, in turn, trigger an alert.[71] In the U.S. context, Guy Thomas has suggested that this is not an insurmountable task.[72] As of 2003, the U.S. customs service's Air and Marine Interdiction

Coordination Center was investigating an average of 2900 anomalous tracks everyday. Careful analysis cleared most of them but some still required an aircraft or boat to be sent for investigation.[73] Since then, the intention has moved beyond the surveillance of North American waters to achieve what is known as "global maritime intelligence integration." However, the size of the oceans means that the scale of the investment required to cover them using technical methods is beyond the means of a single country.[74] Coupled to this is the recognition that the sheer volume of the potential contacts means that, in all likelihood, detailed MDA will be achieved only in areas of critical interest, for example, "hub" ports, sections of vital sea lanes, chokepoints such as the Straits of Dover or Malacca, and sea areas such as the Gulf of Guinea and Horn of Africa where security concerns are currently high.[75]

LIFELINE OR PIPEDREAM?

For most part, merchant vessels do not move in controlled channels and according to fixed parameters in the way that credit card transactions, telecommunications traffic, and aircraft do. Some ships, particularly large container vessels in the liner trades and those fulfilling long-term commodity supply charters, however, do follow established sea-lanes and follow more predictable patterns. However, the suggestion that if a ship deviates from a recognized "motion" pattern it must be doing so for a good business reason that the owner or charterer is willing to reveal, and if one is lacking then the ship must be up to no good, verges on the simplistic.[76] While AIS, LRIT, and MDA all appear to offer surety and reliability, this is at odds with the turbulence and changeability of the sea and the people who use it.

Unquestionably, all three offer benefits to seafarers; if a ship gets into trouble, there is a much better chance that SAR services will know where they are, although in many places this will not necessarily mean that the possibility of help will increase. It will also mean that ships that abide by the rules are more likely to have their port arrivals and departures expedited efficiently whereas those that do not will be delayed. Coast guards and security officials will also have a much better idea of what ships are entering or passing through their territorial waters. If port and fleet managers are granted access to LRIT data, it will give them a tool that will enable them to manage traffic flows more effectively.

From the mariner's point of view, however, there is an inherent contradiction between the emphasis the ISPS Code places on information confidentiality and the "free-to-air" openness of AIS.[77] AIS was initially and specifically designed as an aid to safe navigation and collision avoidance. It was not designed to be an aid to maritime security. Yet, this is what it has increasingly become for those states that are looking to fulfill or bolster their surveillance needs. LRIT was designed to fill the transoceanic security gap. In both cases, mariners are being asked to surrender their traditional anonymity, which often remains their first line of defense. The claim that 'the innocent have nothing to hide' is a false dichotomy. Reluctance to provide information is not contingent on guilt but on the desire for privacy or autonomy. At the heart of the issue is the matter of trust: Can mariners be sure that the information they supply will be treated with discretion and respect? Can maritime authorities be sure that the information mariners supply is truthful and accurate? Although no awareness program will work without an element of compulsion, it cannot work effectively without a clear recognition by all parties that there are benefits to be shared.[78] This is the point at which mariners' concerns can become acute. If anonymity is to be stripped away, then coastal authorities in particular must accept greater responsibility for transiting or inbound vessel protection by providing additional patrols and the resources needed to investigate unidentified targets.[79]

Surveillance and data fusion, which together produce greater awareness, are the first two stages in a four-stage process that culminates in decision and action.[80] Many states, including states in the developed world, have not invested enough in the decision-making process and not provided sufficient boats, aircraft, and personnel to conduct comprehensive maritime security operations effectively.[81] As in so many towns and cities where money has been spent on closed circuit television systems, the investment in surveillance technology has not been matched by more cops on the beat.

Moreover, the hope that states might have been prepared to rein in their political differences in pursuit of a common interest in the suppression of criminal or terrorist activity, appears to have been impeded in some parts of the world such as the Baltic and North Pacific by the reappearance of what might be termed "Cold War" attitudes however muted.

ACKNOWLEDGMENTS

The author would like to thank the interviewees—several of whom wished to remain anonymous— who generously gave their time during the preparation of this chapter. The author would like to mention Dana A. Goward and his team at USCG headquarters in particular. All opinions, errors, and omissions are the author's own.

NOTES

1. Louise Richardson. 2006. *What Terrorists Want: Understanding the Enemy, Containing the Threat.* New York: Random House, p. 167.
2. Martin N. Murphy. 2007. *Contemporary Piracy and Maritime Terrorism.* Adelphi Paper No. 388. Abingdon and New York: Routledge for the International Institute of Strategic Studies.
3. Defence Research and Development Canada has made the point that: "Understanding an SRS (Self-Reporting System such as AIS or LRIT) is less about physics and engineering than it is about social psychology, public relations and law. In short, there is a strong human element to SRS. Security centres should respond by hiring or developing more expertise in these areas." Tim Hammond *et al.* 2006. The implications of self-reporting systems for maritimedomain awareness. Defence R&D Canada—Atlantic. Technical Memorandum, 2006–2232, December, p. iii. http://pubs.drdc.gc.ca/inbasket/hammond.061031_1017.TM%202006-232.pdf.
4. Murphy. *Contemporary Piracy and Maritime Terrorism*, p. 74.
5. IMO. "Automatic Identification System," available at http://www.imo.org/dynamic/mainframe.asp?topic_id=754; USCG Navigation Center. "AIS Overview," available at http://www.navcen.uscg.gov/enav/ais/default.htm.
6. The limitation for ships on domestic voyages is 500 GRT.
7. Andy Norris. 2007. "AIS implementation—success or failure?" *The Journal of Navigation*, 60(1), January, 2.
8. Brian Tetreault. 2006. "Automatic identification system; the use of AIS in support of maritime domain awareness." *US Coast Guard Proceedings*, Fall, p. 27; Wikipedia. "Automatic Identification System," available at http://en.wikipedia.org/wiki/Automatic_Identification_System.
9. Tetreault. 2006. "Automatic Identification System," p. 28.
10. Bernhard Berking. 2003. "Potential and benefits of AIS to ships and maritime administrations." *WMU Journal of Maritime Affairs*, 2(1), April, 63; M.J. Lewandowski and D.J. Pietraszewski. 2002. "Automatic Identification System: A General Discussion of Development, Application, and Implementation." Paper prepared for the USCG Research & Development Center Project 2410.5—Vessel Traffic Management Research, June, pp. 2–3, available at http://www.rdc.uscg.gov/iws/pubs/ais-paper.pdf; USCG Navigation Center. "What AIS Broadcasts," available at http://www.navcen.uscg.gov/enav/ais/what_AIS_broadcasts.htm.
11. William R.Cairns. 2005. "AIS and long range identification & tracking." *The Journal of Navigation*, 58(2), May, 187; interview with LMIU representative, August 2007. Ranges of up to 100 NM (185 km) are achieved regularly in the Persian Gulf and up to 200 NM (370 km) have been achieved in U.K. waters. Interview with DSTL official, September 2007. The USCG reports reception at 220 NM (407 km). "Satellite AIS from USCG." *Digital Ship*, April 2007, p. 26 at http://www.uscg.mil/nais/documents/Article1-APR07.pdf. This phenomenon is known as "atmospheric ducting."
12. Lewandowski and Pietraszewski. "Automatic Identification System: A General Discussion of Development, Application, and Implementation," p. 2; USCG Navigation Center. "How AIS Works," available at http://www.navcen.uscg.gov/enav/ais/how_AIS_works.htm. For more detail on "Class B" see USCG Navigation Center. "Types of AIS," available at http://www.navcen.uscg.gov/enav/ais/types_of_AIS.htm.
13. For background on why this system was chosen see Norris. 2007. "AIS implementation—success or failure?" p. 3.

14. Class B will update data less frequently.
15. Lewandowski and Pietraszewski. "Automatic Identification System: A General Discussion of Development, Application, and Implementation," pp. 2, 4.
16. USCG Navigation Center. "How AIS Works."
17. David Wilson-Le-Moine. "Vessel tracking technologies and their role in the fight against global terrorism." *Presentation to the SMi 'Maritime Security' Conference*, London, February 22–23, 2006.
18. Craig Eason. 2006. "Freedom and security: the dilemma of vessel tracking." *Lloyd's List*, April 21. Available from *SecurityInfoWatch.com*, April 28, 2006, at http://www.securityinfowatch.com/article/article.jsp?siteSection=386&id=7983.
19. Berking. 2003. "Potential and benefits of AIS to ships and maritime administrations," pp. 64–68.
20. Berking. 2003. "Potential and benefits of AIS to ships and maritime administrations," pp. 61–62; on VTS see IMO. "Vehicle Traffic Services," available at http://www.imo.org/Safety/mainframe.asp?topic_id=387 and USCG Navigation Center. "Vehicle Traffic Services," available at http://www.navcen.uscg.gov/mwv/vts/vts_home.htm.
21. Berking. 2003. "Potential and benefits of AIS to ships and maritime administrations," p. 75; Lewandowski and Pietraszewski. "Automatic Identification System: A General Discussion of Development, Application, and Implementation," pp. 4, 10.
22. The IMO guidelines admit that although use of the equipment is mandatory it "might, under certain circumstances, be switched off on the master's professional judgement." IMO. "Guidelines for the Onboard Operational Use of Shipboard AIS," pp. 6–9. According to Robert Allan, who conducted research in 2004, 19 percent of masters definitely turn off their AIS equipment in piracy-prone areas and 47 percent have considered doing so. Robert H. Allan. 2005. "Automatic Identification System: Research from the Bridge," available at http://www.nautinst.org/ais/docs/researchFromBridge.doc. Peter Lehr has suggested that the likelihood of pirates monitoring AIS transmissions is low overall and that only highly organized pirate gangs intent on hijacking whole ships would derive any benefit from such activity. Peter Lehr. 2006. "AIS, pirates and maritime terrorists: how real is the threat?" *Seaways*, June, p. 9.
23. Matt Hilburn. *Broader Picture. Sea Power.* Vol. 50, No. 12, December 2007, p. 33.
24. The IMO itself warns that "the accuracy of AIS information received is only as good as the accuracy of the AIS information transmitted." IMO. "Guidelines for the Onboard Operational Use of Shipboard AIS," p. 9. Also David Patraiko. 2004. "AIS: Operator Feedback Analysed." *Seaways*, October, p. 5.
25. Eason. "Freedom and security: the dilemma of vessel tracking"; Norris. "AIS implementation—success or failure?" pp. 4, 6.
26. Interview with Julio Espin, Managing Director, Lloyd's LMIU, June 2007.
27. Confidential interview with maritime official, July 2007.
28. Hammond et al. 2006. "The implications of self-reporting systems for maritime domain awareness," p. 17. "Reliability of ship-identification system in doubt." *Tradewinds*, September 7, 2007. Steve Carmel, senior vice president, maritime services for Maersk Line has suggested that "upwards of 30 percent" of AIS data is wrong. Hilburn. *Broader Picture*, p. 33.
29. Berking. "Potential and benefits of AIS to ships and maritime administrations," pp. 63–64.
30. "Navigation–A bridge too far?" 2006. *Fairplay*, December 7.
31. Depending on frequency, pulse repetition rate and beam width radar will often achieve only a positional accuracy of 30–50 m; AIS aims to achieve a positional accuracy of 10 m when linked to DGNSS signals. Radar is affected particularly badly by heavy rain or snow. International Association of Lighthouse Authorities (IALA). 2002. VTS Manual. 4.2.3.2, Positional accuracy, p. 51.
32. A close association between radar and AIS had been shown to prevent "target" or "track" swap. International Association of Lighthouse Authorities (IALA). *Guidelines on AIS*, Volume 1, Part I (Operational Issues) Ed. 1.1 4.1.4.2 Improved Vessel Tracking, p. 24.
33. For a detailed review of these issues, see Berking. "Potential and benefits of AIS to ships and maritime administrations," pp. 69–73. The radars, moreover, had to be designed specifically to work with AIS. Norris. "AIS implementation—success or failure?," p. 7.
34. The risk of confusion was revealed in early tests. Lewandowski and Pietraszewski. "Automatic Identification System: A General Discussion of Development, Application, and Implementation," p. 5; for a thorough exposition of the problems, see Norris. "AIS implementation—success or failure?," pp. 4–6.
35. Edmund Hadnett. 2005. "AIS at the Front Line: The View from the Bridge 'One Year On'." *The Journal of Navigation*, 58(2), May, 192–193; "AIS: Operator Feedback Analysed."
36. Confidential interview with maritime official, July 2007; also see Eason. "Freedom and security: the dilemma of vessel tracking."

37. Hadnett. "AIS at the Front Line: The View from the Bridge 'One Year On'," p. 195; Eason. "Freedom and security: the dilemma of vessel tracking;" Norris. "AIS Implementation—Success or Failure?," p. 4 where he makes the point that many ship-owners were under the impression that AIS was a "fix-and-forget" system, pp. 6–7, 9.

38. William R. Cairns. 2006. "Keeping Watch: The new SOLAS regulation on long-range identification and tracking." *US Coast Guard Proceedings*, Fall, p. 35. "Shipping nations agree satellite tracking rules." *Reuters*, May 19, 2006. The relevant IMO Resolutions are 202 (81), 210 (81), and 211 (81).

39. Confidential interview with maritime official, July 2007.

40. Cairns. "AIS and Long Range Identification & Tracking," p. 182. Also IMO "Long range identification and tracking," at http://www.imo.org/Safety/mainframe.asp?topic_id=905.

41. Alice Lipowicz. "Coast Guard plans data center to monitor vessels." Washington Technology, May 1, 2008.

42. Amendments to the International Convention on Safety of Life at Sea, 1974. As amended. Chapter V, Paragraph 7.2. (MSC 81/25/Add.1. Annex 2, p. 4).

43. Confidential interview with maritime official, July 2007.

44. Neville Smith. 2007. "Iridium gains authorisation for LRIT service provision." *Lloyd's List*, March 23; "Bright future for Iridium." 2007. *Fairplay*, February 1.

45. IMO. "LRIT-Related Matters: Billing Issues." MSC 83/6/5, July 2, 2007.

46. The IMSO manages a number of public service communication programs through Inmarsat satellites. See http://www.imso.org/public/whatis.htm.

47. Differences arose over whether coastal states had the right to monitor the movements of vessels passing their coasts if they were sailing in international waters. Hugh O'Mahony. 2006. "Debate still rages over coastal state monitoring." *Lloyd's List*, May 12. These differences have now been resolved. "Shipping nations agree satellite tracking rules." 2006. *Reuters.com*, May 19, available at http://today.reuters.com/News/CrisesArticle.aspx?storyId=L1928035.

48. Cairns. 2006. "Keeping Watch," p. 37. For AUSREP, see http://www.amsa.gov.au/Shipping_Safety/AUSREP/AUSREP_system/; for AMVER, see http://www.amver.com/ and Hammond et al. 2006. "The Implications of Self-Reporting Systems for Maritime Domain Awareness," p. 8; for Pole Star, see http://www.polestarglobal.com/index.html.

49. IMO. "Development of an E-Navigation Strategy." COMSAR 11/14/4, December 22, 2006.

50. IMO Resolution 210 (81) (May 19, 2006) Annex 13. "Performance Standards and Functional Requirements for the Long-Range Identification and Tracking of Ships."

51. Amendments to the International Convention on Safety of Life at Sea, 1974. As amended. Chapter V, Paragraph 9.1. (MSC 81/25/Add.1. Annex 2, p. 5).

52. "A loophole big enough to sail through." 2006. *Fairplay*, July 20.

53. Cairns. "AIS and Long Range Identification & Tracking," pp. 186–188.

54. Hilburn. *Broader Picture*, pp. 32–34.

55. Ibid., p. 188–189.

56. Stew Magnuson and Breanne Wagner. 'Satellite to demonstrate maritime surveillance for Coast Guard.' *National Defense*, January 2008 at http://www.nationaldefensemagazine.org/issues/2008/January/SecurityBeat.htm.

57. "A loophole big enough to sail through," loc. cit.; "Satellite AIS from USCG," loc. cit.; "Orbcomm sat with USCG AIS will launch in 2007." *Micom Monitoring Post*, February 11, 2007 at http://mt-milcom.blogspot.com/2007/02/orbcomm-sat-with-uscg-ais-will-launch.html.

58. George Vance and Paulo Vicente. 2006. "Maritime Domain Awareness: A Structure to Enhance Maritime Decision Making." *US Coast Guard Proceedings*, Fall, p. 7.

59. Ibid.

60. "Long range lunacy." 2007. *Fairplay*, February 1.

61. It is important to note that the U.S. Navy's concept of MDA is much broader than the one described here. Although the Navy defines it as achieving an effective understanding of anything that could affect the security of the United States from the maritime domain, it makes it clear that it is more about building security partnerships than vessel tracking. Office of the Chief of Naval Operations. "Navy Maritime Domain Awareness Concept," 2007 available at http://www.navy.mil/navydata/cno/Navy_Maritime_Domain_Awareness_Concept_FINAL_2007.pdf.

62. Jason Sherman. 2005. "Domain Defense." *Sea Power*, Vol. 48, No. 5, available at http://www.navyleague.org/sea_power/may_05_20.php.

63. For the analogies between MDA and military "battlespace awareness," see Hammond et al. 2006. "The Implications of Self-Reporting Systems for Maritime Domain Awareness," p. 1.

64. "The National Strategy for Maritime Security." 2005. pp. 16–17; David W. Munns. 2006. "121,000 Tracks." *Sea Power*, Vol. 48, No. 7, July.

65. Stew Magnuson. 2006. "Mesh of technologies to provide maritime safety net." *National Defense*, August, available at http://www.nationaldefensemagazine.org/issues/2006/August/MeshofTechnolog.htm.

66. "A loophole big enough to sail through," loc. cit.

67. Interview with maritime official, July 2007.

68. "Terror alert as police seize cargo ship." 2001. *BBC News*, December 21, available at http://news.bbc.co.uk/onthisday/hi/dates/stories/december/21/newsid_2539000/2539557.stm; John Steele. 2001. "Security alert as Channel ship is seized." *Daily Telegraph*, December 22, available at http://www.telegraph.co.uk/news/main.jhtml?xml=/news/2001/12/22/nship22.xml; Martin Bright, Nick Harris and Nick Paton Walsh. 2001. "Hunt for 20 terror ships." *The Observer*, December 23, available at http://observer.guardian.co.uk/international/story/0,6903,624196,00.html.

69. Magnuson. "Mesh of technologies to provide maritime safety net."

70. Sherman. "Domain Defense."

71. Magnuson. "Mesh of technologies to provide maritime safety net."

72. Bobby Junker, a senior official with the Office of Naval Research appeared to contradict this when he said "there is too much data for human intelligence analysts to evaluate and detect potential threats in the maritime domain" and that one particular challenge is "to figure out how to spot 'anomalous behaviour' at sea." Zachary M. Peterson. 'ONR official: Sensors needed to monitor ocean.' *Navy Times*, 2nd August 2007 at http://www.navytimes.com/news/2007/08/navy_maritime_domainawareness_070801w/.

73. Guy Thomas. 2003. "A Maritime Traffic-Tracking System: Cornerstone of Maritime Homeland Defense." *Naval War College Review*, Autumn.

74. "The National Strategy for Maritime Security." 2005, op. cit., p. 16.

75. Michael Bruno. 2006. "US maritime awareness a 'vulnerability'." *Aerospace Daily & Defense Report*, May 16.

76. Kendra E. Moore "Pirates Patterns, and Other Passions." *DARPATech*, August 9–11, 2005, available at http://www.darpa.mil/DARPATech2005/presentations/ixo/moore.pdf.

77. Steven Jones. 2006. *Maritime Security: A Practical Guide*. London: The Nautical Institute, p. 210.

78. Hammond et al. 2006. "The Implications of Self-Reporting Systems for Maritime Domain Awareness," pp. 13–15, 17.

79. Hadnett. "AIS at the Front Line: The View from the Bridge 'One Year On'," p. 196.

80. Thomas. "A Maritime Traffic-Tracking System."

81. Paul Mitchell. 2005. "Network-centric Management of Maritime Security." Institute of Defence and Strategic Studies Commentary, December 30, available at http://www.rsis.edu.sg/publications/Perspective/IDSS942005.pdf.

3 Maritime Forces and Security of Merchant Shipping in the Mediterranean Sea and Northern Indian Ocean

Russell Pegg

CONTENTS

INTRODUCTION

For centuries, the navies and coast guards of nations have been patrolling territorial and international waters to ensure freedom and protect the vital interests of their maritime borders. Today, when 95 percent of the world commerce travels by sea and many (both individuals and organized groups) seek to exploit potential weaknesses in national security, the role of traditional maritime forces has changed to a more constabulary nature; to what extent can a commercial enterprise rely on such support and how can it be called for? This chapter aims to inform the reader as to what assistance may be available and the expected capabilities that may be offered by military and coast guard agencies. In doing so, the chapter discusses some of the background of naval operations and deployments intended to instill greater maritime security in the areas in which they are present; examine some examples of international Maritime Security Operations (MSO) in the Mediterranean

Sea, Red Sea, Arabian Sea, and Arabian Gulf, and comment on the ways in which the efforts of navies and merchant seafarers are complementary, reinforcing, and interdependent in the challenging task of ensuring greater maritime security for all stakeholders in specific maritime spaces.

Advice regarding how merchant seafarers and others within the shipping industry can exchange information with naval operations is provided, where applicable, in appropriate sections of the chapter.

BACKGROUND

The majority of commercial ship owners typically think about the interaction between naval forces and merchantmen only during times of increased tension or conflict (e.g., the Gulf War) with the emphasis being on either protection of shipping from an opposing force or deconfliction from operations by friendly forces. In the current climate of regional conflicts, with increased piracy and a plethora of illicit activities on the sea, there is an appetite for greater interaction and cooperation between legitimate civil and military maritime agencies for the common good.

Maritime security is fundamental to all we do; all mariners are stakeholders. This is a significant departure from the Cold War days when the military focus was on countering the strategic ballistic missile threat. Currently, the greatest threats to peace and stability are the asymmetric threat of terrorism and the destabilizing effects of organized crime, and in this regard, the global maritime highway is not exempt.

CLIMATE

The world has changed—the events of September 11, 2001 and those thereafter introduced a new threat that is yet to manifest itself on that scale in the maritime domain. The most serious maritime security threats today are asymmetric in nature. Although the conventional threat to a nation from opposed naval forces has declined, it is the indeterminate threats that pose the greatest risk to collective security, and in this regard, it is not just terrorism that we need to worry about. In addition to the traditional threats against maritime trade, there are threats to critical national infrastructure and energy supply lines too (bulk fuel carriers are included in this category) that have common boundaries with the maritime environment. For example, the opening of the Baku-Tbilisi-Ceyhan pipeline will add a significant number of crude oil tankers operating in the eastern Mediterranean—the effect of one of these vessels colliding with a key installation such as an oil or gas platform, or worse being deliberately targeted to cause maximum destruction and economic disruption, is unthinkable.

HORIZON

Unlike civil aviation, where the rules and regulations for global flights are protected by international protocols and ratified agreements, the maritime domain is largely unregulated by comparison. However, is this changing? The introduction of the automated identification system (AIS) and long-range identification and tracking (LRIT) may eventually lead to discussions regarding "sailing plans," which in reality is already being developed in some of the world's more congested waterways and busy ports.

Is it too far fetched to consider the ship's navigator filing a sailing plan 24 hours before departure and to wait for international clearance before sailing? Is it unreasonable for company security officers (CSOs) to contact regional maritime hubs (RMH) to initiate a communications link and check on conditions within their area of responsibility?

Economics alone dictates the importance of maritime security as shipping companies seek to move trade from one point to another by the most efficient and economical means possible, without the worry of interference along the way. In this environment, do navies and coast guards and marine police units have a growing role to play? The answer must be yes.

HOW CAN NAVIES HELP?

There are many good examples of where navies have supported the merchant community in times of conflict—convoy protection during the world wars, and later, during the conflict in the Arabian Gulf region. However, there have been far fewer incidences of this kind of support during peacetime. To provide a better understanding of where navies and military organizations can help, the North Atlantic Treaty Organization (NATO) offers a good example.

NAVAL COORDINATION AND GUIDANCE FOR SHIPPING

The Naval Coordination and Guidance for Shipping (NCAGS) organization operates under the guidance of a NATO document titled Allied Tactical Publication 2 (ATP 2), which is an easy-to-read manual that provides general plans, guidelines, and format for providing a service to both the merchant ships and the assigned naval commanders. ATP 2 provides plans for communications and procedural guidelines for ships at sea. For the mariner, it describes the processes for routing, passage, dispersal, emergency movements, and most importantly, for sending reports of position and intended movement (PIM). Similar to many other international guidelines, this document is written in general policy terms to allow variations in scope, specific tasking, and operational procedures. It is highly recommended to be maintained as a shipboard reference.

Although there is an NCAGS functional presence in many navies and various exercise locations from time to time, the NATO Shipping Centre (NSC) is the permanent organization that serves as the focal point. The NSC is colocated with the NATO Maritime Component Command (MCC) Northwood, England, and is tasked with establishing and maintaining links with the military, merchant shipping, National Shipping Authorities (NSA), and other international maritime agencies.

> The aim of the NATO Shipping Centre (NSC) is to provide improved information exchange on merchant shipping, and facilitate increased voluntary co-operation between military commanders and commercial shipping operators. The NSC will collect and process merchant shipping information, develop a surface picture of shipping in areas of interest, support military operational requirements, and advise shipping on the evolving situation.[1]

Normally, the NSC is the best conduit for merchant ship operators initiating communication between civil and military organizations for the purpose of increased cooperation and coordination. Unless otherwise informed through a national Notice to Mariners (NOTAMS) signal, which is part of the naval maritime domain operational process, NSC is the first point of contact that merchant ships can utilize. Serving as a collector and disseminator of issues related to maritime security, the NSC regularly receives "neighborhood watch" type of reports that it passes to the appropriate authorities for vetting and possible further action. In this sense, the NSC is similar to the IMB operations center for piracy, although its remit is not focused on piracy. If the situation warrants, there may be a broadcast message made, which informs mariners of a more appropriate point of contact.

If the maritime security situation warrants, NCAGS officers deploy to the responsible national navy and NATO MCCs, and possibly even to ports within the affected shipping area. In brief, these NCAGS organizational cells will provide adequate information to the naval commander to determine merchant ship locations for maintaining a Recognized Maritime Picture (RMP). During peacetime, most navy commands maintain an RMP as provided by locator data within the SOLAS-mandated Automated Identification System (AIS) radio transmissions. Here, it is important to recognize that in a time of conflict or maritime security threat, it is likely that the merchant ships will switch off their AIS transmitters for their own individual security. Until security-dedicated ship-tracking systems, which provide secure encrypted signals, are in place (e.g., LRIT), and the appropriate information release agreements are made, it becomes a very difficult and manually based task to maintain current plots of merchant ship traffic at sea for the maritime commanders. In such a scenario, there is a need for more direct communication with merchant ships and the associated workload dramatically increases. In essence, it is this additional workload that is the lion share of the NCAGS operational function, and one which the merchant community can greatly assist.

Beyond the procedures described in the ATP 2 handbook, NCAGS officers also provide advice to NATO naval commands on specific aspects of commercial maritime operations. The NCAGS organization speaks the language of both the navies and the merchant marine to provide a linkage for collaboration. For example, NCAGS is facilitating the bridge between the commercial maritime industry and NATO through the establishment of a NATO notification protocol for merchant ship security alerts (ship security alert system [SSAS]) and Global Maritime Distress Signals (GMDSS). Such interorganizational protocols are necessary so that, under such circumstances, NATO assets can render assistance in a rapid but appropriate manner that is completely integrated and coordinated with port and flag state authorities. This should be no different from the present reaction by navies and coast guards to a distress call relayed from a Maritime Rescue Coordination Center (RCC). In the interest of safety and security, it is vital that a close relationship is maintained between like-minded maritime centers.

The NCAGS organization can provide a credible account to naval commands as new operational authorities are assumed in reaction to evolving maritime security threats, provided a degree of separation and impartiality is maintained. This could also include international disaster response and recovery operations. It is within the NCAGS function to serve both the navies and the merchant marine. The NCAGS can help ensure that maritime information gathered for NATO naval commands remains focused on serving the safety and security of international maritime commerce and the environment. This is of course a common mission; however, a merchant navy-based influence can help remind naval commanders of specific details that may be overlooked in times of crisis.

For the seafarer, a security professional, or the government, the value of the NCAGS organization remains based on its evolving role in providing a recognized interface to both the navy and the merchant marine for increased security that shows tangible and measurable benefits to maritime commerce. Similar to many aspects of security, it may be another question that cannot be completely answered unless a given security situation deteriorates and the process can be completely tested.

As highlighted, ATP-2 is a publication, which provides ship owners, operators, masters, and watch-keeping officers with vital details regarding the interaction between naval forces and commercial shipping. In particular, the publication serves as a handbook for the worldwide application of NCAGS principles and procedures that exist to enhance the safety of shipping in times of peace and conflict. The complete ATP 2 document can be downloaded at http://shipping.manw.nato.int.

OPERATION ACTIVE ENDEAVOUR

Operation Active Endeavour (OAE) is NATO's Article V Operation in the Mediterranean established in 2001 to fight terrorism at sea. The NATO Maritime Commander in Naples oversees this operation to deter terrorism and contribute to the peace, stability, and security of all nations in the region. The operation is based on international law, and directly supports the United Nations Security Council Resolutions (UNSCR) against threats to international peace and security caused by terrorist acts. Specifically, Active Endeavour is now focused on the following four areas: It helps deter and disrupt any action supporting terrorism at or from sea; controls "chokepoints" (i.e., the most important passages and harbors within the Mediterranean Sea) by deploying mine-hunters from one of the standing NATO Mine Counter-Measures Groups to carry out preparatory route surveys; provides escorts for designated vessels through the Strait of Gibraltar when necessary; and enhances the ongoing Mediterranean Dialogue program and other NATO programs intended to promote bilateral and multilateral relations.

At all times, NATO units dedicated to OAE are patrolling the Mediterranean basin, collecting information and assessing the situation in their vicinity. They provide the visible presence and potential reaction forces that may respond rapidly if required. The merchant marine community is encouraged to engage with these forces to collectively enhance maritime security.

As a recognized Regional Maritime Hub (RMH) in the Mediterranean, Allied Forces Maritime Component Command HQ Naples (CC-MAR Naples) controls the operation from its highly sophisticated Maritime Operations Center, working round-the-clock with many nonmilitary regional organizations. This operations center has close ties and exchanges information with national agencies of many littoral countries. It can also act on any report fed to the NSC—a sister organization within the Allied Forces Maritime Component Command HQ Northwood (CC-MAR Northwood), which fulfills the same function for the Atlantic region.

Physical presence and interaction go a long way in maintaining security at sea. The Atlantic Ocean and Mediterranean Sea are patrolled by frigates and corvettes specifically dedicated to maritime security operations (MSO) by the NATO allies on a voluntary basis, and are supported by two maritime high readiness forces, if and when needed. In addition to these surface units, submarines provide complementary surveillance by providing discreet monitoring of specific areas to detect suspicious behavior, while Maritime Patrol Aircraft (MPA) provide wide-area coverage across the region using a variety of sensors to detect and classify vessels and other objects of interest.

MARITIME NEIGHBORHOOD WATCH

Everyday, merchant ships sailing the Atlantic and Mediterranean are "hailed" by patrolling NATO naval units and aircraft asking them to identify themselves and their activity. This information is then reported to the Maritime Operations Centers and the NSC in Northwood. If anything appears unusual or suspicious, teams of between 15 and 20 specially trained personnel may board the vessel to inspect documentation and cargo. If there is credible intelligence or strong evidence of any terrorist-related activity, further action may follow. The suspect vessel will then be shadowed until action is taken by a responsible agency, or it enters a country's territorial waters on the way to a port. If a vessel refuses to be boarded, NATO will take all necessary steps to ensure that it is inspected as soon as it enters any NATO country's territorial waters.

The NATO naval commander understands the needs of the merchant operator to maintain focus on the transportation mission without interruption or delay, however, there is benefit to be gained by the commercial operator if formal communication with naval and coast guard forces is established in the event of a security incident while underway. To this end, the RMHs work very closely with national authorities and directly with other naval and coast guard forces operating in the Atlantic and Mediterranean to enable this communication and enhance an appreciation of NATO's activity and purpose in these areas.

To support international interests better, it is vital the merchant community adopts an ethos of a Maritime Neighborhood Watch. Without active participation of all stakeholders, the maritime environment will never be safe from illicit behavior. Apart from reporting suspicious behavior, another area where the merchant marine community can support maritime security is through the voluntary reporting system.

OAE VOLUNTARY REPORTING SYSTEM

A number of nations have been asked to encourage their shipping authorities to voluntarily report the movement of their vessels. The sole purpose of voluntary reporting is simply that an appreciation of ship movement by military authorities reduces the time spent on hailing and conducting inspections at sea and in harbor. For example, merchant vessels reporting their movement 24 hours before passing through the Strait of Gibraltar or the Suez Canal are less likely to be hindered by the many military and coast guard vessels and airplanes operating elsewhere in the Mediterranean.

Reporting is on a voluntary basis, and can be achieved by using the following template and sending a fax, or by downloading a simple reporting program at http://shipping.manw.nato.int/ and e-mailing to info@shipping.nato.int.

FORMAT ALPHA/SHIP DATA CARD

Details should be sent 24 hours in advance. The NSC requests to be kept informed of ships movements and intended ports between Gibraltar and the Suez Canal. Timings should indicate the use of local or UTC/Zulu.

Ship data required

1. Ship's name
2. International call sign
3. IMO number
4. General nature of cargo

Voyage data required

1. Last port of call, departure date, and time
2. Current position, date, and time
3. Next port of call, arrival date, and time
4. Additional ports of call, dates, and times
5. Start canal transit, date, and time
6. Additional information as required

NATO SHIPPING CENTRE

If mariners encounter any suspicious activity in the Atlantic or Mediterranean Sea, it should be reported to the NSC at their toll-free number or via e-mail at shippingcentre@manw.nato.int.

OTHER ALLIED MSO TASK FORCES: CTF 150, 152, AND 158

Active Endeavour is perhaps the best known allied MSO; however, there are several other operations providing vital security for commercial shipping in specific strategic sea areas. The three most notable are the Combined Task Forces 150, 152, and 158 (otherwise known as CTF 150, CTF 152, and CTF 158). It is important to note that although many NATO countries have participated in all three, they are not NATO operations. Rather they are comprised of naval forces from countries that are active participants in the U.S.-led war on terrorism. Essentially, the mission of all three CTFs is to conduct MSO in their respective areas of responsibility (or battle spaces). In this context, MSO is defined as follows:

> Maritime Security Operations (MSO) set the conditions for security and stability in the maritime environment and complement the counter-terrorism and security efforts of regional nations. MSO deny illegal use of the maritime environment as a venue for attack or to transport personnel, weapons, or other material.[2]

The geographical areas of operation of the three CTFs are shown in the map (Figure 3.1).

The most immediate conclusion that can be drawn from the map is the strategic purpose of the three task groups; essentially they are deployed and tasked to ensure the security of the strategic sea

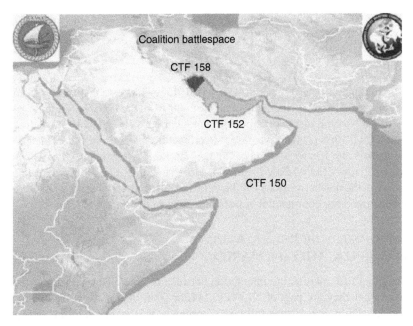

FIGURE 3.1 CTF geographical areas of operation. From http://www.royalnavy.mod.uk/server/show/nav.5561.

lanes of communication (SLOC) between the Mediterranean and the oil-producing regions of the Middle East, principally the Persian Gulf. Essentially, the intention is to ensure that sea trade and the flow of petroleum in the region is secure from any terrorist threats that might exist or have the potential to develop.

CTF 150

CTF 150, with its logistic hub at Djibouti, conducts MSO in the Gulf of Aden, Gulf of Oman, Arabian Sea, Red Sea, and in the northern half of the Indian Ocean. It is coordinated with, and incorporates vessels of, the U.S. Navy's Fifth Fleet. Like CTF 152 and 158, it is under the command of Combined Forces Maritime Component Commander/Commander U.S. Naval Forces Central Command in Bahrain. Essentially, it was established to monitor, interdict, and if necessary, board suspect vessels in support of the war on terrorism. Countries presently contributing to CTF-150 include Canada, France, Germany, Pakistan, the United Kingdom, and the United States. However, other nations that have participated include Australia, Italy, Netherlands, New Zealand, Portugal, Spain, and Turkey. The command of the task force, which usually consists of 14–15 warships and replenishment vessels, rotates between the various participating navies. Since its inception in 2002, CTF 150 has boarded numerous vessels, including dhows, fishing boats, and tankers in its area of responsibility, found and confiscated illicit drugs, and conducted antipiracy and cordon operation off the coast of Somalia.[3]

CTF 152

This multinational force, which was established in March 2004, conducts MSO in the south and central Arabian Gulf. Operating in the shipping lanes and littoral waters in the region, one of its main functions is to support the MSO of the navies of the Gulf Cooperation Council (GCC) nations[4] and complements their wider regional security efforts. The force's capabilities are significant, and it is frequently led by a U.S. Carrier Strike Group.[5]

CTF 158

The third of the international naval task groups—CTF-158—was established as a result of Operation Iraqi Freedom, and consists principally of naval assets from the U.S. Navy, the Royal Australian Navy, and the Royal Navy. It also works in close conjunction with elements of the Iraqi Navy and the Iraqi Marines. CTF-158's primary purpose is to protect Iraqi territorial waters and its offshore oil infrastructure; namely the Khawr al Amayah and Al-Basrah Oil terminals (KAAOT and ABOT), which are located south of the Al-Faw Peninsula. More generally, CTF-158 provides international maritime security in the northern reaches of the Persian Gulf, and in doing so offers greater security for the oil tankers and other commercial vessels operating in the area.[6]

Information Exchange in the Red Sea, Arabian Sea, and Arabian Gulf: U.K. MTO and MARLO

As stated throughout this chapter, the interaction between the merchant navy crews and the naval forces at sea (whether they are part of NATO's OAE or from one of the three coalition CTFs) is not merely encouraged by the various military commands, it is essential to the very purpose and success of these operations. In addition to the interfaces for NATO listed in this chapter, the United Kingdom and the United States have shore-based units dedicated to the exchange of information between merchant vessels and coalition forces in the regions encompassed by the three CTFs. The Royal Navy's U.K. Maritime Trade Operations (MTO), which was established in Dubai in October 2001, functions as an interface between vessels in the aforementioned region through its Merchant Vessel Voluntary Reporting Scheme.[7] Although the MTO's focus is ostensibly to support the U.K.-flagged vessels and U.K. commercial shipping in the area, it also provides support across the entire maritime industry for vessels of all registries and countries of ownership.[8]

Only on a voluntary basis, ships of any flag or ownership are invited to report to MTO on passing the following geographical points:

- Port of Suez for vessels entering or leaving the region via the Red Sea
- 5° S for vessels entering or leaving the region via the Indian Ocean
- 78° E for ships entering or leaving the region via the Indian Ocean

Using ukmtodubai@eim.ae, vessels are requested to pass on the following information:

- Ship's name
- IRCS
- Flag
- IMO number
- MMSI
- Inmarsat telephone number including satellite prefix
- Telex and fax number
- E-mail address
- Company having day-to-day management
- Type of ship
- Current position and speed
- Itinerary in the region with route way points and destination port(s)

MTO reciprocates by posting information for commercial mariners on its Web site. In the past, bulletins have included piracy and security warnings for the Horn of Africa, security sweep procedures for VLCCs loading at Al-Basrah Oil Terminal, medical emergency assistance information, and details of some of the MSO activities by the three CTFs that are of direct interest to merchant shipping in the region.

Maritime Liaison Office (MARLO), the U.S. equivalent of MTO, has a similar function to MTOs, and functions to facilitate the exchange of information between the U.S. Navy and the commercial shipping community in the U.S. Central Command's area of responsibility. MARLO, which is based in Bahrian, essentially serves as a source of information regarding safety and security of shipping in the region. MARLO is staffed by the U.S. Coast Guard, Navy, and civilian personnel, and can be accessed through its Web site, http://www.marlobahrain.org or e-mail at marlo.bahrain@marlobahrain.org.

The purpose and operations of OAE, the aforementioned CTFs, and U.K. MTO and MARLO are admittedly varied. Forces at sea, although focused on the provision of MSO, also have other military capabilities and functions. MTO and MARLO are information exchanges for maritime safety and security in specific waters. In times of peace and periods of fluctuating terrorist, piracy, and criminal risk, the value of all of these operations is clear. However, these forces, operations, and organizations also serve as examples of the kinds of operational effort and effect that would be in existence and available for the provision of MSO and shipping protection in times of more obvious conflict; for this reason, therefore, it is important that commercial seafarers be familiar with what they do, what they provide, and how to communicate with them.

SUMMARY

We all agree that there is a real twenty-first century threat—the maritime domain is yet to be a victim of a terrorist mass atrocity or high consequence attack. Navies and coast guards are, by design, transformational in nature; however, they can better assess and more rapidly respond to calls for help if the "information sharing" barriers are broken down. Many within the military have all been inculcated with the paradigm that information should only be shared with those who have a specific need to know. It is now time to change that paradigm for MSO to one where information is shared, unless there is a specific reason not to do so. Making this shift will require a significant change in both the military–and the civil organizational culture at all levels, from senior executives down to the deck hand. Navies and coast guards are there to help protect the freedom of the high seas and the integrity of territorial waters, but they cannot do so without direct interaction with the maritime community.

NOTES

1. ATP-2(B) Volume II: Naval Co-Operation And Guidance for Shipping Manual (NCAGS) http://www.shipping.nato.int/ATP2Bdownl/file/_WFS/atp-02%2528B%2529v02.pdf.
2. http://www.royalnavy.mod.uk/server/show/nav.5561.
3. http://en.wikipedia.org/wiki/Combined_Task_Force_150.
4. The GCC comprises of the kingdoms of Bahrain and Saudi Arabia, the sultanate of Oman, and the emirates of Kuwait, Qatar, and the United Arab Emirates.
5. http://www.royalnavy.mod.uk/server/show/nav.6482.
6. http://en.wikipedia.org/wiki/Combined_Task_Force_158.
7. http://www.rncom.mod.uk/uploadedFiles/RN/Maritime_Operations/0001-UKMTO.pdf.
8. Ibid.

4 Evolving U.S. Framework for Global Maritime Security from 9/11 to the 1000-ship Navy

Chris Rahman

CONTENTS

In the United States, the events of September 11, 2001, created an impetus for an urgent review of security procedures for ships, ports, and the global seaborne supply chain. In particular, the 9/11 attacks forced the U.S. authorities to reassess the ways in which America's irregular enemies, to conduct further catastrophic attacks against the American homeland, might exploit those elements of the international sea-based trading system. Indeed, Al-Qaeda has been explicit in its threats against not only the United States but also the entire U.S.-led international order. Al-Qaeda's strategy included targeting a presumed American vulnerability, the U.S. economy, which was a focal point for 9/11 mastermind, Khalid Sheikh Mohammed.[1] Attacks against the international economic system were thus viewed as one potential method of targeting the extant global order, including threats to close major sealanes.[2] At least in theory, this type of challenge to the *status quo* raises the stakes and creates a material interest in combating the terrorist threat for all states integrated into the globalized world economy. Nevertheless, clearly it is the United States that remains a primary target of Muslim extremist ire.[3] Coupled with its self-assumed, functional role as the guardian or "sheriff" of world order writ large,[4] Washington has, by seeming necessity, taken the lead both in responding to the 9/11 attack itself and in prosecuting the wider "war on terror," albeit with questionable results so far.

In the maritime sphere, the U.S. Navy's Cold War role of asserting sea control to protect the sea lines of communication connecting the continental United States with its dependent allies in Europe and Asia morphed at the close of that global conflict to the one of a benign preponderance at sea. This condition, which was at least implicitly accepted by most seagoing states at that time, provided a form of "general deterrence" against generic threats to international sea lanes;[5] or, more properly stated, threats to the security of shipping, as Eric Grove reminds us in this context, "one does not defend the sea" *per se.*[6]

The 9/11 attacks and the earlier efforts of Al-Qaeda painfully demonstrated the inability, however, of traditional deterrence mechanisms to prevent the depredations of strongly motivated terrorist groups and, potentially, revolutionary or "rogue" states employing unconventional forms of warfare such as terrorist attacks, even attacks involving the use of weapons of mass destruction (WMD).[7] Indeed, the efficacy of the entire Cold War-era deterrence framework has been called into question in a new security environment inhabited by a relatively unfamiliar (i.e., non-Russian and nonstate) array of adversaries.[8] This very concern, in fact, was one of the underlying drivers of the adoption of the doctrine of preemption—or more accurately stated in the case of Iraq, preventive war—in the *National Security Strategy of the United States of America*, September 2002, the formative strategic policy document of the post-9/11 period.[9]

The 2002 *National Security Strategy* became the umbrella document for further national security policy and strategy formulation, setting out the immediate strategic threats to America and its interests, and its national strategy for responding to these "new" threats of globalized terrorism, rogue states, and the proliferation of WMD. Subsequent documents set out the corresponding frameworks for, *inter alia*, security strategy, military strategy, homeland security, combating WMD proliferation, and the protection of critical infrastructure. The ongoing focus of this chapter is the American policy and strategy framework for security in the maritime domain and, in particular, how strategies formulated to improve the security of the American homeland have impacted maritime security considerations on a truly global scale. In so doing, special attention will be given to the implications of the U.S. Navy's proposed Global Maritime Partnership Initiative—or 1,000-ship Navy—concept,[10] which sets forth a vision of an informal international cooperative network of navies, coastguards, and other relevant agencies to enhance maritime domain awareness and maritime enforcement effectiveness against the spectre of terrorism and other nontraditional (i.e., nonmilitary) threats to safety and security at sea.

MARITIME TRANSPORTATION AND U.S. HOMELAND SECURITY AFTER 9/11

Transportation security in general was a major focus of America's reaction to the 9/11 attacks. This was hardly surprising given the selection by Al-Qaeda of commercial airliners as their weapon of choice for high impact, catastrophic strikes against the United States. The reconfiguration of the American national security apparatus brought on by that fateful September day led, for example, to the creation of new agencies such as the Transportation Security Administration to be situated within the new Department of Homeland Security, the largest and most symbolic creature of Washington's post-9/11 security reorganization. By late 2002, considerable work had been completed tightening security in the American maritime transportation sector with the passing of the Trade Act and the Maritime Transportation Security Act and, in December 2002, the release of the *U.S. Coast Guard Maritime Strategy for Homeland Security*.[11]

Throughout late 2001 and 2002, agencies of the new Department of Homeland Security formulated a series of measures to reduce America's vulnerabilities to terrorist attacks against, or *via*, its maritime transportation sector. The opportunities available to terrorists groups wishing to carry out such an attack on an open maritime transportation system were deemed to be substantial. In the words of the *9/11 Commission Report*, the "Opportunities to do harm are as great, or greater, in maritime … transportation" as they are in the commercial aviation industry.[12] To place the vulnerabilities into perspective, the United States has over 98,000 miles of shoreline and 361 ports, through which almost 95 percent of the U.S. international trade flows. More than 40 percent of the world's fleet of merchant ships may enter American ports annually and approximately 30,000 containers enter daily.[13] This perceived vulnerability also has ramifications far beyond the United States, as so many countries, and the health of the world economy in general, are dependent on the vast American market, with the American proportion of world maritime trade close to 20 percent of the total.[14]

A wide range of maritime terrorist threats and risks were considered possible in the aftermath of 9/11, including attacks against ships and maritime infrastructure, the use of ships as weapons, the use of ships and containers to transport weapons or terrorists, and the exploitation of legitimate shipping operations as a means of financing terrorist groups.[15] However, the most pressing post-9/11 maritime security concern for the United States undoubtedly has been the potential for terrorists to exploit the openness of the international maritime trading system to smuggle a WMD and, in particular, a nuclear or crude atomic device, into a major American port or port city. Although the successful employment of nuclear weaponry may be one of the least likely scenarios for a terrorist attack, the magnitude of the consequences for life, property, and the wider economy would be immense. The nuclear threat thus cannot be ignored in a security climate in which Al-Qaeda has expressed strong interest in acquiring such weapons. The detonation of such a device in or near a major U.S. city would not only cause mass casualties in the tens or possibly even hundreds of thousands and devastate infrastructure in the immediate area, but the impact would also have, at the least, a devastating near-term effect on the U.S. economy and U.S. society as a whole. A study has estimated that the effect of such an attack could conceivably cost the U.S. economy up to $1 trillion.[16] Although such estimates can always be challenged due to their speculative nature, it is certain that the economic consequences of a nuclear attack would be vast; and because of the sheer size of the U.S. economy and its centrality to the globalized world economy, the global economic costs would be even greater. Furthermore, the social and political consequences of the loss of a leading American city, both domestically and internationally, are unpredictable.

U.S. MARITIME SECURITY INITIATIVES

The period following 9/11 witnessed the rapid promulgation of new American maritime security regulations that have reshaped the entire international environment for seaborne trade.[17] All countries and businesses wishing to trade with the United States have had to comply with the new rules or risk losing effective access to the U.S. market. The rationale underpinning these initiatives has been to collect as much information as possible on ships, people, and cargo, before they enter the United States to identify possible risks for further investigation, including cargo inspection and possible enforcement action.

Probably the most stringent measure is the advance electronic cargo information, or 24-hour rule, which requires that the detailed manifest information on all containerized and break-bulk cargo bound for the United States be provided to U.S. Customs and Border Protection (CBP), 24 hours before loading in the foreign port of embarkation. For transhipped cargoes, the process must be undertaken at the last port of embarkation/transhipment before entering the United States, even if the manifest information had already been provided at the port of origin. The 24-hour rule also applies to cargoes not destined for the United States but which transit through American ports. The 24-hour rule requires that cargo manifests be transmitted electronically using the CBP automated manifest system. Cargo should not be loaded for 24 hours following submission of the manifest, lest shippers incur penalties. Noncompliance can lead to a CBP "do not load" instruction or a denial of entry to a U.S. port. Noncompliance also can lead to a targeting of specific cargo as a potential security risk, which would require scanning or a more intrusive inspection.

A further source of information is the requirement for ships to provide advance notification of arrival at a U.S. port. Following 9/11, the advance notification timeframe for ships to inform the U.S. Coast Guard of their scheduled port call was stretched from 24 to 96 hours prior to arrival. Vessels are required to provide schedule, cargo, and crew information.

The information generated by the 24-hour rule is used for targeting suspicious cargoes undertaken by other U.S. initiatives such as the Container Security Initiative (CSI). Based on selected risk criteria, all containerized cargoes destined for the United States are prescreened using the information gathered from the automated manifest system. Containers pinpointed by the U.S. Customs and Border Protection's computerized automated targeting system as high risk are further investigated.

The automated targeting system adds intelligence and historical data from different sources, to the cargo information, which is then integrated and processed, using analytical criteria, to assess the level of risk. Under the CSI, CBP personnel are posted to foreign CSI ports to oversee the prescreening process by local officials of containers bound for the United States. The underlying rationale is to single out cargoes which may pose a potential threat in the prescreening process, and carry out scanning or physical inspection, if necessary, before shipping to the United States.

CSI ports are required to install equipment at their own expense for the nonintrusive inspection of containers, such as large x-ray or gamma ray scanners, to produce imagery of container contents, and radiation detection devices. The development of smart technologies to provide tamper proof container seals is also being pursued. Around 58 of the world's major container ports are now part of the CSI scheme, and other countries have entered into agreements that allow their entire port sector to be rated as CSI compliant. The goal is to have at least 85 percent of containers destined for the United States to be shipped by CSI ports.[18] Compliance can be important if a particular state or port is engaged in direct trade with the United States. The ramifications of not being CSI compliant could include a loss of business to rival ports, the extent of which easily would outweigh the relatively small costs of equipping the port with the necessary scanning devices.

The U.S. Department of Energy also runs a scheme involving the installation of radiation detection equipment to prevent nuclear or radiological weapons or material from being smuggled into the United States via the maritime trading system: the so-called Megaports Initiative. Under this scheme, the Department of Energy's National Nuclear Security Administration intends to install equipment in at least 24 ports and train local officials in its use.

The Customs-Trade Partnership Against Terrorism (C-TPAT) is a voluntary scheme that involves the cooperation of participating members of the private sector along the entire length of the supply chain with certain CBP security procedures. Partner companies agree to apply certain security standards according to a set of C-TPAT minimum security criteria focusing on security standards and procedures at the point of origin, the point of stuffing (of containers), and the development of better container security standards, including the use of "smart" seals. Companies are required to "engage and leverage" other businesses along the supply chain to maximize the security benefits.[19] American importers who are C-TPAT members, for example, can require contracts with foreign suppliers to stipulate security procedures for shipping their goods to the United States. In return, C-TPAT member companies in theory receive expedited processing and clearance of their goods on arrival. However, these companies are not exempted from other U.S. maritime security regulations; it can only lessen members' risk scores in the automated targeting system.

A further U.S. measure with a direct impact on other countries and international cooperation for maritime security is the International Port Security Program, whereby the U.S. Coast Guard teams visit foreign ports to assess those states' compliance with the International Maritime Organization's (IMO's) International Ship and Port Facility Security (ISPS) Code, which lacks its own compliance mechanisms. The U.S. Coast Guard issues regular port security advisories that detail which countries or ports have been found to be in noncompliance with the code and the measures each needs to take to comply. Failure to do so may result in ships that have used such identified, noncomplying ports as one of their last five ports of call being targeted for a range of actions by the U.S. Coast Guard, including dockside boardings, boarding at sea, or denial of entry of the vessel into the United States.

Many of the measures mentioned were codified into U.S. legislation by the *Port Security Improvement Act 2006* (SAFE Port Act). The United States is also attempting to internationalize these regulations by pushing, for example, for international standards for container security and advanced manifest information requirements, through bodies such as the World Customs Organization (WCO) and International Standards Organization. This has the dual benefit of creating international standards for security measures and expanding the scope of security initiatives from a singular applicability to trade only with the United States to seaborne trade on a global basis. As a result of internationalization, the new security measures may also achieve a greater degree of international acceptance and legitimacy in the eyes of those states and bodies that might have been skeptical of perceived American unilateralism or motives. As an example, the WCO's Standards to Secure and Facilitate Global Trade (SAFE Framework of Standards) of June 2005 is a voluntary system to enhance supply chain security by encouraging cooperation among customs authorities. The cooperation includes data exchange and risk profiling of cargoes. In June 2006, a concept analogous to C-TPAT was introduced, the authorized economic operator (AEO) guidelines, to build partnerships with the private sector, whereby businesses will receive expedited customs clearances in return for implementing certain security practices. Further, on a bilateral basis U.S. authorities may accredit the AEO schemes of other customs agencies to facilitate easier trade procedures with the United States, as has occurred with the New Zealand scheme, for example.

Washington has also led the drive for tighter maritime security regulations and procedures in international and regional bodies. For example, the United States has been a leading driver of new IMO measures such as the ISPS Code, the October 2005 amendments to the SUA Convention and its protocol, and the further amendments to the SOLAS Convention to provide for long-range identification and tracking of vessels. At a regional level, the United States has been active in the Asia Pacific Economic Cooperation (APEC) forum, promoting the forum's consideration of transnational security issues, including terrorism. APEC has developed the Secure Trade in the APEC Region (STAR) initiative, with a major focus on the security of ships, their cargoes, and the wider supply chain.[20]

The U.S.-initiated Proliferation Security Initiative (PSI) also has significant maritime security implications by promoting the interdiction of vessels suspected of illegally transporting WMD, their components, or delivery systems, within the limits of existing international law. This includes the signing of eight bilateral ship-boarding agreements with major flag states, which effectively give the United States the right to board and inspect ships flying the flags of those partner states on the high seas suspected of carrying WMD. Washington is particularly attached to the PSI's informal nature—a veritable poster child for the Bush administration's favored "coalitions of the willing" construct of likeminded states cooperating voluntarily against a common threat, unencumbered by the maddening constraints of international bureaucracy, consensus building, majority voting, or the spectre of a United Nations (UN) Security Council veto.

ESTABLISHING A POLICY FRAMEWORK: THE NATIONAL STRATEGY FOR MARITIME SECURITY

In December 2004, a presidential directive for the promulgation of Maritime Security Policy, National Security Presidential Directive 41/Homeland Security Presidential Directive 13 (NSPD-41/HSPD-13), established a Maritime Security Policy Coordinating Committee (MSPCC) representing all relevant government departments and agencies to improve the effectiveness of interagency coordination for, and the practice of, maritime security. The MSPCC was tasked with overseeing the development of a *National Strategy for Maritime Security* (NSMS), which was released in September 2005, as well as the following eight supporting implementation plans, each of which was drafted by the appropriate government department or agency:

- *The National Plan to Achieve Maritime Domain Awareness*
- *The Global Maritime Intelligence Integration Plan*
- *The Maritime Operational Threat Response Plan*
- *The International Outreach and Coordination Strategy*
- *The Maritime Infrastructure Recovery Plan*
- *Maritime Transportation System Security Recommendations*
- *The Maritime Commerce Security Plan*
- *The Domestic Outreach Plan*

NSPD-41/HSPD-13 directed that a "coordinated and integrated," whole-of-government strategy approach be pursued to improve both American national security throughout its own maritime domain and the ability to defend the United States and its vital interests against threats emanating from or *via* the global maritime domain, to be jointly led by the Departments of Defense and Homeland Security. It mandated that the new strategy be build on existing measures for maritime security "centered on a layered, defense-in-depth framework," which should encompass government and private sectors as well as domestic and international elements, and be global in scope.[21] The resulting NSMS and its implementation plans thus became the overarching policy and strategy framework for American maritime security. Those documents demonstrate how the various post-9/11 initiatives, mentioned earlier, have been developed and integrated into a discernible whole consonant with the priorities of the *National Security Strategy*, and establish the framework for the further development of an extensive and integrated system of maritime security.

Perhaps the first interesting point to note about the NSMS is its characterization of the world's oceans as a "largely unsecured medium for an array of threats by nations, terrorists, and criminals."[22] It is therefore constructed around a threat-centric perspective of the maritime domain and, although the categories of threat discussed in the document are inclusive of those posed by nation states, terrorists, pirates, and transnational criminal groups, marine environmental damage, and illegal migration by sea, it is, however, clear that the priority and motivating threat is that of terrorism. In particular, it reemphasizes the "preeminent" security priority of post-9/11 national security policy of protecting the American homeland from attack, especially an attack involving WMD.[23] The NSMS also recognizes the common interest of states to both utilize and protect the global maritime domain, and asserts that the responsibility for this collective security at sea must be shared.[24]

The NSMS establishes four strategic objectives as a framework for the pursuit of improved maritime security, which are themselves informed by three guiding principles.[25] Those principles are, first, maintaining the freedom of the seas; second, ensuring that maritime commerce can continue uninterrupted; and, third, preventing "dangerous people and material" from entering the United States in a way that does not hinder legitimate travel and trade. The four strategic objectives consist of the prevention of terrorist attacks and criminal or "hostile acts" in the maritime domain, protection of population centres and critical infrastructure in or nearby the maritime domain, minimization of damage from any attack and planning for postattack recovery, and the safeguarding of the ocean and its resources. Note the importance given to information—an awareness of possible threats in the maritime domain—and the use of that knowledge to foreclose any attack, whether imminent or incipient, before it occurs. It thus emphasizes prevention, deterrence (when, or if, possible), and preemptive action to interdict threats, with a preference for doing so far from American shores.[26]

To be able to fulfill those strategic objectives, the NSMS establishes five strategic actions, which seek to improve international cooperation, maximize awareness in the maritime domain, "embed security" into the practices of the commercial sector—such as those already discussed regarding container security, "deploy layered security," and ensure that the U.S. maritime transportation system can survive and continue to operate, as a system, following a potentially catastrophic attack on one or more of its constituent parts.[27]

The NSMS reflects the globalized nature of the world economy, the interconnectedness of the maritime trading system, and the multinational nature of the shipping industry itself. It also recognizes the constraints imposed on the power of any one nation to enforce its national security interests throughout the global maritime domain by national sovereignty, maritime jurisdiction, and other elements of international law—which include, in particular, those codified in the United Nations Convention on the Law of the Sea.[28] As a result of these factors, the NSMS emphasizes the need for enhanced international cooperation. In addition to its activities to bolster states' maritime security and counter-proliferation powers in international organizations such as the IMO and WCO, and by further developing measures and procedures to improve the ability of states to target and interdict suspect cargoes such as the CSI and PSI described earlier, the United States also places considerable importance on expanding regional maritime security regimes and initiatives. The NSMS deems such schemes to be of particular importance in choke points such as the Straits of Malacca and Singapore and other narrow seas vital to the free movement of international shipping.[29]

An essential element of America's international strategy is thus to build capacity in developing states and regions deemed to be critical for American, and global, maritime security. Moreover, Washington's international maritime security engagement is designed to reach beyond foreign governments and international and regional organizations, to also encompass the overseas private sector and even "the public abroad," in keeping with its wider approach to maritime security.[30]

MARITIME DOMAIN AWARENESS

The importance of maritime domain awareness (MDA) for an enhanced security environment pervades most U.S. maritime security initiatives. As discussed earlier, information and knowledge are the keys to understanding the security situation throughout the maritime domain and to prevent, through preemption or interdiction, or defend against, any maritime-related threats. The American definition of MDA is itself so pervasive and all-encompassing that the enormity of the task becomes readily apparent: maritime domain awareness "is the effective understanding of anything associated with the maritime domain that could impact the security, safety, economy, or environment of the United States."[31]

The requirements for comprehensive MDA in the current security environment are substantially different from those pursued by the United States for ocean surveillance during the Cold War, which were primarily designed to acquire Soviet naval surface, subsurface, and airborne targets. Some of the "legacy" technologies developed by the United States for intelligence, surveillance, and reconnaissance (ISR) in the maritime domain remain relevant and useful, such as the ship-tracking capabilities designed to assist targeting for the Tomahawk long-range antiship cruise missile.[32] Another Cold War system that is being considered for adaptation to the task of tracking merchant ships is the sound surveillance system (SOSUS) of underwater fixed array acoustic sensors, which were developed to detect, identify, and track Soviet submarines based on each boat's individual acoustic signature.[33]

The demands of the contemporary threat environment require greater awareness and knowledge, in near real time, of merchant ship movements, especially in critical sealanes and coastal waters. The sheer quantity of commercial maritime "targets" that need to be acquired to establish a comprehensive MDA picture is thus somewhat different, both in scale and tactical nature, from the earlier mission of finding and tracking the maritime assets of an often elusive Soviet military adversary spread thinly over vast ocean areas. Nevertheless, the U.S. ambition is to further develop its legacy military sensor systems, combined with the commissioning of new or improved technologies, such as space-based surveillance and analytical computer software, and information generated from international cooperation and the new regulatory environment, to eventually be able to track every ship of the world's entire merchant fleet, in the words of Rear Admiral Tony L. Cothron, the Director of Naval Intelligence, "on a minute-by-minute basis."[34] Today, that scenario is still likely to be an aspiration rather than a reality, yet it seems as if America's maritime security policymakers and boffins are serious enough to at least push the boundaries of what is currently possible.

Greater detailed information relating to the entire commercial maritime supply chain, stretching from the manufacturer and exporter in the country of origin to the importer in the country of final destination also needs to be added to ISR data. It must also include ports, including those used for transshipment, the vessels, and cargo and crew/passenger manifests. The integration of large quantities of ISR, ship, and supply chain data in a temporally meaningful way is an especially challenging task, which requires the application of technology not only to acquire the data but also to process it, as well as highly developed forms of international cooperation for the purpose of information sharing.

The U.S. MDA development plans seek to harness and even shape both the domestic and international regulatory environment, and the commercial sector to generate the information to populate the databases, which will "detect, fuse, and analyze aberrant patterns of activity" in the maritime domain. To accomplish this task, advanced computer-based algorithms are being used as data mining tools to detect anomalous behavior. This may involve anomalies detected in vessel movements based on comparing actual location and heading information compiled from various sensors and the ship's automatic identification system (AIS), for example, with its sailing schedule and advance manifest information, or in detecting patterns of behavior with the ship, cargo manifests, crew, or passengers that might indicate a potential threat. The intent is to fuse information from all relevant sources of data into a common operating picture reaching across all levels of the U.S. domestic jurisdiction, and where possible extending internationally, whereby threat indicators are tagged by the automated targeting system for further investigation and enforcement action, if required.[35]

LAYERED SECURITY

The concept of "layered security" is multifaceted and exists across different levels of analysis. In the NSMS, layered security refers to the application of security measures to all potential areas of vulnerability, such as ships, people, ports, and related infrastructure. Security measures can consist of the physical security of maritime assets, physical cargo inspections, interdiction, and law enforcement agencies and a military capable of mounting an effective response to identified threats.[36]

However, when one examines the NSMS and its implementation plans, *in toto*, it becomes clear that further to that description, layered security can in addition refer to integration and cooperation across different levels of government: federal, state, local, and tribal. It also applies to cooperation between domestic government departments and agencies; and internationally, between U.S. authorities and those of partner nations. A further application of layered security involves enmeshing the private sector into supply chain security practices.

Last, the concept of layered security has a physical and geographical connotation related to the expectation that threats will be appropriately dealt with, where possible, as early and as far from U.S. territory as possible. These layers of maritime security can be categorized as three basic zones: U.S. territory and jurisdiction, ocean areas not under coastal state jurisdiction while vessels are in transit, and the territory and jurisdiction of foreign states. In this way, one can think of layered security as an admixture of physical and legal zones of jurisdiction stretching out from the importing and exporting businesses and maritime industries located on the U.S. mainland, to include the landward areas surrounding ports and the port zones themselves; U.S. internal waters, territorial sea, contiguous zone, and exclusive economic zone; the high seas; shipping companies, and other maritime industries engaged in international trade with the United States; and the waters under the jurisdiction of other states, their ports, and exporting industries in those countries. Thus, in the farthest layer lies the beginning of the supply chain connecting foreign countries to U.S. territory, the security of which is the object of schemes such as C-TPAT and the 24-hour rule.

THE GLOBAL MARITIME PARTNERSHIP INITIATIVE

The U.S. Navy's contribution to the security of the seaborne trading system has increased markedly since 9/11, from providing the reassurance of general deterrence for the world's major SLOCs in the pre-9/11 era to embracing a new mission to contribute to the sea-based defence of the American homeland in the context of the "global war on terror." The difficulty faced by the U.S. Navy in so doing has been in part one of transitioning from a posture of general deterrence to the prevention of specific, unfamiliar challenges, in an operating environment in which political and legal complexity rules, and where pervasive information and situational awareness and numbers of naval platforms rather than the combat power of individual platforms are likely to be leading determinants of effectiveness. The downsizing of the navy from its Cold War peak to its current levels, including the retirement of its frigates, and a concentration on the world's littoral regions—the outer edges of U.S. layered security—where shipping and offshore infrastructure is most vulnerable to unconventional attack, are indicators of U.S. Navy limitations in fulfilling this new role. At least as important, though, is the complex jurisdictional environment in the littorals, whereby the assertion of coastal state sovereignty or sovereign rights, described earlier, limits the ability of the U.S. Navy or other external forces from effectively asserting good order at sea in regions where it is lacking or is at risk.

This complex and difficult operating environment thus demands a high level of international cooperation to overcome the many potential impediments to countering threats to shipping, ports, and both coastal and offshore infrastructure, and other maritime or maritime-related threats. The U.S. Navy's answer to this conundrum of protecting an increasingly vulnerable sea-based trading system, which continues only to grow in importance due to the thickening of international economic interdependence, has been the promotion of a new model for naval, interagency, and private sector cooperation for maritime security: the 1000-ship navy.

This concept was announced in August 2005 and officially launched in September of the same year by the U.S. Navy's Chief of Naval Operations, Admiral Mike Mullen.[37] The concept is built on a foundation of strategic thinking regarding the impact of transnational threats in the globalized, post-9/11 world on the future role of maritime power and, in particular, American naval power.[38] It also builds on the U.S. Navy's post-Cold War focus on operating in the littorals and influencing the fight on land, as set out in operational concepts such as *From the Sea* (1992), *Forward … from the Sea* (1994), and *Sea Power 21* (2002). It has a clear precursor in the U.S. Pacific Command's Regional Maritime Security Initiative (RMSI), released in detail in 2004, which establishes a framework for cooperation to "synchronize and align maritime security activities of willing nations" in the Asia-Pacific region.[39] The concept also reflects the thinking behind the NSMS, while the PSI remains a favored model in Washington for structuring informal "coalitions of the willing" to combat the new threats to international order.

The 1000-ship navy is predicated on an assumption that good order at sea and the integrity of the sea-based trading system is increasingly under threat from the combined scourges of terrorism, piracy, drug smuggling, weapons proliferation, and other transnational criminal activities. These unconventional and irregular threats at sea supposedly represent the "challenges of our age" for navies and other maritime enforcement agencies, and are particularly prevalent in the "ungoverned and under-governed parts of the maritime domain," according to Mullen. Similar to the RMSI, the 1000-ship navy concept has focused on two main objectives: improved MDA and enhanced maritime enforcement capacity. The intended global 1000-ship navy network would combine MDA information from the sensors and sources of participating navies, coast guards, and other government agencies and maritime industry.[40] The technical challenges would thus include not only sensor and data processing, but also protocols and interoperability requirements for information sharing.

The intention to elicit the participation of the private sector follows the explicit understanding of wider maritime security policy, as expounded in the NSMS and various U.S. Customs and Border Protection security regimes, that engaging maritime industry is an essential ingredient to improving security of the maritime transportation and offshore sectors. Although private sector players are likely to be primary beneficiaries, both directly and indirectly, from enhanced security, their participation is also likely to be dependent on commercial considerations; perhaps to the extent that participation in the network will need to be cost neutral. Private sector involvement might include arrangements with major shipping companies, which would see AIS data provided directly to naval platforms or other sea, ground, or air-based assets; perhaps using advanced, and more secure AIS systems. This type of arrangement might overcome the current problems with the security of AIS data, which is either freely available on the Internet, or available at relatively low cost on a subscription basis, in near-real time. This has led to a widespread practice of ships' AIS transponders being switched off in potentially dangerous waters, such as the Strait of Malacca, lest the data is used by pirates or even terrorists to coordinate attacks against shipping. Clearly, the utility of AIS will be undermined if data security continues to be compromised.

The information is likely to be integrated into a future American unlimited track database, which would attempt to verify MDA information by merging and correlating the track data of different information sources and separate databases. Indeed, it is clear that technology will play a leading role in the Global Maritime Partnership Initiative. Although it may be self-evident that effective MDA requires the development and application of technology, there is a danger that what began as a political initiative for greater international cooperation to improve maritime security in the era of global terrorism might devolve into a technology-driven exercise of pursuing what is technically possible. That certainly would be consistent with America's prevailing strategic culture, which tends to treat strategic challenges as mere technical problems to be resolved by engineering solutions.[41] This suspicion is backed by statements by Admiral Mullen, who has claimed that the "promise of significant technological progress" is itself a sufficiently "compelling reason to cooperate," and that "Technology and information technology, in particular, may very well be the single largest contributor to our maritime security in the future."[42]

Mullen announced a set of "first principles" for the 1000-ship navy in December 2005.[43] These principles are somewhat reminiscent of the guiding conceptual and operational framework for that model "coalition of the willing": the PSI and its own Statement of Interdiction Principles.

First Principles of the Global Maritime Network

1. The continued primacy of national sovereignty.
2. States have many common interests at sea and cooperation is the key to resolving challenges to those interests.
3. The network will be limited to the maritime domain.
4. National capabilities will be the building blocks of the network.
5. The network is not limited to navies.
6. States able to provide assistance to others should be willing to do so.
7. States needing assistance should be willing to request it when necessary.
8. The development of regional networks will provide the basis for an eventual global maritime network.
9. Information sharing is a key to effectiveness, preferably on an unclassified basis.
10. The security situation at sea demands that the process of constructing networks begins as soon as possible.

The U.S. Navy's concept thus promotes the "export" of security to, and capacity building programs for, littoral regions in which maritime security is lacking. The construction of regional networks is already happening independently of the 1000-ship navy in many parts of the world—from the Caribbean to the Gulf of Guinea to the Black Sea. However, while it may be relatively easy to build networks in regions such as the Mediterranean, where NATO's Operation *Active Endeavor* has been carrying out maritime security operations to guard against terrorist threats to shipping since October 2001, the difficulties of doing so in regions where there is no preexisting alliance system or cooperative framework in place for multinational operations are manifold. This is certainly the case in areas where outside involvement invokes a high degree of resentment or suspicion, especially when the United States is concerned.

Nowhere does this situation apply more than in archipelagic Southeast Asia, a vital trade route where suspicions of U.S. motives run high, especially within the Muslim states, and where highly expansive views over sovereignty and sovereign rights at sea are held. Security multilateralism is extremely difficult to achieve in such circumstances, making the development of a regional network in this part of the world where terrorists and insurgent groups have actually undertaken maritime attacks unlikely. The RMSI was strongly criticized by Malaysia and Indonesia, for example, and neither of those Straits states has joined the Japanese-initiated Regional Cooperation Agreement on Combating Piracy and Armed Robbery against Ships in Asia (ReCAAP), raising doubts over the ultimate success of that scheme.[44]

Indeed, the skepticism of much of the Muslim world over the U.S. "global war on terror" and the wider international disgruntlement over Iraq is likely to limit the involvement of many states in parts of the world where greater levels of maritime security cooperation are most needed. There are two aspects to this reticence. First, although the U.S. Navy has scoped the 1000-ship navy concept in "feel-good" terms of global cooperation for good order at sea, it seems clear that the driving motivation is the (Islamic) maritime-related terrorist threat to the U.S. homeland and America's wider strategic interests. In this respect, the scheme might be viewed as the U.S. Navy's attempt to make itself more directly relevant to the war on terrorism, which together with the related stabilization campaigns in Iraq and Afghanistan, remains the U.S. Defense Department's primary preoccupation, as is made clear in the 2006 *Quadrennial Defense Review Report.*

Second, the leadership role of the U.S. Navy itself will provide pause to some states. In fact, this is an issue that seems to be causing some confusion. On the one hand, the concept has been spruiked not as an American-led system or as an alliance but as a genuine network, whereby membership is voluntary and states participate to the extent that they are willing and able to do so. On the other hand, however, the guiding hand of the United States is likely to be perceived even if not constantly felt. Although conceptually analogous to a computer network, in which computers can be plugged into the system when required, the fact remains that even regional maritime security networks will require at least one state to take the initiative to build and maintain the system. In the Mediterranean, for example, in addition to *Active Endeavor*, the Italian Navy has taken the initiative in developing the Virtual Regional Maritime Traffic Centre (V-RMTC), a system for the exchange of unclassified shipping data in the Mediterranean and Black Seas. Intentionally a non-NATO project to promote the inclusiveness needed for wider cooperation and sharing of MDA information, the V-RMTC will provide a common maritime operating picture using a Web-based graphic database system. The system provides tracks of merchant ships of 300 gross registered tons (GRT) and above and incorporates AIS information from ships and departure and estimated arrival information from ports in participating states.[45]

The V-RMTC may very well provide a sound model for the type of unclassified regional information–sharing networks envisaged by the Global Maritime Partnership Initiative. However, it is difficult to envisage any one state being able to take the lead in a region such as Southeast Asia. Singapore may well be trying to fulfill that role, for example, by hosting and funding the ReCAAP Information Sharing Centre and promoting use of the Republic of Singapore Navy's Web-based information-sharing system, the Regional Maritime Information Exchange (ReMIX). Nevertheless, it is most unlikely that its neighbors would ever fully accede to any system led by Singapore.

The linking of regional networks to form a global network may be even more problematic politically, for it is only the United States that has the vision, will, and capability to pursue such an arrangement. The fact remains, however, that the U.S. role will be associated with its current strategic priorities, making it a hard sell for many of the world's littoral states. Indeed, one of the contributing drivers of the concept was the need to overcome communications and interoperability problems encountered in coalition operations during earlier stages of Operation *Enduring Freedom* the global campaign against Islamic revolutionary extremism. To this end, the United States has been developing its Combined Enterprise Regional Information Exchange System (CENTRIXS), a Web-based data exchange system that consists of multiple, unconnected coalition "communities of interest," with differing levels of security classification depending on the identity of the community members, as a technology enabler for the 1,000-ship Navy.[46]

Once again, however, the United States may be mistaken in viewing the problems of MDA information exchange in technical rather than political terms. Moreover, to make any global network as inclusive as possible, it would be preferable not to view it in terms of coalition building. Yet the employment of a U.S.-controlled coalition communications tool, whether CENTRIXS or any similar alternative, inevitably will raise questions over whether the Global Maritime Partnership Initiative will be a genuinely inclusive global network working for the common good or an American-led coalition serving primarily American strategic objectives. These are issues that can be overcome, as the example of the V-RMTC demonstrates, but political sensitivities will remain. Some states may even view the accessing or sharing of MDA data regarding activity in their national maritime zones as infringements of sovereignty, even if their arguments would be dubious in legal terms.

The likelihood is that those states (and their respective navies) that already maintain close relationships will continue to develop their systems and protocols for data sharing and interoperability to improve the common MDA picture. The challenge will be to draw other states into the network. Some may increase cooperation with network members without formally joining themselves; others will remain leery of any involvement at all. The same precautions apply in terms of capacity building and the "exporting" of maritime security to regions that need it. In some regions, outside intervention to improve maritime security may be welcomed, as has been the case with the American involvement in the Gulf of Guinea. Relatively low-key maritime security capacity-building programs in Southeast Asia, including those delivered by Australia, Japan, the United States, and Singapore continue to be well received by the recipient states. Any suggestion of operational intervention by outside forces, however, will continue to be strongly resisted. Furthermore, it is not clear whether the 1,000-ship Navy network will actually increase the level of capacity-building activity taking place. A more reasonable perspective might be to treat the concept as a guiding framework for activity already under way. Ultimately, it will be the collection and sharing of MDA information that will be the first true test of the effectiveness of the concept.

THE EVOLVING INTERNATIONAL FRAMEWORK
FOR MARITIME SECURITY: A U.S. SYSTEM

Until 9/11, the international regulatory environment for maritime security was extremely lax, particularly when compared to that for aviation security. Apart from the original 1988 SUA Convention, the provisions in the Law of the Sea Convention dealing with piracy and national customs requirements and other law enforcement efforts to combat maritime-related crime, most of the relevant regulatory framework dealt with matters of maritime safety rather than security. The experience of the 9/11 attacks changed the perceptions of threat regarding the vulnerability of all modes of transportation, particularly in the United States and among other like-minded states. In particular, the maritime transportation system was deemed to be the most likely vector for a WMD attack. Although the threat perception was (and is) not equally shared, any response impacting the international economic system inevitably affects all states and businesses involved in international trade. The response has had the effect of transforming the regulatory environment for seaborne trade by placing security considerations at the forefront of maritime regulation. Whatever shortcomings or gaps that might remain in the international framework for maritime security today, it must be understood that maritime security has been transformed within the period of just a few years: how many industry or government players would have predicted on September 10, 2001, that the maritime security environment would have evolved so far—into today's complex matrix of security regulation and innovation—in such a short period of time?

At least as impressive is that these changes have been driven primarily by one player: the United States. The U.S. authorities have taken a trinitarian approach to the problem of post-9/11 maritime security by, first, introducing a series of unilateral security measures that directly impact all who wish to trade with the United States; second, driving regulatory change within international organizations, especially the IMO; and third, promoting concepts for enhanced cooperation, particularly regarding the sharing of MDA information. An important aspect to the American approach has been to integrate the private sector into maritime security processes—a practical recognition of the central role of industry in the maritime sphere. Many of the American unilateral measures are also being adopted by other states, shaped to their own circumstances, to enhance their own national security; a situation in which the United States has increasingly set the model for international practice.

Although some of the measures discussed in this chapter may have been immediate, *ad hoc* responses to the 9/11 attacks, increasingly the web of American and U.S.-initiated maritime security measures are beginning to appear as parts of an integrated whole. That whole is represented in the U.S. policy and strategy context by the NSMS. However, the evolving international framework for maritime security can also be viewed as a part of the American policy context: it has been driven primarily by the United States for the purpose of safeguarding U.S. homeland security, but with the added advantage of improving the integrity of the entire seaborne trading system. This may be considered as the U.S. "sheriff" fulfilling part of its wider responsibilities to protect the extant world order. If not anything else, the rapid development of the post-9/11 maritime security framework demonstrates what is possible when necessity demands. It also demonstrates the undiminished role of the United States in shaping the international security environment, employing an admixture of unilateral measures, international negotiation within the UN system, and informal cooperative frameworks to achieve the desired ends. It is likely that only the singular attention of Washington could have driven developments so far, so quickly. On the evidence of developments in international maritime security, speculation on the imminent decline of American influence would seem to be, at best, premature.

NOTES

1. The 9/11 Commission Report. *Final Report of the National Commission on Terrorist Attacks upon the United States*. W.W. Norton, New York, n.d., p. 153.
2. Michael Richardson, *A Time Bomb for Global Trade: Maritime-related Terrorism in an Age of Weapons of Mass Destruction*, Institute of Southeast Asian Studies, Singapore, 2004, p. 5.
3. See, for example, the controversial and perhaps overstated, yet insightful, analysis of Michael Scheuer ("Anonymous"), *Imperial Hubris: Why the West Is Losing the War on Terror*, updated edn., Potomac Books, Washington, 2005.
4. This is a role that substantively only the United States can currently fulfill. See Colin S. Gray, *The Sheriff: America's Defense of the New World Order*, University Press of Kentucky, Lexington, KY, 2004; and for the wider debate, Andrew J. Bacevich, ed., *The Imperial Tense: Prospects and Problems of American Empire*, Ivan R. Dee, Chicago, 2003.
5. For general deterrence, see Patrick M. Morgan, *Deterrence: A Conceptual Analysis*, 2nd edn., Sage, Beverly Hills, CA, 1983, pp. 42–46.
6. Eric Grove, *The Future of Sea Power*, Naval Institute Press, Annapolis, MD, 1990, p. 22. The broader issues of marine environmental protection and resource conservation, i.e., safeguarding the sea itself, have been well integrated into a modern theory of sea power by the leading contemporary maritime strategic thinker, Geoffrey Till, as part of his concept of "good order at sea" in his *Seapower: A Guide for the Twenty-First Century*, Frank Cass, London, 2004, chaps. 10–11. Although such concerns are important, they lie beyond the focus of this chapter.
7. The types of currently perceived threats of this nature were presaged in Fred C. Iklé, "The Next Lenin: On the Cusp of Truly Revolutionary Warfare," *The National Interest*, No. 47, Spring 1997, pp. 9–19.
8. See Keith B. Payne, *The Fallacies of Cold War Deterrence and a New Direction*, University Press of Kentucky, Lexington, KY, 2001.
9. *The National Security Strategy of the United States of America*, September 2002, pp. 15–16.
10. The term "Global Maritime Partnership Initiative" was coined to assuage concerns with the military-centric connotations of the "1000-ship Navy." However, both labels are in common use and employed herein.
11. The U.S. Coast Guard had been relocated from the Department of Transportation to the Department of Homeland Security as part of the institutional reorganization.

12. *The 9/11 Commission Report*, p. 391.
13. Cited in the *International Outreach and Coordination Strategy for The National Strategy for Maritime Security*, November 2005, p. 2. The U.S. definition of its maritime domain encompasses all of its navigable waterways, including major rivers and the Great Lakes; therefore the figures cited may also be so inclusive.
14. Cited in the *Maritime Commerce Security Plan for The National Strategy for Maritime Security*, June 28, 2005, pp. 3–4.
15. For a good analysis of the types of terrorist threats possible, see Organization for Economic Co-Operation and Development (OECD), *Security in Maritime Transport: Risk Factors and Economic Impact*, OECD, Paris, July 2003, pp. 8–18.
16. Cited in the *International Outreach and Coordination Strategy*, p. 3.
17. Unless otherwise noted, the following section is based on United Nations Conference on Trade and Development, "Container Security: Major Initiatives and Related International Developments," UNCTAD/SDTE/TLB/2004/1, 26 February 2004, pp. 4–26; the *International Outreach and Coordination Strategy*, Appendix B, pp. 1–7; and the *Maritime Commerce Security Plan*, pp. 9–11.
18. U.S. Customs and Border Protection, *Container Security Initiative 2006–2011 Strategic Plan*, August 2006, pp. 36–37.
19. U.S. Customs and Border Protection, *Securing the Global Supply Chain: Customs-Trade Partnership Against Terrorism (C-TPAT) Strategic Plan*, November 2004, pp. 22–24; and "C-TPAT Security Criteria – Sea Carriers," March 1, 2006.
20. For APEC measures, see Chris Rahman, "The International Politics of Combating Piracy in Southeast Asia," in Peter Lehr, ed., *Violence at Sea: Piracy in the Age of Global Terrorism*, Routledge, New York, 2007, pp. 185–186.
21. National Security Presidential Directive 41/Homeland Security Presidential Directive 13 (NSPD-41/HSPD-13) on Maritime Security Policy, December 21, 2004, pp. 4–5.
22. *The National Strategy for Maritime Security*, September 2005, p. 2.
23. Ibid., p. 7.
24. Ibid., p. 2.
25. Ibid., pp. 7–12.
26. Ibid., pp. 8–9.
27. Ibid., pp. 13–24.
28. For an analysis of how these constraints function to frustrate maritime enforcement activities in the case of piratical attacks against shipping, for example, see Martin Murphy, "Piracy and UNCLOS: Does International Law Help Regional States Combat Piracy?" in Lehr, *Violence at Sea*.
29. *The National Strategy for Maritime Security*, pp. 14–15.
30. *International Outreach and Coordination Strategy*, p. 7.
31. *National Plan to Achieve Maritime Domain Awareness for The National Strategy for Maritime Security*, October 2005, p. 1.
32. Norman Friedman, "Sea Power and Navies: An American View," in Jack McCaffrie, ed., *Positioning Navies for the Future: Challenge and Response*, Halstead Press, Sydney, 2006, p. 40.
33. David W. Munns, "121,000 Tracks," *Seapower*, July 2005, p. 10.
34. Rear Admiral Tony L. Cothron, USN, quoted in note 33, p. 11.
35. *The National Strategy for Maritime Security*, p. 17; and *National Plan to Achieve Maritime Domain Awareness*, pp. 4, 12–17 and Appendix B.
36. *The National Strategy for Maritime Security*, pp. 20–23.
37. Admiral Mike Mullen, USN, remarks delivered at the Naval War College, Newport, RI, 31 August 2005, available at http://www.navy.mil/navydata/cno/speeches/mullen050831.txt; and Mullen, remarks delivered at the *17th International Seapower Symposium*, Naval War College, Newport, RI, September 21, 2005, available at http://www.navy.mil/navydata/cno/mullen/speeches/mullen050921.txt.
38. See, for example, the National Defense University publication, *Globalization and Maritime Power*, Sam Tangredi, ed., NDU Press, Washington, 2002.
39. Commander, U.S. Pacific Command, *Strategy for Regional Maritime Security*, November 2004, p. 9.
40. Vice Admiral John G. Morgan, USN, and Rear Admiral Charles W. Martoglio, USN, "The 1,000-ship Navy: Global Maritime Network," *U.S. Naval Institute Proceedings*, November 2005, pp. 14–17.
41. On U.S. strategic culture, see Gray, *The Sheriff*, p. 126.

42. Admiral Mike Mullen, USN, remarks delivered to the Western Pacific Naval Symposium, Pearl Harbor, HI, October 31, 2006, p. 3.
43. Admiral Mike Mullen, USN, edited remarks to the RUSI Future Maritime Warfare Conference, London, December 13, 2005, available at http://www.navy.mil/navydata/cno/speeches/mullen051213.txt.
44. For further discussion, see Rahman, "The International Politics of Combating Piracy in Southeast Asia."
45. Italian Navy General Staff, "Operational Arrangement Concerning the Establishment of a Virtual Regional Maritime Traffic Centre (V-RMTC) for the Mediterranean and Black Seas," available at http://www.marina.difesa.it/vrmtc/2007/uk/operational.asp.
46. Steven A. Davis, "Designing a Network to Empower the Fleet: Challenges, Opportunities for NNFE Year 2," *CHIPS*, April–June 2007, p. 25.

5 Maritime Terrorism: Locations, Actors, and Capabilities

Peter Lehr

CONTENTS

More than six years after 9/11, the topic of maritime terrorism shares a trait with the topic of cyber-terrorism. Despite all the hype and hysteria surrounding it, acts of maritime terrorism are by no means frequent occurrences,[1] and their impact has been fairly limited—a far cry from the grandiose statements of Osama bin Laden that Jihadists would cut the lifelines of our economies, thereby destroying the very fabric of our societies, and also a far cry from all the doomsday scenarios peddled by interested parties. Obviously, only very few terrorist cells have both the inclination and the capabilities to strike at sea because carrying out such strikes depends on a certain degree of familiarity with the sea. In a sense, one could argue that terrorists would also need a kind of "maritime domain awareness" (MDA) to even think about including maritime attacks into their *modus operandi*—and on the availability of a special set of knowledge and skills.

> Operating at sea requires terrorists to have mariner skills, access to appropriate assault and transport vehicles, the ability to mount and sustain operations from a non-land-based environment, and familiarity with certain specialist capabilities (for example, surface and underwater demolition techniques).[2]

All these formidable obstacles notwithstanding, acts of maritime terrorism do occur, targeting ships, ports, and oil terminals. For this reason, we have to study and analyze them, to prepare ourselves for countermeasures. This is exactly what this chapter is all about. Ignoring the realm of megaterrorism speculation, and all the "high impact, low probability" scenarios, this chapter focuses on acts of maritime terrorism, which actually did take place. It categorizes these acts of maritime terrorism, takes a look at actors, their *modus operandi* and their known skills as well, and then attempts to do some crystal ball gazing in the conclusion. And because I see myself as a terror specialist and not an antiterror expert, I refrain from discussing how to combat such acts of terrorism.

But first, an overview on the historical and political context of maritime terrorism is discussed, to obtain a view of the proverbial "bigger picture."

THE NEW PIRATE WIND AND THE SPECTER OF MARITIME TERRORISM

Virtually all oceans of the world have a long history of maritime piracy from the early days of seafaring in small, coast-hugging vessels all through the age of oared and sailed ships up to the heydays of Imperialism, when British frigates battled with pirate vessels along the East African coast, in the Sulu Sea[3] or in the Caribbean. With the advent of steamships, which usually outran and massively outgunned any pirate ship around, maritime piracy finally met its fate somewhere in the nineteenth century when the last pirate ship had been sunk—or so it seemed. The so-called Barbary states at the northern African coast of the Mediterranean were finally defeated by the fledgling United States Navy; the whole Indian Ocean was turned into a British Lake, courtesy of the Royal Navy; the Caribbean became a backwater of diverse colonial powers; and the waters of the Asia-Pacific, including the South China Sea, were being heavily patrolled by warships of several Western fleets. In the twentieth century, nobody was talking about acts of piracy any longer. Although some opportunistic forms of piracy still existed, it was the East–West conflict that monopolized security discussions, pushing everything else to the sidelines.[4] However, piracy never really ended, and a couple of years after the end of the Cold War, the demise of the so-called evil empire—the Soviet Union, and the inauguration of a new world order of peace (which, of course, died in its infancy), maritime transport had to grudgingly accept that maritime piracy was back with a vengeance. Yet, there might just be a much more sinister threat lurking out there: the threat posed by maritime terrorism.

The suicide attacks launched against the USS *Cole* in October 2000, the supertanker *Limburg* in October 2002, or the attacks against the Al-Basra Oil Terminal (ABOT) and the Khor al-Amaya Oil Terminal (KAAOT) in April 2004 could give us a glimpse of the shape of things to come. After transport by air had been attacked with devastating effects in 9/11 and after transport by rail came under attack in March 2004 in Madrid and July 2005 in London, transport by sea might be the next. Osama bin Laden himself exhorted global Jihadists to target maritime transport on several occasions to disrupt our economic lifelines. And in April 2004, the Jihadist online magazine *Mu'askar al-Battar* (Al-Battar Training Camp) published an anonymous article entitled "Anti-Ship Warfare," which describes the use of "Greek Fire"-style incendiary devices against the crusaders' "large battleships fitted with multi-story towers" during the siege of Acre and compares that to the strikes against the USS *Cole* and the MV *Limburg* (which is discussed later), exhorting the readers to do likewise.[5]

To prevent acts of maritime terrorism from happening, or at least to prevent the worst-case scenarios from happening, a flurry of new maritime security initiatives have been introduced in the wake of 9/11, on both the national and the international levels, such as International Ship & Port Facility Security code (ISPS), Container Security Initiative (CSI), Customs-Trade Partnership Against Terrorism (C-TPAT), and Proliferation Security Initiative (PSI).[6] On the "business end" of maritime security, both hardware and software solutions are on offer, which can assist maritime law enforcement agencies and port authorities to build up a so-called MDA and defend port facilities against terrorist threats. First of all, the Automated Identification System (AIS) and a satellite-based long-range version named Long-Range Identification and Tracking (LRIT) system provide a more or less detailed picture of what is going on at the high seas (LRIT from December 31, 2008 onward) and near our shores or ports (AIS since December 31, 2004). To further assess a potential threat detected by either AIS or LRIT, several software solutions such as Informa's "Vigilance Vessel Profiling System"[7] have been developed to profile ships with regard to their owners, cargo, previous ports of call, future destinations, and more. On the hardware front, unmanned aerial vehicles (UAVs), sonar systems and sophisticated Closed-Circuit Television (CCTV) supervision systems are available to support port authorities in monitoring their usually vast port facilities.

Generally, all these efforts are laudable attempts in increasing both maritime safety and security. However, this flurry of activities in the wake of 9/11 has also resulted in the emergence of a new kind of maritime terrorism industry, where scaremongers seem to be in the lead, for a variety of reasons, which are not discussed here. This new variant of "terrorologists" are busily conjuring up maritime versions of "ultraterrorism" or "megaterrorism," resulting in what I like to call the "maritime terrorism nightmare charts."

Currently, the undisputed leader of the maritime terrorism nightmare charts, at least in the United States, is an attack with a weapon of mass destruction (WMD) voyaging to its target not on the tip of a missile but hidden in a container on board of a large container ship. Number two on the list is the "floating bomb" scenario, that is, a hijacked liquefied petroleum gas (LPG) or liquefied natural gas (LNG) tanker driven into a major port and exploded there, with the intent of disrupting seaborne global trade. The number three position is currently held by the "momentum weapon" scenario, which revolves around a large ship such as an ultra-large crude carrier or a chemical tanker. In such a case, the terrorists would attempt to drive a large vessel into the harbor at high speed to ram either other ships with vulnerable cargoes or oil terminals and the like and then detonate the ship. Such a scenario has been developed, for example, for the port of Singapore—home of Southeast Asia's largest oil refineries.[8] All of these maritime megaterrorism scenarios have one thing in common: they still firmly belong to the realm of fiction.

As stated in the introduction, all these worst-case scenarios are ignored in this contribution. There are several reasons behind the decision to ignore the more dreadful scenarios. First of all, terrorists are copycats. They use tactics that worked for them or worked for other groups before, they adapt them to their own circumstances, honing their skills and then striking continuously. This is the way terrorist groups acted on the land and this is also the way terrorist groups acted against aviation. It is not very plausible to me that they should not attempt to do likewise at sea. Second, it is even less plausible that terrorist groups should go for a "maritime terrorist spectacular" without first trying to get a certain degree of familiarity with this (for them) new environment. And third, it seems to be, for me at least, outright implausible that terrorists would be able to acquire and ship a nuclear weapon—except maybe a comparatively crude radiological dispersal device, also known as "dirty bomb"—into a port or develop the skills necessary to turn a hijacked LNG into a "floating bomb." In a nutshell, even the most determined maritime terrorists have to face a steep learning curve when it comes to embarking on a terror campaign in a new environment, and for them, too, the motto should be "keep it simple ..."

MARITIME TERRORISM I: IMPROVISED EXPLOSIVE DEVICES AND VEHICLE-BORNE IMPROVISED EXPLOSIVE DEVICES IN A NEW ENVIRONMENT

It has been asserted continuously that, when studying acts of terrorism and predicting acts of terrorism in the foreseeable future, the lessons of history could be quite misleading, because terrorist organizations tend to reinvent themselves, change their *modus operandi* quite frequently, and commit more and more audacious attacks to (a) prevent security forces to outguess and outwit them and (b) not to disappoint the rising expectations of their sympathizers and potential recruits as well as to maintain their reputation as being the *avant-garde* of their respective cause intact. However, this assertion is not supported by facts. Despite all the dire predictions of the acts of megaterrorism disrupting the very fabric of our societies, even six years after 9/11, acts of terrorism tend to be rather pedestrian. This is most certainly no consolation to any of the victims of such attacks—approximately 200 people perished in the first Bali attack in 2002, about the same number died in the Madrid bombings of 2004, and 52 were killed in the 7/7 bombings in London in 2005. However, all these attacks centered on explosives either hidden within or nearby their targets (train carriages, cars parked outside) or "transported" to the chosen targets by suicide bombers, concealing the devices beneath their clothing or in their cars. To repeat this important observation, far from reinventing themselves and changing their *modus operandi* frequently, terrorist organizations—often restrained by limited resources—seem to prefer repeating those tactics that worked with a high rate of success for them or other terrorist organizations before. Car bombs are easy to set up, whereas developing new tactics or devising acts of megaterrorism necessitate a long planning cycle and tie up of scarce resources and skilled operatives for a considerable period of time, with a high risk of failure.[9]

If we take a look at the still not-so-frequent acts of maritime terrorism, we get pretty much the same picture: most terror attacks aiming at damaging a vessel or a port facility were launched by using either improvised explosive devices (IEDs) or vehicle-borne improvised explosive devices (VBIEDs). The few remaining attacks made use of standoff weapons such as the ubiquitous RPG-7. Because such attacks are not that difficult to plan and launch, and because explosives and weapons are easily acquired from the black market, it seems to be quite likely that these run-of-the-mill attacks of the past will also be the most probable scenarios that the ship masters and port authorities will have to deal with in the foreseeable future. Such attacks are called "low impact, high probability": low impact, because they are not likely to achieve any long-term interruptions of the maritime supply chain itself—although they may lead to increased insurance rates—and high probability, because they do not require any special skills apart from rigging the explosives, which means such attacks are easy to conduct, comparatively cheap, and the "bang for a buck" ratio is amazing: the attack on the USS *Cole* cost approximately U.S.$50,000, and the repairs of the destroyer amounted to not less than U.S.$250 million. This is asymmetric warfare at its best, and that is why we are examining this type of attack first, using some recent—or not so recent—cases for illustration.

IMPROVISED EXPLOSIVE DEVICES

Smuggling bombs or IEDs on board a ship may still be the easiest way to commit an act of maritime terrorism as long as port security remains lax, which, unfortunately, is the case not only in third world harbors but also in many of the busy Western ports—the ISPS code notwithstanding. Just take a look at the long (car) queues at "our" ferry ports at holiday season, and you will get an impression of the dilemma faced by security personnel: if they screen every car and every passenger as thoroughly as required by regulations, the tight timetables on which the ferries operate would go straight out of the window. Thus, a bombing attack on a channel ferry or a ferry in the Mediterranean would not be too difficult to accomplish. The case study chosen for illustration is an attack that actually happened: the bombing of the *Superferry 14* in February 2004 in the Bay of Manila.

The *Superferry 14* was a large and quite modern "roll on-roll off" (Ro-Ro) ferry employed on a regular service, sailing from Manila to Bacolod and Davao and back. With a weight of little over 10,000 dwt, it could accommodate 1747 passengers. On February 26, 2004, she started her voyage as usual about 23:00 from berth 51 with approximately 900 passengers on board. One hour out of port and still in the Bay of Manila, just off the famous Corregidor Island, a huge explosion tore through the ship. Sixty three people were killed by the blast, and many more died in the fire engulfing the ship after the explosion. Soon after the explosion the ferry started slowly to list, to finally capsize in the early morning hours of the 27th. About 800 passengers and crew members of the ship could be saved during the difficult rescue operation, but all in all, 116 people died in this disaster.

Despite claims from several terrorist groups, the blast was initially thought to have been an accident, caused by a gas explosion. But after divers righted the ferry five months after it sunk, they found evidence of a bomb blast. Also, a man named Redendo Cain Dellosa admitted to planting the bomb on board, hiding it in a television set, on behalf of the Abu Sayyaf Group (ASG). Dellosa purposely placed his deadly TV set filled with 8 lb of trinitrotoluene (TNT) near the cheap seats to maximize the number of victims. It is believed that Abu Sayyaf bombed *Superferry 14* because the company that owned it, WG&A, did not comply with an Abu Sayyaf letter demanding protection money.

It took investigators five months to prove beyond doubt that it actually had been a terror attack—too late to generate any major media coverage for ASG, but that is another story. In the end, *Superferry 14* shows some interesting parallels to the ferry *Estonia*, which sank in the Baltic Sea in December 1997. In both cases, some still believe it was an accident, others are sure it was a terror attack, and others again blame organized crime. If it was intended to be a terror attack as part of the struggle for an independent Mindanao, it resulted in very poor returns for Abu Sayyaf. Nevertheless, it showed how easy it is to target ferries in ports where security checks are virtually nonexistent, and where basically everybody can enter and exit such vessels unchecked before they are finally put to sea. But, as argued earlier, how much more difficult would that be in Western ferry ports?

One does not need to look only at ships as targets for such IED attacks. High-value port facilities such as oil terminals or refineries also qualify as very tempting targets. An early example for such a scenario is the so-called Laju Incident, which took place in the Port of Singapore. This incident happened long before 9/11 during the Third Indochina Conflict and is nearly forgotten now. On January 31, 1974, a terrorist commando armed with submachine guns and explosives approached the island of Pulau Bukom Besar by boat and tried to storm the Shell oil refinery complex situated there. The group consisted of two Japanese nationals from the Japanese Red Army and two Arabs from the Popular Front for the Liberation of Palestine (PFLP). Their plan was to blow up some sensitive parts of the refinery to disrupt the oil supply of the embattled Republic of South Vietnam. However, the terrorists were discovered far too early to do any major damage although they succeeded in exploding three of their twelve explosive charges. While trying to escape, they hijacked the ferry boat *Laju* and its crew members. When the *Laju* was intercepted by Singaporean police boats and navy gunboats, a hostage crisis enfolded, which lasted for not less than one week. In the end, the terrorists were allowed to leave Singapore for Kuwait, where they disappeared without a trace.[10]

Another variant of the IED attack was used by—probably Shiite—insurgents based in Basra against a Tigris river patrol of the British Royal Marines: the insurgents hid an IED at the end of a pier the patrol had to pass, and detonated it at the right moment. Several marines got killed in this riverine adaptation of the ubiquitous roadside bomb. So far, there has been no repetition, and it is not very probable that such an attack would be attempted against targets larger than medium-sized ships. A lack of portside security in certain harbors would rather be exploited for standoff weapon attacks, or for launching a VBIED—also known as suicide boat.

Vehicle-Borne Improvised Explosive Devices

Another way to launch attacks either on shipping or on port facilities, which is fairly established nowadays, is by employing small boats—rigid raiders, dinghies, and the like—as attack vehicles. These boats can transport an explosive load of several hundred pounds at fairly high speed right into the target. Operating these boats is not difficult at all. Basically, anyone can do it, especially so if the distance to the target is short and the weather conditions are not too bad. The following two factors are the only major disadvantages of small boats: one cannot venture out too far in uncertain or difficult weather conditions nor can afford to loiter somewhere far from the shore, waiting for one's prey, which may or may not come. But even these difficulties can be overcome either by using a medium-sized vessel such as a *dhow* or a small freighter as a platform for attack—but then one has to face the problem of low speed—or as a mother ship for attacks launched by speedboats or rigid raiders. All of these different types of attack have already happened, and we will now discuss some case studies.

Because this book on ISPS implementation aims at the civil maritime transport sector, the USS *Cole* attack of October 2000 is ignored and the second most (in-) famous attack on the MV *Limburg* is discussed instead. On October 6, 2002, this vessel, a French-owned supertanker, was lying at anchor in the Yemeni oil port of Mina al-Dabah near the town of Mukallah at the Yemen's Arabian Sea coast, waiting to load 1.5 million barrels of heavy crude oil. The 300,000 dwt "very large crude carrier" (VLCC) was a two-year-old modern double-hulled vessel in good condition, already carrying 400,000 barrels of heavy crude oil from the Iranian oil port of Kharj. After filling up at Mina al-Dabah, the *Limburg* was bound for Malaysia.

After the attack, Mina al-Dabah has frequently been described as a "quiet out-of-the-way corner." Maybe this was the case in earlier times, but nowadays this Yemeni oil port is located amid bustling oil trade with commercial shipping including local vessels and warships of Western origins on their way from the Gulf to the Red Sea and vice versa. The port was deemed to be safe. On that Sunday, however, the ship's master, Hubert Ardillon, and another officer, noticed a small vessel approaching fast. The vessel impacted on the port side, a violent explosion occurred, and the *Limburg* burst into flames. The force of the explosion was strong enough to penetrate the double hull of the ship and create a hole 6–8 m wide. Several crew members were injured by the blast, and 90,000 barrels of oil spilled into the Arabian Sea. The master ordered the ship to be evacuated. In the hasty process of evacuation from the burning tanker, one crew member drowned. The fire could be extinguished within hours, and thanks to its double hull, the *Limburg* did not sink—as it was probably expected by the terrorists.

Immediately after the incident, both Yemeni and French authorities denied that there had been a terrorist attack, claiming the explosion had been caused by accident. This was probably a "last-ditch" effort to prevent a political and economic spillover of the incident. However, rumors about the incident proved to be sufficient to cause the price for crude oil to increase by 1.3 percent within hours after the attack, and another 24 hour later, the insurance costs for a voyage into Yemeni ports had tripled. A statement allegedly issued by Osama bin Laden himself, further discredited the attempts to "sell" the act as an accident.

> By exploding the oil tanker in Yemen, the holy warriors hit the umbilical cord and lifeline of the crusader community, reminding the enemy of the heavy cost of blood and the gravity of losses they will pay as a price for their continued aggression on our community and looting of our wealth.[11]

The strategy of denial, therefore, is not a viable one. Seen from a Yemeni point of view this attempt was hardly surprising, because, in the long term, Yemen's economy was the real victim of the terrorist attack. Because of the high insurance premium of 0.5 percent of the value of the ship's hull and machinery, most traffic was diverted to the nearby Omani port of Salalah. With regard to container shipping, this resulted in a plunge from a transshipment rate of 43,000 TEU (twenty-foot equivalent unit [standard container length]) in September 2002 to as little as 3,000 TEU in November 2002. The earlier prospering Aden Container Terminal was virtually crippled, forcing the Port of Singapore Authority (PSA), which owned 60 percent of it, to write off its stakes and hand its shares back to the Yemeni government just to cut its losses. The attack itself was simple enough: Saudi born Al-Qaeda operator Abdulraheem al-Nashiri, nicknamed "the prince of the sea," prime suspect of the USS *Cole* attack and currently in U.S. custody, financed the venture by paying U.S.$40,000. With this money, another Al-Qaeda operator, Abu Ali al-Harithi, bought the explosives and acquired a small boat. The boat was prepared by Al-Qaeda specialists at a house at Mukalla—a small town near the port of Mina al-Dabah. On October 6, 2002, two suicide bombers drove the boat to the tanker and rammed it into the hull, triggering the explosion. All in all, this attack was not more complicated than rigging a car and driving it to a checkpoint in Baghdad and exploding it there.

Another set of high-value targets for maritime terrorism are port facilities, especially oil or gas terminals. The ABOT and the KAAOT, for example, were attacked by one *dhow* and two explosive-filled speedboats piloted by suicide bombers of Zarqawi's Jamaat al-Tawhid on April 24, 2004. The attack on ABOT showed all the hallmarks of the maritime suicide attacks described earlier. Two zodiac-type speedboats intruded into the inner security perimeter and approached the terminal at high speed. At the time of the attack, approximately at 5:20 local time, two VLCC were moored alongside the oil platform: the unloaded MV *Apollo* and the fully loaded MV *Takasuza*. The leading one of the two approaching boats apparently aimed for the platform itself, whereas the second one went for the *Takasuza*—whether by chance or by intention is not clear. The lead boat came under machine gun fire from a position at the platform and detonated before it could hit the installation. The second one also came under fire but could not be intercepted in time and actually managed to ram the tanker at high speed although the two terrorists piloting it were already dead. However, its deadly cargo of about 700 lb of explosives failed to explode.[12]

The attack on KAAOT, which happened about 20 minutes earlier, is a novelty: the vessel chosen for the attack was a *dhow*—a rather slow and cumbersome vehicle when compared to the speedboats more commonly used. The vessel's slow approach gave the U.S. forces protecting the installation enough time to launch a "vessel boarding search and seizure" (VBSS) team from a nearby patrol boat. However, when the VBSS team attempted to board the *dhow*, it detonated. Two U.S. sailors and one U.S. coast guardsman were killed and five were injured by this blast.[13] It is anybody's guess what the real intention of the terrorists was. Although the powerful blast indicates that the vessel was laden with enough explosives to do serious damage at the terminal, its low-speed approach and the rather obvious unlikelihood of a successful "home run" could also mean that the aim here simply consisted in killing as many U.S. sailors as possible.

After the attack, both terminals were shut down for 24 hours for security reasons, although the damage to the terminals was slight: at the ABOT, an electrical generator was damaged. It is true that a successful attack on both of the terminals "would have brought Iraq's delicate economy to a standstill for months with serious consequences for global oil prices".[14] However, the experience from the later stages of the Iraq–Iran War in the 1980s shows that oil terminals are notoriously difficult targets: Even sustained air attacks from the Iraqi air force failed to destroy the Iranian oil terminal of Kharj in 1984 and 1985. Attacks by seaborne IEDs are also hardly likely to have more than "nuisance value" if proper security measures are taken. But still, the closure of both terminals for security reasons inflicted a cost of U.S.$28 million due to oil not being exported during this time.[15]

Suicide attacks are also the hallmark of the *Kadal Puli* or Sea Tigers. The Sea Tigers are the naval branch of the Liberation Tigers of Tamil Eelam (LTTE), sporting uniforms, ranks, and pennants like a "real" navy, and acting as such. Contrary to state navies, however, the Sea Tigers also have a special branch for suicide attacks, the so-called Black Sea Tigers. Tactically, the Black Sea Tigers rely on wolf pack-style attacks, carried out by fast attack crafts—some of them featuring a crude, self-made stealth design—aiming at overwhelming the defenses of their prey. In his report on a recent encounter between the Sri Lankan Navy and the Sea Tigers/Black Sea Tigers, Tony Birtley explains:

> The Sea Tigers' suicide craft are almost impossible to detect. They are dark, sit low in the water and cannot be detected by radar. The only way for the Sri Lankan navy to find them is through heat-detecting systems, but even then they travel at such speed that they are very difficult to shoot at. The boats, packed with explosives, are modelled on an American stealth bomber, but a more recent development is a human torpedo craft designed especially for suicide attacks.[16]

Although the ominous out-boarder-propelled human torpedo craft is yet to see action, the Sri Lankan Navy lost almost half their fleet to Sea Tigers/Black Sea Tigers suicide crafts. Sri Lanka Navy (SLN) vessels are not the only targets, the Sea Tigers also attack merchant vessels found in Sri Lankan coastal waters claimed by the LTTE. However, no merchant vessel ever came under suicide attack in a Sri Lankan port—although some Western-owned vessels have been shot up during attacks on naval bases situated in ports such as Colombo and Galle—and shipping on the sea lines of communication (SLOCs) leading through the Bay of Bengal has been safe from attacks so far.

At least in theory, light aircraft and small commercial aircraft could also qualify for VBIED attacks on ships and port facilities, but so far, such attacks have not happened. Compared to other types of VBIED attacks, that is, car bombs and suicide boats, the level of expertise needed for such types of attack would be considerably higher: individuals earmarked to carry out these airborne attacks would have to undergo sufficient flying lessons to safely take off, navigate, and descend into a reasonably large—and high-value—target, not too far away from the air strip. Having mentioned this, the LTTE's newly established aviation wing already proved their capability to conduct a bombing run on Colombo Airport, using a light aircraft. Thus, maybe, sooner or later we will see a "Black Air Tiger" squad emerge—but because this is sheer speculation, we better return to the facts.

The fact is that skills needed to carry out VBIED attacks range from fairly low to moderate, depending on the circumstances. Short-range attacks from jetties or other suitable locations at the shore against clearly visible and slow-moving or immobile targets under favorable weather and water conditions require only a very superficial familiarization with the boat used for the attack and certainly no advanced mariner skills as mentioned earlier. However, attacks launched under less-than favorable conditions, that is, choppy waters, fog, and dense traffic, would require at least some basic mariner skills. For example, in Australia, the minimum skill level for this purpose would be that provided by a recreational marine driver license course.[17] This course, which takes a minimum of six hours, includes theoretical and practical lessons.

Still, such inconspicuous and rather cheap courses would not provide operators with enough knowledge and skills to conduct long-range attacks, for which small boats are not feasible anyway. A way around this would be either to use a larger pleasure craft as the assault vessel or to operate from a mother ship. Such attacks have been launched by Somalian pirates, operating as far as 150 Nmi away from their shores from a *dhow*, and were planned by an Al-Qaeda terrorist cell based in Morocco to attack Western naval shipping in the Strait of Gibraltar. This group contemplated to also use their mother ship as a backup. As discussed earlier, a *dhow*, big enough to qualify as a mother ship, has already been used in a suicide attack against KAAOT. The low speed of this type of vessels, however, begs the question of how to approach inconspicuously enough to avoid evasive maneuvering from the targeted vessel. This would restrict the use of such vessels to narrow straits or harbors teeming with all kinds of ships and boats, including, for example, motor yachts, trawlers, or tugboats[18]—depending on the location, the maritime terrorist attack would be planned for. In any case, to strike successfully at locations far away from the shore, the terrorists would need fairly sophisticated skills including advanced navigational skills and the ability to use more or less complicated technology such as automatic radar plotting aid (ARPA)/radio detection and ranging (RADAR) systems or long-range navigation (LORAN) receivers.

SUBSURFACE IMPROVISED EXPLOSIVE DEVICE ATTACKS: SCUBA DIVERS AND LIMPET MINES

As stated earlier, some attack scenarios mentioned in the "maritime terrorism nightmare chart" sound a bit outlandish, and seem to be taken out of some Tom Clancy-style novels. Until recently, I would have also included scuba diving attacks in this category, dismissing the possibility of such attacks out of hand: they seem to be more complicated than they sound, and the rate of failure might be quite high.[19] However, and quite surprisingly, at least three scuba diving attacks directed against naval vessels can be confirmed so far. The better known of those three attacks has been committed by a diver team of LTTE's Sea Tigers in 1994, the lesser known but much earlier two strikes were carried out in 1975 by diver teams of the Argentinean guerrilla organization ironically named "Montoneros"—which translates into "Mountaineers."

The first confirmable subsurface maritime terrorist attack is the Montoneros' scuba attack on the Argentinean Navy's first guided-missile destroyer, *Santisima Trinidad* on August 27, 1975. This audacious operation had been planned since November 1974 by the Montoneros' "Arturo Lewinger Combat Platoon" studying underwater attacks conducted during World War II and adapting them to their capabilities and available equipment.[20] Richard Gillespie vividly describes the attack.

> A celluloid version might have conveyed the scene better than the guerrillas' printed account of it: the vessel lying in Ensenada Río Santiago Naval Shipyards, where it was being outfitted, protected by unsuspecting Naval Guards; the stealthy nocturnal approach of the saboteurs in a collapsible, camouflaged boat; the three-and-a-half-hour labours of Montonero frogmen, close enough to hear the guards chatting as they attached 170kg of underwater demolition charges to the hull; and the climactic explosion [...][21]

Although the Type-42 destroyer survived the powerful detonation, its hull was badly damaged and its electronic war suite completely destroyed. The damages delayed it from entering into service for about a year.[22]

The Montoneros' diver team conducted a similar operation in a mining attack on a yacht used by Argentine's Commander-in-Chief of the Navy, Admiral Emilio Eduardo Massera, on December 14, 1975, seriously damaging the vessel.[23] The series of maritime attacks may have even started a year earlier. On November 1, 1974, the Montoneros successfully bombed the yacht of General Commissioner Alberto Villar, the chief of the federal police. The evidence of this bombing attack that killed Villar and his wife is a bit circumstantial, however, it is an established fact that the bomb exploded soon after Villar steered his yacht away from the Tigre boat dock where it had been moored. However, it is not clear whether the bomb had been smuggled aboard and hidden between the floorboards and the engine by one of their operators, or whether it had been attached to the hull by a diver team. It is also not completely clear how the charge was triggered, some information point at remote control, and other sources claim that the charge was triggered by the heat of the engine. Be that as it may, the data available is too circumstantial to count this act of terror as a scuba diving attack. But still, the Montoneros committed the first two confirmed scuba diving attacks in the history of terrorism, showing that—despite the level of difficulty usually referred to by (combat) diving specialists—such attacks are perfectly feasible, given meticulous planning and training.

Meticulous planning and training is something the *Kadal Puli* or Sea Tigers of the LTTE, mentioned earlier, excel in. It is thus not surprising that—apart from its ubiquitous suicide attacks—they also have launched at least one successful scuba diving attack and attempted several others. The one confirmable successful operation was carried out on April 19, 1995, when a team of LTTE divers blew up two Sri Lankan Navy gunboats in Trincomalee. This successful scuba diving attack was followed up by another attack nearly a year later, again with Sri Lankan Navy ships as the chosen targets. Allegedly, the diver team attempted to attach a limpet mine at the hull of the ship but failed to do so. Instead of aborting the mission, the divers are said to have pressed the mine against the hull by their bodies and then exploded it, turning the mission into a suicide operation. Unfortunately, not much credible information was available on this mission, at least not from open sources. It is difficult to establish facts as there are two completely different reports of this (botched) attack on the port of Colombo on April 12, 1996. For example, a press release of the LTTE stated the following:

> Last Thursday at about 9.30 pm six LTTE Black Tigers from LTTE under water diving divisions set off from Mutuwal which is about two miles from the Colombo port. The team included four male divers from the Sulojan Diving Division and two female divers from the Ankayatkanni Diving Division. Around midnight they reached the entry area of Colombo port. Three of the divers attached timed explosives to a fuel-carrying cargo ship and two general cargo transporters moored 700 m away. Their timers were set to go off together. The divers then swam out to an LTTE speed boat loaded with explosives outside the harbour. The three other divers headed towards the naval yard where six major fighting ships were moored. They secured the bombs to the hulls of three of the vessels and detonated the explosives together at about 1.30 am. All the six vessels were destroyed and were sunk within minutes of each other.[24]

A completely different story emerges in a press report of the Sri Lankan Ministry of Defence, however.

> On April 12, around 0545 hrs, two LTTE cadres were detected under water at the entrance to the Colombo Harbour by naval personnel using sonar equipment. The two LTTE cadres were fired at by the naval personnel killing them instantly. Two Sea Tigers exploded indicating that they were carrying explosives in [sic] their person. Around 0615 hours a white colour vallam [small boat; P.L.] carrying a minimum of three LTTE cadres attempted to gain entry to the Harbour. On detection, naval personnel fired at the vallam sinking it. All three Sea Tigers were killed as a result. [...] Two merchant vessels were slightly damaged due to the cross fire. [...][25]

Although there is more evidence supporting the version of the Ministry of Defence than the claims of the LTTE, fact is that LTTE divers actually attempted to attack the port of Colombo on that day. And, if the Ministry of Defence's report is correct, this would also be the first-ever use of sonar equipment to thwart a scuba diving attack launched by maritime terrorists—or, in this case, guerrillas, if one prefers.

However, as stated earlier, so far only three scuba diving attacks can be confirmed. Apart from them and the unsuccessful attempt described earlier, we know of several other incidents involving limpet mines, of which it is not clear whether the mines were attached to the hull by divers below or near the waterline or whether they were fixed to the hull elsewhere or to parts of the vessel's superstructure. One such attack was launched by the Algerian Front de Libération Nationale (FLN; National Liberation Front) during their war of independence, targeting a French warship at the French naval base of Toulon. Another limpet mine attack by activists of the Sea Shepherds sunk the Cypriot-registered whaler *Sierra,* in the port of Lisbon on February 6, 1980.[26]

Both expertise and equipment needed for such attacks are, in theory at least, easy enough to acquire. With regard to equipment, even rebreathers—formerly strictly for military use—can now be bought without raising an alarm because rebreathers do not produce bubbles and they are perfect for fish watching and photographing, which is why there is a certain demand among recreational divers nowadays. Of course, the absence of bubbles also means that there are no visible traces of diving activity on the surface, which is why rebreathers have been used by combat divers in the first place and which is why they would also be perfect for maritime terrorists. As a matter of fact, the LTTE's Sea Tigers already acquired rebreathers and trained some of their commandos in the use of these systems. Also, diver propulsion vehicles, starting at bargain price levels, are widely available. For example, I remember having seen some of the entry-level models at the duty-free zone of Heathrow Terminal 3.

The know-how needed to make use of such technology is provided by scuba diving schools, catering for more tourists, especially during holiday season as it is a popular sport. A Professional Association of Diving Instructors (PADI) Advanced Open Water Diver course, for example, includes practical and theoretical lessons on the use of diver propulsion vehicles, on night diving (including underwater navigation by night), and even the art of lifting and moving heavy material underwater in its search and recovery diver module.[27] The course costs a couple of hundred U.S. dollars only and takes about two days, five dives included. PADI also offers specialty courses for each (and many more) of the specialties described earlier, in which the respective skills can be honed. Other scuba diving organizations offer similar courses so that, again, in theory, individuals planning acts of maritime terrorism could acquire quite sophisticated skills, which would enable them to plan, organize, and carry out a scuba diving attack with a degree of confidence. Interestingly, circumstantial evidence points at a more professional support at least for Sea Tiger divers—allegedly, their commandos are trained by ex-Norwegian Special Forces members in "techniques and tactics of underwater demolitions" on "a small island in the Andaman Sea".[28]

The "iffy" questions remaining in this context are how to acquire the explosives needed—but that is a problem every terrorist cell has to solve—and how to turn them into a limpet mine, that is, an explosive charge, which will stay attached to the hull and explode after being triggered, or just the latter if we are talking about an underwater suicide attack. Also, the problems posed by navigating at night in a busy harbor in very low visibility should not be underestimated.[29] Nevertheless, the Montoneros' frogmen team and the Sea Tigers' scuba diving commando—again, the Sea Tigers may well enjoy professional support in this regard as well—proved beyond any reasonable doubt that such obstacles can be overcome. Scuba diving attacks have been conducted in the past, so we may have to face them in the future as well.

Standoff Weapon Attacks

Another way of attacking ships that actually have been used once or twice is firing at them from short to medium range with certain kinds of standoff weapons. In theory, standoff weapons range from heavy-caliber sniper rifles such as the famous Barrett to machine guns to rocket-propelled grenades to mortars and other unguided missiles. In a landmark study conducted by Clark et al., rifles, machine guns, and mortars were discounted as feasible standoff weapons: rifles and machine guns for lack of impact on big ships, and mortars for lack of accuracy in regard to hitting a moving target.[30] Clark's assumptions in regard to rifles and machine guns are borne out by the fact that assault rifle fire is frequently used in piracy attacks to cow the targeted crews into submission, but not in an attempt to seriously damage the vessel, whereas machine guns have been used by the LTTE's Sea Tigers, for example, in a daring attack on the port of Colombo, during which several ships' superstructures have been raked by machine gun salvoes. The damages inflicted in such attacks were inconsequential, however. Rocket-propelled grenades and antitank missiles are an entirely different story—at least in theory.

The *Seabourn Spirit*, a cruise ship of Seabourn Cruises, came under such a standoff weapon attack on November 5, 2005, approximately 100 sea miles off Somalia's coast. The attackers were a gang of pirates on board of two 25-ft long fiberglass boats, who attempted to stop the vessel with a barrage of AK-47 rounds and at least two RPG-7 grenades. Usually, Somalian pirates are quite successful in hijacking ships and crews by such a show of brute force. This time, however, their attack was unsuccessful, thanks to the determined counteractions by the crew: while the captain and his crew on the bridge first tried to ram and capsize one of the boats to prevent the pirates from boarding and then increased the speed to outrun them, other crew members under the command of the ship's security officer successfully deployed a sonic gun to frighten away the attackers. This "long range acoustic device" (LRAD) was developed after the attack on the USS *Cole* in October 2000 as a nonlethal weapon to keep small boats from approaching U.S. warships.[31] None of the passengers were harmed during the action, but one crew member suffered minor injuries by shrapnel. One of the RPGs actually penetrated the hull, damaging a stateroom, whereas another RPG was reported as having bounced off the stern. Further minor damages were caused by the pirates' gunfire.

Three months before this attack, on August 19, 2005, an Al-Qaeda cell had already used standoff weapons in an attempt to attack two large U.S. Navy vessels. The targeted vessels are high-value targets for maritime terrorists. One of them, USS *Kearsarge* (LHD 3), being a Wasp-class amphibious assault ship with a displacement of 40,500 t and an overall length of 257 m,[32] looks like an aircraft carrier. The other one, USS *Ashland* (LSD 48), is a Whidbey Island-class dock landing ship with a displacement of nearly 17,000 t and an overall length of 186 m.[33] Both vessels came under fire by two unguided missiles—probably the ubiquitous *Qassam* or a derivative—while visiting the Jordanian port of Aqaba. Neither of the two warships was hit. However, one Jordanian soldier was killed and another injured by this attack. The *Abdullah al Azzam Brigades*, affiliated with Al-Qaeda, claimed responsibility for this unsuccessful attack, and a video clip appeared soon after, showing several operatives firing missiles at an undisclosed location against an equally undisclosed target. It is doubtful whether the clip is authentic, but in any case, the attempted attack rather serves to reinforce the point made by Clarke et al. that mortar rounds and unguided missiles are not nearly precise enough to attack naval or maritime targets.

There is yet another category of standoff weapon attacks, even if we are pushing it a little now. If a high-value target such as an LNG tanker cannot be attacked from land, sea, or subsea due to exclusion zones, coast guard cutters, and police patrol cars along the shore, a light aircraft could be used as a vehicle of attack in a "conventional" bombing run. However, this scenario is mentioned only because the LTTE obviously has acquired both the light planes and the skills necessary to operate them, as demonstrated by their air raid on Colombo Airport. Apart from that, such a scenario is purely speculative at the time of writing.

MARITIME TERRORISM II: NON-IMPROVISED EXPLOSIVE DEVICE ATTACKS

Apart from IED attacks, other devastating attacks on ships with the intention of sinking them have been reported, which did not involve the use of explosives, but the time-honored tactics of ramming and sabotaging the targeted vessels. These types of attacks are not very well known to the public, therefore, are discussed first. Much better known because of the *Achille Lauro* incident are cases of hijacking of ships—also known as "shipjacking." Here, the targeted vessel is not necessarily attacked to sink it, but to take the crew or, in the case of cruise liners, the crew and passengers hostage for ransom or for coercing governments to release certain prisoners. This category of attack forms the last part of our analysis of maritime terrorist attacks.

RAMMING ATTACKS AND SABOTAGE

In the introduction, the "momentum weapon" scenario was briefly mentioned in which big ships could be used to ram either other vessels or port facilities to be exploded there, and it was also mentioned that the PSA considers such a scenario to be credible. However, we preferred to call it "high impact, low probability." Still, it should be pointed out that such attacks took place quite frequently, although in a very narrow context and restricted to just one actor and one special set of targets: the Sea Shepherds as actors, and trawlers involved in illegal fishing and whaling operations as targets. A case in point is the sustained attack on the Cypriot-registered whaler *Sierra*, which was rammed twice by a Sea Shepherd vessel in the harbor on July 16, 1979, "tearing the hull open to the waterline and forcing the ship into port for repairs,"[34] and finally sunk "by Sea Shepherd operatives in Lisbon harbour on February 6, 1980"[35] by limpet mines[36]—an act for which the Sea Shepherds openly claimed responsibility. The Sea Shepherds also claim to have sunk two other whalers in 1980, claiming that

> Sea Shepherd successfully shut down all pirate whaling operations in the North Atlantic within a year after a dozen years of failure by the International Whaling Commission. The IWC has no enforcement division to insure its laws are upheld.[37]

All in all, since 1980, the Sea Shepherds have attacked and sunk or damaged at least six whalers and trawlers by ramming them. As Richard Lloyd Perry reports, "[their] flagship, *Farley Mowat*, is equipped with a "hydraulic can opener," which could seriously damage the hull of another vessel".[38] Obviously, this "can opener" works perfectly fine.

Another tactic employed by the Sea Shepherds is sabotaging vessels at quayside or dockside by sneaking aboard and opening the seacocks. An example for this tactic is the scuttling of two Icelandic whaling ships—half of their fleet, as the Sea Shepherds comment—in November 1986 by two Sea Shepherd engineers.[39] Both tactics so far have only been used by the Sea Shepherds, for obvious reasons: scuttling a ship by opening the seacocks requires an intimate knowledge of the ships' architecture and design to find and recognize them without delay; ramming a ship to seriously damage its hull requires an intimate knowledge of one's own vessel's capabilities and an ability to use these capabilities to the maximum along with advanced navigational skills and a familiarity with harbor and port piloting. If the targeted ship is moving, its course and speed in relation to the attacking ship has to be calculated as well as to hit it hard enough to damage it without risking one's own vessel. Such operations, meant to damage ships without hurting anyone, are very obviously an order of magnitude more complex than the perpendicular speedboat suicide attacks on slowly moving ships or ships not moving at all[40]—which is why, in all probability, we will not see such highly sophisticated and usually victimless attacks launched by maritime terrorists.

HIJACKING SHIPS: AT THE NEXUS BETWEEN POLITICAL PIRACY AND MARITIME TERRORISM

Much more likely to happen (again) are scenarios built around the hijacking of ships. Such acts did occur even before 9/11, and they still occur on a regular basis, albeit in the context of piracy. The attack on the *Seabourn Spirit*, for example, most probably was an attempt to hijack the ship and hold the passengers at ransom. Frequent attacks on local trawlers in the Straits of Malacca usually have the same purpose, but sometimes, ships simply disappear after having been hijacked. So far, these "phantom ships" have fallen prey to the most serious acts of piracy—high-level armed assault or robbery (HLAAR), better known as "major criminal hijack" (MCHJ). In the relatively new context of maritime piracy, it is not impossible that hijacked tugs or trawlers might reappear as suicide vessels as described earlier.

In theory at least, large vessels such as oil tankers, LNG carriers, chemical tankers, and the like could be hijacked to scuttle them in a narrow strait, or, less likely with regard to heightened security in basically all of the major hub ports, use them as "momentum weapons," that is, drive them at high speed into other high-value ships or port facilities. And, even more into the realm of theory, a cruise liner could be hijacked by a group of maritime terrorists because such a brazen act, if successful, would give them immediate 24-hour global news coverage. The hijacking of the Italian cruise ship *Achille Lauro* is a case in point.

The hijacking of the *Achille Lauro* was actually not the first act of maritime terrorism—there had been a hijacking in 1961 in the port of La Guaria, Venezuela, when the Portuguese cruise liner *Santa Maria* was temporarily taken over by 25 armed men in a protest against Portugal and Spain—but it is the first spectacular one: 450 crew members and 97 passengers of the 631-ft long cruise ship were taken hostage by just 4 terrorists, and 1 person got killed.[41]

On October 3, 1985, the *Achille Lauro* left the port of Genoa for an 11-day cruise through the Strait of Messina to Egypt and Israel with 748 passengers and 450 crew members on board. Also on board were four young men, of whom eyewitnesses said after the hijacking that they behaved suspiciously, always sticking together. On October 7, the ship reached Alexandria, and 651 passengers took the opportunity to participate in a bus tour to the pyramids. These passengers were meant to reembark some hours later in Port Said. Soon after the majority of the passengers had left the ship, the four young men, members of a faction of the Palestine Liberation Front (PLF), took over. They fired their assault rifles, which they had smuggled on board to frighten the crew, rounded up the remaining 97 passengers, and ordered the captain to get the ship out of the port. They made the captain and the crew believe that there were, all in all, 20 hijackers on board.

The four hijackers then demanded the immediate release of 50 Palestinians being held in Israeli prisons. Because Israel did not respond to their demands, they threatened to kill their hostages. On Tuesday, October 8, they shot dead Leon Klinghoffer, a U.S. citizen, and threatened to kill a second passenger. After protracted negotiations with Italian, Egyptian, and Syrian authorities, the four hijackers agreed to end their action and to leave the ship on Wednesday, October 9. A small boat took them aboard in Egyptian waters near Port Said. It later emerged that their original intention might have been to attack Ashdod, Israel, which would have been the next port of call after Port Said. Some news reports claimed that when a cabin steward spotted their concealed weapons, the four terrorists panicked, which resulted in them hijacking the ship.[42] Whatever their intention may have been, the hijacking prompted the International Maritime Organization to complement the U.N. Law of the Sea Convention with an addendum, the "Suppression of Unlawful Acts at Sea" Convention, also known as "Rome Convention."

Major cruise lines will be quick in pointing out that security measures have been vastly improved after this incident, therefore, a repetition of such an act is highly unlikely. That may be true, but it is also true that all these "floating cities" or "floating casinos" are highly visible and irresistible targets for maritime terrorists. The expected gains from a successful hijacking of one of these ships—which often stop at destinations where security measures are rather lax—may outweigh the risks the maritime terrorists would have to take by a margin wide enough to make them at least think about it. A terrorist cell affiliated to Al-Qaeda based in Morocco allegedly planned such an operation when they were arrested by the police.

The level of difficulty of such operations, however, is an order of a magnitude higher than suicide attacks. The terrorist group would have to solve the problem of smuggling weapons and explosives on board, as well as getting their operatives there—if they are not already aboard acting as crew members. They would need to be familiar with the ship's design, and with the route taken by the ship on that particular cruise. Several commando-style scenarios have been offered to me by members of certain maritime special forces, ranging from the rather simple and straightforward to the overly complicated. They need not be discussed here. Suffice it to say that cruise liners stopping in ports prone to corruption, organized crime activity, and piracy are much more at risk than high-profile cruise liners such as the *Queen Mary*.

CONCLUSION

Basically, all naval or maritime specialists dealing with maritime terrorism are convinced that, given Al-Qaeda's propensity for patient and intricate preparation, a sustained maritime terrorism campaign in the near future seems to be highly likely.[43] Not being so sure about that, it is argued in this chapter that even if such a campaign would be launched, the types of attack chosen by Al-Qaeda and affiliated groups as the most likely actors would be "high probability, low impact" variant strikes rather than "low probability, high impact" acts of maritime megaterrorism. It is plausible that terrorists embarking on a terror campaign in an unknown environment would draw on their existing capabilities and skills to minimize their risks instead of immediately going for a "maritime big bang." Thus, working under the assumption that terrorists (a) are copycats and (b) have to make do with limited resources, this chapter examined maritime terror attacks both pre- and post-9/11 because these attacks can be seen as the shadow of the future: they already worked for terrorist actors, the special set of maritime expertise and skills is rather modest, and the attacks are comparatively cheap, especially with regard to the damage inflicted on the targets.

If one takes a look at the statistics, seaborne suicide attacks (both successful and unsuccessful ones) against ships by ramming them with small vessels are the most frequent of all such known acts of maritime terrorism. Apart from frequent suicide attacks committed by the LTTE Sea Tigers against ships of the Sri Lankan Navy, there were several attempts to attack Western—usually United States—warships in the Gulf, Arabian Sea, and Strait of Gibraltar. So far, only one attempt was successful—the October 2000 attack on the USS *Cole,* killing 17 sailors. All other attempts either misfired like the attack on the USS *The Sullivans* in January 2000 due to technical problems or were prevented from taking place at all by successful counterterrorist operations such as the uncovering of a plot to attack Western ships in the Strait of Gibraltar by Moroccan law enforcement authorities. There was one suicide attack in November 2002 by members of the "Islamic Jihad" on a patrol boat of the Israeli Defence Force, which suffered only minor damage. There was also one successful suicide attack on Western commercial shipping, targeting the tanker *Limburg* in October 2002, and one unsuccessful attempt on two oil terminals in the Persian Gulf, ABOT and KAAOT, as described earlier.

Very surprisingly, scuba diving attacks follow as the second most frequent type of maritime terrorist attacks: so far, there have been three confirmed and at least two probable underwater attacks, as discussed earlier. Knowing that Al-Qaeda and Al-Qaeda-affiliated groups such as Jemaah Islamiyah and the ASG have already been trying to acquire scuba diving expertise, we can expect this type of clandestine maritime terrorist attacks to be attempted in the near future.

Successful or attempted nonsuicide bombing attacks relying on IEDs are the third most common method of attack, but only if one lumps together the *Superferry 14* bombing, the failed attempt to bomb an oil refinery in Singapore, and the Basra bombing attack on a British river patrol in one category.

Nonlethal attacks such as ramming ships or sabotaging them in ports without injuring crew members or anybody else have been and should be treated as a category of its own. They are acts of ecological terrorism, so far restricted to one actor and one group of targets: on the one hand, the Sea Shepherds as actors, and on the other hand, whalers and trawlers involved in illegal fishing or whaling operations. However, it can be expected that such acts of ecoterrorism will increase in frequency over the next couple of years, affecting other types of ships more and more. Vessels transporting hazardous cargoes such as nuclear waste or chemicals readily come to mind, and so do offshore installations such as oil rigs or mobile drilling platforms, especially so if they are intended for explorative drilling in the previously "pristine" Arctic or Antarctic waters. Acts of ecoterror would probably continue to be conducted in such a fashion that nobody gets injured and that the environment does not get polluted, which points at attempts to sabotage vessels at anchor, ramming attacks or attempts of boarding/hijacking targeted vessels or oil rigs.

It is noteworthy that all acts of maritime terrorism so far have been short-range attacks against ships moored in a port or against port facilities—the *Seabourn Spirit* attack being the only incident where a ship has come under attack more than 150 Nmi offshore. This brazen act of maritime piracy rather than terrorism will probably remain the proverbial exception confirming the rule because maritime terrorists—again, so far—neither have the capability nor the inclination of launching attacks on the high seas, for a variety of reasons.

Some acts of maritime terrorism could be prevented by taking the provisions of ISPS serious: acts of sabotage, for example, or acts of boarding/hijacking. Both categories of maritime terrorism could be prevented by a vigilant crew—that is, if there is not just a skeleton crew of a dozen or less persons on board to drive down operating costs. The bad news is, even the best ship's security plans notwithstanding, there is not much commercial shipping could do to fend off suicide attacks launched by a determined actor. A targeted ship's crew would rather be in the position of the master of the *Limburg*, seeing a dinghy approaching at high speed, and unable to do anything about it. Even if the targeted ship is not moored to any facility, it is unlikely that the officer of the watch could react in time to dodge a fast-moving small boat. Even the vaunted "sonic gun" would probably not be good enough to fend off such an attack—although it would be better than nothing. Also, there is nothing much shippers could do to prevent scuba diving attacks from happening: commercial ships are not equipped with any sonar system, and crews are nowadays so small that there are not enough sailors on board to constantly monitor pitch-black waters for traces of bubbles—in case the submarine attackers do not use rebreathers. Interestingly, sonar systems tailor-made to detect scuba diving attacks are already available, a few ports already have installed them, and the port of Colombo allegedly even used one to fend off a scuba diving attack. But because scuba diving attacks are usually perceived to be highly unlikely to ever happen, cash-strapped ports are not in a hurry to routinely install them—which may well turn out to be a costly mistake.

The good news is, in case a commercial vessel is a high-value target such as an LNG carrier, a chemical tanker, an oil tanker, or a cruise ship, the likelihood is quite high that the port establishes an exclusion zone around it, patrolled by some maritime law enforcement agencies. They might even deploy a floating barrier to prevent suicide attacks from happening. Unfortunately, and that is bad news again, not all ports in all parts of the world will be that quick in addressing their security problems: signing up to the ISPS Code or CSI is one thing, implementing all the nice plans that look good on paper is another. Therefore, the only consolation that readers can get out of this contribution is that acts of maritime terror have been few and far between up to now, and that in all probability, the number of such attacks will not rise dramatically in the foreseeable future—there are simply too many targets at land that can be attacked with a high probability of success so that terrorist groups need not dabble in a territory that is unfamiliar to them. The chances are good that crew members can spend their entire professional life at sea without them or their ship ever being a victim of a maritime terrorist attack. This only leaves the odd act of piracy to worry about.

NOTES

1. Greenberg and Chalk et al. state that according to the Research and Development (Corporation) (RAND) Terrorism database, maritime terrorist attacks constitute only 2 percent of all international incidents of terrorism during the last three decades. See Greenberg, Michael D. Chalk, Peter et al., *Maritime Terrorism. Risk and Liability.* Santa Monica, CA: RAND Corporation, 2006, p. 9. Depending on the definition of terrorism chosen (i.e., is the attack on the USS *Cole* a terrorist attack or a guerrilla incident?), incidences of maritime terrorism could even constitute less than 1 percent over the same period.
2. Greenberg and Chalk et al., ibid., p. 10.

3. The expression "Pirate Wind" refers to the easterly winds which in the seventeenth and eighteenth centuries brought the Sulu pirate fleets to the coasts of Borneo. See Rutter, Owen, *The Pirate Wind. Tales of the Sea-Robbers of Malaya.* Singapore, Oxford and New York: Oxford University Press, 1986.

4. This is the argument of Peter Chalk, put forward in his monograph *Grey-Area Phenomena in Southeast Asia: Piracy, Drug Trafficking and Political Terrorism.* Canberra: Strategic Defence Centre, 1997 (Canberra Papers on Strategy and Defence No. 123), p. 24.

5. Translated by Ulph, Stephen and Heffelfinger, Christopher, in "Anti-Ship Warfare and Molotov Cocktails at the Siege of Acre, 1190," in Sirrs, Julie; Abedin, Mahan and Heffelfinger, Christopher (eds.) *Unmasking Terror: A Global Review of Terrorist Activities. A Compendium of Articles from Jamestown's Terrorism Monitor, September 11, 2003 – September 11, 2004.* Washington: The Jamestown Foundation, 2004, pp. 86–90.

6. These initiatives are covered in several other chapters of this book, which is why they will be ignored here.

7. More information can be found at the Lloyd's Marine Intelligence Unit. See at http://www.lloydsmiu.com/lmiu/products.htm (accessed on August 15, 2007).

8. LaMoshi, Gary, "How It Could Happen ..." *Asia Times Online*, August 11, 2004 (see this and related articles at http://www.atimes.com; accessed on August 9, 2007).

9. This is also the opinion of Greenberg and Chalk et al., op. cit., pp. 10–11.

10. The story of the Laju Incident can be found at the Web site of the Ministry of Defence Singapore at http://www.mindef.gov.sg/imindef/about_us/history/birth_of_saf/v06n01_history.html (accessed on August 9, 2007).

11. As cited in Herbert-Burns, Rupert, "Terrorism in the Early 21st Century Maritime Domain," in Ho, Joshua and Raymond, Catherine Zara (eds.) *The Best of Times, The Worst of Times: Maritime Security in the Asia-Pacific.* Singapore: World Scientific, 2005, pp. 155–178.

12. A Jewish Institute for National Security Affairs (JINSA) online report argues that both boats exploded before they could hit their targets. See Howland, Jonathan, "Countering Maritime Terror, U.S. Thwarts Attacks, Builds Up Foreign Navies," *JINSA Online*, June 17, 2004 (http://www.jinsa.org/articles/print.html/documentid/2567; accessed on November 07, 2006).

13. Ibid.

14. Ibid.

15. Whether this is a "real" cost or not depends on the ability of both terminals to make up for the delay.

16. Birtley, Tom, "Sri Lanka Battles Tigers at Sea," *Aljazeera.net*, 11 June 2007 (see at http://english.aljazeera.net/NR/exeres/F827D082-514A-42B8-BF43-03DA00F6FA7E.htm, accessed on August 9, 2007). The article includes a link to a video clip on this engagement on *You Tube* (direct link: http://www.youtube.com/watch?v=HFp0bjSgwe4, accessed August 8, 2007).

17. For example, see the requirements for Queensland, Australia at http://www.msq.qld.gov.au/Home/Licensing/Recreational/Boatsafe_course (accessed on August 9, 2007).

18. During the last couple of years, quite a few trawlers and tugboats have been hijacked by local pirates. Maritime terrorists could be tempted to do the same, using the hijacked vessel for their own purpose.

19. See, for example, the failed mock attack in the port of Rotterdam conducted by experienced scuba diving instructors, as described in Richardson, Michael, *A Time Bomb for Global Trade. Maritime-related Terrorism in an Age of Weapons of Mass Destruction.* Singapore: ISEAS, 2004, pp. 20–22.

20. Gillespie, Richard, *Soldiers of Peron: Argentina's Montoneros.* Oxford, U.K.: Clarendon Press, 1982, p. 196.

21. Ibid., with further references.

22. Gillespie, Richard, op. cit., pp. 196–197. Ironically, the Santísima Trinidad being a British design, it played a lead role during the first stage of Argentine's "Operation Azul"—the amphibious landing on April 1 and 2, 1982 near Mullet Creek, East Falkland Islands, to capture Government House.

23. Gillespie, Richard, op. cit., p. 197.

24. Athas, Iqbal, "LTTE Willing to Lose Space But Not Men," *The Sunday Times Situation Report*, Sunday Times, Colombo, 21 April 1996 (see at http://www.sundaytimes.lk/960421/sitrep.html; accessed on October 22, 2007).

25. Ibid.

26. Sea Shepherd Conservation Society, "Defending Whales. The History of Sea Shepherd Conservation Society and Whaling." See at http://www.seashepherd.org/whales/whales_SSCS_history.html (accessed on August 21, 2007).

27. See the description of available advanced open water diver modules at PADI's website at http://www.padi.com/english/common/courses/rec/continue/aow.asp (accessed on August 10, 2007).

28. Chalk, Peter, "Liberation Tiger of Tamil Eelam's (LTTE) International Organization and Operations—A Preliminary Analysis," *Commentary*, SCG International Business Risk Consultancy, February 2003. See at http://www.scgonline.net/special/WIB/No19/TamilNo19.htm (accessed on October 22, 2007).

29. For this reason, in June 2007, the FBI issued another alert to the U.S. scuba industry with regard to requests to dive in murky waters or sewer pipes, and other requests inconsistent with ordinary recreational diving, including the use of rebreathers and propulsion vehicles, extra navigation training and conducting kick-counts (a navigation aid). See the FBI alert at the Web site of the Underwater Times at http://www.underwatertimes.com/news.php?article_id=64810251370 (accessed on August 8, 2007).

30. See Clarke, Richard A. et al., *LNG Facilities in Urban Areas. A Security Risk Management Analysis for Attorney General Patrick Lynch Rhode Island.* Rhode Island: Pro Bono Publications, May 2005, pp. 84–96.

31. For more information on LRAD, see http://www.defense-update.com/products/l/LRAD.htm (accessed on November, 18, 2005).

32. Information from Wikipedia, "USS Kearsarge (LHD-3)," available at http://en.wikipedia.org/wiki/USS_Kearsarge_(LHD-3) (accessed on August 25, 2007).

33. Information from Wikipedia, "USS Ashland (LSD-48)," available at http://en.wikipedia.org/wiki/USS_Ashland_%28LSD-48%29 (accessed on August 25, 2007).

34. Sea Shepherd Conservation Society, "Defending Whales. The History of Sea Shepherd Conservation Society and Whaling," http://www.seashepherd.org/whales/whales_SSCS_history.html (accessed on August 21, 2007).

35. Ibid.

36. "Sea Shepherd's Record of Violence," *The High North News Extra*, No. 7, April 10, 1994, available online at http://www.highnorth.no/Library/Movements/Sea_Shepherd/se-sh-re.htm (accessed August 21, 2007).

37. Sea Shepherd Conservation Society, "Defending Whales. The History of Sea Shepherd Conservation Society and Whaling," http://www.seashepherd.org/whales/whales_SSCS_history.html (accessed on August 21, 2007).

38. Parry, Richard Lloyd, "Whalers Aid in Antarctic Rescue of Environmentalists," *Times Online*, February 9, 2007, http://www.timesonline.co.uk/tol/news/world/asia/article1358479.ece (accessed on August 21, 2007).

39. Sea Shepherd Conservation Society, "Defending Whales. The History of Sea Shepherd Conservation Society and Whaling," http://www.seashepherd.org/whales/whales_SSCS_history.html (accessed on August 21, 2007).

40. The same view is expressed by Pelkofski, James, "Before the Storm: Al Qaeda's Maritime Campaign," *Proceedings*, Annapolis, MD: U.S. Naval Institute, December 27, 2005.

41. See, for example, Bohn, M. K., *The Achille Lauro Hijacking. Lessons in the Politics and Prejudice of Terrorism.* Washington: Brassey's, 2004.

42. Bohn, M. K., ibid., p. 15.

43. Pelkofski, James, "Before the Storm: Al Qaeda's Maritime Campaign," *Proceedings*, U.S. Naval Institute, December 27, 2005.

6 Distinctions in the Finer Shades of Gray: The "Four Circles Model" for Maritime Security Threat Assessment

Hans Tino Hansen

CONTENTS

Maritime security threats are currently often labeled by the type of attack or criminal acts, with piracy and terrorism being the two most widely used. The media, for the sake of simplifying argument, labels these acts as being carried out either by "pirates" or by "terrorists." However, deeper understanding of security threats in the maritime domain is much more complex, and careful analysis of the potential perpetrators is necessary. These threats should be seen in a total perspective where all relevant security threats are addressed and the gray areas between these threats are identified and explained. Focusing on individual and specific parts of these threats may be an academic interest, but will not in itself provide a useful foundation for risk management methodology for the people who are responsible for tasking, chartering, operating, or indeed protecting vessels and facilities in the shipping and offshore domain.

The Four Circles Model[1] has been developed for the utilization of a methodology where all relevant security threats can be compartmentalized to help the stakeholder better understand the ultimate aim of the organization behind the threat and, therefore, motivation, intent, and tactics selection. In the process, the model reveals that much of today's acts of maritime crime are carried out by organized crime organizations and syndicates and insurgency groups rather than the traditional pirates or terrorists.

Analysis in the last ten years has mainly been driven by the threat of terrorist attacks against maritime targets, also labeled as "maritime terrorism." In the past, acts of terrorism have been carried out against a number of maritime targets with the majority perpetrated against passenger-carrying vessels such as ferries and cruise ships as these targets resulted in the highest level of publicity for the cause of the terrorists where the objective is political in nature. Examples of such incidents include *Santa Maria* in 1961, *Achille Lauro* in 1985, the *City of Poros* in 1998, *Our Lady of Mediatrix* in 2000, and the recent *SuperFerry 14* in 2004. Other attacks have also been directed against military targets such as the USS *Cole* and USS *Ashland* in 2002 and 2005, respectively. However, comparatively few attacks have been carried out against commercial shipping vessels, nevertheless, notable examples of attacks against nonpassenger merchant shipping includes the Liberian-registered tanker *Coral Sea* in 1971, Greek freighter *Vory* in 1974, and the well-known attack against the VLCC tanker *Limburg* in 2002.

Generally, maritime targets have had a low attraction for terrorist groups because they offered less publicity and a less dramatic impact or net gain in relation to the level of complex planning and execution required. Aeroplanes, public buildings, trains, and other similar nonmaritime targets have traditionally offered a more effective output ratio for terrorists, and therefore less than 2 percent of registered terrorist attacks have so far been carried out against maritime targets.[2]

Nevertheless, terrorism has been a powerful element in shaping the design, and the singular driver behind, development, and implementation of the International Ship and Port Facility Security (ISPS) Code and has also been the most widely discussed maritime security threat in international media as well as in expert studies by academics, think tanks, and analytical institutes since 2000. A great number of restricted as well as public studies have been produced discussing various forms of maritime terrorism, developed from case studies as well as hypothetical threats constructed for analytical reasons, or in rare cases, to provide a basis for specific planning and practical agenda. In some of these studies, the potential threat level for types of maritime terrorism has been widely exaggerated due to personal, political, or other reasons. Other studies have followed the American One Percent Doctrine[3] and analyzed worst-case scenarios with nuclear bombs of different types, although openly contending that the probability of such an attack is extremely low.

Terrorism, thus, is perhaps the most widely analyzed threat among the wider list of security concerns confronting governments and the commercial sector. Wider studies and the more focused technical case-study analysis continue to concentrate on assessing worst-case scenarios at the point of impact (to the company or vessel), whereas at the same time, conversely, highlighting very low levels of probability.

However, the total threat picture in the maritime domain consists of a number of levels of threats that are distinctive and represent different types of criminal activities directed toward the maritime sector. Understanding the levels themselves as well as the interrelationship between them is equally important; this holistic approach will result in greatly improved and useful threat intelligence. This approach can similarly lead to improved threat and risk assessments for the commercial sector, resulting in more finessed security risk management at the operational level. At the strategic and political levels, a more nuanced and sophisticated understanding of maritime threats will enable improved, better-coordinated countermeasures, and the ability to more specifically determine the effects of such measures in the short-, medium-, and long-term.

This chapter presents the analytical model, which has been developed by Risk Intelligence to explain the character of maritime security threats and their relation to the maritime domain. The Four Circles Model has been developed with the aim of producing an analytical framework that can present the complex set of threats in an illustrative manner, although simultaneously allowing for a more detailed analysis of organizational characteristics and interaction between them.

THE FOUR CIRCLES MODEL

Today's media has not only a tendency to generalize the threats from terrorism and piracy to make it more understandable to the general public but also because they do not have enough knowledge about the subjects they are writing on. This leads to stereotypes that alter the public's image of the threats. Furthermore, it also contributes to the terminology used by officials and politicians, which can also be misleading or erroneous. Defining terrorism today is a different undertaking when compared to 10–20 years ago when, for instance, only attacks against civilian targets were considered as acts of terrorism. Practical use of the term "terrorism" has had an important impact on the understanding of the concept where attacks against military targets are now also—in the broader sense of the term—included in the general perception of terrorism.[4]

In understanding maritime security threats from groups conducting unlawful acts, it is important to understand their motivation, organizational structure, and tactics. Understanding their background will enable the analyst to assess the threats from these types of organizations, at the same time providing fundamental insights about the characteristics defining the future potential of a given organization. This will, in turn, provide a basis for forecasting as well as providing suggestions for countermeasures and solutions to address the root causes of the threats. Without these insights, credible threat assessment is much harder to produce and use for further analysis or threat-mitigation planning.

DEFINITIONS

PIRACY

Piracy can be seen as either a type of organization, where the entire group is organized for piracy activities with financial gain being the singular objective, or a tactic to obtain financing employed by organizations with other aims, such as insurgency groups or organized crime syndicates.

The definition for piracy used by the International Maritime Bureau (IMB) is as follows and includes certain low-level crimes such as robbery. However, it describes the act in itself and not the intention of the perpetrator.

> An act of boarding or attempting to board any ship with the apparent intent to commit theft or any other crime and with the apparent intent or capability to use force in the furtherance of that act.

The International Maritime Organization (IMO) definition in the 1982 United Nations Convention on the Law of the Sea (UNCLOS) (article 101) explicitly underlines piracy as those acts carried out for private ends, which excludes acts of terrorism, insurgency, or those of environmental activists for that matter.

Piracy consists of any of the following acts:

1. Any illegal act of violence or detention, or any act of depredation, committed for private ends by the crew or passengers of a private ship or private aircraft and directed
   a. To the high seas against another ship or aircraft, persons or property on board such a ship or aircraft
   b. Against a ship, aircraft, person, or property in a place outside the jurisdiction of any state
2. Any act of voluntary participation in the operation of a ship or aircraft with knowledge of facts making it a pirate ship or aircraft
3. Any act inciting or of intentionally facilitating an act described in subpoints 1 or 2.[5]

Armed robbery against ships is defined in the Code of Practice for the Investigation of the Crimes of Piracy and Armed Robbery Against Ships (resolution A.922 (22), Annex, paragraph 2.2) as follows:

> Armed robbery against ships means any unlawful act of violence or detention or any act of depredation, or threat thereof, other than an act of "piracy", directed against a ship or against persons or property on board such ship, within a State's jurisdiction over such offences.

In other words, according to the IMO, it is as follows:

- Piracy involves a criminal act of violence, detention, or depredation.
- Piracy is committed on the high seas or in places outside the jurisdiction of any state.
- Piracy involves using a ship to attack another ship (which excludes mutiny and barratry), according to the "two-ship rule."
- Piracy is committed for private ends (which excludes the acts of terrorists or environmental activists).
- Piracy is committed by the crew or passengers of a privately owned vessel (which excludes attacks by naval craft).

For the purpose of this model, which focuses on the motivation for the incidents, the IMO definition does not apply as this form of maritime crime is also carried out by some groups that are also politically motivated at a strategic level, yet carrying out the act itself at a tactical level for largely financial reasons.

Piracy consists of the following main forms of criminal activity:

- Harbor and anchorage attacks
- Attacks against vessels at sea—(sea) robbery, sometimes also referred to as "Asian piracy"
- Attacks against vessels at sea—hijacking accompanied by the neutralization of the crew (a variation of this can include the permanent seizure of a vessel by pirates)
- Kidnap for ransom

TERRORISM

Terrorism can refer to either a type of organization where the entire group is organized for terrorist activities with a political aim or a tactic to realize certain subgoals employed by organizations with other aims such as insurgency groups or organized crime syndicates. Terrorism is a form of struggle in which violence is deliberately used against civilians to achieve political goals (nationalistic, socioeconomic, ideological, and religious) and is, rather, intentionally and specifically directed at civilians.[6]

Terrorism is violence, or the threat of violence, committed to create an atmosphere of fear and alarm. These acts are designed to coerce others into actions they would not otherwise undertake or refrain from actions they desired to take. All terrorist acts are crimes. Many of them can also be regarded as violations of the rules of war, provided a state of war existed. This violence or threat of violence is generally directed against civilian targets. The motives of all terrorists are political, and terrorist actions are generally carried out in a way that will achieve maximum publicity. Unlike other criminal acts, terrorists often claim credit for their acts. Finally, terrorist acts are intended to produce effects beyond the immediate physical damage of the attack or operation, having long-term psychological repercussions on a particular target audience. The fear created by terrorists may be intended to cause people to exaggerate the strengths of the terrorists and importance of their cause, provoke governmental overreaction, discourage dissent, or simply intimidate and thereby enforce compliance with their demands.[7]

INSURGENCY

Those carrying out an insurgency are "insurgents." Insurgents engage in regular or guerrilla combat against the armed forces of an established authority, government, or administration. Insurgents usually are in opposition to a civil authority or government primarily to overthrow or obtain autonomy or independence for a certain geographical area, a share in government, to further a separatist or revolutionary agenda, or improve their condition. In addition to military activity, insurgency groups may use terrorist attacks to increase awareness of their cause as well as criminal activities such as weapons, drugs, commodity and human smuggling, counterfeit, fraud, illegal money laundering, cargo theft, and other forms related to and often in cooperation with organized crime syndicates. Furthermore, insurgency groups in proximity to coastal areas and straits have been active in piracy as a financial tactic.

Insurgency can be defined as

A protracted political-military activity directed toward completely or partially controlling the resources of a country through the use of irregular military forces and illegal political organisations.[8]

ORGANIZED CRIME

Criminal activities relevant to the model include a wide range of areas with illegal (sometimes in combination with legal) ventures for a financial purpose. The activities included, among others, are smuggling, human trafficking, theft, robbery, drugs and arms running, counterfeit, and fraud.

Organized crime is defined as a nonideological enterprise that involves a number of persons in close social interaction, organized on a hierarchical basis for the purpose of securing profit and power by engaging in illegal and legal activities. Positions in the hierarchy and those involving functional specialization are assigned according to skill. Permanency is assumed by the members who strive to keep the enterprise integral and active in pursuit of goals. It eschews competition and strives for monopoly over particular activities on an industrial or territorial basis. There is willingness to use violence and bribery to achieve ends or maintain discipline. Membership is restricted, although nonmembers may be involved on a contingency basis.[9]

ORGANIZATIONAL CHARACTERISTICS

Groupings considered in the following can be viewed as anything between an *ad hoc*, or loosely connected, body of individuals to a highly structured entity. Examples of a low level of organizational structure are the "subsistence pirates," who function as fishermen for most part of the year but gather to attack targets of opportunity. At the other end of the organizational spectrum are the "criminal syndicates" in Asia as well as some of the terrorist groups in this region.

The aim of the organization and its actions will determine the group's typology—pirates, organized crime syndicates, insurgents, or terrorist organizations.

MOTIVATION

One of the primary identifiable characteristics of a group is its aim or *raison d'etre,* which defines its long-term objectives. This may be purely financial as in the case of most piracy groups and organized crime syndicates, or purely political[10] as for most terrorist groups. There are exceptions where organized crime syndicates are also involved in politics; however, this is usually a necessary facilitating adjunct to the overriding long-term objective of pure financial gain.

TACTICS

An organization will employ a number of tactics such as piracy (including hijacking and kidnaping or ransom at sea) or a terrorist attack as distinct ways of achieving their overall strategic objective (financial or political). An insurgency organization engages in a military or guerrilla campaign, whereas at the same time mounting terrorist attacks against governmental or public targets as well as conducting a range of illegal activities to finance its operations. Some of these activities are in the maritime domain. Similarly, organized crime syndicates are engaged in piracy operations including hijacking, kidnaping and ransom, or cargo theft. For example, an organization such as Movement for the Emancipation of the Niger Delta (MEND) in Nigeria employs both piracy and terrorism to achieve its goals.

PUBLICITY LEVEL

Another important characteristic of an organization is the level of publicity aspired for. It is low or nonexistent in the case of pirates or organized crime syndicates who in general do not want any public or media attention focused on their activities. However, it is very high for international terrorist groups where publicity is the "oxygen" they live on. However, as with all definitions in this model, there are gray zones and some piracy groups are also known to use the media to further their aims. The following Table 6.1 illustrates the distinctions:

TABLE 6.1
Various Organizational Types and Their Motivational and Tactical Tendencies

Organization	Piracy	Terrorist	Insurgency	Organized crime
Motivation and Objectives	Financial	Political[a]	Political	Financial
Tactics Employed	Piracy	Terrorist	Terrorist Piracy	Terrorist Piracy
Publicity Aims	None	High	Medium	Low
Examples	Somali Marines	Al Qaeda (AQ), Jemaah Islamiyah (JI), Popular Front for the Liberation of Palestine (PFLP)	MEND, Moro Islamic Liberation Front (MILF)	Abu Sayyaf [b]

[a] Political, religious, idological, nationalistic.
[b] Started as an insurgency group but has migrated to organized crime.

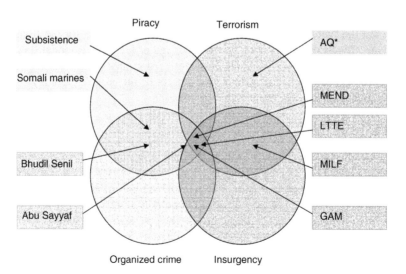

FIGURE 6.1   The Four Circles Model ("*" Represents the old AQ core and not the present AQ, which is an umbrella organization for the core (the old AQ). Regional entities include AQIM, affiliates in Iraq, Saudi Arabia, as well as the mid-level "emirs" and loosely connected self-radicalized networks in these countries.)

ORGANIZATIONAL DYNAMICS

Insurgent groups are generally permanently fixed to a geographical area of operation and will not, for any substantial amount of time, move its activities to other areas due to the primacy of its fundamental objectives such as the overthrowing of an unwanted government or polity.

Terrorist groups are usually associated to certain areas and a political aim; however, transnational or international exceptions with more mobile tendencies or endemic aspirations also exist. One of these is the global jihad with Al Qaeda as its core element, that is, in a generic sense, not related to a geographical region; although some of its important elements are related to a specific geographical area such as the Al Qaeda in the Islamic Maghreb or AQIM (formerly known as Groupe Salafiste pour la Prédication et le Combat [GSPC; Salafist Group for Preaching and Combat]) in North Africa.

Organized crime syndicates are dynamic and highly adaptable fluid organizations, which can change its geographical area of operations as well as the types of crimes perpetrated. As a number of criminal syndicates also have legitimate business, or operate under the guise of brass plate companies, they are even more flexible in conducting operations encompassing a number of geographical areas as well as different types of illegal activities.

Piracy groups are usually organized in certain coastal areas, but are relatively flexible in changing and adapting their organization to changing scenarios. This can include moving around in coastal areas if the external pressures such as increased patrols and interdiction by coast guards increase to unpermissive levels. The Somali piracy groups, having the apparent ability to adapt quickly to the changing internal situations as well as those on the water are good examples.

MIGRATION AND DYNAMICS

There are notable examples of organizations that depart from their original ideas and morph into other forms of criminal organization due to specific changes in strategy adopted by the command elements or more slowly through the political degradation of its leadership. In the latter case, financial gains and financial control replaces ideological and political aims. A well-known example of this is Revolutionary Armed Forces of Colombia (FARC), which today has very little to do with the revolutionary Marxist–Leninist ideology, but a great deal more to do with drug production and trafficking. Today, FARC is entirely an organized crime syndicate.

ABU SAYYAF GROUP

Another example is the Abu Sayyaf Group (ASG), which originated in 1990 as a splinter group of radical members of the main insurgency group in the southern Philippines—the Moro National Liberation Front (MNLF), which moderated somewhat and turned into more of a political party by 1989. From its inception, this group, under the leadership of Abdurajik Abubakar Janjalani, embarked on an ideological aim for creating an Islamic state in the southern Philippines, including the islands of Jolo, Basilan, and Western Mindanao.

ASG carried out a number of high-profile terrorist bombings and attacks, whereas simultaneously conducting a range of criminal activities to finance their operations. However, on December 18, 1998, Janjalani was killed in a firefight with the police and his younger brother, Khadaffy Janjalani, succeeded as the leader of the group and quickly consolidated his power. This also marked the turning point for ASG, shifting from its ideologically driven aspirations to a financially motivated strategy characterized by increased kidnappings, murders, and robberies. One of the main maritime attacks by the group was the bombing of *SuperFerry 14* on February 27, 2004, where 117 people were killed. The bombing was reportedly committed against the ferry line for not complying with a demand to pay protection money, and not as a politically motivated act against the government as part of the struggle for an Islamist state. The ASG has transformed from an insurgency group, using different types of crimes to finance the ideological struggle, into an organized crime group with financial gain as the primary motive.

SUBSISTENCE PIRATES

These are poor, ill-equipped fishermen or villagers from coastal areas. Their activities are often a result of relative desperation and their opportunistic attacks are aimed at maintaining a subsistence level, or to improve this level. In some parts of the world, generations of coastal communities have carried out these types of attacks for centuries (and communitarian crimes) where the spoils have been distributed among the local population (have been an important part of daily life).

Counterpiracy measures have had their greatest effect on these types of attackers. Local and regional military and law enforcement campaigns have a substantial impact, but long-term effects in reducing crime at sea from these types of perpetrators are only possible through increasing the relative income and wealth in these coastal communities such as Dumai in Indonesia. However, improved socioeconomic factors alone is not enough to adequately suppress this type of piracy considering the ingrained tendencies and historical background of these communities. Also, these pirates are hired by organized crime syndicates to carry out their "dirty work." This potentially opens up new ways of earning within organized crime, offering far greater financial return than legitimate employment ashore, not withstanding the obvious increased risks.

SOMALI MARINES

This particular group, which is known by several names, including the "defenders of the Somali territorial waters," had a base in the Harardhere area in the Mudug region of Somalia before the Islamic Courts Union took control of central Somalia during the summer of 2006. Until this development, the group had carried out a number of long-range hijackings in the waters off the coast of Somalia and was behind the majority of larger hijackings that were executed in the central and northern sea areas off the coast. In December 2006, the Ethiopian Army and Transitional Federal Government occupied the region and removed all influence of the Islamic Courts Union. However, by January 2007, the government and Ethiopian forces had withdrawn toward central Somalia and away from the coastal areas. Not surprisingly, from the end of January 2007, reports started to emerge from Harardhere that the pirates had returned to the area and begun to take advantage of the fact that there was no government control or other form of authority, and hence no law enforcement or militia forces. Furthermore, according to international law, international forces monitoring the Somali coast, such as the Task Force 150, could not enter territorial waters, and the government did not have any naval or coast guard assets to protect the area. This led to a zone with no central control. Also, with the absence of militia forces from the local clans, the region quickly became a safe area for the pirates to prepare and execute their operations. The local leaders have expressed that they would like to get rid of the pirates but they have no means at their disposal to do so.

The group is well organized. Although it has a flow of people and assets, it no longer has a formal base of operations; however, moves around in the Mudug region, mostly between the two coastal areas of Harardhere and Hobyo. The leaders are from the semiautonomous Puntland region, but the rank and file are multiclan and as such the group is not directly connected to any clan structure. Besides the leadership, the organization is fluid and people join in and out of the group constantly. However, the *modus operandi* of the group is highly professional, with its own intelligence networks that gather information on vessels and has one or more mother ships that can operate up to 250 Nmi from the coastline with two to four open motorboats embarked. The group also has quite sophisticated methods for the delivery of ransoms, which are paid for the release of the vessels in their possession. Although certain sources claim that the group has killed members of hijacked crews, only one killing has been confirmed till date; indeed, the crew members of the Danish vessel, *Danica White*, hijacked on June 1, 2007, were treated relatively well during their captivity.

Although other pirate groups have been more connected to Somali political entities, it does not seem as if this group is connected to particular clans, but rather may be connected to individual stakeholders in Somalia's internal politics.

GERAKAN ACEH MERDEKA

Gerakan Aceh Merdeka (GAM) struggled against the Indonesian government for many years until the Tsunami in 2004 damaged large parts of coastal Aceh and forced the group and central government to cooperate to get relief aid to the inhabitants of the Aceh province. The cooperation paved the way for successful peace negotiations, which resulted in a peace accord in August 2005, which ultimately led to local elections and the election of the GAM leader as the province governor on December 11, 2006. On December 27, 2006, the group officially disbanded the military wing and disarmed.

The organization had run a military and guerrilla campaign against the government forces and financed its operations with, among other activities, a long list of organized crimes and acts of piracy. Activities included drug and arms running, human trafficking, smuggling, and other types of crime in close cooperation with organized crime syndicates in neighboring countries and further afield in Thailand. In addition, GAM was directly behind a large proportion of vessel hijackings in the northern part of the Strait of Malacca off the coast of Sumatra, including several against transiting product tankers.

On the basis of its activities before the end of 2006, the group was placed in the main group of insurgency groups with supporting activities in organized crime and piracy. As is generally seen with insurgency groups that enter a peaceful path, some renegade individuals (or splinter elements) who have been previously engaged in the group's criminal activities have continued with criminal activities, or parts of it, outside the organization. On October 1, 2007, one such individual was arrested by the Indonesian police.

GAM is a good example of an organization with a political aim of financing its activities with a number of criminal activities, but which also largely ended these activities when a peace accord had been signed, with it gaining power in the Aceh province through peaceful elections.

BHUDIL SENIL SYNDICATE

The Bhudil Senil Syndicate has conducted a number of different criminal activities with piracy as one of their main activities in the maritime arena. Based on Batam Island, near Singapore, the Bhudil Senil Syndicate was behind a number of the high-profile piracy attacks in the Strait of Malacca till 2005. However, the syndicate, in light of increased coordinated patrols during the War Risk rating of the straits (2005–2006), broadened its activities and began to refocus on other illegal maritime acts. The group was a key player in illegal bunkering in the Singapore strait in 2005, throughout late 2006 and into 2007. Specifically, the group has concentrated on its gravel or sand smuggling operations from Indonesian islands to Singapore due to official export bans imposed by both Malaysia and Indonesia. This syndicate is an ideal example of a criminal organization that not only uses piracy as a tactic, but is highly adaptable and can engage in numerous criminal activities concurrently in response to changes in policy or security situation, such as taking advantage of granite export bans to the city–state or imposition of more regular and widespread antipiracy patrols in the strait.

MOVEMENT FOR THE EMANCIPATION OF THE NIGER DELTA

MEND is an umbrella organization for a number of subgroupings in the Niger Delta that have a common political aim of increasing the distribution of wealth from oil production among the inhabitants of the delta. However, this goal is also mixed with immediate financial aims, and some of its suborganizations are showing signs of greater inclination toward financial rather than politically motivated activity. For analytical purposes, MEND is defined as an insurgency group because of its publicly stated aim as being one that is predominantly political in nature. Support for this argument also lies in the fact that MEND, in most cases, does not ask for a ransom for the kidnapped persons from the oil industry or shipping community, but demands political concessions or freeing of certain individuals. In a number of cases, MEND kidnaps individuals from rigs or oil installations in the morning only to set them free in the evening. This is clearly intended to send a message that they have this capacity and can use it at will. However, the organization has also used a combination of terrorist and piracy tactics to achieve its goals; and in some cases, even both have been employed to achieve its tactical objectives.

Finally, MEND has played a very clever game in reducing oil output with 20–30 percent as a result of its actions in the delta; but it has stopped doing it as it would also harm the revenue streams to the Niger Delta area and its inhabitants. Being an insurgency organization, MEND is linked to a given territorial area as well as certain political groups and subsequently will be difficult to defeat militarily as well as politically.

CONCLUSION AND PERSPECTIVES

The difference between facing a threat from pirates and that from an insurgency group or organized crime syndicate carrying out piracy activities is perhaps not that distinct from the perspective of the attacked crew. However, the significance of this distinction is certainly more telling from the perspective of industries, governments, and international organizations that confront these groups. Essentially, the vital difference lies in the range of the most effective options available to combat the threat. Subsequently, some of the methods employed to deal with the threat in a given incident are the same regardless of the typology of the group, whereas the broader strategies available to get rid of the threat in the long-term perspective are quite diverse. An insurgency group with support from the population, including those that have been coerced into giving support, cannot be easily persuaded to give up its activities unless it achieves its political goal or is fully defeated. Separately, geography also plays an important role in determining the outcome of the struggle between pirates, insurgents or criminals, and the security forces ranged against them. Trying to combat piracy in the Indonesian Archipelago of some 14,000 islands poses extreme logistical as well as operational challenges. Geography can also be a defining feature in the struggle to contain piracy in Somalia where most of the pirate groups can be prevented from conducting their activities by occupying critical areas of the coastline and few coastal cities if possible.

For the ship owner or company security officer in both the shipping and offshore industries, this model provides a framework for understanding maritime threats; it offers a tool for the correct assessment of scenarios and improves the ability to better determine possible outcomes of applied contingencies at the company and vessel or platform level, when an attack has occurred or is occurring. For the master, officers, and crew on a seized vessel, greater knowledge about the motivation of the attackers may provide insights into how they are to be treated during a hijacking or kidnapping.

For industry, governmental, and other international stakeholders, the model provides an analytical platform for understanding maritime-based threats in a more intuitive and sophisticated way. Media and governments talk of the dangers of piracy and terrorism and their prevention, yet the major activities conducted against the maritime domain are ultimately those conducted by insurgents and crime syndicates. The nuanced distinctions of threat typology also affect supply-chain stakeholders, but have a different implication when it comes to prevention and resolution. There are different viable solutions for the various types of crimes. Media and government agencies, in using only terrorism and piracy as defining terms, can limit options for accurate understanding and mitigating strategies because of this. This can also alter the perception of the public as to the true nature of the problem and how to deal with it. Careful application of the Four Circles Model can provide a potent tool for those that need to pin down precisely the threat they are dealing with and thus better design of the optimum and most realistic security solutions.

ACKNOWLEDGMENTS

The author would like to thank senior analysts Atle Mesøy and Karsten von Hoesslin of Risk Intelligence as well as Rupert Herbert-Burns for their contributions in developing the Four Circles Model. This also applies to all external experts and partners who have been commenting on the model including, among others, Thomas Weik of Det Norske Veritas (DNV) and Bob Reeve and Dirk Steffen of Aegir Security Solutions.

NOTES

1. Four circles model of Risk Intelligence was developed initially as an internal methodology to map the different organizations carrying out criminal acts in the maritime domain. Later it was conveyed to their clients and partners during the company's piracy and maritime terrorism workshops and now it is the main framework in the Risk Intelligence's analysis of these threats.
2. MIPT Terrorism Knowledge Base (Tkb), www.tkb.org.
3. The One Percent Doctrine (also called the Cheney doctrine) was developed in November 2001 as an U.S. administration response to terrorist threats. Vice President Dick Cheney stated that "If there's a 1% chance that Pakistani scientists are helping al-Qaeda build or develop a nuclear weapon, we have to treat it as a certainty in terms of our response. It's not about our analysis ... It's about our response." From Ron Suskind, 2006, *The One Percent Doctrine: Deep Inside America's Pursuit of its Enemies Since 9/11*, Simon & Schuster, New York.
4. Originally official U.S. terminology by U.S. State Department allowed attacks against military targets to be included in the terrorism statistics if the geographical area in question was not in a state of military hostilities. However, global jihadist terrorism has changed the playing field from regions and nations to the global arena.
5. http://www.imo.org/TCD/mainframe.asp?topic_id=362.
6. Dr Boaz Ganor, ICT (International Institute for Counter-Terrorism), Israel.
7. Tkb (Terrorism Knowledge Base).
8. This definition was used by the U.S. Central Intelligence Agency during the 1980s, and it still remains useful (William Rosenau, 2007, *Subversion and Insurgency*, RAND National Defence Institute, Occasional Papers 2, RAND Corporation).
9. Definition by Howard Abadinski, 1994, *Organised Crime*, Nelson-Hall, Chicago, IL by André Standing in "*Rival Views of Organised Crime*," Institute for Security Studies, South Africa, 2003.
10. Political is understood in the context of this model as political, ideological or religious, or other nonfinancial aims.

Section 2

Industry Sectors:
Threats and Responses

7 Implications and Effects of Maritime Security on the Operation and Management of Merchant Vessels

Steven M. Jones

CONTENTS

It is fair to say that at present "security" is neither a popular word, nor a terribly popular concept across certain areas of the maritime industry. Since 2004, and the adoption of the International Ship and Port Facility Security (ISPS) Code, the demands of maritime security have been met with a wave of apathy, and in some circles even antipathy. Some of this aversion is perhaps understandable, but nevertheless it is disappointing that within many companies, on many ships, and in the minds of countless individuals, security appears to be something to be endured, rather than something to explore, develop, and harness positively. It is therefore important to remember that even aside from the commercial and regulatory imperative, anything that sees individual seafarers arrive home safe, sound, and in one piece cannot be all bad.

The adoption of the ISPS Code and the heightened global focus on maritime security has introduced a slew of new roles, responsibilities, and interactions within shipping companies and onboard ships. In assessing the realities, implications, and effects of maritime security on merchant shipping, it is important to consider all parts of the chain, and to look not solely at the requirements placed onto companies and vessels, but also the leadership and management of the security regimes, and the resources dedicated to implementing the requirements.

THE COMPANY

INTERNATIONAL SHIP AND PORT FACILITY SECURITY (ISPS) CODE RESPONSIBILITIES

The ISPS Code applies to all the safety of life at sea convention (SOLAS) vessels over 500 gross registered tonnes (GRT) engaged on international voyages and all port facilities serving such ships. Under the terms of the ISPS Code, shipping companies are required to designate a company security officer (CSO) for the company and a ship security officer (SSO) for each of its ships. The CSO's responsibilities include ensuring that a ship security assessment (SSA) is properly carried out, ship security plans (SSPs) are prepared and submitted for approval by (or on behalf of) the administration and thereafter are placed on board each ship. The SSP should indicate the operational and physical security measures that the ship itself should take to ensure it always operates at a minimum of security level 1. The plan should also indicate the additional, or intensified, security measures the ship itself can, and will, take to move to and operate at security level 2, when instructed to do so. Furthermore, the plan should indicate the possible preparatory actions the ship could take to allow prompt response to instructions that may be issued to the ship at security level 3.

After satisfying the requirements of SOLAS chapter XI-2 and part A of the ISPS Code, ships will be issued with an International Ship Security Certificate (ISSC). This is to be retained on board and available for inspection at all times. The ISSC is prima facie evidence of compliance, and will be inspected by port State officials. Such inspections will not normally extend to examination of the SSP itself, except in specific circumstances in which "clear grounds" are identified to indicate that the vessel is not in compliance and the only means to verify or rectify the noncompliance is to review the relevant requirements of the SSP. In this case, limited access to the specific sections of the plan relating to the noncompliance may be allowed, but only with the consent of the maritime administration of the flag state or the master.

Under the provisions of regulation XI-2/9, ships using port facilities or proceeding to a port may be subject to port State control inspections and additional control measures, as the contracting government has the right to exercise various security measures if there is a reason to believe that the security of the ship has, or the port facilities it has served have been compromised. The relevant authorities may request the provision of information regarding the ship, its cargo, passengers, and ship's personnel before the ship's entry into port. Circumstances have arisen in which entry into port has been delayed and even denied.[1,2]

WIDER RESPONSIBILITIES

It is important to understand that above and beyond the requirements of mere legislation there exists a moral responsibility upon the shipowner/operator to provide adequate security protection for their seafarers, passengers, hull, machinery, and cargo. This is a clear duty and is no different from the traditional responsibility to provide the correct and adequate safety measures in case of fire, collision, or bad weather.

In this case, the shipowner/operator and the master need to know what is the likelihood of an attack, what is the probable nature of the attack, and how best to provide practical protection within the requirements of the relevant legislation and within their commercial budget. So we can see there is a pressure to comply and to provide adequate and effective security provisions. However, the path from owners and managers having the freedom to interpret security on an *ad hoc* basis pre-2004 to the present situation has not been a comfortable journey for many to make.

Aside from this moral and commercial responsibility, ISPS requires that the "company," at least should assure that all their vessels comply with the requirements of part A of the ISPS Code, and that in achieving this they have taken into account the guidance contained in part B.

For the purposes of ISPS, the responsibilities apply to the owner of the ship or any other organization or person such as the manager, or the bareboat charterer, who has assumed the responsibility and any duties associated with the operation of the ship from the owner, and who has agreed to take over all the responsibilities imposed by the ISPS Code. The company will appoint CSOs and SSOs and ensure that each vessel undergoes an SSA, while developing an SSP for each vessel. In addition, the company will provide training and make sure that the security regimes are afforded all necessary resources.

Shipowners have been under intense pressure over the past decade to respond to international legislation to make the shipping industry safer, cleaner, and now more secure. It has been seen that many of the lessons learnt in complying with the International Safety Management (ISM) code have been transferred within many companies to their security regimes. The companies that are able to adopt the ISM code in a thorough and all encompassing manner will have systems and procedures in place, which enable their personnel to absorb these new security requirements in a more straight-forward and logical way. Such companies have found that while the aims of safety and security are different, there is a large crossover and elements of harmonization between the two. The lessons of a robust ISM safety management system (SMS) can be transferred to security, and the training, reporting, and onboard resource elements all mesh well with the ISPS requirements.

When one compares safety to security there are, naturally, very different philosophies to adhere—although safety requires openness, security opposes this, and requires control and constraint of movement. So although transferring the lessons of safety management can work and a company with a proper functioning SMS is half way there, we have to remember that safety is no longer enough, a secure ship may be safe, yet a safe ship may be far from being secure.[3]

FINANCIAL AND COMMERCIAL IMPLICATIONS

The very nature of the ISPS Code as a response to a perceived security threat to shipping has meant that the commercial and operational needs of companies, ships, ports, and international trade were not a seeming priority when drafting the code. As a result, we see that in addition to extending the way a company's operational department, its vessels, and personnel need to evolve and adapt to security demands so too the commercial department. The ISPS Code poses a vast array of potential pitfalls from a commercial perspective, and it is vital that these are recognized and responded to. Most important in these is the fact that the ISSC (security certificate) is necessary to trade into SOLAS contracting states—effectively "no certificate, no entry!".[4]

Trading under ISPS is understandably not as free and easy as once it was. Many port State control regimes have now tightened and the chance of detention, expulsion, or refusal of entry for vessels that are deemed to pose a risk has inevitably increased. This can have enormous effect on a vessel's commercial viability and of course the owners' views on the associated commercial risks. Aside from these new risks, there are also potential associated costs—whether more people are needed, new equipment is fitted, or consultants are appointed to draw up plans, all have cost implications and therefore a commercial element, and the need to be budgeted for is a reality of this more security-conscious environment.

One of the most potentially serious implications from a commercial perspective is that of potential delay. Although most ports have so far coped quite well in maintaining the flow of trade, it will only take one security alert for delays to occur. Though at present the use of either the ISM or the ISPS Codes in legal cases is still very much in its infancy, this is an area for exploitation by lawyers, and many more cases as time progresses will perhaps hinge on the compliance with the requirements of not merely the old standard of seaworthiness, but of the far-reaching safety, environmental, and security management.[5]

KEY PERSONNEL

Although the security industry at large is awash with technical solutions and computer-based management tools, the real cornerstone of an effective ISPS regime is the people, across all levels of the chain of command. Despite all these hardware and software tools, there are still many security basics which, to be rolled out effectively, need a fully trained, truly committed, and motivated workforce.

Although the basic "letter of ISPS" and its listed components, as explained later, can perhaps be subsumed by someone with only the minimum of security awareness, to harness the true "spirit of ISPS" requires something more. To train, monitor, and lead; to effectively delegate; and to manage limited and finite resources in the face of onerous legislative demands, and of any potential incidents, takes the highest caliber people possible. It takes people who not only know what to do, but also who understand why and how to use this knowledge to get the best out of the law, their plans, and their people.

THE COMPANY SECURITY OFFICER (CSO)

One of the primary features of ISPS compliance is the designation of a CSO. The CSO has the pivotal role of managing security and consolidating the demands of the legislation with the commercial and operational realities of the companies, and with the management of vessel security. The duties of the CSO, as laid down within the ISPS Code include, but are not limited to:

- Advising the level of threats likely to be encountered by the ship, using appropriate security assessments and other relevant information
- Ensuring that ship security assessments are carried out
- Ensuring the development, the submission for approval, and thereafter the implementation and maintenance of the SSP
- Ensuring that the SSP is modified, as appropriate, to correct deficiencies and satisfy the security requirements of the individual ship
- Arranging for internal audits and reviews of security activities
- Arranging for the initial and subsequent verifications of the ship by the administration or the recognized security organization
- Ensuring that deficiencies and nonconformities identified during internal audits, periodic reviews, security inspections, and verifications of compliance are promptly addressed and dealt with
- Enhancing security awareness and vigilance
- Ensuring adequate training for personnel responsible for the security of the ship
- Ensuring effective communication and cooperation between the SSO and the relevant port facility security officers (PFSOs)
- Ensuring consistency between security and safety requirements
- Ensuring that, if sister-ship or fleet security plans are used, the plan for each ship reflects the ship-specific information accurately
- Ensuring that any alternative or equivalent arrangements approved for a particular ship or group of ships are implemented and maintained

The code does not impose any requirement as to the rank or seniority of the person appointed to the CSO role, other than a CSO qualification. However, it is implied through the job requirements that it should be someone with a heightened level of knowledge, experience, and standing within the company. The list of responsibilities does not really capture the essence of what a "good" CSO should provide for the company, vessels, SSO, crews, and clients—that is to ensure that security is taken seriously, and that the threats are not only just noted but also fully understood and managed.

It is possible to meet many different types of CSO, and the most effective are not those who simply switch their normal focus for a few minutes a day onto security. The most effective CSO are those able to anticipate threats, mange their resources, and engender a real enthusiasm for security across their whole organization.[6] Security is a hugely important part of any company's risk management strategy, and it needs to be honestly viewed, not with a jaundiced, dismissive eye, but with dynamism to harness the many positives that security can bring to any existing management structure.[7]

THE SHIP SECURITY OFFICER (SSO)

Under the requirements of the ISPS Code, an SSO has to be designated on each ship. The duties and responsibilities of the SSO shall include, but are not limited to:

- Undertaking regular security inspections of the ship to ensure that appropriate security measures are maintained
- Maintaining and supervising the implementation of the SSP, including any amendments to the plan

- Coordinating the security aspects of the handling of cargo and ships stores with other ship-board personnel and with the relevant PFSOs
- Proposing modifications in the SSP
- Reporting to the CSO regarding any deficiencies and nonconformities identified during internal audits, periodic reviews, security inspections, and verifications of compliance and implementing any corrective actions
- Enhancing security awareness and vigilance on board
- Ensuring that adequate training has been provided to shipboard personnel, as appropriate
- Reporting all security incidents
- Coordinating implementation of the SSP with the CSO and relevant PFSO
- Ensuring that security equipment is properly operated, tested, calibrated, and maintained, if any

The Code does not specify the rank of the officer to be given the security role, but it has become increasingly a common practice to give the role to a senior deck officer, either the master or the chief officer, once they have completed their SSO training.

The introduction of the SSO role has caused a large degree of concern among the seafaring community. The shipping industry has long been accused of trying to reduce the number of people on each vessel. Although in some instances the overall workload can be absorbed by fewer people, the fact that ISPS has imposed a large degree of additional paperwork, training, and management responsibilities onto the ship, and specifically the SSO, has been a major concern. As with the CSO role, to really succeed in making the security relevant, active, and effective it takes a complete devotion and alteration of mindset. However, these things are not easy when the individual in question has to juggle competing demands, and sometimes even conflicting philosophies.[8]

THE MASTER

The basic challenges that the masters are facing today are in some ways the same as they have always been, that is, "getting the cargo to the right place at the right time." However, with the additional legislative demands the master now has to "get the cargo to the right place at the right time, safely, securely, in an environmentally sound way, and with a full record to demonstrate how they did what we have done".[9] In listing the CSO and the SSO before the master was in no way intended to denigrate this vital role, but it does perhaps hint at some of the difficult balancing acts and shifts of power that ISPS has unwittingly borne.

One area of great concern has been the exact extent of a master's powers, especially when faced with the setting of security levels. The ISPS Code clearly states that the responsibility for setting the security level, applicable to any particular time and also to ships and port facilities, belongs to contracting governments. So we can see that a ship is required to act upon the security levels set by contracting governments. We can, however, envisage circumstances in which the master may be forced to take rapid decisions regarding the level of security employed on the vessel, before any contact with contracting governments has been initiated. After all, the master of a vessel will be in a much better practical position to assess threats to his/her vessel.

In SOLAS chapter XI-2 "Special Measures to Enhance Maritime Security," Regulation 8 stresses the master's discretion for ship safety and security. Part 2 of this regulation states "If, in the professional judgment of the Master, a conflict between any safety and security requirements applicable to the ship arises during its operations, the Master shall give effect to those requirements necessary to maintain the safety of the ship. In such cases, the master may implement temporary security measures and shall forthwith inform the Administration and, if appropriate, the Contracting Government in whose port the ship is operating or intends to enter. Any such temporary security measures under this regulation shall, to the highest possible degree, be commensurate with the prevailing security level. When such cases are identified, the Administration shall ensure that such conflicts are resolved and that the possibility of recurrence is minimized."[10]

This regulation means that the master can increase the security provisions on board the vessel as a "temporary measure," and await further instruction from the contracting government as to the official security level to be adopted. The master in such instance may have instructed personnel to "act as at security level 2"—it is important to note that any such informal arrangements can only raise security levels, not lower them—and the vessel must follow the minimum security standards laid down within the SSP for the security level, the vessel has been instructed to adopt.[11] The CSO, SSO, and master should be in discussion regarding the requirements for these temporary measures and the administration should be contacted for assistance and a formal security level notification. Also, if a vessel is to trade into a noncompliant port, it may be advisable to contact the administration, before arrival and request they formally impose an increase to a minimum of security level 2.[12]

There are many things for the master to consider in balancing the traditional demands and responsibilities with the new—and in managing the relationship with the SSO. For this reason, many observers have agreed that although it may be possible to install the master as SSO, it probably is not the most effective way to manage any potential conflicts between safety and security. The master remains in command of the vessel regardless of the management structure imposed beneath him/her—for that reason it is vital that the SSO is able to keep the master fully briefed, but also respond flexibly and quickly to all instructions and to remove any potential barriers to safety.[13]

SHIPBOARD PERSONNEL

Aside from the more senior shipboard positions such as master and SSO, there are of course numerous new responsibilities stemming from ISPS for the rest of the shipboard personnel as well. Within the SSP there will be duties such as gangway watches or security patrolling, along with searching and escorting visitors. These security matters will place further pressure on sea staff, and with smaller crew numbers being used on some vessels it appears that manpower from all departments will be called upon to fulfill the requirements of ISPS. This can introduce increased potential for accidents on board the vessel, and as such shipboard personnel should be mindful of the tasks they are required to perform, and of the training they are given.

Operations such as entering enclosed spaces, working with mooring ropes, and working aloft are familiar to an experienced deck crew, who are trained in the work and also the personal protective equipment used. However, these may be alien surroundings to members of the catering or engineering departments, who may be utilized to assist in unfamiliar surroundings, as the master and departmental managers try to juggle their resources. They may not be adequately trained and familiarized and it is important for management, both ashore and on board, to accept that accidents are likely to occur if unfamiliar personnel are placed under difficult and unusual circumstances. It is vital that each crewmember is adequately briefed and trained to perform the tasks for which they are appointed.

The subject of the increased workload is one that has been discussed at length both before and after the adoption of ISPS. The International Maritime Organization (IMO) has stated that the smaller crew numbers now found onboard ships favor attackers and place ships at a great disadvantage.

A small crew engaged in ensuring the safe navigation of their ship through congested or confined waters will have the additional onerous task of maintaining high levels of security surveillance for prolonged periods. It should be remembered that personnel are still limited by the hours of rest provisions within the Standards of Training, Certification and Watch keeping (STCW) Convention. If the crew of a vessel cannot do all that is required of them, then it is imperative that they are provided with additional resources. The IMO state that shipowners should consider enhancing security watches if their ship is in waters or at anchor off ports, where attacks occur. Shipowners will wish to consider providing appropriate surveillance and detection equipment to aid their crews and protect their ships. There can be no excuses, ships need to meet all requirements incumbent upon them, and security is no different.

One of the more complex and wider issues that has stemmed from the introduction of the ISPS Code is the question of vetting of seafarers. In the main although most companies rightly insist on checking the professional credentials of employees, it has always been something of a sticking point to develop a global system of security vetting, and it seems increasingly unlikely that a universal system of vetting and checking will be introduced.

Although vetting from a wholly security perspective may be a challenge too far for some administrations, there have been huge strides taken in providing a new form of seafarers identification document. During the initial IMO sessions that led to the creation of the ISPS Code, an invitation was extended to the International Labour Organization (ILO) to continue the development of a seafarers' identity document as a matter of urgency.[14] The brief was to produce a document for professional purposes, a verifiable security document, and a certification information document. This led to the introduction of C185 Seafarers' Identity Documents Convention (Revised), 2003.[15] The seafarer's identity document contains particulars about the holder and are restricted to the following:[16]

1. Full name (first and last names where applicable)
2. Sex
3. Date and place of birth
4. Nationality
5. Any special physical characteristics that may assist identification
6. Digital or original photograph
7. Signature

SUPERNUMERARIES, CONTRACTORS, AND RIDING GANGS

Across many vessel types, there are increasing instances of contractors and riding gangs being placed on board. As the time spent by most vessels in port has been reduced, it is, in many instances, the only option to get certain maintenance work performed. In addition to this increasing trend of having such personnel on board, there has always been vessels which regularly and frequently carry external personnel, one thinks of dive support vessels, cable ships, and crew boats in particular.

Although having additional personnel on board is often necessary, it can have repercussions for the management of security on the vessel. There are also issues of vetting to consider, and it should be stressed that any security system can be compromised more easily from the inside. Thus, it is vital that the CSO can be satisfied of the credentials of those intending to join the vessel, and of the company supplying them.

Aside from the potential dangers posed by placing an externally controlled workforce onto the vessel, it is vital that the SSO is able to instill the message to these workers regarding the way in which they are to conduct themselves while on board. This naturally applies for safety as well as security, and it is important that the company recognizes the importance of managing these personnel, as well as the ability to impose some form of sanctions upon them, if they ignore the requirements of the management systems in place. It may also be advisable to develop a reporting system to monitor the conduct while on board to enable the SSO to report objectively back to the CSO, and to better avoid any conflicts on board.

Supernumeraries are a slightly different case, but they still require management, and whether they be family of crew or office personnel, they will require some form of introduction to the conduct expected from them with regards to security.[17]

OFFICE PERSONNEL

The companies that appear to have greater success in adopting the measures required by ISPS are those, which have developed a company-wide security strategy, not just a vessel-based scheme. The best thing about these systems is the involvement of office staff at all levels. In such a system the office personnel are briefed on the requirements of maritime security and of the challenges that the sea-going staff, their vessels, and the company are facing, and also the ways in which their assistance, appreciation, and understanding can aid all. This unified approach galvanizes all those trying to drive the security culture, and also mitigates the risk of conflicting instructions or responses. It is often a fact that a company, which is able to bring all its resources together in advance can overcome the business hurdles it faces in much better ways, and is able to get the positive results it needs to operate.

The demands of ISPS and of maritime security are in general quite onerous and have imposed a great deal upon sea staff. It is, therefore, a sign of a progressive company in which office personnel are encouraged and trained to help those at sea, and understand the constraints and difficulties faced by them.

MANAGEMENT

It is often difficult for many SSOs to manage all shipboard personnel in their security roles; particularly, as many SSOs themselves are only equipped with the basic notions of safety management. This "cascade training," where one person is formally instructed, and then joins the ship and has to pass on all their knowledge to colleagues has caused problems across shipping before, and it is regrettable that we are seeing it once again.[18]

To teach shipboard personnel the skills of managing the tasks they will be instructed to perform, respond in the correct way, and through the correct reporting lines would be a difficult task for even the best-equipped, professional trainer. Therefore, it is important that the potential for a weakness in the chain is identified within this part of the system. The shipboard personnel are only as good as their SSO and perhaps we are expecting too much in this hard pressed individual to create the positive and effective security regime, the ISPS Code requires.

THE SHIP SECURITY PLAN (SSP)

When one looks at the security resources in place and means of effectively ensuring, monitoring, and recording security compliance, one realizes that the systems developed and contained with the SSP are the foundation upon which any effective security regime is built. However, it can also be the stumbling block for those that fail.

With many SSPs now having been in place for a number of years, we are now seeing that crew and officers are becoming increasingly comfortable with their duties and a more security conscious mindset. Of course, there are still some "bad" SSPs around. Just as with ISM Code SMSs it can take considerable time to identify and remove problems. Regrettably, some operators also, occasionally, ignore the plain fact that their systems are ineffective.[19] If a crew is burdened with poor, ambiguous, and incorrect advice they can waste a lot of time and effort attempting to decipher it, and will inevitably make mistakes as they go.

To assess an effective SSP, it is important to look at who wrote it, and the nature of the process undertaken to produce it. In the early days of ISPS adoption there were many plans drawn up, which simply rehashed old advice given to secure cruise ships, with very little real understanding, appreciation, or adaptation given to make them relevant to the vast number of more mainstream merchant vessels. The SSP must address issues such as:[20]

- Measures to prevent weapons, dangerous substances, and devices from being taken aboard ship
- Identification of restricted areas

- Measures for prevention of unauthorized access to the ship
- Procedures for responding to security threats
- Procedures for evacuation in case of security threats
- Duties of shipboard personnel assigned security responsibilities
- Procedures for auditing security activities
- Procedures for security training, drills, and exercises
- Procedures for interfacing with port facility security activities
- Procedures for the periodic review of the SSP
- Procedures for reporting security incidents
- Identification of the SSO
- Issues related to ship security equipment

The full list of what should be covered within the SSP is detailed within the ISPS Code, it is also vital to assess whether each of the responsibilities has been honestly viewed and the day-to-day operations of the specific ship and its crew has been taken into account.

One of the major problems is found within SSPs which impose overly rigorous security measures upon vessels when security levels are raised.[21] While many ships are already pushing the limits of what is possible and what is credible while operating at Security Level 1, it seems incredible that they would then be able to absorb all the measures stated in some rather imaginative SSPs. When a vessel with a relatively small number of people on board talks of doubling gangways watches, deck patrols, and bridge watches, one wonders whether the CSO and consultants have actually taken the opportunity to count the number of people on board. In addition, it must be remembered that in some cases the increase of security levels, certainly from 1 to 2, can last for days, perhaps weeks, and not just hours.

The SSP can be the best ally any ship and its crew can have, but a poor system can become a noose around their neck, far more damaging than even a terrorist or pirate attack could be. The key to security is making it work, and to do that requires the development of a system that is actually capable of working. Some SSPs sadly are not fit for purpose and the CSO, SSO, master, and Flag State need to work together to make sure the ship cannot simply comply, but can realistically respond in the face of an incident or attack. This honest and pragmatic view of a vessel's security provisions can aid the ship not only in the face of attack but also in the event that port State control (PSC) deems there to be "clear grounds" to view the SSP. It also reflects the fact that the SSP needs to be a living document, one which is maintained, and kept contemporary and up to date.

Once the PSC officer makes such a statement, and is subsequently granted access by the master and the Flag State, there are a number of points to be remembered and applied. It is evident that many companies are not aware of the fact that the SSP must be maintained "current and applicable" to the vessel's trading pattern and routes. Thus, it is vital that the SSP reflects the ship's operation and the threats and vulnerabilities it actually faces. Within the vessel's security regime must be a means of accessing contemporary threat information. As Without this the PSCO could deem the SSP to be noncompliant. Also, as per the requirements of the code the SSP needs to include details of security records, covering:[22]

- Training, drills, and exercises
- Security threats and incidents
- Breaches of security
- Changes in security levels
- Communications related to the direct security of ship—such as specific threats to the ship, or within port facilities the ship is in or has visited

Failure to maintain the SSP in this fashion will contribute to the possibility of detention and delay. Having a classification society or recognized security organization (RSO)-approved SSP does not mean that the plan is current and valid, it simply means that the procedures and processes outlined in the plan were acceptable and satisfied the compliance requirements at the time of approval.

Just as in the case of appointment of the right people, and the allocation of the necessary resources, it is vital that the SSP is recognized as a vital part of the security of the vessel. ISPS is not just a paper exercise, and needs to be managed properly through an effective, practical, and realistic system.

PORTS AND TERMINALS

The ISPS Code imposes responsibilities on port authorities to undertake detailed security assessments of port facilities to identify threats and vulnerabilities and to produce incident response plans. Each government who has a port in its jurisdiction must, for their part, identify the level of threat and provide appropriate intelligence and advice to ports and ships. Contracting governments are also responsible for inspecting ports and ensuring ISPS compliance. Ports are vulnerable to attacks and criminal activity, and as such assessments of port vulnerability, restricted personnel entry, background checks of port employees, and regular training for port security personnel are all critical.

Although securing a ship imposes certain burdens, to secure a port takes much greater investment and use of resources. Therefore, the need to exploit technology is vital; security equipment, regular boat patrols, cameras, and vessel-tracking devices all contribute to the security of a port. This security must be in place if vessels within the port are to be kept safe from attack.

Among the many areas of conflict to arise have been the divergent views on security from shipping and ports. It has been a source of much dissatisfaction among the shipping fraternity that in many cases, the major ports aside, the levels of investment in training and of procedural changes made by shipping companies have not been matched as readily by the majority of ports they trade into.[23] Many ports seemingly see seafarers, ships, and cargoes as a security threat, whereas on the other side, shipping sees that a vast majority of ports have not made the investment to become truly secure. Stories abound of lax gate controls, broken fences, and free and unfettered access from the sea for all manner of small craft. Thus, while shipping companies feel pressed on all sides, and while some seafarers have their civil liberties quashed there are criticisms that ports have not done all they can to secure themselves—despite the fact that ports in most major trading nations are subjected to government inspections. In the European Union, this would be Regulation (EC) No 725/2004,[24] and in the United States the Maritime Transportation Security Act (MTSA)[25] and NVIC 11-02.[26]

Such a debate is obviously best judged from both sides. However, what is not disputed is the effect a port call to an "unsecured port" can have on the security profile of a vessel. Vessels are required to record details of all port calls, and the status of their own security and that of the port. This is kept within a "Continuous Synopsis Record" (CSR). The CSR of a vessel is intended to provide an onboard record of the history of the ship, and is issued by the flag state. Additionally, if a port facility does not have a port facility security plan, then details should be provided of a suitably qualified person who can arrange appropriate security measures for the ships visit, including a declaration of security (DoS) if necessary. Once a vessel lists a port of concern on its CSR, this entry will cause problems over a minimum of the next 10 port calls. Full details of both the DoS and the CSR are to be found in the ISPS Code, including guidelines on their usage.[27]

In the light of any serious security concerns, there may be decisions to be made by the CSO, SSO, and master as to whether they choose to enter a port they deem to pose a security hazard. Because such a decision would have potentially significant commercial, legal, and insurance implications, it should also perhaps include the commercial and chartering departments of the shipping company. Guidance from the relevant Protection and Indemnity (P&I) Association may also be advisable.

THE PORT FACILITY SECURITY OFFICER (PFSO)

In keeping with companies and ships, the ISPS Code has introduced a new role within ports, the PFSO. Full details of the specific requirements and listed minimum duties of the PFSO role can be found in the ISPS Code, but in essence these mirror the requirements of the CSO role, but with a natural port-based emphasis.

One of the most basic requirements for any PFSO is to act as first point of contact for the security, and this naturally imposes a degree of contact and liaison with the CSOs and SSOs of inbound and berthed vessels. There is, however, a growing catalogue of anecdotal evidence to suggest that many SSOs have "never seen a PFSO," let alone maintaining ongoing prearrival dialogue with the CSO. This is of great concern, and should perhaps force some ports to reassess their security plans, roles, and responsibilities.[28]

SECURE PORTS

Not all the ports seemingly perceive security to be a real priority. However, there are some major ports in which security integrity has become a real market asset, and as such they vigorously apply both the letter and spirit of the ISPS Code. Such ports include the major container ports that make up the container security initiative (CSI) scheme,[29] and also many large oil and gas terminals.

In the light of market imperative for some sectors to demonstrate security excellence, Lloyd's register quality assurance (LRQA), an independent international auditing body, has been promoting its security auditing system. As an example of this standard, they have been auditing terminals for compliance with the international standard—ISO/PAS 28000:2006.

PRACTICAL CONSIDERATIONS

It is vital for vessels entering port to recognize any potential security threats well before arrival. The CSO, SSO, and master should be aware of the threats posed and should be able to implement any necessary actions. Many of the threats stem from slight additions or extensions to the normal hazards to navigation. Areas which involve tight turns, shallows, or increased vessel movements will be managed by the normal safety management procedures, and by the bridge team resources. However, it is always useful for all personnel to remain alert to any security implications and threats that only surface when the vessel approaches port, and which are far removed from those faced during ocean transits. Such threats can include the movement of small craft, the "tourist or terrorist" issue, and issues of public access close to vessels or close to areas of maneuvering. There are issues surrounding anchorage areas, and also specific forms of riverine or shallow water threat as well as instances of piracy, drug and people smuggling, and stowaways. These are the concerns that the port and the PFSO should assist all vessels with. If there does not appear to be sufficient guidance or support then the SSO, master, and CSO should issue a protest, as this can severely impact the effective provision of security.

CONTRACTING GOVERNMENTS

The conception, debate, adoption, and subsequent introduction of the ISPS Code was driven very much by a political agenda, one created not by the industry to protect itself, its crews, and ships, but by governments who see shipping and seafarers as a potential threat. It has been suggested that ships themselves could be seen as a means of delivering weapons of mass destruction, or that the vessels themselves could be the weapon used. Scenarios range from collisions with shore structures to collisions with other vessels to scuttling them in sensitive sea-lanes. Hence, obviously, port and coastal states are concerned with the security of their borders, and as such are putting a burden to shipping to prove that vessels are not a threat. This means that all vessels must prove their security credentials and do their utmost to ensure they do not pose a threat to the countries and ports that they visit.

Aside from the fact that governments are demanding security improvements from shipping and each other's ports, Flag States have also been given responsibilities through ISPS. It is for Flag States to set security levels and provide guidance for protection from security incidents for the vessels flying their flag, and where they impose heightened security measures and levels, contracting governments must issue appropriate instructions and provide security-related information to the ships and port facilities that may be affected. Contracting governments have various responsibilities, including:

- Setting applicable security levels
- Approving SSP and amendments
- Verifying the compliance of ships with SOLAS chapter XI-2 and part A of the ISPS Code
- Issuing the ISSC
- Determining which port facilities are required to designate a PFSO
- Ensuring completion and approval of the port facility security
- Assessment and the port facility security plan and amendments
- Exercising control and compliance measures
- Issuing the statement of compliance of a port facility
- Communicating security information to the IMO and to the shipping and port industries

When we look at all these new responsibilities, it seems obvious that certain marine administrations will simply not have adequate resources to take on these tasks. To do this they are allowed to delegate certain responsibilities to RSO, a role that many classification societies have been quick to absorb into the many other functions they already provide to many maritime administrations, globally.

PORT STATE CONTROL

The development of the PSC system to police the standards of vessels arriving into certain geographic areas has been one of the real success stories of recent times. Although the regimes around the world may be far from perfect, they have certainly laid down the groundwork to slowly force substandard ships and operators from the seas. Naturally, this role of inspection has been extended to include security and a form of screening similar to the normal PSC-targeting processes has been developed and implemented in many areas to target vessels for security risk and ISPS-related compliance examination.

Initially the PSCO will simply look at whether an ISSC is produced, if this is not available then there will be rounds of intensified inspection and severe sanctions will be imposed. Such sanctions would possibly include some of the following control measures:

- Inspection of the vessel
- A requirement to rectify the noncompliance
- Delay of the vessel
- Denial of entry into port
- Detention of the vessel
- Restriction of operations including movement within the port
- Expulsion of the ship from the port
- The contracting government may also apply alternative or additional lesser administrative or corrective measure

This list represents the "recommended control measures" as promulgated within the United Kingdom to PSCO, and constitutes the responses that should be given to any security infringements. These are mirrored across other regimes, and the fallout and stigma of such sanctions could remain with a vessel for some time.

There are a whole host of factors affecting the fundamental security of seafarers and companies that have, in the main, been sidestepped by the wording contained within the ISPS Code. Profiling a vessel on purely a security perspective is still not the norm, as access to most targeting resources is spread over numerous agencies and departments. There are naturally some security agencies that will monitor and control certain pieces of data and information but due to the sensitive nature of the organizations, their information and potential responses, the wider industry has never been fully instructed as to what would trigger a security force, or law enforcement reaction.

When one views the security screening parameters we see that there are certain fundamentals, which any owner/operator would be well advised to pay close attention to. Many of these however, mirror the targeting factors used with regards to safety and so the prudent operator should have systems in place to ensure that their vessels are not unduly harassed when arriving into port.

MARITIME SECURITY CONSIDERATIONS AND ISSUES

FLAG STATE PERFORMANCE

The performance of a vessel's Flag State will affect the likelihood of a vessel being subjected to inspection by PSC, the immigration services, or by law enforcement and customs officials. Flags with a poor safety, environmental, or security profile will bring all their vessels higher up the targeting database when they attempt to enter the port or territorial limits of a particular jurisdiction. If a Flag State makes the so-called "targeted list," it can have major repercussions for the vessel flying that particular flag. The vessel may be subjected to an ever-increasing amount of port State scrutiny due to the negative standing of the Flag State. At a minimum, there will be a loss of time and, as we have seen in previous sections the likelihood of enforcement measures [18].

OWNERS' PERFORMANCE

As with Flag States, there are owners of certain vessels who are targeted for increased attention. The likelihood of such an increased attention is heightened if the same owner has a history of casualties, or of safety or environmental violations, or has suffered from the imposition of past security control measures. There are other issues relating to ownership, which can see a vessel targeted for inspection, such as change of name or flag.

CHARTERER PERFORMANCE

Charterers, depending on the exact terms of the charter party agreement, can have a huge bearing on the conduct of a vessel—as such this is another area that will be closely viewed when assessing the degree of threat, or of interest posed by the vessel or its cargo. Although the ship itself may have a pristine record of compliance, and is casualty free, if it is chartered by a company or individual of "interest," then this can affect the treatment meted out to the vessel.

CARGO

In the United States, the fear has long been of a "weapon of mass destruction" being secreted in a container and smuggled into the country and detonated. The cargo being carried, therefore, has a great bearing on the way a vessel is viewed by the port of entry, and the degree of attention it is afforded by the security services. There has also been an increasing degree of attention afforded to the arrival into ports of LNG tankers, and although there may be some debate over the exact degree of threat posed, it is interesting to see just how such a vessel can affect the port security response. The Port of Boston is an interesting case in point.

When an LNG tanker arrives into the Distrigas natural gas storage facility, near Boston, Massachusetts it heralds an incredible flurry of security activity.[30] When the tanker reaches waters approximately 2 miles from the harbor, five United States Coast Guard (USCG) vessels meet it and establish a 500-yard perimeter or "bubble" around it. The two forward vessels are equipped to ram an offending vessel if needed but are charged with herding suspect vessels away from the hull of the tanker. The two aft USCG vessels are equipped with heavy weaponry and are charged with disabling a suspect vessel if the forward USCG vessels fail to stop the advance. The fifth USCG vessel is the command vessel (OTC) from where all decisions regarding the security of the transport are made.

This vessel is free to move wherever it needs but generally stays aft of the transport tanker. Another security "bubble" or perimeter is established at the 1000-yard mark, from the transport tanker. This 1000-yard bubble is comprised of four Massachusetts State Police boats (two forward and two aft), one Boston Police Department boat to the port side, and one environmental police boat on the starboard side. These vessels will approach a suspect vessel and attempt to "chase" it from the area. These vessels operate under existing rules of engagement with respect to the use of deadly force previously established by their respective agencies.

In addition to water assets, the Massachusetts State Police has the responsibility to shut down traffic on the Tobin Bridge while the tanker is in close proximity to it. A state police helicopter hovers and provides observation from the time the tanker is met outside the harbor until it is docked. Boston Police Department has the responsibility of closing all adjacent roads and wharfs that lead to the harbor. There are police units stationed at each of these access points from the time the tanker enters the harbor to the time it docks, approximately two hours. Boston Police Department estimates that it ties up 20–30 police officers per trip (inbound/outbound).

CLASSIFICATION SOCIETY

Classification society detention records are viewed in much the same way as Flag State performance. A classification society with a poor safety and detention record will, therefore, impose a greater risk of inspection on its vessels than a vessel whose construction is monitored by a member of the International Association of Classification Societies (IACS).

NATIONALITY OF CREW

It is a regrettable fact, but many security decisions are seemingly made on a discriminatory basis. As such there have been many instances affecting seafarers of particular race or religion and these can cause problems to vessel owners in certain ports and countries.[31] For example, there is much anecdotal evidence to suggest that seafarers of Pakistani origin have been faced with many difficulties when their vessels have arrived in ports around the United States. Although it is likely that a port State would deny taking a decision to act against a vessel based on the nationality of its crew, it remains something that the prudent ship operator would be advised to consider before sending a particular vessel to certain areas.

The introduction of ISPS has been blighted by the shoddy treatment afforded to many seafarers, particularly in the United States, where many spurious immigration decisions have seen seafarers confined to their vessels instead of being granted shore leave, and access to the social facilities they deserve, demand, and need.[32] In many areas crews have been treated as potential terrorists, rather than professional mariners simply doing their job. It is important to embrace the seafaring community to ensure that security measures are effective. With the support and respect of seafarers imposing universal, unified security constraints can work—something far from guaranteed when this vital link in the security chain is derided and abused.

RECORD KEEPING

When considering inspections and targeting, it is important to stress the importance of keeping security records to demonstrate a vessel's compliance with ISPS. Details of the following activities addressed in the SSP must be kept on board for at least the minimum period specified by the administration:

- Training, drills, and exercises
- Security threats and security incidents
- Breaches of security
- Changes in security level

- Communications relating to the direct security of the ship such as specific threats to the ship or to port facilities the ship is, or has been
- Internal audits and reviews of security activities
- Periodic review of the ship security assessment
- Periodic review of the SSP
- Implementation of any amendments to the plan
- Maintenance, calibration, and testing of any security equipment provided on board including testing of the ship security alert system

The records must be protected from unauthorized access or disclosure. They can be stored in an electronic format, but must be appropriately protected.[33,34]

WIDER ISSUES

COASTAL STATE INVOLVEMENT

Over the years since the adoption of the ISPS Code, many coastal States have vied to gain access to information relating to the maritime domain and the movement of vessels in their vicinity. One area of heavy pressure has been from the United States to allow monitoring of vessels passing in, or near their coastal waters. The U.S. Coast Guard met its April 2007 deadline mandated by the SAFE Port Act of 2006 to track all large commercial vessels within the U.S. waters.[35]

Traditionally, the rights of free passage handed down over time, and codified in the United Nations Convention on the Law of the Sea (UNCLOS) has kept that ships were allowed free, unmolested passage through such waters, but not for much longer. With the advent of automatic identification systems (AIS), the nature of ship movements has moved very much into the mainstream, and the roll out of long-range identification and tracking (LRIT) adds to the monitoring of every vessel. Coastal States play an ever wider role in the management of security of vessel movements, and this may ultimately see the traditional freedoms of navigation eroded when coastal states decide to deny entry into their waters of certain vessels.

INSURANCE

In a very basic sense the maritime industry exists in its present form due to willingness of insurers to allow ship and cargo owners to transfer financial risk through insurance policies. This means that when any threats to trade emerge insurers take a very dim view and seek to protect themselves. This naturally has a huge effect on those they provide cover to. As a result the introduction of the ISPS Code has caused some consternation for insurers. Meeting the requirements of the legislation and of operating in a prudent manner are more important than ever, even when faced with threats beyond the control of the insured.

LIABILITY ISSUES

SHIPBOARD PERSONNEL

There has been a rapidly growing market for protection devices on ships. Devices such as searchlights, cameras, and "sonic guns" (long-range acoustic devices, LRAD) as used to such high acclaim on the "Seaborn Spirit" when attacked off Somalia in 2005, have become commonplace. However, it is not simply enough to buy the most popular equipment. It is vital to make whatever is fitted onboard work, from considerations of the crew, positioning, and the protection afforded. Most merchant crews will not have had any "warlike" scenario training, and are not to be considered as "battle-hardened marines," so any response to violence needs to be implemented in a way that supports, coordinates, and protects crew effectively.

There is an important point here, in fighting off pirates and repelling boarders, merchant crews are being exposed to "low-level warfare." This raises the question of proper preparation for such conflict. It may seem obvious, but a hard hat, boiler suit, and gloves are not providing adequate protection when facing enemy fire. The increased use of defensive devices means that crew can be exposed to injury, and without the correct protective clothing the likelihood of serious casualty is greatly increased. No military organization would send troops into battle without a proper helmet and bullet-proof vest, so should shipboard personnel be asked to put their lives on the line for companies that will not provide them with the necessary protective equipment? Perhaps it would be better to avoid the question, and to instead simply provide the right kit for the job.

There are serious liability issues here for shipowners. If a crew member was placed in a position of danger, that is, ordered to operate some form of protective security device, and was then injured as a result of inadequate safety protection, there would be a case for compensation, and these areas need to be explored in greater detail by companies.

DAMAGE TO THIRD PARTIES

With the seemingly popularity of such equipment as the LRAD, the question of rules of engagement arises. It seems likely that sooner or later, some seafarers will inadvertently "blast" some innocent third party with their sonic gun, and it is important that the company can defend itself from allegations of improper usage. So it is important that the security management system guards against such accidents, or at least demonstrates that the crew have been made aware of the potential for accidents using protective devices. Of course, training is also a vital consideration for such equipment.

CHARTERERS

Risk is increasing across all parts of the maritime supply chain and this is not solely due to the values carried on ever larger ships and to increasing commodity prices. It rather rests with the significant claims inflation. Claims are today seemingly more likely to occur, and also likely to be more expensive when they do. Legal and regulatory changes, the approach of port authorities, and court decisions have effectively meant an increase in charterers' legal liabilities across a wide spectrum of marine incidents. It is a major concern for any charterer that they may become embroiled in a dispute based on some ISPS or security oversight.

Whereas it is relatively easy to vet owners for all other forms of compliance, security is more difficult to assess, other than sighting the ISSC, it is impossible to know what they should be doing about security (as laid down in the SSP), or what they are actually doing. This has led many more charterers to look to cover their third party liabilities, and has led P&I cover to meet possible exposure. Increasingly, according to the U.K. P&I club,[36] charterers are looking for cover tailored to their particular situations, which integrates hull and other covers, provides pure liability protection for nonoperational charters and offers pollution liability without sublimit. It seems that it may also be prudent to also seek coverage to guard against the potential effects of security liabilities.

Without due care and attention to security matters it would be all too easy for a charterer to be left exposed. According to Dr Chao Wu, Legal Director, Thomas Miller P&I Ltd., "[a] charterer needs standard P&I cover for the same risks as are usually insured by an owner. However, a charterer may need to widen the scope of cover for direct liabilities if he agrees to take on contractual risks that would not fall to him as a matter of law. He will also need cover for liability where he indemnifies the owner for such risks".[37]

EQUIPMENT

The installation of security equipment may be seen as a positive step, and many of the tools available today can indeed supplement and underpin the shipboard security system. However, it is not enough to merely supply and install the equipment: personnel need to be properly instructed in the operation, maintenance, and also the identification of faults. Many devices may not be common to seafarers, and if they are not provided with the necessary levels of instruction either the equipment will not be used to its full potential, or it will lay idle. Good equipment is only as good as the training and support given to the crew for operating it.

ONBOARD SECURITY ORGANIZATION

SECURITY LEVELS

The most fundamental element of the ISPS Code has been the introduction of a three-tier threat assessment system, which are as follows:

- *Security Level 1*. Normal. The level for which the minimum appropriate protective security measures shall be maintained at all times.
- *Security Level 2*. Heightened. The level for which appropriate additional protective security measures shall be maintained for a period of time as a result of heightened risk of security incident.
- *Security Level 3*. Exceptional. The level for which further specific protective security measures shall be maintained for a limited period of time when a security incident is probable or imminent, although it may not be possible to identify the specific target.

These three levels allow the security management regime to align itself with the level of threat, and in theory the three levels also allow resources to be effectively managed and applied. At security level 1 the minimum measures shall ensure:

- The performance of all ship security duties
- Control of access to the ship
- Control of the embarkation of persons and their effects
- The monitoring of restricted areas to ensure that only authorized persons have access
- The monitoring of deck areas and areas surrounding the ship
- Supervision of cargo handling and ship's stores
- Security communications are readily available

At security level 2, the additional protective measures, specified in the SSP, shall be implemented. At security level 3, further specific protective measures, specified in the SSP, have to be taken.

The vessel must respond to any increase of security level by acknowledging receipt of the instructions, and then by implementing the necessary measures appropriate as laid down within the SSP. Before entering a port, or while in a port that has set security level 2 or 3, the ship shall acknowledge receipt of this instruction and shall confirm to the PFSO that the necessary steps, as per the SSP, or in the case of security level 3, that any additional government instructions have been taken. The ship shall report any difficulties in implementation, and where the vessel does have difficulties the PFSO and SSO shall liaise and coordinate the appropriate actions. If a ship is at a higher security level than the port it intends to enter, or where it is already located, then the ship must immediately advise the contracting government, within whose territory the port facility is located, and the PFSO of the situation. Where such instances occur, the Flag State requiring its ships to set security level 2 or 3 in a port of another contracting government shall inform that contracting government without delay.

Thus, one of the major issues of security management remains the ability to increase security when a rise of level is imposed. This can be in the provision of resources, and also in the systems to enact the change.

It has been a fact that security level changes have not been very common. Even in the wake of terrorist attacks it seems that there has been a relaxed view taken by many States to increase the levels. In some instances this hesitation stems from the application of intelligence, whereas in others it appears to be a decision taken to avoid any undue political fallout. Many port and Flag States do not want to give the impression that security is a concern for them, or that they pose a heightened threat, and so elect to keep their level of changes to an absolute minimum. From a practical perspective this has been useful for shipping, but it does call into question the usefulness of a global security regime in which certain parties are hesitant to act, to save face.

Despite the low frequency of security level change, it is very sensible for the CSO and SSO to remain aware and alive to the possibilities of an increase, say if they are trading into a particularly sensitive area or region. This anticipation can make the process much easier to handle and manage, as too can drills held to simulate the requirements of an increase in levels.[38]

Training Issues

Training of personnel is vital to create and apply a working security regime, and to comply with the demands of the ISPS Code. The needs of training are fairly straightforward in the major ISPS roles of CSO, SSO, and PFSO all have specific training and certification demands imposed on them. IMO has developed three model courses:

- ISPS—Company Security Officer, 2003 edition
- ISPS—Port Facility Security Officer, 2003 edition
- ISPS—Ship Security Officer, 2003 edition

The model courses aim to provide knowledge to those who may be designated to perform the duties and responsibilities of a CSO, a PFSO, and an SSO.

Despite the emphasis on training there are exceptional circumstances under which an unqualified person can hold the role of an SSO. If a person holding a certificate of proficiency as an SSO is temporarily unavailable, the administration may permit a seafarer having an understanding of the SSP to serve as the SSO until the next port of call or for a period not exceeding 30 days, whichever is greater. In such circumstances, the company should inform the competent authorities of the next port(s) of call of the arrangements in place. Under STCW.6/Circ.9 the amendment came into effect on January 1, 2008.

Once personnel are in possession of their qualifications, and the SSP is installed on the vessel, it is important to remember that security is not neglected and as such drills and exercises are a vital part of the security effort. From changes in security levels, bomb alerts, piracy attacks, etc., there are many and varied scenarios which can be introduced and drilled against. In addition to these smaller shipboard efforts, it is important to involve other parts of the security chain, and real or desktop exercises involving the CSO and PFSO are a natural extension of the security training system.

Drills and exercises are not only important in developing the response to a security threat, but they can also help to motivate staff and provide them with an opportunity to openly assess the role they can play in helping to secure the vessel. In most cases it helps if the drills and exercises contain an element of realism, and capture the likely events that will threaten the vessel. For instance, if a vessel trades in pirate hot spots, drug-exporting nations, or into ports with a known stowaway problem it would seem churlish to ignore these facts when developing the drill schedule.

The reactions of personnel to drills are all important and in some instances SSOs have attempted to engender some enthusiasm for the exercises through the use of "incentives." A number of vessels reportedly secreted U.S.$50 in cabins and around spaces to encourage crews to search more thoroughly. Although this is a positive and imaginative step, it may not actually serve the purposes of training people to search for, say, explosives. If the crew are used to rampaging into a space and ripping fittings apart to find their cash reward they may learn techniques that could seriously affect whether a bomb or improvised explosive device would detonate. Hence, although it is a good idea to encourage staff, the steps used must be conducive to the correct and safe procedures necessary.

Standards of Training, Certification and Watch Keeping (STCW) and Security

The importance of security in day-to-day maritime operations saw security provisions in revisions of the International Convention on STCW.[39] According to the demands for security training, the following measures included:

- Shipboard personnel to undergo appropriate security-related training, irrespective of whether they have been assigned any security-related duties or not, before commencing any seagoing service.
- Appropriate provisions requiring shipboard personnel who have been assigned security-related duties to undergo appropriate training before commencing any seagoing service.
- Before being assigned shipboard duties, all seafarers should receive approved security training familiarization, instructions for the prevention of security-related incidents, and familiarization with their security-related duties contained in the SSP. Such familiarization should be provided by the SSO or other equally qualified person.

As a result of this recognition of the need for harmonized security training standards, the amendments were adopted in May 2006 and entered force on January 1, 2008, adding new minimum mandatory training and certification requirements for persons to be designated as SSOs.[40]

Barriers to Compliance

When one looks at the issues associated with security training, it is important to understand and consider the numerous "barriers" which can exist, and which can prevent even the most committed company from achieving their security aims. For example, many forget that the ship is not simply a vessel for the carriage of goods, it is also a seafarer's home. To break down some of the apathy and miscomprehension regarding security it is vital that the CSO, SSO, and master work hard to instill positive new habits across all personnel. The open days of the past are sadly gone, and now we are forced to embrace fully a regime based on

- *Locking.* Keeping cabins and all areas secured, while balancing the needs for safe evacuation.
- *Controlling.* Access onto and around the vessel needs to be controlled and monitored.
- *Thinking.* All personnel need to "think securely," their actions affect the security of the vessel and all must be encouraged to live and work in a new manner.

Communication

The shipping industry has long grappled with problems of language. Although English is the basic tool for maritime communications, there can be issues associated on board if the SSP is not communicated effectively across the working language(s) of the vessel. While SSPs may be in Spanish and French, there is a strong argument for some basics to be translated and communicated to crew who may otherwise struggle to grasp the finer points of security, and of the aims of ISPS.

Another issue is that of "culture." Some seafaring nations have seemingly not coped well with implementing the requirements of the code. When companies have looked harder at the issues and failures it has been seen that culturally, security is not something which comes naturally. For instance, a member of the crew stopping an official and questioning them for ID, and so on, is something many have struggled with.[41] In such cases it was and is a case of breaking down the cultural barriers, and empowering and supporting the crew to act as per the SSP. This is not always an easy step, but once the process is implemented and completed then the crew will be able to ensure the vessel is not only compliant, but is working to its full potential. Most important in fostering a security culture and in breaking down these barriers is the need to ensure that personnel have the resources to actually achieve what is required of them. If the resources are in place and easily applicable, and if there is a security culture crew members can understand and respect, then the aims are more likely to be achieved.[42]

PRIVATE SECURITY GUARDS

Ships, while in port or operating within certain geographical areas, are regularly and routinely required to use additional protective security from shore-based providers. Often this is done without too much thought to the standards of the companies being used. This is an oversight that must be addressed, as it is vital that background checks are performed on all third-party security contractors.

In some ports the PFSO will already have a list of vetted suppliers. However, this will not always be the case, and companies are encouraged to introduce procedures to ensure that private security contractors provide standards of service and personnel fit for purpose. The International Marine Contractors Association (IMCA) has produced a simple audit checklist to evaluate a security contractor's suitability before being contracted. The checklist includes such matters as the security company structure, their recruitment standards, training procedures and the ability of their guards.[43] The checklist should be sent to the company's shipping agent for completion and immediate return to the CSO before the arrival of the vessel in port; or when additional security measures and use of contracted guards are to be implemented at sea or at anchor.

In addition to this it is also vital that the SSO understands the exact nature and extent of the security to be provided by these external companies. The SSO must be satisfied as to which areas of the vessel they will cover, and also the main focus of security, whether they are tasked to stop people accessing the vessel, or, as is the case in some ports, whether they are purely meant to ensure that seafarers do not leave.[44]

EXPANDED SKILLS

NEGOTIATION AND SUPPORT

A major security concern has been the increasing prevalence of kidnapping for ransom by many pirate gangs. People and vessels are becoming currency, and off the coasts of Somalia and Nigeria the taking of entire ships and their crews is becoming worryingly commonplace. Insurance policies exist, and provide a welcome mechanism for reacting to such terrifying events, but perhaps we should be more concerned with the provision of advice on dealing with the event, and even more vitally the provision of proper support and counseling afterwards.

The response of shipping to hostage situations is not always consistent and fully formed. Many crews simply do not receive any training in negotiating with hostage takers and are, therefore, placed in extremely dangerous situations with little or no experience of the techniques to best protect themselves and their colleagues. A hostage situation places innocent seafarers directly in harm's way, and negotiation quickly becomes one of the most important aspects of such a crisis.

A skilled negotiator must find out what the hostage taker wants, who he or she is, and what it will take to achieve a peaceful outcome, all while ensuring the safety of the crew involved. Since it may take time to establish lines of communication with formally trained and experienced negotiators, often shipboard personnel become "accidental or reluctant negotiators." Despite the lack of training any respite, calm and clarity that can be brought through negotiation by a master or SSO can save lives.

The primary objectives of a negotiator are:

- *Prolong the situation*. The longer an incident lasts the less likelihood of bloodshed.
- Ensure the safety of the hostages.
- Keep things calm.
- Foster relationships between negotiator, hostages, and hostage taker.

The skills necessary to achieve these objectives are not easily gained, and as such masters and SSOs should be trained to deal with them. At the very least they should have some idea of who and what may face them and have practiced techniques to fall back on.[45]

INTERNATIONAL SAFETY MANAGEMENT (ISM) CODE AND INTERNATIONAL SHIP AND PORT FACILITY SECURITY (ISPS) CODE

Throughout the earliest days of the ISPS Code there were calls that it should simply have been an extra annex to the International Management Code for the Safe Operation of Ships and for Pollution Prevention (ISM Code). There are fundamental differences, however, between the ISM and ISPS Codes. In essence security is concerned with the risks associated with protection against intentional acts of disturbance, damage or destruction. Safety, however, concerns the risks associated with protection against accidental disturbance, damage, or destruction. The ISM Code is a management system containing the overarching principles that cover the day-to-day operations aboard ship, and within companies. The reason that the ISM Code is so thin is that it needs to stay aloof from detail. It is the principles of what to do, not an instruction guide of how to do them.[46]

So what of the future? What we will see, and this is an initiative that is gathering pace, is the natural harmonization of ISM and ISPS. It is sensible to have an integrated safety and security management system within a company and aboard ship but the components pertaining to ISM and ISPS compliance need to be clearly identifiable and traceable so as to be able to demonstrate compliance with each Code. Also, ISM audits are not to duplicate or replace other surveys or verifications so ISM and ISPS verification audits also need to be distinct. That is, an ISM audit cannot replace an ISPS audit. The ISPS verification audits can be done distintcly and during the same ship visit by suitably qualified auditors, but each survey or audit is done distinctly and sequentially. The truth remains that ISM Code is the umbrella over all of the vessel's requirements—it ensures personnel do what has to be done, that tasks are performed correctly, and are then recorded as being done. These basic operational tenets are as true to safety, security, pollution, training, manning, and all aspects of the proper and effective management of a vessel, company, and personnel.

The most effective security regimes are able to take advantage of the system management approach, they are able to develop and implement best practice and tap into the discipline which many across shipping have grown into since the advent of the ISM Code.

SAFETY *VERSUS* SECURITY

The IMO MSC 82 Human Element Working Group considered the report of the Group of Independent Experts (GIE) established by the secretary general to analyze the impact of the ISM Code and its effectiveness in the enhancement of safety of life at sea and protection of the marine environment. The committee noted that the industry had identified common areas between the ISM and the ISPS codes and that resolution A.852 (20) on guidelines for a structure of an integrated system of contingency planning for shipboard emergencies may provide guidance to handle or manage common areas of the ISM and ISPS Codes. It was noted that, to properly motivate seafarers, companies should take into account feedback from shipboard personnel, including the outcome of shipboard safety committees to improve their operations and procedures relating to safety and environmental protection and it was essential for the company to respond in a constructive and timely fashion to any feedback received from seafarers operating the SMS. Since seafarers are integral to the effective operation of the SMS they should, therefore, be involved in the development and improvement of the system to ensure that the manuals are proportionate, concise and relevant.

Although the GIE advice stopped short of mentioning feedback from seafarers on security, it is important to stress that safety meetings should be expanded to include security topics and concerns and the feedback from all involved is vital to ensure continuous improvement of the security regime in place.[47]

Self-Assessment

MSC.1/Circ.1217 is the interim guidance on voluntary self-assessment by companies and CSOs.[48] It has been stated that with the maritime industry being subjected to so many pieces of legislation over the past decade that there should now be a period of reflection to make the rules we currently have worked. As part of this reflective process it has been recognized that self-assessment could be a positive way of managing both compliance and continuous improvement. The Tanker Managers Self Assessment Scheme (TMSA) has been a seeming portent for the future management of many operational facets of shipping, and as the lessons have disseminated across other vessel types we have seen IMO rolling out MSC.1/Circ.1217. This voluntary self-assessment tool is intended to help to identify any aspects of SOLAS chapter XI-2 and the ISPS Code that the company and CSO can address to enhance the SOLAS chapter XI-2 and ISPS Code implementation process.

Search and Rescue (SAR)

On July 1, 2006, amendments to two IMO conventions entered into force (SOLAS) and the Search and Rescue (SAR) Convention of 1979.[49] As the IMO has stressed, the amendments concerning the treatment of persons rescued at sea are particularly appropriate as seemingly more migrants and refugees are involved in accidents at sea.

The amendments do of course have a large effect on a number of areas of ship operations—most important would be the effect on the vessel's security provisions. The master's responsibility for security under ISPS Code and the responsibility to render assistance to persons rescued at sea[50] are, at first glance, seemingly incompatible aims. It may seem obvious, but one cannot maintain effective security while bringing any number of unknown persons onto a vessel, especially if this is done in an uncontrolled way. In a rescue situation it is likely that other matters aside from security will be taking precedence. As stressed in the ISPS Code, the master has ultimate responsibility and must make decisions at the time of the event, with the understanding that the traditional undertaking to rescue persons in distress takes priority. Once the decision to rescue persons at sea has been made, the master may have unwittingly been forced to compromise the SSP—as designed for the vessel. This is particularly true if there are large numbers of people coming aboard (all things are relative, but for these purposes we shall assume that a "large number" would be $\geq 1/3$ ships complement).[51] In such an event the security provisions of the vessel will not be designed, or not likely, to adequately cope with such an influx of people. There is of course a world of difference between rescuing a lone yachtsman, and bringing hundreds of refugees from a sinking hulk on board. We have to understand and recognize the differences, and develop a rescue plan that at once satisfies the demands of saving lives with the need to ensure that the vessel remains as secure as possible.

The provisions within the ISPS Code do not cover an operation such as the large-scale rescue of persons at sea. Regarding such events the ISPS Code simply states[52]

in the event that persons or goods rescued at sea are on board, all known information about such persons or goods, including their identities when known and the results of any checks run on behalf of the ship to establish the security status of those rescued. It is not the intention of chapter XI-2 or part A of this Code to delay or prevent the delivery of those in distress at sea to a place of safety. It is the sole intention of chapter XI-2 and part A of this Code to provide States with enough appropriate information to maintain their security integrity.

These ISPS requirements are relatively simple to implement—even if the gathering of the information may ultimately prove problematic. At the same time the lack of clear guidance in the ISPS Code places the master, SSO, and CSO at a disadvantage, as they must develop a strategy that will allow them the flexibility to save lives, but one that will also ensure that the ship remains secure. Regrettably this strategy may also have to ensure that in the event of port state interrogation, or any subsequent legal or commercial disputes, the master demonstrates that every possible step was taken to marry seemingly conflicting demands of ISPS and for the responsibility to save lives.

Seen from a purely ISPS perspective there is surprisingly little a master and crew must do to conform. However, to keep the vessel secure there are a number of steps that can be taken. The first would be to develop a plan. The SSA should view all potential conflicts between safety and security, and there is an increasing area of operations that the rescue of migrants might be seen as a foreseeable risk. The CSO should be keeping the vessel informed on security risks, and this should include the likelihood of encountering large numbers of migrants. Seemingly vessels in the vicinity of the African Coast and the Canary Islands are likely to be placed in a rescue scenario as discussed here.

Once the risk is identified, the CSO must issue instructions to mitigate the security risk. Though we recognize that it is vital to get the injured parties on board as quickly, and as safely as possible, it may be advisable to consider the following minimum measures:

- *Those rescued should be embarked into a secure "quarantine" area.* This should be an area that the ships personnel can secure from the rest of the ship, but which is comfortable and where assistance and humanitarian aid can be administered.
- This "quarantine area" will allow the crew to contain those rescued and also to control movement around the vessel. Those rescued, just as with stowaways, should not have free movement around the vessel. This is to guard the security of the vessel, and also for the safety of those on board. As we know, ships can be dangerous places—and we do not want injuries.
- *It is advisable to monitor the "quarantine area."* This can be done physically, but the use of CCTV would place less demand on an already strained crew.
- It is vital to take advice, from flag and port states, and also from the vessels P&I club. The CSO must continually monitor the situation and provide the necessary advice and support to the ship—while also keeping external agencies availed of the circumstances and events.
- The vessel, certainly in the first day or so of the rescue, would be advised to work at an increased security level. Further guidance can be gained through CSO and flag state dialogue.
- The rescue of large groups of migrants has become a huge political stumbling block. It is, therefore, sometimes advisable for the CSO to make contact with the media, as this can help speed the response of certain states in accepting the entry of the migrants.

It should be remembered that often migrants are desperate, and having placed their lives at risk will often take drastic actions to secure their dreams of a relocation. The risk of hostage taking within the crew is strong, and crewmembers should never work alone within the security quarantine area. There should be a sufficient strength in numbers (where and when possible) to deter attack by those rescued.[53]

Rescues at sea are difficult and there are many elements that place a vessel and her crew at risk. In the past, perhaps we looked only at the safety and operational risks of performing such a task. Regrettably, in this modern climate of fear and suspicion there is a security risk posed by bringing unknown persons onto the vessel. We must juggle the demands of rescue and aid, with the responsibility to secure the vessel. There are some who do use nefarious means to get onto, or closer to ships. Somali pirates have become most adept at raising false alerts to bring ships closer to their trap. We must also recognize the potential for undesirables to take advantage of the traditions of rescue and aid that ships are bound to provide. It is a fact that under ISPS, ship personnel will do all possible to keep people off the ship, but once there is an issue of safety, the crew themselves will actually help people onto the vessel. This is a dangerous and difficult dichotomy to manage.

BREACHES OF SECURITY

To date there have been relatively few terrorist attacks on shipping, but that does not mean we should allow any complacency. The fact that piracy, drug smuggling, people smuggling, and instances of stowaways are still an everyday problem means that there are times when systems can fail, and security is compromised. In appreciating that ships are vulnerable to attacks (of whatever form), we need to put in place thorough, effective and simple contingency plans to deal with the fallout of any likely event.

It is perhaps human nature, but sometimes people do not know how to act, and more likely when to act—and a properly trained and resourced crew will be able to understand when to implement measures and what they should do. For this reason, much of the ISPS Code deals with the measures to mitigate the risk of attack. However, very little guidance is given on what to do if the worst happens, and a security incident or breach has occured.

If the security system fails, and if the vessel security is compromised, the CSO, SSO, and master need to be able to initiate a proper response, one that reflects the equipment and the people actually available. The contents of the SSP can give any crew the upper hand in dealing with such a situation, but only if it reflects the vessel realistically. There are many plans drawn up by consultants who are not adequately familiar with seafarers, ships, or the equipment they may be likely to have on board. Many simply drew up plans for cruise ships, and tried to superimpose these plans onto other vessels. When the general alarm sounds it is not the time to find out that you do not have blast containment equipment, or that the SSO has never actually been able to understand how to create a blast path.

Incident control in the event of a security breach is vital, just as it is for any normal incident. There is a very fine line in shipping—once a security incident occurs it is the training and skills relating to safety which again come to the fore. Safety of life, pollution control and the safety of vessel all then depend on the more traditional seamanship skills, and of the responses laid down not necessarily within the SSP, but within the SMS. There are a host of survivability basics to consider such as:

- Navigation
- Propulsion
- Stability
- Fire fighting
- First aid

There are also issues relating to potential evacuation of the vessel, and these will need to be assessed by the remaining senior officers. Such issues may be:

- Should you abandon ship?
- Can you get off?
- Who should evacuate? All personnel or just non-essential?
- What are the means of escape? Lifeboat/Liferaft?

It seems that in applying the lessons of safety management when security procedures are established we are better placed to respond. In the event of an incident we come full circle and rely again on the mainstays of maritime safety knowledge, skills, instincts, and training. ISPS should not interfere with safety. It needs to mesh with it to provide a seamless solution.

The Aftermath

In the event of a security breach there are numerous responsibilities to be satisfied, and most impotant in them is the reporting and investigation. However, there has long been one area which has been neglected, and which is only now starting to become an issue. Aside from the actual events surrounding maritime attacks and kidnap, be they by pirates, terrorists, or criminal gangs, there are also issues to be explored in the aftermath, such as the matter of counseling and support of seafarers after an event.[54]

Quite often after a vessel has been freed from a hostage situation, little time or effort is made to rehabilitate or counsel the victims. Many of the vessels freed off over the past years off Somalia appear to simply head off to Dubai or Djibouti where some crew are repatriated, and others remain on board, end of the story. This cannot be the right thing for the people, or for the business. A vessel left under the control of a master with undiagnosed "post-traumatic stress disorder" is a real concern, and companies must do more to assess the psychological damage caused and how to relieve it. This means that companies should establish a formal system of trauma counseling. Perhaps in the "macho" world of shipping this has been considered unnecessary, but aside from the compassionate nature of such assistance there are also commercial and liability issues.

It is imperative that ship operators understand the complex relationship they have with freed hostages and have a policy to help close the incident out. Anticipation and planning will allow a company to refine its own ideas about good practice, and develop a coherent, integrated, yet adaptable counseling plan. It is likely that after an event, insurers may start to ask some rather searching questions—especially if the P&I Association is facing damages or compensation claims. As many of these aspects of security are not mandatory, they would be seen as operating outside of the normal ISPS provisions, and would be perhaps found within the auspices of a complete company security plan. Such likely questions would include the following:

- Do owners have hostage crisis management plans, a designated crisis management team, and a training program for ships crews? How are these plans exercised and tested?
- Do these plans specifically reflect the unique elements of maritime hostage taking and piracy?
- Do crews receive advice and guidance on how to survive as a hostage and during an armed military rescue?
- Does an owner's duty of care extend to the provision of medical and psychological support for the hostages and their families both during and after an incident?
- In the event of a hostage taking who debriefs the officers and the ships crew?
- Who records their experience in an evidential form for later use?
- Who gathers evidence?
- Who gathers information about the pirates' tactics, numbers, knowledge, equipment, nationality, and motivation to develop intelligence?
- How are hostage crisis management plans adjusted as a result of lessons learned?
- How do owners manage any ransom demands?

If the answer to any of these questions is blank bemusement, or the belief that such an event cannot happen, it would seem that the contingency plans may need revision.

Future of Security

The overall perception of maritime security within the shipping industry still appears to remain as being "against seafarers," rather than "for them".[55] To counter the negative perceptions of security, it is important to develop a new sense of purpose and focus, tempered with a sense of reality and perspective in seafarers' minds. It is vital to show those charged with making security work that threats do indeed exist, but that they do not necessarily consist of the terrorist "bogeyman" blowing their ship to pieces. The focus needs to be on the ever-present maritime threats, such as piracy, drug smuggling, and stowaways. With the right attitude to security and by following robust, practical guidance, shipping companies and their valuable assets will have a chance to succeed and to make security a true everyday function of their operations.[56]

We have seen too many seafarers embarrassed by the measures they employ on board—crew meekly asking for identification, and then apologizing and explaining that it is all because of the ISPS Code. We need to support, empower, and encourage all those engaged in security. That is the task that the entire shipping industry, from navies, Flag and port States, to professional bodies, shipowners, and personnel, all need to embrace as one. It has long been recognized throughout many different industries that being secure makes us more efficient, and shipping is no different.[57] A ship viewed in isolation is nothing, just steel and machinery—it is the crew that makes it, and they are the heart and soul of any vessel. If you walk up the gangway and are stopped by a confident, knowledgeable, and empowered member of the crew, we can perhaps assume that the whole crew will be positive in all aspects of their work.

To secure or defend their ship the crew must know it intimately. The crew that knows its vessel will care more about the ship and will, therefore, look after it better throughout every facet of its operation. Two of the most straightforward facets of security are awareness and good basic "housekeeping" in and around the vessel. These seem very basic, but they are the foundations upon which security will succeed or fail, and to make these essentials work needs the full support of the crew.

In many quarters it has been seafarers that have been criticized for not accepting security and not treating it seriously, which is unfair. Seafarers are not resistant to change, but as professionals they have to see that there are tangible benefits to this transformation. We, therefore, have to educate them and make sense of security—it has to be relevant and sensible. Other parties then need to recognize these improvements and afford seafarers and shipping companies the respect and freedoms they deserve, such as shore leave for crews and commercial incentives for owners. If harnessed correctly, ISPS can have a huge positive effect, resulting in safe and secure vessels operated by enthusiastic and motivated crews.

Thus, there are obviously benefits associated with the correct application of the ISPS Code—as long as certain preconditions are fulfilled. To conclude, we shall look at the preconditions first and then turn to the benefits.

KEYS TO THE FUTURE OF MARITIME SECURITY

- *Understanding security.* Ship's personnel need better understanding of both the letter and the spirit of the ISPS Code. This knowledge will aid their sense of where ISPS fits into their day-to-day operations and what they can do to better secure their vessel.
- *Acceptance of ISPS and maritime security.* To accept security it is important that personnel are able to follow the logical evolution of ISPS and see where it harmonizes with their other onboard roles, particularly those contained within the vessel's SMS.
- *Bringing security to life.* In the past, outside of certain piracy hot spots, security was not a real issue in shipping. As such many see it as simply another burden, and another set of activities to keep them from their much-needed rest. We have to change this perception, by stressing how simple it can be to make real and effective security change without undue load on the crew.
- *Improved security procedures.* Inspections and searches on board have to evolve, and crew must learn to inspect and search correctly, quickly, effectively, and safely. Searching correctly can be a difficult and dangerous task—there is the risk of disturbing threatening material or indeed not finding it—so it has to be done properly. It is vital that seafarers understand the right, safe, and thorough way of responding to security alerts.

- *Increased security reporting.* Understanding what constitutes a security risk, breach, or threat will allow the crew to document the security incidents—this will assist the CSO and will reinforce the company, fleet, and vessel security regimes.
- *Introduction of a security culture.* The birth of a proper and functioning security culture paralleling the safety philosophy is the next vital step. In a true safety and security culture, officers and crew will understand what they are doing and why, and in this way will start to think in a secure manner. This will allow the requirements of the ISPS Code and of their own SSP to become an accepted and welcome part of everyday shipboard operations.
- *Dealing with people.* The crew is faced with many new challenges; the biggest of these is in the form of people. From agents, chandlers, inspectors, surveyors, and so on, the crew has to be capable and confident in controlling access and assessing what steps need to be taken to protect the secure integrity of the vessel.[58]

BENEFITS OF CORRECT INTERNATIONAL SHIP AND PORT FACILITY SECURITY CODE IMPLEMENTATION

Despite the widespread operational changes there are a whole host of benefits associated with the correct application of the ISPS Code:

- *Reductions in incidents.* With security comes a greater awareness of the vessel. This understanding and appreciation can be harnessed to enhance the safety culture already on board, which will lead to a reduction in lost time and total recordable incident rates.
- *Harder target.* While many do not see ships as being at risk, the harder a target appears, the more likely any would-be protagonists will simply look for a softer option. So a proper security regime may see a vessel ignored by terrorists, pirates, stowaways, and smugglers in favor of an alternative, easier target.
- *Reductions in insurance claims.* A reduction in incidents (whether safety- or security-based) will lead to a decrease in insurance claims, which in turn will save outlay on deductibles. This will positively impact a company's claims profile, which in turn may lead to reduced premium increases. One P&I Club has already recorded a 50 percent drop in stowaway incidents, and also a massive reduction in spurious gangway "slip-and-trip" claims.
- *Reduction in commercial disputes.* The shipowners' very existence depends on the relationship with their clients, the cargo owners. The introduction of a proper and effective ISPS regime through the provision of a trained and knowledgeable crew will lead to a reduction in negative incidents that may impact on this business relationship. Detentions, delays, expulsions, and banning orders can lead to a breakdown in a vessel's trading capacity, and these must be guarded against.
- *Reduction in legal disputes.* When commercial relations break down, legal disputes inevitably arise. These are costly and can negatively impact any ship or company. Security breaches affect the flow of trade, but they can be reduced with the provision of a crew with the right skills.
- *Improved relations with flag state.* Any company or vessel seen to be taking positive and effective steps to make its plans and people more secure will be treated with greater respect, and afforded even greater assistance from their flag state authority. The Flag State wants owners to take the necessary steps to make ISPS work, and will recognize any genuine efforts made.
- *Improved relations with port state.* An effective ISPS regime is vital in satisfying PSC inspectors of the secure integrity of the vessel. The proper and effective implementation of ISPS on board will mean an increased likelihood of successfully passing PSC inspections, thus avoiding delays and detentions.

- *Reputation*. Today, more than ever, a positive business reputation is vital. To gain and maintain this industry standing takes time, effort, and investment. Clean, safe, and secure ships are the answer and all these aspects have an equal and vital role to play in any ship management regimen.
- *Financial benefits*. Security should be seen as an investment, not a burden. The benefits of effective ISPS adoption can be translated into financial gains. We have seen that security can add to the knowledge, skills, and effectiveness of a crew, and that this well trained and efficient crew is an obvious positive aspect when operating the vessel. This becomes "a good crew," and as we have seen this can mean a "good ship." Good vessels, with no detentions, arrests, or negative publicity attached have a better trading profile than others, so we can say that a "good ship" is a more attractive asset and will attract more cargo, thus more profit for the owner.

NOTES

1. ISPS: International Ship and Port Facility Security Code. *IMO Maritime Safety*, The International Maritime Organization, 2004.
2. Steven Jones, *Maritime Security: A Practical Guide*, (London: The Nautical Institute), 2006.
3. Ibid.
4. Peter Moth, *ISPS Code: A Practical Guide*, Foreshore Books, 2004 edition.
5. "Ship Security—ISPS Code Briefing," *Signals* (special issue), North of England P&I Association, 2003.
6. *Creating a Security Culture*, by John Ramage, Managing Director, International Registries (UK) Ltd, February 2004, p. 2.
7. ISPS: International Ship and Port Facility Security Code, *IMO Maritime Safety*, 2004.
8. ISPS: International Ship and Port Facility Security Code. *IMO Maritime Safety*, 2004.
9. Conversation with Captain Nicholas Cooper, Nautical Institute President, *UKHO ECDIS Today*, Issue 7, 2006.
10. The IMO: "Amendments to the Annex to the International Convention for the Safety of Life at Sea (SOLAS), 1974, pp. 10–11. The full text can be found, for example, online at http://www.admiraltylaw guide.com/conven/amendsolas2002.pdf (accessed on 07/10/2007).
11. Master's Discretion for Ship Safety and Security. Notice to Members No. 3, West of England P&I Association, 2003–2004.
12. North of England P&I Association Presentation to Ship-owners, Iran 2004.
13. *Signals Newsletter* 55, (Newcastle, UK: North of England P&I Association), 2004, p. 1.
14. IMO Conference resolution 8: ILO to establish a joint ILO/IMO Working Group, www.imo.org.
15. C185 Seafarers' Identity Documents Convention (Revised), International Labour Organization, 2003, http://www.ilo.org/ilolex/cgi-lex/convde.pl?C185.
16. *Maritime Security: A Practical Guide*, by Steven Jones, 2006.
17. Transportation Worker Identification Credential (TWIC) Implementation in the Maritime Sector. US Transportation Security Administration (TSA), 2005.
18. IMO, MSC/Circ.1091, Issues to be Considered When Introducing New technology on Board Ship, (London: The IMO), June 6, 2003.
19. Dr Phil Anderson, *Cracking the Code: The Relevance of the ISM Code and Its Impact on Shipping Practices*. Nautical Institute, 2003.
20. ISPS: International Ship and Port Facility Security Code. *IMO Maritime Safety*, 2004.
21. IMO, ISPS Code status update 05, www.imo.org.
22. Peter Moth, *ISPS Code: A Practical Guide*, 2004 edition.
23. Greaves, Europe makes 'mockery' of ISPS Code, *Lloyd's List*, April 27, 2007.
24. Regulation (EC) No 725/2004 of the European Parliament and of the Council of 31 March 2004 on enhancing ship and port facility security.
25. U.S. Maritime Transportation and Security Act of 2002.
26. Navigation and Vessel Inspection Circular No. 11-02, Subject: Recommended Security Guidelines For Facilities.
27. ISPS: International Ship and Port Facility Security Code, *IMO Maritime Safety* 2004.
28. E-mail correspondence to author from Seagoing personnel.
29. CSI: Container Security Initiative, US Customs and Border Protection, www.cbp.gov.

30. LNG Security at Distrigas Facility. US Department of Homeland Security.
31. Alexandros M. Goulielmos, Agisilaos A. Anastasakos, Worldwide security measures for shipping, seafarers and ports: An impact assessment of ISPS code, September 2005.
32. "Access Denied: Implementing the ISPS Code." The International Transport Workers Federation, www.itfglobal.org/infocentre/pubs.cfm/detail/1446.
33. ISPS: International Ship and Port Facility Security Code, *IMO Maritime Safety*, 2004.
34. Paris MOU targeting system www.parismou.org.
35. "Coastguard meets SAFE PORT Act Deadline." USCG Press Release, April 2007.
36. "Advice for Charterers as Legal Liabilities Grow." Thomas Miller & Co. Ltd Press Release, May 2007.
37. Ibid.
38. ISPS: International Ship and Port Facility Security Code, *IMO Maritime Safety*, 2004.
39. STCW regulation VI/5—Requirements for the issue of certificates of proficiency for ship security officers, and STCW Code section B-VI/5—Guidance regarding training for ship security officers.
40. May 2006 amendments to STCW Convention and STCW Code—security officers, fast rescue boats www.imo.org.
41. Steven Jones, *Maritime Security: A Practical Guide*, 2006.
42. Alert! *Human Element Bulletin*, 14 2007, www.he-alert.org.
43. International Marine Contractors Association's (IMCA) Security Task Force.
44. US Coast Guard Port Security Advisory (2-05), May 20, 2005.
45. Conversation between author and Graham C. Clifford, Security Risk Management Consultant, 2006.
46. Dr Phil Anderson, Cracking the code: The relevance of the ISM Code and its impact on shipping practices, Nautical Institute, 2003.
47. MSC 82, The Joint MSC/MEPC Working Group on Human Element, 2006, www.imo.org.
48. MSC.1/Circ. 1217, Interim guidance on voluntary self-assessment by companies and company security officers (CSOs) for ship security, www.imo.org.
49. SOLAS and SAR amendments strengthen international rescue regime, www.imo.org.
50. Justin Stares, "Migrant rescue 'a legal must," *Lloyd's List*, May 30, 2007.
51. Steven Jones, "Security and the 1st July Amendments to SOLAS and SAR Conventions." *The Nautical Institute Seaways Magazine*, September 2006.
52. ISPS: International Ship and Port Facility Security Code, *IMO Maritime Safety*, 2004.
53. Michael Pugh, "Drowning not waving: Boat People and Humanitarianism at Sea," *Journal of Refugee Studies*, Oxford University Press, Vol. 17, No. 1, 2004, pp. 50–69.
54. Conversation between author and Graham C. Clifford, Security Risk Management Consultant, 2006.
55. ISPS: Two Years On, by Steven Jones. *Shiptalk News Special Report*, ISPS Special Report 1, 2006, p. 1, www.shiptalk.com.
56. International Chamber of Shipping and International Shipping Federation, *Pirates & Armed Robbers: Guidelines on Prevention for Masters and Ship Security Officers* (4th Ed.), (London: International Shipping Federation), 2004.
57. Finnlines Group, A new look at security, *Finnlines Magazine*, 1, 2004, p. 2.
58. Steven Jones, *Maritime Security: A Practical Guide*, 2006.

8 Maritime Terrorism: Threat to Container Ships, Cruise Liners, and Passenger Ferries

Peter Chalk

CONTENTS

INTRODUCTION

With the collapse of the Soviet Union and the European Communist Eastern Bloc in the late 1980s, it was confidently assumed that the international system was on the threshold of an era of unprecedented peace and stability. Politicians, academics, and diplomats alike increasingly began to forecast the imminent establishment of a new world "order" that would be managed by liberal democratic institutions, and which would develop within the context of an integrated global economy based on the principles of the free market.[1] As this unprecedented interstate structure emerged and took root, it was assumed that destabilizing threats to national and international security would decline commensurately.

However, the initial euphoria that was evoked by the end of the Cold War has been systematically replaced by a growing sense of appreciation that global stability has not been achieved and has, in fact, been decisively undermined by transnational security challenges, or the so-called gray area phenomena. These threats, which cannot be readily defeated by the traditional defenses that states have erected to protect both their territories and populaces, bear off the remarkable fluidity that currently characterizes international politics—a setting in which it is no longer exactly apparent who can do what, to whom, and with what means. Moreover, it has become increasingly apparent that in the contemporary era, violence and the readiness to inflict death is being used by the weak not so much as a means of expressing identity, but more intrinsically as a way of creating it.[2]

Stated more directly, the geopolitical landscape that presently confronts the global community lacks the relative stability of the linear Cold War division between East and West. Indeed, few of today's dangers have the character of overt military aggression stemming from a clearly defined sovereign source. In contrast, security, conflict, and general threat definitions have become far more opaque and diffuse in nature, taking the form of amorphous challenges, whose source is internal rather than external to the political order that the concept of "national interest" has conventionally represented.[3]

The maritime realm is particularly "conducive" to these types of threat contingencies, given its vast and largely unregulated, opaque nature. Covering 139,768,200 mi^2,[4] most of this environment takes the form of high seas that lie beyond the strict jurisdiction of any one state—meaning they are, by definition, anarchic. These "over the horizon" oceans are fringed and linked by a complex lattice of territorial waters, estuaries, and riverine systems, which in many cases, are poorly monitored, and in terms of internationally recognized jurisprudence exist as entirely distinct and independent entities.[5] Combined, these various traits and practices have served to ingrain the planet's aquatic expanse with the type of unpredictable and lawless qualities that Thomas Hobbes once famously wrote ensured life as "brutish, nasty, and short."

One particular threat that academicians, intelligence analysts, law enforcement officials, and politicians have begun to take increasingly serious note of during the past several years is the exploitation of the maritime realm to simultaneously facilitate terrorist logistical and operational designs. Indeed, commentators in various countries now appear to believe that the next major strike against Western interests is as likely to emanate from a nonterritorial theater as a land-based one.

Three types of vessels have garnered particular attention in terms of future potential maritime terrorist[6] risk contingencies: container carriers, cruise liners, and passenger ferries. The focus on these crafts stem from a variety of factors including their potential use to smuggle weapons and operatives, disrupt the mechanics of global oceanic freight, and facilitate mass casualty attacks. No less saliently, fund-raising hijackings and strikes against passenger vessels have already occurred, with the latter constituting the most frequent manifestation of terrorism in the maritime realm. This chapter discusses the respective vulnerabilities and attractiveness of commercial and passenger shipping to extremist aggression, discussing different attack contingencies and likely implications that might thereby result. A brief assessment of some of the major international initiatives that have been enacted to better safeguard the world's sea ways and some tentative policy recommendations for guiding and enhancing future maritime security drives are also provided.

CONTAINER SHIPS

Approximately, 112,000 merchant vessels, 6,500 ports and harbor facilities, and 45,000 shipping bureaus constitute the contemporary international maritime transport system, linking about 225 coastal nations, dependent territories, and island states. This expansive network caters to about 80 percent of commercial freight, which in 2001 included an estimated 15 million containers that collectively registered 232 million point-to-point movements across the world's seas.[7]

VULNERABILITIES AND ATTRACTIVENESS TO TERRORISM

The global container-shipping complex has been the focus of considerable attention, largely because it is widely seen to represent a viable logistical conduit for availing the covert movement of terrorist weapons and personnel. There are at least four factors that underscore this perceived vulnerability.

First, the sheer volume of commercial freight that is moved by container ships effectively eliminates the possibility of comprehensive checks once the cargo reaches its port of destination. Indeed, experts universally acknowledge that trying to inspect all incoming cargo—or even a significant random sample—without unduly interrupting the contemporary dynamic of oceanic exchange is neither possible nor economically tenable, given the number of boxed crates involved.[8] Even in countries with advanced x-ray and gamma scanning technologies, inspection rates remain minimal. In the United States, for instance, a mere 10 percent of the approximately 6 million boxed crates that arrive in the country every year can be expected to have undergone some sort of scrutiny; this equates to about one to two containers out of every twenty.[9]

Second, the highly complex nature of the containerized supply chain creates a plethora of opportunities for terrorist infiltration. Unlike other cargo vessels that typically handle payloads for a single customer loaded at port, container ships deal with goods and commodities from hundreds of companies and individuals, which in most cases, are received and transported from inland warehouses characterized by varied (if not highly questionable) on-site security. For even a standard consignment, numerous agents and parties would be involved, including the exporter, the importer, the freight forwarder, a customs broker, excise inspectors, commercial trucking firms, railroad, dockworkers, and possibly harbor feeder craft and the ocean carrier itself. Each point of transfer along this spectrum of movement represents a potential source of vulnerability for the overall security and integrity of the cargo, providing terrorists with numerous opportunities to "stuff" or otherwise tamper with the boxed crates.[10]

Third, is the rudimentary nature of the locks that are used to seal containers. Existing devices offer little, if any protection, and often consist of nothing more than a plastic tie or bolt that can be quickly cut and then reattached using a combination of superglue and heat.[11] Most commercial shipping companies have been reluctant to develop more resistant mechanisms, given the costs involved. A standard seal can be purchased for a few cents if ordered in bulk, whereas more robust versions might run to several hundreds of dollars. Moves to develop so-called smart boxes equipped with global positioning systems (GPS) transponders and radio frequency identification devices (RFIDs) that emit signals if they are interfered with have run into similar problems and had not, at the time of writing, been embraced with any real degree of enthusiasm by the international maritime industry.[12]

The overall vulnerability of crated cargo is further exacerbated by the "Trans International Routier" (TIR) haulage system, which is used to transport such merchandise from warehouse to port. Any container bearing the TIR logo is assumed to have had its contents inspected and sealed at source by relevant authorities—a designation that precludes any additional checks before dockside loading. There are a variety of ways in which terrorists could compromise and exploit this internationally recognized arrangement for their own purposes, ranging from spray painting a false logo on the outside of a generic; preloaded crate, to bribing officials to issue a TIR designation for a container that had already been tampered with; to stealing and "stuffing" one en route to a port.[13]

Fourth, the effectiveness of point-of-origin inspections for containerized freight is highly questionable. Many resource-constrained states in Asia and Africa fail to routinely vet dockworkers, do not require that truck drivers present valid identification before entering an off-loading facility, and frequently overlook the need to ensure that all cargo is accompanied by an accurate manifest. Even richer nations in Western Europe and North America are not devoid of these types of deficiencies. Privacy regulations in the Netherlands, for instance, preclude the option of comprehensive security vetting for dockworkers without first gaining their permission. In the words of one Dutch expert, "I would be amazed if harbor employees at Rotterdam, Antwerp, or Amsterdam were required to undergo any form of mandatory background criminal check." In the United States, about 11,000 truck drivers enter and leave the Long Beach terminal in Los Angeles with only a standard driver's license, whereas Singapore, which runs arguably one of the world's most sophisticated commercial maritime terminals, does not require shipping companies to declare goods on their vessels if they are only transiting through the country's port[14]—meaning that the government does not know what is being transported on the vast bulk of carriers that transship through the city-state.[15]

The absence of uniform and concerted safeguards is problematic as it is virtually impossible to inspect containers once they are on the high seas, while delaying checks until after they arrive at their destination may be too late to prevent a terrorist event from occurring. The enactment of the International Ship and Port Facility Security (ISPS) Code is designed to offset some of these problems by mandating a minimum set of requirements to govern the integrity of the maritime export–import chain; however, the initiative suffers from a number of serious gaps, which are explicated in the section on Maritime Security Initiatives.

ATTACK CONTINGENCIES AND IMPLICATIONS

As suggested earlier, terrorist contingencies against container ships are more likely to revolve around exploitation of the cargo supply chain than attacks directed against the crafts themselves. Merchant carriers are not only large, but they also have a high waterline, which means that a considerable amount of explosives would be needed to cause a critical breach. Just as importantly, there would be little immediate impact associated with sinking a commercial carrier of this sort, either in terms of attracting media attention or eliciting public angst (far less terror). The one possible exception would be an attack that is aimed at destroying a vessel to block a narrow sea-lane of communication (SLOC), and thereby disrupt maritime trade. However, there are very few critical choke points that are truly nonsubstitutable for ocean-bound freight (bypassing the Malacca Straits, for instance, would require only an extra three days of "steaming") and other than oil, highly perishable foodstuffs, and critical medical supplies, most commodities would not be unduly affected by short delays in delivery.[16]

Container vessels could certainly be used as a "Trojan horse," however, to covertly transport terrorist weapons and personnel. Not only does commercial shipping represent a tried and tested means of moving people to distant shores without being detected, illegal migrants have frequently been able to enter a third country by posing as sailors—a status that gives them the right to go ashore (while their vessel is docked) without being subjected to the type of standard immigration procedures that are normally used to check disembarking passengers. There is no reason why terrorists could not mimic this latter procedure to facilitate the placement of their own cadres around the world. Equally as relevant to container carriers is the possibility of an operative stowing away in an onboard crate. One case just after 9/11, which involved an Egyptian who had transformed an empty container bound for Halifax, Canada into a sophisticated living area complete with a bed, food-making facilities, and a rudimentary latrine system highlights the potential. The individual, who was apprehended in possession of American airport maps and security passes, disappeared after being granted bail.[17]

Although all of these scenarios are both plausible and worrying, it is the possibility of a crate being used to hide a radiological dispersal device (RDD, commonly referred to as a "dirty bomb") that is giving most cause for concern.[18] An attack of this sort that targets a major port could have enormous political and economic ramifications, irrespective of the number of people actually killed. Depending on the size and the sophistication of the weapon used, a resulting explosion could theoretically contaminate the terminal at levels well above tolerable civilian exposure limits. At the very least, this would precipitate the immediate termination of all operations at the facility in question; more seriously, it could also generate severe pressure for a general shutdown of the country's intermodal transportation system until it could be determined that it was safe.[19] As Stephen Flynn remarks, the immediate and latent economic fallout from such a contingency would be acute, if not catastrophic.

> Examining cargo in tens of thousands of trucks, trains and ships to ensure that it poses no threat would have devastating economic consequences. When containers stop moving, assembly plants go idle, retail shelves go bare and workers end up in unemployment lines. A [comprehensive] three-week shut down [across the board] could well spawn a global recession.[20]

The closure of all 29 seaports along the American West Coast in October 2002 provides an empirical indication of the damage that could occur. These terminals handle approximately 42 percent of U.S.'s maritime imports and exports by value. The 14-day lockdown, which was caused by a labor dispute between dockworkers and management, disrupted more than 200 ships carrying

300,000 containers, resulting in cargo delays, costly diversions to alternative ports, and unemployment lines as businesses laid off workers and cut production. The direct cost to the U.S. economy has been estimated at U.S.$467 million, whereas the subsequent effort to clear freight backlogs is thought to have removed between 0.4 and 1.1 percent of nominal gross domestic product (GDP) from prominent Asian exporters including Hong Kong, Malaysia, and Singapore.[21]

The disruptive economic dimension of maritime terrorism has been singled out as having specific pertinence to transnational Islamist extremism, precisely because "Al-Qaeda" has specifically emphasized that attacking key pillars of the Western commercial and trading system is integral to the self-defined "jihadist" war on the United States and its major allies. Repeated statements to this effect have been issued by Bin Laden and his cohorts post-9/11, the main thrust of which have been to denigrate America as a paper tiger on the verge of financial collapse and ruin. This stance was perhaps best exemplified in an Al-Qaeda communiqué that was issued following the bombing of the *M/V Limburg*[22] in October 2002.

> By exploding the oil tanker in Yemen, the holy warriors hit the umbilical cord and lifeline of the crusader community, reminding the enemy of the heavy cost of blood and the gravity of losses they will pay as a price for their continued aggression on our community and looting of our wealth.[23]

CRUISE SHIPS

As of January 1, 2004, there were 339 active oceangoing cruise liners operating around the world with a combined weight of some 10.9 million gross tons. Vessels capable of carrying well in excess of a thousand people were included in this global fleet, although most ships (65 percent) were of the lower berth category with an average passenger load of 224. Ten companies controlled 64 percent of the market, three of which were in clear domination: "Carnival," "Royal Caribbean," and the "Star/NCL." Approximately 12 million paying customers were projected to have taken a cruise in 2004, 78 percent of whom were from North America, 18 percent from Europe, and 4 percent from Asia and the South Pacific. The bulk of this traffic was concentrated in the Caribbean (46 percent), followed by the Mediterranean (21 percent) and Alaska (8 percent).[24]

VULNERABILITIES AND ATTRACTIVENESS TO TERRORISM

There are several facets of the luxury-oriented, yet highly popular cruise liner industry that would appear to have particular relevance for future terrorist attack contingencies.

Most fundamentally, these vessels constitute an attractive target that directly resonates with the underlying ideological and operational rationale of Al-Qaeda and the wider internationalist Islamist movement. Not only do cruise ships cater to large numbers of people who are confined to a single geographic space—which make them ideal venues for carrying out assaults intended to maximize civilian casualties (a hallmark of jihadist terrorism in the post-9/11 era)—they are also highly iconic in nature, reflecting the type of explicit Western materialism, affluence, and discretionary spending that Bin Laden–inspired extremists are so opposed to.[25] Moreover, the fact that the vast bulk of passengers originate from well-to-do North American middle class Judeo-Christian backgrounds means that indiscriminate attacks can be carried out with little or no risk of negatively impacting on wider Muslim interests.[26] This is not necessarily the case with land-based incidents, as bombings of Western embassies in Kenya and Tanzania (1998), tourist resorts in Bali (2002 and 2005), and hotels in Jakarta and Amman (2003 and 2005, respectively) have clearly demonstrated.[27]

On a more general level, a decisive strike against a major oceangoing carrier such as the *Queen Mary II*, *Queen Elizabeth II* (QEII), *Freedom of the Seas*,[28] or *Crown Odyssey* would almost certainly result in a global Cable Network News (CNN) effect. Indeed, as the November 2005 attack against the *Seaborne Spirit* off the coast of Somalia[29] demonstrates, even comparatively small-scale events have the potential to elicit considerable international media attention and interest. Generating this type of publicity is critical to the dynamics of any terrorist entity, not least because it can be readily exploited to demonstrate operational vibrancy, which is vital both for attracting recruits and boosting the morale of existing cadres.

In addition, there are a number of vulnerabilities pertinent to the cruise industry that could be potentially exploited by terrorists. Although more rigorous since 9/11, security checks remain somewhat lax and are far less stringent than those used for commercial aviation. According to officials in the United Kingdom, prominent British companies such as "Cunard" physically inspect only about 2 percent of boarding passengers (however, they are required to pass through a metal detector and all carry-on luggage is x-rayed), and under normal circumstances, generally, do not scan hold bags before they are transferred to cabins. Equally, although virtually all major operators thoroughly vet their own crew and maintenance staff, many of the service employees who have access to ships at overseas docks may not have undergone any form of comprehensive background checking. These personnel, who are often highly receptive to bribes and other forms of co-option (given the low wages they are routinely paid), offer terrorists' a ready conduit to smuggle and stash weapons/explosives for subsequent attacks. Exacerbating these problems is the very nature of oceanic recreation, which necessarily precludes (or at least limits) the extent to which forceful mitigation measures can be instituted: specifically, strident confrontational security does not sit well with the pleasurable holiday experience cruise firms are striving to provide.[30]

There are also certain operational traits that could conceivably open up cruise ships to possible terrorist risks. Vessels frequently anchor offshore for extended periods of time (sometimes up to 24 hours) to allow those on board an opportunity to take day trips. It is during these prolonged stops that a liner would be most exposed to a collision assault—either from a fast approach and explosive-laden suicide craft or a more sizeable boat (2000+ tonnage), which is deliberately smashed into its side.[31] The traditional practice of passengers congregating on upper decks and waving to onlookers, friends, and relatives at a departing port could be just as problematic in terms of inviting attacks, particularly land-based standoff strikes involving flat trajectory weapons such as rocket-propelled grenades (RPGs), missiles, shoulder-launched missiles, and sniper rifles.[32]

Finally, virtually all luxury liners sail according to precise schedules and preplanned itineraries, which are readily available through the Internet, advertising brochures, or travel agents. This information constitutes a highly valuable source of intelligence for terrorists, allowing a perpetrating group to pick the time and place where it will be easiest to covertly expedite the transfer of explosives and operatives to a targeted vessel or when a ship will be most susceptible to a mid-sea assault. Such advanced knowledge, if adroitly exploited, would help to greatly offset the uncertainty that is normally associated with preattack planning and logistics.[33]

ATTACK CONTINGENCIES AND IMPLICATIONS

As with container ships, most experts agree that sinking a cruise liner would be extremely difficult. These vessels are built with safety as the foremost priority. Hulls are double-lined and, in most cases, interiors are compartmentalized with largely watertight systems in place.[34] Attempting to overcome these safeguards through an onboard explosion would require several, highly powerful bombs; a sophisticated understanding of the structural integrity of the target in question (particularly in terms of being able to quickly and accurately discern weak points in the craft's "skeletal" design); and sufficient time to appropriately rig the vessel for detonation.[35] For most terrorists, such logistical, skill and temporal requirements are not readily available.

An external small-boat ramming attack, which would combine (and amplify) a blast's shock wave with the energy of momentum, has a far greater prospect of causing extensive damage. However, even here, the possibility of a critical breach is questionable. Certainly, the suicide strikes on the USS *Cole* and *M/V Limburg*, which although not specifically directed against a passenger liner, nevertheless do demonstrate the general difficulty of fatally destroying a major oceangoing carrier.

The only other option would be to try and bring down a liner through an underwater attack, specifically by attaching mines or other "parasitic devices" to a berthed[36] ship's hull.[37] Although possible, this type of combat diving requires considerable training and skill with regard to swimming undetected and avoiding the high volume of traffic, which typically traverses major maritime terminals.[38] Moreover, in the case of a shallow water port such as Rotterdam, the net effect of a submersible strike would merely be to cause the stricken vessel to settle on the bottom of the seabed, not to sink it.[39]

There are several other terrorist scenarios, however, which, although somewhat less dramatic in manifestation, could still elicit considerable fear, damage, or publicity. For instance, a group could bomb venues where passengers routinely congregate for relaxation and recreation, including restaurants, casinos, and cinemas. Plastic/C4 explosive would be "ideal" for this type of attack as it is both hard to detect and highly malleable in nature (which means bombs can be broken down and repackaged in everyday items that are unlikely to raise suspicions).[40] A series of random killings or hostage takings could also be staged, either using basic weapons that are accessible on board (e.g., knives stolen from kitchen galleys) or more lethal assault rifles and pistols, which had already been predeployed by co-opted members of the crew.[41] Equally, an organization could carry out localized acts of arson in areas where fire doors are absent or where sprinkler systems and alarms had first been disabled.[42] Finally, various biological assaults might be possible, ranging from high-tech releases of airborne viruses through a ship's ventilation system to more rudimentary (and, hence, arguably more probable) disseminations of foodborne contaminants such as *Salmonella*, *Escherichia coli*, botulism, and mercury.[43]

Depending on the size of the vessel and the scale and sophistication of the operation, a concerted strike against a cruise ship could result in a casualty count of several hundred, if not more. Quite apart from the widespread physical pain and psychological trauma that this would necessarily engender, it could also have genuinely disruptive political and fiscal effects. Critics, albeit with the benefit of hindsight, would undoubtedly demand why the sector was left exposed and why the intelligence services in the relevant flag nation failed to foresee that an attack was imminent. In an age where counterterrorism has emerged as one of the state's most pressing responsibilities, such a reaction could easily precipitate a subsequent chain of events that, if not carefully managed, works to fundamentally erode popular perceptions of governing credibility, if not legitimacy (as it did in Spain following the catastrophic commuter trains bombings of 2004).

The economic fallout could be every bit as serious, especially given the highly concentrated character of the cruise business and the fact that this mode of transportation is not integral to an individual's day-to-day life, travel needs, or, indeed, leisure pursuits.[44] As one maritime security analyst in London put it, "If a major cruise liner was hit, the industry will be in big trouble. People just won't sail anymore—either with the company owning the vessel or with one of its [few] competitors."[45] In the United States, this could result in considerable losses, jeopardizing not only $30 billion in direct monetary benefit but also the revenue base of major tourist ports—notably, Miami, Galveston, Canaveral, New York, Los Angeles, Honolulu, Tampa, Seattle, and (assuming a post-Katrina recovery) New Orleans—as well as some 315,000 full- and part-time jobs.[46]

PASSENGER FERRIES

Passenger ferries are extensive throughout the world, providing a cheap, highly accessible, and ubiquitous mode of transport that many people have come to rely on as not only a cost-effective alternative to flying, but often also as their principal means of national and international movement. Journey times can be as long as 24 hours or as short as 10 minutes, with routes embracing everything from major sea sailings to inter-island transits and harbor/river crossings. Many of the larger vessels currently in operation are able to accommodate a customer base numbering in the tens of hundreds, if not thousands, and at least in the developing world, it would not be uncommon for these

TABLE 8.1
Traffic Passing through the Port of Dover, June 2005

Form of Traffic	Numbers
Passengers	1.3 million (5.6 million between January and June)
Cars	259,000
Freight vehicles	180,000
Coaches	12,000

Source: U.K. Customs and Excise, September 2005.

ships to sail well over designated capacity limits. Besides civilians, ferries frequently cater to a wide array of vehicles. Colloquially known as "ro-ros" (roll on, roll off), these crafts are designed with expansive open decks immediately above their hull that allow for the rapid loading and debussing of cars, tourist coaches, buses, minivans, and freight trucks. As is exemplified by the Port of Dover (which acts as Britain's principal maritime gateway to the English Channel and European continent) in Table 8.1, the total volume of traffic passing through a particular hub can quickly add up.

VULNERABILITIES AND ATTRACTIVENESS TO TERRORISM

Although certainly not an iconic or prestige target in the manner of cruise ships, there are several traits inherent to passenger ferries that make this specific form of maritime transportation especially vulnerable or attractive to terrorist aggression. First, extant security measures at passenger terminals vary greatly and even in developed littoral states such as the Netherlands, Canada, the United Kingdom, and United States are not nearly as extensive as those employed for cruise liners (much less aircraft). Specifically, the need to move high volumes of embarking traffic in as efficient a manner as possible means that protective measures must minimize the disruptive impact of any security thereby instituted; in other words, the latitude for carrying out concerted checks on baggage, cars, trucks, and people is very limited.[47] Indeed, the institution of even minimal precautionary measures can have the effect of generating huge delays and backlogs. Dover provides a case in point. In the immediate aftermath of the July 2005 London underground bombings, all motorists bound for Calais were subjected to a slightly more rigorous regime of predeparture scrutiny and examination. Although individual inspections and questions generally took no more than a few minutes per vehicle, combined, they served to create tailbacks that extended over 4 miles.[48]

Second, vetting of those working onboard ferries is *ad hoc* and partial, reflecting the seasonal and highly transient nature of these personnel. Background checks, to the extent that they occur, are generally aimed at verifying past employers and rarely embrace wider criminal investigations. Throughout much of Asia and Africa it is unlikely that any consistent form of examination takes place, largely because owner-operators lack the means (and frequently the willingness) to do so, something that is particularly true for foreign nationals. Maritime experts generally concur that the absence of effective staff/crew scrutiny represents a significant point of vulnerability for commercial ferry companies, providing extremists with an ideal opening to covertly place insiders on board targeted vessels for strike or logistical purposes. Several commentators argue that dangers are further exacerbated—at least in the context of the post-9/11 international Islamist threat—by the overwhelming number of North Africans, Arabs, Filipinos (Catholic and Muslim), and Indonesians owner-operators typically hire to fill service positions on their ships. This employment bias is viewed as potentially worrisome in that it affords Al-Qaeda cohorts and affiliates with a perfect cover and allows them to take advantage of one of the key principles emphasized in jihadist field/training manuals—to "hide in plain sight" whenever possible.[49]

Third, and in common with cruise liners, ferries sail along predefined routes according to set departure and arrival times. By definition, these schedules have to be made widely available to the paying public and, as a result, are easily accessed through a broad array of mediums and conduits, ranging from travel guides and port terminals to the Internet.[50] Itineraries are, in short, both fixed and highly transparent, availing terrorists with a reasonably accurate cartographic picture, which can be used to gauge the point at which vessels are most susceptible to attack and interception. The Abu Sayyaf Group (ASG) in the southern Philippines provides a good example of an organization that has conspicuously planned many of its maritime assaults around information of this sort.[51]

Finally, there are certain features in the specific construction of ferries that serve to weaken their wider structural integrity and safety. As noted earlier, ro-ros are deliberately built with large open car decks to avail the efficient embarkation/disembarkation of vehicles. Crucially, this particular design format makes these vessels acutely sensitive to subtle shifts in their center of gravity, largely because they necessarily lack stabilizing bulkheads on their lower sections. Undue movements of improperly secured automobiles or sudden accumulations of even small amounts of water[52] are especially likely to trigger such effects and could, depending on the severity of the situation at hand, cause a ship to list or fully capsize.[53] As one high-ranking official with the IMB in London put it, "One [event] and that's it; these boats have no damage limitation at all."[54]

Fast cats, a rapid passenger-only ferry that is used extensively in many parts of the world for short inter-island crossings or river trips, suffer from different, but potentially as serious vulnerabilities. To facilitate speed, these crafts have a minimal superstructure, which is typically developed from lightweight metal alloys such as aluminum. Hulls, consequently, tend to be paper thin, which makes them extremely susceptible to critical beach from either external or internal sources. Moreover, because outer shells are based on a material (aluminum) that has a relatively low ignition temperature, the possibility of a primary attack spawning a large-scale secondary fire (together with all the smoke and heat that this would entail) is high.[55]

ATTACK CONTINGENCIES AND IMPLICATIONS

Of all the types of shipping covered in this chapter, ferries are probably the most vulnerable to terrorist aggression, given the structural nature of the vessels and the highly open environment in which they operate. The range of potential contingencies is, hence, fairly extensive and could embrace any one of the following:

- A bomb attack carried out either on one of the lower car decks or in one of the principal passenger-holding areas
- Arson (which could manifest both as a primary act of aggression or as a by-product of an explosive detonation)
- A suicide strike (such as the use of a small boat that is deliberately rammed into the side of a targeted vessel)
- Mid-sea interception and seizure to elicit ransom (political or monetary) demands
- A random shooting spree using weapons covertly smuggled on board during the embarkation process or predeployed by co-opted crew/staff members

The implications of a concerted strike on a ferry could be extensive. As with cruise liners, a mass casualty event is likely to have acute political ramifications and may well elicit strong domestic pressure for the initiation of mitigation measures that extend far beyond the maritime realm. In the Philippines, for instance, the 2004 strike against *Super Ferry 14*—which resulted in 116 deaths[56]— had a profound effect on perceived domestic terrorist threat contingencies and was a central factor in subsequent moves that have been made to promulgate legislation that will, for the first time, allow the government to detain a suspect on the specific charge of terrorism, bar those convicted of such crimes from plea bargaining and probation, and prescribe additional penalties for any individual who directly or indirectly is linked to designated terrorist acts.[57] Attempts to introduce measures of this sort are noteworthy in the light of the country's relatively recent martial past under Ferdinand Marcos and the extreme sensitivity this experience fostered—within the governing establishment as well as among the population at large—toward sanctioning any type of extrajudicial processes or legal practices.

Significant economic externalities could also eventuate. Attacks that result in widespread fatalities and injuries would almost certainly expose owner-operators to large-scale compensation or liability payouts—both of which would have import for subsequent maritime insurance coverage. Various major ferry accidents that have occurred provide an indication of just how great these fiscal fallouts could be. The 1994 sinking of the *Estonia* in the Baltic Sea (852 deaths), for instance, generated victim claims in excess of U.S.$110 million, whereas the (known) legal costs associated with the capsizing of the *Herald of Free Enterprise* outside the Belgian port of Zeebrugge in 1987 (193 fatalities) have been calculated at U.S.$70 million.[58]

Beyond these direct costs, decisively interrupting ferry traffic may well have an impact on the stability of the targeted state's wider economy. This is particularly true in the developing world where geographic factors often dictate the need for cheap, high-volume passenger vessels to avail travel between island archipelagos as well as to compensate for the lack of viable surface infrastructure such as a functioning road and bridge system.[59] Even in more economically advanced states such considerations can have relevance. In the United Kingdom, for instance, repeated acts of terrorism in the Dover Straits would probably encourage trucking companies to use the "Chunnel" as their primary conduit to the European continent. This underwater rail route, although rapid, is far more expensive and less expansive than the sea crossing, which would inevitably raise the overall rate charge for freight shipments—creating a price burden that would ultimately fall on the individual consumer.[60]

MARITIME SECURITY INITIATIVES

Growing international concern for the safety and integrity of global shipping has generated increased pressure for structured multilateral agreements to better secure the world's oceanic environment. Some of the more notable initiatives that have subsequently ensued include[61]

- The Container Security Initiative (CSI), which involves a series of bilateral, reciprocal accords that, among other things, allow for the forward deployment of U.S. Coast Guard and Border Protection (CBP) officers and their foreign counterparts to prescreen container ships bound for and departing from U.S. shores. As of July 2004, the CSI was operational at 20 overseas ports.[62]
- The ISPS Code, which was adopted by the International Maritime Organization (IMO) at its December 2002 conference, outlines minimum security procedures that all ships (above 500 tons) and ports must meet to improve overall maritime security. Any vessel which does not meet these requirements or which leaves a port that does not, can be turned away by relevant authorities at the destination terminal.
- The Proliferation Security Initiative (PSI), which aims to combat the proliferation of weapons of mass destruction (WMD) by sanctioning the right to stop, board, and, if necessary, seize a vessel on the high seas if it is suspected of smuggling chemical, biological, radiological, or nuclear materials. At the time of writing, the PSI had been adopted by 13 countries: Australia, France, Germany, Italy, Japan, the Netherlands, the Marshall Islands, Poland, Portugal, Singapore, Spain, the United Kingdom, and the United States.[63]
- The Customs-Trade Partnership Against Terrorism (C-TPAT), which offers international importers expedited processing of cargo if they comply with CBP guidelines for securing their entire supply chain. Over 45,000 companies have so far agreed to participate in C-TPAT.[64]

In addition to these measures, the United States has taken the lead in formulating and underwriting several maritime security and capacity-building initiatives in regions that are either viewed as a vital component of the Global War on Terror (GWOT) or recognized as integral to Western commercial and energy interests. A good example was the 2004 establishment of the Combined Task Force-Horn of Africa (CTF-HOA), which, among other things, has a remit to detect, disrupt, and detect transnational terrorist groups operating in the vicinity of the coastal waters of Djibouti, Ethiopia, Eritrea, Kenya, Somalia, Sudan, and Yemen.[65] Other parts of the globe that have received similar attention include West Africa, especially Nigeria and the wider Gulf of Guinea (which over the coming decade is estimated to account for up to 20 percent of U.S. oil imports),[66] and the Malacca Straits (one of the key maritime corridors connecting Southeast Asia with the economic hubs of China, Japan, and South Korea, as well as, more broadly (through the Indian Ocean), the Middle East).

A complete discussion on the strengths and weaknesses of these measures is beyond the scope of this chapter. However, a few preliminary remarks can be made. On the positive side, the initiatives have helped to lend a degree of transparency to what has, hitherto, been a highly opaque theater. Specifically, they lay the parameters for regulated intestate action in the maritime realm, both by enumerating rules, principles, and attendant responsibilities for international cooperation and, more importantly, by providing a common framework in which joint policies over the medium to long term can be further developed and refined. This type of contextual foundation simply did not exist before 9/11.[67]

On the negative side, the programs outlined earlier suffer from three critical shortfalls as presently configured.

- First, they are limited in functional and geographic scope, tending for the most part to be confined to a narrow set of like-minded allies.
- Second, most of the emphasis is on initiatives aimed at increasing the security "wall" around commercial seaborne traffic, paying scant regard for contingencies that do not involve containerized cargoes (such as ferry bombings) or modalities designed to counter the root source of threats to the oceanic environment, or, indeed, terrorist organizations themselves.
- Finally, and with particular reference to ISPS, the code's stipulations extend to neither small craft nor coastal rivers/tributaries; most oceanic trading countries have consistently failed to meet these regulations[68]; and there is, as yet, no definitive means to effectively audit how well extant measures are being implemented by participating states or, indeed, to gauge their overall utility in terms of dockside security.[69] Moreover, there are presently 43,000 carriers in the global shipping industry that weigh 500 tons or more. This means that approximately 130 vessels need to be certified each day—a task that according to Lord Westbury, the Chief Executive Officer (CEO) of Global Marine Security Systems, will lead to a number of smaller companies and ports going out of business.[70]

Given its expanse, lack of regulation, esoteric character, and general importance as a critical conduit for international trade, it is reasonable to assume that the maritime environment will remain of interest to terrorist organizations—both for logistical and attack purposes. There are several ways by which the world's principal maritime nations could help to offset some this threat quotient. Areas where multilateral input would be particularly useful include

- Further expanding the nascent regime of post-9/11 maritime security, both in terms of pressing littoral states to sign up to multilateral protocols and instituting effective structures for measuring and ensuring compliance with their stipulations
- Boosting the coastal monitoring capabilities of states in areas of strategic maritime importance or endemic pirate activity through the provision of surveillance assets, training, and technical support[71]

- Informing the parameters of bilateral and multilateral maritime security collaboration by conducting regular and rigorous threat assessments aimed at delineating high probability risk scenarios and quantifying their costs
- Investigating ways of encouraging owner-operators and other third-party stakeholders to institute more effective security measures at ports and implement better documentation and screening procedures for vessel crew and support staff
- Sponsoring research into cost-effective initiatives for better securing ships and oceanic freight, especially with regard to developing innovations such as commercially viable satellite tracking systems, tamperproof container locks and "smart" crates that are capable of emitting warnings if their contents are disturbed after being sealed

NOTES

1. See, for example, The International Monetary Fund, *World Economic Outlook* (Washington: IMF), 26–27, 1991.
2. "Terrorism and the Warfare of the Weak," *The Guardian* (United Kingdom), October 27, 1993.
3. Peter Chalk, *Non-Military Security and Global Order: The Impact of Extremism, Violence and Chaos on National and International Security* (London: Macmillan), pp. 1–2, 2000.
4. This equates to some 2.42 times the planet's terrestrial surface area.
5. Rupert Herbert-Burns, "Terrorism in the Early 21st Century Maritime Domain," in Joshua Ho and Catherine Zara Raymond, eds., *The Best of Times, the Worst of Times: Maritime Security in the Asia-Pacific* (Singapore: World Scientific Publishing), p. 157, 2005.
6. For the purpose of this chapter, maritime terrorism is defined as "the undertaking of terrorist acts and activities (1) within the maritime environment; (2) using or against vessels or fixed platforms at sea or in port, or against any one of their passengers or personnel; (3) against coastal facilities or settlements, including tourist resorts, port areas, and port towns or cities." This conceptualization is based on the one developed by the Council for Security Cooperation in the Asia Pacific's (CSCAP) Working Group on Maritime Security. See S. Quentin, "Shipping Activities: Targets of Maritime Terrorism," *MIRMAL* 2, January 20, 2003, available online at http://www.derechomaritimo.info/pagina/mater.htm, last accessed October 18, 2005.
7. Author interview, Lloyds of London, September 2005. See also Herbert-Burns, "Terrorism in the Early 21st Century Maritime Domain," pp. 158–159; Joshua Sinai, "Future Trends in Worldwide Maritime Terrorism," *Connections: The Quarterly Journal* 3/1 (March): 49, 2004; "Maritime Security Measures to Amplify Cost for Shipping," Transport Security World, July 29, 2003; Organization for Economic Cooperation and Development (Washington, DC: OECD), *Security in Maritime Transport: Risk Factors and Economic Impact* (OECD), July 2003; Central Intelligence Agency (CIA), *CIA World Fact Book*, available online at http://www.cia.gov/cia/publications/factbook/geos/xx.html, last accessed November 4, 2005.
8. Author interviews, maritime experts and intelligence officials, Singapore, London, and Rotterdam, September 2005. See also John Fritelli et al., *Port and Maritime Security: Background and Issues for Congress* (Washington: Congressional Research Service, RL31733), p. 4, December 30, 2004; Catherine Zara Raymond, "Maritime Terrorism, A Risk Assessment," in Joshua Ho and Catherine Zara Raymond, eds., *The Best of Times, the Worst of Times: Maritime Security in the Asia-Pacific* (Singapore: World Scientific Publishing), p. 187, 2005; N. Brew, "Ripples from 9/11: The U.S. Container Security Initiative and Its Implications for Australia," *Current Issues Brief* 28: 5, 2003; and Customs and Border Protection (CBP), *Fact Sheet: Cargo Container Security—U.S. Customs and Border Protection Reality*, October 2004, available online at http://www.cbp.gov/linkhandler/cgov/newsroom/fact_sheets/2004/5percent_myth.ctt/5percent_myth.doc, last accessed November 6, 2005.
9. Robert Block, "Security Gaps Already Plague Ports," *The Wall Street Journal*, February 23, 2006.
10. Fritelli, *Port and Maritime Security: Background and Issues for Congress*, p. 9; James Hoge and Gideon Rose, eds., *How Did This Happen* (New York: Public affairs), p. 188, 2001.
11. See, for instance, J Saunders, "Marine Vulnerability and the Terrorist Threat," *International Maritime Bureau* (London: International Chamber of Commerce), p. 4, 2003.

12. Author interviews, Department of Homeland Security Liaison Officials, U.S. Embassy, Singapore and London, September 2005. In bulk order form, these types of technologies would cost at least U.S.$500 per container. Shipping companies have also been reluctant to make such investments given that even more advanced boxes cannot offer anything approaching 100 percent infallibility.

13. Author interview, former British defense intelligence official, London, September 2005.

14. This is largely due to a fear that if declarations on all cargoes were made mandatory irrespective of whether or not Singapore was the final port of call, the resulting red tape would deflect trade north to Malaysia.

15. Author interviews, maritime security analysts and government officials, Amsterdam and Singapore, September 2005. See also Block, "Security Gaps Already Plague Ports."

16. Author interviews, maritime experts and intelligence analysts, Singapore, London, and Amsterdam, September 2005. The one major exception to this is the Suez Canal. However, this waterway is heavily monitored and patrolled, given its strategic proximity to the Persian Gulf, which currently acts as one of the principal naval theaters for supporting the conflict in Iraq and wider Global War on Terror (GWOT).

17. Author interview, Control Risks Group and U.K. Customs and Excise, London, September 2005. See also Sinai, "Future Trends in Worldwide Maritime Terrorism," 57 and Philip Shenon, "U.S. Expands Plan for Cargo Inspections at Foreign Ports," *The New York Times*, June 12, 2003.

18. A 2006 acquisition proposal by the Dubai-based Ports World incorporated to take over the commercial running of five major U.S. ports from the U.K.-based Peninsula and Oriental Steam Navigation (since abandoned) galvanized American concerns in this regard, not least because the United Arab Emirates (UAE) served as one of the jumping off points for the 9/11 hijackers and have since been connected both to financing of the residual *Al-Qaeda* network as well as the nuclear procurement efforts of Iran. See Bill Spindle, Neil King and Glenn Simpson, "In Ports Furor, A Clash Over Dubai," *The Wall Street Journal*, February 23, 2006.

19. Author interview, Department of Homeland Security Liaison official, U.S. Embassy, Singapore, September 2005.

20. Stephen Flynn, "The Neglected Homefront," *Foreign Affairs* (September/October): 25, 2004; see also Peter Chalk et al., *Trends in Terrorism: Threats to the United States and the Future of the Terrorism Risk Insurance Act* (Santa Monica, CA: RAND), p. 34, 2005.

21. Michael Richardson, *A Time Bomb for Global Trade: Maritime-Related Terrorism in an Age of Weapons of Mass Destruction* (Singapore: Institute for Southeast Asian Studies), p 66, 2004; OECD, *Report on Security in Maritime Transport: Risk Factors and Economic Impact* (Paris: OECD), pp. 17–18, July 2003; Department of Foreign Affairs and Trade (DFAT), *Global Issues Brief on Economic Costs of Terrorism* (Canberra: DFAT Economic Analytical Unit), April 7, 2003.

22. The attack against the *M/V Limburg* involved a small, explosive-laden suicide boat that was rammed into the side of the tanker. Although the incident resulted in only three deaths (two of whom were the bombers), it directly contributed to a short-term collapse of international shipping business in the Gulf, led to a 48 cent/barrel hike in the price of Brent crude oil, and as a result of the tripling of war risks premiums levied on ships calling at the Aden caused the Yemeni economy to lose an estimated U.S.$3.8 million a month in port revenues. See Ben Sheppard, "Maritime Security Measures," *Jane's Intelligence Review* (March): 55, 2003; Richardson, *A Time Bomb for Global Trade*, p. 70; Herbert-Burns, "Terrorism in the Early 21st Century Maritime Domain," p. 165; Chalk et al., *Trends in Terrorism*, p. 22, f/n 20-21.

23. Alleged Bin Laden statement cited in Herbert-Burns, "Terrorism in the Early 21st Century Maritime Domain," p. 165. See also Brian Whitaker, "Tanker Blast was Work of Terrorists," *The Guardian* (United Kingdom), October 17, 2002.

24. William Ebersold, "Industry Overview: Cruise Industry in Figures," *Touch Briefings*, 2004, available online at http://www.touchbriefings.com/pdf/858/ebersold.pdf, last accessed November 9, 2005.

25. A dossier captured with Nashiri in 2003 specifically listed cruise liners sailing from Western ports among *Al-Qaeda's* targets of opportunity, highlighting their "attractiveness" in terms of mass casualty attacks. See Ali Koknar, "Maritime Terrorism: A New Challenge for NATO," *Energy Security* (January 24), 2005, available on-line at http://www.iags.org/n0124051.htm, last accessed December 8, 2005; and Ben English, Ian Gallagher and Jeff Sommerfield, Al Qaeda Blueprint Exposed," *The Courier-Mail* (Australia), December 29, 2003.

26. Author interviews, maritime analysts and intelligence officials, Singapore, London, and Amsterdam, September 2005.

27. All of these attacks resulted in inordinately high casualty rates for local Muslims, which at least in the case of the embassy bombings far outweighed Western fatalities and injuries.

28. The Royal Caribbean owned *Freedom of the Seas*, which came into service in 2006, is the largest cruise liner currently in operation, capable of carrying 4370 passengers and 1360 crew. See Linda Garrison, "Royal Caribbean International Names New Ultra-Voyager Cruise Ship," Abou.com, available online at http://cruises.about.com/od/cruisenews/a/041109rci_p.htm, last accessed November 8, 2005.

29. The liner, which was en route from Egypt to Mombassa, Kenya with 302 passengers and crew, was attacked with machine gun fire and rocket-propelled grenades after it strayed too close to the Somali shore. Although no one was seriously injured in the assault, the incident caught the headlines of major newspapers around the world, many of who focused on the fact that the ship was carrying mostly Western tourists.

30. Author interviews, U.K. Customs and Excise officials, London, September 2005.

31. Author interview, Lloyds of London, London, September 2005.

32. Author interview, former British defense intelligence official, London, September 2005.

33. Author interviews, U.K. Customs and Excise, London, September 2005.

34. It would be impossible to construct a cruise liner that has a fully compartmentalized watertight system in place as the recreational and luxury-oriented nature of these vessels necessarily requires an onboard configuration that is open and accessible (within the constraints of allowable safety limits).

35. Author interviews, Ministry of Foreign Affairs, Singapore and International Maritime Bureau, London, September 2005.

36. It would be highly difficult to carry out an attack of this sort against a ship that is moving given the extremely strong currents and undertow that its engines would necessarily generate.

37. The U.S. government issued a warning in the Spring of 2002 specifically highlighting the threat posed to cruise liners by "swimmers" attaching incendiary devices to ship hulls. See Sinai, "Future Trends in Worldwide Maritime Terrorism," 65 and Rick Newman, "Full Steam Ahead: In the New Age of What Ifs. Here is What Cruise Liners Are Doing To Keep You Safe," *National Geographic Traveler* (January/February): 12, 2003.

38. Author interview, U.K. Customs and Excise, London, 2005. One group that is acknowledged to have mastered combat scuba techniques is the LTTE. Indeed, the Tigers are known to have developed their own two-man mini submarine specifically for the purpose of covertly debussing divers inside Sri Lankan harbors. Author interview, Sri Lankan intelligence officials and western diplomats, Colombo, May 2004. See also Anthony Davis, "Tracking Tigers in Phuket," *Asiaweek* (June), 2000; and "Lanka Suspects Submarine in Thailand to be LTTE's" *Times of India*, July 16 2000.

39. Author interview, Control Risks Group, Amsterdam 2005.

40. Author interviews, U.K. Customs and Excise, London, September 2005.

41. Author interview, Raytheon International and Glenn Defense Marine Asia, Singapore, September 2005.

42. Author interview, Maritime Intelligence Group (MIG) analyst, Washington, August 2005.

43. Author interviews, U.K. Customs and Excise, Lloyds of London and former British defense intelligence official, London September 2005. See also Sinai, "Future Trends in Worldwide Maritime Terrorism," 65 and Eric Watkins, "Shipping Fraud Heightens Terror Threat," *The Guardian* (United Kingdom), February 6, 2002.

44. See, for instance, Admiral James Loy, "Seaports, Cruise Ships Vulnerable to Terrorism, *Guest Commentary* (July 28), 2001, available online at http://www.politicsol.com/guest-commentaries/2001-07-28.html, last accessed November 7, 2005.

45. Author interview, Control Risks Group, London, September 2005.

46. Figures derived from International Council of Cruise Lines (ICCL), "A Partner in U.S. Growth," available online at http://www.iccl.org/resources/economicstudies.cfm, last accessed November 7, 2005.

47. In Britain, for instance, cars and coaches are inspected on a random, selective basis. Freight vehicles are rarely, if ever checked (especially those bearing the TIR insignia—see section on container shipping). As one former defense intelligence official opined: "Ferries are their own worst enemies: [the industry is] designed to transport a high volume of people as conveniently, cheaply and quickly as possible. Most operators simply do not have the infrastructure—or willingness—to carry out a comprehensive regimen of security checks." Author interview, former U.K. defense intelligence official, London, September 2005.

48. Author interviews, U.K. Customs and Excise officials, London, September 2005.

49. Author interviews, maritime analysts and intelligence officials, Singapore, London, Amsterdam and Washington, August and September 2005.
50. In the United Kingdom, for instance, the schedules and itineraries of all ferry companies operating out of the country can be accessed on the web through www.ferries.com.
51. Author interviews, Ministry of Home Affairs and Ministry of Foreign Affairs, Singapore, September 2005.
52. According to one U.S.-based maritime security analyst, as little as a foot of water accumulated in a single location could upset a ship's center of gravity through the so-called free surface effect. Author interview, Washington, August 2005.
53. It should be noted that certain countries have moved to address this specific structural vulnerability. In the United Kingdom, for instance, ferries are now constructed with drains in their car decks to prevent the free surface effect. Many also have additional buoyancy devices such as air-filled tanks strapped to either side of the vessel. Author interviews, U.K. Customs and Excise officials, London, September 2005.
54. Author interview, IMB, London, September 2005.
55. Author interviews, U.K. Customs and Excise officials, London, September 2005.
56. For more on this incident see Peter Chalk, "JTIC Terrorism Case Study No. 5: The Super Ferry 14 Bombing, 2004," *Jane's Intelligence Review*, 2006.
57. These measures are contained within a proposed Human Security Act that at the time of writing had already been approved by the Senate and was expected to be signed into law later in 2007. See Carlos Conde "Philippine Senate Approves Anti-Terrorism Legislation," *International Herald Tribune*, February 8, 2007.
58. "Insurance Claims To Exceed $110m," *Lloyds List*, September 29, 2004, 1; Rory Knight and Deborah Pretty, "The Impact of Catastrophes on Shareholder Values," *Oxford Executive Research Briefings*, available online at http://www.e-ternity.ca/papers/whitepaper/sedgewickreport.pdf, last accessed December 2, 2005.
59. See Catherine Lawson, "Ferry Transport: The Realm of Responsibility for Ferry Disasters in Developing Nations," *Journal of Public Transportation* 8/4: 20, 2005.
60. Author interviews, U.K. Customs and Excise officials, London, September 2005.
61. The list does not cover multilateral agreements that are primarily designed to address the piracy problem such as the "Eye in the Sky Initiative" (EIS, enacted in 2004 between Indonesia, Malaysia, Singapore, and Thailand to facilitate limited airborne surveillance over the Malacca Straits) and the Regional Cooperation Agreement on Combating Piracy and Armed Robbery Against Ships in Asia (ReCAPP, a 2004 Japanese-sponsored initiative that aims to provide a legal framework for apprehending and prosecuting those who engage in piratical attacks in the Asia-Pacific). It should be noted, however, that there is obvious scope for these and other similar accords to be modified in the future so that they are able to play a more definitive role in the realm of maritime terrorism.
62. U.S. Customs and Border Protection, "Keeping Cargo Safe: Container security Initiative," available online at http://www.cbp.gov/xp/cgov/border_security/international_activities/csi/ last accessed October 26, 2004; Fritelli et al., *Port and Maritime Security: Background and Issues for Congress*, pp. 12–13; General Accounting Office (GAO), *Summary of Challenges Faced in Targeting Oceangoing Cargo Containers for Inspection* (Washington: GAO-04-557T), March 31, 2004.
63. U.S. Department of State, "The Proliferation Security Initiative," June 2004, available online at http://usinfo.state.gov/products/pubs/prolif, last accessed October 26, 2005; Richardson, *A Time Bomb for Global Trade*, pp. 97–108.
64. Fritelli et al., *Port and Maritime Security: Background and Issues for Congress*, p. 13.
65. Clive Schofield, "Horn of Africa Conflicts Threaten US Anti-Terrorism Efforts," *Jane's Intelligence Review* (June): 46, 2004.
66. Currently, some 17 percent of Washington's non-Gulf oil imports are derived from the Central/West African basin, which also accounts for over 80 percent of American trade and investment on the continent. Nigeria, itself, is the world's sixth largest petroleum producer and with European and U.S. dependence on imported oil is projected to grow to more than 70 and 60 percent respectively by 2010, the security of such reserves will become increasingly important. See Stephen Morrison, "Africa and the War on Global Terrorism," testimony given before the House International Relations Subcommittee on Africa, November 15, 2001, available online at http://www.yale.edu/lawweb/avalon/sept_11/morrison-001.htm, last accessed February 10, 2007; and Tamara Makarenko, "Terrorist Threat to Energy Infrastructure Increases," *Jane's Intelligence Review* (June): 8–13, 2003.

67. See, for instance, Stephen Flynn, "On the Record," *Government Executive Magazine*, October 1, 2003.

68. At the time of writing, only 10 percent of port facilities around the world were in compliance with ISPS stipulations. See "ISPS Code Status Update 01," available online at http://www.imo.org/home.asp, last accessed November 7, 2005.

69. As one maritime analyst summed up with respect to the Rotterdam—the world's busiest terminal for oceangoing freight—although the facility is compliant on paper and relatively secure compared to most other international ports, the whole verification procedure remains weak, constituting not much more than "a tick in the box exercise." Author interview, maritime security analysts, Control Risks Group, Amsterdam, September, 2005.

70. Sheppard, "Maritime Security Measures," 55.

71. Because many littoral states in need of coastal surveillance support also suffer from high rates of corruption (e.g., Nigeria, the Philippines, Indonesia, Thailand, and Kenya), the provision of material, as opposed to financial assistance is generally regarded as preferable.

9 Tankers, Specialized Production Vessels, and Offshore Terminals: Vulnerability and Security in the International Maritime Oil Sector

Rupert Herbert-Burns

CONTENTS

INTRODUCTION

When viewed in a holistic sense, from the perspective of the global trade of petroleum by sea, where the vast majority of cargoes are transported safely, the security of the maritime environment is in a generally healthy state. This is important to consider when tackling issues relating to the security of tankers, floating production units, and coastally situated infrastructure, because dramatic headlines relating to piracy attacks against tankers and the aforementioned infrastructure can sometimes give the erroneous impression that threat levels are endemically high and worsening. For the most part, this is not the case. However, unfortunately, some regional concerns persist. One maritime area, for example, that continues to warrant constant vigilance is the offshore exploration and production area off the Nigerian coast, where tankers, offshore support vessels, and production facilities continue to be regularly attacked by well-armed militants and pirates. In a recent high-profile incident in June 2008, Movement for the Emancipation of the Niger Delta (MEND) guerrillas managed to attack the Shell-operated floating production, storage and off-loading unit (FPSO), Bonga, which was located 75 Nmi from the coast. On a broader scale, it is also important to bear in mind that this "operational-level" security perspective is not the only level of concern. Governments must always continue to plan for the implications of possible "strategic-scale" petroleum supply disruptions in the event of a wider intra- or interstate conflict in an oil-producing region.

The strategic importance of crude oil, products, liquefied petroleum gas (LPG), and increasingly, liquefied natural gas (LNG), to the global economy renders any major threat to the security of the maritime trade of petroleum of significant importance. This extant reality has been conflated in the past six years or so because of the steady mean increase in benchmark crude oil prices since early 2002,[1] and the tightening of the supply–demand margin over the same period. Indeed, this amplification has been further enhanced since the beginning of 2007 due to the steady upward momentum of all three nominal benchmark crude price listings—WTI, Brent, and Dubai, caused by an increasingly lean supply–demand margin; geopolitical brittleness in the Middle East (specifically due to the war in Iraq and tensions between the United States and Iran); shut-in production and supply disruptions in Nigeria; high-volume arbitrage of crude oil on the future market; and a weakened dollar.[2] This sharpened condition has given rise to the paradoxical situation wherein despite the predominantly sanguine picture of the macro operational-level security situation for tankers, cargo infrastructure, and personnel, any fresh or durable threat to security at this level will trigger a virtually reflexive spike in oil pricing. Furthermore, a very serious incident involving a high-consequence target, such as a major oil terminal in the Persian Gulf, could give rise to the sustained disruption of crude oil flows and alter the geostrategic imperatives governing end-to-end petroleum supply security.

This chapter does not intend to highlight and analyze the whole spectrum of causal variables that impact on the oil and gas supply–demand flux, basket pricing, and the geopolitical variables that shape the global petroleum system. This is best reserved for a far larger and more complex project, which also embraces the terrestrial environment and the wider geopolitical ontology of the major producing and transit regions. Nevertheless, amid the aforementioned context, the intention of this chapter is, however, to examine and discuss the operational-level security realities that concern the loading and discharging of oil cargoes at coastal and offshore terminals, and the operations of tankers, FPSOs, and drillships in littoral waters, which are typically more prone to security risks. Although there are areas of operational confluence with regard to the security of petroleum trades, this chapter concentrates on the oil sector rather than on both oil and gas, as the scale and nuances of the liquefied gas trades warrant distinct attention, which is examined in Chapter 10.

This chapter is divided into the following sections: first, a concise examination is offered concerning the current and possible future axes of security risk, primarily from a geographical perspective. This is followed by a commentary on the International Ship and Port Facility Security (ISPS) Code and the Suppression of Unlawful Acts (SUA) Convention as they explicitly and implicitly pertain to the security of the processing and trade of bulk oil cargoes. Thereafter, specific sections explore the factors that give rise to the vulnerability of tankers, floating production units, drillships, and coastal and offshore terminals. Each section also provides examples, and discusses some of the measures and operations designed to mitigate security risks and threats to these vessels, facilities, and associated maritime spaces.

CONTEMPORARY THREAT AND RISK OVERVIEW

Vessels that lift petroleum cargoes, including LNG and LPG, and all of the associated coastally located refining, storage, and loading/receiving infrastructure, are vulnerable to attack in times of war, and also to acts of sabotage and terrorism in the same way as other vessels and maritime trade facilities. However, it is the "strategic premium" of petroleum to the global economy, the way "Big Oil" is seen by some as synonymous with Western rapaciousness and exploitation in certain parts of the world, and the extant security concerns in several of the most important oil-producing regions that arguably places this industrial and shipping sector highest on the list of desirable targets. In stark terms, the oil industry and associated shipping draws far greater attention to itself than others, as it has done since oil and gas became the inescapable underpinning of political, military, and economic power in the early twentieth century.

Extant and emergent security threats directed at infrastructure and shipping within the littoral spaces of sources of supply and processing are incubated within, and can certainly be expressed from, these terrestrial spaces. The causes and outcomes of this turbulence and associated risks and threats are many and varied: Failed, failing, or structurally weak states in sub-Saharan Africa such as Somalia, Sudan, and Nigeria; the presence of anti-Western Islamic fundamentalist terrorist groups, intrastate conflict, and balance of power challenges in the Middle East; and enduring political turbulence and insurgency in parts of Latin America have all had, and some continue to have, security implications for the petroleum industry and the shipping that services its exports.[3] The unfortunate reality is that many of the problems in these regions (and in some cases, the waters proximate to them) are enduring, and moreover, the exact forms and trajectories of associated threats at any given time are problematic to quantify. Furthermore, it is impossible to precisely predict how systemic risks will manifest themselves over the next two decades or so, which complicates the measurement of similar precise security measures designed to confront them.

Nevertheless, what is certain is that there are themes of risk and putative threats that will persist and emerge, and governments, corporate oil, and shipping operators must continue to cater to this reality. Except in the most extreme cases of a wider regional war that could render whole coastlines and bodies of navigable water hostile (an instance that is fortunately less probable), the petroleum production and trading system can certainly function amid insurgencies, terrorist attacks, piracy, and armed robbery at sea, albeit with interruptions and cost. However, to do so, the need for measures designed to mitigate risks and absorb the effects of attacks and interruptions is as essential as ever. Indeed, there is also room for improvement in certain areas.

As stated earlier, for the majority of the world's coastal and littorally-sited oil infrastructure and for the tankers operating in these waters, the current security "risks" are low, but credible. Identifiable "threats" (as ascertained by government intelligence, military, or other security forces) are generally still lower. This is important to note because effective security in the maritime domain is costly, manpower intensive, and can be diplomatically and politically delicate to instigate once the need for deployed naval units have been deemed necessary. What is needed, thus, is deliberate concentration of attention and effort in those oil-producing and transit spaces where elevated security risk have been specifically identified, especially those where intelligence has also identified definitive threats such as terrorist operations in the planning phase, refocused insurgent activity directed against tankers and terminals, or more sophisticated grades of organized crime-directed piracy and armed-robbery attacks. From the point of view of vessel crews and terminal owners and operators, this attention must take the form of developing a thorough and continuously updated appreciation of the security risks—essentially the development of successive intelligent pictures, which can complement and shape the physical risk and danger-mitigating procedures such as extra security bridge watches, radar watches, upper-deck patrols, terminal patrols, water patrols, vessel escorts, locked-down accommodation space access points, hull inspections by divers, alarms, and easily accessible communications.

The intensity of counterterrorist/insurgent operations or anti-piracy patrols must be sufficiently calibrated to the risk and threat level, and also in terms of the type of forces deployed if this becomes necessary. In high-risk areas, at governmental and intergovernmental levels, deterrent patrols by naval, coast guard, and police units (including maritime patrol aircraft) can be very effective depending on the classification of the waters (international or territorial). However, experience shows that multinational efforts such as the successful trilateral MALSINDO initiative in the Strait of Malacca by the Indonesian, Malaysian, and Singaporean governments can still run into operational obstacles, for example, the right of "hot pursuit" into another's territorial waters.

Owing to the sensitivity of territorial water sovereignty between the littoral states, MALSINDO does not provide for "hot pursuit."[4] In instances where a naval or coast guard ship of one country is the only asset available on scene and is in pursuit of a pirate or even a suspected terrorist, under current protocols, the chase will have to be abandoned once the suspects enter the territorial waters of another state. This is a reality known only too well to experienced pirates. In complex archipelagos and straits with multiple bordering countries and joining sovereign littorals, comprehensive multinational security operations must have the flexibility that is required to give criminals no quarter. Such protocols will also be essential if endemic maritime security is sought for the waters off the Horn of Africa and the Gulf of Guinea. Unfortunately, these facilitating agreements do not come easily.

Lower-risk waters around the world may only require the presence of coast guard or marine police units, whereas high-threat areas will necessitate naval units (ships and aircraft) to support the civil forces. The need for increased naval presence in international waters off the coast of Somalia, as mentioned earlier, is a good example of the latter. Clearly, in some areas such as in the Gulf of Guinea, the nominal scale and capabilities of maritime security forces from countries in the region will probably be insufficient to meet extant and possible future threat levels. Under these circumstances, in accordance with international and national laws and with the necessary diplomatic protocols in place, the participation of all the stakeholder countries in the region as well as other available foreign forces should be seriously considered. In those areas where the potential exists for concerns in the future, subtle long-range monitoring of the area is prudent, and specifically tasked surveillance operations to identify and classify threats should be deployed if matters appear to be changing or deteriorating.

At the company and vessel level, company security officers (CSOs), masters, and ship security officers (SSOs) should strive to obtain as much information as possible about high-risk areas before arrival. The key is preparation. Company teams ashore tasked with vessel and infrastructure security tend to have more time, greater resources, and greater accessibility to government sources of security warnings. Thus, they are in the best position to compile complete and more regularly updated security intelligence briefs for the security managers at the terminals or SSOs onboard vessels. Therefore, Managers and SSOs should continue to monitor the security situation in the waters they are operating in for any changes, and exchange information with other ships in the company fleet.

Most of these professionals at the company and vessel or terminal level are well accustomed to doing this; however, some useful sources of maritime security information and risk warnings are worth noting.

- U.S. Navy Office of Naval Intelligence (ONI)—worldwide threat to shipping mariner warning information
- U.K. Ministry of Defence (MoD)—worldwide threat to shipping monthly report
- Maritime Security Council (MSC), United States
- International Maritime Bureau (IMB)—weekly, quarterly, and annual piracy reports
- ReCAAP—monthly, quarterly, and halfyearly reports

- North Atlantic Treaty Organization (NATO)—shipping information center
- Maritime Liaison Office (MARLO), Bahrain—advisory bulletins
- U.K. Maritime Trade Operations (MTO), Dubai
- National agencies (e.g., TRANSEC, MCA, USCG, MARAD, and DHS)
- Lloyd's Market Association—http://www.the-lma.com/lma_public/default.asp?id=374
- News updates and other more maritime and energy-specific reports from AFP, AP, BBC, BIMCO, Bloomberg, CNN, Fairplay, Lloyd's List, and Reuters are also good sources of generic situational changes in regions and countries around the world, if not always for more maritime-focused or type-specific security warnings in selected areas.

CURRENT ELEVATED-RISK WATERS

The current elevated-risk littoral and coastal areas for shipping, designated by the Lloyd's Joint War Risk Committee as listed in the recent "Hull War, Strikes, Terrorism and Related Peril Listed Areas" on August 7, 2006 are shown in Table 9.1. Areas of particular significance for the loading of oil cargoes and the transit of tankers are marked in bold. Additional areas of concern are highlighted by the IMB and Regional Cooperation Agreement on Combating Piracy and Armed Robbery against Ships in Asia (ReCAAP). It should be noted that not all of these areas exhibit elevated risk at all times,

---

TABLE 9.1

Elevated Security-Risk Waters, Coastal Areas and Ports in 2007/08

Africa

- **Djibouti (excluding transit through Bab el Mandeb Straits) (choke point)**
- **Ivory Coast**
- **Nigeria, including all Nigerian offshore installations**
- Somalia, including waters up to 200 Nmi off the East African (Indian Ocean) coast. Vessels or craft are not to approach within 100 Nmi of the **Socotra archipelago**. Vessels or craft are to stay at least 40 Nmi to the north of the Somalian coast when transiting the Gulf of Aden

Middle East

- **Bahrain excluding transit**
- **Iraq, including all Iraqi offshore oil terminals (ABOT and Khor al Amaya Terminal)**
- Israel
- Lebanon
- **Qatar excluding transit**
- **Red Sea**
- **Saudi Arabia excluding transit**
- **Yemen (including the Gulf of Aden)**

South Asia

- **Bangladesh**: Chittagong anchorage and approaches
- **Pakistan**
- Sri Lanka
- Thailand, but only the **southern Gulf coast between the ports of Songkhla and Narathiwat**

Southeast Asia

- The island of Ambon (Seram)
- The port of **Balikpapan** (Southeast Borneo), including waters out to 25 nm
- Borneo, but only the northeast coast between the ports of Kudat and Tarakan inclusive
- The port of Jakarta
- The port of Poso (Sulawesi)
- Sumatra, but only the northeastern coast between 5°40′ N and 0°48′ N, excluding transit
- Philippines, but only Mindanao, between the ports of Polloc and Mati
- **Sulu Archipelago including Jolo**
- **Malacca Straits and Singapore Straits [Choke point][a]**

[a] The Strait of Malacca was officially removed from the LJWRC listed areas on April 20, 2007, but has been retained here for precautionary reasons.

Source: Lloyd's Joint War Risk Committee, IMB, and ReCAAP.

but have done so at some point in the recent past or continue to do so at varying intervals and intensities. Furthermore, situations and risk levels change and, thus, the latest information must always be sought. Nevertheless, the table reasonably captures the general situation at the time of writing.

The areas encompassed in this table are extensive and many are important regions for tanker traffic operating near coastlines, at coastal terminals, and in various littoral regions either as destinations for loading and discharging products and crude or as transit areas. Possible future areas of concern in the coming years could include the following:

- The eastern Mediterranean
- Strait of Hormuz
- The Gulf of Thailand
- Contested parts of the Arctic Ocean, potentially rich in hydrocarbon deposits
- Guyana–Suriname maritime boundaries/exclusive economic zone (EEZ)
- Tunb Islands and Abu Musa Island
- Shatt al-Arab
- Caspian Sea
- East China Sea (Senkaku-shoto Islands, Japan's unilaterally demarcated EEZ)
- South China Sea (Paracel Islands and Spratly Islands)
- Taiwan Strait (although many tankers bound for Japan tend to steam to the east of Taiwan to avoid dense fishing vessel traffic)

There are other chapters in this book that examine typological threats in some detail and, thus, are not examined in detail here. Furthermore, certain risks and threat methods are considered in the remainder of the chapter. However, in general, the types of risk and threats to the security of tankers and infrastructure are as follows: terrorist use of a vessel as a makeshift "weapon system" (embracing ramming and deflagration properties of vessel); total or partial sabotage of the vessel or facility; a suicide attack from a boat, vessel, or vehicle (VBIED); a piracy attack in international waters; robbery (especially armed robbery) inside territorial waters; insurgent or guerrilla attacks as part of wider land-based campaigns; tankers and infrastructure deliberately targeted or caught in a war zone (attacks from air-launched, shore-fired, or ship-launched/fired ordnance and sea mines); tankers as victims of illicit trafficking operation; and vandalism.[5]

Several of these scenarios such as piracy, robbery, and vandalism are far more common, whereas the more exotic and certainly more dangerous ones in terms of likely wider consequences, such as terrorist attacks against tankers, are fortunately very rare. Others such as the use of a tanker as a destructive instrument by a terrorist cell constitute only putative scenarios and these, although admittedly high-consequence events, must not dominate security assessments and planning. Vessels and infrastructure attacked in war zones, as mentioned earlier, is clearly not an extant threat but should be borne in mind for future contingency planning. Arguably, the greatest current concern is the attacks against tankers, FPSOs, and terminals by guerrillas and criminals in the Gulf of Guinea. However, the intensity of these attacks will flux in keeping with the political situation in Nigeria, the capability and intentions of groups such as Movement for the Emancipation of the Niger Delta (MEND), and the effectiveness of the maritime security forces available to deter and interdict. Constant monitoring by all stakeholders of the situation in this area is not merely prudent, it is essential.

ISPS CODE AND THE SUA CONVENTION AND THE SECURITY OF TANKERS, FPSOS, FSOS, DRILLSHIPS, AND FIXED PLATFORMS

ISPS CODE

There is no need to provide a preamble of the International Ship and Port Facility Security Code (ISPS Code), which is addressed in detail elsewhere in this book. Instead, I will start by stating that as far as the more specific requirements and considerations required for the secure production, loading, conveyance, and discharging of bulk petroleum cargoes (including LPG and LNG) are concerned, the protocols, provisions, and guidelines within the code are frankly insufficient. Indeed, they are arguably not fit for purpose, given the security risks that currently exist and potential threats that could evolve. This reality is all the more important to expose and discuss, given that the code was initially conceived and implemented to address terrorist threats in the maritime domain, and bulk shipments of these flammable, toxic, and potentially explosive cargoes (under the correct fuel–air mixture and containment conditions), and the facilities that process them, clearly represent vulnerable and attractive targets.

On scanning the entire ISPS document, no specific references to petroleum cargoes, flammable cargoes, product tankers, very large crude carriers (VLCCs), ultra large crude carriers (ULCCs), LNG, LPG, oil terminals, gas terminals, pirates, piracy, kidnapping of crew, or suicide attacks (boat or personnel-delivered) were found. There is only a single reference to oil tankers, gas carriers, and chemical tankers in Appendix 2 Form of a Statement of Compliance of a Port Facility Statement of Compliance of a Port Facility.[6] Fixed or floating platforms or mobile offshore drilling units are mentioned; however, no specific guidelines regarding the fortification of security at either these facilities or the vessels interfacing with them are laid down. The provisions simply state that

> Contracting Governments should *consider establishing* appropriate security measures for fixed and floating platforms and mobile offshore drilling units on location to allow interaction with ships which are required to comply with the provisions of chapter XI-2 and part A of this Code.[7]

It should be noted that it merely states that governments should "consider" establishing appropriate measures. What are the appropriate measures? Should there not be some thoroughly conceived guidelines to assist governments in advising on, or implementing, sufficient security measures? The threats and attacks being experienced by terminal and platform operators and ship crews in the Niger Delta is an example of the clear need for direction on this. Registered Security Organizations (RSOs) that are hired by shipping companies and terminal operators to advise in the design of security plans and standard operating procedures at the three security levels should be given at least some direction as to the minimum standards and designs necessary for these special and vulnerable facilities.

With respect to FSOs and FPSOs, there is a single reference under Annex 2 Conference Resolution 3—Further Work by the International Maritime Organization Pertaining to the Enhancement of Maritime Security that "invites" the International Maritime Organization to "review the aspect of security of ships to which chapter XI-2 of the Convention applies when interfacing with floating production storage units and floating storage units and take action as appropriate."[8] In June 2004, further attention was paid to these facilities with regard to security and the ISPS Code within a document entitled Guidance Relating to the Implementation of SOLAS chapter XI-2 and the ISPS CODE. Significantly, the document stated that

> MSC 77 decided that neither of the two types of floating production, storage and offloading units (FPSOs) and floating storage units (FSUs), were ships subject to the provisions of SOLAS chapter XI-2 and of part A of the ISPS Code, but, however, they should have some security procedures in place to prevent contamination of ships and port facilities which are required to comply with the provisions of chapter XI-2 and of part A of the ISPS Code.[9]

Essentially, this means that what scant mention is afforded to these vulnerable facilities in the code, governments and operators are not obliged to establish security measures for them as they are not covered under the protocols. The advice that some security should be implemented is encouraging, but it is only raised as a concern that an unsecured facility might "contaminate" the vessels that are covered under the code and have reason to interface with the FPSO or FSU (FSO) for operational reasons (cargo transfers). Furthermore, the document states that

> MSC/Circ.1097 offers no advice as to the specific security measures or procedures that should be taken by a ship which is required to comply the provisions of SOLAS chapter XI-2 and of part A of

the ISPS Code (SOLAS ship) when such a ship is engaged in ship-to-ship activities with either an FPSO or an FSU. If a SOLAS ship interfaces with an FPSO or an FSU it is deemed to be equivalent to interfacing with a non-SOLAS ship ... Conference resolution 7 ... invites Contracting Governments to establish, as they may consider necessary ... appropriate measures to enhance the security of ships and of port facilities other than those covered by SOLAS chapter XI-2. This invitation covers both FPSOs and FSUs.

On balance, even allowing for the deliberately elastic and broad interpretability of international conventions generated by the United Nations (UN) and the provisions relating to the vulnerable and high-consequence infrastructure (in the event of an attack) and vessels that interact in the carriage of petroleum are not reassuring. In the first instance, how are governments and vessel operators (particularly those with limited financial and material resources available for security) supposed to provide even fundamental security for these facilities and vessels, if little or any specific mention is made for them in the code? How can they be expected to achieve the minimum security needed in the absence of decent guidelines? Secondly, despite being a complex fusion of vessel and oil terminal functionality (both of which are covered separately under the code), FPSOs and FSOs (or FSUs) are not covered by the code when operating in that capacity, and thus, are nominally exempt from governments and operators providing the security they so obviously require. Notwithstanding the latter, it would be fair to say that in areas where security risks are elevated or threats identified, prudent owners and operators of these facilities will certainly take all the precautions they can, and governments will tend to provide additional security and deterrent sea and air patrols if they are able to do so. But the lack of specific allowance for these facilities remains a concern, and their inherent operational ambiguity between being a vessel and a nonfixed terminal needs to be looked at deliberately as security requirements and parameters can change significantly depending on the vessel/facility operational status and location.

The ISPS Code is a broad "framework" designed to establish benchmarks for security across the commercial maritime spectrum and across the globe. In that capacity, the regime is arguably sufficient, and has improved the security of those vessels and facilities that fall under its remit. However, given their vulnerability, and the likely high-consequence nature of a terrorist, guerrilla, insurgent, or criminal strike against a petroleum facility or tanker, it is unfortunate that sufficient, specially calibrated security provisions and guidelines for these facilities and vessels were not included. Owners, operators, and where applicable and appropriate—governments can impose some basic security on these facilities and vessels by drawing from the minimum standards stipulated by the code. However, for a sufficiently thorough program, particularly in higher-risk waters and coastlines, additional protocols and resources must be brought to bear. This reality is further enforced because of the insufficiently precise inclusion in the code regarding possible terrorist threat types and axes, nor any mention of the more common problem of piracy, vessel hijacking, or kidnapping of crews.

SUA CONVENTION

The Convention for the Suppression of Unlawful Acts against the Safety of Maritime Navigation, 1988 and the Protocol for the Suppression of Unlawful Acts against the Safety of Fixed Platforms Located on the Continental Shelf, 1988 were both adopted on March 10, 1988 and entered into force on March 1, 1992. The latter protocol essentially extended the requirements of the convention to those fixed drilling and production platforms that were engaged in the exploitation of offshore oil and gas.[10] The convention was conceived in direct response to a concern regarding "unlawful acts which threaten the safety of ships and the security of their passengers and crews."[11] These concerns of the international community were the result of a series of incidents and reports in the 1980s of crews being kidnapped, vessels being hijacked or being damaged, destroyed, and threatened by explosives planted by terrorists. In some instances, people on board attacked or seized vessels had been threatened or killed.[12]

In November 1985, in accordance with the IMO's 14th Assembly Resolution A.584(14), the IMO's Maritime Safety Committee (MSC) was instructed to develop "detailed and practical technical measures, including both shoreside and shipboard measures, to ensure the security of passengers and crews."[13] Fundamentally, the main purpose of the SUA Convention and the protocol is to ensure that sufficient and appropriate action is taken against those who have committed unlawful acts against vessels and offshore oil and gas infrastructure. Acts that include vessel seizure by force, acts of violence against those on board the vessel of facility, and the placing of explosives on vessels and facilities that are intended to destroy or damage it.

In the wake of 9/11, the implementation of the ISPS Code, a noticeable elevation in the number and frequency of pirate attacks, and a series of terrorist attacks in the maritime arena, most notably, the attacks against the VLCC *Limburg*, the USS *Cole*, and *Superferry 14*, the 2005 Protocol to the SUA Convention was adopted on October 14, 2005. The protocol, specifically Article 3bis, expanded SUA to more specifically address the acts of terrorism, particularly acts involving the use of biological, chemical, and nuclear materials and weapons of mass destruction (WMD). Specific to the topic at hand, however, Article 2bis of the 2005 Protocol gives specific provision for acts of terrorism involving offshore platforms on the continental shelf. The article states that

> A person commits an offence if that person … when the purpose of the act, by its nature or context, is to intimidate a population, or to compel a government or an international organization to do or abstain from doing any act, uses against or on a fixed platform or discharges from a fixed platform any explosive, radioactive material or BCN weapon in a manner that causes or is likely to cause death or serious injury or damage; or discharges from a fixed platform, oil, liquefied natural gas, or other hazardous or noxious substances, in such quantities or concentration, this it causes or is likely to cause death or serious injury or damage …

What is encouraging about SUA, and specifically, the protocols that address offshore oil and gas infrastructure, and the 2005 Protocol that further highlights terrorist acts on, against, or using offshore infrastructure, is that it has given consideration for vulnerable elements of the maritime-based oil and gas industry, and drawn attention to potential acts of terrorism that might involve the industry. SUA provides an international regime and framework for addressing potentially serious security threats in this arena, and has highlighted *a priori* that special consideration must be given to this vulnerable infrastructure. It gives implicit, if not explicit, warning that the consequences of an attack against or using this infrastructure is likely to have serious consequences and that their specific technical, operational, and locational characteristics warrant specific attention and accommodation.

Furthermore, under Article 8, the protocol also establishes mechanisms to enable the boarding (with the consent of the flag state) in "international waters" of vessels suspected of being involved in a SUA-designated offense, including terrorism. This will provide security forces the legal framework essential for conducting preemptive operations in international waters against terrorist cells that have boarded and taken control (or intend to do so) of tankers or terminals when good intelligence has provided sufficient warning.

The SUA Protocol, thus, effectively provides the first international treaty and framework for combating and prosecuting those criminals and terrorists who have attacked (or intend to attack), or used a tanker or fixed oil or gas installation as part of a terrorist operation. Although the protocol has been open for signature since February 2006, it only enters force after the twelfth country (three countries in the case of the Fixed Platforms Protocol) signs without reservation as to ratification, acceptance, or approval.[14]

ISPS and SUA represent the most direct and comprehensive international regimes and facilitating mechanisms yet conceived that address security in the maritime domain. As indicated, however, there are some notable omissions in the ISPS Code relating to tankers and petroleum industry infrastructure, and this should arguably be viewed with some concern, given the inherent vulnerabilities of these vessels and facilities, their clear attractiveness as targets, and the likely scale of the consequences of an attack against these vessels or infrastructure. Given the limitations of the ISPS Code examined earlier, the ensuing discussion concentrates on the specifics of security as it relates to coastal and littoral oil loading and discharging infrastructure, and crude and product tankers. Although SUA does not make any specific provision for oil tankers, gas carriers, or FPSOs and FSOs, it makes special accommodation for fixed offshore installations, which could include terminals. The 2005 Protocol is a further step in the right direction, but is yet to come into force.

CRUDE AND PRODUCT TANKER VULNERABILITY AND SECURITY

For the purpose of clarity, Table 9.2 reveals the types of tanker and their cargo capabilities included in this analysis.

Overview: VLCCs and ULCCs

As of October 2007, there were 501 "live" VLCCs listed in the Lloyd's Marine Intelligence Unit's (Lloyd's MIU) Shipping Information Database (SID) ranging from the 320,000 dwt *Aquarius Voyager* to the only slightly smaller 213,855 dwt vessel, *Mediterranean*. This large number compares with only 13 live ULCCs ranging from the 564,650 dwt *Knock Nevis* to the *Younara Glory*, which at 320,050 dwt, just enters the ULCC category. The total operational or "live" VLCC and ULCC tonnage for the global fleet amounted to an impressive 145,730,192 dwt. Looking ahead, there are 141 VLCCs on order and under construction around the world, totaling about 43,583,980 dwt; however, there were no ULCCs listed as "on order" or "under construction" at the time of writing.[15]

These tankers represent the essential "moving parts" of what is essentially a petroleum "sea bridge" of strategic dimensions for fuel oil, condensates, and crude oil (although the majority of lifts are crude) connecting the major export terminals with the primary markets in North America, Europe, and increasingly Asia. Sea trade of crude oil amounts to approximately 2.2 billion tons per year, representing 89 percent of the total volume of global crude trade. The remaining volume is conveyed by pipeline, which amounts to approximately 231 million tons per year, and about 17 million tons are transported overland through rail tankers and a far smaller proportion of road tankers.[16] The clear dominance of the quantity moved by sea has long rendered this trade of inescapable strategic importance to the global economy and the energy security of major importing states. If the perpetual free movement of this class of ships were to be impeded in terms of major volume or prolonged duration, refineries would run out of feedstock, prices would spike and remain high, and economies would suffer deep and long-term damage.

Before commenting on issues pertaining to tanker security and concerns over their vulnerability on the world's oceans, it is important to remind that the overwhelming majority of this tonnage

TABLE 9.2
Tanker Types and Associated Displacement Ranges

Type	Displacement Range (dwt)	Cargo
Coastal	Up to 16,500	Products
General purpose	16,500–25,000	Crude or products
Handy size	30,000	Crude or products
Aframax	Specifically 79,990, but generally accepted range is 75,000–120,000	Crude or products
Panamax	55,000–70,000	Crude or products
Suezmax	120,000–200,000	Crude or products
VLCCs	200,000–320,000	Crude oil
ULCCs	Over 320,000	Crude oil

transits from source to market securely, and this reality should be used to contextualize identifiable concerns and threats. Crucially, it should be used to moderate the tendency by some to focus on the dramatic "what if" hypothetical scenarios very heavily. In the absence of recent attacks, conventional or terrorist, much of the commentary in the media, some private security consultants, and even among some government security officials regarding tanker security has tended to focus on the impact of putative scenarios involving terrorist attacks against crude tankers. More spectacular scenarios have highlighted the possibility of the deliberate use of one of these vessels as a makeshift "weapon system" utilizing its cargo and size (and perhaps also its momentum) as the instrument of destruction against a port or amid a trading choke point such as the Strait of Malacca. This kind of commentary is arguably valuable to guide consequence analysis and precautionary action to help ensure/enforce security, but it should not dominate the analysis nor necessarily determine the often expensive measures taken to mitigate the dangers of such unlikely possibilities. Moreover, it is unnecessary and dysfunctional to credit terrorists or insurgents as a broad collective with the operational capabilities necessary for such an attack, which very few possess. Overly imposing security measures can constrain day-to-day shipping operations, and also incur greater financial burden on ship owners and shippers alike. Thus, balance is the key, and the points raised earlier in the chapter with regard to the arguable inadequacies of the ISPS Code must also be given due consideration.

VLCCs and ULCCs are vulnerable for three main reasons: What are they and what do they represent? The nature of their structural and operational characteristics. And, from where and through which sea areas and regions are they operating? Vessels of this class of ship, rather than the more modestly sized product tankers, are iconic as critical instruments of the global petroleum trading system. They are seen by some as the "capital ships" of tanker fleets and (where applicable) as among the most conspicuous elements of the oil companies, both international and national, which operate or charter them, particularly the so-called "super majors" or "Big Oil" companies based within some states belonging to the Organization for Economic Cooperation and Development (OECD). As such, these vessels and their cargoes also have definitive political capital as targets in the eyes of those terrorists or insurgents (actual or aspiring) with maritime operations capabilities.

Thus, seen as vital synapses between oil-producing countries (the governments of which can have delicate relationships with their clients, or indeed often inimical relationships with the latter in the eyes of indigenous insurgents or terrorists), VLCCs and ULCCs are rendered far more attractive as targets than other classes of ships from the outset. Thusa successful attack on a crude oil tanker by a terrorist or insurgent team would be an isolated and infrequent event; the attack against the *Limburg* in October 2002 is yet to be repeated. A successful operation of this kind requires good intelligence, detailed planning, expertise, great determination, and logistical support from shore. VLCCs and ULCCs are more vulnerable on a day-to-day basis to pirate and armed robbery attacks while at anchor rather than to a terrorist operations cell, even in high-density oil operations and transport areas such as the Arabian Gulf, the Gulf of Suez, and the Gulf of Guinea. This is largely due to their inherent vulnerability to assault resulting from their structural and operational features, and because of the nature of the littoral areas through which they must pass.

A great deal has been written on piracy methodology in the wider maritime security literature, and has also been discussed and analyzed in detail elsewhere in this book, therefore, I will not go into exhaustive detail on piracy attacks on VLCCs here except for a few key issues that are worth noting. Between 1994 and 2006, 472 pirate attacks against crude oil tankers worldwide have been reported to and logged by the IMB.[17] What is interesting is that this represents 12.8 percent of the total reported attacks against "all" vessel types during the same period, yet VLCCs and ULCCs comprise just 1.96 percent of the total global merchant fleet by number of hulls.[18] Thus, the figures suggest that these vessels are not only comparatively more vulnerable to determined assault from a practical perspective, but also because they transit and lie at anchor in sufficient numbers in areas prone to piracy and robbery; these vessels, thus, constitute an above-average number of "targets of opportunity."

The vulnerabilities and security concerns of VLCCs and ULCCs from an operational perspective is explored alongside product tankers in the section on VLCC, ULCC, and Product Tanker Vulnerability. However, advancing from the context established earlier, some strategic-level security issues are worth mentioning. A single event is unlikely to change the market and supply *status quo* for long—prices will spike, then resettle. A tanker on its own, while vulnerable, is not as effective a target as a tanker undergoing loading/discharge operations berthed at a terminal. The potential for a far greater net destructive yield, in this case, would probably result in the halting or long-term interruption of terminal supply. If the export volume capacity were high, such as at the sea island terminal at Ras Tanura, a successfully debilitating attack would have enormous consequences for supply volumes and basket pricing. Some estimates suggest that Ras Tanura is responsible for 10 percent of the world's daily exported crude oil total. Wider extrapolation of that figure tells the whole story.

EVOLVING REFINING HUBS AND PRODUCT TANKER FLEET DEVELOPMENT AND TRADE: IMPLICATIONS FOR POTENTIAL SECURITY RISK?

The vulnerability of product tankers from an operational perspective is examined in the following text; however, some general points on this class of ship are noteworthy. As of October 2007, there were 429 product tankers between 1,400 and 157,700 dwt under construction and on order around the world, totaling about 23,134,529 dwt. This constitutes an increase of almost 10 percent on the live fleet of 4400 vessels.[19] Of these, 354 are Handy size tonnage and above, and 131 are either the larger Suezmax or Aframax; representing over 30 percent of new-build tonnage. Alongside this expansion in the fleet of the larger product tanker classes, there are also some interesting developments in the geographical patterns of future primary distillation refining capacity as shown in Table 9.3. Expanded capacity in the Middle East and Asia are marked in bold.

What is immediately revealing is that of the total projects currently under construction, 50.32 percent of this new refining capacity is in Africa and the Middle East. This is clearly illustrative of the geographical shift in the new global refining capacity toward the main sources of supply, and toward the regions experiencing accelerating consumption growth. Viewed in a holistic sense, the future trend will be toward greater numbers of large product tankers lifting refined fuels (such as gasoline, diesel, avgas, and Jet-A) from major refining hubs in the Middle East and Asia (and to a lesser extent Africa) directly to markets. Given the smaller amount of additional capacity expansion in Europe and North America, this is likely to result in more, large-displacement product tankers lifting refined fuels around the world, and in the process, displacing some of the traditionally intense crude shipments along these sea lanes of communication and through the major choke points, particularly the Straits of Hormuz, Bab el Mandeb, the Suez Canal, and Malacca.

TABLE 9.3
New Refining Capacity Under Construction

Region	Number of New Refineries	Number of New Expansions	Refining Capacity (Thousand barrels per day)	Refining Capacity Expansion of the Total (percent)
Europe and Eurasia	4	1	1,198	9.68
North America	2	5	1,530	12.36
South and Central America	3	0	700	5.66
Africa	7	1	1,420	11.48
Middle East	**14**	**3**	**4,806**	**38.84**
Asia-Pacific	**8**	**4**	**2,720**	**21.98**
Total	38	14	12,374	100

Source: Petroleum Economist.

The potential security implications of this evolving shift in refining concentrations and vessel/trade type are not straightforward to ascertain and much less to conclude. Nevertheless, some interesting points are worth noting. Very large aggregations of refining and product export in specific countries and regions raises important strategic-level security questions of the geographically concentrated vulnerability of both infrastructure and supply. Singapore, for example, has been a high-volume refining hub for the whole of Southeast Asia for many years and constitutes an economically vital strategic facility for the entire region as well as for the country itself. Needless to say, the security it has afforded is significant.

Expansions in the Arabian Gulf/peninsula—Abu Dhabi, Iran (although expansion of infrastructure there is less certain), Kuwait, Oman, Qatar, Saudi Arabia, and UAE—are of particular interest from this perspective. Once it becomes clear that consumers are relying far more heavily on refineries, export terminals, and refined products based in, and emanating from, this region, it will render the infrastructure, access waters, choke points, and associated shipping potentially even more "valuable" as political targets. Nevertheless, refineries are generally well protected (particularly from the landside access), therefore, terrorists might look for "softer" targets, which means that product tankers, nearby deepwater anchorages, narrow approach channels where vessels are compelled to maneuver at reduced speeds, and loading terminals could be perceived as easier targets, particularly at the tanker–terminal interface during loading operations. In actuality, these areas are also far better protected than they once were. Nevertheless, the emerging picture is clear.

From a design perspective, product tankers are typically more vulnerable to assault than crude tankers are, and if they are lifting more volatile cargoes such as avgas, Jet-A, diesel, and particularly gasoline and naphtha, their cargoes are more easily prone to deliberate ignition (if deflagration of the vessel is the objective). Although it is impossible to determine the effectiveness or consequences of deliberately using the potentially destructive properties of a product tanker through deflagration as a result of a terrorist operation, the increasing number of these vessels loading more volatile cargoes from expanding refining hubs in elevated risk sea areas should be viewed in a more appropriately nuanced sense, rather than merely seeing the vulnerability and security implications of all tanker types in the same light. This changing situation in the nature of trade of these more volatile liquid cargoes, specifically greater traded volumes and vessel number concentrations, could arguably be compared to the potential implications for large export nodes for LPG, such as Juaymah in Saudi Arabia.

PRODUCT TANKER DESIGN AND OPERATION

Product tankers, generally smaller than their crude-lifting cousins, are structurally more complex (due to the ability of many to convey different grades of refined product fuels simultaneously, which requires complex pumping-system architecture). As oil refinery production capacity has increased and the demand for refined products has grown, so too has the size of vessels and those under construction and on order. Many of the new-build product tankers are approaching the size of some crude oil tankers.

There are two main types of product tankers: "clean" or "white" ships and "dirty" or "black" ships. Clean tankers lift products with color specifications, such as gasoline, Jet-A, naphtha, and lubricating oils. These high-grade products tend to be more volatile, and their vaporous forms can be explosive under the correct fuel–air ratios and containment conditions. Dirty tankers are configured for the conveyance of heavy fuel oils, bitumen, and asphalts. The two variants tend not to interchange between the different products. However, most product tankers are designed specifically to lift different products simultaneously in separate tanks, divided by intricate valve and pumping systems. Most vessels will be fitted with inert gas generators, bottled nitrogen cargo tank top-up systems, and closed-loading vapor-return cargo-handling systems. Not all product tankers are designed to lift petroleum-based cargoes; others convey palm oil, juices, water, and molasses among others.

Because of their structural design, product tankers have tank decks that are near the waterline when the vessel is fully laden. Also, product tankers tend not to be fast compared to other types of merchantmen. Most, if not all, younger vessels are double-sided or double-hulled, which further increases safety margins in the event of grounding or collision.

VLCC, ULCC, AND PRODUCT TANKER VULNERABILITY

Besides geographical risk drivers and threat concentrations, there are some key reasons for the inherent vulnerability of these vessels. These include: limitations in speed, maneuverability, visual blind spots, radar sector-blanking astern and on the quarters for both S and X bands (particularly for tankers with large funnel casings), low freeboards (when laden), dangerous cargoes (flammable/ toxic), and small crews. Tankers are slow and unmaneuverable, particularly when laden. Although VLCCs, when at full sea speed "in ballast," can sail approximately 24–26 percent faster than when they are laden and when weather conditions permit; they are also more responsive to helm orders in this state, although sea state and wind can affect the rate of turn and transfer. After calculating across the entire global fleet, crude oil tankers have a mean speed of 14.96 kn. The slowest ships can sail at just 9.0 kn, whereas the fastest vessels launched in 2006 can achieve about 24.25 kn.[20] Despite their slower full sea speed as a class, VLCCs are more vulnerable to assault and attack when at dead slow, slow, and half-ahead, such as when entering terminal approach channels, in the Suez Canal, and when embarking/disembarking pilots.

Product tankers, in contrast, have an average speed of only 12.28 kn across the fleet. The slowest parcel tankers built in the 1960s sail at just 9 kn or so; however, the fast modern ships can achieve 22 kn.[21] The mean speeds across both classes are revealing for their conclusiveness; these vessels will not be able to outrun attacking pirates, robbers, or a suitably equipped and experienced terrorist cell. Generally, tankers will not be able to outrun anything but the slowest *dhows* and fishing boats. Any boat used as an explosively rigged suicide platform (VBIED), even a modern *dhow*, will be sufficiently fast if selected to attack a tanker, that is, making way.

Because of their very low freeboards, more volatile cargoes and slow speeds, laden product tankers are more vulnerable and arguably more attractive as targets, particularly when in high-risk littoral areas. Crude tankers are more complex to assault, board, and impose total control over than smaller product tankers due to their increased deck expanse, superstructure size, increased number of decks, and freeboard. However, attempted and successful boardings of VLCCs off the coast of Brazil and in the Strait of Malacca are well documented.[22] VLCCs sailing in ballast are less vulnerable due to their elevated full sea speed and greatly increased freeboards.

Larger tankers, particularly when in ballast, have more areas at the forward end (specifically on either side of the stem, where the anchor chain leads to the hawse pipe) and the stern of the vessel (proximate to the ship's side) that are out of sight from the bridge. This is of concern as it means an attacking small craft or assault team can approach an anchored tanker at night largely unobserved. This can be mitigated by more extensive upper-deck floodlighting clusters to complement the exterior lighting on the accommodation superstructure. Some lights on the upper deck that also project into the surrounding waters is advisable, as is the use of bridge-wing mounted spotlights. Clearly, all lighting is essential for closed-circuit television (CCTV) coverage of the upper deck at night. However, a CCTV system with panning cameras that can establish interlocking fields of view and that cover visual blind spots is the optimum system. Security fences such as "Secure Ship" are an option, and extra upper-deck patrols and dedicated radar watches in high-risk waters are also fundamental parts of security procedures at level 3 and also at level 2 under certain circumstances and in specific waters today.

Laden tankers (particularly VLCCs and ULCCs) navigating deepwater, marked channels that lead to and away from offshore terminals, and single-point moorings (SPMs) are frequently restricted in their ability to maneuver or are constrained by their draft. In elevated risk areas, this is a vulnerable time for the vessel and intense visual and radar vigilance is essential to spot any approaching small craft that may pose a threat. Watch keepers must be mindful of radar blind arcs astern and on the quarters as these are well known and favored approaches. A similar situation exists in busy traffic separation schemes (TSS), although there is generally more room to maneuver.

Frankly, in high-threat waters, unless the deepwater channels and TSS have been sanitized by naval or coast guard escorts, there is little a tanker could do to avoid an attacking craft.

Tankers undergoing ship-to-ship (STS) cargo transfers are highly vulnerable in high-risk waters as evidenced by several attacks by pirates in the Niger Delta area in recent years. Vessels engaged in STS have the benefit of being able to deploy more lookouts, patrols, and response teams in an aggregate sense, but suffer from an obvious inability to maneuver and evade. The important thing is to try and avoid boarding if at all possible; once assailants are on board, they will be able to take advantage and gain control of the situation. Boarding prevention is the best and frankly, the only means of defense. A summary of general precautions is listed in Table 9.4.

TABLE 9.4
Vessel Security Precautions in Elevated Risk Waters

Vigilance	Majority of the attacks will be deterred if the assailants are aware they have been seen and the crew is prepared to resist boarding. Ensure more, visible and irregularly timed patrols of upper deck and around superstructure.
24-Hour visual, radar, and security watch	Maintenance of a 24-hour visual and short-range radar watch in high-risk waters form the bridge. X-band radars are useful for close proximity coverage of small targets with smaller radar cross-sections. S-band is superior in adverse weather and for longer-range monitoring in open water.
Enhanced watches in hours of darkness	Preferred approaches by assailants tend to be in blind spots at the bows and stern. Increased watches of these areas (especially anchor chains and mooring lines) between 01:00 and 06:00 hours (when most attacks occur) by patrols equipped with radios is advised.
Sealed access	Fit hawse pipe plates and lock all doors and hatches, while ensuring consideration for escape and movement in case of fire or other emergency.
Radio communications	Establish and maintain radio contact with all stations and patrols and shoreside authorities
Lighting	Deck and over-side lighting, especially at the bow and stern should be provided to illuminate surrounding waters and "dazzle" would-be assailants. Searchlights on the bridge wings should also be available. Additional or enhanced lighting should not be so bright or extensive so as to interfere with safe navigation if the vessel is under way.
Fire hoses and other equipment/systems	In high-risk waters, fire hoses should be charged and laid out to be used to repel borders. Water should be sprayed on deck where attackers are likely to try and board, such as the poop deck. Consider fitting intruder-detection systems, CCTV, night-vision equipment, and link these systems to a central alarm system.
Secure areas	If assailants have managed to get on board, the crew should be able to retreat to secure areas. This could be the accommodation spaces as a whole or in security restricted areas such as the bridge and engine control room. It may also be advisable to secure the cargo control room if possible.

Source: U.K. Department of Transport (TRANSEC).

ULCCs, VLCCs, and product tankers are most vulnerable to attack and boarding when engaged in cargo operations, at anchor, embarking pilots, in pilotage channels, and to a slightly lesser extent while under way inshore and in littoral waters. There are two main reasons for this: First, as already mentioned, they are slow and the larger vessels are often restricted in their ability to maneuver; and second, because these water areas lie within easy reach of would-be assailants (pirates, terrorists, or insurgents), operating in small crafts. Essentially, the further offshore tankers sail, the safer they become. In 2006, the total number of reported actual and attempted robberies against vessels berthed or at anchor in roads was 150 versus 88 incidents against vessels that were under way.[23] It would be fair to point out that these are robberies not piracy incidents, and thus, one cannot prudently extrapolate for terrorist or insurgent actions or capabilities. However, it is a reasonable representation of the comparative ease of assaulting vessels that are static. The incidents listed in the following text highlight the vulnerability of tankers at anchorages waiting to load.

In the early hours of June 16, 2005, three men armed with knives and assault rifles boarded a VLCC at anchor in the deepwater anchorages located to the southeast of the Al Basrah Oil Terminal (ABOT) in Iraq. Fortunately, the vessel was in a heightened security state (likely to have been ISPS Level 2), which meant that the assailants were spotted by the watch keeper and were unable to gain access to the secured superstructure and designated restricted areas (all access doors are locked at this level). Once the alarm had been sounded, the assailants fled and escaped in a high-speed boat waiting alongside.[24]

However, this incident took place two weeks earlier when men armed with AK-47 assault rifles boarded the Cypriot-registered 310,428 dwt VLCC *Nordmillenium* on May 31 anchored some 10 Nmi from ABOT at the same deepwater anchorage in position 29°27′ N, 48°56′ E.[25] The men managed to gain access to the bridge, assaulted the master, and escaped with thousands of dollars in cash. The IMB reported that "They tried to enter the bridge claiming to be policemen. The master denied them entry and the pirates became violent ... they assaulted the master causing him injuries and demanded money."[26] A U.S. naval warship patrolling the security zone around ABOT arrived after the attack after responding to the mayday alert that was sent out over very high frequency (VHF). The warship arrived too late to apprehend the assailants.

Following this incident, Jayant Abhyankar, deputy director of the IMB, stated that the incident raised serious questions about security at the oil terminal. In a statement that was revealing of the anchorages in this area, Lieutenant Commander Charlie Brown of the U.S. Navy's Fifth Fleet said the Coalition Maritime Security Force (CMSF) was only directly responsible for security at the oil terminals themselves. "We are patrolling the [terminal] area and we do want to set those conditions for security and stability ... But those ships that are transiting to and from, that are not at the terminals, need to provide some of their own security as well."[27]

Competent assailants will use a wide array of skills and techniques to effect a successful attack or robbery, including:

- Approaching under cover of darkness
- Exploiting blind spots
- Use of deception (pretending be officials boarding legitimately)
- Use of high-speed boats
- Being well-armed and prepared to use lethal force if necessary
- An awareness of patrolling patterns and likely response times
- Good knowledge of upper-deck and accommodation space layouts

FSO, FPSO, AND DRILLSHIP VULNERABILITY AND SECURITY

Before examining the security of these specialized facilities in greater detail, some clarification regarding their definitions are essential as these facilities are distinct in some import ways.

FLOATING STORAGE AND OFF-LOADING UNITS

FSOs (which can also be considered a subset of FPSOs) are sizeable floating storage devices (usually for crude oil), which are typically employed in oil fields where it is not feasible to lay long subsurface pipelines from the production facilities and wellheads to shoreside processing plants, tank farms, and terminals. This can be due to several factors: the extreme depth of water (or unfavorable seabed topography), project financial constraints, or, because the expected life span of the play is too short to warrant the investment in fixed-pipe infrastructure. Most FSOs tend to be retired or retasked single-hulled VLCCs and ULCCs, which have been specifically converted for this purpose. Currently, the largest FSO in operation is the 564,650 dwt *Knock Nevis* (ex-*Seawise Giant*), which is moored at the Al Shaheen oil field/terminal off the northeast shoulder of Qatar. According to the LMIU, there are 41 vessels listed as operational FSOs worldwide.[28]

In terms of operational sequence, the production platform transfers oil to the FSO by a short pipeline where it is stored until a tanker comes alongside the FSO and loads directly from it. This off-loaded oil is then replaced on board the FSO and the sequence begins again.

FLOATING PRODUCTION, STORAGE, AND OFF-LOADING UNITS

These facilities, sometimes referred simply as "units" or "systems," are the more complex cousins of FSOs, wherein a production capability has been added on board—essentially oil/water/gas separation modules, power generation capacity, water injection pumps, and gas compression units. The oil or gas is then accumulated in sufficient quantities in the unit's storage tanks until it can be transferred to a tanker moored astern, the cargo is then conveyed ashore to a refinery or to desired market destinations around the world. FPSOs are either new-builds that are constructed to order, or conversions of decommissioned tankers of varying sizes. Of the 115 live FPSOs listed by LMIU, the largest is the 400,000 dwt *FPSO Dalia*, located off Angola, with the smallest being the 3,659 dwt *Bourbon Opale*, moored in Frontera on the Mexican Gulf coast.[29] FPSOs range in length between 390 and 64 m.

FPSOs are particularly effective in deepwater blocks where it is economically or practically unfeasible to lay oil-transfer pipelines ashore. FPSOs are favored over more permanent, high-cost, fixed, or semisubmersible platforms in smaller oil fields, where extraction and production times are likely to be too short to warrant an expensive dedicated facility. Once extraction has reached its economically feasible limit, the unit is simply relocated to another site. FPSO's have been in operation in offshore fields around the world since the late 1970s; predominately in the North Sea, Brazil, Southeast Asia (particularly in the South China Sea), the Mediterranean, in Australian waters, and off the west coast of Africa. Some FPSOs now have a production capacity of about 250,000 barrels per day with as many as 50 risers coming up from wellheads on the seabed.

From a structural/technical standpoint, FPSOs are a fusion of vessel and petroleum production functions, and are thus, complex in nature. The system comprises the following main features: the accommodation and helideck superstructure, upper-deck-located production systems (oil/water/gas separation units), storage tanks located in the hull, mooring system, off-loading pumping systems, gas flare tower or boom, and the mooring turret (internal or external), which gathers and houses the risers. The turret structures, in addition to anchoring the vessel, are designed to allow "weather vaning" of the FPSO to accommodate changing wind and wave direction and conditions. They also enable the uninterrupted flow of oil and production fluids from vessel to undersea field wellheads. External turrets facilitate quick disconnection of the main facility in the event of an emergency.

Recent events in the waters off Nigeria have highlighted the vulnerability of FPSOs. In the dawn of May 3, 2007 at 03:30 hours, a group of MEND guerrillas assaulted and boarded the FPSO vessel *Mystras* (also referred to as *Okono Terminal*), which was moored 55 Nmi off the coast of Port Harcourt in Nigeria.[30] The *Mystras* produces crude from the Okono and Okpoho fields at the rate of 65,000 barrels per day. At the time of the attack, there were 85 people on board of which 22 were foreign nationals.[31] Following the assault and subsequent kidnapping of six expatriate workers, the terminal operators were forced to declare *force majeure*. The incident prevented crude-loading operations during the days that followed. Fortunately, the abducted workers were released the following day.

The incident demonstrates the extensive reach of the MEND guerrillas much further offshore in the Gulf of Guinea, rather than just the inshore and coastal areas where they tend to concentrate their operations. They have developed a capability and preference for operations under the cover of darkness, and are sufficiently adept at approaching and boarding a facility of this kind: one that has a high freeboard; is extensively lit along the upper deck and superstructure; and, has a complex topside deck layout. Furthermore, it seems the assailants met little or no resistance, and that once on board, they quickly gained the initiative and maintained control of the situation.

This case also demonstrates the vulnerability of these high-value facilities although they are situated so far offshore. In an expansive and intensively productive area such as the Niger Delta and the wider reaches of the oil-rich regions of the Gulf of Guinea, the sheer number of offshore facilities makes endemic security coverage difficult, if not impossible to provide round the clock. It was first thought that the further FSOs and FPSOs ventured offshore to service oil production from the more remote exploration blocks, the more secure from the threat of shore-based guerrillas they would become; however, this is no longer necessarily the case. Their isolation has in effect induced greater vulnerability as protective or reactionary assistance, if it were not already on-station, would take time to reach the unit in the event of an assault.

From the perspective of the vulnerability of the facility (its location notwithstanding), its high capital value, the quantity of oil in storage (the larger units can store 2 million barrels of oil), and the oil being lifted from the seabed, this is an attractive target for would-be terrorists or insurgents with sufficient offshore reach and operational finesse. Security personnel on board could deter (and perhaps prevent) boardings and subsequent kidnappings if in sufficient numbers; however, given that the finite space available on board, the addition of extra accommodation for a sizeable security force would be unlikely. Furthermore, the operational crews on board are unlikely to have either the training or spare manpower to mount robust security operations should the need arise. Thus, in high-threat waters, these units must be protected externally by naval or coast guard forces to assure security. Although the large-scale impact to the host country and the world oil market of an attack or hostage-taking on an FPSO would probably be very limited in scale and duration in the event production was halted, the destruction of such a facility could likely cause extensive loss of life on board, have serious consequences for the operating IOC or NOC, and send shockwaves through the marine insurance market. Such an attack would also probably result in a serious environmental problem in the form of an oil spill.

As these facilities proliferate and their importance and contribution become more widely appreciated, due consideration must be given to affording them sufficient security in high-risk/threat waters. There should be a commensurate effort in line with the perceived scope and sophistication of the threat, the net vulnerability of the units in operation given any existing security on board, and the value of the facility's contribution to the overall oil production of the country or company in question. This is not an inexpensive undertaking; however, the coast of neglect could be far higher. As mentioned earlier in the section addressing ISPS Code limitations, FSOs and FPSOs stand out, as the ambiguity over their status as part vessel and part platform leaves them in somewhat of a "blind spot" as far as being embraced by the code's protocols, much less being considered as special cases given their rather unique characteristics and vulnerability. Currently, it is left to owning/operating companies and host governments to provide the security required. Sophisticated and continuous assessments of the maritime security situation and the security required for these facilities is currently of the greatest importance in the Gulf of Guinea, particularly within Nigerian waters and adjacent international waters. Many of the precautions for VLCCs in elevated risk waters as mentioned earlier are applicable to FSOs and FPSOs; however, their obvious high values, far larger numbers of personnel on board, and their clear inability to maneuver away from danger necessitates additional security measures that directly reflect the threat level.

DRILLSHIPS

A drillship is a monohulled vessel that has been fitted with a drilling apparatus. It is most often used for the drilling of exploratory oil or gas wells located in deepwater blocks. However, some drillships have also been used for scientific research that requires collecting seabed geological core samples. LMIU currently has 94 operational drillships listed around the world in its SID.[32] However, by no means are all of these under contract at any one time. Drillships, however, constitute a fairly small portion of the overall offshore drilling facilities.

Modern drillships range in displacement from 127,209 dwt to as small as 32 dwt, and vary in size from 280 m length overall to only 20 m.[33] The central operational/structural feature of these vessels, besides their accommodation superstructure and main propulsion machinery, has dominated the drilling platform and derrick located amidships, which connects the drill string through the hull into the water and the seabed below. These vessels can drill exploratory, wildcat, or production wells in water depths of up to 12,000 ft and drill depths of 35,000 ft, giving a total drill-string depth of some 47,000 ft (almost 8 mi). To drill in such a necessarily precise and sustained fashion, these vessels must be moored in such a way that they essentially "hover" in precisely the correct position over the wellhead. Earlier, this was achieved using a ring of anchors that moored the vessel over the well. However, the modern vessels use dynamic positioning systems (DPS)—a system using hull-mounted thrusters that continuously adjust the vessel's position for variances of wind, sea state, and current. The thrusters are controlled by a computer system that obtains referential position data from the ship's differential global positioning system (DGPS), operating in conjunction with sensors mounted on the drilling template on the seafloor.[34]

Despite their obvious complexity, unrivaled operational versatility, and capital value (which means that drillships can command the highest daily leasing rates of all offshore drilling platforms), and because of their vessel shape (which results in greater movement in heavier sea and wind conditions), drillships are best suited for operations in typically calmer or sheltered waters near the shore. Nevertheless, Table 9.5 shows the areas of the world where these unique vessels are drilling under contract. The remainder of the global fleet is either in port, undergoing maintenance or refit, or in passage to or from exploration or production areas.

In much the same way as FPSO and FSOs, drillships are vulnerable to security threats due to two main criteria—their structural and operational characteristics and their location (if they are operating in elevated risk waters). From a structural stance, these vessels are less easy to board from the waterline due to their comparatively high freeboard (especially when under way), but the "moon pool" aperture in the hull also renders them vulnerable to infiltration from beneath the water. This latter approach would only be significant if the assailants were highly skilled, supported from a nearby dive boat, and frankly, daring. When the vessel is drilling, it is essentially static,

TABLE 9.5
Drillship Locations

Region	Drillships
East coast of South America—Brazil	7
Mediterranean—North African coast	1
North Sea	1
South Asia—Arabian Sea and Bay of Bengal	7
Southeast Asia	2
U.S. Gulf of Mexico	6
West Africa—Gulf of Guinea & Angola	9
Total	33

Source: Rigzone.

and thus, vulnerable to assault from pirates and other would-be assailants, although the lack of anchoring lines and cables in the case of those vessels fitted with DPS reduces the axes of boarding. However, unlike ordinary merchant vessels, the complexity of the upper-deck drilling and auxiliary machinery configuration and below-deck layout means that these vessels are more problematic to secure and control from the point of view of the assailants, unless they were in sufficient numbers and adequately familiar with the deck and superstructure configuration. Also on the positive side, vulnerabilities are offset by the fact that these vessels are comparatively fewer in number as "targets of opportunity" worldwide, and less attractive from a point of view being able to initiate a more spectacular and debilitating attack as would be the case with an FPSO, given that the latter is often producing from multiple wells and loaded with stored crude, associated gas, or condensate.

Table 9.5 reveals that many of the drillships currently under contract are operating in elevated-risk maritime areas, namely in West Africa, South and Southeast Asian waters. Drillships off West Africa will be more vulnerable to assault by groups such as Niger Delta People's Volunteer Force (NDPVF) and MEND if they are within their operational reach. However, for these groups, the destruction of facilities is seldom the objective; rather it is the personnel on board who are targeted for kidnap and ransom. In June 2006, the semisubmersible rig, *Bulford Dolphin*, was attacked 60 km offshore, and eight men were taken hostage and held in captivity ashore. In March 2007, another worker was seized from the same facility. Although a rig, the incidents highlight the potential vulnerabilities of drillships offshore, particularly when viewed alongside similar assaults on FPSOs that are also located in the same region. Given the logistical obstacles of assaulting facilities far offshore and returning with captives, these incidents are relatively infrequent. However, as with FPSOs and rigs, drillships located in the littoral and necessarily sheltered waters will remain vulnerable; the security they have afforded must be viewed commensurately.

TERMINAL VULNERABILITY AND SECURITY

As mentioned earlier, tankers are most vulnerable and constitute an optimal target when they are loading and discharging. Depending on the specific threat profile of the country, if it is elevated at the time, a VLCC or ULCC loading at a vital exporting country such as Saudi Arabia, Russia, Iran, the UAE, Kuwait, Nigeria, Venezuela, Iraq, or Algeria is rendered a valuable "strategic" target due to the likely widespread repercussions of an attack, provided the combined (tanker/terminal) destructive impact of the attack cripples or seriously disrupts the export capability of the terminal. A crude tanker will be more vulnerable in these circumstances than at a discharge terminal, where the impact on the global market of a similar attack would be less acute or potentially long lasting.

As highlighted earlier, geopolitically vital facilities in a high-threat area, such as Iraq, will be well protected. However, some terminals in critical exporting countries where the dangers of a "latent" threat that has not yet manifested itself could be very vulnerable due to the lack of sufficient protective cover. Vulnerability will be exacerbated if the facility is isolated far from shore support, such as an FSO or FPSO.

From an operations perspective, the vessel–terminal interface is more vulnerable during certain times. During berthing operations, when all personnel are otherwise engaged getting the tanker alongside and the vessel is attached to both the terminal dolphins and the attending tugs, there is little or no available manpower to function in a lookout or counteroffensive capacity. Moreover, there is no chance the vessel can be moved out of position fast enough in the event of an attack. Terminals operate round the clock; berthing and loading arm-manifold connection operations at night are at greater risk to a successful attack given the "inwardly directed" attention by vessel and terminal personnel, and reduced visibility beyond the cover of the terminal's and tanker's lighting. Extensive and intense lighting is a must, as is the deployment of additional personnel to watch the surrounding waters. If available, a radar watch should also be maintained. Also, tankers are alongside for an extended period when loading and discharging. Even at export terminals with high pump rates, tankers can expect to be alongside for 18–24 hours. At older, less sophisticated facilities, VLCCs can take up to 48 hours to load; this expands the time window of opportunity for would-be attackers.

KHAWR AL AMAYA OIL TERMINAL AND AL BASRAH OIL TERMINAL

Although unique in its intensity, and certainly not indicative of the nominal levels of security for most of the offshore facilities (Figure 9.1) in the oil-producing countries around the world, the security afforded the two offshore terminals off the Al-Faw peninsula in southern Iraq by Task Force 158 is an example of what can be provided if the threat is sufficiently enduring and the strategic importance of the facility is commensurately high.

(a)

(b)

FIGURE 9.1   Al Basrah Oil Terminal.

Berthing and loading operations security at the Al Basrah terminal begin when the tankers arrive at the deepwater anchorage. Tankers are boarded by CMSF Vessel Boarding Search and Seizure (VBSS) teams comprising marines and sailors. These teams secure the vessel's crew, check documentation, and carry out a thorough search of the accommodation spaces and superstructure. The essential purpose of the VBSS is to ensure that the tankers have not been compromised by a terrorist cell, there are no explosives or weapons on board, and the crew is legitimate and all are accounted for. When the vessel is ready to go alongside, another combined U.S. Navy/Iraqi Marines security team from the terminal's Navy Mobile Security Force (MSF) board with the berthing pilot to ensure that the crew is not interfered with as they carry out berthing operations. This team stays on board until the tanker is secured alongside.

The security on the terminal itself is of a high order, as is the protective screen provided by TF-158, and increasingly the Iraqi maritime forces. Besides the well-armed personnel on the terminal itself, Maritime Security Operations (MSO) in the Northern Arabian Gulf (NAG), which center on the protection of the Khawr Al Amaya Oil Terminal (KAAOT) and ABOT, are directed from *Ocean 6*—an "Afloat Forward Staging Base" (AFSB) that is moored to one of the terminals. *Ocean 6* is a chartered barge that features the command, control, communications, intelligence, and surveillance capabilities similar to those found in a coalition warship's combat information center (or operations room), and can thus act as a command and control platform in support of personnel and warships assigned to protect the terminals.[35]

VULNERABILITIES

From a structural perspective, offshore terminals are vulnerable for a variety of reasons, and specifically in certain ways. Shore-located terminals can be threatened from landside, air, and seaward. Assuming a non-conventional conflict environment (e.g., major interstate war), given that most fixed-installation security systems and protocols tend to be focused toward landside approaches, the greatest vulnerability is generally from the seaward axis. Long jetty structures (which accommodate supply pipes from shore) are common in the Persian Gulf, where shallow coastal waters force loading infrastructure further offshore; consequently, these facilities and any berthed tankers are isolated and vulnerable. However, causing sufficient damage with an improvised explosive device (IED) to an offshore terminal (which is fixed to the seafloor by a steel jacket) or to the crude/product lines running from shore-based supplies is problematic, even for very experienced operatives. On the other hand, the equipment on the platform itself is easier to destroy successfully; provided of course, access to the platform can be effected.

Among the most vulnerable features at a terminal are the loading arms that connect to the tanker's manifold system amidships. These loading arms are exposed and would be conspicuous targets for sabotage, particularly when connected and feeding crude or products to the vessel. The pressure under which the cargo is transferred (some can transfer up to 25,000 barrels per hour) would amplify the likelihood of a serious fire should an explosive charge or IED be placed, or if they are struck by a well-aimed portable antiarmor weapon. Another vulnerable area is where the oil feed lines from shore rise from the waterline and connect to the base of the terminal trestle. These areas must be thoroughly protected by nets, which prevent access by swimmers/divers. They should be well lit at night and, if possible, covered by CCTV.

The attacks against KAAOT and ABOT in April 2004 demonstrate the capability of a determined team to inflict damage against offshore infrastructure, to the extent where loading operations can be interrupted for a significant period. However, the incidents also demonstrate limitations. The initial attack was approximately 500 m from KAAOT's No. 7 berth, which did not result in any structural damage. The second and third attacks against ABOT were rather more serious, with both assault teams exploding their VBIEDs some 20 m from a tanker's exposed seaward side at the No. 2 berth. There was limited damage to the vessel, but not to the terminal itself. Furthermore, the quantities of high-grade explosives (C-4, PE4, Formex, Semtex, etc.) used would need to be sufficiently large. (The quantity used against the USS *Cole* was estimated at 400 lb of C-4.)[36] Clearly, for a successful attack, a craft would need to approach undetected. At the Iraqi terminals, this is highly unlikely in view of the pervasive security today. However, an approach to an unprotected terminal and loading tanker would be more straightforward. Any major terminal located in elevated risk waters must be afforded security commensurate to the threat and its export importance.

Terminals are also vulnerable to assault and boarding, particularly at night and in instances where the facility is isolated. In this instance, it is also the personnel who are vulnerable as the following example reveals.

At approximately 06:00 hours on May 1, 2007, a team of MEND guerrillas in six fast boats assaulted the Chevron-operated "Pennington" offshore oil terminal, and abducted six foreign workers. (Pennington is one of the six main export terminals servicing Nigeria, the others being "Bonny," "Brass River," "Escravos," "Forcados," "Kwa Iboe," and "Odudu.")[37] In the course of the operation, the militants claimed to have overpowered the security personnel stationed on board. Interestingly, MEND announced on May 23 that the hostages would be released unconditionally on May 30 provided the oil companies made no offers for the return of the hostages in exchange for a ransom. The attack and subsequent kidnapping was specifically intended as a political message and a warning to the incoming government following the recent elections. Chevron "shut in" production at its 15,000 barrels per day Funiwa field following the kidnappings.[38] This incident demonstrates how a large, well-armed and determined force of guerrillas can overpower a small security force on an offshore facility, and control the situation sufficiently to take hostages without the necessity of a large-scale, violent confrontation. Once an attacking force has gained access to the terminal or berthed tankers, it is very problematic to regain the initiative and force off the facility. It also shows the obvious and continuous (and stated) linkage between these kinds of guerrilla operations, oil, and politics.

Single-Point Moorings

ULCCs and the larger, deeper-draft VLCCs often take on crude cargoes at SPMs that are located in deepwater offshore such as at Juay'mah in Saudi Arabia, the Louisiana Offshore Oil Platform (LOOP) in the United States, and Ain Sukhna[39] in the Gulf of Suez. SPMs are vulnerable to sabotage due to their isolation and also because they tend not to be as thoroughly protected as the more conspicuous fixed, sea island-type terminals. However, a successful sabotage operation would require the assailants to get on to the buoy or access the feed line beneath it. Such an attack could result in a conflagration; however, another concern would also be the induced oil spill that would disrupt loading operations while repairs were affected. Explosives or an IED placed and detonated on an SPM while attached to a loading tanker could have more serious consequences than if the valve equipment on the top of the SPM was simply vandalized. It should be stressed that if several SPMs were to be destroyed completely and in unison at a facility, this could have serious consequences for the export capacity of the terminal in question. Delays of several months could be induced, if the destruction caused significant oil spills, and if the buoys and the feed lines themselves had to be replaced. In established high-threat areas, these facilities must be afforded the same level of protection as their more physically obvious jacket platform/trestle terminal cousins.

CONCLUSION

This chapter attempts to examine and discuss the extant and potential risks and possible threats to a broad range of vessel types, specialized production and storage facilities, and the export terminals engaged in the production and conveyance of crude oil, condensates, and products around the world. As highlighted earlier in the chapter, it is important to remember that notwithstanding the existence and potential for a range of risks and threats such as piracy, armed robbery, kidnap and ransom of personnel, vandalism, and terrorism, the vast majority of these vessels, facilities, and terminals do not fall victim to attacks and operate normally, despite some having to function in elevated risk regions and waters. Nevertheless, security concerns exist and will continue to do so for tankers and terminals, given the range of inherent operational and technical vulnerabilities described earlier and the persistence of extant risks and putative threats in certain well-known parts of the world.

This reality is further compounded by the specter, however diffuse and infrequent, of the attractiveness of tankers and petroleum infrastructure as potential targets for terrorist operators with the necessary skill sets, determination, and opportunity. It is this latter issue of "opportunity" that is the easiest to capitalize on from the point of view of the assailants and would-be terrorists, provided they are afforded the room to do so. Also, it is simultaneously the only area where stakeholders, security forces, and governments can realistically mitigate against likely risks and threats. If tanker crews, terminal operators, security forces, and governments can reduce the opportunity through the continuous development of good intelligence to facilitate warning of impending threats, and the adoption of precautionary measures to enhance and maintain security, then the outlook is positive. It can also be argued that there is always more that can be done, and perhaps, this is true. However, prudence also demands that expenditure in financial, material, and operational terms is commensurate with the security reality on the ground. In the end, however, given the likely wide and long-term repercussions of a successful attack on a high-consequence target (such as a major export terminal) in a time of tight supply–demand dynamics and high oil prices, there is an argument that perhaps there is no such thing as too much security and that costs must be borne. The notion of "opportunity cost" takes on a rather more sober, if ironic, meaning in this light.

NOTES

1. *Petroleum Economist*, August 2007.
2. Ibid.
3. Duncan Clarke, *Empires of Oil: Corporate Oil in Barbarian Worlds* (Profile Books: London), pp. 174–181, 2007.
4. Gurpreet S. Khurana, Cooperation Among Maritime Security Forces: Imperatives for India and Southeast Asia.
5. *Petroleum Economist*, Fundamentals of Energy Infrastructure Security: Risk Mitigation in the International Environment, 2005.
6. International Maritime Organization, Consideration and Adoption of the International Ship and Port Facility Security (ISPS) Code Consideration and Adoption of the Resolutions and Recommendations and Related Matters—Conference Resolution 2 and related amendments to the 1974 SOLAS Convention and Conference resolutions 3–11.
7. Ibid.
8. Ibid.
9. International Maritime Organization, MSC/Circ.1111, 7 June 2004: Guidance Relating to the Implementation of Solas chapter XI-2 and the ISPS Code.
10. International Maritime Organization, Convention for the Suppression of Unlawful Acts Against the safety of Maritime Navigation, 1988, http://www.imo.org/Conventions/mainframe.asp?topic_id=259&doc_id=686.
11. Ibid.
12. Ibid.
13. Ibid.
14. http://usinfo.state.gov/is/Archive/2005/Oct/28-980286.html.
15. Shipping Information Database (SID), Lloyd's Marine Intelligence Unit, London.
16. Lloyd's Marine Intelligence Unit, Analysis of Petroleum Exports Service (APEX) analysis.
17. International Maritime Bureau, Piracy and Armed Robbery Against Ships Annual Reports 1994–2006.
18. Ibid.
19. Shipping Information Database (SID), Lloyd's Marine Intelligence Unit, London.
20. Figures calculated from the Lloyd's Marine Intelligence Unit (LMIU) Shipping Information Database (SID).

21. Ibid.
22. Fundamentals of energy infrastructure security, *Petroleum Economist*, August 2005.
23. International Maritime Bureau, Piracy and Armed Robbery Against Ships Annual report 2006.
24. http://www.alertnet.org/thenews/newsdesk/L16679135.htm.
25. Shipping Information Database (SID), Lloyd's Marine Intelligence Unit, London.
26. http://www.indybay.org/newsitems/2005/06/08/17464821.php.
27. Ibid.
28. International Maritime Bureau, Piracy and Armed Robbery Against Ships Annual report 2006.
29. Ibid.
30. http://www.nga.mil/MSISiteContent/StaticFiles/MISC/wwtts/wwtts_20070516100000.txt.
31. Ibid.
32. Shipping Information Database (SID), Lloyd's Marine Intelligence Unit, London.
33. Ibid.
34. http://www.globalsecurity.org/military/systems/ship/offshore-drillship.htm.
35. http://www.cusnc.navy.mil/articles/2006/186.html; http://www.marinelink.com/Story/Ocean-6-Conducts-Operations-with-BOXESG-205230.html.
36. *Petroleum Economist*, Fundamentals of Energy Infrastructure Security, 2005.
37. http://www.unitedijawstates.com/mend.htm.
38. http://uk.reuters.com/article/topNews/idUKL0149368920070501.
39. Ain Sukhna is the Egyptian terminal at the southern end of the Sumed (Suez-Mediterranean) pipeline that links the Red Sea with the Mediterranean. Sumed pipeline is a 320 km long line that comprises two parallel 42″ lines with a capacity of approximately 2.5 million barrels per day. It enables VLCCs to partially discharge their cargo before transiting the Suez Canal, which has a draft restriction. On reaching the Mediterranean, the tankers reload oil at Sidi Kerir.

10 Security in the Maritime Sector of the Liquefied Natural Gas Industry

Peter Martin

CONTENTS

Despite the relatively rapid response to terrorism in the maritime sphere, particularly though the new regulations in chapter XI of the Safety of Life At Sea (SOLAS)[1] (International Maritime Organization 1974) and International Ship and Port Facility Security (ISPS) Code,[2] there remains a perception that liquefied natural gas (LNG) carried by sea in bulk is a threat to communities living adjacent to LNG facilities. Public anxiety about the potential of a terrorist attack on LNG shipping or facilities drives risk assessment plans to consider the possibility of piracy,[3] sabotage, and terrorism. Of particular concern is the possibility that an LNG vessel (Figures 10.1 and 10.2) could be the direct target of a terrorist attack or hijacked and used as a weapon.[4]

LNG is an energy resource with significant advantages over other fossil fuels. It is the cleanest burning fossil fuel, producing half of the carbon dioxide emissions of coal when used for electric power generation, and provides strategic diversity in an energy portfolio that also seeks to reduce green house gas emissions in today's "climate change" environment. Coupled with an impressive safety record, the LNG industry is ideally placed to make a significant contribution to energy demands at present although the world seeks alternative energy options for the future.

Natural gas is the fuel of choice in the Asia-Pacific region where security of supply, relative price stability, and environmental friendly qualities are key considerations for power generation facilities. However, although Asian interests in LNG flourish along a finely balanced supply and demand equation in a region that consumes more than three quarters of the world's trade in LNG, interest on the west coast of the United States is timid, despite the benefits of this energy resource. California's Ventura County proposed Cabrillo Port facility includes an LNG receiving facility 22 km offshore where the cargo is regasified and piped ashore into the California Gas Company's

FIGURE 10.1   Moss spherical tank LNG carrier.

FIGURE 10.2   Membrane tank LNG carrier.

onshore gas pipeline system. Security of supply at this terminal would provide an estimated 10–15 percent of California's daily natural gas requirements and make the state less vulnerable to variations in supply and price.

Yet the project was rejected by the state lands commission, which also decided not to certify the environmental impact report. The perceptions of celebrities about the LNG industry drew media attention and public interest to scuttle the project[5] (Business Monitor International 2007, NGI's Daily Gas Price Index 2007). Even with the assurance of demonstrated safe practice, reduced greenhouse gas emissions, an alternative energy resource, and increased maritime security measures following the September 11, 2001 attack, the LNG industry still fails to convince those which are potentially affected by terrorism.

In view of California's rejection of what is otherwise a viable energy industry in other sectors of the world, this chapter explores the measures that have been put in place to improve safety and mitigate concern about the risk posed by LNG to adjacent shore-side communities. Initiatives to improve safety in the maritime sector of the LNG industry are considered in four parts in this chapter. The first partprovides a brief historical overview of LNG development in the United States and what is an impressive safety record. The second part provides the detailed international maritime initiatives to improve safety standards for providing an indication of the depth of protection afforded by maritime regulation. The third part examines LNG vulnerability and risk and highlights the safety measures taken to mitigate risk. The fourth part briefly compares the implication of maintaining security of oil supply at the expense of a diversified energy portfolio that includes LNG.

HISTORICAL OVERVIEW

In broad terms, the established components of LNG production are receiving terminals and regasification facilities, liquefaction facilities at a supply source, and the critical linkage between these two components, shipping. LNG is a natural gas that is refrigerated, not pressurized, for shipping long distances as a cryogenic[6] liquid. When the LNG carrier reaches an import terminal, the cargo is discharged and stored in large tanks until it is revaporized for distribution as natural gas through an existing pipeline network (Figure 10.3).

The requirement to transport natural gas by sea was stimulated by a growing appreciation in the late 1940s and early 1950s that the widespread practice of oil companies flaring off "unwanted" associated gas at the oil fields was both a waste of energy and potential income.[7] Two options considered at the time were to pump the gas back into the reservoir or pipe it to the nearest industrial customer. A third consideration was to transport the gas by sea; however, this was the least attractive option as there was no known technology to achieve this.[8] The commercial potential of gas stimulated technological development such that international commercial LNG shipments began in the late 1950s.[9] The first LNG cargo transited the Atlantic Ocean in 1958; and by 1964, the first purpose-built LNG carriers were in service under a long-term gas purchase agreement (McGuire and White 2000, p. 11).[10]

The United States's relationship with LNG began in the early 1970s with small gas projects providing early confidence to pursue larger gas contracts in 1978 followed by the trunk line project for Lake Charles in 1982. This development occurred during a period of rapid change in the international energy market, which included two oil price shocks, widespread nationalism of international oil companies within Organization of the Petroleum Exporting Countries (OPEC), and restructuring of the North American gas industry.[11] Even as the industry gained early momentum, reliance on gas was undermined in the late 1970s and early 1980s when trade from Indonesia to California and Algeria to

| Gas field | Liquefaction facility | LNG storage tank | LNG tanker | LNG storage tank | Vaporizers | To pipeline system |

Producing region   Consuming region

FIGURE 10.3   Components of LNG production. (From CMS Energy.)

Cove Point, Elba Island, and Lake Charles collapsed resulting in the shut down of the operation after less than two years. Fifteen tankers were laid up and three import terminals were mothballed.[12]

The ill-fated Algeria project was to be the largest LNG transportation project in the world and the first to transport large quantities of natural gas to the United States by ship. However, contractual disagreements, failure at the trials of the first of three conch-designed ships in May 1979, and the grounding of the LNG tanker El Paso *Paul Kayser* at full speed off Gibraltar, resulted in diminished confidence in the gas industry. Although the groundings of El Paso *Paul Kayser* and *LNG Taurus* in the late 1970s were both serious events, each confirmed the inherent strength of their design of vessel, which incorporates additional barriers and physical separation of the cargo to the sea. Cove Point and Elba Island remained closed for more than 20 years.[13] Cove Point reopened in July 2003 and waves of enthusiasm for LNG led to proposals for new receipt and regasification terminals.[14]

The impact of 9/11 led to public concern about LNG, particularly on the west coast. Possible terrorist attacks on hazardous and flammable ship cargoes such as LNG stimulated imaginative scenarios about the effect of a traumatic LNG shipping disaster on public safety and property. This concern arose despite an accumulation of evidence to suggest that terrorist attacks against maritime targets have been rare[15] and, during a period when more than 33,000 LNG tanker voyages have been conducted worldwide, LNG tankers have not been attacked by terrorists or pirates. Indeed, in terms of cargo loss, the LNG shipping industry has an exemplary safety record with only eight marine incidents in the past 40 years.[16] The number of serious LNG and liquefied petroleum gas (LPG) incidents reported annually since 1980 has reduced significantly and this is attributed to a wide range of regulatory, design, crew competence, and ship management improvements.[17]

INTERNATIONAL MARITIME INITIATIVES TO IMPROVE SAFETY STANDARDS

There are a number of international treaties, conventions, laws, regulations, standards, and guidelines to enhance the safety of LNG tanker operations. These include codes, classification society rules,[18] and state-based regulation, some of which also affect LNG facilities' design, construction, operation, and maintenance. All LNG vessels in international service must comply with the major maritime treaties agreed according to the International Maritime Organization (IMO), such as

- Conventions for the SOLAS, 1974 and 1981
- Convention for the prevention of pollution from ships (MARPOL)
- International Maritime Dangerous Goods (IMDG)[19] Code[20]
- Convention on the international regulations for preventing collisions at sea, 1972 and 1981
- International Convention on Standards of Training, Certification and Watchkeeping (STCW) for seafarers, 1978 and 1995
- International management code for the safe operation of ships and for pollution prevention (International Safety Management [ISM] Code), 1994

However, LNG carriers are unique in that it is a cryogenic liquid; accordingly, specialized materials, construction methods, and operating procedures are needed to safely handle this cargo. The general rules and regulations that govern ships at sea do not address the particular concerns of LNG; therefore, specific rules and regulations have been developed by the various entities to ensure the safety of LNG tankers and their ports of call.[21] The IMO has adopted approximately 40 conventions and protocols (codes) that detail a common set of standards for ships to comply with. Compliant vessels are issued with a certificate of fitness and periodically inspected to ensure that the requirements of the code are met during the lifetime of the ship.[22] The three IMO Codes specific to gas carriers are

- Code for existing ships carrying liquefied gases in bulk (the Existing Ships Code). This code generally applies to ships delivered before December 31, 1976.

- Code for the construction and equipment of ships carrying liquefied gases in bulk (the GC Code). This code generally applies to ships built on or after December 31, 1976 but before July 1986.
- International Code for the Construction and Equipment of Ships Carrying Liquefied Gases in Bulk (IGC Code). This code is mandatory under the provisions of chapter VII of the 1974 SOLAS convention. It applies to ships in which the keels are laid on or after July 1, 1986.[23]

Other professional and trade organizations that contribute to the safe operation of gas carriers and terminals include the

- Society of International Gas Tanker and Terminal Operators (SIGTTO)
- Oil Companies International Maritime Forum (OCIMF)
- International Association of Ports and Harbors (IAPH)
- World Shipping Council
- International Navigation Association (PIANC)

In addition, state initiatives to identify hazard zones for a range of maximum credible events due to puncture, normal accidents, terrorism, and jetty loading arm failure contribute to the safety of gas operations. These zones are based on current vessel design considerations and incorporate procedures adopted by operators and port authorities to address the risks and hazards associated with LNG. General security and operating procedures that prevent security breaches include general security zones around ships, exclusion zones around the facility equipment, surveillance, tug assistance, constant communication, continuity of crew with strict selection and security procedures, and frequent inspections.

Following 9/11, the 1974 SOLAS convention was amended to include the ISPS Code. This code was implemented in July 2004 and fundamentally affected every ship owner conducting blue-water trade in ships. Numerous countries, the United States in particular, concluded that terrorists were likely to use ships as weapons or create chaos in international trade and the international economy. The ISPS Code is the first multilateral security standard created to strengthen maritime security by impressing regulatory requirements to prevent and suppress acts of terrorism against shipping and ports. It follows risk management principles to provide a consistent framework for evaluating risk and enable governments to best determine how to reduce vulnerabilities.

The code requires security threat assessments to be made by the government of a country or a designated authority within government. Measures taken to provide port security are increased from level 1 to 3.[24] Shipboard security requirements are similarly designated but determined by the appropriate authority of the ship's flag. Security plans should suit the individual company, ship, and conditions under which the company is trading but also recognize port security levels. Other features of the code that affect shipping are the requirement for a company security officer, ship security assessment, ship security plan, ship security officer, declaration of security, training, and drills; records are to be kept.

With respect to keeping terrorists off ships, the salient feature of the code is the requirement for a ship security plan to detail measures for controlled access to the ship and prevention of weapons and other dangerous devices being embarked. Consistent with the ISPS code, other security initiatives include port access control both at the import (regasification) and export (liquefaction) terminals with gated access control and surveillance assets; well trained, vetted, and specialist crews; and traffic monitoring and reporting systems. Further ISPS Code initiatives to enhance maritime security include the requirement to

- Fit automatic identification systems (AIS)[25]
- Make the ship identification number readily visible
- Fit a ship security alert system
- Use SAT C information for long range tracking

The ship security alert system is designed to alert the company and authorities ashore. It should be capable of activation from the bridge and other place on the ship in the event of a security threat. However, the amendments to SOLAS only require that ships be able to send an alert and authorities ashore be able to receive them. The response to be taken is not specified, which raises some uncertainty as to how this system will work in practice. Yet, despite the initiatives to enhance maritime safety, the perceived vulnerability and risk of the LNG industry still outweigh an impressive, and demonstrated, safety record. But, what are the vulnerabilities and risks in the LNG industry?

LIQUEFIED NATURAL GAS VULNERABILITY AND RISK

LNG is transported and stored as a cryogenic liquid and when regasified to natural gas, it is flammable in certain concentrations of air. Risks identified for the operation and handling of LNG have been scientifically examined and reported at many of the sources given in this chapter. However, conflicting expert opinion and the absence of a litany of LNG disasters to support scientific argument leaves room for skepticism. The more evident hazards assessed by experts for the conduct of LNG operations are

- Collision
- Methane
- Freezing liquid
- Explosion
- Pool fires

COLLISION

LNG tankers[26] are designed to have additional strength built-in than double-hull oil tankers. There are typically four to five physical barriers between the LNG cargo and external environment. This design and construction feature of LNG vessels suggests that collision velocities for equivalent hole sizes in other cargo carriers will be one to two knots higher than for a LNG vessel. The Sandia report suggests that an LNG tanker collision with a large ship even at 10 knots is expected to produce an effective hole size of no more than approximately 1 m^2 for an LNG spill.[27] If collision at 10 knots establishes a benchmark for consideration, then operational measures taken to mitigate such an event would include proactive vessel traffic management to coordinate ship movements in inner and outer harbors, where the consequences of a potential LNG spill might be most severe.[28]

METHANE

The Sandia report suggests that in the event of a large-scale LNG release, the cryogenic LNG will begin to vaporize. LNG concentrations in the atmosphere could present an asphyxiation hazard to personnel exposed to the vaporization plume as it displaces breathable air. However, methane is considered a simple asphyxiant with low toxicity to humans.[29] There has not been any injury associated with the production of LNG since 1979 and although this incident resulted in one death and a serious injury, neither was the result of methane asphyxiation.[30,31]

FREEZING LIQUID

In an unlikely event of skin contact with LNG, the cryogenic fluid will freeze the skin at the point of contact, which is a human hazard. An incident of this nature is only likely to occur to those operating closely with LNG on the ship; therefore, there is no danger of this hazard affecting an adjacent port community.

EXPLOSION

As LNG is stored at $-160°C$, no pressure is required to maintain the gas in its liquid state. The sophisticated design of LNG containment systems prevents ignition sources making contact with the liquid; and as LNG is stored at atmospheric pressure, any puncture of the cargo hold does not create an immediate explosion.[32] Although scientific methodology suggests that an LNG explosion is not a threat, perception about the potential trauma of terrorist activity seems to outweigh the potential of LNG.

POOL FIRES

Expert opinion suggests that if LNG spills near an ignition source, the evaporating gas in a combustible gas–air concentration will burn above the LNG pool. The resulting "pool fire" will spread as the LNG pool expands away from its source and continues evaporating. Such pool fires are intense, burning far more hotly and rapidly than oil or gasoline fires; and the LNG must be consumed to extinguish the fire.[33] The threat of a pool fire is considered the most serious LNG hazard; but although the nature of the hazard is real, even in this case, there is conflicting evidence concerning its magnitude.

Notwithstanding the regulations that govern the operations and conduct of LNG operations, design initiatives to mitigate identified risks within the LNG tanker include monitoring systems for

- Sophisticated radar and positioning systems to monitor the ship's position and any nearby traffic
- Global maritime distress system to signal an onboard emergency
- Gas detectors to pick up the presence of minute quantities of methane
- Fire detectors to sense heat or flames

Collectively, the overall safety regime for operations with LNG reflects the significant intellectual engagement of LNG shippers to ensure that commercial imperative is undertaken in conjunction with safe practice. If this effort fails to convince some sectors of the community, then what are the alternatives?

THE IMPLICATIONS OF MAINTAINING SECURITY OF OIL SUPPLY AT THE EXPENSE OF POTENTIAL LIQUEFIED NATURAL GAS IN THE ENERGY MIX

Environmental concerns and increasing focus on global warming issues are significant motivators for an interest in LNG.[34] Gas is essentially free of sulfur and particulate matter and has a higher hydrogen-to-carbon ratio, minimizing CO_2 emissions. In comparison to oil and coal, the environmental performance of natural gas favors its use for power generation as the costs of meeting air pollution standards are generally the lowest for natural gas; technological advances have raised the thermal efficiency of gas-fired units to 50 percent, whereas the average thermal efficiency of electricity generation in Organization for Economic Cooperation and Development (OECD) country fossil fuel plants is around 38 percent; and the planning horizon and lead time required for the construction of gas-fired units are shorter.[35]

The alternative to LNG tankers shipping this energy resource is the import of other fossil fuels such as oil in tankers. Although the Exxon Valdez oil spill accident occurred in 1989 and many IMO initiatives have been implemented to mitigate the risk of a similar environmental disaster,[36] oil tankers by design have less protective hull barriers than the LNG tanker. LNG will dissipate in air whereas oil has the potential to cause significant environmental damage.

The Exxon Valdez accident alone caused the death of thousands of animals and destruction of billions of salmon and herring eggs. The long-term effects include reductions in ocean animal populations, stunted growth in pink salmon populations, higher death rates for sea otters and ducks that ingested contaminated creatures, and contaminated mussel beds that will take up to 30 years to recover.[37] Alarmingly, the Exxon Valdez was not the largest spill of all times but the thirty-fifth of a litany of oil spills from shipping that occurs every year.[38] It seems that any opportunity to reduce the inshore movement of oil tankers by displacing this fossil fuel with natural gas carried in more robust tankers is not feasible but necessary.

Although LNG facilities have the potential to be high-profile terrorist targets, LNG storage facilities are few in number when compared with similar targets such as oil refineries, fuel pipelines, and hazardous cargo vessels.[39] On the basis of data from the U.S. Office of Hazardous Materials Safety, 1000 LNG tanker shipments account for less than 1 percent of total annual U.S. shipments of hazardous marine cargo such as ammonia, crude oil, LPGs, and other volatile chemicals.[40] Many of these hazardous cargoes represent less of a risk than LNG, but many are just as dangerous and pass through the same waters as LNG.[41] Perhaps, this statistic reveals less about LNG's small comparative movement in the U.S. shipping but more about the lack of LNG tanker visibility, which (in conjunction with fear of terrorism) helps to feed anxiety about the potential of LNG to be used to create trauma in a shore-side community.

CONCLUSION

Although the world's LNG industry is expanding rapidly with economic and environmental benefits, there is still a perception in some quarters that the LNG tanker and facilities pose risks disproportionate to alternative energy resources. Like other fossil fuels, LNG poses its own challenges in terms of the shipboard and port management of hazards unique to operation and transportation of this cargo. Although law makers and the general public are concerned about these hazards and how they might be exploited by terrorists, the LNG industry does not have the history of operations to indicate that pirates or terrorists have the maritime experience to conduct operations in support of trauma at sea or in harbor.

Indeed, it is the author's view that it would take considerable maritime and specific LNG-tanker knowledge to effectively overrun and hijack such a vessel. As an aircraft cockpit necessarily has centralized control of all mechanical functions, the bridge equipment of an LNG tanker is also complex with the capability of centralized control but with a number of other options for controlling machinery at stations separate to the bridge. Also with more expert crews in LNG tankers, it would be a challenging prospect for pirates or terrorists to rapidly gain control throughout the vessel. Even with the eventual control of the crew, knowledge of machinery and cargo monitoring systems would be needed to sustain an intention to traumatize with confidence.

The transportation of oil in tankers has a litany of environmental disasters to support research and mitigating action to stem the possibility of further events. In the absence of such disasters, the LNG industry appears to suffer reverse discrimination despite the considerable regulatory, design, and operational measures implemented to mitigate vulnerability and risk. In response to shore-side anxiety about LNG operations adjacent to some communities, recent scientific studies on LNG transportation and facilities have, arguably, highlighted the risks of operating this cargo but with somewhat ambiguous conclusions. The LNG tanker, like other shipping, is vulnerable to an attack. However, regulatory measures taken to mitigate vulnerability and risk in the industry from its earliest days, coupled with new maritime security regimes implemented by the IMO through the ISPS code, have failed to convince some sectors of the community about the benefits of living and working with LNG.

The rejection of the proposed LNG facility at Cabrillo Port based on community concern over environmental and possible terrorism issues are noteworthy as they highlight two conditions that continue to perennially influence the maritime sector. The first is the political leverage afforded by mention of terrorism or piracy at sea, whether real or perceived, to sway argument. The second is the continued relationship between safety standards, commercial imperative, and community concern.[42] Regulation and safety requirements governing the conduct of shipping operations, and more specifically LNG operations, are extensive and there is arguably little more that can be done to enhance safety and security in the maritime sphere. The encouraging aspect of the rejection of the Cabrillo project is that alternative options for energy must still be available in California; the project was not a crisis of choice. Although the threat of terrorism disproportionably affects perception, energy choices, scientific research, impressive safety record, robust LNG tanker design, considerable environmental advantages, and the integrity of IMO, and state regulatory systems fail to gain traction where anxiety in sectors of a community have constituent power.

NOTES

1. International Maritime Organization (IMO), International Convention for the Safety of Life at Sea (SOLAS), 1974. See http://www.imo.org/Conventions/mainframe.asp?topic_id=250.
2. The Code was incorporated into SOLAS chapter XI in two parts. Part A contains the mandatory requirements and part B provides guidelines on how to meet them. See http://www.imo.org/Newsroom/mainframe.asp?topic_id=583&doc_id=2689#code.
3. Piracy activity has three main themes: attacks on vessels at sea, harbor and anchorage attacks, and hijacking merchant ships at sea. In the Pacific basin LNG trade, LNG tankers regularly ply sea lines of communication adjacent to piracy hot spots in Southeast Asia. However, while piracy and the specter of maritime terrorism may be an international concern to blue-water shipping, it is the commercial imperative of the LNG operation itself that drives studies to convince affected populations of LNG safety close inshore.
4. "International and National Efforts to Address the Safety and Security Risks of Importing Liquefied Natural Gas": A Compendium, prepared for California Energy Commission; Prepared by ASPEN Environmental Group Consultant Report; CEC-600-2005-002, Phinney, S., D. Env. Sacramento, CA, Contract No. 700-99-014, January 2005, p. v.
5. See NGI's Daily Gas Price Index, "CA Governor Rejects BHP Billiton LNG Project," Intelligence Press, Sterling, VA, May 21, 2007, and *Business Monitor International*, "Industry News—California LNG Project Terminated," May 21, 2007. The project was ostensibly terminated by California's Governor on environmental grounds; however, large protests by Malibu residents led by Hollywood celebrities also included terrorism as a concern.
6. "Cryogenic" refers to low temperature and low temperature technology. There is no precise temperature for an upper boundary but $-100°F$ ($-73°C$) is often used. LNG is transported and stored at temperatures below methane's atmospheric boiling point $-162°C$. A volume of LNG is approximately 1/600th of the volume of natural gas.
7. Fflooks, R., "Natural Gas By Sea," Second Edition, London: Witherby and Co. Ltd., 1993, p. 8.
8. Ibid.
9. In January 1959, the world's first LNG tanker, Methane Pioneer, carried LNG from Lake Charles, LA to Canvey Island, United Kingdom.
10. McGuire, J.J. and White, B., "Liquefied Gas Handling Principles On Ships and in Terminals," Third Edition, London: Witherby & Company Limited, 2000, p. 11. Today the majority of LNG tankers are between 125,000 and 135,000 m^3 in capacity. The current fleet of LNG vessels has grown to 257 with 122 on order, 2 new orders and 7 LNG tankers scheduled for delivery in 2008. See http://www.lngoneworld.com (retrieved 8 May, 2008).
11. Jensen, J. T., "The Development of a Global LNG Market. Is it Likely? If So When?" NG 5, Oxford Institute For Energy Studies, Oxford, 2004, p. 8.
12. Ibid.
13. See Ffooks, R., "Natural Gas by Sea—The Development of a New Technology," Second Edition, London: Wetherby and Co. Ltd., 1993. p. 212.
14. Jensen, J. T., op.cit., p. 81.
15. Terrorist attacks against merchant shipping have generally been focused on passenger and cruise ship operations such as the 1985 attack on the *Achille Lauro* off Egypt and the 1989 attack on the *City of Poros* off Greece. Subsequent attacks on merchant ships included the *Limburg* off Yemen in October 2002, apparently confirming the fears of nations about the vulnerability of all merchant shipping.
16. Incidents occurred where LNG was spilled but there was no containment failure, release of cargo, or loss of life. See, SANDIA Report, SAND2004-6258, "Guidance on Risk Analysis and Safety Implications of a Large Liquefied Natural Gas (LNG) Spill Over Water"; Hightower, M., Gritzo, L., Luketa-Hanlin,

A., Covan, J., Tieszen, S., Wellman, G., Irwin, M., Kaneshige, M., Melof, B., Morrow, C., Ragland, D.; prepared by Sandia National Laboratories, contract DE-AC04-94AL85000; Unlimited Release, printed December 2004, p. 99.

17. "Consequences of LNG Marine Incidents," Pitblado, R.M., Baik, J., Hughes, G.J., Ferro, C., Shaw, S.J., Det Norske Veritas (USA) Inc., Houston, TX 77084, CCPS Conference Orlando, June 29 to July 1, 2004. p. 5.

18. For example, Det Norske Veritas (DNV), American Bureau of Shipping (ABS), and Lloyds. Ship Classification Societies (Class) set industry standards that considerably influence the safe design, construction, hull maintenance, and engineering systems in ships. Class inspections and ratings for ships are an integral component of the maritime adventure where commercial opportunity necessarily attracts the attention of voyage underwriters.

19. See also: http://www.imo.org/Safety/mainframe.asp?topic_id=158.

20. SANDIA Report, op.cit., p. 58.

21. "Consequence Assessment Methods for Incidents Involving Releases from Liquefied Natural Gas Carriers," 131-04, GEMS 1288209. This work was compiled by ABSG Consulting Inc. for the Federal Energy Regulatory Commission (Washington DC) under contract number FERC04C40196, May 13, 2004, p. 41.

22. *Tanker Safety Guide—Liquefied Natural Gas*, Second Edition, London: International Chamber of Shipping, 1995. pp. 171–172.

23. See http://www.imo.org/Environment/mainframe.asp?topic_id=995.

24. The three-tier security systems are level 1 (low risk), level 2 (medium risk), and level 3 (high risk).

25. The original intention of the AIS was to enhance navigation safety by providing an automated VHF ship/ship and ship/shore interface for monitoring and tracking purposes. However, serious concerns about the system were evident as the transmitted information is available to any receiver be it that of terrorists, pirates, or belligerent nations wanting to attack or approach a particular ship.

26. There are three types of LNG carriers—membrane ships, independent prismatic tank ships, and independent spherical tank ships.

27. SANDIA Report, op.cit., p. 44.

28. Ibid., p. 45.

29. SANDIA Report, op.cit., p. 37.

30. See "LNG Safety and Security," Centre for Energy Economics, Sugar Land, TX, Foss, M. M., Ph.D, October 2003, Table 4, pp. 77–79.

31. On the basis of volume, LNG is typically 85–96 percent methane, with the balance being mostly other light hydrocarbons such as ethane, propane, butane, and up to 1 percent nitrogen. Methane is colorless, odorless, and tasteless and is flammable in air at 5–15 percent (by volume).

32. "LNG Safety and Security," ibid., p. 17.

33. "Liquefied Natural Gas (LNG) Infrastructure Security: Background and Issues for Congress," Parfomak, P.W., Congressional Research Service—The Library of Congress, Washington, September 9, 2003, p. CRS-8.

34. It is ironic that despite this apparent enthusiasm, the California governor rejected the LNG project on advice from state agencies that the project would result in "significant and unmitigated" impacts on air quality and marine life. See NGI's Daily Gas Price Index, "CA Governor Rejects BHP Billiton LNG Project," May 21, 2007.

35. "The Growth of Japan's LNG Industry: Lessons for China and Hong Kong," ibid., p. 331.

36. The U.S. Congress subsequently enacted legislation requiring all tankers to be double-hulled by 2015.

37. See http://en.wikipedia.org/wiki/Exxon_Valdez_oil_spill (retrieved August 2, 2007).

38. See http://www.isaa.org.uk/downloads/oilspillstats.pdf (retrieved August 2, 2007).

39. "Liquefied Natural Gas (LNG) Infrastructure Security: Background and Issues for Congress," loc. cit., CRS–20.

40. Office of Hazardous Materials Safety, Department of Transportation, *Hazardous Materials Shipments*, Washington, October, 1998, Table 2. p. 2.

41. "Liquefied Natural Gas (LNG) Infrastructure Security: Background and Issues for Congress," ibid.

42. Broken Hill Proprietary (BHP) Billiton spent four years working with state and federal officials to address the concerns of regulators and members of the public. See NGI's Daily Gas Price Index, "CA Governor Rejects BHP Billiton LNG Project," May 21, 2007.

11 Offshore Oil and Gas Industry Security Risk Assessment: An Australian Case Study

Lee Cordner

CONTENTS

INTRODUCTION

World energy consumption is forecast to increase by more than two-thirds over the three decades to 2030, with oil remaining the dominant energy source. Asia, particularly China and India, accounts for almost half of the projected increase in world oil demand.[1] World natural gas consumption is projected to grow at 2.3 percent per annum, almost doubling by 2030, accounting for approximately one-quarter of world energy consumption over the same period,[2] and displacing coal as the world's second most important energy source.

In the evolving world energy scene, the offshore oil and gas industry has become increasingly important. It is a significant component of the global maritime sector and a major factor in the global economy. The exploration for, and extraction of, oil and gas offshore has increased in priority as onshore resources have become harder to obtain, the onshore security environment has become more challenging, and technological advances make offshore extraction technically feasible and economically viable. The offshore oil and gas industry, with its vast investment in large fixed and floating platforms and vessels, in locations extending to the edge of continental shelves and beyond, presents a range of unique factors for international and national security regulation and enforcement.

The purpose of this chapter is to analyze security risk assessment, with particular regard to terrorism threats, as they affect the offshore oil and gas industry in the context of the International Ship and Port Facility Security Code (ISPS Code) and related international conventions and protocols, utilizing the Australian approach as a case study.

THE AUSTRALIAN CASE IN CONTEXT

Australia is a net importer of oil products with very small domestic reserves, producing primarily light sweet crude. Australian natural gas reserves, exported as liquefied natural gas (LNG), are more significant. Although with less than 1 percent of world reserves,[3] Australia represents 6 percent of world production and 10 percent of the Asia-Pacific LNG market,[4] and is predicted to be the world's third largest LNG exporter by 2010.[5] Significant gas reserves are located offshore to the northwest and north of the country in Australia's exclusive economic zone (EEZ) and in the joint petroleum development area (JPDA) shared with East Timor. Australia's major customers are Japan, South Korea, and China, and LNG is shipped by tankers passing through the archipelagic waters of Southeast Asia.

Exports of LNG are currently provided primarily from the North West Shelf Venture (NWSV), operated by Woodside Petroleum Ltd. (Woodside) on behalf of a consortium. In 2006, NWSV delivered 205 cargoes of LNG, including its 2000th cargo since commencement of operations and its first cargo to the Guangdong terminal in southern China.[6] Domestic energy needs in parts of Australia are also largely met by natural gas, with the state of Western Australia heavily reliant on gas piped overland from the North West Shelf. The JPDA offers the vastly increased potential for natural gas production when fully operational (Figure 11.1).

There are also offshore gas facilities to the south of Australia, mainly in Bass Strait, supplying gas primarily to the state of Victoria. Bass Strait is geographically distant from the main sources of regional Islamist terrorism in Southeast Asia, and the associated potential security risks are deemed to be lower. This analysis therefore concentrates mainly on security risks to the oil and gas areas to the north of Australia.

Australia is a developed western power and was quick to emphatically support the United States following the Islamist extremist terrorist attacks on September 11, 2001. Australia provided military forces for operations against the Taliban in Afghanistan and, along with the United Kingdom, committed military forces to the U.S.-led invasion of Iraq. Australia has maintained modest forces in both countries since then. Australia has been specifically identified as a target by Al-Qaeda in numerous public statements.[7]

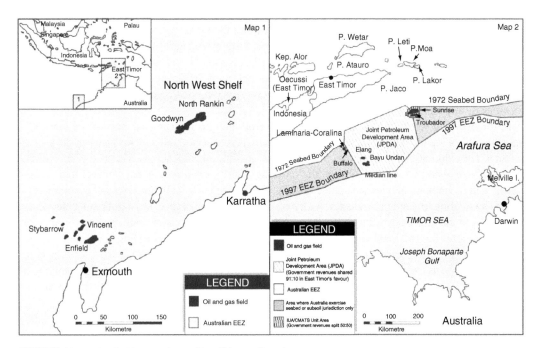

FIGURE 11.1   North Western Australia offshore oil and gas areas.

Australia is located next to Indonesia, the most populous Islamic country in the world. Indonesians very largely practice a moderate form of Islam, and relations with Australia are mostly positive. However, there have been several terrorist incidents perpetrated by extreme Islamist elements in Indonesia directed at Australia and the West, including the Bali bombings in October 2002, which took the lives of 88 Australians, 3 Australian residents, and 111 people from other countries;[8] the bombing of the Australian Embassy in Jakarta in September 2004; and the October 2005 Bali bombings resulting in the death of 20 more people, including 4 Australians. Australia's actions in support of East Timorese independence have been the subject of strident criticism from Al-Qaeda, along with Islamic elements within Indonesia and other parts of Southeast Asia. Although the incidence of maritime-related terrorist attacks have been limited in number globally, of regional relevance in February 2004, Abu Sayyaf Group, a Muslim extremist, Al-Qaeda-linked organization, claimed responsibility for an attack on a Philippines passenger ferry, which caused significant loss of life.[9]

In summary, although Australia is a relatively small player in the global oil and gas equation, it has significant offshore gas interests, primarily to the north of the country, and is expanding its regional exports of LNG. Further, Australia's identification as a terrorist target by Al-Qaeda, its geographic location next to Southeast Asia and strong alignment against Islamist-supported terrorism have compelled the Australian Government, along with the key industry players involved, to take a proactive and determined stance to address potential terrorist security risks to its offshore oil and gas industry. These factors underpin the utility of Australia's approach as a case study for this analysis.

APPLICABILITY OF THE ISPS CODE TO OFFSHORE OIL AND GAS

The December 2002 International Maritime Organization (IMO) Conference of Contracting Governments adopted the ISPS Code and International Convention for the Safety of Life at Sea, 1974 (SOLAS 74) amendments to chapter XI-1 and a new chapter XI-2, all to be implemented by July 1, 2004. SOLAS 74 was extended to cover port facilities noting that "provisions relating to port facilities should relate solely to the ship/port interface".[10]

Of direct relevance to the oil and gas industry was the inclusion of cargo ships of "500 gross tonnage and upward," "mobile offshore drilling units," and requirements that ship security plans should contain provisions for a ship when interfacing with "fixed or floating platforms or a mobile drilling unit on location".[11] IMO Conference Resolution 7 recognized the need to establish measures to enhance the security of mobile offshore drilling units on location and fixed and floating platforms not covered by chapter XI-2 of SOLAS 74. However, the ISPS Code and SOLAS 74 fell short of encompassing such offshore facilities. The IMO only went as far as encouraging contracting governments, when exercising their responsibilities for mobile offshore drilling units and for fixed and floating platforms operating on their continental shelf or within their exclusive economic zone, to ensure that security arrangements applying to those offshore facilities would allow interaction with ships covered by the convention. Contracting governments were requested to inform the IMO of any actions they have taken in this respect.[12]

The IMO, in responding to requests for advice on the application of SOLAS chapter XI-2 and the ISPS Code to floating production, storage, and off-loading units (FPSOs) and floating storage units (FSUs) reiterated the view that such facilities were not "ships subject to the provisions of the ISPS Code." However, they should have security procedures in place to prevent "contamination" of ships and port facilities subject to the code.[13] Further, the IMO advised that "As FPSOs and FSUs operate as part of offshore oil production facilities, it can be expected that the State on whose continental shelf or within whose Exclusive Economic Zone the activity is being undertaken will have developed appropriate security measures and procedures under its national law to protect offshore facilities".[14]

The onus is clearly placed on nations to provide legislation that addresses security arrangements for offshore oil and gas facilities operating within a national EEZ or on a continental shelf. One question that appears to remain unanswered at this stage is what security requirements apply for fixed facilities operating outside a national jurisdiction. Technological advances and rising prices mean that oil and gas is being sought and extracted in waters of ever-greater depths. Operations beyond national jurisdictions are increasingly feasible. The IMO may have to further consider its position on offshore oil and gas facilities in the future.

In summary, the ISPS Code and SOLAS 74 amendments apply directly to the offshore oil and gas sector only in respect to cargo ships and mobile offshore drilling units. However, the importance of the compatibility of the security regimes of vessels involved in the oil and gas industry and the offshore facilities they often interface with are recognized and emphasized. National governments are encouraged to take this into account when formulating related national legislation.

THE SUA TREATIES

The United Nations Convention for the Suppression of Unlawful Acts against the Safety of Maritime Navigation (SUA 1988)[15] and Protocol for the Suppression of Unlawful Acts against the Safety of Fixed Platforms Located on the Continental Shelf (SUA Protocol 1988)[16] were initially formalized at Rome on March 10, 1988. The SUA treaties were developed in response to the Achille Lauro hijacking in 1985.[17] SUA 1988 and SUA Protocol 1988 both entered into force generally on March 1, 1992 and came into force in Australia on May 20, 1993. As on March 31, 2007, 144 and 132 contracting states had ratified SUA 1988 and SUA Protocol 1988, respectively. Only since recent terrorist events and since the ISPS Code was developed, has there been wide ratification.[18]

The SUA convention (SUA 2005) and protocol (SUA Protocol 2005) were amended at an IMO Conference in London in October 2005.[19] SUA 2005 requires the ratification by 12 states[20] before it can come into force. The SUA Protocol 2005 requires ratification by three of those twelve states and can only come into force once SUA 2005 has entered into force.[21] As on March 31, 2007, only two contracting states (Cook Islands and St. Kitts and Nevis) had ratified SUA 2005, and none ratified the SUA Protocol 2005.[22]

The main purpose of the SUA treaties is to ensure that appropriate action is taken against persons committing unlawful acts against ships. These include the seizure of ships by force; acts of violence against persons onboard ships; and the placing of devices on board a ship that are likely to destroy or damage it. The convention obliges contracting governments either to extradite or prosecute alleged offenders. Article 8 of SUA 1988 covers the responsibilities and roles of the master of a ship, the flag state, and the receiving state in delivering to the authorities of any state party, any person believed to have committed an offense under the convention, including the furnishing of evidence pertaining to the alleged offense.[23]

The 2005 amendments to the SUA treaties impose a range of expanded provisions specifically targeted at international terrorism. For example, it is an offense to unlawfully and intentionally seek to intimidate a population, or to compel a government or an international organization to do or to abstain from any act; to use against or on a ship or discharging from a ship, or transport in a ship, any explosive, radioactive material or a BCN (biological, chemical, nuclear) weapon in a manner that causes or is likely to cause death or serious injury or damage; to discharge, from a ship, oil, LNG, or other hazardous or noxious substance, in such quantity or concentration that causes or is likely to cause death or serious injury or damage; or use a ship in a manner that causes death, serious injury, or damage. It is an offense to attempt to commit an offense; participate as an accomplice; organize or direct others to commit an offense; or contribute to the commissioning of an offense. Parties are required to take necessary measures to enable a legal entity (e.g., this could be a company or organization) to be made liable when a person responsible for management of control of that legal entity has, in that capacity, committed an offense under the convention.[24]

Importantly, for this analysis, the SUA 1988 Protocol (and the SUA protocol 2005 amendments) extends the provisions of the SUA treaties, as they apply to shipping, to offshore oil and gas platforms on the continental shelf. Contracting governments are authorized to enact legislation for dealing with unlawful acts of violence against such platforms. However, the question of application beyond national jurisdictions remains (i.e., to fixed platforms possibly operating beyond the continental shelf in the future). The inconsistency of the IMO's approach with the ISPS Code and SOLAS 74 amendments, in not including offshore platforms, is underlined by the SUA treaties.

In April 2007, at a summit in Australia, a senior IMO representative stated that these inconsistencies were recognized and were part of a long list of matters to be considered by the IMO in the coming years. He advised that the initial formulation of the ISPS Code and SOLAS 74 amendments focused attention on making expeditious changes to improve shipping and port security due to concerns about vulnerabilities to terrorism. He advised that offshore platforms were of less concern to the contracting governments at the time because those who had responsibility for such platforms indicated that they had adequate national provisions in place for the security of platforms under their jurisdiction.[25]

This analysis is primarily concerned with provisions for the "prevention" of terrorist acts against offshore oil and gas facilities. The SUA treaties provide the international basis for "responding" to acts or threats of terrorism and other criminal acts against ships and fixed offshore platforms. In Australia, the SUA treaties are enacted in the "Crimes (Ships and Fixed Platforms) Act 1992",[26] which provides the legal basis for authorities to respond to such crimes under Australian jurisdiction, and bring offenders to justice. Importantly, the SUA provisions apply to all vessels, not just those over 500 t.

THE AUSTRALIAN RESPONSE

The Australian response to offshore oil and gas industry security must be seen in the context of a broader, whole of government approach when dealing with the threat of terrorism. The post-September 2001 Australian domestic legislative and organizational response was initially slow; however, the Bali bombings in October 2002 prompted a rapid acceleration in responsiveness. The National Security Committee of Cabinet (NSC), chaired by the prime minister and comprising key Australian government ministers, and the Council of Australian Governments (CoAG), also chaired by the prime minister and comprising the premiers and chief ministers from each state and territory, oversaw a broad range of new and enhanced legislative, coordination, and security capability measures designed to ensure effective national counterterrorism prevention and response arrangements were in place. The Secretaries Committee on National Security (SCNS)[27] was directly involved, and in October 2002, a new peak body, known as the National Counter-Terrorism Committee (NCTC), was created to provide coordination and advice across commonwealth and state jurisdictions.

In Australia, the responsibilities, authorities, and mechanisms to prevent, and if necessary manage acts of terrorism and their consequences are outlined in the National Counter-Terrorism Plan (NCTP).[28] The security of the Australian offshore oil and gas industry is affected by many aspects of the NCTP and related arrangements, which are summarized as follows:

1. Australian government responsibilities include the maintenance of counterterrorism capabilities, prevention strategies, and operational responses to threats, leading the management of intelligence, and determining and promulgating the national counterterrorism alert level. State and territory responsibilities are also specified.[29]
2. The Australian government regulates security arrangements for Australian ports, port facilities, ships, and offshore oil and gas facilities. This is administered by the Commonwealth Department of Infrastructure, Transport, Regional Development and Local Government, Office of Transport Security (OTS). Specifically, the "Australian Government has direct responsibility for offshore maritime counterterrorism prevention

and response (that is seaward of the territorial sea baseline), including the protection of oil and gas facilities ...".[30] Of significance here is the fact that state governments have long exercised administrative jurisdiction over adjacent offshore oil and gas facilities. For example, the North West Shelf comes under the jurisdiction of the Western Australian (WA) government. Before these arrangements, responsibility for North West Shelf security rested with the WA government, who had little capacity to discharge that responsibility.

3. A coordinating and controlling entity known as Border Protection Command (BPC), renamed from Joint Offshore Protection Command in January 2007, is the lead agency for offshore security. Commander BPC has joint responsibilities with the chief executive officer (CEO) of customs for coordinating civil maritime surveillance and response, and the chief of the defense force (CDF) for military offshore maritime protection functions.[31] (Note: Australia does not have a separate coast guard, as is the case in some other countries. BPC is a coordinating agency for civil maritime surveillance and response services provided to the many Australian government agencies responsible for activities that extend offshore, for example, fishing, immigration, quarantine, and offshore resources.)

4. Responsibilities for critical infrastructure (CI) protection are outlined. These apply to offshore oil and gas facilities that contribute significantly to meeting Australia's energy needs or contribute significantly to export income (i.e., the North West Shelf and Bass Strait facilities). A National Committee on Critical Infrastructure Protection (NCCIP) coordinates arrangements between commonwealth, state and territory governments, with a Critical Infrastructure Advisory Council (CIAC), which includes energy industry advice, and a Business Government Advisory Group on National Security also in place.[32]

5. Importantly, a Trusted Information Sharing Network (TISN) has been established to facilitate the sharing of security information (including intelligence, where necessary) between the Australian government and owners and operators of CI.[33]

ARRANGEMENTS SPECIFIC TO THE OFFSHORE OIL AND GAS INDUSTRY

The Australian government responded in a timely and proactive manner to the implementation of the ISPS Code and SOLAS 74 amendments. The Maritime Transport Security Act (MTSA) 2003 was quickly developed and passed by Parliament to take effect on July 1, 2004 at the same time as the ISPS Code. However, like the ISPS Code, the MTSA did not extend to offshore oil and gas facilities.

In 2004, the Australian Government Task Force on Offshore Maritime Security concluded that there was a need for security regulations to cover the offshore oil and gas industry. The Maritime Transport Security Amendment Act 2005 provided the remedy, directing that the MTSA be amended and renamed the Maritime Transport and Offshore Facilities Security Act (MTOFSA) 2003.[34] Concomitantly, Maritime Transport and Offshore Facilities Security Regulations 2003[35] were put in place. Effectively, the amended act and regulations meant that ISPS Code requirements similar to those for ships and port facilities were also applied to offshore oil and gas facilities and offshore service providers operating under Australian jurisdiction. In 2006, a plain language summary of the MTOFSA and regulations called "Strengthening Maritime Security: Who, what and where?",[36] was published to aid communication of these significant maritime security changes across the broader Australian maritime and offshore community.

The MTOFSA and regulations establish the regulatory framework for Australian offshore oil and gas security. The MTOFSA makes compliance by offshore industry participants mandatory, just as Australia, as a contracting government, has an obligation to set in place arrangements to comply with the ISPS Code and SOLAS 74 amendments. All offshore industry participants[37] are required to have government-approved offshore security plans in place,[38] and failure to comply satisfactorily with all or parts of the MTOFSA requirements is an offense. Approval for offshore security plans that are deemed to be inadequate can be cancelled.[39] Further, demerit points are accrued if an offshore industry participant is convicted or found guilty of an offense against the act or if the participant pays a penalty as an alternative to prosecution. Accumulation of demerit points to a certain level may result in government approval for an offshore security plan to be cancelled.[40] Cancellation of an offshore security plan effectively means the participant can no longer operate.

SECURITY RISK ASSESSMENT AND MANAGEMENT

The Australian government has been proactive in promoting a consistent and professional approach to security arrangements for the offshore oil and gas industry, which reflects the national importance placed on the sector. Risk management processes fundamentally underpin the offshore oil and gas industry security processes. Offshore facility operators are required to have a valid security assessment as part of an offshore security plan that must include, *inter alia*, details of the risk management process adopted; the risk context or threat situation for each facility; identification of possible risks or threats, with the likelihood and consequences of their occurrence; and the identification of possible risk treatments and their effectiveness in reducing risk levels and vulnerabilities.[41]

In addition to the legislative, regulatory, and information documents already cited, OTS issued the "Offshore Oil & Gas Risk Context Statement" (OGRCS)[42] in April 2005 and the "Offshore Security Assessments Guidance Paper" (OSAGP)[43] in June 2005. Together these documents outline a coordinated approach to security risk management from a national level through enterprise and organizational levels down to individual operations and operators. Specific risk management guidance for the oil and gas sector is provided utilizing generic approaches defined by Australian and New Zealand standards and guidelines.[44] The adequacy of these documents and the approaches prescribed are considered in the following paragraphs.

THE RISK CONTEXT

The OGRCS provides an overview of the transnational terrorism security environment in 2005, as relevant to the Australian oil and gas industry. The document is intended only to supplement threat and risk assessment information from other sources. The onus remains on specific owner/operators to determine their own security risks, utilizing risk assessment processes.[45] The OGRCS establishes the strategic and economic importance of the offshore oil and gas industry to Australia by stating "protecting it from the threat of terrorism is a national priority for the immediate and foreseeable future."[46]

The OGRCS assesses the international terrorism threat to Australia's oil and gas industry in the context of Al-Qaeda's identification of Australia as a legitimate target, and threats and actions intended to damage Western economies, particularly by targeting the global oil and gas industry.[47] When assessing the comparative threat and attendant risks of terrorist attacks on offshore oil and gas facilities, it must be observed that apart from attacks primarily against onshore oil facilities in the Middle East and Africa, there has been little direct evidence of attacks or attempts to attack offshore facilities, particularly gas facilities, and particularly those located in Southeast Asia. Furthermore, if terrorists did choose to target offshore oil and gas facilities in the Asia-Pacific region, the abundant facilities in the South China Sea are probably more readily accessible. These and other factors must be taken into account in the risk assessment process.

The OGRCS recognizes that terrorist attacks on the oil and gas sector anywhere in the world affects the energy sector's operating costs, particularly protective security and insurance costs. An attack on an offshore oil or gas facility anywhere would impact on global and regional security and economic well-being.[48] While the impact of attacks anywhere will be felt across the global oil and gas industry, not stated in the OGRCS is the prospect that companies operating in the relatively remote and (so far) benign Australian environment may find this presents them with a net commercial advantage. This also reinforces the view that it is in the interests of all parties involved in Australia to take all reasonable precautions to keep the risks as low as possible.

The likelihood of terrorist attacks on offshore facilities is less than that for land-based targets because, generally, they offer less attractive and more difficult targets. For example, if Australia was to be directly attacked, a greater terror impact for effort could be achieved by targeting populous urban areas, government infrastructure, or financial centers in the major cities. The OGRCS identifies several inherent features of the offshore oil and gas industry that act as deterrents to attack including difficulty in inflicting significant damage on robust structures with safety shutdown procedures; the logistics involved in attacking geographically distant and isolated facilities; and the generally small crew size offering reduced prospects for mass casualties. This must be balanced against the vulnerability of facilities in isolated, open-water settings which are also located in potentially large distances from interdiction and response capabilities.[49] The latter factor can be compensated by intelligence and maritime surveillance efforts, enabling the prepositioning of capable maritime response forces, which are able to remain on station in distant geographic locations for significant periods.

In the Australian case, with its vast maritime geography, including 12,000 Nmi of coastline and large offshore jurisdictions, maintaining effective surveillance and response presents major challenges. However, under the direction of BPC, reasonably comprehensive aerial surveillance of the north and northwest approaches to Australia is routinely conducted against illegal immigration, smuggling, and fishing activities using primarily contracted civil surveillance aircraft. This effort is supported by Australian Defence Force (ADF) maritime patrol aircraft and rotary wing assets. Surface response assets are coordinated from Australian Customs Service (ACS) and ADF (Navy) sources. An example of what can be achieved has been the Australian government–directed surveillance and interdiction operations against illegal immigration. These operations encompass large ocean areas off northwest Australia around Christmas Island reaching as far as Indonesian waters, and have been maintained almost continuously for several years. The NWSV has also received coincidental security benefits as there has been higher levels of maritime surveillance by, and presence of, naval forces in the area than otherwise might have been the case.

The OGRCS identifies several potential terrorism scenarios including:

- Direct attack, primarily using small craft packed with explosives or standoff weapons
- Armed intrusion by pirates or terrorists, primarily against tankers under way
- Hijacked vessels or aircraft driven or flown into an offshore facility
- Sabotage, underwater attack, or computer network attack[50]

Clearly, geography and logistics are major factors in determining the likelihood of various scenarios and the vulnerability of certain assets in the Australian context. For example, the prospect of small craft attack in the JPDA, 100–200 km south of East Timor, must be taken seriously. The area is relatively close to Indonesian West Timor, and Indonesian and other fishing vessels are frequently observed close to oil and gas facilities. In contrast, the likelihood of small craft attack in the NWSV, is much lower, as it lies 130–190 km northwest of Karratha, Western Australia with more than 1000 km of open sea separating it from the Indonesian Archipelago.[51] A problem for oil and gas facility operators is that there is very little they can legally do about such vessels in their vicinity. They have no powers to exercise law enforcement functions, and facilities are often very remote from assistance. However, so far there has been no indication of intent to conduct attacks using fishing vessels.

Armed intrusion by pirates or terrorists is more likely to occur in the navigationally constrained waters of the archipelagic straits plied by LNG and oil tankers proceeding between Australia and North Asian markets. The capability and intent of the attackers are significant factors, when combined with more favorable geography and the level of tanker vulnerability. However, most piracy incidents occur in or around the high-traffic density waters of the Malacca Straits rather than the straits to the east used by vessels transiting to and from Australia, and so far terrorists have shown very little capability or intent for this type of attack. In June 2004, Indonesia, Malaysia, and Singapore entered into an arrangement to conduct coordinated security surveillance and patrols of the Malacca Straits, partly in response to pressures from the United States, who were promoting a Regional Maritime Security Initiative (RMSI).

The consequences of terrorist attacks are likely to be more severe for petroleum tankers because of their volatile cargoes. As seen in the attack on the *MV Limburg*, it is difficult to inflict damage on modern, double-hulled tankers; however, such attacks can have significant, wider implications.[52] LNG tankers are inherently more difficult to attack and the cargo more problematic to ignite in the way many outside the industry have erroneously perceived.[53]

The OGRCS considers the prospect of a hijacked tanker or offshore tender vessel being used to ram a platform, FPSO, FSU, or another tanker with dire consequences.[54] However, the OGRCS does not mention or assess any changes to the likelihood of tanker hijacking once ISPS Code and MTOFSA-mandated risk treatment measures are introduced.

An attack by a hijacked aircraft is given greater emphasis in the OGRCS, suggesting "All substantial offshore oil and gas facilities are vulnerable ..." and that "There are no preventive measures that offshore facilities can reasonably take to prevent such attacks".[55] Again, this could be seen as presenting an overly alarmist and simplistic perspective. Although "offshore facilities" may have very limited capacity themselves to prevent such attacks, the overall national and international security system, employing intelligence and broader national defense capabilities, combined with counterterrorism measures imposed in the aviation sector, along with the remote geography of areas such as the NWSV, means that the risks when fully assessed, may be considerably less than implied.

The OGRCS states' offshore facilities are potentially vulnerable to acts of sabotage with the likelihood reduced as most employees' transit to platforms by helicopter or company-operated vessels. Risks can be further reduced by effective security screening of employees. The likelihood of underwater attack is mitigated by the difficulty of acquiring and applying the highly specialized capabilities required. A computer network attack can be mitigated by imposing appropriate network security controls.[56]

The OGRCS correctly asserts that heightened security awareness can be a major factor in reducing the likelihood of a terrorist attack being successfully mounted.[57] The inherent remoteness of the NWSV and JPDA facilities is advantageous here. Given the recent emphasis on security across the offshore oil and gas sector, the likelihood of suspicious activity being reported should be considerably improved. Anecdotal reports in recent years of light aircraft, chartered and flown by foreign nationals, conducting joy flights over the NWSV facilities and not being reported should be a thing of the past. The other side of this issue is, of course, the need to have communication arrangements, procedures, and response capabilities in place to ensure that responsible authorities will deal promptly with such reports.

In summary, the OGRCS provides a useful and mainly balanced, although in some respects limited, contextual overview of the Australian offshore oil and gas sector security risks from international terrorism. As stated in the introduction to the OGRCS, it does not alleviate the requirement for detailed, specific, and ongoing security risk assessments by local operators.

OFFSHORE SECURITY RISK ASSESSMENTS

The OSAGP[58] provides concise guidance on an indicative security risk assessment process to assist offshore oil and gas operators to meet the security assessment requirements of the MTOFSA and regulations. It is not the intention of this analysis to review the OSAGP in detail. General points relevant to the wider application of offshore security risk assessments are discussed where appropriate.

Clearly, it is in the interests of industry participants to follow the processes outlined. They are obliged to submit offshore security plans to OTS for approval, and OTS is the author of the guidelines. The OSAGP implies that the OTS assessment and review process may be delayed if security plans are not presented in an easy-to-read format.[59] Further, the prescribed process is generally consistent with risk management processes practiced across the industry for other aspects of operations, including safety.

The OSAGP prescribes a nine-stage risk assessment process designed to establish effective risk management that begins with communication and consultation, and includes risk identification, analysis, evaluation, treatment, monitoring, reviewing, and recording.[60] The process further allows for facility operators to cover more than one facility where appropriate and to be called a "network security assessment" or "joint security assessments" where, for example, collective facilities exist in a common geographic area serviced by common offshore service providers.[61] This approach would seem to be applicable for operators such as Woodside with the NWSV, which covers many facilities across a large geographic area. FPSOs and FSUs are required to have two sets of security assessments and plans: one when operating as an offshore facility and another when operating as a ship.[62]

The Australian and New Zealand standard[63] risk management process is essentially designed for dealing with safety and technical risks that offer a reasonable opportunity for assessing the probability of an event occurring. A significant challenge to the validity of the security risk assessment process for terrorism arises in the risk analysis phase, which is based on effective assessment of likelihood. Assessing likelihood is particularly problematic when attempting to define the prospect of a terrorist attack.

Security environment factors such as geography, known terrorist capabilities, social and cultural factors, and intelligence reports are important. However, in determining the likelihood of a terrorist event occurring, analysts are faced with the challenge of assessing the intent of actors whose actions, by reasonable standards of human behavior, are irrational and random. This means that the risk analysis process must focus more on vulnerabilities than likelihood, and risk treatment options must address vulnerability reduction. Determining priorities for managing vulnerabilities presents many challenges, and approximate judgments can often be the only option. Treatment options designed to reduce the prospect of major consequences from random events can be costly and difficult to justify to senior management. This can lead to untreated vulnerabilities presenting opportunities for terrorists. Security risk assessment against terrorism has more in common with the human uncertainties posed by political risk assessments than the safety or technical risks the prescribed process was designed to address.

Establishing the internal risk context is identified in the OSAGP as being particularly important. The major risk for organizations is failure to achieve strategic, business, or project objectives, or to manage stakeholder risks.[64] Identification of critical assets and their risk controls and treatments and stake in particular operations relative to a company's overall operations and commitments is vital.

For example, Woodside operates the NWSV, which includes two of the world's largest gas production platforms: North Rankin A (a central hub of the offshore activity) and Goodwin A, along with the *Cossack Pioneer* FPSO, connected by pipelines to onshore processing facilities at Karratha. The NWSV is a joint venture and Woodside has a 16.7 percent interest, with a 50 percent interest in the domestic gas joint venture.[65] Woodside is a relatively small oil and gas company by international standards and although it has expanding international interests, its major revenue-earning operations are in Australia. Continuing successful operation of the NWSV is therefore of critical importance to the viability of Woodside.

Chevron Australia Pty Ltd. also has a 16.7 percent equity interest in the NWSV, which is a relatively small commitment, given the size of the parent Chevron Corporation's massive global oil and gas interests. Chevron is also leading development of the Gorgon LNG Project, situated off northwest Australia, and has a 50 percent interest across the Greater Gorgon area, therefore, the internal risks to the company here are potentially higher.[66]

The OSAGP lists terrorist risk factors that should be considered when identifying offshore security risks. It advises that security risk assessments should generally be framed in the context of the current security environment[67] as outlined in the OGRCS, and with regard to State and Territory Government CI risk assessments, where applicable.

In Australia, there is a notable administrative conflict involving security alert levels that must be managed by the offshore oil and gas industry. There are four national security alert levels in the system used throughout Australia: low, medium, high, and extreme.[68] The ISPS Code specifies

Security levels 1, 2, and 3 for maritime-industry participants. Australian government regulations[69] direct that offshore security plans for operators and service providers must address security measures to be enacted for the three ISPS Code levels. The OSAGP attempts to deal with this lack of consistency by advising offshore industry participants to "readily understand the two alert systems" and presents a table showing national security alerts low and medium align with maritime security level 1, high with 2, and extreme with 3.[70]

The OSAGP recognizes that risk analyses can be qualitative, quantitative, or semiquantitative. It advises that qualitative risk analyses are sufficient for offshore oil and gas security risk assessments as they provide satisfactory indicators of risk levels,[71] which appear to be sound guidance in the circumstances. Further guidance is provided on risk categories, likelihood and consequence estimates, and risk treatments and other factors in the risk management process, along with basic templates that may assist those preparing risk assessments.

In summary, the OSAGP presents useful basic guidance for offshore security risk assessment. However, when analyzing the risks posed by international terrorism, there are some inherent and critical shortcomings in the prescribed process. Assessing vulnerabilities to terrorist attack offers greater utility than the likelihood of an attack occurring. Involvement of experienced security risk assessment professionals, knowledgeable about the offshore oil and gas sector, is necessary to ensure that effective security plans are developed and maintained.

INDUSTRY RESPONSE

The Australian government-mandated counterterrorism security arrangements have been strongly welcomed by the principal companies operating in the Australian offshore oil and gas industry. At an early stage, offshore facility operators were concerned about the potential vulnerability of their facilities to terrorist attack. However, before recent developments, they were not in a position to fully understand and assess the risks themselves, nor did they have the authority or security capabilities to effectively address the risks. Intelligence, surveillance, and response capabilities, and the authority for their employment primarily lie with Australian government agencies. Both government and industry recognize that they have vital interests in a secure oil and gas industry, and an effective partnership is required to ensure that this is provided.

Offshore industry participants are very familiar with, and in many cases deeply experienced in the application of, risk management processes. Woodside, for example, has highly developed risk management processes and a risk management culture that has long been applied across all aspects of the company's business and operations. It permeates all levels of decision making from the board to local operations. Comprehensive approaches to risk management in the oil and gas sector have been driven by the need to comply with stringent occupation health and safety (OH&S) requirements, as well as the need to address political, technical, and financial risks for projects often requiring large investment outlays.

There are, however, a number of challenges for offshore operators when dealing with security risk management. Although they may be very conversant with risk management processes and have risk treatment arrangements in place, some supporting service providers may not. For example, during construction phases of large oil and gas facilities, many contractors and large numbers of employees are engaged.[72] Ensuring adequate security controls by all participants, including the vetting of personnel in these circumstances, poses particular challenges. Setting and maintaining common security standards across the offshore and onshore oil and gas industry would require legislation with similarly powerful compliance requirements and penalties to that for OH&S in Australia; however, this is not the case as yet.

Importantly, embracing formal risk management approaches in some parts of the government sector in Australia has lagged behind industry. Oil and gas companies may find themselves interfacing with public organizations that are less proficient in risk management processes than themselves. There are also organizational culture and perception differences that have to be managed. In the

Australian case, the recent creation of several bodies that facilitate the industry–government security interface, for example, CIAC, will improve communication and understanding. Similarly, the establishment of the TISN has been an essential development as intelligence and information sharing between government and nongovernment participants is vital to counterterrorism efforts.

Although many oil and gas companies have long-standing and well-developed risk management and OH&S arrangements in place, approaches to security have been less consistently developed. Companies who operate in unstable and dangerous security environments around the world will have developed strong local security arrangements. However, companies operating in the relatively stable and secure Australian environment have not been compelled earlier to impose security measures there, other than at a low level. For example, Woodside only recently appointed a general manager security.[73] The management of security had previously been included with health and safety. Effective security against terrorism requires all participants in the security system to play their part because terrorists may attempt to exploit any weak links. Creating a security culture within companies will take time and effort, but is now recognized as an essential part of the security risk treatment process.

CONCLUSIONS

The ISPS Code and SOLAS 74 amendments have revolutionized ship and port security arrangements. Their focus is on prevention of terrorist events in the maritime domain, however, their direct application to the offshore oil and gas sector is limited. The SUA treaties apply to offshore oil and gas facilities on the continental shelf and these have recently been amended. The SUA treaties enable contracting governments to develop response mechanisms for dealing with acts or threats of terrorism by enacting criminal legislation. The inconsistency of approach by the IMO to offshore oil and gas security regulation is highlighted. This will require further consideration by the international community in coming years.

The IMO has encouraged national governments to develop security measures for offshore facilities that will not compromise the security of associated vessels. Australia, as a contracting government, has been proactive in imposing similar counterterrorism security arrangements for the offshore oil and gas sector to those for shipping and ports within its national jurisdiction.

The Australian government has developed a comprehensive set of legislation, regulations, guidelines, and mechanisms to enhance maritime security against international terrorism within a broader national counterterrorism framework. These also apply to operators and facilities in the Australian offshore oil and gas industry. A significant aspect of the Australian government–directed approach to maritime security is the application of risk assessment processes in developing mandated security plans. The approach recognizes that there must be a partnership between government and industry; however, the onus is placed on individual operators to develop complying security plans, utilizing commonly understood risk management processes.

The Australian case study presents a useful tool for analyzing the application of the ISPS Code and risk assessment processes to the offshore oil and gas industry in one national jurisdiction. Although geographical, political, cultural, and other factors will vary greatly around the world, there exists a common requirement to effectively manage the security risks to the global oil and gas industry posed by international terrorism.

NOTES

1. U.S. Government, Energy Information Administration, *International Energy Outlook 2006*, Office of Integrated Analysis and Forecasting, U.S. Department of Energy, Washington, June 2006, pp. 1, 25, and 37, available at http://www.eia.doe.gov/oiaf/ieo/index.html. IEO 2006 projections for overall energy consumption are to increase by 71 percent between 2003 and 2030, with oil demand increasing 47 percent and non-OECD Asia, including China and India accounting for 43 percent of the increase. The natural gas share of total world energy consumption is forecast to increase from 24 percent in 2003 to 26 percent in 2030.

2. International Energy Agency, *World Energy Outlook 2004*, Paris, France, 2004, pp. 33 and 129, available at http://www.iea.org//textbase/nppdf/free/2004/weo.2004.pdf.

3. *International Energy Outlook 2006*, op. cit., pp. 39–40.

4. Australian Government, *Offshore Oil & Gas Risk Context Statement*, Department of Transport and Regional Services, Canberra, April 2005, p. 5, available at http://www.infrastructure.gov.au/.

5. Australian Government, *Securing Australia's Energy Future: July 2006 Update*, Commonwealth of Australia, Canberra, 2006, p. 1, available at http://www.pmc.gov.au/initiatives/docs/energy_update_july2006.pdf.

6. Woodside Petroleum Ltd, *Concise Annual Report 2006*, p. 8, available at http://www.woodside.com.au. The first cargo to southern China was delivered in May 2006.

7. *Offshore Oil & Gas Risk Context Statement*, op. cit., p. 10.

8. Australian Government, *Transnational Terrorism: the Threat to Australia*, Commonwealth of Australia, Canberra, 2004, p. xi, available at http://www.dfat.gov.au/publications/terrorism.

9. Bergin A. and Bateman S., *Future Unknown: The Terrorist Threat to Australian Maritime Security*, The Australian Strategic Policy Institute Limited, Canberra, 2005, pp. 12–13, available at http://www.aspi.org.au/. The Philippines ferry, *Superferry 14* was sunk reportedly by a bomb that was planted in the engine room before the vessel sailed. Maritime-related terrorist attacks include attacks on the USS *Cole* in Aden in October 2000, the French tanker *Limburg* off Yemen in October 2002, and the oil refinery in Yanbu, Saudi Arabia, and the Al-Khobar Petroleum Centre, Saudi Arabia both in May 2004. One hundred and eleven people were reported confirmed dead or missing (presumed dead) from the *Superferry 14* incident.

10. IMO, *ISPS Code 2003 Edition: International Ship & Port Facility Security Code and SOLAS Amendments 2002*, London, December 9–13, 2002, Annex 1, pp. 3 and 9, available at http://www.infrastructure.gov.au/.

11. Ibid., Annex 1, pp. 6, 63, and 83.

12. Ibid., Annex 2, pp. 8–9, Conference Resolution 7.

13. IMO, *Guidance Relating to the Implementation of SOLAS Chapter XI-2 and the ISPS Code*, MSC/Circ.1097, London, June 6, 2003, available at http://www.imo.org/.

14. IMO, *Guidance Relating to the Implementation of SOLAS Chapter XI-2 and the ISPS Code*, MSC/Circ.1111, London, June 7, 2004, available at http://www.imo.org/.

15. United Nations, *Convention for the Suppression of Unlawful Acts against the Safety of Maritime Navigation* (SUA Convention), Australian Treaty Series 1993 No. 10, Australian Government Publishing Service, Canberra, 1995.

16. United Nations, *Protocol for the Suppression of Unlawful Acts against the Safety of Fixed Platforms Located on the Continental Shelf*, Australian Treaty Series 1993 No. 11, Australian Government Publishing Service, Canberra, 1995.

17. On *October 7, 1985*, four men representing the *Palestine Liberation Front* (PLF) took control of the liner off *Egypt* . They directed the vessel to sail to *Tartus, Syria*, and demanded the release of 50 *Palestinians*, then in Israeli prisons. When refused permission to dock at Tartus, the hijackers shot one passenger and threw his body overboard. The ship headed back toward Port Said, and after two days of negotiations the hijackers agreed to abandon the liner for safe conduct and were flown toward *Tunisia* aboard an *Egyptian* commercial airliner. The plane was intercepted by *U. S. Navy* fighters on *October 10* and directed to land at a *NATO* base in *Sicily*, where the hijackers were arrested by the *Italians* after a disagreement between United States and Italian authorities. Available at http://en.wikipedia.org/wiki/Achille_Lauro.

18. For example, only Singapore, Vietnam, and the Philippines (along with Australia and New Zealand) of Association of South East Asian Nations (ASEAN) had ratified SUA 1988 before 2003.

19. IMO, *Final Act of the International Conference on the Revision of the SUA Treaties*, LEG/CONF.15/23, London, October 19, 2005, available at http://www.imo.org/.

20. IMO, *Protocol of 2005 to the Convention of Unlawful Acts against the Safety of Maritime Navigation*, LEG/CONF.15/21, London, November 1, 2005, available at http://www.imo.org/.

21. IMO, *Protocol of 2005 to the Protocol for the suppression of Unlawful Acts against the Safety of Fixed Platform Located on the Continental Shelf*, LEG/CONF.15/22, London, November 1, 2005, available at http://www.imo.org/.

22. From http://www.imo.org/.

23. From IMO summary information about the SUA Convention and Protocol available at http://www.imo.org.

24. Ibid.

25. This is a summary of remarks made by Captain Hartmut Hesse, Senior Deputy Director, Sub-Division for Operational Safety and Human Element, Maritime Safety Division of the IMO, at the Port and Maritime Security and Counter-Terrorism Summit, Melbourne, Australia on April 30, 2007.

26. Australian Government, *Crimes (Ships and Fixed Platforms) Act 1992*, Act No. 173 of 1992 as amended, Commonwealth of Australia, Canberra, May 2001, available at http://www.comlaw.gov.au.

27. Chaired by the Secretary of the Department of Prime Minister and Cabinet, SCNS is the senior body of Australian Government officials advising the NSC.

28. Australian Government, *National Counter-Terrorism Plan*, Second Edition, Commonwealth of Australia, Canberra, September 2005, available on http://www.nationalsecurity.gov.au.

29. Ibid., pp. 2:2–2:3.

30. Ibid., p. 3:5.

31. Ibid.

32. Australian Government, *Protecting Australia Against Terrorism 2006: Australia's National Counter-Terrorism Policy and Arrangements*, Commonwealth of Australia, Canberra, 2006, pp. 16 and 29, available at http://www.nationalsecurity.gov.au.

33. *National Counter-Terrorism Plan*, op. cit., p. 3:6.

34. Australian Government, *Maritime Transport and Offshore Facilities Security Act 2003*, Act No 131 of 2003 as amended, Commonwealth of Australia, Canberra, 2006, available at http://www.infrastructure.gov.au/ and http://www.comlaw.gov.au.

35. Australian Government, *Maritime Transport and Offshore Facilities Security Regulations 2003*, Statutory Rules 2003 No. 366 as amended, Commonwealth of Australia, Canberra, March 27, 2007, available at http://www.infrastructure.gov.au/ and http://www.comlaw.gov.au.

36. Australian Government, *Strengthening Australia's Maritime Security: Who, what and where?* Department of Transport and Regional Services, Canberra, 2006, available at http://www.infrastructure.gov.au/.

37. *Maritime Transport and Offshore Facilities Security Act 2003*, op. cit., p. 16. "Offshore industry participant means: an offshore facility operator; a contractor who provides services to an offshore facility operator; or a person who: conducts an enterprise connected with a security regulated offshore facility; and is prescribed by the regulations."

38. Ibid., pp. 89–103.

39. Ibid., p. 101.

40. *Maritime Transport and Offshore Facilities Security Regulations 2003*, op. cit., pp. 179–180.

41. Ibid., pp. 75, 78, and 79. Details of security assessment requirements are contained in Regulations 5A.05 and 5A.45.

42. *Offshore Oil & Gas Risk Context Statement*, op. cit.

43. Australian Government, *Offshore Security Assessments Guidance Paper*, Department of Transport and Regional Services, Canberra, June 24, 2005, available at http://www.infrastructure.gov.au/.

44. *AS/NZS 4360:2004 Risk Management* and *AS/NZS HB 436:2004 (Guidelines to AS/NZS 4360:2004) Risk Management Guidelines Companion*, available through http://www.standards.com.au.

45. *Offshore Oil & Gas Risk Context Statement*, op. cit., p. 3.

46. Ibid., p. 11.

47. Ibid.

48. Ibid., p. 12.

49. Ibid., p. 14.

50. Ibid., pp. 14–20.

51. Ibid., pp. 14–16.

52. Congressional Research Service Report for Congress, *Maritime Security: Potential Terrorist Attacks and Protection Priorities*, January 9, 2007, Paul W. Parfomak and John Frittelli, Resource, Science and Industry Division, Order Code RL 33787, available at http://www.fas.org/sgp/crs/homesec/RL33787.pdf. The MV Limburg in 2002 was probably attacked by a rocket-propelled grenade fired from a small boat. The attack penetrated both its double hulls. Although the bombing killed only one member of the *Limburg's* crew, it caused insurance rates among Yemeni shippers to rise 300 percent and reduced Yemeni port shipping volumes by 50 percent in the month after the attack. The bombing also caused significant environmental damage, spilling 90,000 barrels of oil into the Gulf of Aden.

53. *Offshore Oil & Gas Risk Context Statement*, op. cit., pp. 16–18.

54. Ibid., pp. 18–19.

55. Ibid.

56. Ibid., pp. 19–20.

57. Ibid., pp. 22–23.
58. *Offshore Security Assessments Guidance Paper*, op. cit.
59. Ibid., p. 5.
60. Ibid., pp. 7–8. The nine stages of the risk process are communicate and consult, a continuous part of the process; establish the context, which includes developing the risk criteria in the context of existing controls; risk identification, what can happen, when, and where; analyse risks, estimate likelihood and consequences; evaluate risks, using an agreed risk rating scale and set priorities; treat risks, factors to reduce the likelihood or consequences of unacceptable risks; monitor and review risks, checking for effectiveness of controls; recording the risk management process, to allow for audit and review, and compliance monitoring; and establishing effective risk management, which should be the sum outcome of the whole process.
61. Ibid., p. 8. The definition of offshore service providers includes, for example, helicopter services for transporting crew or freight and supply vessels or workboat services, both of which may be normally based outside the boundary of the security-regulated offshore area.
62. Ibid.
63. *AS/NZS 4360:2004 Risk Management* and *AS/NZS HB 436:2004*, op. cit.
64. *Offshore Security Assessments Guidance Paper*, op. cit., p. 10.
65. Woodside Petroleum Ltd., *Concise Annual Report 2006*, op. cit., p. 8.
66. Chevron Corporation, *Australia Fact Sheet*, San Ramon, California, United States, updated March 7, 2007, available at http://www.chevron.com/.
67. *Offshore Security Assessments Guidance Paper*, op. cit., pp. 13–15.
68. *National Counter-Terrorism Plan*, op. cit., p. 3:2.
69. *Maritime Transport and Offshore Facilities Security Regulations 2003*, op. cit., pp. 81, 88, and 89.
70. *Offshore Security Assessments Guidance Paper*, op. cit., pp. 19–20.
71. Ibid., p. 17.
72. Construction of the fourth and fifth LNG trains at Woodside's onshore Karratha plant required thousands of additional workers, while existing parts of the plant kept operating.
73. The current general manager security at Woodside was appointed in 2005. Information is available at http://www.woodside.com.au/Profile/Executive+management.htm.

Section 3

Legal Frameworks for Maritime Security

12 The 1988 SUA Convention and 2005 SUA Protocol: Tools to Combat Piracy, Armed Robbery, and Maritime Terrorism

Robert C. Beckman

CONTENTS

INTRODUCTION

This chapter traces the development of the modern international conventions for combating piracy and armed robbery against ships and maritime terrorism. It begins with a brief analysis of the piracy provisions in the United Nations Convention on the Law of the Sea, 1982[1] (1982 Convention). It then examines the background to the development of the first United Nations (UN) terrorism convention on the safety of international maritime navigation, the Convention for the Suppression of Unlawful Acts Against the Safety of Maritime Navigation,[2] 1988 (1988 SUA Convention). It then turns to the protocol of 2005 to the Convention for the Suppression of Unlawful Acts Against the Safety of Maritime Navigation[3] (2005 SUA Protocol), which was drafted by the Legal Committee of the

This chapter was first published in *Maritime Affairs*, the journal of the National Maritime Foundation of India, Vol. 2, No. 2, Winter 2006, pp. 29–52. It is republished with the permission of that foundation and the author.

International Maritime Organization (IMO) to deal with the threat of maritime terrorism and illicit transfer of weapons of mass destruction (WMD) by sea.

At the same time that the 1988 SUA Convention was adopted, the Protocol for the Suppression of Unlawful Acts Against the Safety of Fixed Platforms Located on the Continental Shelf,[4] 1988 (1988 SUA Platforms Protocol) was adopted. Similarly, at the same time that the 2005 SUA Protocol was adopted, the Protocol of 2005 to the Protocol for the Suppression of Unlawful Acts Against the Safety of Fixed Platforms Located on the Continental Shelf[5] (2005 SUA Platforms Protocol) was adopted. Because this chapter focuses on the international conventions dealing with piracy, armed robbery against ships, and maritime terrorism involving ships, the 1988 SUA Platforms Protocol and the 2005 SUA Platforms Protocol will not be examined.

PIRACY UNDER THE 1982 CONVENTION

All states have an obligation under the 1982 Convention to cooperate to the fullest possible extent in the repression of piracy on the high seas.[6] If an attack on a ship constitutes piracy as defined in the 1982 Convention, every state has the right to seize the pirate ship, arrest the pirates, and seize the property on board.[7] This is an exception to the general principle governing jurisdiction on the high seas, which provides that ships on the high seas are subject to the exclusive jurisdiction of the flag state.[8]

Unfortunately, the rules on piracy in the 1982 Convention have not been effective in dealing with attacks on merchant ships. There are several reasons for this. The most important is that piracy under the 1982 Convention is limited to attacks on the high seas or in an exclusive economic zone.[9] Most attacks on ships take place near the coast, either when the ships are in port or at anchor, or when they are transiting in the territorial sea. Attacks on ships in these areas are classified as armed robbery against ships,[10] not piracy, and the special jurisdictional rules on piracy are not applicable. Although the Straits of Malacca and Singapore have been notorious for "piracy attacks," most of the attacks on ships in these straits are not piracy. Because the southern half of the Malacca Strait and the entire Singapore Strait are within the territorial sea of the littoral states, attacks on ships exercising transit passage in these areas must be classified as armed robbery against ships. Therefore, no state has the right to exercise police power to arrest the "pirates" involved in such attacks except the coastal state in whose territorial sea the attacks took place.

There are other problems with respect to the definition of piracy under the 1982 Convention. First, piracy must be for private ends.[11] Therefore, attacks on ships for terrorist purposes or for the purpose of supporting a separatist movement are not piracy, and the special rules on piracy do not apply. Second, piracy under the 1982 Convention requires an attack by one ship against another ship, thereby excluding cases where the passengers hijack a ship.[12]

Therefore, even though the 1982 Convention has been universally accepted, its provisions on piracy have not been effective in dealing with piracy and armed robbery against ships or acts of maritime terrorism.

BACKGROUND TO THE 1988 SUA CONVENTION

The 1988 SUA Convention[13] was prepared by the IMO in response to the 1985 hijacking of the Italian-flag cruise ship *Achille Lauro* by extremists in the Mediterranean Sea. The attack on the *Achille Lauro* demonstrated the weakness of the piracy provisions in the 1982 Convention. The problem was considered by IMO's 14th assembly in November 1985, which supported a proposal by the United States that measures to prevent such unlawful acts should be developed by the IMO.

The models that were used in drafting the new convention were the Hague Convention for the Suppression of Unlawful Seizure of Aircraft, 1970[14] (1970 Hague Convention) and the Montreal Convention for the Suppression of Unlawful Acts against the Safety of Civil Aviation, 1971[15] (1971

Montreal Convention). The 1970 Hague Convention and the 1971 Montreal Convention were the first of the UN terrorism conventions. The scheme of the 1988 SUA Convention is the same as the scheme in those two conventions. The scheme has the following features.

First, specific acts are defined in the conventions as criminal offenses, and states parties agree to make these acts criminal offenses under their domestic law punishable by serious penalties.[16] Second, states parties agree to establish jurisdiction over the offenses when they take place in their territory, when the offense takes in other places where they have criminal jurisdiction (e.g., on a ship or aircraft registered in their state), and when an alleged offender is present in their territory.[17] Third, if persons who are alleged to have committed an offense under the convention enter the territory of a state party, that state party is required to take the alleged offenders into custody,[18] and to either extradite them to another state party, or prosecute them in its courts. This is referred to as the obligation to "extradite or prosecute."[19] Fourth, states parties agree that the convention itself can serve as the legal basis for the extradition of alleged offenders to another state party, so that extradition is possible even if there is no extradition treaty between the two states parties.[20] Fifth, states parties are obligated to afford one another the greatest measure of cooperation in connection with criminal proceedings to prosecute the offenders.[21]

The rationale behind these UN terrorism conventions is simple. If all the states in a region are parties to the convention, persons who commit an offense under that convention will have no place of refuge. If they enter the territory of any state party to the convention, they will be taken into custody, and they will either be prosecuted in that state or extradited to another state party.

OFFENSES IN THE 1988 SUA CONVENTION

The offenses defined in Article 3 of the 1988 SUA Convention involve acts that endanger the safety of international maritime navigation, including

- Seizure of or exercise of control over a ship by any form of intimidation
- Violence against a person on board a ship
- Destruction of a ship or the causing of damage to a ship or to its cargo
- Placement on a ship of a device or substance that is likely to destroy or cause damage to that ship or its cargo
- Destruction of, serious damaging of, or interference with maritime navigational facilities

An important feature of the 1988 SUA Convention is that it is not limited to offenses committed on the high seas or in an exclusive economic zone. It applies to offenses committed in maritime zones under the territory sovereignty of coastal states (territorial sea and archipelagic waters) as well as in maritime zones outside the territorial sovereignty of coastal states (high seas or exclusive economic zone). The convention applies so long as the ship is scheduled to navigate beyond the limits of the territorial sea of a single state.[22] Therefore, an attack against a ship exercising the right of transit passage through the Straits of Malacca and Singapore would be an offense under the 1988 SUA Convention if the attackers seize control of the ship or use violence against a person on board the ship. Even an attack on a ship at anchor off the coast of a state would be an offense under the 1988 SUA Convention if the attackers seize control of the ship or use violence against a person on board the ship.

The 1988 SUA Convention does not contain any provisions giving additional powers to states to interdict and board ships and arrest offenders. The enforcement of the convention is dependent on coastal states arresting offenders within their territorial sea, as well as states parties arresting alleged offenders who are present in their territory. In addition, to the extent that an offense under the SUA convention also constitutes an act of piracy as defined in Article 101 of the 1982 Convention, any state could arrest and seize the pirates on the high seas or in an exclusive economic zone.[23]

STATUS OF THE 1988 SUA CONVENTION

The 1988 SUA Convention was adopted on March 10, 1988 and entered into force on March 1, 1992.[24] Despite the fact that the 1988 SUA Convention is a useful tool to combat some cases of attacks, piracy, and armed robbery against ships, states were slow to ratify it or accede to it. On December 31, 2000, there were only 52 states parties to the convention. The 52 states parties included three states from South Asia (India, Pakistan, and Sri Lanka) and two states from Northeast Asia (China and Japan). None of the Association of Southeast Asian Nations (ASEAN) countries were parties on December 31, 2000.[25]

After the attack on the World Trade Center in New York on September 11, 2001, the IMO urged its members to become parties to the 1988 SUA Convention. Consequently, the number of states parties to the 1988 SUA Convention increased significantly. On November 30, 2006 there were 142 states parties. In south Asia, four states are parties (Bangladesh, India, Pakistan, and Sri Lanka), whereas only the Maldives is not. In northeast Asia four states are parties (China, Japan, Mongolia, and South Korea), whereas only North Korea is not. Six members of ASEAN are parties (Brunei, Cambodia, Myanmar, Philippines, Singapore, and Vietnam) and four members of ASEAN are not (Indonesia, Laos, Malaysia, and Thailand). Unfortunately, three of the states that are not parties border the piracy-prone Malacca Strait—Indonesia, Malaysia, and Thailand.[26]

SYSTEM OF COMPULSORY BINDING DISPUTE SETTLEMENT

The 1988 SUA Convention contains a procedure for the settlement of disputes between states parties concerning the interpretation or application of the convention. Article 16(1) provides that if the dispute cannot be settled by negotiation within a reasonable time, it shall at the request of one of the states parties to the dispute, be submitted to arbitration. If, within six months from the date of the request for arbitration, the parties are unable to agree on the organization of the arbitration, any one of those states parties may refer the dispute to the International Court of Justice.

Article 16(2) permits states to formally declare to the IMO secretary general that they wish to opt out of the compulsory binding dispute settlement system in Article 16(1). Four states in Asia (China, India, Myanmar, and Vietnam) have made formal declarations stating that they do not consider themselves bound by Article 16(1) on dispute settlement.[27] Therefore, any dispute concerning the interpretation or application of the convention involving any of these four states will not be subject to the system of compulsory binding dispute settlement in Article 16(1).

CASES WHERE THE 1988 SUA CONVENTION WOULD BE USEFUL

If all of the states in the region were parties to the 1988 SUA Convention, attacks on ships in the region that involve violence or the takeover of a ship would be offenses under the convention, and the flag state and the state in whose territorial sea the attack took place would both have jurisdiction over the offense. If the perpetrators entered the territory of another state party, that state would also have jurisdiction over the offense. The 1988 SUA Convention would cover the most serious type of attack on ships—planned activities by international organized crime syndicates to "hijack" merchant ships for the purpose of stealing the ship as well as its cargo.

An example of an incident is the hijacking of the *MV Petro Ranger* in April 1998. The *Petro Ranger* was owned by a Singapore national and was flying the flag of Malaysia. While enroute from Singapore to Vietnam with a cargo of diesel fuel, it was attacked by Indonesians off the coast of Malaysia. While at sea, the cargo was transferred to another ship. The *MV Petro Ranger* was reflagged as a Honduran ship and renamed the *MV Wilby*. The hijacked ship then proceeded to Hainan, China. The Chinese authorities arrested the "pirates" for smuggling, but they were released after only a few months in jail. At the time of the hijacking of the *MV Petro Ranger*, China was a party to the 1988 SUA Convention, but Malaysia and Indonesia were not. If Malaysia had been a state party, it could have demanded that China take the alleged offenders into custody and either prosecute them for an offense under the SUA Convention or extradite them to Malaysia. If Indonesia had also been a state party, it would have been under an obligation to give assistance to the prosecuting state in connection with the criminal proceedings, including assistance in obtaining evidence at their disposal necessary for the proceedings.[28] However, if a dispute had arisen between China and either Malaysia or Indonesia concerning the interpretation or application of the convention, the dispute would not be subject to compulsory binding dispute settlement under Article 16(1) because China has officially declared that it does not consider itself bound by Article 16(1).

The *MV Alondra Rainbow* incident[29] is another case where the 1988 SUA Convention would have been applicable if all the states concerned had been states parties at the time of the incident. The *MV Alondra Rainbow* was owned by a Japanese and was flying a Panama flag. It was hijacked off the coast of Indonesia in the Malacca Strait. Acting on information provided by the Piracy Reporting Centre of the International Maritime Bureau (IMB), India interdicted, boarded, and arrested the pirates in its exclusive economic zone. The seizure by the Indian authorities of the ship in its exclusive economic zone was lawful under international law either because the ship was a pirate ship or because the ship was stateless, as it was not registered in the state whose flag it was flying when it was intercepted. The pirates were charged and convicted in India for several offenses under the penal code. If India had been a party to the 1988 SUA Convention at the time of the incident, the pirates could have been charged under one of the offenses set out in the 1988 SUA Convention. Also, if Indonesia had been a state party to the 1988 SUA Convention at the time of the incident, Indonesia would have been under a legal obligation to cooperate with India in connection with the criminal proceedings against the pirates under the 1988 SUA Convention.

BACKGROUND TO THE 2005 SUA PROTOCOL

After the 9/11 attacks, the IMO adopted Assembly Resolution A.924(22)[30] calling for a review of the existing measures and procedures to prevent acts of terrorism that threaten the security of passengers and crews and the safety of ships. In October 2001, the Legal Committee of the IMO decided to review the 1988 SUA Convention (and the 1988 SUA Protocol) in the wake of the terrorist attack on the United States. The Legal Committee agreed to include the review of the SUA Convention as a priority item in its work program.[31]

In April 2002, the Legal Committee agreed to establish a Correspondence Group led by United States with the short-term aim of developing a working paper on the scope of possible amendments for consideration at the 85th session of the Legal Committee in October 2003. The longer-term aim was to draft the amendments and make a recommendation to the IMO Assembly that it convene an international diplomatic conference to consider and adopt amendments to the 1988 SUA Convention.[32] All states and interested international organizations were invited to participate in the work of the group.

The delegation of the United States, as lead country for the Correspondence Group, prepared and introduced a document containing draft amendments to the 1988 SUA Convention. Among the most important amendments proposed by the United States were the following: (1) the addition of seven new offenses into Article 3 of the 1988 SUA convention, four of which were concerned with activities taking place on the ship or directed toward the ship that involve a terrorist purpose and (2) new provisions permitting the boarding and search of a suspect ship by law-enforcement officials of another when such ship is in international waters (located seaward of any state's territorial sea), and is reasonably suspected of being involved in, or reasonably believed to be the target of, acts prohibited in Article 3 of the Convention.[33]

The Legal Committee continued to work on a revised draft protocol prepared by the Correspondence Group over the next three years. The Correspondence Group received comments and suggestions from numerous states and organizations that participate in the work of the IMO. Most delegations expressed support for the revision. However, concerns were expressed that the draft boarding provisions should not intrude into the principles of freedom on navigation on the high seas and the exclusive jurisdiction of flag states over their vessels on the high seas.[34] Delegations also stated that the SUA protocol must not impinge on the operation of international commercial shipping. The two articles that were the subject of major debate and disagreement were Article 3*bis*, which sets out new offenses to be added to the convention, and Article 8*bis*, which establishes new provisions for the boarding and search of suspect ships.

After three years of study and deliberation, the Legal Committee completed its work at its 90th session in April 2005.[35] An International Conference on the Revision of the SUA Treaties (2005 Conference) was held in October 2005 to adopt amendments to the 1988 SUA Convention (and to the 1988 SUA Platforms Protocol). The 2005 SUA Protocol was formally adopted at the 2005 Conference on October 14, 2005.[36]

The 2005 SUA Protocol will enter into force 90 days after the date on which 12 states formally ratify or accept it by giving official notice to the IMO secretary general of their consent to be bound by its provisions.[37] To become a party to the 2005 SUA Protocol, a state must first become a party to the 1988 SUA Convention.[38] As of March 31, 2008, only two states have ratified the 2005 SUA Pratocol.

Articles 1–16 of the 1988 SUA Convention, as revised by the 2005 SUA Protocol, together with Articles 17–24 of the 2005 SUA Protocol and its annex, are to constitute and be called the Convention for the Suppression of Unlawful Acts against the Safety of Maritime Navigation, 2005.[39]

NEW CATEGORIES OF OFFENSES IN THE 2005 SUA PROTOCOL

One of the significant aspects of the 2005 SUA Protocol is that it broadens the list of offenses by adding three categories of new offenses.

The first category of new offenses concerns acts of maritime terrorism such as using a ship as a weapon or as a means to carry out a terrorist attack.[40] These new offenses require a specific knowledge and intent. They also require a "terrorist motive"—the purpose of the acts must be to intimidate a population or compel a government to do or abstain from doing an act.[41] These new offenses update the categories of acts that might endanger the safety of ships engaged in international maritime navigation.

The second category of new offenses are nonproliferation offenses that are intended to strengthen the international legal basis to impede and prosecute the trafficking on the high seas in commercial ships of WMD, their delivery systems, and related materials. The nonproliferation provisions require states parties to criminalize transport on the high seas of WMD and certain related materials, as well as nuclear material and equipment.[42] This category of new offenses goes beyond the scope of the 1988 SUA Convention, which dealt only with acts that threaten the safety of maritime navigation. It establishes a new tool to combat the proliferation of WMD. The United States justified the inclusion of this category of offenses by pointing out that it was a response to the measures called for in UN Security Council Resolution 1540 on the nonproliferation of WMD.[43] The offense for trafficking in WMD or related materials on the high seas requires certain "knowledge and intent." However, no "terrorist motive" is required because the proliferation offenses are intended to cover the proliferation of WMD by sea for profit as well as for terrorist purposes.

The third category of new offenses establishes a new tool for dealing with persons who commit offenses under the other UN terrorism conventions. It makes it an offense to transport any person by sea who has committed an offense under the 1988 SUA Convention, the 2005 SUA Protocol, or any of the other UN terrorism conventions when intending to assist that person to evade criminal prosecution.[44] This category of offenses also goes beyond the scope of the 1988 SUA Convention, which was focused exclusively on acts that endangered the safety of maritime navigation. This offense also requires specific "knowledge and intent" to ensure that innocent seafarers and masters are not made criminals. The UN terrorism conventions concerned are listed in an annex. The list is as follows:

1. Convention for the Suppression of Unlawful Seizure of Aircraft, done at The Hague on December 16, 1970
2. Convention for the Suppression of Unlawful Acts against the Safety of Civil Aviation, done at Montreal on September 23, 1971

3. Convention on the Prevention and Punishment of Crimes against Internationally Protected Persons, including Diplomatic Agents, adopted by the General Assembly of the UN on December 14, 1973

4. International Convention against the Taking of Hostages, adopted by the General Assembly of the UN on December 17, 1979

5. Convention on the Physical Protection of Nuclear Material, done at Vienna on October 26, 1979

6. Protocol for the Suppression of Unlawful Acts of Violence at Airports Serving International Civil Aviation, supplementary to the Convention for the Suppression of Unlawful Acts against the Safety of Civil Aviation, done at Montreal on February 24, 1988

7. Protocol for the Suppression of Unlawful Acts against the Safety of Fixed Platforms Located on the Continental Shelf, done at Rome on March 10, 1988

8. International Convention for the Suppression of Terrorist Bombings, adopted by the General Assembly of the UN on December 15, 1997

9. International Convention for the Suppression of the Financing of Terrorism, adopted by the General Assembly of the UN on December 9, 1999

A provision is included to allow new UN terrorism conventions to be added to the list in the annex.[45] Also, if any state is not a party to any of the UN terrorism conventions listed in the annex, it may declare that in the application of the 2005 SUA Protocol to it, that convention shall be deemed not to be included in the list.[46]

CONTROVERSIES RELATING TO THE NEW OFFENSES

One of the main goals of the international shipping organizations and major flag states was to ensure that the new offenses were not so broadly worded that they would make innocent masters and seafarers criminals for carrying particular items or persons. For this reason, the knowledge and intent provisions were carefully scrutinized and debated. International shipping organizations such as the International Chamber of Shipping, International Association of Independent Tanker Owners (INTERTANKO), and The Baltic and International Maritime Council (BIMCO) made representations to the Legal Committee. On September 20, 2005 the United States and the International Confederation of Free Trade Unions (ICTFU) submitted comments on the provisions of the draft protocol, pointing out how the final draft of the new offenses incorporated provisions on knowledge and intent, which would ensure that the interests of innocent seafarers and carriers were protected.[47]

The new offenses relating to nonproliferation provoked much controversy and debate in the Legal Committee. Some delegations expressed concern about the scope of the nuclear materials offense, the definition of "transport," and the definition of "dual-use" items in the transport offense. The final language with respect to dual-use is the result of multiple rounds of intense discussions in which various proposals were considered and debated. The United States maintains that the language in the final document is consistent with UN Security Council Resolution 1540 and the international nonproliferation treaties.[48]

The consistency of the new offenses with the international nonproliferation treaties was another subject of controversy. The final draft contains a "savings clause" in Article 3*bis* 2 that is intended to preserve the right of persons in the states parties to the Non-Proliferation Treaty[49] (NPT) to transport nuclear and nuclear-related dual-use items consistent with the NPT. The savings clause in Article 2*bis* 3 is intended to provide that the provisions creating offenses preserve the rights and obligations of parties to the biological weapons convention[50] and chemical weapons convention.[51] Therefore, the nonproliferation offenses are intended to be consistent with existing international NPTs, as the savings clauses provide that the provisions do not affect the rights, obligations, and responsibilities of states under international law and the NPTs.[52]

India objected to the NPT savings clause on the ground that it discriminates against the handful of non-NPT states because it would not protect nuclear commerce among those states. The United States responded to this point as follows:

> One delegation has argued that the NPT savings clause discriminates against the handful of non-NPT States because it would not protect nuclear commerce among those States (document LEG/CONF.15/12) refers.) However, the savings clause would protect nuclear commerce between that handful of States and all NPT Parties, so long as the nuclear material, if destined for a non-NPT Party, will be under IAEA safeguards in that country, as required in the NPT, or if from a non-NPT Party, so long as the recipient NPT Party complied with its NPT obligations in regard to that material. Moreover, the savings clause would not criminalize nuclear commerce among the handful of non-NPT States that was concluded aboard non-SUA ships, or by air.[53]

India was not satisfied with this statement, and made its objections known at the conference. It submitted a formal statement to the 2005 Conference explaining why it was not able to join the consensus on the draft protocol because its concerns had not been addressed. It requested that its statement be circulated and its reservations recorded in the official documents of the 2005 Conference. On the point about discrimination against non-NPT parties, India made the following point in its statement:

> We have also expressed, at this Diplomatic Conference as well as in the past meetings, our concerns related to the proposed Article 3*bis* 2 (Savings Clause). This article curtails the rights of a State not Party to the NPT to pursue peaceful uses of nuclear energy and to transport including on its own civil/commercial vessels, nuclear or nuclear-related dual-use materials for peaceful purposes. This is clearly a discriminatory and exclusive provision and we cannot accept it. Since nuclear energy is a safe, secure and environmentally clean source of energy, it is a vital component for meeting the developmental needs of a large and growing economy like ours. We are committed to exploring its full potential for peaceful purposes.[54]

Pakistan, a second nuclear state that is not a party to the NPT, expressed similar concerns as India at the 2005 Conference. It stated that it could not accept the NPT-related obligations that are reflected in the 2005 SUA Protocol. Like India, Pakistan requested that the statement setting out is position by circulated as an official document of the 2005 Conference.[55]

BOARDING PROVISIONS

The most significant and most controversial aspect of the 2005 SUA Protocol is that it introduces provisions for the boarding of ships seaward of the outer limit of the territorial sea (on the high seas or in an exclusive economic zone) where there are reasonable grounds to suspect that the ship or a person on board the ship is, has been, or is about to be, involved in the commission of an offense under the 2005 SUA Protocol.

The boarding provisions in Article 8*bis* were controversial because they establish a new mechanism for enforcing a UN terrorism convention. Most states accepted the need for a provision allowing suspect vessels to be boarded and searched on the high seas, but many insisted that the provision be narrowly drafted, and that it contain detailed safeguards to prevent abuse. States also maintained that any new boarding provisions must be consistent with the 1982 Convention, and must not infringe either the rights or jurisdiction of coastal states in their territorial sea or the principle that ships on the high seas are subject to the exclusive jurisdiction of the flag state. As a result, Article 8*bis* went through numerous drafts and substantial revisions, as the United States, as the head of the Correspondence Group, which prepared the draft, attempted to meet the concerns for safeguards and consistency with the 1982 Convention.

The boarding provisions that were eventually agreed upon in Article 8*bis* are consistent with the 1982 Convention. Boarding can only take place seaward of the outer limits of any state's territorial sea (on the high seas or in an exclusive economic zone), and only with the express consent of the flag state. Also, if the flag State does decide to give its consent to the boarding, it may impose conditions on the boarding state.[56]

Many states and organizations argued that the new boarding provisions must not unduly interfere with the economic interests of flag states and ship owners or with the rights of seafarers. As a result, the new boarding provisions contain the most comprehensive set of "safeguards" ever included in any international agreement of this nature. Among the safeguards are the following:

- Use of force must be avoided except when necessary to ensure the safety of its officials and persons on board or where the officials are obstructed in the execution of authorized actions, and any use of force must not exceed the minimum necessary and reasonable in the circumstances.[57]
- The boarding state must take into account the dangers and difficulties involved in boarding a ship at sea.[58]
- The boarding state must take due account of the need not to endanger the safety of life at sea and of the safety and security of the ship and its cargo,[59] and must take reasonable steps to avoid a ship being unduly detained or delayed.[60]
- The boarding state take due account of the need not to prejudice the commercial and legal interests of the flag state,[61] and must advise the master of its intention to board and afford him the opportunity to contact the owner and the flag state.[62]
- For all boardings, the flag state retains the right to exercise jurisdiction over a detained ship, cargo, or other items and over persons, including seizure, forfeiture, arrest, and prosecution.[63]
- The boarding state is liable for damage, harm, or loss attributable to it when the grounds for the boarding prove to be unfounded or when the measures taken are unlawful or exceed those reasonably required in the circumstances.[64]

The boarding provisions also contain safeguards relating to human rights and protection of the environment. The boarding state must ensure that all persons on board are treated in accordance with international human rights law.[65] Also, the boarding state must ensure that any measure taken with regard to the ship and its cargo is environmentally sound under the circumstances.[66]

Given the comprehensive safeguards, there is little likelihood that the boarding provisions will be open to abuse by the major powers. In fact, if all the states in a region were to become parties to the 2005 SUA Protocol, it would ensure that boardings, if authorized, will be conducted according to procedures that afford appropriate protections to flag states, seafarers, and carriers.

CONTROVERSIES RELATING TO THE BOARDING PROVISIONS

One provision in the original draft submitted by the United States that caused particular concern was a "tacit authorization" provision. The original U.S. draft of Article 8*bis* provided that if the authorities in the flag state do not respond within four hours to a request from law-enforcement officers to take appropriate measures, the law-enforcement officers may proceed to board and search the suspect ship.[67] This provision providing for "tacit authorization" to board and search if there is no objection within four hours generated much discussion and debate.

The tacit authorization provision was included by the United States because there are a small minority of flag states that do not carry out their obligations or responsibilities as flag states seriously, and it may not be possible to contact the appropriate authorities in such flag states within a reasonable amount of time. It argued that the tacit authorization provision was the best way to deal with this problem. However, the clause met serious opposition because states felt it would erode the exclusive jurisdiction of flag states over their ships on the high seas. In the end, it proved so controversial that it was dropped. States were simply unwilling to create a new exception to the general principle that ships on the high seas are subject to the exclusive jurisdiction of the flag state. Therefore, the final version of Article 8*bis* does not deal with the problem identified by the United States. If a flag state fails to respond to a request to verify the flag of a suspect ship, boarding is not permissible, because boarding can only take place with the express consent of the flag state.[68]

The 2005 SUA Protocol contains two provisions permitting states parties to declare in advance that they authorize the boarding of ships flying their flag under certain conditions. First, a state party can submit a declaration to the IMO secretary general authorizing boarding and search by another state party of a ship flying its flag when the boarding state has reasonable grounds to suspect that the ship or a person on board the ship is, has been, or is about to be, involved in the commission of an offense under the 2005 SUA Protocol.[69] Second, state parties can submit a declaration to the IMO secretary general authorizing the boarding and searching of ships flying their flag by another state party if they fail to respond within four hours to a request to verify the registration of a vessel flying their flag.[70] Because these are "opt in" provisions that apply only if the state party declares that it accepts them, they were not controversial.

PROVISIONS FOR UPDATING SUA IN THE LIGHT OF OTHER TERRORISM CONVENTIONS

The 2005 SUA Protocol also contains provisions designed to update the 1988 SUA Convention so that its provisions are consistent with those in the recent UN terrorism conventions, including the International Convention for the Suppression of the Financing of Terrorism,[71] 1999, and the International Convention for the Suppression of Terrorist Bombings,[72] 1997. First, the savings clauses in Article 2*bis* (1) and (2) were added to provide that nothing in this convention shall affect other rights, obligations, and responsibilities of states and individuals under international law, and to provide that the convention does not apply to the activities of armed forces during an armed conflict. Second, Article 3*quater* was added to update the provision on accessories to offenses. Third, Article 5*bis* was added to provide that legal entities other than persons might be liable for offenses. Fourth, Article 11*bis* was added to make it expressly clear that extradition may not be refused on the grounds that it was a political offense. Fifth, Article 11*ter* was added to allow the requested state to deny a request for extradition or for mutual legal assistance in specific circumstances. Finally, Article 12*bis* was added to the mutual legal assistance provisions regarding the testimony of prisoners.

RELATIONSHIP TO THE PROLIFERATION SECURITY INITIATIVE

It should be noted that the 2005 SUA Protocol is consistent with the U.S.-led proliferation security initiative (PSI)[73] and is complementary to it. The 2005 SUA Protocol specifically provides that state parties may conclude agreements or arrangements between them to facilitate law-enforcement operations carried out under the boarding provisions.[74] The PSI would arguably be such an arrangement. In addition, the 2005 SUA Protocol specifically provides that state parties are encouraged to develop standard operating procedures (SOPs) for joint operations and to consult with other states with a view to harmonizing SOPs.[75]

The link between the PSI and the boarding provisions in the 2005 SUA Protocol could be a very significant development. The PSI statement of interdiction principles is very general.[76] The United States has negotiated bilateral ship boarding agreements with several of the major flag states,[77] but the safeguards in Article 8*bis* are much more extensive than in the bilateral agreements. Therefore, if states cooperating in the PSI used the procedures for boarding that are set out in Article 8*bis* as their SOPs, it would ensure that any interdictions and boardings under the PSI follow common procedures that contain extensive safeguards. This would alleviate some of the concerns in certain states that interdictions and boardings under the PSI might be abused.

This link between the interdiction and boarding procedures in Article 8*bis* and the PSI could develop independent of the process of ratification or accession to the 2005 SUA Protocol. If states participating in the PSI and states cooperating with the PSI were to follow the procedures and safeguards in Article 8*bis* as SOPs under PSI, Article 8*bis* procedures could be incorporated into the PSI through practice. This would be a very positive development.

CONCLUSIONS

The 1988 SUA Convention and the 1988 SUA Protocol create offenses and cooperative arrangements for combating acts that endanger the safety of maritime navigation. The 1988 SUA Convention is a useful tool to combat the hijacking of ships by international organized crime groups. It is also a useful tool for combating attacks on ships involving violence against persons on board the ship when the offenders are present in the territory of another state party. However, the effectiveness of the 1988 SUA Convention depends upon all of the states within a region becoming parties.

States were slow to become parties to the 1988 SUA Convention. However, the 9/11 attacks made the international community realize that further measures must be taken to ensure the safety of international maritime navigation. One result was that the number of states parties to the 1988 SUA Convention increased dramatically. At the same time, the IMO initiated measures to update the 1988 SUA Convention in light of the increased threat of maritime terrorism.

After three difficult years of negotiation with active participation from many member states of the IMO, the 2005 SUA Protocol was adopted. It creates important new offenses to deal with the threat of maritime terrorism and the illicit transport of WMD by sea. In addition, it creates a new offense for the illegal transport of fugitives by sea who are accused of violating any of the UN terrorism conventions. The new offenses were the subject of long and difficult negotiations to ensure that they did not make criminals of innocent masters and seafarers or infringe on the rights and obligations of states under other conventions such as the NPT, the Biological Weapons Treaty and the Chemical Weapons Treaty. The new offenses expand the scope of the 1988 SUA Convention, but the mental element required for the transport offenses is such that innocent masters and seafarers should be protected.

The 2005 SUA Protocol contains new boarding provisions that create an important new mechanism to combat maritime terrorism and the illicit transport of WMD by sea. The new boarding provisions were the subject of intense negotiations over a period of three years. The provisions that were finally agreed upon are consistent with the 1982 Convention and with the principles of international law governing ships on the high seas.

The boarding provisions in the 2005 SUA Protocol are significant for several reasons. First, they demonstrate that the international community is very reluctant to create new exceptions to the principle of flag state jurisdiction on the high seas. Article 8*bis* provides that suspect ships on the high seas or in an exclusive economic zone can only be boarded with the express consent of the flag state. Second, they include extensive safeguards that are designed to facilitate the boarding of suspect ships whereas at the same time protecting the interests of seafarers, carriers, and flag states. The elaborate procedures and safeguards are likely to serve as a model for future international agreements relating to the boarding of ships on the high seas. Third, there is a possibility that the boarding procedures and safeguards set out in Article 8*bis* will become the SOPs for cooperative arrangements like the PSI on the interdiction and boarding of ships. They may also have an impact on the kinds of safeguards flag states will insist upon if there is a request to board one of their ships that is suspected of carrying materials in violation of the UN Security Council Resolution on North Korea.[78]

As the IMO secretary general Efthimios E. Mitropoulos made it clear in his statement at the close of the conference, early acceptance of the 2005 SUA Protocol should be a priority for all states. He stated that

The usual request for States to become Parties to any new IMO treaty is, in the case of the two Protocols adopted today, an urgent plea, the importance of which, beyond any doubt, is clearly understood by all.

We are running a race against time in our efforts to prevent and suppress unlawful acts against the safety of maritime navigation and to bring to justice the perpetrators of the unlawful acts covered by the 2005 SUA Protocols. Early entry into force of the Protocols is therefore of the essence. And, while early deposits of instruments of ratification will send a strong message that the maritime community is eager and willing to protect the industry against acts of terrorism, on the other hand, any delays in so doing will send a wrong signal to all those who, at this time, are profiting from the present legal vacuum which the Protocols aim to fill.[79]

All states should give a high priority to the ratification and implementation of the 2005 SUA Protocol. Even states such as India and Pakistan that have problems with the provisions relating to states not parties to the NPT, should seriously consider acceding to the 2005 SUA Protocol. India and Pakistan might consider making a reservation regarding the provisions that they believe do not adequately address their concerns. This is because the success of the 1988 SUA Convention and the 2005 SUA Protocol depends to a large extent on their becoming universally accepted by the leading states in the region.

There are still situations where the 2005 SUA Protocol will be of no assistance in combating maritime terrorism at sea. Because no exception was made to the principle of flag state jurisdiction, suspect ships cannot be boarded without the express consent of the flag state. The so-called rogue states who are most likely to engage in activities contrary to the 2005 SUA Protocol are not likely to become parties to it. Therefore, in the end, what the 2005 SUA Protocol will do is to create expedited procedures for the boarding of suspect ships on the high seas among states with common interests in combating activities such as piracy, armed robbery against ships, and maritime terrorism.

NOTES

1. Adopted in Montego Bay on December 10, 1982, entered into force on November 16, 1994. As of November 8, 2006, there are 152 states parties to the convention. Text and status are available online at http://www.un.org/Depts/los/index.htm.
2. Adopted in Rome on March 10, 1988, entered into force on March 1, 1992. For text, see Australian Treaty Series 1993 No. 10, http://www.austlii.edu.au/au/other/dfat/treaties/1993/10.html.
3. Adopted in London on October 14, 2005 [2005] ATNIF 30, For text, see http://www.austlii.edu.au/au/other/dfat/treaties/notinforce/2005/30.html.
4. Adopted in Rome on March 10, 1988, entered into force on March 1, 1992. For text, see Australian Treaty Series 1993, No. 11, http://www.austlii.edu.au/au/other/dfat/treaties/1993/11.html.
5. Adopted in London, October 14, 2005 [2005] ATNIF 31, For text, see http://www.austlii.edu.au/au/other/dfat/treaties/notinforce/2005/31.html.
6. Article 100, 1982 Convention, *supra* note 1.
7. Article 105, 1982 Convention, *supra* note 1.
8. Article 92, 1982 Convention, *supra* note 1.
9. Articles 101 and 58(2), 1982 Convention, Ibid. Article 101 refers to acts on high seas. Article 58(2) provides that the provisions on piracy also apply in the exclusive economic zone.
10. The term "armed robbery against ships" is used by the United Nations when referring to attacks on ships in areas within the territorial sovereignty of coastal States. For information, see the IMO home page on "piracy and armed robbery against ships," www.imo.org.
11. Article 101, 1982 Convention, *supra* note 1.
12. Ibid.
13. *Supra* note 2.
14. Adopted at the Hague on December 16, 1970, entered into force on October 14, 1971. For text, see Australian Treaty Series 1972, No. 16, http://www.austlii.edu.au/au/other/dfat/treaties/1972/16.html.
15. Adopted in Montreal on September 23, 1971, entered into force on January 26, 1973. For text, see Australian Treaty Series 1973, No. 24, http://www.austlii.edu.au/au/other/dfat/treaties/1973/24.html.
16. Article 3, 1988 SUA Convention, *supra* note 2.
17. Article 6, 1988 SUA Convention, *supra* note 2.
18. Article 7, 1988 SUA Convention, *supra* note 2.

19. Article 10, 1988 SUA Convention, *supra* note 2.
20. Article 11, 1988 SUA Convention, *supra* note 2.
21. Article 12, 1988 SUA Convention, *supra* note 2.
22. Article 4, 1988 SUA Convention, *supra* note 2.
23. S*upra* note 9.
24. Article 18 provides that it enters into force 90 days after the 15ht state deposits an instrument of ratification or accession or otherwise expresses its consent to be bound.
25. Status of multilateral conventions and instruments in respect of which the IMO or its secretary general performs depositary or other functions, as at December 31, 2000, pp. 319–326.
26. Status of IMO conventions is available online at the IMO home page. See www.imo.org.
27. Declarations submitted by states are also available online at the IMO home page under "Conventions." See www.imo.org.
28. Article 12(1), 1988 SUA Convention, *supra* note 2.
29. This case is well known in India. Information on this incident is available on the Internet by searching the name of the ship.
30. Assembly Resolution A.924(22), Review of Measures and Procedures to Prevent Acts of Terrorism which Threaten the Security of Passengers and Crews and the Safety of Ships, adopted on November 20, 2001.
31. IMO Legal Committee, 83rd Session, October 8–12, 2001. A summary of the work of the Legal Committee is available on the IMO home page under Committees. See www.imo.org.
32. IMO Legal Committee, 84th Session, April 22-26, 2002. Ibid.
33. IMO Legal Committee, 85th Session, October 21-25, 2002.
34. IMO Legal Committee, 88th Session, April 19-23, 2004.
35. IMO Legal Committee, 90th Session, April 18-29, 2005.
36. 2005 SUA Protocol, s*upra* note 3.
37. Article 18, 2005 SUA Protocol, *supra* note 3.
38. Article 17(4), 2005 SUA Protocol, *supra* note 3.
39. Article 15(2), 2005 SUA Protocol, *supra* note 3.
40. Article 3*bis* (1)(a), 2005 SUA Protocol. *supra* note 3.
41. Ibid.
42. Article 3*bis* (1)(b), 2005 SUA Protocol, *supra* note 3.
43. Security Council Resolution 1540, adopted on April 28, 2004.
44. Article 3*ter*, 2005 SUA Protocol, *supra* note. 3
45. Article 22, 2005 SUA Protocol, *supra* note 3.
46. Article 21, 2005 SUA Protocol, *supra* note 3.
47. LEG/CONF.15/14, Comments on the protections afforded to the shipping industry, September 20, 2005.
48. LEG/CONF.15/15, Comments on counter-terrorism, non-proliferation and boarding provisions, submitted by the United States, September 22, 2005.
49. Treaty on the Non-Proliferation of Nuclear Weapons, done at Washington, London and Moscow on July 1, 1968, entered into force on March 5, 1970. For text, see Australian Treaty Series 1973, No. 3, http://www.austlii.edu.au/au/other/dfat/treaties/1973/3.html.
50. Convention on the Prohibition of the Development, Production and Stockpiling of Bacteriological (Biological) and Toxin Weapons and on their Destruction, done at Washington, London, and Moscow on April 10, 1972, entered into force on March 26, 1975. For text, see Australian Treaty Series 1977, No. 23, http://www.austlii.edu.au/au/other/dfat/treaties/1977/23.html.
51. Convention on the Prohibition of the Development, Production, Stockpiling, and Use of Chemical Weapons and their Destruction, done at Paris on January 13, 1993, entered into force on April 29, 1997. For text, see Australian Treaty Series 1997, No. 3, http://www.austlii.edu.au/au/other/dfat/treaties/1997/3.html.
52. Comments on counter-terrorism, *supra* note 48.
53. Ibid., paragraph 15.
54. LEG/CONF.15/19, Statement by India, November 15, 2005.
55. LEG/CONF.15/20, Statement by Pakistan, November 15, 2005.
56. Article 8*bis* (5) (c), 2005 SUA Protocol, *supra* note 3.
57. Article 8*bis* (9), 2005 SUA Protocol, *supra* note 3.
58. Article 8*bis* (c), 2005 SUA Protocol, *supra* note 3.

59. Article 8*bis* (10) (a) (iv), 2005 SUA Protocol, *supra* note 3.
60. Article 8*bis* (10) (a) (ix), 2005 SUA Protocol, *supra* note 3.
61. Article 8*bis* (10) (a) (v), 2005 SUA Protocol, *supra* note 3.
62. Article 8*bis* (10)(a)(viii), 2005 SUA Protocol, *supra* note 3.
63. Article 8*bis* (8), 2005 SUA Protocol, *supra* note 3.
64. Article 8*bis* (10)(b), 2005 SUA Protocol, *supra* note 3.
65. Article 8*bis* (10)(a)(ii), 2005 SUA Protocol, *supra* note 3.
66. Article 8*bis* (10)(a)(vi), 2005 SUA Protocol, *supra* note 3.
67. Article 8*bis*, paragraph 3, LEG 88/3, Annex I, February 13, 2004.
68. Article 8*bis* (5)(c), 2005 SUA Protocol, supra note 3.
69. Article 8*bis* (5)(d), 2005 SUA Protocol, *supra* note 3.
70. Article 8*bis* (5)(e), 2005 SUA Protocol, *supra* note 3.
71. Adopted in New York, December 9, 1999, entered into force, April 1, 2002. For text, see Australian Treaty Series 2002, No. 23, http://www.austlii.edu.au/au/other/dfat/treaties/2002/23.html.
72. Adopted in New York, December 15, 1997, entered into force, May 23, 2001. For text, see Australian Treaty Series 2002, No. 17, http://www.austlii.edu.au/au/other/dfat/treaties/2002/17.html.
73. For information on the PSI, see the United States State Department web site at http://www.state.gov/t/np/c10390.htm.
74. Article 8*bis* (13), 2005 SUA Protocol, *supra* note 3.
75. Article 8*bis* (12), 2005 SUA Protocol, *supra* note 3.
76. For the text of the principles, see http://www.state.gov/t/isn/rls/fs/23764.htm.
77. The texts of the U.S. bilateral ship-boarding agreements are available on the U.S. State Department web page at http://www.state.gov/t/np/c12386.htm.
78. Security Council Resolution 1718, adopted on October 14, 2006. The text is available on the UN home page at http://www.un.org/Docs/sc/unsc_resolutions06.htm.
79. IMO Press Briefing No. 42, October 17, 2005. Available on home page of IMO at www.imo.org.

13 Interdiction and Boarding of Vessels at Sea: New Developments and Old Problems

Stuart Kaye

CONTENTS

INTRODUCTION

The practical aspects of maritime security consist of many elements including port security measures, vessel monitoring, intelligence collection, and cooperation. One aspect of maritime security that is an essential element, which regardless of other developments can never be entirely dispensed with, is the interdiction and boarding of vessels. There will always be a necessity on the part of governmental vessels to intercept, board, and bring under control ships at sea. This chapter considers the relevant international law to the interdiction and boarding of vessels at sea, including some recent developments designed to widen the circumstances where a boarding might take place.

The law of the sea has traditionally not been sympathetic to measures toward the interdiction of vessels other than that of the flag state, except in extremely limited circumstances. The grundnorm point is the basic principle of noninterference with vessels at sea, unless they are flying your state's flag or have engaged in behavior giving rise to universal jurisdiction, such as piracy or the slave trade. This has been the situation for many years, as is borne out by a statement by Lord Stowell almost two centuries ago:

> In places where no local authority exists, where the subjects of all States meet upon a footing of entire equality and independence, no one State, or any of its subjects, has a right to assume or exercise authority over the subjects of another. No nation can exercise a right of visitation and search upon the common and unappropriated parts of the sea, save only on the belligerent claim.[1]

Even if a jurisdictional basis can be found, international law circumscribes the means available to compel a vessel to comply with an order to heave to. This chapter also explores the relevant authority dealing with the use of force at sea during peacetime to indicate what range of action can be used by a commander to compel compliance.

JURISDICTION TO BOARD VESSELS

Lawfully, boarding vessels at sea usually requires a state to have some form of jurisdiction over the vessel, and the boarding has to be undertaken by a warship or appropriately marked government vessel. The Law of the Sea Convention (United Nations Convention on Law of the Sea)[2] indicates the scope of jurisdiction available to states within the different maritime zones and beyond on the high seas, and is a logical starting point for considerations of jurisdiction.

There are three types of jurisdiction that are relevant to the exercise of an enforcement jurisdiction at sea, although not all three will necessarily be available to a state in any given situation. The relevant types of jurisdiction for boarding are as follows:

- Coastal jurisdiction
- Flag state jurisdiction
- Universal jurisdiction

COASTAL STATE JURISDICTION

Coastal state jurisdiction is derived from proximity to the territory of the coastal state. The Law of the Sea Convention organizes maritime jurisdiction under a series of maritime zones, where the extent of jurisdiction increases, the closer the relevant zone is to the coastal state. For example, the waters closest to the coastal state, internal waters enclosed by bays, fringing islands, or in ports or roadsteads, give the coastal state a jurisdiction that almost equates to the jurisdiction on land.[3] On the contrary, in the waters of the exclusive economic zone (EEZ), the coastal state's jurisdiction is limited to specific activities only, and boarding of vessels for enforcement purposes would be limited to those purposes.[4]

Before considering jurisdiction in each of the maritime zones, it is important to note that some vessels are exempt from the operation of coastal state law, regardless of the maritime zone the vessel is in. Warships and government vessels engaged in noncommercial service are described as being sovereign immune, and are not subject to enforcement action under the law of the coastal state, although present in internal waters or the territorial sea. In the event such a vessel contravenes the laws of the coastal state, it may be asked to leave the territorial sea, but the only other recourse a coastal state has is to make a claim against the flag state.[5]

In jurisdictional terms, the internal waters of a state are treated as equivalent to land. They are part of the sovereignty of the coastal state, and foreign vessels in these waters have no guaranteed right of navigation. Vessels in internal waters that are not sovereign immune are subject to the full jurisdiction of the coastal state, although traditionally coastal states do not apply laws related to the internal economy and operation of the vessel.[6]

The territorial sea is also part of the sovereignty of the coastal state, but a foreign vessel may not necessarily be subject to the complete jurisdiction of the coastal state. This is because foreign vessels have a right of innocent passage through the territorial sea, and coastal state jurisdiction over such vessels is restricted to specific subject areas. These vary depending on the type of jurisdiction and the matter the coastal state wishes to regulate, and are considered individually later in this section.

The coastal state always retains a "right of protection" to prevent passage through its territorial sea that is not innocent and ensure that vessels bound for its internal waters do not breach their conditions of entry. This right is dealt with under Article 25 of the Law of the Sea Convention, and it appears to legitimize efforts by a coastal state to remove vessels from its territorial sea if their passage is not innocent.[7] In addition, the coastal state may impose laws relating to innocent passage. These may be directed at the following areas under Article 21:

a. The safety of navigation and the regulation of maritime traffic
b. The protection of navigational aids and facilities and other facilities or installations
c. The protection of cables and pipelines
d. The conservation of the living resources of the sea
e. The prevention of infringement of the fisheries laws and regulations of the coastal state
f. The preservation of the environment of the coastal state and the prevention, reduction, and control of pollution thereof
g. Marine scientific research and hydrographic surveys
h. The prevention of infringement of the customs, fiscal, immigration, or sanitary laws and regulations of the coastal state

Criminal jurisdiction can be exercised by the coastal state in the territorial sea in relation to a vessel passing through the territorial sea, but is restricted to a number of defined circumstances. Article 27 of the Law of the Sea Convention provides for the exercise of criminal jurisdiction by the coastal state:

1. The criminal jurisdiction of the coastal state should not be exercised on board a foreign ship passing through the territorial sea to arrest any person or conduct any investigation in connection with any crime committed on board the ship during its passage, except only in the following cases:
   a. If the consequences of the crime extend to the coastal state
   b. If the crime is of a kind to disturb the peace of the country or the good order of the territorial sea
   c. If the assistance of the local authorities has been requested by the master of the ship or by a diplomatic agent or consular officer of the flag state
   d. If such measures are necessary for the suppression of illicit traffic in narcotic drugs or psychotropic substances

As criminal jurisdiction can be awakened where the coastal state is requested to provide assistance, whether from the flag state or by the master of the ship, there is potentially no restriction as to the subject matter of the jurisdiction. The coastal state is also able to impose measures on vessels in its territorial sea that have been within its internal waters under Article 27(2) of the convention. There is a restriction, however. Criminal jurisdiction can only be applied to offences that have occurred in the territorial sea, and not before entering it, provided the ship is foreign and is proceeding from a foreign port without entering internal waters.[8]

Beyond the territorial sea, a coastal state may also claim a contiguous zone to a distance of 24 Nmi. The contiguous zone has its origins in the "hovering acts" used by Britain and the United States in the nineteenth and twentieth centuries to combat smuggling.[9] Coastal states have enhanced jurisdiction over customs, fiscal, immigration, and sanitary matters, although it would be incorrect to assume that the contiguous zone gives a state complete jurisdiction over these matters. Article 33 of the Law of the Sea Convention provides:

1. In a zone contiguous to its territorial sea, described as the contiguous zone, the coastal state may exercise the control necessary to
   a. Prevent infringement of its customs, fiscal, immigration, or sanitary laws and regulations within its territory or territorial sea
   b. Punish infringement of the aforementioned laws and regulations committed within its territory or territorial sea

It is significant that Article 33 only gives a state jurisdiction to "prevent" infringement of customs, fiscal, immigration, and sanitary law within its territory or territorial sea. As Shearer points out, this may be sufficient to give a coastal state the right to engage in warnings or inspections of an infringing vessel, but not sufficient to be able to take enforcement action against an infringing vessel.[10] Whether prevention could be stretched to permit a boarding is a moot point, but it seems clear that such a boarding could not lead to the arrest of a vessel and its crew without the ship having entered the territorial sea at some point.

Beyond the territorial sea, to a maximum distance of 200 Nmi, a state may claim an EEZ. Within the EEZ, the coastal state has jurisdiction over economic activities in the water column and on the seabed, environmental protection, and installations and artificial islands. The coastal state can undertake enforcement action in support of these areas.[11]

In the context of marine living resources, the coastal state's rights of enforcement are contained in Article 73. The coastal state has a right to board, inspect, and arrest vessels as necessary to ensure compliance with its laws operating in the EEZ. Limitations on the rights relate to guarantees that vessels and crews arrested should be able to be released on the posting of a reasonable bond, and that crews, in the absence of an agreement with the flag state, ought not to be liable to imprisonment.[12]

Jurisdiction over environmental matters in the EEZ also gives the coastal state an enforcement jurisdiction in certain circumstances over foreign-flagged vessels in these waters. There is a specific provision dealing with enforcement against ocean dumping by vessels, as well as a more general provision. To deal with the specific provision first, Article 216 provides that laws and regulations implemented in accordance with the convention and applicable international standards can be enforced by the coastal state with respect to dumping in its territorial sea, EEZ, or on its continental shelf. Although this provision gives a coastal state a wide reach, it also specifically empowers the flag state with the same jurisdiction, and notes that once proceedings have begun in one state, the other state cannot take action. As such, flag states could limit the ability of a coastal state to take action by doing so themselves.

With respect to more general environmental protection in the EEZ, enforcement is pursuant to Article 220, and in part provides:

3. Where there are clear grounds for believing that a vessel navigating in the EEZ or the territorial sea of a state has, in the EEZ, committed a violation of applicable international rules and standards for the prevention, reduction, and control of pollution from vessels or laws and regulations of that state conforming and giving effect to such rules and standards, that state may require the vessel to give information regarding its identity and port of registry, its last and its next port of call, and other relevant information required to establish whether a violation has occurred.

4. States shall adopt laws and regulations and take other measures so that vessels flying their flag comply with requests for information pursuant to paragraph 3.

5. Where there are clear grounds for believing that a vessel navigating in the EEZ or the territorial sea of a state has, in the EEZ, committed a violation referred to in paragraph 3 resulting in a substantial discharge causing or threatening significant pollution of the marine environment, that state may undertake physical inspection of the vessel for matters relating to the violation if the vessel has refused to give information or if the information supplied by the vessel is manifestly at variance with the evident factual situation and if the circumstances of the case justify such inspection.

6. Where there is a clear objective evidence that a vessel navigating in the EEZ or the territorial sea of a state has, in the EEZ, committed a violation referred to in paragraph 3 resulting in a discharge causing major damage or threat of major damage to the coastline or related interests of the coastal state, or to any resources of its territorial sea or EEZ, that

state may, subject to Section 7, provided that the evidence so warrants, institute proceedings, including detention of the vessel, in accordance with its laws.
7. Notwithstanding the provisions of paragraph 6, whenever appropriate procedures have been established, either through the competent international organization or as otherwise agreed, whereby compliance with requirements for bonding or other appropriate financial security has been assured, the coastal state if bound by such procedures shall allow the vessel to proceed.

This means that different scope for enforcement action will occur based on an assessment of the severity of the pollution incident. A violation that is rated as causing or threatening significant pollution permits the coastal state to undertake a physical inspection of a vessel if the vessel has failed to provide adequate information in the circumstances. Only what is considered major pollution damage or a pollution threat will entitle a coastal state to detain a polluting vessel. The subjectivity in assessing what will constitute major damage to some extent vitiates from a coastal state's point of view, the restriction in this case.

Flag State Jurisdiction

In waters beyond national jurisdiction, the principal mode of asserting jurisdiction is through the jurisdiction based on registration, commonly referred to as flag state jurisdiction. Flag state jurisdiction is one of the oldest principles within the law of the sea, and it occupies the pivotal role in the regulation of matters at sea beyond national jurisdiction. Article 92 of the Law of the Sea Convention retains the basic notion that ships are only subject to the jurisdiction of a single state when on the high seas, or are stateless:

1. Ships shall sail under the flag of one state only and, save in exceptional cases expressly provided for in international treaties or in this convention, shall be subject to its exclusive jurisdiction on the high seas. A ship may not change its flag during a voyage or while in a port of call, save in the case of a real transfer of ownership or change of registry.
2. A ship that sails under the flags of two or more states, using them according to convenience, may not claim any of the nationalities in question with respect to any other state, and may be assimilated to a ship without nationality.

This provision makes it very clear that in the ordinary course of events, ships on the high seas beyond national jurisdiction will only be subject to the jurisdiction of their flag state, and therefore will not generally be able to be boarded by other states' vessels.

If there is a flag state concurrence permitting enforcement, then such action can also be taken, as envisaged in Article 92. The Law of the Sea Convention does not, beyond the reference in Article 92, explicitly contemplate enforcement under the authority of another state against vessels flying its flag, with the agreement of the flag state and enforcing state, but there is no impediment to such an arrangement. Most flag states would be reluctant to permit enforcement by another state, but there are examples of ship-boarding agreements where this authority does exist. For example, the United States has concluded ship-boarding agreements with a number of flag states including Liberia and Panama[13] to allow ships to be stopped and searched for weapons of mass destruction (WMD), or related materials, in certain circumstances. Similarly, there is a limited ability of states to board vessels flagged in other states, where both are parties to the United Nations Straddling and Highly Migratory Fish Stocks Agreement and are participating in a common regional fisheries management organization.[14] It is worth noting that in these examples, the right to stop and board a third state vessel is very limited, and would certainly not equate to the powers a warship or government vessel would have over a vessel flagged in its own state.

Universal Jurisdiction

International law does permit the exercise of jurisdiction by states over foreign vessels beyond national jurisdiction except in limited circumstances. These are outlined in Article 110 of the Law of the Sea Convention:

1. Except where acts of interference derive from powers conferred by treaty, a warship which encounters on the high seas a foreign ship, other than a ship entitled to complete immunity in accordance with Articles 95 and 96, is not justified in boarding it unless there is reasonable ground for suspecting that
   a. The ship is engaged in piracy
   b. The ship is engaged in the slave trade
   c. The ship is engaged in unauthorized broadcasting and the flag state of the warship has jurisdiction under Article 109
   d. The ship is without nationality
   e. Although flying a foreign flag or refusing to show its flag, the ship is, in reality, of the same nationality as the warship

In the cases of piracy and the slave trade, the rationale for placing these under universal jurisdiction was that they represent serious international crimes, and it is preferable that any member of the international community ought to be able to take action against vessels involved in their perpetration. This rationale seems less defensible for unauthorized broadcasting, but strong British pressure during the negotiation of the convention was able to bear fruit.[15] The remaining categories deal with vessels that have no nationality, and therefore should be able to be regulated by all, and vessels of the flag state seeking to disguise their identity. What is clear is that warships, and other vessels appropriately marked as being on government service, can exercise jurisdiction over vessels beyond coastal state jurisdiction in these limited circumstances, without the concurrence of the flag state.[16]

There is some scope, under the convention and in older international authority, that states do possess a right of visit to vessels, to ascertain their status. As is evident from Article 110, the ambit of this right of visit is very limited. Article 110(2) of the Law of the Sea Convention restricts it to the cases in Article 110(1), meaning that a right of visit to establish a ship's right to its flag can only be exercised on the rare occasions a ship may be suspected as being a pirate vessel, a slaver, engaging in unauthorized broadcasting, without nationality, or feigning another nationality when in reality it holds the nationality of the inspecting ship.

NEW DEVELOPMENTS

In the years since the terrorist attacks against the United States on September 11, 2001, there have been a number of developments that potentially have implications with respect to boarding ships at sea. The implications of each of these measures will be considered in turn.

International Ship and Port Facility Security Code

The International Ship and Port Facility Security (ISPS) Code[17] has been instituted under the auspices of the International Maritime Organization (IMO) to provide greater security for ships and port facilities in an environment more conscious of the risks of terrorist attack. In the context of boarding and interdiction of vessels, the ISPS Code does not provide for boarding of vessels at sea by other states than the flag state.

Suppression of Unlawful Acts against the Safety of Maritime Navigation Convention

Negotiated in the wake of the hijacking of the cruise liner *Achille Lauro* in the 1980s, the convention for the Suppression of Unlawful Acts against the Safety of Maritime Navigation (SUA convention)[18] provides a framework for dealing with terrorist acts and the like against ships at sea. It was negotiated in part because the traditional definition of piracy, as reflected in Article 110 of the Law of the Sea Convention required the activities to have been committed for private ends, which may not include terrorist acts as perpetrators might be motivated by a political cause.

Parties to the SUA convention have a wide jurisdiction to deal with offences against shipping, including seizing a ship, performing acts of violence against individuals on a ship, or damaging a ship or its cargo to endanger its safe navigation. Although jurisdiction to make laws to create offences for these activities is widely construed, being based on flag or the physical presence of a vessel in the territorial sea, or even attempted coercion of the state concerned or its nationals, the SUA Convention does not authorize boarding of a ship at sea by any state other than the flag state. Furthermore, the Preamble of the SUA convention provides "matters not regulated by this convention continue to be governed by the rules and principles of general international law," which would appear to limit nonflag state intervention to acts covered under Article 110 of the Law of the Sea Convention, which would essentially be acts of piracy. The only mechanism that might permit another state to have a role is in Article 8 of the SUA convention, which provides the master of a vessel may hand individuals over to a "receiving state," other than the flag state.

The adoption of the SUA convention by states was initially slow, but gathered pace strongly in the years following the terrorist attacks against the United States on September 11, 2001. In addition, since that time, further diplomatic efforts to extend the scope of the convention have been pursued within the IMO, leading to the adoption of a protocol to the SUA convention in late 2005.[19]

The principal focus of the 2005 SUA Protocol is on WMD and their nonproliferation, but the amendments also create additional offences of using a ship as a platform for terrorist activities[20] as well as the transportation of an individual who has committed an offence under the SUA convention,[21] or any of another nine listed antiterrorism conventions.[22] However, for the purposes of this discussion Article 8*bis* potentially widens the scope for third-party boarding of ships and needs to be specifically considered.

The operative provision for a third-party boarding of a vessel at sea is Article 8*bis*(5) of the 2005 SUA Protocol. It provides:

5. Whenever law enforcement or other authorized officials of a state party (the requesting party) encounter a ship flying the flag or displaying marks of registry of another state party (the first party) located seaward of any state's territorial sea, and the requesting party has reasonable grounds to suspect that the ship or a person on board the ship has been, is or is about to be involved in the commission of an offence set forth in Article 3, 3*bis*, 3*ter*, or 3*quater*, and the requesting party desires to board,
   a. It shall request, in accordance with paragraphs 1 and 2 that the first party confirm the claim of nationality
   b. If nationality is confirmed, the requesting party shall ask the first party (hereinafter referred to as "the flag state") for authorization to board and to take appropriate measures with regard to that ship which may include stopping, boarding, and searching the ship, its cargo, and persons on board, and questioning the persons on board to determine if an offence set forth in Article 3, 3*bis*, 3*ter*, or 3*quater* has been, is being, or is about to be committed
   c. The flag state shall either
      i. Authorize the requesting party to board and to take appropriate measures set out in subparagraph (b), subject to any conditions it may impose in accordance with paragraph 7
      ii. Conduct the boarding and search with its own law enforcement or other officials
      iii. Conduct the boarding and search together with the requesting party, subject to any conditions it may impose in accordance with paragraph 7
      iv. Decline to authorize a boarding and search

The requesting party shall not board the ship or take measures set out in subparagraph (b) without the expressed authorization of the flag state.

This provision provides that a third state may board after ascertaining the nationality of a vessel suspected of committing an offence under Article 3 or its related amendments, notifying the flag state and obtaining the consent of the flag state. In the absence of this consent from the flag state, a boarding cannot take place. A mechanism does exist to try to avoid intransigence by the flag state, where the flag state may lodge a declaration in Article 8*bis* granting a right to board four hours after request to board, or a declaration permitting boarding by other state parties.

If evidence of a past, current, or imminent offence is discovered in the course of a boarding, the flag state still retains jurisdiction, but it may authorize the boarding state to detain the vessel, its cargo, and crew, pending further instructions. It is clear from the text that the flag state is to remain in control, and that a boarding and subsequent discovery of an offence does not act as a basis for the boarding state to take over the matter. Article 8*bis* in part states:

7. The flag state, consistent with the other provisions of this convention, may subject its authorization under paragraph 5 or 6 to conditions, including obtaining additional information from the requesting party, and conditions relating to responsibility for and the extent of measures to be taken. No additional measures may be taken without the express authorization of the flag state, except when necessary to relieve imminent danger to the lives of persons or where those measures derive from relevant bilateral or multilateral agreements.

8. For all boardings pursuant to this article, the flag state has the right to exercise jurisdiction over a detained ship, cargo, or other items and persons on board, including seizure, forfeiture, arrest, and prosecution. However, the flag state may, subject to its constitution and laws, consent to the exercise of jurisdiction by another state having jurisdiction under Article 6.

The practical upshot of these measures is that state parties to the SUA convention and 2005 SUA Protocol, when the latter enters into force, will be able to board each other's vessels at sea, with each other's consent. This consent may be expedited through declarations being made, but will still be required to start any further action. The 2005 protocol also envisages cooperation between states with respect to how such boardings and subsequent action might take place.[23]

PROLIFERATION SECURITY INITIATIVE

The proliferation security initiative (PSI) is an informal international understanding that provides a basis for cooperative action at sea to deal with vessels suspected of carrying WMD or related equipment to nonstate actors. It is not a treaty and, therefore, is not binding, but rather a statement of intention indicated by states, indicating how they plan to cooperate and what steps might be taken to intercept a suspected cargo. A number of states have indicated their strong support for the PSI, while many more have shown an interest in participating.[24]

In the context of boarding and interdiction, there has been a Statement of Interdiction Principles made by the PSI states, and a portion of this is directly relevant to the boarding and interdiction of vessels at sea:

Take specific actions in support of interdiction efforts regarding cargoes of WMD, their delivery systems, or related materials, to the extent their national legal authorities permit and are consistent with their obligations under international law and frameworks, to include:

a. Not to transport or assist in the transport of any such cargoes to or from states or nonstate actors of proliferation concern, and not to allow any persons subject to their jurisdiction to do so.

b. At their own initiative, or at the request and good cause shown by another state, to take action to board and search any vessel flying their flag in their internal waters or territorial seas or areas beyond the territorial seas of any other state that is reasonably suspected of transporting such cargoes to or from states or nonstate actors of proliferation concerns, and to seize such cargoes that are identified.

c. To seriously consider providing consent under the appropriate circumstances to the boarding and searching of its own flag vessels by other states and to the seizure of such WMD-related cargoes in such vessels that may be identified by such states.

d. To take appropriate actions to (1) stop or search in their internal waters, territorial seas, or contiguous zones (when declared) vessels that are reasonably suspected of carrying such cargoes to or from states or nonstate actors of proliferation concern and to seize such cargoes that are identified and (2) to enforce conditions on vessels entering or leaving their ports, internal waters, or territorial seas that are reasonably suspected of carrying such cargoes, such as requiring that such vessels be subject to boarding, search, and seizure of such cargoes before entry.[25]

This statement provides for two distinct jurisdictional bases for boarding a vessel. The first is flag state jurisdiction, where a flag state undertakes to board and search vessels flying its flag reasonably suspected of carrying WMD or related material and seize such cargo if found. This is clearly consistent with international law as such enforcement is restricted to the flag state's waters or waters beyond its jurisdiction, but outside the territorial sea of another state. Flag state jurisdiction is also available to third states where the flag state undertakes to "seriously consider" providing consent to the boarding states to board, search, and if necessary, seize the cargo. It is significant that while the possibility of third state action is clearly contemplated, states supporting the statement are only obliged to "seriously consider" rather than to acquiesce to a third state boarding.

The second basis of jurisdiction for boarding and interdiction is territorial jurisdiction, where the flag state of the vessel concerned is not relevant. This has the coastal state asserting jurisdiction over a vessel because of its presence in the territorial sea, without necessarily obtaining the consent of the flag state. There has been significant academic debate over the legality of this territorial basis for stopping and boarding ships, and seizing cargos. Certainly, it would not *prima facie* seem consistent with a right of innocent passage and the restrictions on the exercise of criminal jurisdiction by a coastal state over vessels passing through their territorial sea.

Although a number of arguments can be raised in support of the legality of such an interception, including the right of a coastal state to act in its individual or collective self-defense, there has not been support for this mode of action to date in the United Nations Security Council. The council may make a resolution pursuant to chapter VII of the United Nations Charter, if it feels the application of force would assist in combating a threat to international peace and security,[26] and therefore could provide legitimate authority for a coastal state to stop and board a suspect vessel in its territorial sea, or even outside it. Security Council Resolution 1540 urges states to prohibit the transit of WMD to nonstate actors, but it does not create any positive duty on states to undertake interdiction of such vessels. The resolution only authorizes such action as is "consistent with international law,"[27] and therefore, boarding a suspect vessel in the territorial sea may not be legitimate.

One development that has occurred with the development of the PSI has been the conclusion of ship-boarding agreements between the United States and a number of flag states with open registries. These agreements permit the United States to stop and board vessels flagged in the participating states, often with short-term notice and permission periods, to search and seize WMD, associated materials, and delivery systems. The agreements are mostly reciprocal, therefore, theoretically, participating states could exercise identical powers over suspect U.S. flagged vessels, but practically, the prospect of this occurring is remote. At the time of writing, seven such agreements had been concluded, with states such as Panama, Liberia, the Marshall Islands, Croatia, Belize, Cyprus, and Malta.[28]

INTERDICTION

A critical issue exists in relation to the use of force against vessels during peacetime. States, through their warships or other government vessels, may be able, under international law, to assert a right to board a vessel at sea. This may be through an assertion of jurisdiction over the vessel, the permission of the flag state, or through a mere right to visit the vessel. If the vessel in question refuses to comply to permit a boarding to take place, the question is raised as to what degree of force may be imposed to compel compliance.

The Law of the Sea Convention says very little as to what level of force may be imposed by a state to uphold its rights and jurisdiction at sea. The convention notes that the exercise of jurisdiction should be by a warship or other marked government vessel, which may imply that some degree of force might be used as most vessels fitting these descriptions are armed, but it is submitted that this is too much to read into the convention. As the convention does not deal with the issue, it is necessary to apply older principles of international law.

There have been a number of cases dealing with offshore maritime enforcement and the use of force. In the case of *I'm Alone*, a joint commission dealt with matters surrounding the pursuit and destruction of a Canadian vessel suspected of smuggling alcohol during prohibition by the U.S. Coast Guard. The commission, after dealing with issues of hot pursuit, held that the sinking of *I'm Alone*, which had offered no threat to the pursuing coast guard vessels, was contrary to international law. The commission was satisfied that a pursuing vessel might use necessary and reasonable force for the purpose of boarding, searching, seizing, and bringing a vessel to port, and if in such circumstances the vessel was to sink, then that might be acceptable, providing the sinking was incidental to necessary and reasonable action. However, where an unarmed vessel had been deliberately sunk, such action would be contrary to international law.[29]

In the *Red Crusader*, an international inquiry between the United Kingdom and Denmark had to consider an incident between a Scottish trawler and a Danish fisheries patrol vessel in the waters around the Faroe Islands. After having been stopped by the Danish patrol vessel *Neils Ebbesen* on suspicion of fishing, the *Red Crusader* fled, taking two Danish crewmembers with it. The *Neils Ebbesen* gave chase, and ultimately fired upon *Red Crusader*, initially with 40-mm gunfire directed at the mast, radar scanner, lights, and then into the vessel's stern. When this proved ineffective, *Neils Ebbesen* fired its 127-mm solid shot from its main armament at the *Red Crusader*. The incident was brought to a close with the intervention of a Royal Navy ship interposing itself between the two vessels.

The court of inquiry held that the force used against the *Red Crusader* was contrary to international law. It considered the firing of solid shot into the *Red Crusader* without warning, and firing in such a way as to endanger human life exceeded the legitimate use of force.[30]

The most recent significant international case dealing with the use of force in enforcement actions at sea was that of the *M/V Saiga (No. 2)* before the International Tribunal for the Law of the Sea. The *Saiga* was a tanker, registered in St. Vincent and the Grenadines, which was engaged in bunkering fishing vessels off the coast of Guinea. A Guinean patrol vessel pursued the *Saiga* and fired at it, although it was disputed before the tribunal what caliber of weapon was used. The tribunal held that the level of force used by Guinea was excessive and stated:

155. In considering the force used by Guinea in the arrest of the *Saiga*, the tribunal must take into account the circumstances of the arrest in the context of the applicable rules of international law. Although the convention does not contain express provisions on the use of force in the arrest of ships, international law, which is applicable by virtue of Article 293 of the convention, requires that the use of force must be avoided as far as possible and, where force is unavoidable, it must not go beyond what is reasonable and necessary in the circumstances. Considerations of humanity must apply in the law of the sea, as they do in other areas of international law.

156. These principles have been followed over the years in law enforcement operations at sea. The normal practice used to stop a ship at sea is first to give an auditory or visual signal to stop, using internationally recognized signals. Where this does not succeed, a variety of actions may be taken, including the firing of shots across the bows of the ship. It is only after the appropriate actions fail that the pursuing vessel may, as a last resort, use force.[31]

This places a substantial restriction on the use of force in maritime enforcement. Aside from an exception in relation to self-defence; which was touched upon in *M/V Saiga (No.2)*, but deemed inapplicable by the Tribunal in the circumstances, it certainly makes it explicit that the use of force is only permissible after a variety of other measures have been implemented, including warning shots across the bow. Together with *Red Crusader* and *I'm Alone*, it makes it most unlikely that the application of force that could potentially cause physical harm to humans in the arrest of a vessel at sea can be lawfully used.

Such an approach is largely duplicated in the 2005 protocol to the SUA convention. Article 8*bis*(9) provides:

9. When carrying out the authorized actions under this article, the use of force shall be avoided except when necessary to ensure the safety of its officials and persons on board, or where the officials are obstructed in the execution of the authorized actions. Any use of force pursuant to this article shall not exceed the minimum degree of force that is necessary and reasonable in the circumstances.

It is significant that the language used in the last sentence of this paragraph is identical to the phrase used by the International Tribunal for the Law of the Sea in paragraph 155 of its joint judgment in the *M/V Saiga*.

Notably, where a boarding is undertaken, under Article 8*bis*(10) of the 2005 SUA Protocol, the scope of the duty is described in detail, perhaps reflecting the heightened concern of states regarding the exercise of a power to board and arrest against their flagged vessels:

10. Safeguards:
    a. Where a state party takes measures against a ship in accordance with this article, it shall
        i. Take due account of the need not to endanger the safety of life at sea
        ii. Ensure that all persons on board are treated in a manner that preserves their basic human dignity, and in compliance with the applicable provisions of international law, including international human rights law
        iii. Ensure that a boarding and search pursuant to this article shall be conducted in accordance with applicable international law
        iv. Take due account of the safety and security of the ship and its cargo
        v. Take due account of the need not to prejudice the commercial or legal interests of the flag state
        vi. Ensure, within available means, that any measure taken with regard to the ship or its cargo is environmentally sound under the circumstances
        vii. Ensure that persons on board against whom proceedings may be commenced in connection with any of the offences set forth in Article 3, 3*bis*, 3*ter*, or 3*quater* are afforded the protections of paragraph 2 of Article 10, regardless of location
        viii. Ensure that the master of a ship is advised of its intention to board, and is, or has been, afforded the opportunity to contact the ship's owner and the flag state at the earliest opportunity
        ix. Take reasonable efforts to avoid a ship being unduly detained or delayed

These provisions reinforce the basic position with respect to the use of force, but also flesh out detail on how a vessel and its crew must be dealt with. The level of detail would seem to go well beyond the previously discussed cases.

CONCLUSION

Although some developments, particularly the 2005 protocol to the SUA convention, have widened the potential scope of third-party boarding and interdiction of vessels at sea, it is apparent that the scope of the right to board suspect vessels is still quite limited. Similarly, the level of force able to be used in support of enforcement operations is also extremely limited. Even under the pressure of the international fight against terrorism and the risk of proliferation of WMD, states still appear very reluctant to cede their rights as a flag state to permit enforcement by other states against vessels flying their flag. Whether this state of affairs proves sufficient to meet the needs of the international community for increased peace and security remains to be seen.

NOTES

1. *Le Louis* (1817) 2 Dods 210; 165 ER 1464.
2. United Nations Convention on the Law of the Sea, done at Montego Bay on December 10, 1982, entered into force November 16, 1994: 1833 UNTS 396 (hereinafter LOSC).
3. See Part II, Section 2, LOSC.
4. Part V, LOSC.
5. Articles 30 and 31, LOSC.
6. *Patterson v. The Eudora* (1903) 190 US 169.
7. See I.A. Shearer, Problems of Jurisdiction and Law Enforcement against Delinquent Vessels, *International and Comparative Law Quarterly*, 35, 320 at 325, 1986.
8. Article 27(5), LOSC.
9. See C.J. Colombos, *The International Law of the Sea*, Longman, 1968, pp. 136–140; M.S. McDougall and W.T. Burke, *The Public Order of the Oceans: A Contemporary International Law of the Sea*, New Haven, 1987, pp. 585–603.
10. Shearer, *supra* note 7, p. 437.
11. Article 73, LOSC.
12. Articles 73(2) and 73(3), LOSC.
13. See http://www.state.gov/t/isn/c12386.htm.
14. For example, see Article 20, Agreement for the Implementation of the Provisions of the United Nations Convention on the Law of the Sea of December 10, 1982, Relating to the Conservation and Management of Straddling Fish Stocks and Highly Migratory Fish Stocks, done at New York on December, 4, 1995, entered into force December 11, 2001: (1994) 33 ILM 968.
15. M.H. Nordquist (ed.), *United Nations Convention on the Law of the Sea, 1982: A Commentary*, Dordrecht, 1995, Vol. 3, p. 233.
16. Article 110, LOSC.
17. International Ship and Port Facility Security Code, IMO, 2003.
18. Convention for the Suppression of Unlawful Acts Against the Safety of Maritime Navigation, done at Rome on March 10, 1988, entered into force on March 1, 1992: 1678 UNTS 221 (hereinafter SUA Convention).
19. Protocol of 2005 to the Convention for the Suppression of Unlawful Acts Against the Safety of Maritime Navigation, IMO Doc. LEG/CONF. 15/21, done at London on February 14, 2006 (hereinafter 2005 SUA Protocol).
20. Article 3*bis*, 2005 SUA Protocol.
21. Article 3*ter*, 2005 SUA Protocol.
22. Annex, 2005 SUA Protocol.
23. Article 8*bis*(12), 2005 SUA Protocol.
24. See http://fpc.state.gov/documents/organization/48624.pdf.
25. Reprinted at http://www.dfat.gov.au/globalissues/psi/psi_statement.html.
26. Article 42, United Nations Charter.

27. Operative paragraph 10 provides:

Further to counter that threat, *calls upon* all States, in accordance with their national legal authorities and legislation and consistent with international law, to take cooperative action to prevent illicit trafficking in nuclear, chemical or biological weapons, their means of delivery, and related materials.

28. See http://www.state.gov/t/isn/c12386.htm.
29. *Claim of the British Ship "I'm Alone" v United States Joint Interim and Final Reports of the Commissioners*, 1933 and 1935. *American Journal of International Law* 29, 326 at 330, 1935.
30. *Red Crusader, International Law Reports*, 35, 485 at 497–499, 1962.
31. *M/V Saiga (No.2)* ITLOS, http://www.itlos.org/case_documents/2001/document_en_68.pdf.

14 Long-Range Identification and Tracking Systems for Vessels: Legal and Technical Issues

Martin Tsamenyi and Mary Ann Palma

CONTENTS

INTRODUCTION

When the International Ship and Port Facility Security (ISPS) Code and amendments to the International Convention for the Safety of Life at Sea (SOLAS), 1974 were adopted by the International Maritime Organization (IMO) in December 2002, one of the issues that remained to be resolved was the long-range identification and tracking (LRIT) of ships. Resolution 3 of the 2002 SOLAS conference called on the IMO to carry out, as a matter of urgency, an impact assessment of the proposals to implement the LRIT of ships and develop and adopt appropriate performance standards and guidelines for the LRIT system.[1] The establishment of the LRIT system aims to complement and support the implementation of the ISPS Code by detecting security threats and taking preventive measures against security incidents affecting ships or port facilities used in international trade.

Since the adoption of the ISPS Code, significant progress has been made in developing the legal, technical, and administrative mechanisms for the adoption of the LRIT system for vessels. Resolutions were adopted by the Maritime Safety Committee (MSC) of IMO on May 19, 2006 pertaining to the amendments to SOLAS chapter V, performance standards and functional requirements for the implementation of the LRIT for ships, and arrangements for the timely establishment of the LRIT system.[2] Unlike the ISPS Code which was adopted under SOLAS chapter XI on maritime security, the LRIT system has been introduced as regulation 19-1 under chapter V of SOLAS amendments on the safety of navigation to emphasize not only its maritime security but also its search and rescue (SAR), safety, and environmental applications.

To elaborate on the specific provisions of SOLAS regulation V/19-1 and MSC resolutions adopted in 2006, the *ad hoc* Engineering Working Group of the IMO drafted six technical documents on the LRIT system for adoption of the Maritime Safety Committee (MSC) of the IMO. They are the draft technical specification for the international LRIT data exchange, draft technical specifications for the international LRIT data center, revised draft technical specifications for communication in the LRIT system, draft LRIT technical costing and billing standard, draft protocols for the development testing of the LRIT system and for testing the integration of new LRIT data centers into the system, and draft guidance on setting up and maintaining the data distribution plan.[3] Legal, policy, and technical debates continued after the adoption of these technical specifications. At its 84th session held in May 2008, the MSC amended the standards and functional requirements for the LRIT of ships and adopted documents providing guidance on the implementation of the LRIT system, including the receipt of LRIT information by SAR services and compliance of ships to transmit LRIT information. The MSC also revised the interim technical specifications for the International LRIT Data Exchange, International LRIT Data Centre, communications within the LRIT system, and the LRIT Data Distribution Plan.*

Negotiations within the IMO have resulted in agreement on a number of key issues; particularly, the types of vessels to be tracked, LRIT information to be transmitted, who can receive LRIT information and at what distance, timeframe for the implementation of the LRIT system, basic aspects related to the technical and administrative requirements of the LRIT system, confidentiality of the LRIT information, and cost of access to LRIT information. However, there are still concerns about some aspects of these issues that require clarification and resolution among the contracting governments of IMO so that the LRIT system can be implemented effectively. These concerns include the sharing of LRIT information among states, measures to be taken in case of breach of confidentiality of information, cost sharing among states, and penalties in case of nonpayment of dues.

This chapter provides analysis of the status of the LRIT system and legal, administrative, and practical implications of its implementation for states.[4] It also discusses concerns with respect to the draft technical standards for the LRIT system and concludes by highlighting the measures that the IMO and its contracting governments would need to take to advance the implementation of the LRIT system.

TYPES OF VESSELS INCLUDED IN THE LONG-RANGE IDENTIFICATION AND TRACKING SYSTEM

Under SOLAS regulation V/19-1, the obligation to transmit LRIT information applies to the following types of ships engaged in international voyages:

- Passenger ships, including high-speed passenger craft
- Cargo ships, including high-speed craft of 300 gross register tons (GRT) and above
- Mobile offshore drilling units[5]

---

* IMO, Maritime Safety Committee, Resolution MSC.263(84) (adopted in May 2008), Revised performance standards and functional requirements for the long-range identification and tracking of ships; Resolution MSC.264(84) (adopted in May 2008), Establishment of the International LRIT Data Exchange on an Interim Basis; Guidance on the Implementation of the LRIT System, MSC.1/Circ.1256, June 5, 2008; Guidance on the Survey and Certification of Compliance of Ships with the Requirement to Transmit LRIT Information, MSC.1/Circ.1257, June 5, 2008; Guidance to Search and Rescue Services in Relation to Requesting and Receiving LRIT Information, MSC.1/Circ.1258, June 5, 2008; and Interim Revised Technical Specifications for the LRIT System, MSC.1/Circ.1259, June 5, 2008. The revised interim technical specifications has yet to be published by IMO as at 25 June 2008.

The limit of 300 GRT is a departure from the requirements under the ISPS Code, which applies to vessels of 500 GRT and above.[6] The difference in the application of SOLAS regulation V/19-1 and the ISPS Code can be explained based on the adoption of the LRIT system under SOLAS chapter V on the safety of navigation, which generally requires all vessels of 300 GRT and above engaged in international voyages to carry shipborne navigational equipment and systems.[7]

The ships that will be fitted with an LRIT system include ships constructed on or after December 31, 2008, or ships constructed before December 31, 2008, and certified for operations in sea areas A1, A2, A3, and A4, depending on when the first survey of radio installation occurs for these vessels.[8] Ships, irrespective of the date of construction, fitted with an automatic identification system (AIS) and operated exclusively in sea area A1 are exempt from these regulations.

APPLICATION TO NONSAFETY OF LIFE AT SEA VESSELS

Considering that the LRIT system only applies to large merchant vessels, the fact that security threats may also come from smaller vessels should be counted. Such vessels are numerous compared to large vessels, transit waters closer to shore, and access remote port areas without undergoing extensive security checks unlike the inspections conducted on large ships. The LRIT system also does not apply to fishing vessels. Identification of fishing vessels proves useful particularly in cases where such vessels are used to threaten the security of a state or the maritime environment. The possibility that fishing vessels may compromise the security of offshore installations and platforms should also be viewed as a concern, given that such vessels sometimes fish very close to installations and platforms. Although there are fishing vessels, which are under national or regional vessel monitoring systems (VMS) and some states request AIS information from vessels that have obtained fishing licenses under their jurisdiction,[9] there is still a considerable number of fishing vessels, particularly small fishing vessels, which cannot be tracked or are not under any surveillance systems.

Although current SOLAS regulations do not apply to vessels, which are generally less than 300 GRT, the ISPS Code recognizes the need to address and establish measures to enhance the security of such ships. Paragraph 4.46 of the ISPS Code provides that nonparty ships and ships below the SOLAS convention size are subject to measures by states to maintain security. Such measures should be developed with due regard to the requirements in chapter XI-2 of the regulations and guidance provided in the ISPS Code. It is clear from these provisions that the regulation of smaller vessels is still left to the discretion of individual states.

In March 2005, Japan hosted a seminar and study on maritime security measures for non-SOLAS vessels and requested the IMO MSC to look into the matter. Subsequently, the ministerial conference on International Transport Security held in Tokyo, Japan in January 2006 invited the IMO to undertake a study and make recommendations to enhance the security of ships other than those already covered by SOLAS chapter XI-2 and the ISPS Code to protect such ships from becoming targets of terrorism, piracy, and armed robbery.[10]

Subsequently, the MSC, in its 82nd session, agreed that non-SOLAS vessels share the same operational environment as ships, which fall within the scope of SOLAS chapter XI-2 and the ISPS Code. The MSC agreed to establish a Correspondence Group on security aspects of the operation of ships to undertake a scoping study and develop recommendation guidelines on the matter and, in particular, ships which do not fall within the scope of SOLAS chapter XI-2 and the ISPS Code. The specific terms of reference for the Correspondence Group are to:

- Define the scope of the threats to non-SOLAS ships, posed by non-SOLAS ships to SOLAS ships, and posed by non-SOLAS ships to port, onshore, and offshore facilities
- Categorize the types of non-SOLAS ships that the guidelines are intended for, and prioritize, if possible, given the different national perceptions of risk

- Prepare draft guidelines, including a list of possible security measures and best practices such as procedural and physical measures
- Identify what additional guidance, if any, might be offered to ISPS Code compliant ships and port facilities in relation to the interface with non-SOLAS ships[11]

The MSC agreed that the guidelines to be developed must be nonmandatory in nature and applied proportionate to assessed levels of threat and risk under the purview of the concerned individual contracting governments.

At the 83rd session of the MSC in July 2007, the correspondence group, coordinated by the United Kingdom, reported that it has received examples of best practices from several states, which could potentially be applied to non-ISPS vessels.[12] However, because of the divergent views expressed on the matter during the session, the correspondence group was tasked to continue to work and develop a set of draft guidelines for consideration by the MSC.[13]

INFORMATION TO BE TRANSMITTED

The class of ships to which the LRIT system applies are required to automatically transmit their identity, position, and date and time of position.[14] LRIT positions may be transmitted at intervals ranging from 15 minutes to periods of six hours.[15] Apart from these pieces of information and transmission of a notice that a ship is proceeding to a particular port, no additional information is required from ships under the LRIT system,[16] except when specifically requested by the flag state of a vessel. The international LRIT data center may upon request, collect additional information from ships entitled to fly the flag of an administration on the basis of specific arrangements concluded with the concerned administration.[17] However, apart from the identity, position, and date and time of position, no other information may be transmitted by that LRIT data center to other LRIT data centers.[18]

Identifying and tracking ships on the basis of positional data will provide more information than what is currently being collected. One of the advantages for implementing the LRIT system is that it obtains and provides information at the global level, which would otherwise be gathered individually by states with little possibility of sharing. In practice, however, it is doubtful that the extent to which the agreed information to be collected through the LRIT system is sufficient to enable an assessment to be made by states of possible security threats posed by a particular ship.[19] Information from other sources such as intelligence from bilateral and regional cooperation is critical for enhancing the practical utility of the LRIT system. The successful implementation of the requirement for ships to transmit up to four position reports per day will also depend on the cost of the transmission of information. This issue is further discussed in the following sections.

TECHNICAL AND ADMINISTRATIVE REQUIREMENTS OF THE LRIT SYSTEM

As a global scheme, the LRIT system consists of the shipborne LRIT information transmitting equipment, communication service provider (CSP), application service providers (ASP), the LRIT Data Centers, including any related vessel monitoring systems, LRIT data distribution plan, and international LRIT data exchange.[20] The technical components of the LRIT system such as the installation of shipborne equipment and subscriptions to a CSP and an ASP entail specific and minimum requirements particularly with respect to the transmission, security, and confidentiality of LRIT information.[21] The administrative aspect of the LRIT system as stipulated in the adopted performance standards involves the establishment of LRIT data centers and execution of particular functions including the collection, transmission, dissemination, exchange, archival, maintenance, and securing of LRIT information.[22] All LRIT information are provided to contracting governments and SAR services entitled to receive the information, upon request, through a system of national, regional, cooperative, and international LRIT data centers by using the international LRIT data exchange.[23]

In detail, the LRIT system consists of the following components and functionalities:[24]

A. *The shipborne LRIT information transmitting equipment.* In addition to the general IMO requirements for shipborne radio equipment forming part of the global maritime distress and safety system (GMDSS), the shipborne equipment under the LRIT regulations should automatically, and without human intervention on board the ship, transmit the ship's LRIT information at six-hour intervals to an LRIT data center. The equipment should configure remotely to transmit LRIT information at variable intervals and interface directly to the shipborne global navigation satellite system equipment or have internal positional capability.

B. *The CSPs.* CSPs provide services that link the various parts of the LRIT system using communication protocols to ensure the end-to-end secure transfer of the LRIT information.

C. *The ASPs.* ASPs provide the communication protocol interface between the CSPs and the LRIT data centers. ASPs provide an integrated transaction management system for the monitoring of LRIT information throughput and routeing and ensure that LRIT information is collected, stored, and routed in a reliable and secure manner. ASPs provide services to the national, regional, cooperative, and international LRIT data centers.

D. *LRIT data centers.* All data centers are required to establish and continuously maintain systems which ensure, at all times, that LRIT data users are only provided with the LRIT information they are entitled to receive in accordance with SOLAS regulation V/19-1. LRIT data centers are responsible for collecting, storing, and disseminating information as instructed by administrations and in accordance with the SOLAS regulations and relevant standards agreed by IMO governments.

A contracting government is allowed to establish a national LRIT data center, whereas a group of contracting governments can establish either a regional or a cooperative LRIT data center. The relevant details concerning such centers should be provided to the IMO without undue delay and information provided is to be updated as and when changes occur.

The international LRIT data center is an element of the international LRIT system that receives, stores, and disseminates LRIT information on behalf of governments. It should receive and process LRIT information from all ships, other than those that are required to transmit LRIT information to a national, regional, or cooperative LRIT data center. It should also accommodate any LRIT data user not participating in a national, regional, or cooperative LRIT data center. The international LRIT data center ensures that LRIT data users are only provided with the LRIT information they are entitled to receive as specified in SOLAS regulation V/19-1.

E. *The LRIT data distribution plan.* The LRIT data distribution plan contains the critical tombstone information, different polygons, distances, and standing orders that are involved with flag state, port state, coastal state, and SAR access to the LRIT information. Particularly, it should include a list of contracting government and SAR services entitled to receive LRIT information and their points of contact; information on the boundaries of geographic areas within which each contracting government is entitled to receive LRIT information about ships in the area; information on any standing orders given by a contracting government with respect to the criteria for receiving LRIT information, such as the distance from the coast or port within which the provision of LRIT information is required. Resolution MSC.263(84) provides the definition of the geographical area within which each contracting government is entitled to receive LRIT information.*

F. *The international LRIT data exchange.* The international LRIT data exchange is the message handling service that facilitates the exchange of LRIT data among data centers to enable LRIT data users to obtain the LRIT positional data, which they are entitled to receive. The international LRIT data exchange does not provide information directly to a LRIT data user.

Resolution MSC.264(84) provides for the establishment and operation of the International LRIT Data Exchange by the United States on an interim basis. Until permanent arrangements are established, the International LRIT Data Exchange will be provided by the US at their own expense and neither IMO nor any of the LRIT Data Centers nor any of the other Contracting Governments would be required to make any payment to the US for its services.

G. *LRIT data users.* LRIT data users primarily consist of flag states, port states, coastal states, and SAR services.

Tracking of any applicable ship begins with LRIT positional data being transmitted from the shipborne equipment. The information transmitted from the ship travels across the communication path set up by the CSP to the ASP. The ASP, after receiving the LRIT information from the ship, adds additional information to the LRIT message and passes the expanded message to its associated LRIT data center. The LRIT data centers then store all incoming LRIT information from ships instructed by their administrations to transmit LRIT information to the concerned data center. The LRIT data centers disseminate LRIT information to LRIT data users according to the data distribution plan. The LRIT data centers process all LRIT messages to and from the international LRIT data exchange. The international LRIT data exchange will process all LRIT messages between LRIT data centers and route the message to the appropriate data center based on the information contained within the data distribution plan. However, the LRIT data exchange neither processes nor stores the positional data contained within LRIT messages. LRIT data users are entitled to receive or request LRIT information in their capacity as a flag state, port state, coastal state, or SAR service. Figure 14.1 illustrates the architecture of the LRIT system.

The international LRIT data center is expected to process data from about 50,000 SOLAS class ships. On the basis of the requirement for ships to transmit LRIT information four times a day, the total number of reports that would be generated from SOLAS ships is around 200,000/day.[25]

---

* Section 11.2.2 of MSC.263(84) provides that "for the purpose of the implementation of the provisions of SOLAS Regulation V/19-1.8.1, each Contracting Government should provide a list of geographical coordinates of points, based on the WGS 84 datum defining the geographical area:

(a) of the waters landward of the baselines for measuring the breadth of the territorial sea of the Contracting Government concerned;

(b) of the territorial sea of the Contracting Government concerned;

(c) between the coast of the Contracting Government concerned and a distance of 1000 Nmi from its coast. The Contracting Government concerned may, in lieu of defining the aforesaid area with reference to the geographical co-ordinate points defining its coast, define the area with reference to the geographical coordinate points of the baselines for measuring the breadth of the territorial sea of the Contracting Government; and

(d) within which the Contracting Government concerned is seeking the provision of LRIT information other than those provided above."

The geographic coordinates of points that determine the waters landward of the baselines and the territorial sea of the Contracting Government concerned include the baselines for measuring the breadth of the territorial sea in accordance with international law, as well as the lines of delimitation between the Contracting Governments concerned and States with adjacent coasts. The waters landward of the baselines also includes the coast of the Contracting Government concerned including any landward waters within which any ships required to comply with SOLAS Regulation V/19-1 is able to navigate. Such geographical information does not prejudice the rights, jurisdiction or obligations of States under international law nor the position of Contracting Governments in relation to land or maritime claims or disputes. Although this provision attempts to address the issue of the receipt of LRIT information among States with overlapping land and maritime boundaries, it is silent on the matter of undelimited maritime zones. This is a grey area that could potentially lead to disagreements between States with adjacent coastal areas and territorial seas.

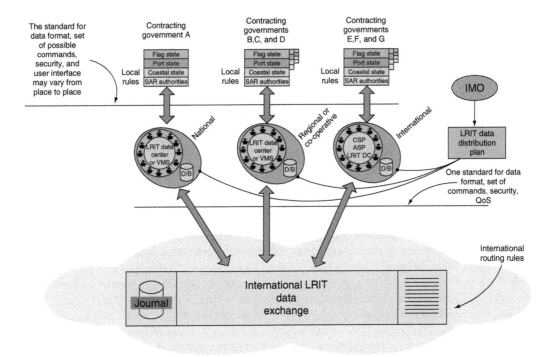

FIGURE 14.1 LRIT system architecture. (From IMO, Annex to Resolution MSC.263(84), Revised Performance Standards and Functional Requirements for the Long-Range Identification and Tracking of Ships, adopted in May 2008.)

The international LRIT data center must process and handle any input within 60 s and receive and store at least five reports per second.[26]

As for the need for an LRIT coordinator, the MSC invited the International Mobile Satellite Organization (IMSO) to undertake the review of the performance and auditing of the LRIT system on behalf of IMO.[27] The IMSO reported that it is willing to act as the LRIT coordinator, at no cost to the IMSO parties, in accordance with the decision of the IMO.[28] This commitment has been adopted as an amendment to the IMSO convention.[29] Further, in July 2007, IMSO has reported on its review and audit of the performance standards and functional requirements of the LRIT system, including an evaluation of proposals submitted by states for the establishment, operation, and maintenance of the international data exchange and international data center.[30]

The establishment of the LRIT system is more technical in scope; nevertheless, its implementation requires states and relevant international organizations such as the IMO and IMSO to enter into a series of agreements, for example,

- Agreement between the SOLAS governments and the LRIT coordinator
- Agreement between the SOLAS contracting governments, international data center, and international data exchange
- Agreements between the SOLAS governments and the LRIT data centers (national, regional, and cooperative) governing access to the LRIT data distribution plan
- Service contracts between IMSO and every data center, international data center, and any other node in the LRIT system with which IMSO has a mandatory relationship[31]

These legal arrangements need to be set in place to ensure the effective implementation of the system. Such arrangements would also need to include the settlement of financial obligations, particularly between the LRIT Data Centers and the SOLAS Contracting Governments.

In addition to these legal arrangements, internal administrative procedures are also required to ensure that shipping companies, shipowners, and vessel masters and crew are aware of their obligations to implement the LRIT system. Administrations would need to provide companies and owners of ships entitled to fly their flag relevant guidance on all pertinent LRIT-related matters, and in particular information relating to the LRIT Data Center to which ships should transmit LRIT information, the recognized ASPs, and the recognized organizations which may be authorised to survey and certify the compliance of the ships with SOLAS Regulation V/19-1 and the revised performance standards.* Administrations should also have in place directions to companies with respect to the transfer a flag to another Contracting Government to ensure proper decommissioning of the shipborne equipment used for LRIT transmission.†

WHO CAN RECEIVE LRIT INFORMATION AND FROM WHAT DISTANCE

After intense negotiation, agreement has been reached on access to LRIT information by various categories of states, including the distance from their shores from which such information may be received. LRIT information will be made available to flag, port, and coastal states.[32]

SOLAS regulation V/19-1/8.1 provides that as a flag state, a contracting government is entitled to receive LRIT information from ships flying its flags anywhere in the world. A port state is also entitled to receive LRIT information, but only from ships which have communicated an intention to enter its port facility, irrespective of the location of the ship. However, a contracting government acting as a port state is not entitled to receive LRIT information about ships located within the internal waters or archipelagic waters of another contracting government. It was also agreed that a contracting government acting as a coastal state is entitled to receive LRIT information on ships permitted to fly the flag of other contracting governments even when such ships are not intending to enter a port facility or place under the jurisdiction of that coastal state. Coastal states can obtain LRIT information from such ships when they are navigating within a distance of up to 1000 Nmi off their coast, provided that such ships are not located within the waters landward of the baselines of another contracting government. A coastal state is not entitled to receive LRIT information on ships located within the territorial sea of the contracting government whose flag the ship is entitled to fly. Finally, SOLAS regulation V/19-1/12 also provides that LRIT information be made available to SAR services of contracting governments for use in relation to rescuing persons in distress at sea.

In early discussions within IMO on the powers of flag, coastal, and port states to receive LRIT information, the issue of providing LRIT information to a coastal state on ships transiting waters within a distance of up to 1000 Nmi off its coast invited the most controversial legal debate among IMO contracting governments. Among the IMO members favoring the receipt of LRIT information from a distance more than 200 Nmi from the shores of the coastal state included the European Commission (EC),[33] Australia,[34] and the United States.[35] However, there are states, which maintain the view that coastal states should be allowed to receive LRIT information only within 200 Nmi because it will otherwise impair the exclusive jurisdiction of a flag state over its ships and create additional rights for coastal states outside the exclusive economic zone (EEZ). These states include Iran,[36] China,[37] the Russian Federation,[38] and Brazil.[39]

The prescriptive powers of coastal states in various maritime zones of jurisdiction under international law, particularly the United Nations Convention on the Law of the Sea (LOSC), provide the legal basis for allowing such states to receive LRIT information beyond 200 Nmi from the coast. Providing LRIT information to states from a distance of up to 1000 Nmi from their shores does not impinge on freedom of navigation under international law.[40]

---

* MSC.1/Circ.1256, para. 7.1.1; *See also* MSC.1/Circ.1257.
† MSC.1/Circ.1256, para. 7.2.

In terms of technical application, contracting governments have responsibility with respect to obtaining LRIT information. If a government wishes to receive LRIT information, it needs to give the LRIT data center a standing order regarding the criteria for receiving such information.[41] To which LRIT data center should the LRIT information be transmitted by ships entitled to fly its flag should be decided by each contracting government. A flag state that wishes to receive LRIT information on one of its registered ships can either send a request message to the data center to which it is connected or submit standing orders regarding the criteria for receiving LRIT information to its LRIT data center. The standing order information should include the ship name, IMO ship identification number, and reporting rate. The contracting government uses LRIT messages to start tracking, stop tracking, or alter the reporting rate of the LRIT information.[42] If the ship transfers to another flag, both the state which originally flagged the ship and state to which the flag is transferred to should report the effective date and time of transfer and state whose flag the ship was formally entitled to fly.[43] Contracting governments are also responsible for the validity of the information within the data distribution plan.[44]

The request for LRIT information by a port state is triggered by a notice of arrival. After receiving a notice of arrival, a port state that wishes to receive LRIT information can send either a request message including all applicable port state parameters or a request message referring the receiving data center to the standing orders applicable to that port state contained in the data distribution plan. The standing order may include a combination of the ship name, IMO ship identification number, flag, reporting rate, and the distance from the contracting government's port or distance from the coastline, or a point in time. If a port state wishes to stop receiving LRIT information, it must send a request message to the ship's data center instructing the data center to stop sending reports.[45]

A coastal state that wishes to receive LRIT information is required to submit standing orders regarding the criteria for receiving LRIT information. The standing order criteria should include the distance from its coast within which the coastal state wishes to track ships, reporting rate, and, optionally, the flag of ships it does not (or does) wish to track. This will enable the data center to filter the data reports based on a ship's distance from the coast as well as the flag of the ship. If the coastal state wishes to stop receiving LRIT information, it must either actively send a request message to the ship's data center or within the data distribution plan only request that the first regular position message inside the coastal state area be transmitted to the coastal state.[46]

For the purposes of SAR, a contracting government that wishes to receive LRIT information as a SAR entity can use either a SAR surface picture (SURPIC) request message or a poll request message to obtain the required information. The SAR SURPIC provides the SAR authority with information of the ships within a requested vicinity and the message is sent to the international LRIT data exchange by the data center associated with the SAR authority. SAR authorities can use a SAR poll request message to retrieve additional positional data on ships in the vicinity of a SAR incident.[47] The IMO has issued MSC.1/Circ.1258 which includes the obligations of SAR services with respect to the implementation of SOLAS Regulations V/19-1 on the confidentiality and security of information, the process of requesting LRIT information, and limitations during the phased-in implementation of the LRIT system. The international LRIT data center is required to provide SAR services with LRIT information transmitted by all ships located within the geographic area specified by the SAR service requesting the information to permit the rapid identification of ships that may be called to provide assistance in relation to distress at sea.[48]

Figure 14.2 illustrates how a contracting government may seek LRIT positional data from its LRIT data center.

The rights of flag, coastal, and port states to obtain LRIT information from ships as well as obligations to provide standing orders with respect to the criteria for receiving such information are not governed by technical and administrative rules only. Legislative action at the domestic level is needed to compel vessels to submit LRIT information and regulate the relationship between the state and the data center through which LRIT information is transmitted.

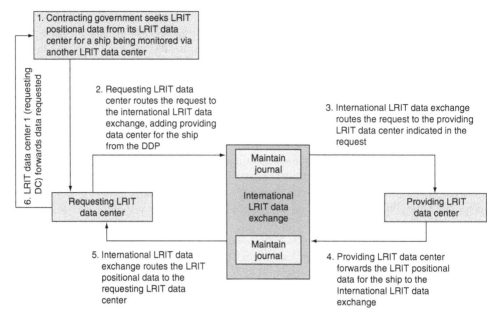

FIGURE 14.2 Recommended process of seeking LRIT data by a contracting government. (From IMO, Interim LRIT Technical Specification and Other Matters, MSC.1/Circ.1219, IMO, London, December 15, 2006.)

ENFORCEMENT POWERS IN RELATION TO THE LRIT SYSTEM

The right of coastal states to receive LRIT information does not automatically translate into the right to take enforcement action. The legal limits on taking enforcement action in the event that a state has, on the basis of LRIT information, identified a vessel as a threat to its national security are regulated by general rules of international law, particularly the LOSC. Regulation 19-1/1 of SOLAS chapter V provides that

> Nothing in this regulation or the provisions of performance standards and functional requirements adopted by the Organization in relation to the long-range identification and tracking of ships shall prejudice the rights, jurisdiction or obligations of States under international law, in particular, the legal regimes of the high seas, the exclusive economic zone, the contiguous zone, the territorial seas or the straits used for international navigation and archipelagic sealanes.

It is clear from this provision that the SOLAS regulation does not create nor affirm any new rights of states over ships beyond those existing in international law, particularly the LOSC, nor does it alter or affect the rights, jurisdiction, duties, and obligations of states in connection with the LOSC.

SECURITY AND CONFIDENTIALITY OF LRIT INFORMATION

Confidentiality considerations have always been the key concern of flag states and industry in relation to the adoption of any vessel tracking system. This was the case much earlier during the 1980s and 1990s in relation to the introduction of satellite VMS for fishing vessels. Concerns by flag states and the fishing industry resulted in the establishment of comprehensive legal provisions, policies, and strategies by regional fisheries management organizations and coastal states to assure the fishing industry and individual fishers that the information collected by fisheries management authorities through the VMS will be kept confidential.[49]

Similar to the VMS much earlier, confidentiality concerns were voiced by some flag states and industry groups during the negotiation of the LRIT system. A number of ship owners associations, principally, the International Chamber of Shipping (ICS), Baltic and International Maritime Council (BIMCO), International Parcel Tanker Association (IPTA), International Association of Independent Tanker Owners (INTERTANKO), International Council of Cruise Lines (ICCL), Society of International Gas Tanker & Terminal Operators (SIGTTO) argued strongly for the need to address the confidentiality issues associated with the collection and receipt of LRIT information.[50] The key concerns were that the allowing of all ships to be tracked and identified anywhere in the world would be detrimental to maritime security, the very purpose for which the LRIT system is being created. It was argued that unless LRIT information was kept secured, it would allow the dissemination of unwanted or unauthorized information, which may be used to adversely affect the commercial activities of vessels; and encourage discrimination and victimizing of certain ships without appropriate clear grounds.[51] The protection of confidential information, it was argued, is essential to ensure that a port or coastal state will not discriminate without clear grounds against the ships of any state or against ships carrying cargoes to, from, or on behalf of any state.[52]

SOLAS regulation V/19-1 on the LRIT of ships addressed the foregoing confidentiality concerns by imposing a number of requirements on states that receive LRIT information. States are required to recognize the importance of LRIT information and respect the commercial confidentiality and sensitivity of any such information they may receive. Contracting governments must also protect the information they may receive from unauthorized access or disclosure and use the information they may receive in a manner consistent with international law.[53] These requirements under the SOLAS amendments, however, are very general in nature.

Paragraph 12 of the Resolution MSC.263(84) on the performance standards and functional requirements for the LRIT for ships provides specific methods to ensure the security of data in LRIT communications. These methods are authorization, authentication, confidentiality, and integrity. The resolution provides that access must only be granted to those who are authorized to receive the specific LRIT information. Any party exchanging information within the LRIT system should require authentication before exchanging information. Contracting governments should also protect the confidentiality of the LRIT information to ensure that it is not disclosed to unauthorized recipients although it is being transmitted across the LRIT system. Contracting governments are further required to ensure that the integrity of the LRIT information is guaranteed and that no data has been altered. The draft technical specifications for communications in the LRIT system states that data exchanged between LRIT components must not be disclosed to unauthorized entities during transit across the LRIT network.[54] Exchange of information must be accomplished through standard cryptography techniques featuring an encryption strength equivalent to or better than 128 bits. Any access or release of information must include an audit trail of access to, modification of, or deletions made.[55]

An important issue is the consequences of breach of the confidentiality requirements by contracting governments. In relation to this issue, paragraph 13 of the amendment to the SOLAS regulations provides that "Contracting Governments may report to the Organization any case where they consider that provisions of this regulation or of any other related requirements established by the Organization have not been or are not being observed or adhered to." What is not clear is the range of possible actions that may be taken by the organization in such circumstances. Ultimately, the flag state has the power to deny access to LRIT information from its vessels to coastal states that are found to be in breach of their obligations. In this regard, the SOLAS LRIT amendments provide that

> the Administration shall be entitled, in order to meet security or other concerns, at any time, to decide that long-range identification and tracking information about ships entitled to fly its flag shall not be provided pursuant to the provisions of paragraph 8.1.3 to Contracting Governments. The Administration concerned may, at any time thereafter, amend, suspend or annul such decisions.[56]

In such circumstances, the administrator is required to communicate its decision to IMO, which in turn is required to "inform all Contracting Governments upon receipt of such communication together with the particulars thereof."[57] To guard against ships being subjected to additional security measures by some contracting governments, it is a requirement that a lawful decision by the administrator to withhold LRIT information from contracting governments shall not prejudice the rights, duties, and obligations of such ships under international law.[58]

To implement these undertakings, it is necessary for IMO contracting governments to put in place additional legal and administrative measures at the national level such as the development of legislation to protect confidentiality and protocols for the management of LRIT information that they may receive. Similarly, any agreement that will be concluded between international organizations such as the IMO and IMSO, LRIT data centers, and contracting governments and SAR services would need to include provisions on the protection of data and information and integrity and secure handling of data.

COST OF IMPLEMENTING THE LRIT SYSTEM

The cost to IMO contracting governments arising from the establishment and operation of the LRIT system was a major issue during the negotiations of the amendment to SOLAS chapter V. The negotiations resulted in a four-point consensus on the issue. The first is that contracting governments will bear all costs associated with any LRIT information they request and receive. Second, contracting governments are not entitled to impose any charges on ships in relation to the LRIT information they may seek to receive. Third, unless the national legislation of the administration provides otherwise, ships entitled to fly its flag shall not incur any charges for transmitting LRIT information in compliance with the provisions of this regulation.[59] Finally, SAR services of contracting governments are entitled to receive, free of any charges, LRIT information in relation to the SAR of persons in distress at sea.[60]

There are two issues related to the cost of implementing the LRIT system. The first issue relates to the cost of installing the shipborne equipment and testing the conformance of that equipment with LRIT system specifications. MSC.1/Circ.1257 provides that the conformance test should be conducted either by a recognized ASP or by an authorised testing ASP. However, such testing is not free, and there have been suggestions that the cost be borne by the shipping company and not the contracting government.* This recommendation appears to be inconsistent with paragraph 11.1 of SOLAS Regulation V/19-1.

The second issue relates to the cost associated with the receipt of LRIT information. Although the costing and billing standard for the receipt and transmission of LRIT information is yet to be finalized by IMO, the overall costing and billing framework has been described by the *ad hoc* working group on engineering aspects of LRIT. After studying different billing scenarios, the *ad hoc* working group proposes three possible options of sharing the minimum four position reports per day between data centers. The first option is no cost sharing or no charge for the cost of the position report except the overhead cost of the international LRIT data center. This implies that the regular position reports are being paid for by the flag state and provided free of charge to requesters. The second option is for cost to be shared and third option is for the source contracting government to make profit. For the second and third options, costs can be either

- A position report by report. For example, if one report is requested by five data centers, then each data center pays 20 percent of the cost
- A calculation based on the total volume over a time period. The total number of position reports out of the data center over the time period shares total cost.[61]

The *ad hoc* working group recommends that policy decisions be made by the IMO MSC on these options. It also recommends that contracting governments do not pursue variable pricing for requesting and obtaining LRIT information and a simple billing system be selected for costs between data centers as well as from the international data centers and connected contracting governments.

---

* See Polestar, LRIT Equipment Conformity Testing, Available at www.lrit.com. Accessed on June 26, 2008.

As the LRIT coordinator, IMSO has drafted an implementation plan for the LRIT system, part of which is the estimated budgetary requirement. For the IMSO to recover its costs for the LRIT services, the following general charging policies have been adopted

- As a general principle, IMSO will charge participating LRIT data centers in the international LRIT data exchange, on an annual basis and in advance, for the performance review and audit services they require for continuing participation in the LRIT system.
- Additionally, IMSO will charge ASPs providing services to the international data center an administrative charge, on an annual basis and in advance, for the costs incurred in providing certification and annual review, at the beginning of every year.
- Additional fixed fees apply for evaluating and testing of new and modified elements of the LRIT.[62]

It was also suggested that the cost of the LRIT coordinator be shared equitably among all the data centers within the LRIT system based on the level of effort that the LRIT coordinator will expend to perform its duties.

Contracting governments may opt to establish their own national data centers or cooperate in a regional or cooperative data center and are expected to bear all, or a proportion if coopting, of any associated costs. However, those contracting governments not wishing to establish a data center must inform their ships that they will be reporting to the international data center, and consequently bear any start up or operational costs. In the case of access to LRIT information by SAR services, overhead costs would need to be shared between contracting governments in a data center.

The cost of acquiring LRIT information is enormous and requirement that contracting governments would bear all costs associated with any LRIT information they may request and receive would seriously harm many developing countries. In practice, this would mean that developed countries would end up being the major beneficiaries of the LRIT system.

To illustrate the financial capacity required of developing states to identify and track vessels, a number of states are examined. The United States estimates that 3000 ships transit within 1000 Nmi off the coast of the United States on any given day. Of this number, approximately 450 are U.S.-flagged ships and the remaining are foreign flags that transit internationally. On the basis of the performance standards and functional requirements for LRIT, one transmission would be made every six hours, or four times a day, 365 days a year. The United States estimates that the foreign flag whips within 1000 Nmi off the coast or bound for U.S. ports would result in approximately 10,200 transmissions per day (2550 ships × 4 transmissions per day) for a total of 3,723,000 transmissions per year. The U.S.-flagged ships would require approximately 1800 transmissions per day (450 ships × 4 transmissions per day). With a cost of U.S.$ 0.25 per transmission, the United States would incur LRIT information costs of approximately U.S.$ 930,750 annually from foreign flag ships and U.S.$ 164,250 annually from U.S.-flagged ships.[63]

Canada estimates that it will be tracking approximately 1000 ships on any given day (60 of which are entitled to fly its flag, 140 ships intending to enter into its ports every six hours, and approximately 800 ships navigating within 1000 Nmi off its coast at least every 12 hours). On the basis of the estimated cost of CA$ 0.27 (U.S.$ 0.25) per transmission, the estimated annual cost of LRIT information for Canada is CA$ 236,500, or U.S.$ 219,000.[64]

For Australia, it is estimated that 2500 ships transit within 1000 Nmi off the Australian coast in any 24-hour period and would be affected by LRIT. At a cost of AU$ 0.17 per transmission, it is estimated that Australia would include the cost of approximately AU$ 602,500 annually. However, after considering the requirements and benefits of receiving LRIT information, Australia has determined a requirement for reports every 12 hours, halving the earlier mentioned cost.[65] For India, the cost of tracking 700 foreign flag ships and 300 Indian flag ships amounts to a total of U.S.$ 365,000 annually.[66]

The costs associated with implementing an LRIT system will depend on the number of ships being tracked by a state and amount of LRIT information that a state would require from these ships

to determine a potential threat to its maritime security. However, the LRIT information cost estimates provided by the United States, Canada, Australia, and India would indicate the huge amount of money that developing states would need to identify and track vessels. Such need for substantial financial capacity might hinder states from implementing the LRIT system.

There are also other issues related to the cost of the LRIT system that are yet to be discussed by the IMO MSC. These issues include the following:

- Are contracting governments entitled to recover costs or realize profits?
- Can a contracting government establishing a national data center or group of contracting governments establishing a regional or cooperative data center not pay for the regular LRIT information transmitted by ships entitled to fly its or their flag?
- If a regional or cooperative data center or the international data center receives the same message multiple times in accordance with the LRIT data distribution plan entries, how many times should it pay for it?
- Under what circumstances can a contracting government share with other entities outside its data center LRIT information that it is entitled to, has requested or has received, and are there any cost implications associated with the sharing of such information?
- How should costs be differentiated, that is, by requestor, message type, or volume?
- How will overhead costs be apportioned?
- How should nonpayment of dues be addressed?[67]

These issues would need to be resolved by IMO contracting governments to provide a costing and billing framework for the LRIT system that is reliable and would not create disproportionate burden among states. There is also a need to ensure that contracting governments establishing national, regional, and cooperative data centers would subscribe to a minimum or regular amount of transmission of LRIT information for the system to be financially sustainable. The emphasis on the maritime safety and marine environmental protection application of the LRIT system would assist in increasing the demand for LRIT information and would contribute to its financial viability. Aside from establishing procedures for the settlement of accounts, measures would also be needed to be adopted within the costing and billing framework to address concerns such as nonpayment of LRIT costs.

TIMEFRAME FOR IMPLEMENTATION

The SOLAS regulations on LRIT entered into force on January 1, 2008, giving SOLAS Contracting Governments a year to establish and test the LRIT system. Similarly, the regulations provide ship operators a year to start fitting or upgrading the necessary equipment in order for their ships to transmit LRIT information. The IMO has also adopted a phased approach to the implementation of the regulation which will allow for compliance not later than the first radio survey after 31 December 2008 or in the case of ships operating in Sea Area A4 not later than the first radio survey after 1 July 2009. However, due to pending practical, financial, and legal concerns associated with the LRIT system, it would not be surprising if such concerns would affect the timely implementation of the system.

CONCLUSION

This chapter shows that despite significant progress in adopting legal and technical mechanisms to implement the LRIT system, much is left to be addressed before the system becomes functional. Aside from some technical specifications on the overall LRIT system that need some adjustments, there are also issues about the confidentiality and security of information and the cost and billing of LRIT information that would still require some further consideration by IMO contracting governments.

To ensure the timely and effective implementation of the LRIT system, IMO contracting governments, with the collaboration of IMSO, would need to establish legal arrangements between the IMO and the IMSO and contractor for the international data center and international LRIT data exchange; international data center and the national, regional, or cooperative data centers; international data center and states; and national, regional, or cooperative data centers and states. Agreements between these parties or entities would need to take into account the security and handling of LRIT information. Legislation and administrative procedures at the national level are also needed to ensure that proper mechanisms are established for the acquisition of LRIT data from ships and transmission of such data to the data Centers. The shipping industry, including vessel owners, masters and crew would need to be fully aware of their obligations to implement the LRIT system.

Among the various unresolved issues on the LRIT system, the costing and billing standards for the LRIT system requires urgent deliberation. The costing and billing framework that would need to be put in order requires provisions on determining the cost of LRIT information, cost of sharing such information among states, procedure for the settlement of accounts, and measures to be taken against states failing to discharge their financial obligations with respect to the LRIT system. Not only should the costing and billing standards for the LRIT system exhibit financial viability but it should also be formulated in an equitable manner so as not to impose a disproportionate burden on states, particularly developing states.

NOTES

1. Conference Resolution 3, Further Work by the International Maritime Organization Pertaining to the enhancement of maritime security, adopted on 12 December 2002, para. 2, in the Conference of Contracting Governments to the International Convention for the Safety of Life at Sea, 1972, Agenda items 7 and 8, SOLAS/CONF.5/34, Consideration and adoption of the International Ship and Port Facility Security (ISPS) Code consideration and adoption of the resolutions and recommendations and related matters, SOLAS/CONF.5/34, December 17, 2002.
2. Resolution MSC.202(81) (adopted on May 19, 2006), Adoption of Amendments to the International Convention for the Safety of Life at Sea, as Amended, in IMO, MSC, 81st Session, Agenda item 25, Report of the Maritime Safety Committee on its 81st Session, MSC 81/25/Add.1, June 1, 2006, Annex 2; Resolution MSC.210(81) (adopted on May 19, 2006), Performance Standards and Functional Requirements for the Long-Range Identification and Tracking of Ships, in MSC 81/25/Add.1, Annex 13; Resolution MSC.211(81) (adopted on May 19, 2006) Arrangements for the Timely Establishment of the Long-Range Identification and Tracking System, in MSC 81/25/Add.1, Annex 14.
3. IMO, Maritime Safety Committee, 83rd Session, Agenda item 6, LRIT-related matters, Report on the outcome of the intersessional meetings of the *Ad Hoc* Working Group on engineering aspects of long-range identification and tracking of ships, submitted by the Chairman of the *Ad Hoc* Working Group, MSC 83/6/1, July 9, 2007, 6 Annexes.
4. For detailed analysis of the legal issues associated with the LRIT, see Martin Tsamenyi and Mary Ann Palma, "Legal Considerations in the Implementation of Long-Range Identification and Tracking Systems for Vessels," *The Journal of International Maritime Law* 13:1, Jan–Feb 2007, 42–55.
5. SOLAS Regulation V/19-1/2.1.
6. IMO, International Ship and Port Facility Security (ISPS) Code, 2003, para. 3.1.
7. SOLAS Regulation V/19/2.4.
8. See SOLAS Regulation V/19-1/2.1. For purposes of GMDSS, the world's oceans are divided into four areas. Area A1 lies within range of shore-based VHF coast stations (20–30 Nmi). Area A2 lies within range of shore based MF coast stations (excluding A1 areas) (approximately 100–150 Nmi). Area A3 lies within the coverage area of Inmarsat communications satellites (excluding A1 and A2 areas—approximately latitude 70° north to latitude 70° south). Area A4 comprises the remaining sea areas outside areas A1, A2, and A3 (the polar regions).
9. Joint 2nd Session of the FAO/IMO Joint *Ad Hoc* Working Group on Illegal, Unreported and Unregulated Fishing and Related Matters, Rome, Italy, July 16–18, 2007, Use of AIS and Possible Future Use of LRIT as a Tool to Track IUU Fishing Vessels, submitted by Norway, FI:JWG/FAO/IMO/IUU/2007/INF.17, July 3, 2007, para. 6. Norway suggests the possibility for coastal states without national VMSs to require fishing vessels to transmit LRIT data.

10. Ministerial Conference on International Transport Security, Tokyo, Japan, January 12–13, 2006, Ministerial Statement on Security in International Maritime Transport Sector. Available at www.mlit.go.jp. Accessed on September 28, 2007.
11. IMO, MSC, 82nd Session, Agenda item 24, Report of the Maritime Safety Committee on Its Eighty-second Session, MSC 82/24, December 18, 2006, para. 4.75.
12. See IMO, MSC, 83rd Session, Agenda item 4, Measures to Enhance Maritime Security, Correspondence group on security aspects of the operation of ships which do not fall within the scope of SOLAS chapter XI-2 and the ISPS Code, submitted by the United Kingdom as co-ordinator of the correspondence group, MSC 83/INF.7, July 25, 2007.
13. IMO, MSC, 83rd Session, Agenda item 4, Measures to Enhance Maritime Security, Correspondence group on security aspects of the operation of ships which do not fall within the scope of SOLAS chapter XI-2 and the ISPS Code , submitted by the United Kingdom as co-ordinator of the correspondence group, MSC 83/4/2, July 25, 2007, paras. 12–13.
14. SOLAS Regulation V/19-1/2.1; See also IMO, Subcommittee on Radiocommunications and Search and Rescue (COMSAR), Measures to Enhance Maritime Security, Long-Range Identification and Tracking of Ships, submitted by the Rapporteur of the Correspondence Group on Long-Range Identification and Tracking of Ships, COMSAR 8/13/4, December 12, 2003, p. 5.
15. Annex to Resolution MSC.263(84), para. 4.2.
16. IMO, MSC, 81st Session, Agenda item 5, Measures to Enhance Maritime Security, Outcome of the MSC/ISWG/LRIT, Note by the Secretariat, MSC 81/5/1, October 25, 2005, para. 24.
17. Annex to Resolution MSC.263(84), para. 9.4.
18. Annex to Resolution MSC.263(84), para. 8.4.
19. See statements by The Netherlands, Sweden, and the International Association of Marine Aids to Navigation and Lighthouse Authorities (IALA), IMO, MSC, 78th Session, Agenda item 7, Measures to Enhance Maritime Security, Long-range Identification and Tracking of Ships, submitted by the Netherlands and Sweden, MSC 78/7/8, March 19, 2004; IMO, COMSAR, 8th Session, Agenda item 13, Measures to Enhance Maritime Security, Long-range identification and Tacking of Ships, submitted by the Netherlands, Sweden, and IALA, COMSAR 8/13/7, December 17, 2003.
20. Annex to Resolution MSC.263(84), para. 1.2.
21. Annex to Resolution MSC.263(84), paras. 4–6.
22. Annex to Resolution MSC.263(84), para. 7.
23. Annex to Resolution MSC.263(84), para. 1.3.
24. See Annex to Resolution MSC.263(84) and MSC.1/Circ.1259.
25. Annex 2 of MSC 83/6/1, Draft Technical Specifications for the International LRIT Data Centre, para. 2.2.2.1.
26. Annex 2 of MSC 83/6/1, Draft Technical Specifications for the International LRIT Data Centre, para. 3.3.1.1.
27. IMO, MSC, 81st Session, Agenda item 25, Report of the Maritime Safety Committee, on Its Eighty-First Session, MSC 81/25, May 24, 2006, para. 5.121.
28. MSC, 82nd Session, Agenda item 8, Radiocommunications and Search and Rescue: Long-Range Identification and Tracking of Ships, submitted by the IMSO Secretariat, MSC 82/8/9, para. 5.1.
29. MSC 82/8/9, para. 5.1, citing Assembly/18/Record of Decisions paragraph 4.2.9.
30. See documents of the 83rd Session of IMO Maritime Safety Committee: MSC 83/6/7, MSC 83/6/11 and MSC 83/6/13 and 2nd Session of the Intersessional MSC Working Group on Long-range Identification and Tracking MSC/ISWG/LRIT 2/3/2.
31. IMO, Sub-Committee on Radiocommunications and Search and Rescue, 11th Session, Agenda item 14, Development of an E-Navigation Strategy: Report of the E-Navigation Strategy and LRIT Issues Working Group, COMSAR 11/WP.4/Add.1, February 21, 2007, paras. 16–19.
32. SOLAS Regulation V/19-1/8.1.
33. IMO, Intersessional MSC Working Group on Long-range Identification and Tracking, 1st Session, Agenda item 3, Development of the Draft SOLAS Amendments on Long-Range Identification and Tracking, submitted by Austria, Belgium, Bulgaria, Cyprus, Czech Republic, Denmark, Estonia, Finland, France, Germany, Hungary, Ireland, Italy, Latvia, Lithuania, Luxembourg, the Netherlands, Malta, Norway, Poland, Portugal, Romania, Slovakia, Slovenia, Spain, Sweden, the United Kingdom, and the European Commission, MSC/ISWG/LRIT 1/3/2, September 19, 2005, para. 4.6.
34. IMO, MSC, 79th Session, Agenda item 5, Measures to Enhance Maritime Security, LRIT of Ships, submitted by Australia, MSC 79/5/12, September 24, 2004, para. 8.

35. IMO, MSC, 80th Session, Agenda item 5, Measures to Enhance Maritime Security, submitted by the United States, MSC 80/5/8, March 4, 2005, para. 4. See also other submissions of the United States to IMO, MSC 77/6/16, MSC 78/3/5, COMSAR 8/13, COMSAR 8/13/5, COMSAR 9/12/8, and MSC 80/3/3.
36. MSC/ISWG/LRIT 1/3, para. 4.
37. MSC 80/WP.7/Add.1, para. 38.
38. IMO, Intersessional MSC Working Group on Long-range Identification and Tracking, 1st Session, Agenda item 3, Development of the Draft SOLAS Amendments on Long-range Identification and Tracking, submitted by the Russian Federation, MSC/ISWG/LRIT 1/3/4, September 20, 2005.
39. IMO, Sub-committee on Radiocommunications and Search and Rescue, 9th Session, Agenda item 12, Measures to Enhance Maritime Security, LRIT of Ships, submitted by Brazil, COMSAR 9/12/3, December 3, 2004.
40. See Martin Tsamenyi and Mary Ann Palma, "Legal Considerations in the Implementation of Long-range Identification and Tracking Systems for Vessels," *The Journal of International Maritime Law* 13:1, Jan–Feb 2007, 49–55.
41. Annex to Resolution MSC.263(84), para. 16.
42. Annex 2 of MSC 83/6/1, Draft Technical Specifications for the International LRIT Data Centre, para. 4.2.1.1.
43. Annex to Resolution MSC.263(84), paras. 15.3 and 15.5.
44. Annex 6 of MSC 83/6/1, Draft Guidance on Setting Up and Maintaining the LRIT Data Distribution Plan, para. 3.3.
45. Annex 2 of MSC 83/6/1, Draft Technical Specifications for the International LRIT Data Centre, para. 4.3.1.
46. Annex 2 of MSC 83/6/1, Draft Technical Specifications for the International LRIT Data Centre, para. 4.4.
47. Annex 2 of MSC 83/6/1, Draft Technical Specifications for the International LRIT Data Centre, para. 4.5.
48. Annex 2 of MSC 83/6/1, Draft Technical Specifications for the International LRIT Data Centre, paras 3.2.4.3 and 3.2.5.1.10.
49. Food and Agriculture Organization, Fisheries Management, *FAO Technical Guidelines for Responsible Fisheries No. 4*, Rome, 1997, p. 30.
50. IMO, Maritime Safety Committee, 76th Session, Agenda item 4, Measures to Enhance Maritime Security, Consideration of Comments on Draft Conference Resolution 10, submitted by ICS, BIMCO, IPTA, INTERTANKO, ICCL, and SIGTTO, MSC 76/4/21, November 1, 2002, paras 3.b and 4.
51. IMO, Intersessional MSC Working Group on Long-range Identification and Tracking, 1st Session, Agenda item 3, Development of the Draft SOLAS Amendments on Long-Range Identification and Tracking, submitted by the Islamic Republic of Iran, MSC/ISWG/LRIT 1/3, September 15, 2005, para. 4.2.
52. MSC/ISWG/LRIT 1/3, para. 4.3.
53. SOLAS Regulation V/19-1/10.
54. Annex 3 of MSC 83/6/1, Draft Technical Specifications for Communication in the LRIT System, para. 5.2.4.
55. Annex 1 of MSC 83/6/1, Draft Technical Specification for the International LRIT Data Exchange, para. 4.1.4.1.
56. SOLAS Regulation V/19-1/9.1.
57. SOLAS Regulation V/19-1/9.2.
58. SOLAS Regulation V/19-1/9.3.
59. SOLAS Regulation V/19-1/11.1 and 11.2.
60. SOLAS Regulation V/19-1/12.
61. Annex 4 of MSC 83/6/1, Draft LRIT Technical Costing and Billing Standard, subsection 2.4.1.1 and 2.4.1.1.
62. IMO, MSC, 83rd Session, Agenda item 6, Performance Review and Audit of the LRIT system, MSC 83/6/7, 6 July 2007, paras. 23–24.
63. IMO, MSC, 83rd Session, Agenda item 6, LRIT-Related Matters. Comments on the Outcome of COMSAR 11, submitted by the United States, MSC 83/6/4, July 2, 2007, para 3.
64. IMO, MSC, 83rd Session, Agenda item 6, LRIT-Related Matters. Comments on the Outcome of COMSAR 11 and MSC/ISWG/LRIT 2, submitted by Canada, MSC 83/6/15, August 14, 2007, para. 6.

65. IMO, MSC, 83rd Session, Agenda item 6, LRIT-Related Matters. Comments on the Outcome of COMSAR 11, submitted by Australia, MSC/ISWG/LRIT 2/3/1, 6 July 2007, paras. 4–5.

66. IMO, MSC, 83rd Session, Agenda item 6, LRIT-Related Matters. Comments on the outcome of COMSAR 11 and MSC/ISWG/LRIT 2, submitted by India, MSC 83/6/16, August 14, 2007, paras. 5–6.

67. IMO, MSC, LRIT-Related Matters: Report on the Outcome of the Intersessional Meetings of the *Ad Hoc* Working Group on Engineering Aspects of Long-Range Identification and Tracking of Ships, submitted by the Chairman of the *Ad Hoc* Working Group, MSC 83/6/1, July 9, 2007, Annex 7; See also IMO, Intersessional MSC Working Group on Long-Range Identification and Tracking, 2nd Session, Agenda item 3, Consideration of Issues for the Timely Establishment of the LRIT System, Information in Relation to the submission and circulation of documents, Outcome of the *Ad Hoc* Working Group on engineering aspects of LRIT, Note by the Secretariat, MSC/ISWG/LRIT 2/3/Add.1, July 5, 2007, Annex 2.

15 International Legal Regulatory Framework for Seafarers and Maritime Security Post-9/11

Martin Tsamenyi, Mary Ann Palma, and Clive Schofield

CONTENTS

INTRODUCTION

The terrorist attacks on the United States on September 11, 2001 have undoubtedly transformed the global security environment, and these changes necessarily extend to the maritime domain. Maritime security concerns encompass not only the security of maritime spaces, ships, and ports, but also security in respect of those charged with operating in the maritime environment and facilitating global seaborne trade—seafarers.

The world seafaring industry is considered as an area of vulnerability in the security of the maritime transport sector. This view stems from research, such as those conducted by the Seafarers

International Research Centre (SIRC) at Cardiff University, which indicates that many international seafarers have fraudulent documentation.[1] Indeed, in 2001 alone, there were 12,635 detected cases of forgery in certificates of competency and equivalent endorsements.[2] These numbers and the potential vulnerability of ships and ports to maritime security risks have provoked concerns that it would not be difficult for a terrorist to assume the identity of a seafarer to gain the skills required to operate a ship or move around the world.

Contemporary concerns over maritime security issues relating to seafarers have also provoked media attention. For example, in September 2007, on the eve of a regional leaders summit[3] in Sydney, Australia, a newspaper report warned that during the meeting almost 1500 t of explosives would be shipped in and out of port facilities in proximity to Sydney Airport, on "unregulated" ships manned by crews that had "undergone no background checks".[4] Although the news report was somewhat sensationalist in tone, it nonetheless serves to further highlight an important maritime security concern—ensuring security in relation to seafarers.

Accordingly, and particularly in response to the 9/11 terrorist attacks, the assembly of the International Maritime Organization (IMO) adopted a resolution at its 22nd session calling on states to review measures and procedures to prevent acts of terrorism that threaten the security of passengers and crews and the safety of ships.[5] Besides the security of passengers and crews onboard ships, concerns were also raised about the associated risks of terrorist attacks to ports, offshore terminals and the marine environment, and the people on shore and in the vicinity of port areas. The resolution further prompted the International Labor Organization (ILO) to take measures to enhance maritime security through the improvement of security of seafarers' identification and complementary port security measures. These significant concerns have given rise to efforts designed to improve maritime security by ensuring that seafarers have positive verifiable identification documents.[6]

This chapter outlines the pre-9/11 international regulatory framework for seafarer identification before examining post-9/11 developments, notably the conclusion of the Seafarers' Identity Documents (SID) Convention 2003, with specific focus on the limitations of the regulatory framework from a maritime security perspective. The introduction of mechanisms for the positive verification of seafarer identities, for example, the application of innovative technologies such as biometrics, is addressed. The need to ensure security while simultaneously facilitating maritime trade and protecting the rights of the individual seafarers concerned is also highlighted. The chapter concludes by calling for a wider implementation of the SID Convention 2003 to enhance security in maritime transport.

THE ROLE OF SEAFARERS IN INTERNATIONAL SHIPPING

Over 90 percent of world trade is transported by sea, and the international shipping industry is crucial to an increasingly globalized and interdependent world economy.[7] According to the United Nations Conference on Trade and Development (UNCTAD) the world merchant fleet comprising oil tankers, bulk carriers, general cargo, container ships, and other types of vessels stood at 960 million deadweight t as of January 1, 2006, representing a 7.2 percent increase from 2005.[8] The growth in the volume of seaborne trade is also complemented by a significant increase in port traffic. The UNCTAD review further noted that for developing countries alone, container port throughput reached 336.9 million 20 ft equivalent units (TEUs) in 2004, reflecting an increase of 12.4 percent from 2003.[9]

Seafarers provide the backbone to this globalized maritime transportation industry. There are about 1.3 million seafarers in the world, accounting for about 409,000 officers and 825,000 ratings.[10] Seafarers are directly involved in the international transportation of goods, including sensitive, high-value and dangerous goods as well as the carriage of passengers. A particular noticeable feature of the industry is that the majority of seafarers come from developing states. Table 15.1 shows the major seafarer-producing states in the world.

TABLE 15.1

Major Suppliers of Seafarers in the World, 2005

Country	Officers	Ratings	Total
China	42,704	79,504	122,208
The Philippines[a]	46,359	74,040	120,399
Turkey[a]	22,091	60,328	82,419
India[a]	46,497	32,352	78,849
Ukraine	28,908	36,119	65,027
Russia	21,680	34,000	55,680
Indonesia[a]	7,750	34,000	41,750
Greece	17,000	15,000	32,000
Myanmar	6,000	23,000	29,000
Egypt[a]	3,970	17,999	21,969
Italy	9,560	11,390	20,950
The United States	6,433	14,127	20,560
Japan	12,968	6,856	19,824
Honduras	4,239	15,341	19,580
Croatia	10,300	9,200	19,500
The United Kingdom	14,050	4,500	18,550
Latvia	7,515	10,027	17,542
Brazil	4,504	12,194	16,698
Canada	4,557	10,076	14,633

[a] Estimated numbers of officers or ratings for certain countries were reduced using an activity rate factor of 50 percent.

Note: The original data provided for the following countries are as follows: (1) Indonesia—officers, 46,497; ratings, 64,704. (2) Philippines—officers, 97,842; ratings, 158,934. (3) Turkey—officers, 22,091; ratings, 241,309.

Source: Adapted from: Warwick Institute for Employment Research, *BIMCO/ISF Manpower 2005 Update: The Worldwide Demand for Supply of Seafarers, Main Report*, University of Warwick, Coventry: Team Impression Ltd., December 2005, Appendix C.

PRE-9/11 REGULATORY FRAMEWORK

Given the international character of seaborne trade and seafarers, traditionally, the regulatory framework for the movement of seafarers has been international in scope. Before September 11, 2001, the international regulatory framework comprised the SID Convention 1958 and the Convention on Facilitation of Maritime Traffic, 1965 (FAL Convention) as amended.

SID CONVENTION 1958

The SID Convention 1958 was adopted on May 13, 1958 and came into force on February 19, 1961.[11] The purpose of the SID Convention 1958 was to create an internationally recognized seafarers' document that would be acknowledged by immigration officials to facilitate entry by seafarers into the territories of contracting parties for shore leave and transit purposes.[12] SIDs serve two main purposes. First, although SIDs do not have the same effect as passports, they are intended to provide for positive identification that the document holder is the person to whom it is issued and for the verification of the authenticity of the document to a source. In this respect, Article 2 of SID Convention 1958 provides that if it is not practicable for a party to issue an SID to its national, a passport indicating that the holder is a seafarer should be issued instead. Positive and verifiable identification is intended to assist in the recognition of seafarers by immigration officials, port administrations, customs officials, consular offices, and health and security services, to enable them to have legitimate access to shore facilities while the vessel is in port.

Second, SIDs are intended to facilitate the entry of a seafarer into the territory of a state without the need to apply for a visa, whether for the purpose of temporary shore leave or when in transit to join a ship or to be repatriated. Article 6(1) of the SID Convention 1958 requires its party to permit the entry of a seafarer holding a valid SID into its territory. The SID Convention 1958 does not require a seafarer to possess a visa when requesting for temporary shore leave. Each party is also required to permit the entry of a seafarer holding a valid SID when entry is requested for the purpose of joining his ship, transferring to another ship, passing in transit to join his ship in another country, or for repatriation.[13] However, the right of the seafarer to be granted entry into a party's territory is not absolute. Article 6(3) provides that any party to the SID Convention 1958 may, before permitting entry into its territory, require satisfactory evidence, including documentary evidence, of a seafarer's intention to enter the territory of a party or ability to carry out that intention. Such evidence is obtained from the seafarer, the owner or agent concerned, or from the appropriate consul. This provision implies that a party may legally require the presentation of a visa and other documents other than the SID from the seafarer. This power is further strengthened by Article 6(4) of the SID Convention 1958 which provides that "(N)othing in this Article shall be construed as restricting the right of a Member to prevent any particular individual from entering or remaining in its territory."

Implementation of SID Convention 1958

State practice with regard to SIDs has been far from uniform. Some parties to the SID Convention 1958 such as Norway and Brazil provide exemptions to visa requirements of holders of SIDs issued in accordance with the convention.[14] However, in general, especially for nonparties to the SID Convention 1958, immigration-related national legislation often conflicts with the provisions of the convention concerning the possession of SIDs, obtaining visas for entry into a country's territory, and presentation of passports in lieu of SIDs. For example, New Zealand issues SIDs under the SID Convention 1958, but also requires their nationals to hold valid passports.[15] Conversely, its legislation exempts foreign crew of merchant ships (and commercial aircrafts) from requirements for entry permits, and allows, in some circumstances, for the acceptance of other certificates of identity apart from passports.[16]

In China, foreign crew are required to hold valid crew embarkation cards or boarding cards issued by relevant public authorities before being granted shore leave. For France, shore leave passes are required. In Italy, certain consular conventions may require reciprocal visa endorsement of the sailors' passports, certificates of navigation, or similar documents. In such cases, if the holder of the certificate of navigation or of a similar document is not provided with the reciprocal visa, the Italian authorities will issue the holder with a *laissez-passer* of limited validity.[17]

There are also differences between national practice and the provisions of the SID Convention 1958 on transit and repatriation. In the Netherlands, for example, a Schengen visa is issued to a foreign seafarer after confirmation that the ship and employing company exist and after indicating the port of call. The ship's agent or the manning agent is required to sign a guarantee for possible claims in and by the Netherlands. The seafarer's passport is then stamped and is directed to the ship's agent who must provide transport to the seafarer to the ship. For departure or repatriation, the ship's agent is required to report to the border control authorities that a seafarer is signing off or is to be repatriated. The agent also has the obligation to take the seafarer to the airport.[18]

Some parties to the SID Convention 1958 even have more stringent measures applied to foreign seafarers who are transiting to join ships or are about to be repatriated than those adopted under the convention. In accordance with Greece's Ministerial Decision No. 4803/13/10 of 2000 on conditions and procedures for the entry and exit of foreign seafarers in cases of recruitment and discharge, the seafarer is required to possess a Schengen visa specifying the name of the vessel, the flag, and the ship registration number.[19] At least two days before the entry of the seafarer in the Schengen zone, the shipowner or agent must also provide two documents to the Greek passport control of the port where the ship is located. The first document is a statement confirming the recruitment of the foreign seafarer and guaranteeing all expenses and liability for repatriation. The second is a certificate from the local coast guard that the ship is not detained or under arrest. In the case of the transfer of a seafarer to another ship administered by the same company, the passport control office issues a transit visa. For repatriation, the Greek passport control office issues a transit visa for the time required for exit on presentation of a ticket, a statement from the shipowner assuming liability for repatriation, and a coast guard certification that the seafarer was an active crew member.[20]

It may be seen from the practice of some states that the entry of foreign seafarers to national territories is subject to more rigorous measures than the provisions of the SID Convention 1958. The requirement to obtain and present other documents besides SIDs, such as visas and shore leave or transit passes, is an assertion of the basic right of states to govern the admittance of anyone in their territories for any purpose. However, in the case where a seafarer is not able to comply with the requirements of the state for reasons beyond his or her control, the seafarer may be detained on the ship or in port. In such a case, the SID Convention 1958 will prove insufficient to uphold the basic right of seafarers to shore leave and access facilities in ports. It can therefore be argued that the right of members of the SID Convention 1958 to impose additional requirements on the entry of seafarers in their territories almost render the provisions of the convention with respect to shore leave, transit, and transfer to another ship ineffectual because the admittance of seafarers into a state's territory will always be subject to the exclusive discretion of the state concerned.

Maritime Security Concerns Relating to the SID Convention 1958

Under the SID Convention 1958, the precise form and content of the SID is decided by the party issuing it. The inevitable consequence is that the identification cards for each state are different in appearance. Besides the requirement that the SIDs be designed in a simple manner, be made of durable material, and be produced in a manner that any alterations are easily detectible, there are no other security features specific to the issuance of SIDs under the SID Convention 1958. Given the lack of standardization in developing and issuing SIDs, the authenticity of various formats of identification cards becomes difficult to ascertain. A number of other security-related concerns have been raised about the SID Convention 1958. Some of the major concerns are summarized in the following:

- SIDs often have poor quality and security features.
- SIDs do not necessarily state the sex of the holder and there is no requirement as to the language in which the document must be written.
- In many cases, the bearers' details are handwritten, raising concerns on authenticity and forgery.
- There are no requirements to stipulate the expiry dates of the SIDs.
- The bearer's details are usually incomplete and do not offer the level of information available on a national passport.
- Information within the document is not updated and documents that do not have an expiry date are rarely renewed with a current photograph.
- Personal details of the bearer of the SID may be subsequently different from that stated on the same person's passport (e.g., some countries issue SIDs in the official names of the holders, whereas others issue SIDs in unofficial names).[21]
- Disclosure of the nationality of the bearer of the SID is not mandatory. Article 4(4) of SID Convention 1958 states that "(I)f a Member issues a seafarer's identity document to a foreign seafarer it shall not be necessary to include any statement as to his nationality, nor shall any such statement be conclusive proof of his nationality."

- SIDs may be issued outside the bearer's country with the consequence that immigration authorities are often unsure if an SID is genuine or counterfeit, or whether the issuing state has even ratified the convention.
- SIDs issued under the SID Convention 1958 are not machine-readable.[22]

CONVENTION ON FACILITATION OF INTERNATIONAL MARITIME TRAFFIC 1965

To meet the growing international concern about excessive documents required for merchant shipping, the FAL Convention was developed under the IMO. The objective of the FAL Convention is to facilitate and expedite international maritime traffic and prevent unnecessary delays to ships, persons, and property on board by minimizing the formalities; documentary requirements and procedures associated with the arrival, stay, and departure of ships;[23] and by securing the highest practicable degree of uniformity in such requirements and procedures.[24] It addresses the need to simplify the requirements of customs, immigration, health, and other authorities with respect to ships, its crew and passengers, baggage, and cargo. To date, the FAL Convention has been ratified or acceded to by 110 states or 68.31 percent of the world tonnage.

Under the FAL Convention, a valid SID or a passport is legally considered as the basic document providing public authorities with information relating to the individual member of the crew on arrival or departure of a ship.[25] Under the FAL Convention, states that have not ratified the SID Convention 1958 but have ratified the FAL Convention may issue national identity documents meeting the same standard as required by the SID Convention 1958. Public authorities are also given the right under the FAL Convention to require information from seafarers similar to those required under the SID Convention 1958.[26]

The FAL Convention provides that part of the formalities required of shipowners by public authorities on the arrival, stay, and departure of the ship is the submission of a number of documents, among which are a general declaration, the crew list, and crew's effects declaration.[27] Section 2.2.2 of the FAL Convention states that with respect to the crew, public authorities are not allowed to require more than the number of crew to be stipulated in the general declaration. Section 2.6.1 further provides that in the crew list, public authorities may only require the following information:

- Name and nationality of ship
- Family name
- Given names
- Nationality
- Rank or rating
- Date and place of birth
- Nature and number of identity document
- Port and date of arrival
- Arriving from

In terms of security, the requirement to submit these documents and information may be seen as a measure to verify the details that will be obtained from the ship and its seafarers at ports.

Paragraph 3.10.2 of the FAL Convention states that when it is necessary for a seafarer to enter or leave a country as a passenger by any means of transportation for the purpose of joining a ship, transferring to another ship, or for repatriation, authorities are required to accept from that seafarer a valid SID in place of a passport. This is the case when the SID guarantees the readmission of the bearer in question to the country that issued the document. It is a recommended practice under the FAL Convention for public authorities not to require the presentation of individual identity documents or of information supplementing the SID in respect of members of the crew other than that given in the crew list.[28]

The FAL Convention also adopts measures to facilitate shore leave of foreign crew. Section 3.44 of the FAL Convention states that

> (F)oreign crew members shall be allowed ashore by the public authorities while the ship on which they arrive is in port, provided that the formalities on arrival of the ship have been fulfilled and the public authorities have no reason to refuse permission to come ashore for reasons of public health, public safety or public order.

This measure is similar to that provided in Article 6 of the SID Convention 1958, which provides for the right of the member state to deny entry of a seafarer into its port or territorial waters. Additionally, foreign crew members shall not be required to hold a visa, or special permit such as a pass for the purpose of shore leave.[29] The FAL Convention recommends that crew members, before going on or returning from shore leave, must not be subjected to personal checks.[30] A further recommendation is that authorities provide a system of prearrival clearance to allow the crew of ships that call regularly at their ports to obtain advance approval for temporary shore leave.[31]

Implementation of the FAL Convention

State practice, as can be illustrated with reference to a few examples selected among parties, has shown substantial differences from the requirements of the FAL Convention. Argentina, for example, requires that SIDs establish the sex of the seafarer. The United Kingdom accepts SIDs in lieu of passports, if such documents establish the nationality as well as the identity of the seafarers. In the case of SID issued to a nonnational of the issuing country, the United Kingdom also requires a guarantee of returnability to the issuing country. India accepts the SID as a valid travel document in lieu of a national passport, but a seafarer traveling to India as a passenger is required to possess a visa for India. In Poland, the acceptance of a valid SID in place of a passport requires obtaining permission or visa from the relevant authority. Similarly, Thailand does not accept SIDs without valid visas in lieu of passports.[32]

The United States requires seafarers to obtain transit and crew visas called individual C-1/D visas. The C-1 part of the visa allows a seafarer to remain in U.S. waters for up to 29 days. This allows them to travel from port to port, and when necessary, to transit from the airport to the seaport and vice versa. The D part of the visa identifies the seafarer to U.S. immigration authorities as a crew member working on board a vessel. Some of the documentary requirements for the application of the individual C-1/D visas are the seafarer's ID or registration card, employment history of the seafarer, employment contract, training certificates, and college diplomas. Visas are also issued to the crew of international vessels operating on the outer continental shelf. Seafarer recruitment agencies also have to be accredited before being able to submit transit and crew visas on behalf of their seafarers.

The United States has also adopted security measures on the identification of seafarers as part of the formalities on the arrival of ships. Section 402 of the Enhanced Border Security and Visa Entry Reform Act provides the requirement for commercial aircraft or vessels arriving at, or departing from, the United States to provide border officers with specified passenger and crew manifest information 96 hours before arrival in the port. Manifest information would need to include the complete name, date of birth, citizenship, sex, passport number and issuing country, country of residence, and information on U.S. visa. Similar to the SID Convention 1958, the practice of states with respect to seafarers' identification diverges from the requirements of the FAL Convention.

POST-9/11 REGULATORY FRAMEWORK

After September 11, 2001, the international regulatory framework for seafarers has been substantially modified to address global maritime security concerns, resulting primarily in the adoption of the International Ship and Port Facility Security (ISPS) Code and the SID Convention 2003.

THE INTERNATIONAL SHIP AND PORT FACILITY SECURITY CODE

The ISPS Code was adopted by IMO governments in December 2002 as an amendment to the International Convention on the Safety of Life at Sea (SOLAS), 1974 as amended. The ISPS Code aims at establishing an international framework for cooperation to detect and assess security threats and take preventive measures against security incidents affecting ships or port facilities used in international trade. The ISPS Code recognizes in its preamble the need for seafarers to take shore leave and have access to shore-based seafarer welfare facilities. It also requires the development of port facility security plans in compliance with the code to address, among other things, procedures for facilitating shore leave for ship's personnel or personnel changes, as well as access to visitors to the ship, including representatives of seafarers' welfare and labor organizations.[33]

SID CONVENTION 2003

In December 2002, the conference of contracting governments to the SOLAS convention adopted Conference Resolution 8 on the enhancement of security in cooperation with the ILO. This resolution recognized that the development and use of a verifiable SID would enhance and positively contribute toward international efforts to ensure maritime security and prevent and suppress acts threatening the security of maritime transport.[34] Conference Resolution 8 invited the ILO to continue the development of an SID comprising a document for professional purposes, a verifiable security document, and a certification information document.[35] As a result, the SID Convention 2003 was adopted on June 19, 2003 to revise the SID Convention 1958. Article 12.2 of the convention requires ratification by only two members for the convention to come into force. Only 11 states have ratified the Convention as on August 31, 2007.[36]

The SID Convention 2003 has introduced more comprehensive measures for the issuance of SIDs compared to either the SID Convention 1958 or the FAL Convention. The SID Convention 2003 provides a definition for a seafarer, contains provisions on the facilitation of shore leave and transit and transfer of seafarers, establishes a model for the content and form of SIDs, provides for the use of a biometric template, and requires states to develop national electronic databases on seafarers.

Under the SID Convention 2003, members of the convention are required to issue to each of its seafarer nationals a seafarers identity document. Article 2 of the SID Convention 2003 also provides that members may issue SIDs to seafarers who have been granted the status of permanent residents in its territory. As an important first step, the SID Convention 2003 clearly defined the term *seafarer* as "any person who is employed or is engaged or works in any capacity on board a vessel, other than a ship of war, ordinarily engaged in maritime navigation."[37] Finally, unlike the SID 1958 and the FAL Conventions, the SID Convention 2003 also applies to commercial maritime fishing. The key aspects of the SID Convention 2003 are analyzed in the succeeding subsections.

Content and Form of SIDs under the SID Convention 2003

The SID Convention 2003 provides a common international standard for the issuance of SIDs. It provides the requirement for SIDs to be designed in a simple manner, be made of durable material, and be machine-readable to avoid tampering or falsification, and enable easy detection of alterations. Parties to the SID Convention 2003 are given the right to determine the maximum validity of SIDs in accordance with national laws and regulations; however, the validity should not exceed ten years, subject to renewal after the first five years.[38] Article 3 and Annex I of the SID Convention 2003 provide the details that are required to be entered on the data page(s) of an SID, as follows:

- Name of the issuing authority
- Telephone number(s), e-mail, and Web site of the authority
- Date and place of issue of the document

- Digital or original photograph of the seafarer
- Full name of the seafarer
- Sex
- Date and place of birth
- Nationality
- Any special physical characteristics of the seafarer that may assist identification
- Signature
- Date of expiry
- Type or designation of document
- Unique document number
- Personal identification number (optional)
- Biometric template based on a fingerprint printed as number in a bar code (conforming to the standards developed by the ILO)
- A machine-readable zone conforming to International Civil Aviation Organization (ICAO) specifications
- Official seal or stamp of the issuing authority

The SID Convention 2003 therefore provides significantly more information to be included in SIDs compared to the requirements of the SID Convention 1958 and the FAL Convention. A statement is also required to be placed on the SID emphasising that the document is a stand-alone document and not a passport.

Requirements for Biometrics

The most significant feature of SIDs under the SID Convention 2003 is the inclusion of a biometric template. Biometrics is the use of a physiological or behavioral characteristic unique to each individual for positive and verifiable identification.[39] The SID Convention 2003 requires the development of a global interoperable standard for the biometric template based on a fingerprint as numbers in a bar code. In March 2004, the ILO adopted the technical standard, ILO SID-0002 Finger Minutiae-Based Biometric Profile, for SIDs.[40]

A biometric template is the digital representation of a biometric record that cannot be reverse-engineered back to the initial biometric representation record.[41] Under Article 3(8) of the SID Convention 2003, a template or other representation of a biometric of the holder will be included in the SID provided that it meets certain conditions. First, the biometric needs to be captured without any invasion of privacy of the persons concerned, without causing discomfort to them, risk to their health, or offense to their dignity. Second, the biometric must be visible on the document and it should not be possible to reconstitute it from the template or other representation. Third, the equipment needed for the provision and verification of the biometric, once developed, will need to be user-friendly and generally accessible to governments at low cost. Such equipment needs to be conveniently and reliably operated in ports and in other places, including onboard ships, where verification of identity is normally carried out by the competent authorities. Fourth, the system in which the biometric is to be used, including the equipment, technologies, and procedures for use, should provide results that are uniform and reliable for the authentication of identity.

There are various technical issues related to the application of biometrics in issuing SIDs, which the ILO has tried to resolve when it conducted its biometric testing campaign and established the standards for acquiring fingerprints as biometric representation of seafarers. Questions have also been raised about the interoperability of the system. However, the major issue in implementing the provisions on biometrics under the SID Convention 2003 is the cost to developing states. Some critics maintain that although biometric technology improves security in some situations, its costs more frequently far outweigh its benefits.[42] Most of the developing seafaring nations of the world such as the Philippines, Indonesia, India, and Eastern European countries would require substantial financial capacity to be able to procure the technology required to implement the standards for biometrics under the new convention.

National Electronic Databases

Article 4 of the SID Convention 2003 requires every party to ensure that a record of each SID issued, suspended, or withdrawn is stored in an electronic database. Annex II of the SID Convention 2003 provides the types of information that need to be recorded in a national electronic database. These are:

- Issuing authority named on the identity document
- Full name of the seafarer as written on the identity document
- Unique document number of the identity document
- Date of expiry or suspension or withdrawal of the identity document
- Biometric template appearing on the identity document
- Photograph
- Details of all inquiries made concerning the SID[43]

Such information is deemed sufficient under the SID Convention 2003 to verify the authenticity of the SIDs, their contents, and the status of seafarers. Article 4 of the SID Convention 2003 requires members to maintain the national database system for SIDs consistent with data protection requirements and seafarers' right to privacy. Article 4(3) further entails the adoption of procedures that will enable a seafarer to examine and check the validity of all the data held or stored in the electronic database and provide correction, if necessary, at no cost to the seafarer concerned. The establishment of a national electronic database on SIDs is intended to assist states in facilitating the exchange of information in cases where additional verification of the details of a seafarer is needed.

Similar to the acquisition of the product for biometrics, the costs of administering the national electronic database of thousands of seafarers are also likely to be high for developing seafaring nations. Maintaining a national database involves implementing measures to protect and secure biometric information while providing access to immigration offices and other competent authorities of other states. There may also be legal impediments to the provision of access to information as different states have different laws and regulations with respect to personal privacy and confidentiality of information.

Shore Leave and Transit and Transfer of Seafarers under SID Convention 2003

Shore leave is one of the fundamental rights of a seafarer. It is often the only opportunity for seafarers, particularly ratings, to contact their families and receive social services.[44] Lack of shore leave means confinement on ships that affect the well-being of a seafarer, causes fatigue in the long run, and affects the ability of the seafarer to perform his or her work, with obvious safety implications. Article 6(4) of the SID Convention 2003 requires parties to permit the entry of a seafarer holding a valid SID into its territory with minimal delay when entry is requested for temporary shore leave while the ship is in port, unless clear grounds exist for doubting the authenticity of the SID. Entry is to be permitted provided that the formalities related to the arrival of the ship have been fulfilled and the competent authorities have no reason to refuse permission to come ashore on grounds of public health, public safety, public order, or national security.[45]

In cases of transit and transfer of seafarers, parties to the SID Convention 2003 may require the presentation of SIDs, supplemented by passports.[46] Similar to granting entry to a seafarer for the purpose of shore leave, entry is permitted for the purposes of transfer and transit unless clear grounds exist for doubting the authenticity of the SID and that competent authorities have no reason to refuse entry on grounds of public health, public safety, public order, or national security. Parties may also require satisfactory evidence, including documentary evidence of a seafarer's intention, and ability to carry out that intention, and may further limit the seafarer's stay to a period considered reasonable for the purpose in question.

Similar to the provisions of the SID Convention 1958 and FAL Convention, the provisions of the SID Convention 2003 clearly suggest that a state has the discretion to allow or refuse the entry of a seafarer into its territory, even if that seafarer is in possession of a valid SID. If a seafarer is suspected to be a threat to the national security of a state, such a state may exercise its power to prevent the entry of such person to its territory. The key provision in the SID Convention 2003 that partially balances the right of states to deny entry of a foreign seafarer into their national territories for grounds of public health, safety, order, or national security is found in Article 6(6) of the SID Convention 2003. The article provides that "(f)or the purpose of shore leave, seafarers should not be required to hold a visa. Any Member which is not in a position to fully implement this requirement shall ensure that its laws and regulations or practice provide arrangements that are substantially equivalent."[47] This implies that a state may actually require a visa from a seafarer for purposes of shore leave, although it has the obligation to facilitate the delivery of such visa.

An example of a state that has adopted measures to facilitate the delivery of visas to seafarers to assist in their shore leave, at the same time protect its national security, is Australia.[48] On December 22, 2005, the Australian government announced funding of AUS$100.3 million (about U.S.$87 million) over five years to implement the maritime crew visa (MCV) that aims to strengthen Australia's border control mechanisms through increased security checks of maritime crew entering Australia.[49] As a result, Migration Act 1958 was amended by replacing the special-purpose visa with a new temporary visa called the MCV.[50] From January 1, 2008, a crew is required to hold a valid national passport, an MCV granted for the same passport, and another document that establishes the crew member's employment on the vessel such as a crew list, seaman's book, or contract. An application for an MCV requires a formal visa application process that brings the arrangements for foreign crew in line with other temporary entrants to Australia.

In terms of practical application, a seafarer may apply for an MCV via the Internet or by sending a paper application to Brisbane, Australia. A third party such as a shipping agent may also complete and submit an application based on the information provided by the applicant seafarer. Some of the features of an MCV are:

- Foreign sea crew (other than New Zealand citizens) will be required to hold an MCV for arrival and stay in Australia.
- Visa applicants must be outside Australia at the time of applying for an MCV.
- MCV will be free of charge.
- MCV will be granted for three years.
- MCV will only be valid for the travel to Australia by sea as ship's crew, and not by air.
- MCV will allow multiple entries to Australia by sea during the three-year validity.
- MCS will only permit work associated with the duties performed as crew with the vessel.[51]

By providing three-year validity to the MCV, access to port facilities by legitimate seafarers who are not threats to the security of Australia are facilitated. However, certain conditions will render MCVs to automatically cease or become invalid. These conditions are:

- If the crew leave a vessel on arriving in Australia without being immigration-cleared by Australian Customs
- If the crew do not sign on to a ship within five days of arriving in Australia by air on a transit visa and hold no other visa other than an MCV to remain in Australia
- If another visa held by the crew is cancelled by the department
- If a person is in Australia on another type of visa other than an MCV and that visa expires

- If the crew sign off a ship and do not depart Australia within five days, obtain another type of visa or sign on to another nonmilitary ship in that time
- If the ship on which the crew travel to Australia is ceasing its international voyage status and is declared "imported" by Australian Customs, and within five days the crew do not depart Australia, or sign on to another nonmilitary ship, or do not obtain another suitable visa from the department to authorize their continued lawful stay in Australia
- If the crew no longer satisfy the legal requirements under which they are granted the MCV
- If the crew perform work while in Australia other than work that is required in relation to the usual operational requirements of their ship
- If the presence of a crew member is determined to be "undesirable" by the department[52]

In addition to these security measures, Australia implements other measures to enhance maritime security with respect to seafarer identification. Australia requires vessels to provide prearrival passenger and crew reports no later than 96 hours before arriving in Australia. The Australian Customs Service requires vessels to fill out a number of crew report forms. For international cruise ships and container cargo vessels, electronic passenger and crew reports are required to be transmitted through the Advance Person Processing (APP). APP is an online system through which prearrival reports of shipping passengers and crew traveling to Australia are sent, and the Australian Customs Service notifies the relevant authorities of persons on their way to Australia. APP also allows shipping operators and agents to verify if persons on board hold valid visas or travel authorities to enter Australia. Although APP only applies to international cruise ships and container cargo ships, it would only be a matter of time before all commercial ships traveling to Australia will be expected to use the online APP to replace manual reporting using paper forms. Australian Customs is also planning to develop a vessel profile capability within Information Network to Enhance Response, Control, Enforcement and Prevention Techniques (INTERCEPT)—a computer system recording details of all vessel and crew movements, including recording of ship security information for the Department of Transport and Regional Services (DOTARS).[53] However, due to the MCV initiative, the plan has been delayed. INTERCEPT requires significant changes to capture the required information on crew visa details and adapt the system to the new requirements on maritime crew visa. These initiatives also complement the proposed implementation of the Australian Maritime Identification System (AMIS) to enhance maritime surveillance for purposes of border and fisheries protection and counterterrorism response and interdiction. Under the AMIS, ships intending to enter an Australian port will be requested to provide basic advanced arrival information up to 1000 Nmi from the Australian coast regarding identity, crews, cargo, and ship movements.[54]

OTHER MARITIME SECURITY MEASURES

Because the general objective of adopting new measures with respect to SIDs is to improve maritime security, it remains crucial to address not only the issue of seafarers' identification, but also other security-related issues involving the seafaring industry, such as fraud and forgery of certificates and regulating the access of seafarers to port areas. Most fraudulent certificates are issued to misrepresent the holder's identity, competency, training, experience, age, or medical fitness.[55] Therefore, the international community through the IMO and ILO have adopted measures and standards that address these issues. These measures, however, are nonbinding in nature.

GUIDANCE ON ANTIFRAUD MEASURES AND FORGERY PREVENTION FOR SEAFARERS' CERTIFICATES

The Sub-Committee on Standards of Training and Watchkeeping, at its 34th session in 2003, developed antifraud measures and forgery-prevention features for seafarers' certificates. This guidance was endorsed by the Maritime Safety Committee as MSC/Circ.1089. The aim of MSC/Circ.1089 is to provide information on the various antifraud and antiforgery measures and procedures that may be adopted by IMO member governments.[56] To obtain this objective, IMO member governments are encouraged to use modern technology features to prevent fraud and protect the integrity of certificates in a way that makes replication of the certificates extremely difficult and attempts to alter data that is easily detectable. In compliance with Regulation I/8 of the International Convention on Standard of Training, Certification, and Watchkeeping (STCW Convention), 1978 as amended, and Section A-I/8 of the STCW Code, parties are required to develop and implement appropriate structured antifraud and forgery-prevention policies and procedures that may include various measures such as procedures for the printing, storage, handling, and distribution of blank certificates; maintenance of records of certificates issued; prevention of unauthorized access to databases on certificates; and investigation of alleged frauds or forgeries.[57] Member governments are further required to protect and ensure confidentiality of personal information of seafarers. MSC/Circ. 1089 recognizes that a number of member governments have in place measures or procedures addressing the issue of fraud and forgery. It is up to each member government to decide how to make use of the guidance provided in the circular or at which stage it will revise existing or introduce new measures or procedures in this respect.

GUIDANCE FOR ADMINISTRATIONS, COMPANIES, MASTERS, AND MANNING AGENTS IN DETECTING AND PREVENTING UNLAWFUL PRACTICES

This guidance was also adopted by the Sub-Committee on Standards of Training and Watchkeeping in 2003 as MSC/Circ.1090 to complement MSC/Circ.1089. It aims to assist administrations, shipping companies, manning agents, and shipmasters in identifying the nature and forms of some of the most common unlawful practices related to certificates of competency. MSC/Circ.1090 also provides general recommendation to address the problems. The types of unlawful practices discussed in the circular are:

- Tampering with or unlawful manufacturing of certificates of competency
- Impersonating of a genuine seafarer
- Falsifying information provided to employers
- Forging of, or tampering with, ancillary certificates to apply for a certificate of competency
- Falsifying records of seagoing service to apply for a certificate of competency
- Employing various methods of "cheating" when undertaking examinations required before the issue of a certificate of competency[58]

In the case of the problem of impersonation of seafarers, MSC/Circ.1090 made direct reference to the SID Conventions and emphasized the need for administrations and shipping industries to establish robust procedures to ensure the security of national identity documents.

Both the MSC Circulars 1089 and 1090 were adopted after a review was conducted on the current national database standards, record system, and antifraud measures used by STCW parties. In the study conducted by SIRC on fraudulent practices associated with certificates of competency, it was found that the implementation of IMO member governments on antifraud measures is beset by a number of problems. First, the technology used by states to protect the integrity of certificates and verify the authenticity and identity of the holder is inadequate. Second, there is a lack of harmonization in certificates that makes it difficult for port state inspectors and foreign authorities to detect fraudulent certificates. Third, there is a lack of formal antifraud programs in place across IMO governments and little exchange of information occurs among administrations.[59] It would, therefore, be beneficial for states to consider adopting and implementing some of the recommended measures developed under MSC Circulars 1089 and 1090.

CODE OF PRACTICE ON SECURITY IN PORTS

This Code of Practice was adopted by the ILO to provide guidance in maintaining security in ports and in identifying the roles and responsibilities of governments, employers, and workers in achieving this objective. It embodies the practice and principles of SOLAS chapter XI-2 on special measures to enhance maritime security and the ISPS Code. More specifically, one of the aims of port security measures is to prevent access to the port by persons without a legitimate reason to be there and prevent those persons with legitimate reasons from gaining illegal access to ships or other restricted port areas for the purpose of committing unlawful acts.[60]

Based on the ISPS Code, the Code of Practice provides for the adoption of a Port Security Plan (PSP). One of the requirements under the PSP to promote the physical security of ports is to define procedures for the issuance, verification, and return of port access documents. It is emphasized in the Code of Practice that SIDs issued in accordance with the SID Convention 2003 would meet all the requirements of the code for the purposes of identification and access to ports of seafarers.[61]

Australia and the United States are examples of states that have adopted measures that establish the identification of people working in ports. The Maritime Transport and Offshore Facilities Security Amendment Regulations 2005 of Australia provides for a scheme under which a maritime security identification card (MSIC) is issued to identify a person who has been the subject of a background check.[62] The MSIC is a nationally consistent identification card that shows that the holder has met the minimum security requirements to remain unmonitored within a maritime zone.[63] Section 6.07A of the regulations provide that a maritime industry participant will not allow a person to enter, or remain in, a maritime security zone unless he or she displays a valid MSIC or is escorted by the holder of an MSIC. The MSIC scheme became effective in August 2006 and applies to port, port facility and port service workers, stevedores, transport operators such as train and truck drivers, seafarers on Australian regulated ships, and people who work or supply offshore oil and gas facilities.

Similarly, the United States recognizes that biometric identification procedures for individuals having access to secure areas in port facilities are important tools to deter and prevent port cargo crimes, smuggling, and terrorist actions.[64] There is a requirement under the U.S. Maritime Transport Security Act 2002 to prescribe regulations to prevent unauthorized entry in an area of a vessel or a facility that is designated as a secure area unless that person holds a transportation security card or is accompanied by another individual who holds such a security card.[65] To implement these provisions, the Transportation Worker Identification Credential (TWIC) program has been launched by the Transportation Security Administration and the U.S. Coast Guard. The TWIC program provides a tamper-resistant biometric credential to maritime workers requiring unescorted access to secure areas of port facilities, outer continental shelf facilities, and vessels regulated under the Maritime Transportation Security Act 2002 and all U.S. Coast Guard credentialed merchant mariners.[66]

CONCLUSION

The September 11, 2001 attack on the United States resulted in an international effort to address issues to improve security in the maritime arena. One of the key issues in this context is the security of seafarers' identity documents. As a consequence of the call for an improvement of the security of seafarers' identification and related port security measures, more restrictions apply on the admission of foreign seafarers in national territories that impact on the basic rights of seafarers to access services and facilities in ports. The only provision in the SID Convention 2003 that attempts to balance the right of states to exercise their right to regulate entry of seafarers into their territory and the right of seafarers to shore leave is the requirement for states to establish arrangements that would facilitate the issuance of visas to seafarers in the event that national laws and regulations require the acquisition of a visa for a seafarer to enter the territory of such states. This measure is not widely practiced by states.

Although the SID Conventions and the FAL Convention attempt to provide uniform standards in issuing SIDs and implementing measures related to seafarers' identification, the fact remains that parties to these international conventions retain their unrestricted right to deny entry of any seafarer into their territories if such a person is believed to be a threat to national security. Exercising such right contributes to the inconsistencies not only among national practices, but also between national laws and the implementation of the conventions on SIDs. Such divergence in practice defeats the very purpose that the SID Convention 2003 has been adopted for—which is to enhance the security of seafarers' identification.

Apart from the issues on the access of seafarers to port facilities, there are two other major challenges in implementing the SID Convention 2003. The first is the cost of adopting the prescribed biometric technology and establishing national electronic databases on seafarers. This is a particular concern for developing states. The second concern relates to balancing national policies and regulation on personal privacy and confidentiality of information with provision of access to seafarers' information to foreign states.

These concerns would need to be dealt with to address security concerns on seafarers' identification and effectively implement the SID Convention 2003. There is also a need for a wider application of the SID Convention 2003 including the development of the legislative, administrative, and technical mechanisms for its implementation. It would be critical that the SID Convention 2003 be adopted by at least all the major maritime and seafaring nations, including those that have not ratified the SID Convention 1958.

NOTES

1. Peter Lehr, ed., *Violence at Sea: Piracy in the Age of Global Terrorism*, New York: Routledge Taylor & Francis Group, 2007, p. 253.
2. Seafarers International Research Centre (SIRC), *A Study on Fraudulent Practices Associated with Certificates of Competency and Endorsements: Abridged Report*, Wales: Cardiff University, www.imo.org. Accessed on July 10, 2007, p. 22.
3. The meeting in question was the Asia Pacific Economic Cooperation (APEC) summit, which took place in Sydney on September 2–9, 2007. The 21 member economies of APEC are Australia, Brunei Darussalam, Canada, Chile, People's Republic of China, Hong Kong, China, Indonesia, Japan, Republic of Korea, Malaysia, Mexico, New Zealand, Papua New Guinea, Peru, Republic of the Philippines, Russian Federation, Singapore, Chinese Taipei, Thailand, the United States, and Vietnam.
4. L. Besser, "Explosive cargoes steam by airport," *Sydney Morning Herald*, September 5, 2007. The threatening material referred to in the report were shipments of "explosive grade ammonium nitrate," which was pointed out to be the same explosive used in the terrorist bombings in Oklahoma City in 1995 and Bali in 2002.
5. IMO Assembly, 22nd Session, Agenda item 8, Resolution A.924(22), adopted on 20 November 2001 (Agenda item 8), Review of Measures and Procedures to Prevent Acts of Terrorism which Threaten the Security of Passengers of Crews and the Safety of Ships, A 22/Res.924, January 22, 2002.
6. ILO Governing Body, 283rd Session, Sixteenth Item on the Agenda, Report of the Director General, Third Supplementary Report: Urgent Item on the Agenda on the 91st Session (June 2003) of the International Labour Conference, *Concerning Improved Security of Seafarers' Identification*, GB.283/16/3, Geneva, March 2002, para. 4.
7. International Chamber of Shipping and International Shipping Federation Website. Overview of the International Shipping Industry. www.marisec.org. Accessed on September 20, 2007.
8. United Nations Conference on Trade and Development (UNCTAD), *Review of Maritime Transport 2006*, Geneva: UNCTAD, 2006, p. 19.
9. UNCTAD, *Review of Maritime Transport 2006*, p. 75.
10. Warwick Institute for Employment Research, *BIMCO/ISF Manpower 2005 Update: The Worldwide Demand for Supply of Seafarers, Main Report*, University of Warwick, Coventry: Team Impression Ltd., December 2005, Appendix C.
11. ILO, C108 SID Convention 1958, Geneva, Switzerland, May 13, 1958. The SID Convention 1958 was ratified by 61 member states comprising 60.7 percent of the world fleet. Three of the 61 member states, namely, Azerbaijan, France, and Republic of Moldova denounced the Convention. Article 9 of C108 provides that a member that has ratified the convention may denounce it after the expiration of ten years from the date on which the Convention first comes into force. See the ILO Website http://www.ilo.org/ilolex/cgi-lex/ratifce.pl?C185. Accessed on 15 August 2007.
12. ILO, *Third Supplementary Report Concerning Improved Security of Seafarers' Identification*, para 3.

13. SID Convention 1958, Art. 6(2).
14. ILO, *Submission by the Australian Government to the Consultation Meeting on Improved Security of Seafarers' Identification* (May 9–10, 2002), Seafarers' Identification—Comments by Australian Customs and Department of Immigration and Multicultural Affairs, Geneva: ILO, 2002, p. 3.
15. ILO, *Submission by the Australian Government to the Consultation Meeting on Improved Security of Seafarers' Identification*, p. 3.
16. ILO, *Submission by the Australian Government to the Consultation Meeting on Improved Security of Seafarers' Identification*, p. 4.
17. Convention on Facilitation of International Maritime Traffic (FAL Convention), London, April 9, 1965, Appendix 6, para. 3.47.
18. ILO, *Third Supplementary Report Concerning Improved Security of Seafarers' Identification*, p. 10.
19. ILO, *Third Supplementary Report Concerning Improved Security of Seafarers' Identification*, p. 9.
20. ILO, *Third Supplementary Report Concerning Improved Security of Seafarers' Identification*, p. 10.
21. ILO, *Submission by the Australian Government to the Consultation Meeting on Improved Security of Seafarers' Identification*, p. 2.
22. ILO, *Third Supplementary Report Concerning Improved Security of Seafarers' Identification*, para 7.
23. FAL Convention Art. I and II.
24. FAL Convention, Art. III.
25. FAL Convention, para. 3.10.
26. FAL Convention, para. 3.10.1. Such information are the family name, given names, date and place of birth, nationality, physical characteristics, photograph (authenticated), signature, date of expiry (if any), and issuing public authority.
27. FAL Convention, Annex, Sec. 2.1, 2.10, and 2.11.
28. FAL Convention, para. 3.10.3.
29. FAL Convention, Annex, Sec. 3.44 and 3.47.
30. FAL Convention, Annex, Sec. 3.46.
31. FAL Convention, Annex, Sec. 3.49.
32. FAL Convention, Appendix 6.
33. International Ship and Port Facility Security (ISPS) Code and SOLAS Amendments adopted on December 12, 2002, London, 2003 Part A, para. 16.3.15.
34. Conference Resolution 8 (adopted on December 12, 2002), Enhancement of Security in Co-operation with the International Labour Organisation, (Seafarers' identity documents and work on the wider issues of port security), in ISPS Code 2003 Edition, International Ship and Port Facility Security Code and SOLAS Amendments adopted on December 12, 2002.
35. Conference Resolution 8, para. 1.
36. Azerbaijan, Bahamas, France, Hungary, Jordan, Republic of Korea, Lithuania, Madagascar, Republic of Moldova, Nigeria, Pakistan, and Vanuatu. Azerbaijan and Lithuania declared provisional application of Article 9 of the SID Convention 2003.
37. ILO, C185 Seafarers' Identity Documents Convention (Revised), 2003 (SID Convention 2003), Geneva, Switzerland, June 19, 2003, Art. 1(1).
38. SID Convention 2003, Art. 2(6).
39. ILO, 91st Session, Report VII(1), *Improved Security of Seafarers' Identification*, Seventh Item on the Agenda, Geneva: ILO, 2003, p. 21.
40. ILO, *Seafarers' Identity Documents Convention (Revised), 2003 (No. 185): The Standards for the Biometric Template Required by the Convention*, Geneva: ILO, 2004, p. 3.
41. ILO, *Third Supplementary Report Concerning Improved Security of Seafarers' Identification*, p. 2.
42. S.M. Jones, *Maritime Security: A Practical Guide*, London: The Nautical Institute, 2006, p. 171.
43. SID Convention 2003, Art. 4(2) and Annex II.
44. ILO, *Improved Security of Seafarers' Identification*, p. 9.
45. SID Convention 2003, Art. 6(5).
46. SID Convention 2003, Art. 7.
47. There are also other relevant loopholes in the existing international legal framework on the identification of seafarers outside the purview of this chapter that merit some attention. For one, the SID Convention 2003 does not provide a mechanism that would enable the seafarers to seek reparation in case they have been mistakenly identified as a threat to the security of a member state. Another loophole in SID Convention 2003 is found in Article 7 on the continuous possession of SIDs. Paragraph 1 states that the SID must remain in the seafarer's possession at all times, except when it is held for safekeeping by the master of the

ship concerned, and with the written consent of the seafarer. It has been a standard practice in ships for the master to hold the documents of the seafarers to avoid desertion. However, such provision poses security problems, that is, if a seafarer deserts a ship, it may be difficult for authorities to obtain documentary evidence of the seafarer. These issues should also be addressed if a balance is to be struck between security of seafarers' identification, facilitation of maritime commerce, and protection of workers' rights.

48. Australia is party to the FAL Convention but not to the 1958 and 2003 SID Conventions.
49. Media Release by Amanda Vanstone, Former Minister for Immigration and Multicultural Affairs (2003–2007), *Tougher Checks for Foreign Sea Crew in $100m Border Security Boost*, December 22, 2005. www.immi.gov.au. Accessed on April 10, 2007.
50. Australia, *Migration Amendment (Maritime Crew) Bill 2007*, Outline, para. 2. Special purposes visas will otherwise remain in place for other nonmaritime crew purposes.
51. Australian Government, Department of Immigration and Citizenship, *About the Maritime Crew Visa*. www.immi.gov.au. Accessed on April 13, 2007.
52. Parliament of Australia, Bills Digest No 109 2006-07, *Migration Amendment (Maritime Crew) Bill 2007*. www.aphc.gov.au. Accessed on April 20, 2007.
53. DOTARS, Output 2, *Border Compliance and Enforcement, Operational Performance and Improvement Initiatives*, INTERCEPT, www.customs.gov.au. Accessed on April 14, 2007.
54. Prime Minister of Australia, John Howard, Press Release, *Strengthening Offshore Maritime Security*, December 15, 2004. www.pm.gov.au/News/media_releases/media_Release1173.html. Accessed on January 25, 2005.
55. SIRC, *Study on Fraudulent Practices Associated with Certificates of Competency and Endorsements*, p. 8.
56. IMO, *Guidance on Recommended Anti-fraud Measures and Forgery Prevention Features for Seafarers' Certificates*, MSC/Circ.1089, June 6, 2003, para. 1.2.
57. MSC/Circ.1089, para. 3.1.
58. IMO, *Guidance for Administrations, Companies, Masters and Manning Agents in Detecting and Preventing Unlawful Practices*, MSC/Circ.1090, June 6, 2003, section 2.
59. See SIRC, *Study on Fraudulent Practices Associated with Certificates of Competency and Endorsements*, pp. 17–18.
60. ILO, *Code of Practice on Security in Ports*, MESSHP/2003/14, Tripartite Meeting of Experts on Security, Safety and Health in Ports, Geneva, 2003, para. 3.3.1.
61. *Code of Practice on Security in Ports*, para. 9.4.
62. Australia, *Maritime Transport and Offshore Facilities Security Amendment Regulations 2005 (No. 1)*, Sec. 6.07A.
63. DOTARS, *Maritime Security Identification Cards*, www.dotars.gov.au. Accessed on November 14, 2006.
64. 46 USC§ 70101, added by s. 101 of the *Maritime Security Transportation Act 2002*.
65. 46 USC§ 70105, *Maritime Security Transportation Act 2002*.
66. See U.S. Department of Homeland Security, Transportation Security Administration, U.S. Coast Guard, *Transportation Worker Identification Credential (TWIC) Implementation in the Maritime Sector*, Federal Register, 9110-05-P, January 25, 2007. www.tsa.gov. Accessed on August 30, 2007.

Section 4

Regional Responses

16 Maritime Security Threats in Post-9/11 Southeast Asia: Regional Responses

Rommel C. Banlaoi

CONTENTS

INTRODUCTION

Since the aftermath of the September 11, 2001 (9/11) terrorist attacks on the United States, maritime security threats have been major sources of global anxieties considering the vulnerability of the world's oceans to maritime terrorism. Although historical and empirical evidences have indicated less terrorist attacks on seas before and after 9/11, there is a tremendous fear that maritime vessels and facilities are facing the awesome risks of maritime terrorism.[1] This risk is aggravated by the fact that compared with the land and air, the "sea has always been an anarchic domain" that it is "barely policed, even today."[2] Moreover, the seas have become the medium of various transnational threats that undermine regional and global security.[3]

    This chapter discusses that although terrorism poses a real threat to maritime security in the post-9/11 era, centuries-old security concerns of piracy, smuggling, trafficking, and armed robberies pose greater challenges to the security of the maritime domain, particularly in the South China Sea and other waters in Southeast Asia such as the Strait of Malacca, Sulu Sea, and the Celebes Sea. Although it has been argued that Southeast Asia is fast becoming the world's maritime terrorism hotspot because of a very high incidence of piracy in the area and a burgeoning threat of terrorism posed by armed groups with known maritime abilities such as the Jemaah Islamiyah (JI), the Abu

Sayyaf Group (ASG), the Gerakan Aceh Merdeka (GAM), and even the Moro National Liberation Front (MNLF), nontraditional maritime security issues continue to be main sources of threats in the vital waters of Southeast Asia.

THREAT OF MARITIME TERRORISM IN SOUTHEAST ASIA

Since most Southeast Asian countries are maritime nations, it is argued that it is only natural that terrorist-related activities in the region be considered as maritime terrorism.[4] Singaporean Minister for Home Affairs Wong Kan Seng once opined that piracy in Southeast Asia should be declared as maritime terrorism arguing, "we do not know whether it's pirates or terrorists who occupy the ship so we have to treat them all alike."[5] But the distinction between piracy and terrorism[6] is very blurred because "pirates collude with terrorists, terrorists adopt pirate tactics and policymakers eager for public support start labeling every crime as maritime terrorism."[7] Terrorists can also use piracy as a cover for maritime terrorist attacks.

Motives of pirates and terrorists are arguably different from a conventional perspective. Pirates pursue economic gains, whereas terrorists advance political objectives.[8] But it is said that terrorists have developed some capabilities to either adopt pirates' tactics or "piggyback" on pirates' raid.[9] It is also viewed that maritime terrorists, rather than simply stealing, could either blow up the ship or use it to ram into another vessel or a port facility.[10] Terrorist groups even regard seaports and international cruise liners as very attractive terrorist targets because they reside in the nexus of terrorist intent, capability, and opportunity.[11]

The threat of maritime terrorism started to cause panic in Southeast Asia in the aftermath of 9/11 when Dominic Armstrong of the Aegis Defense Services (ADS) reported that the robbery of an Indonesian chemical tanker, the *Dewi Madrim*, off the coast of Sumatra on March 26, 2003 appeared to be the handiwork of terrorists who were learning how to drive a ship, in preparation for a future attack at sea.[12] The *Economist* even described the *Dewi Madrim* incident as "the equivalent of the Al-Qaeda hijackers who perpetrated the September 11 attacks going to flying school in Florida."[13] The ten hijackers, after driving the ship for almost an hour through the Strait of Malacca, fled and abducted the ship's first mate and captain with no request for ransom money.[14] There were speculations that the victims might be forced to instruct terrorists on ship-handling. What interests analysts on the incident was the observation that the *Dewi Madrim* case has failed to conform to the established patterns or customary practices of piracy attacks. The perpetrators were completely armed with automatic weapons that attacked the ship through the bridge rather than the safe room, and instead of ransacking the crew's goods, they steered a laden tanker for almost one hour.[15]

Another important case that raised the global apprehensions on maritime terrorism was the gruesome bombing of *Superferry 14* on February 27, 2004 after it left Manila Bay. The incident resulted in the death of 116 passengers and the wounding of about 300 others. Because of the human and physical damages caused by the explosion, it was argued that the *Superferry 14* blast was the most violent man-made disaster in Philippine waters since 9/11 and the worst terrorist attack in Asia since the 2002 Bali bombing. Although the ASG claimed responsibility for said explosion, it was actually carried out by Redendo Cain Dellosa, a Muslim convert associated with the Rajah Solaiman Islamic Movement (RSIM). The RSIM, organized by Ahmad Santos in 2001, represents a very minuscule fraction of Muslim converts in the Philippines advocating for the establishment of an Islamic state in the Philippines. An operative of the RSIM, Dellosa was one of those arrested in the coastal town of Anda, Pangasinan in May 2002 for illegal possession of firearms and explosives. But he posted bail and went into hiding until he was arrested again and put to jail in March 2004 in connection with the *Superferry 14* bombing and other criminal charges.

The administration of President Gloria Macapagal Arroyo initially denied ASG's involvement in the *Superferry 14* incident. However, the ASG declared that the bombing of the ferry was a "just revenge" of the group for the "brutal murder" of Bangsamoro people amidst the "on-going violence" in Mindanao. On October 10, 2004, the Marine Board Inquiry tasked to investigate the explosion submitted a report to President Arroyo. This report confirmed that based on the confession of Dellosa, the ASG had indeed deliberately planted the bomb that sank the *Superferry 14*. Dellosa admitted during investigation that he placed about 8 lb of trinitrotoluene (TNT) in a television set, which he carried onto the ferry. The bombing of the said commercial vessel was an excellent case of a maritime terrorist attack in Southeast Asian water in the post-9/11 era.

Maritime terrorism is causing tremendous insecurities in Southeast Asia because most of the countries in the region depend on seaborne trade. The lack of strong regional land transport infrastructure in Southeast Asia compels trading states to rely extremely on air and sea transportation.[16] In fact, half of the world's shipping activities pass through the waters of Southeast Asia. The Strait of Malacca alone carries more than a quarter of the world's maritime trade each year. More than 50,000 large ships pass through the strait annually, not to mention that 40–50 oil tankers sail in the strait daily.[17] Almost all ships that pass through the Strait of Malacca also pass through the South China Sea, which is considered as one of the world's busiest maritime superhighways. Thus, shipping activities in Southeast Asia largely occur in the Strait of Malacca and the South China Sea areas. Close to the South China Sea are the Sulu and the Celebes Seas, which are known important transport routes for trade and commerce in Southeast Asia and the wider Asia Pacific region. The Sulu Sea is separated from the South China Sea in the northwestern portion of Palawan, whereas the Celebes Sea, also an important international shipping lane, is located in the western Pacific Ocean.

It is forecasted that the tremendous growth in the cruise line industry and the emergence of high-speed ferries would be the key developments in the maritime passenger transport business through 2020 and this would greatly increase shipping activities in Southeast Asia.[18] The increasing trends of commercial shipping in Southeast Asia render the challenges of maritime terrorism in the region even more acutely. The JI, ASG, GAM, and MILF are the four major groups that have been identified to have the intent and capability to mount maritime terrorism in Southeast Asia.

THE JEMAAH ISLAMIYAH

JI has been labeled as the "Al-Qaeda" in Southeast Asia. It promotes the idea of establishing an "Islamic Caliphate" in the region encompassing Indonesia, Malaysia, Singapore, the southern Philippines, and southern Thailand.[19] JI traces its origins in the Darul Islam separatist rebel movement in the 1950s and 1960s in Indonesia. It started as a local Indonesian association of militant Muslim but mushroomed in the 1990s into a regional organization of militant Muslims in Southeast Asia with reported followers in Malaysia, Singapore, and the Philippines.

JI had a notorious history of planning to attack American naval warships cruising the Strait of Malacca and the port of Singapore in 2001.[20] The plan was a suicide mission that aimed to attack Western ships. It is viewed that JI poses a real threat to the maritime security of Southeast Asia, particularly in the Strait of Malacca, because of seaborne capabilities of its key operatives. A maritime security expert argues that "the group that would appear to be the only real threat to shipping in the Malacca Straits is JI" that "has shown an interest in attacking shipping in the Straits and vessels visiting Changi Naval Base in Singapore and is suspected of developing more expertise in this area."[21]

There was a contention that the maritime terrorist capability of JI "remains underdeveloped when compared to its land capability."[22] But Philippine intelligence reports indicated that JI conducted joint underwater training with the ASG to conduct maritime terrorist attacks. Based on the interrogation of Gamal Baharan, a captured ASG member involved in the 2005 Valentine's Day bombings of three major cities in the Philippines, some ASG members took scuba diving lessons in southwestern Palawan as part of a plot for an attack at sea. Baharan said that the training was in preparation for a JI bombing plot on unspecified targets outside the Philippines that require underwater operation.[23] Baharan also said that the slain ASG Emir Khadafy Janjalani and the slain ASG spokesman Abu Solaiman were on top of the maritime training.

GERAKAN ACEH MERDEKA

GAM or the Free Aceh Movement is the largest independence movement in Aceh, Indonesia. Founded in 1979 by Tengku Hasan di Tiro, the group has been allegedly linked with Al-Qaeda. But GAM leaders continue to deny their links with any terrorist organizations using economic and religious issues to promote their independence cause. Although there were reports that Al-Qaeda attempted to penetrate Aceh, GAM leaders rejected the religious fundamentalist agenda of Al-Qaeda because their "nationalist impulse appears to have been more durable."[24] Libya was identified to have provided initial support to the GAM. Reportedly, Libya trained about 600 Acehnese who formed the core of GAM fighters. It was also documented that Malaysia supported GAM.

Through the mediation of the Swiss government, GAM signed a Cessation of Hostilities Framework Agreement on December 9, 2002. After the onslaught of the tsunami in Aceh in December 2004, GAM entered into a peace agreement with the Indonesian government in August 2005, agreed to end the insurgency, and expressed its interests in participating in the political process. But "given the presence of fundamental political, economic and social grievances in the province, which have never been satisfactorily rectified or addressed, fears have already been expressed over whether the peace agreement will last."[25]

GAM is believed to have developed maritime terrorist capabilities. GAM has been accused of masterminding several piracy attacks in the northern stretch of the Strait of Malacca, which were linked to Al-Qaeda and JI.[26] GAM admitted to have carried out an attack on a chartered boat of Exxon Mobil in 2002 in Aceh, Indonesia. GAM is also suspected to have carried out a number of kidnap-for-ransom attacks on vessels in Indonesian waters.[27] On October 26, 2003, GAM reportedly intercepted a fishing trawler, PKFA 8588, in the Strait of Malacca, to wit

> While underway, several armed uniformed men suspected to be GAM rebels in a fishing boat hijacked the fishing trawler and sailed it towards Indonesian waters, where Indonesian Marine Police confronted them. A shootout ensued in which two of the suspected GAM members on board the trawler were shot dead and another was injured. Several others in the boat escaped. The crew of the trawler and the suspected GAM members were taken for investigation.[28]

Although GAM piracy attacks were economically motivated, "the biggest fear in the region is that GAM may choose to make a political statement or assist another group in the terrorist brotherhood—such as Jemaah Islamiyah—by setting fire to or detonating an oil or liquefied natural gas tanker in a port or heavily trafficked portion of the Malacca Strait."[29] Since GAM has been labeled as a foreign terrorist organization by the United States, its acts of piracy were viewed as maritime terrorist attacks, although other scholars are challenging this perspective because of the difficulties to draw a clear line between piracy and terrorism.

THE MORO ISLAMIC LIBERATION FRONT

The Moro Islamic Liberation Front (MILF) is another armed group in Southeast Asia that has been considered to have developed maritime terrorist capabilities. The MILF is a breakaway faction of the MNLF. The late Hashim Salamat, known before as the vice chairman of the MNLF, founded the MILF in 1978. Although Salamat traced the origin of the MILF in 1962 when he founded the Moro Liberation Front (MLF) in Cairo, it was only in 1984 when he officially used the name MILF to describe his resistance group.[30] Unlike the MNLF, which is secular in orientation, the MILF is strictly Islamic or fundamentalistic to use the Western label. But Salamat argues, "There is no such thing as Islamic Fundamentalism."[31] Although the MILF aims to establish a separate Islamic state in the southern Philippines through *jihad*, Salamat contends, "Fundamentalism is alien to Islam."[32] The MILF has a military arm called Bangsamoro Islamic Armed Forces (BIAF).

As on July 2007, the Armed Forces of the Philippines (AFP) reported that the MILF has a personnel strength of about 12,000 with firearms of about 9,000. They operate in almost the whole area of southern Philippines, particularly in the province of Maguindanao. But according to Salamat, the MILF has registered more than 70,000 participants from BIAF and more than 100,000 trained but not armed fighters. He even claims that the MILF constitutes 70–80 percent of all fighting forces in Mindanao with a modest navy, short of warships, and some members trained as fighter pilots.[33] Although there were allegations that the MILF has established strong linkages with Al-Qaeda and JI, the Philippine government has not officially tagged the MILF as a terrorist organization in order not to undermine the on-going peace talks are not undermined, which as of now is suffering *impasse* because of the controversial issue of ancestral domain. Many Philippine politicians believe that tagging the MILF as a terrorist organization will cause the termination of the peace negotiations and the escalation of armed conflict in the Philippines.

The MILF has renounced terrorism, but persistently arguing that it has a legitimate cause to wage armed struggle against the government to liberate the Moros from the bondage of Filipino colonialism. But intelligence sources have established MILF link with Al-Qaeda, which was traced to the Afghan war in the 1980s. Osama bin Laden reportedly instructed his brother-in-law, Mohammad Jamal Khalifa, to go to the Philippines in 1988 to recruit fighters. Salamat was reported to have sent 1000 Filipino Muslim fighters to Afghanistan to undergo military training. Salamat saw the training of these Muslim fighters as vital to the strengthening of the MILF.

In July 2007, the MILF was reportedly involved in the beheading of ten of the fourteen Philippine Marines fatalities after a military clash in the coastal town of Tipo-Tipo in Basilan province while on their way back to the military camp to search for the kidnapped Italian priest, Giancarlo Bossi. Although the MILF leadership condemned the beheadings, the military reported that MILF operators, aided by some ASG members, were responsible for the incidents. Like some ASG members, there are members of the MILF who have developed extreme familiarity of the maritime domain. The MILF demonstrated its maritime terrorist capability in February 2000, when it attacked the vessel *Our Lady Mediatrix*, killing 40 people and wounding 50.

The Abu Sayyaf Group

Among these four groups, the ASG has proven its intent and capability to wage maritime terrorism. The bombing of the *Superferry 14* in February 2004 was the most gruesome maritime terrorist attack of the ASG so far.

The forerunner of the ASG was the *Jamaa Tableegh*, an Islamic propagation group established in Basilan in the early 1980s by Abdurajak Janjalani, who at that time was still a member of the MNLF. The *Jamaa Tableegh* gained popularity not only in the island provinces of Basilan, but also in Zamboanga and Jolo.[34] The involvement of some of its followers in antigovernment rallies prompted the military to put the group under surveillance. Key followers of *Jamaa Tableegh* formed the nucleus of the ASG, which Abdurajak Janjalani initially called *Al-Harakatul Al-Islamiyah* (AHAI) or the Islamic Movement. Janjalani organized the ASG to establish an Islamic state in the southern Philippines.

As of July 2007, the AFP reported that the strength of the ASG was estimated at 450, down from its peak of 4000 members in 2001. There has been a decrease in the number of ASG members mainly due to the relentless military pursuit operations mounted against them. But there is no certainty on the real current strength of the ASG as its members overlap with some members of the MILF, and the Misuari Break Away Group (MBG) of the MNLF and the RSIM. It is very important to emphasize, however, that most ASG members and followers belong to Muslim families and communities of fishermen with a century-old seafaring tradition. Because ASG members live very close to the waters of Basilan, Sulu, and Tawi-Tawi, they have gained tremendous familiarity of the maritime environment. In fact, most Muslim Filipinos living in coastal communities are experienced divers. ASG members' deep knowledge of the maritime domain also gives them ample capability to conduct piracy and wage maritime terrorist attacks.

Because of its embedded seaborne abilities, ASG's first terrorist attack was, in fact, maritime in nature. On August 24, 1991 the ASG bombed the *M/V Doulous*, a Christian missionary ship and a European floating library docked at the Zamboanga port. At that time, the missionaries were holding their farewell program after conducting their evangelization project. Two foreign missionaries were killed and eight others were wounded in the blast.

The ASG proved its maritime terrorist mettle when it waged another attack on April 23, 2000, kidnapping some 21 tourists, including 10 foreigners, from a Malaysian beach resort in Sipadan. These foreigners included three Germans, two Japanese, two Finns, two South Africans, and a Lebanese woman. The hostages were eventually taken to Jolo Island of Mindanao. This incident demonstrated ASG's capability of operating outside its usual maritime turf. It also displayed ASG's creativity in waging maritime terrorist attacks because some of its members were disguised as diving instructors. ASG member Ruland Ullah, who is now a state witness to the Sipadan hostage crisis, successfully disguised as a diving instructor in this Malaysian resort before the said incident. An intelligence source revealed that Ullah trained some ASG members in scuba diving before the attack. In fact, the Philippine military recently confirmed that ASG members were trained in scuba diving to prepare for possible seaborne terror attacks not only in the Philippines, but also outside the country. On May 22, 2001, ASG guerrillas raided the luxurious Pearl Farm Beach Resort on Samal Island of Mindanao. This incident resulted in the killing of two resort workers and the wounding of three others. Although no hostages were taken during this attack, the Samal raid demonstrated anew the willingness of ASG to pursue maritime targets.

On May 28, 2001, the ASG waged another maritime terror when it abducted three American citizens and seventeen Filipinos while spending a vacation at the Dos Palmas Resort in Palawan. The Dos Palmas incident convinced the American government that the ASG was a deadly foreign terrorist organization. To increase the capability of the Philippine military to destroy the ASG, American and Filipino forces conducted the controversial joint military exercise called *Balikatan 02-1*. In April 2004, just two months after the *Superferry 14* incident, the Philippine National Police Maritime Group reported that the ASG hijacked a boat and kidnapped two Malaysians and one Indonesian in the southern Philippines near Sabah. Their abduction came on the heels of the escape of 23 ASG members from a Basilan jail. In July 2005, ASG and JI fighters reportedly took underwater training in Sandakan, Malaysia to attack maritime targets such as ports and commercial vessels. In August 2005, military intelligence disclosed that ASG leaders and some foreign terrorists met in Patikul, Sulu to plan an attack of some beaches in Palawan. This prompted the Philippine government to intensify the security of major ports and beaches in the country preventing any planned maritime terrorist attacks to happen.

VULNERABILITIES OF THE SEAS ON MARITIME TERRORISM

Although maritime targets are considered less attractive than land and air targets because assaulting the maritime domain requires highly specialized skills and capabilities, seas are more vulnerable to terrorist attacks because of embedded difficulties to guard the waters. Southeast Asian countries have a combined coastline length of 92,451 km, which is 15.8 percent of the world's total. The archipelagos of Indonesia and the Philippines (the two largest in the world with more than 20,000 islands combined) alone contribute 59 and 24 percent, respectively, to the region's coastlines.[35] Such a coastline makes achieving maritime security in Southeast Asia very difficult and expensive.

Kenneth Button, an American academic, said that Britain and the United States alone spent billions to protect their coastlines. If this were the case, then most Asian countries would not have the money to protect their coastlines as their coastlines are longer than the United States and Britain and their countries poorer. Indonesia, the world's largest archipelago, has a weak maritime force and Indonesia's defense budget is the lowest in Southeast Asia.[36] With the scourge of the Asian financial crisis, the value of the Indonesian defense budget has also declined by 65 percent from 1997 to 1998. This worsened the already tight fiscal problems and prevented the country from allocating more to its maritime security force.[37] The Philippines, the world's second largest archipelago, has one of the most ill-equipped maritime forces in Asia. The American military withdrawal in 1991 aggravated the already poor state of Philippine maritime forces. Although the Philippine military ventured into a force modernization program in 1995, the 1997 Asian financial crisis prevented its implementation and prompted even one own naval officer to lament that the Philippine Navy "lags both in quality and quantity among the other navies in the region."[38]

MARITIME SECURITY THREATS IN SOUTHEAST ASIAN WATERS: BEYOND MARITIME TERRORISM

Beyond maritime terrorism, however, the more serious security threats confronting Southeast Asian waters are the perennial issues of piracy and armed robberies against ships, people smuggling and human trafficking, small arms trafficking, and drugs trafficking. Unlike maritime terrorism, these threats almost occur on a daily basis although actual incidents are monitored and reported on a regular basis.

PIRACY AND ARMED ROBBERIES AGAINST SHIPS

Piracy has been a major maritime security concern in Southeast Asia since the ancient times. It continues to be a gargantuan problem in Southeast Asia, especially in Indonesian waters along the Strait of Malacca and the Celebes Sea and also in Singaporean and Philippine waters adjacent to the Sulu Sea.[39] In fact, Southeast Asia has a long-standing reputation of being the piracy hotspot of the word. It remains the most prone region to acts of piracy and has accounted for about 50 percent of almost all attacks worldwide.[40]

During the third quarter of 2006, however, the International Maritime Bureau (IMB) noted with enthusiasm the decline of reported piracy attacks worldwide from 205 in 2005 to only 174 in 2006.[41] Piracy in Southeast Asia also declined from 84 during the third quarter of 2005 to only 65 during the same period of 2006. This prompted Lloyd to drop the Strait of Malacca from the list of dangerous waterways of the world, which accounted only for eight attacks in 2006 compared to ten in 2005.

It is sad to note that although piracy attacks in Indonesia declined from 61 to 40 during those periods, the country still accounted for more attacks than any other country in the world (Table 16.1). Thus, the IMB still warned mariners worldwide "to be extra cautious and to take necessary precautionary measures" when transiting to waterways of Southeast Asia.[42] The recent statistics released by the IMB indicated that the number of reported piracy attacks in the first quarter of 2007 worldwide

TABLE 16.1
Actual and Attempted Piracy Attacks in Southeast Asia, 2001–2006

Location	2001	2002	2003	2004	2005	2006
Cambodia	—	—	—	—	—	—
Indonesia	71	72	87	70	61	40
Strait of Malacca	14	11	24	25	10	8
Malaysia	15	9	5	8	3	9
Myanmar	1	—	—	1	—	—
Philippines	7	7	12	3	—	3
Singapore	6	4	—	8	7	3
Thailand	6	2	1	4	1	1

Source: ICC International Maritime Bureau, *Piracy and Armed Robbery against Ships*, Report for the Period January 1–September 30, 2006.

declined significantly compared with the same period for 2006.[43] Reported incidents of piracy also dropped significantly in Southeast Asia. Indonesia recorded only nine incidents, down dramatically from 19 in 2006. Only two incidents were recorded in the Strait of Malacca.[44]

It must be noted that there are two major types of pirates operating in Asia in general and Southeast Asia in particular. One type comprises common sea robbers operating in a hit-and-run fashion. They attack ships for no longer than 15–30 minutes, and their operations require a minimum level of organization and planning.[45] Although they engage in simple armed robberies against ships, they have the ability to resort to a high level of violence.

The other type is more organized and virulent. It comprises pirates involved in organized crimes. They are organized pirates gangs or syndicates that attack medium-sized vessels, including cargo ships, bulk carriers, and tankers.[46] This validates the earlier observation that pirates in Southeast Asia range from opportunistic fishermen and the common criminal to members of sophisticated Asian crime syndicates.[47] Piracy also occurs mostly in ports or anchorages. Although piracy is largely a criminal issue, it has been securitized because of its potential nexus with maritime terrorism. The successful comeback of piracy problem after the end of the Cold War and the rise of terrorism after 9/11 make piracy in the age of global terrorism a serious national, regional, and global security issue.[48] Its impact on human security also led to the securitization of piracy.

The cost of piracy in Southeast Asia is very alarming.[49] Piracy in the region is costing the world economy a staggering amount of U.S.$25 billion a year.[50] Piracy is also costing the region about U.S.$500 million a year.[51] Studies show that new maritime security measures to counter the threat of attacks will require an initial investment of at least U.S.$1.3 billion by ship operators, and will increase annual operating costs by U.S.$730 million thereafter.[52] The cost of piracy in Southeast Asia is projected to increase in the future, as the trend in modern piracy points toward more bloody, ruthless, and terrifying attacks.

PEOPLE SMUGGLING AND HUMAN TRAFFICKING

People smuggling and human trafficking continue as serious maritime security problems confronting Southeast Asia. The region has emerged as a key transit region for human smuggling from Iraq and Afghanistan to Australia and elsewhere.[53] Most of the victims involved are women and children who are forced to work as sex workers. Thus, people smuggling and human trafficking are also associated with sex trafficking or white slavery, child prostitution, and forced labor. They are also closely linked with the issue of illegal migration.

At least 200,000–225,000 are trafficked from Southeast Asia annually.[54] From about 45,000–50,000 women and children being trafficked into the United States each year, 30,000 are believed to have come from Southeast Asia.[55] The "third wave" of Chinese illegal migration to the United States, Australia, Japan, and even Europe uses waters of Southeast Asia as a transit point.[56] Much of the human trafficking in Southeast Asia centers on the coastal areas of Thailand, where the sex trade accounts for 2–14 percent of the gross national product.[57]

Although people smuggling, human trafficking, and illegal migration are old criminal problems in the region, the aggravation of the problem in the aftermath of the Cold War has led to the securitization of the issue. Australia, for example, has securitized the issue of people smuggling from Southeast Asia because of the threat it poses to Australian national security and Southeast Asian regional security.[58] The shocking escalation of violence in Southeast Asian countries with ongoing internal armed conflicts and the prevalence of poverty have been identified as some of the factors leading to people smuggling, human trafficking, and illegal migration.

The business of human smuggling and trafficking generates U.S.$8–$10 billion every year.[59] The cost of human smuggling and trafficking worldwide ranges from U.S.$203 to $26,041 per person, depending on the point of origin and the point of destination.[60] In Asia, the average cost is U.S.$15,000. The involvement of organized criminal groups with links with corrupt immigration officials makes human smuggling and trafficking obviously a serious maritime security concern.[61]

SMALL ARMS TRAFFICKING

Illicit trafficking of small arms and light weapons (SALWs) has been a regional menace and decades-long criminal problem in Southeast Asia.[62] The region is viewed as the international hub for small arms trafficking.[63] There is no reliable source, however, on the exact quantity of SALWs being trafficked in the region. But there are at least 639 million small arms in the world today, about 60 percent of which are legally held by civilians.[64] If 40 percent are illegally acquired, about 256 million small arms may have been involved in trafficking.

It has been estimated that SALWs account for about 60–90 percent of more than 100,000 human deaths involved in violent conflicts each year and tens of thousands of additional deaths outside of war zones.[65] There is a view that SALWs cause more human damages than weapons of mass destruction (WMD). SALWs are not only weapons of choice of persons who are involved in organized crimes, but are also of terrorist organizations. Out of 175 terrorist attacks worldwide, approximately half were committed with SALWs.[66] The International Action Network on Small Arms laments that Southeast Asia has been very sluggish in taking effective action to curb illegal arms transfers.[67] But three factors make South East Asia susceptible to small arms trafficking.

- The region is the scene of numerous intrastate conflicts, including Indonesia, Burma, and the Philippines, that draws the demand for weapons from nonstate actors. Unable to afford new arms or find sellers on the legal arms market, nonstate actors often turn to arms dealers and brokers who will supply used or "surplus" arms.
- South East Asia has ready stockpiles of existing weapons. The region has several postconflict states, where vast numbers of military SALW can easily be obtained. Postwar estimates of 500,000 and 1 million military small arms in Cambodia alone, although this has certainly dropped today due to some in-country collection and destruction, and outflow from the country onto the black market. Weapons left over from the wars in Vietnam and Laos as well as imported arms from China and the Middle East are also finding their way to insurgents, criminals, and terrorists throughout the region.
- Southeast Asia is a region with long maritime and continental frontiers that are extremely difficult to monitor and police. Many of Association of Southeast Asian Nations' (ASEAN) members are also "weak states" and lack the capacity to effectively control their borders and interdict arms traffickers. Such states also often store national inventories of legally owned small arms in insecure and poorly managed facilities, making theft, loss and consequently smuggling possible. Many also lack adequate domestic gun control legislation and enforcement. Sales from Thai Army arsenals feature in the local papers on a somewhat regular basis, and those are only the ones caught by the police.[68]

TRAFFICKING IN ILLICIT DRUGS

Drug trafficking is known to be the largest international crime problem in the world with an estimated value of U.S.$400 billion annually.[69] About 200 million people reportedly consume illegal drugs worldwide, mostly cannabis.[70] The United Nations Office on Drugs and Crime (UNODC) has reported that about 15 million people worldwide abused opium and heroin.[71] Southeast Asia, which has grown and sold narcotics for centuries, serves not only as one of the major transits of illegal drug trade in the world, but also as one of the major factories of global narcotics production. Two-thirds of the world's opium production was reportedly based in Southeast Asia through the Golden Triangle of Thailand, Myanmar, and Laos (Figure 16.1). In fact, the Golden Triangle is in reality a "quadrangle" because the Yunnan Province of China, which produces more opium than anywhere else in the world, represents the fourth side of the illegal drug trade network in Southeast Asia.

The Golden Triangle has an opium trade network with the Golden Crescent of Afghanistan, Iran, and Pakistan and opium-producing countries of Mexico and Columbia. Cannabis grows widely in

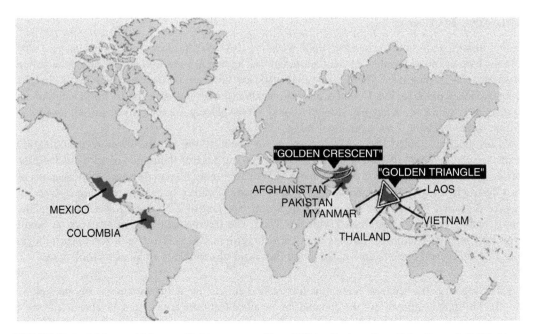

FIGURE 16.1   Major world drug-trafficking centers. (From Wikipedia, http://en.wikipedia.org/wiki/Golden_Triangle_(Southeast_Asia), accessed on November 28, 2006.)

Cambodia, whereas amphetamine-type stimulants are produced mostly in Eastern Myanmar and Northern Laos. Thailand has been the most favored route for drug trafficking in Southeast Asia prompting the Thai government to declare drugs problem as a threat to national security.[72] Illegal drug trade also involves other transnational crimes such as arms smuggling and human trafficking confounding the maritime security challenge.[73]

ASEAN POLICIES AND OPERATIONAL RESPONSES TO MARITIME SECURITY THREATS

The ASEAN is rich with numerous declarations aiming to promote regional cooperation on maritime security, which is subsumed under the issue of nontraditional security (NTS). Since 1967, the bulk of ASEAN maritime security cooperation has always been in the area of NTS.

REGIONAL COOPERATION ON NTS THE ASEAN WAY

ASEAN has two major types of cooperation on NTS. One is cooperation in functional areas that include cooperation in culture and information, disaster management, drugs and narcotics, education, health and nutrition, human immunodeficiency virus/acquired immunodeficiency syndrome (HIV/AIDS), labor, rural development and poverty eradication, severe acute respiratory syndrome (SARS), science and technology, women, youth, and children as well as the ASEAN University Network.[74] The other is cooperation on transnational issues that include environment, transboundary haze, transnational crime and terrorism, legal cooperation, migration, drugs, and civil services.[75] In the past, ASEAN regarded these issues as public, social, criminal, or political issues. Because these issues affect the security of human beings, they have been securitized in the context of human security.

At the policy level, each of these types of cooperation has produced various declarations, agreements, plans of actions, and working groups. But at the heart of all these types of cooperation in Southeast Asia is the ASEAN way of noninterference in the domestic affairs of member states enshrined in the 1976 Treaty of Amity and Cooperation in Southeast Asia. The ASEAN way is a diplomatic norm in Southeast Asia upholding the practice of intense dialogues and exhausting consultations (*musyawarah*) to generate consensus (*mufakat*) on contentious issues facing the region. This practice, called *musyawarah dan mufakat*, encourages all ASEAN members to cooperate on various areas through informal and incremental mechanisms.

The idea of ASEAN Security Community (ASC) in the Bali Concord II signed in October 2003 is a clear demonstration of its members' strict adherence to the ASEAN way. Instead of challenging the ASEAN way of noninterference, the concept of ASC strongly affirms it by stressing that "ASEAN shall continue to promote regional solidarity and cooperation. Member Countries shall exercise their rights to lead their national existence free from outside interference in their internal affairs."[76] The Bali Concord II also reaffirms the principle of the sovereign rights of each member of ASEAN by dismissing the speculation that ASEAN is building a defense pact or military alliance. To promote regional security, the Bali Concord II states that

> The ASEAN Security Community, recognizing the sovereign right of the member countries to pursue their individual foreign policies and defense arrangements and taking into account the strong interconnections among political, economic and social realities, subscribes to the principle of comprehensive security as having broad political, economic, social and cultural aspects in consonance with the ASEAN Vision 2020 rather than to a defense pact, military alliance or a joint foreign policy.[77]

One very important characteristic of the ASC is the strong recognition of ASEAN as a regional security complex where the security of one state is inextricably linked with the security of other states. The Bali Concord II vividly underscores

> The ASEAN Security Community is envisaged to bring ASEAN's political and security cooperation to a higher plane to ensure that countries in the region live at peace with one another and with the world at large in a just, democratic and harmonious environment. The ASEAN Security Community members shall rely exclusively on peaceful processes in the settlement of intra-regional differences and regard their security as fundamentally linked to one another and bound by geographic location, common vision and objectives.[78]

The major ASEAN document that defines the parameters of regional cooperation in the area of NTS in the maritime domain is the ASEAN Declaration on Transnational Crimes signed as early as December 20, 1997 in Manila, Philippines. This declaration was a response to the 29th ASEAN Ministerial Meeting (AMM) in Jakarta in July 1996, which stressed the need "to focus attention on issues such as narcotics and economic crimes, including money laundering, environment and illegal migration that transcend borders and affect the lives of the people in the region." The declaration was also in pursuance of the 30th AMM in Kuala Lumpur in July 1997, which stressed "the need for sustained cooperation in addressing transnational concerns including the fight against terrorism, trafficking in people, illicit drugs, and arms and piracy." Apparent in this declaration is the urgent need to combat transnational crimes that affect human security. Table 16.2[79] lists some of the major declarations, joint communiqué, and other documents signed by ASEAN to combat transnational crimes and promote regional cooperation in NTS.

Because transnational crimes and NTS threats are usually committed at sea, ASEAN issued a communiqué at the conclusion of the 37th AMM held June on 29–30, 2004 in Jakarta where ASEAN foreign ministers urged the need to "explore the possibility of establishing a maritime forum" in Southeast Asia. ASEAN, through the ASEAN Regional Forum (ARF) also issued the Statement on Cooperation against Piracy and other Threats to Maritime Security at the 36th AMM and the 10th ARF Post-Ministerial Conferences in Cambodia on June 16–20, 2003. This statement aims to promote maritime security cooperation not only in Southeast Asia, but also in the entire Asia Pacific region.

Beyond the ASEAN way, Admiral Thomas Fargo of the U.S. Pacific Command launched the controversial concept of Regional Maritime Security Initiative (RMSI) during his testimony before

TABLE 16.2

Major Declarations, Joint Communiqué, and Other Documents Signed by ASEAN to Combat Transnational Crimes and Promote Regional Cooperation in NTS, 1998–2005

Manila Declaration on the Prevention and Control of Transnational Crime (1998)

Joint Communiqué of the Second ASEAN Ministerial Meeting on Transnational Crime (AMMTC), Yangon, June 23, 1999

Joint Communiqué of the Third ASEAN Ministerial Meeting on Transnational Crime (AMMTC), Singapore, October 11, 2001

2001 ASEAN Declaration on Joint Action to Counter Terrorism, Bandar Seri Begawan, November 5, 2001

Joint Communiqué of the Special ASEAN Ministerial Meeting on Terrorism (AMMTC), Kuala Lumpur, May 20–21, 2002

Declaration on Terrorism by the Eighth ASEAN Summit, Phnom Penh, November 3, 2002

Joint Declaration of ASEAN and China on Cooperation in the Field of NTS Issues, Phnom Penh, November 4, 2002

Joint Declaration on Co-operation to Combat Terrorism, 14th ASEAN-EU Ministerial Meeting, Brussels, January 27, 2003

Joint Communiqué of the Fourth ASEAN Ministerial Meeting on Transnational Crime (AMMTC), Bangkok, January 8, 2004

Joint Communiqué of the First ASEAN Plus Three Ministerial Meeting on Transnational Crime (AMMTC+3), Bangkok, January 10, 2004

Joint Communiqué of the 24th ASEAN Chiefs of Police Conference, Chiang Mai, Thailand, August 16–20, 2004

Joint Communiqué of the 25th ASEAN Chiefs of Police Conference, Bali, Indonesia, May 16–20, 2005

Joint Communiqué of the Second ASEAN Plus Three Ministerial Meeting on Transnational Crime (AMMTC+3), Ha Noi, November 30, 2005

Joint Communiqué of the Fifth ASEAN Ministerial Meeting on Transnational Crime (AMMTC), Ha Noi, November 29, 2005

Source: ASEAN Secretariat Web site at http://www.aseansec.org.

---

the U.S. House of Representatives Armed Services Committee on March 31, 2004.[79] The RMSI specifically aims to promote cooperation among navies of the region "to assess and then provide detailed plans to build and synchronize interagency and international capacity to fight threats that use the maritime space to facilitate their illicit activity."[80] It was widely reported in the media that the RMSI intended to combat transnational crimes in the Strait of Malacca through the mobilization of U.S. Marines.[81] Fargo also argued that the RMSI aimed to operationalize the Proliferation Security Initiative (PSI) and the Malacca Straits Initiative (MSI) to promote regional security in the midst of the growing maritime security threats. But ASEAN did not accept the RMSI, PSI, and MSI because of the strong objection of Indonesia and Malaysia who are cautious of American strategic intentions. Marty Natalegawa, spokesman of the Indonesian foreign ministry, stressed that the security of the Strait of Malacca was the joint responsibility of Indonesia and Malaysia. The deputy prime minister of Malaysia, Najib Razak, supported this view when he told the Bernama news agency that Malaysia and Indonesia were responsible for ensuring security in the straits.[82] Razak underscored that Indonesia and Malaysia "do not propose to invite the United States to join the security operations we have mounted there (Malacca Strait)" and "even if they wish to act, they should get our permission as this touches on the question of our national sovereignty."

OPERATIONAL REGIONAL RESPONSES TO MARITIME SECURITY THREATS IN SOUTHEAST ASIA

To address maritime security threats in Southeast Asia at the operational level, ASEAN signed the ASEAN Plan of Action to Combat Transnational Crime (2001) followed by the work program to implement the ASEAN Plan of Action to Combat Transnational Crime (May 17, 2002). In May 2002, Indonesia, Malaysia, and the Philippines signed the Agreement on Information Exchange and Establishment of Communication Procedures, otherwise known as the Trilateral Agreement, to enhance regional cooperation and promote the interoperability among participating countries in curbing transnational crimes and other illegal activities occurring within their territories.

Participating countries have started the formulation of Standard Operating Procedure (SOP) to vigorously implement the Trilateral Agreement. The Trilateral Agreement also inspired the drafting of the proposed ASEAN Counter Terrorism Convention, which was approved at the 12th ASEAN Summit in Cebu, the Philippines. Laos and Thailand have acceded to the Trilateral Agreement.

Besides numerous multilateral mechanisms found in ASEAN, the region also has a complex web of bilateral cooperation among Southeast Asian countries aiming to combat transnational crimes and other maritime security threats. There have been bilateral maritime border security agreements between Indonesia and Malaysia, the Philippines and Malaysia, Singapore and Malaysia, and the Philippines and Indonesia.[83] These maritime border agreements not only aim to promote regional cooperation against maritime security threats in Southeast Asia, but also to ease bilateral tensions in the post-Cold War ASEAN.[84] To strengthen operational response against transnational crimes and maritime security threats, Singapore even proposed the holding of maritime security exercises among navies in Southeast Asia.

But among all initiatives in Southeast Asia, the implementation of round-the-clock coordinated patrols of the Strait of Malacca by Malaysia, Indonesia, and Singapore is the most encouraging. With the code name Operation MALSINDO (Malaysia, Singapore, and Indonesia) launched in July 2004, it is by far the biggest patrolling exercise in the Strait of Malacca by the three littoral states. Although there has been no concrete evidence to suggest that MALSINDO has directly reduced the scale of piracy in the Strait of Malacca,[85] the initiative is an exemplary operational response that can contribute to the reduction of NTS threats in Southeast Asian waters.[86] MALSINDO's best practices can provide useful lessons for future initiatives of claimant states in the South China Sea. As stated earlier, piracy attacks in the Strait of Malacca were reduced during the first quarter of 2007. Moreover, the MALSINDO presents an ASEAN alternative to the American-proposed RMSI. There is a need to emphasize, however, that the MALSINDO is still hampered by the sensitivity of littoral states over protecting sovereignty and a lack of national operational capacity.[87]

Despite the lack of national capacity, the increased attention on maritime security issues have encouraged maritime states in Southeast Asia to venture into naval modernization programs to varying degrees in the mid-1990s. But this does not equate with military effectiveness to address various threats, including maritime, to their national security.[88] The 1997 Asian financial crisis aborted most of these force modernization efforts, particularly in Indonesia, the Philippines, and Thailand. Although Singapore, Brunei, Myanmar, and to a certain extent Malaysia are pushing ahead with their force modernization programs in the aftermath of the financial crisis,[89] present capabilities of littoral states in Southeast Asia remain limited to address the growing maritime security problems in the region. These limitations will be reflected in the present quality and quantity of their maritime forces.[90,91]

CONCLUSION

After 9/11, maritime terrorism became a major source of maritime security anxieties in Southeast Asia because of the terrorist threats posed by JI, ASG, GAM, and the MILF. But the greatest maritime security challenges confronting Southeast Asia are old issues of piracy and armed robberies against ships, people smuggling and human trafficking, small arms trafficking, and drugs trafficking. To address maritime security threats in Southeast Asia, ASEAN promotes regional cooperation in the maritime domain through various multilateral initiatives. ASEAN members also pursue a complex web of bilateral cooperation that aims to secure the waters of Southeast Asia.

But the sensitivity of Southeast Asian states on the issue of national sovereignty slows down the process of regional cooperation in the maritime domain. Even national capacities to manage maritime security threats in Southeast Asia remain very weak. Although maritime states in the region have ventured into naval modernization projects, financial difficulties prevent most littoral states in the region to sustain their efforts.

To overcome the maritime security threats confronting Southeast Asia, there is a need to address threats beyond military approaches. Maritime security problems of piracy and armed robberies against ships, human trafficking, small arms trafficking, and drugs trafficking have deep underlying causes that cannot be solved by military means alone. Addressing maritime security threats in Southeast Asia must be informed by root causes that require political, economic, and sociocultural solutions.

NOTES

1. Michael D. Greenberg, Peter Chalk, Henry H. Willis, Ivan Khilko, David S. Ortiz, *Maritime Terrorism: Risk and Liability* (Santa Monica, CA: RAND), 2006.
2. Gal Luft and Anne Korin, "Terrorism Goes to Sea," *Foreign Affairs*, Vol. 83, No. 6, November/December 2004.
3. *The National Strategy for Maritime Security*, September 2005.
4. Ishak Bin Yeop Hamzah, *Maritime Terrorism and Its Impaction On South East Asian Regional Security* (Kuala Lumpur: University Kebangsaan Malaysia), 2004.
5. Graham Gerald Ong, "Southeast Asian Pirates Bear the Marks of Terrorists," *Institute of Southeast Asian Studies Viewpoints*, January 1, 2004, p. 1, available at http://www.iseas.edu.sg/viewpoint/ggojan04.pdf (accessed on April 27, 2005). See also Agence Prance Presse "Piracy and Equals Terrorism in Troubled Waters: Minister," December 21, 2003, available at http://www.singapore-window.org/sw03/031221af.htm (accessed on April 26, 2005).
6. This portion is largely based in Rommel C. Banlaoi, "Maritime Security Outlook for Southeast Asia," in Joshua Ho and Catherine Zara Raymond (eds.), *The Best of Times, The Worst of Times: Maritime Security in the Asia-Pacific* (Singapore: World Scientific), 2005.
7. Rubert Herbert-Burns and Lauren Zucker, *Malevolent Tide: Fusion and Overlaps in Piracy and Maritime Terrorism* (Washington, DC: Maritime Intelligence Group), July 30, 2004, p. 1.
8. Tamara Renee Shie, "Ports in a Storm? The Nexus Between Counterterrorism, Counterproliferation, and Maritime Security in Southeast Asia," *Issues and Insights*, Vol. 4, No. 4 (Pacific Forum CSIS), July 2004, p. 13.
9. Patrick Goodenough, "Maritime Security Takes Center Stage in SE Asia," *CNSNews.COM*, June 29, 2004, available at http://www.cnsnews.com/ (accessed on July 27, 2004).
10. Ibid.
11. Tanner Campbell and Rohan Gunaratna, "Maritime Terrorism, Piracy and Crime," in Rohan Gunaratna, (ed.), *Terrorism in the Asia Pacific: Threat and Response* (Singapore: Eastern University Press), 2003, p. 72.
12. Michael Richardson, "Terror at Sea: The World's Life Lines are at Risk," *Strait Times*, November 17, 2003.
13. Ibid.
14. Charles Glass, "The New Piracy," *London Review Bookshop*, Vol. 25, No. 24, December 18, 2003, p. 1.
15. Ibid.
16. Sam Bateman, "Assessing the Threat of Maritime Terrorism: Issues for the Asia Pacific Region," *Security Challenges*, Vol. 2, No. 3, October 2006, pp. 77–91.
17. Zachary Abuza, "Terrorism in Southeast Asia: Keeping al-Qaeda at Bay," *Terrorism Monitor*, Vol. II, No. 9, May 6, 2004, p. 4.
18. Ibid.
19. Maria Ressa, *Seeds of Terror: An Eyewitness Account of Al-Qaeda's Newest Center of Operations in Southeast Asia* (New York: Free Press), 2003; Zachary Abuza, *Militant Islam in Southeast Asia: The Crucible of Terror* (London: Lynne Rienner Publishers, Inc.), 2003; and Dirk J. Barreveld, *Terrorism in the Philippines: The Bloody Trail of Abu Sayyaf, Bin Laden's East Asian Connection* (New York: Writers Club Press), 2001.
20. Catherine Zara Raymond, "The Threat of Maritime Terrorism in the Malacca Straits," *Terrorism Monitor*, Vol. 4, Issue 3, February 9, 2006, p. 8.
21. Ibid.
22. Ibid.
23. See Associated Press, "Terrorist Train for Seaborne Attacks" available at http://www.ldslivingonline.com/stories/30_ds_330924.php (accessed on April 27, 2005).

24. Andrew Tan (ed), *A Handbook of Terrorism and Insurgency in Southeast Asia* (U.K. and United States: Edward Elgar Publishing Limited), 2007, p. 55.
25. Ibid., p. 56.
26. Barry Desker, "Protecting the Malacca Straits," *IDSS Commentaries*, March 3, 2005.
27. Raymond, "The Threat of Maritime Terrorism in the Malacca Straits," loc. cit.
28. Quoted in Dana Dillon, "Maritime Security: Defining the Problem," *SAIS Review*, Vol. 25, No. 1, 2005, pp. 155–165.
29. Dana Dillon, "Southeast Asia and the Brotherhood of Terrorism," *Heritage Lecture*, No. 860, November 2004.
30. Hashim Salamat, *Referendum: Peaceful, Civilized, Diplomatic and Democratic Means of Solving the Mindanao Conflict* (Camp Abubakre As-Siddique: Agency for Youth Affairs-MILF), 2002, p. 30.
31. Ibid., p. 32.
32. Ibid. See also Salamat Hashim, *The Bangsamoro Mujahid: His Objectives and Responsibilities*, (Mindanao: Bangsamoro Publications), 1984.
33. Ibid. See also Salamat Hashim, *The Bangsamoro People's Struggle Against Oppression and Colonialism* (Camp Abubakre As-Siddique: Agency for Youth Affairs-MILF), 2001.
34. Abu Hamdie, "The Abu Sayyaf Group" (undated and unpublished manuscript).
35. For more discussions, see "Southeast Asia as the Global Center of Marine Biodiversity" at http://www.pemsea.org/info%20center/articles/tropcsts0797_globlcntrmrnbiodiversity.htm"(accessed on May 4, 2004).
36. Dillon, p. 1.
37. Ibid.
38. Cdr Jose Renan C. Suarez, "Towards a Navy of Substance: A Modernization Program," *Navy Digest*, Vol. 3, No. 1, January–June 2003, p. 32. Also see Lt. Antonio F. Trillanes, "An Implementation Analysis of the Philippine Navy Modernization Program," *Navy Digest*, Vol. 3, No. 1, January–June 2003, pp. 21–28. Trillanes is one of the principal actors in the July 2003 *Oakwood Mutiny*. He is presently in military custody awaiting court martial.
39. Graham Gerald Ong, *Ships Can Be Dangerous Too: Coupling Piracy and Maritime Terrorism in Southeast Asia's Maritime Security Framework*, ISEAS Working Paper No. 1 (Singapore: Institute of Southeast Asian Studies, 2004, p. 1.
40. For the author's elaborate thoughts on this issue, see Rommel C. Banlaoi, "Maritime Security Outlook for Southeast Asia," in Joshua Ho and Catherine Zara Raymond (eds.), *The Best of Times, The Worst of Times: Maritime Security in the Asia-Pacific* (Singapore: World Scientific for the Institute of Defence and Strategic Studies), 2005, pp. 59–80.
41. ICC International Maritime Bureau, *Piracy and Armed Robbery Against Ships*, Report for the Period January 1 to September 30, 2006.
42. Ibid., p. 15.
43. "IMB Piracy Report Notes Decline in Piracy" available at http://www.icc-ccs.org/main/news.php?newsid=83 (accessed on July 8, 2007).
44. Ibid.
45. For elaboration, see Carolin Liss, *Private Security Companies in the Fight Against Piracy in Asia*, Working Paper No. 120 (Australia: Asia Research Centre, Murdoch University), September 2005, p. 2.
46. Ibid.
47. Banlaoi, "Maritime Security Outlook for Southeast Asia," p. 61.
48. For an excellent examination of the nexus of piracy and maritime terrorism, see Peter Lehr (ed.), *Violence at Sea: Piracy in the Age of Global Terrorism* (New York and London: Routledge), 2007.
49. This is based in Banlaoi, "Maritime Security Outlook for Southeast Asia," op. cit.
50. See "Asia Piracy Costs $25 bln a year, says experts," *Reuters News Service*, Singapore, December 11, 2002, available at http://www.planetark.com/dailynewsstory.cfm/newsid/18987/newsDate/11-Dec-2002/story.htm (accessed on April 27, 2004).
51. Bintan Eric Ellis, "Piracy on the High Seas is on the Rise in Southeast Asia," *Fortune*, September 29, 2003. Also available at http://www.singapore-window.org/sw03/030919fo.htm (accessed on April 27, 2004).
52. See Report of the Organisation for Economic Cooperation and Development, "Price of Increased Maritime Security is Much Lower than Potential Cost of a Major Terror Attack," available at http://www.oecd.org/document/30/0,2340,en_2649_201185_4390494_1_1_1_1,00.html (accessed April 27, 2004).

53. Asia Pacific Center for Security Studies, "Executive Summary Transnational Violence and Seams of Lawlessness," February 19–21, 2002, available at http://www.apcss.org/core/Conference/CR_ES/020219ES.htm (accessed on November 27, 2006).

54. Annuska Derks, *Combating Trafficking in Southeast Asia: A Review of Policy and Programme Response* (Geneva: International Organization for Migration), 2000, p. 5.

55. Ibid.

56. Bertil Lintner, "Illegal Aliens Smuggling To and Through Southeast Asia" (Budapest: The European Science Foundation, Asia Committee and the Economic and Social Research Council), May 26–27, 2000, p. 1.

57. Public Broadcasting Service, *Dying To Leave, Handbook: The Business of Human Trafficking*, 2003, available at http://www.pbs.org/wnet/wideangle/shows/dying/handbook.html (accessed on November 27, 2006).

58. Ralf Emmers, *Non-Traditional Security in the Asia Pacific: The Dynamics of Securitization* (Singapore: Eastern Universities Press), 2004, pp. 61–81.

59. Public Broadcasting Service, *Dying To Leave, Handbook: The Business of Human Trafficking*, loc. cit.

60. Melanie Petros, "The Cost of Human Smuggling and Trafficking," *Global Migration Perspectives*, No. 31. April 2005, pp. 4–5.

61. For more discussions, see Hamisch McCulloch, "Assessing the Involvement of Organized Crime in Human Smuggling and Trafficking," *122nd International Training Course*, available at http://www.unafei.or.jp/english/pdf/PDF_rms/no62/UK(2).pdf, (accessed on November 27, 2006).

62. Small arms refer to revolvers and self-loading pistols, rifles and carbines, submachine guns, assault rifles and light machine guns. Light weapons refer to heavy machine guns, hand-held under barrel and mounted grenade launchers, portable antiaircraft guns, portable antitank guns and recoilless rifles, portable launchers of antitank missiles and rocket systems, portable launchers of antiaircraft missile systems, and mortars of calibers less than 100 mm caliber. See Gina R. Pattugalan, "Small Arms Proliferation and Misuse: Human Security Impact and Policy Actions in Southeast Asia," *Kasarinlan: Philippine Journal of Third World Studies*, Vol. 19, No. 1, 2004, pp. 62–91.

63. For an excellent reference, see Philips Jusario Vermonte and Philips Jusario Vermonte (eds.), *Small is (not) Beautiful: The Problem of Small Arms in Southeast Asia* (Jakarta: Center for Strategic and International Studies), 2004.

64. For more information on this topic, see UN Security Council, "Press Release on Small Arms Debate Support Action Programme," November 10, 2002, avialable at http://www.un.org/News/Press/docs/2002/sc7528.doc.htm (accessed on November 27, 2006).

65. Small Arms Survey, *Small Arms Survey 2005: Weapons at War* (Geneva, Switzerland: Small Arms Survey), 2005.

66. See, for example, U.S. Department of State, *Patterns of Global Terrorism 2003* (Washington: Department of State), April 2004. Also see Federation of American Scientist, "Illicit Arms Trade" at http://www.fas.org/asmp/campaigns/smallarms/IssueBrief3ArmsTrafficking.html (accessed on November 27, 2006).

67. International Action Network on Small Arms, "Small Arms in Southeast Asia and the Pacific," available at http://www.iansa.org/regions/asiapacific/asiapacific.htm (accessed on November 27, 2006).

68. David Capie, *Small Arms Production and Transfers in Southeast*, Paper No. 146 (Canberra: Australian National University), 2002.

69. Ralf Emmers, *NTS in the Asia Pacific: The Dynamics of Securitization*, p. 9.

70. Ibid.

71. United Nations Office on Drugs and Crime, *Global Illegal Drug Trends 2003* (New York and Vienna: UNODC), 2003, p. 11.

72. Ralf Emmers, "Securitisation of Drug Trafficking: A Study of Thailand" in *NTS in the Asia Pacific: The Dynamics of Securitization*, pp. 9–34.

73. This particular section of this chapter is based on Rommel C. Banlaoi, Non-Traditional Security Issues in Southeast Asian Maritime Domain: Implications for the Indian Ocean. Paper presented to the International Symposium, "The Changing Oceanic Landscape in the Indian Ocean Region: Issues and Perspectives of Debate" organized by the Centre for Security Analysis (CSA), Chennai, India on December 14, 2006.

74. See ASEAN Cooperation on Functional Areas at http://www.aseansec.org/8558.htm.

75. See ASEAN Cooperation on Transnational Issues at http://www.aseansec.org/4916.htm.

76. *Declaration of ASEAN Concord II*, October 7, 2003.

77. Ibid.

78. *Declaration of ASEAN Concord II*, October 7, 2003.

79. For an excellent commentary on the RMSI, see Joshua Ho, "Operationalising the Regional Maritime Security Initiative," and IDSS Commentaries, May 27, 2004.

80. Testimony of Admiral Thomas B. Fargo, United States Navy Commander U.S. Pacific Command before the House Armed Services Committee, United States House of Representatives regarding U.S. Pacific Command Posture, March 31, 2004. Also available at http://www.pacom.mil/speeches/sst2004/040331housearmedsvcscomm.shtml (accessed on July 27, 2004).

81. Tamara Renee Shie, "Ports in a Storm? The Nexus between Counterterrorism, Counterproliferation, and Maritime Security in Southeast Asia," *Issues and Insights*, Vol. 4, No. 4 (Pacific Forum CSIS), July 2004, p. 23.

82. Patrick Goodenough, "Maritime Security Takes Center Stage in SE Asia," *CNSNews.com*, June 29, 2004. Available online at http://www.cnsnews.com/ (accessed on July 27, 2004). p. 2.

83. For an earlier study, see Amitav Acharya, "Regional Military–Security Cooperation in the Third World: A Conceptual Analysis of the Relevance and Limitations of ASEAN (Association of Southeast Asian Nations)," *Journal of Peace Research*, Vol. 29, No. 1, January 1992, pp. 7–21.

84. N. Ganesan, *Bilateral Tensions in the Post-Cold War ASEAN* (Singapore: Institute of Southeast Asian Studies), 1999.

85. Graham Gerard Ong-Webb, "Piracy in Maritime Asia: Current Trends," in Peter Lehr (ed.), *Violence at Sea: Piracy in the Age of Global Terrorism* (London: Routledge), 2007, p. 79.

86. On July 14, 2005, the Singapore-based Institute of Southeast Asian Studies held a seminar to assess the implementation of MALSINDO after one year. The title of the seminar was "One Year after MALSINDO: Regional Developments, Accomplishments and Further Challenges in the Malacca Straits." See at http://www.iseas.edu.sg/14jul05.html (accessed on March 16, 2005).

87. Chris Rahman, "The International Politics of Combating Piracy in Southeast Asia," in Peter Lehr (ed.), *Violence at Sea: Piracy in the Age of Global Terrorism* (London: Routledge), 2007, p. 194.

88. Andrew Tan, "Force Modernization Trends in Southeast Asia," *IDSS Working Paper*, No. 59, January 2004, p. 1.

89. Ibid. p. 37.

90. For an excellent analysis of conventional military balance in Southeast Asia, see Anthony H. Cordesman, *The Conventional Military Balance in Southeast Asia: An Analytic Overview: A Comparative Summary of Military Expenditure; Manpower; Land, Air, and Naval, Forces; and Arms Sales* (Washington: Center for Strategic and International Studies), February 27, 2000. Also see Sheldon Simon, "Asian Armed Forces: Internal and External Tasks and Capabilities," *NBR Analysis*, Vol. 11, No. 1, 2000, pp. 1–19 and Derek Da Cunha, "ASEAN Naval Power in the New Millennium" in Jack McCaffire and Alan Hinge (eds.), *Sea Power in the New Century: Maritime Operations in the Asia Pacific Beyond 2000* (Canberra: Australian Defence Studies Centre), 1998, pp. 73–83.

91. This particular section of this paper is based on Rommel C. Banlaoi, Non-Traditional Security Issues in Southeast Asian Maritime Domain: Implications for the Indian Ocean. Paper presented to the International Symposium, "The Changing Oceanic Landscape in the Indian Ocean Region: Issues and Perspectives of Debate" organized by the Centre for Security Analysis (CSA), Chennai, India on December 14, 2006.

17 Maritime Dynamism in Indo-Pacific Region

James A. Boutilier

We are currently witnessing what is, arguably, the most dynamic maritime era in living memory. Virtually by any metric—container flows, shipping schedules, shipbuilding tempos, port development, energy flows, naval construction, coast guard activity, submarine acquisition, maritime terrorism, and piratical attacks—this is an era without equal. The forces of globalization, and more specifically the economic vitality of nations like China and India, have contributed directly to this dynamism. Moreover, Asian nationalism has added a Mahanian dimension to the maritime realm, encouraging states to express their new-found power and self-confidence in uncharacteristically bold naval programs. This chapter explores these phenomena, focusing primarily on the state of commercial shipping in the Pacific and Indian oceans and prospects for mid- and big-power navies in the same domain.

The inexorable forces of globalization, with all these phenomena in terms of economic integration, rapidity of transactions, and "just-in-time" door-to-door delivery cultures, have provided an enormous impetus to worldwide export-driven economies. This is particularly apparent in Asia where China, and to a lesser degree India, have developed powerful export-oriented economies. In fact, it is important to note that in the past 25 years, India and China have fundamentally reoriented their axes of national interest away from the interior of Asia toward the sea. This historic shift highlights the critical importance of maritime transport and security to these two great nations. Of particular importance is the growing dependency of both nations on seaborne energy flows, a theme explored at greater length in the following text. This dependency, among other things, will link the Indian and Pacific Ocean complexes in an unprecedented way. These complexes are fundamentally different and yet tanker traffic (not to mention the overlapping naval ambitions of China and India) across the Indian Ocean and through the Strait of Malacca (or neighboring Indonesian Straits) to Asian destinations has had a powerful integrative impact on the two oceans.

China has largely replaced Japan during the past quarter century as the great spark plug energizing Asian economies. Indeed, it could be argued that Chinese economic dynamism helped in lifting the Japanese economic ship of state off the rocks early in the 21st century after more than a decade of debilitating recessions and depressions. Curiously, Japan's economy remains far greater and more developed than China's, but it is Beijing's stellar accomplishment that has captured—even mesmerized—the public imagination. That is, China is rich on the one hand but poor on the other. Although the coastal regions of China, and the Pearl River and Yangtze River deltas in particular, are booming powerhouses, half a billion Chinese remain mired in a state of poverty, existing on less than U.S.$2.00/day. Ironically, China's economic achievements constitute as much of a dilemma for China's leaders as they do for rival powers like the United States. The former are increasingly concerned about the profoundly asymmetric distribution of wealth within the nation. The latter, uncertain about China's end game, is unclear whether China constitutes a threat or an opportunity. Cogent arguments can be advanced to support both position. Certainly, China is a nation on the rise and conventional wisdom dictates that such states have a destabilizing effect on the status quo.

More specifically, Washington and other international capitals have to assess the degree to which China's commercial and naval ambitions may constitute a direct threat to their economic and security well being.

What is inescapably obvious is the fact that China's leaders have embraced the importance of the sea and dedicated themselves to building the infrastructure and acquiring the assets necessary to buttress and reflect their emerging great power status. We can see this clearly when we look at the growth of the Shanghai megaport. Traditionally, Singapore was the greatest container port in Asia, but Shanghai is intent on overhauling Singapore in the short- to mid-term. Singapore handled over 23 million standard twenty-foot equivalent (TEU) unit containers in 2006 and this number is scheduled to rise to over 50 million roughly by 2018. The Shanghai port complex is likely to exceed this figure (building on the great Yangtze riverine highway and burgeoning economies of the Shanghai hinterland) by the same year. Much of the growth stems from transpacific traffic but an even greater proportion is now derived from intra-Asian trade. Trade overall is scheduled to grow at breathtaking rates. Two examples will suffice. It is calculated that 141,000 ships a year will pass through the Strait of Malacca and Singapore by 2018, up from the current figure of 65,000. At the same time, Canadian and American authorities need to add port capacity on the west coast of North America equivalent to one Port of Vancouver (a bulk port that handled 1.7 million containers in 2006) every year for the foreseeable future.

In third place, behind South Korea and Japan, China is committed to surpassing these two countries in shipbuilding capacity by 2015. And this is not merely a case of dead-weight tonnage. The Chinese are moving slowly upmarket in terms of mastering the complex and sophisticated maritime architecture associated with such vessels as liquefied natural gas (LNG) carriers. These ships have been a traditional Japanese and Korean reserve but not any longer.

Ships are also getting bigger and bigger. Each container ship carried 1000–1500 containers (TEUs) 30 years ago. Now there are 10,000-TEU ships on the stocks and plans afoot between Germanischer Lloyd and Hyundai Heavy Industries to build vessels that will carry over 13,400 containers. Ships of this size will be rarities for the moment but they imply a gradual reordering of global shipping patterns, with a handful of megaports (and the top six are now in east Asia) acting as the nodes because they have the requisite depth of water and gantry capacity, whereas more and more feeder lines spread out from them to service lesser ports.

Tankers are increasingly central to the Indo-Pacific maritime arena. As the states of the Indian and Pacific oceans make the transition from agricultural to oil-fueled economies, the demand for energy has become insatiable. This is particularly true in the case of China, a nation that became a net importer of energy in 1993. China's appetite for oil, which stood at 20 million tons in 1996, is likely to grow to 300 million tons by 2020. Accordingly some years ago, Beijing embarked on a worldwide diversification program in search of international sources of energy. The result has been a series of bilateral arrangements that saw China acquiring oil from Columbia, Peru, Sudan, Angola, Iran, Saudi Arabia, and western Canada. So far so good, but the Chinese leadership has grown increasingly concerned that a significant proportion of the imported energy is obliged to transit the Strait of Malacca, a narrow waterway that could be the subject of advertent or inadvertent closure. This concern has led in turn to the articulation of a number of terrestrial strategies that see the Chinese negotiating for oil from the central Asian republics and Russia.

The Chinese, of course, are not the only players in east Asia dependent on imported energy. The Japanese and South Koreans have long been dependent on unimpeded tanker traffic. More recently, New Delhi has also been attempting to diversify its energy sources, in some cases in direct competition with the Chinese. Of particular interest to security analysts in New Delhi has been China's role in stimulating the growth of the new port of Gwadar, west of Karachi, on the Pakistani coast not far from the Strait of Hormuz. Beijing is reported to have contributed U.S.$400 million to the port development scheme and there are some who speculate that, in times to come, Gwadar will be a point *d'appui* for elements of the People's Liberation Army Navy (PLAN), ostensibly to oversee the security of China's trans-Indian Ocean sea-lanes of communication (SLOCs) (that are increasingly important not merely in terms of energy flows but in terms of China's importation of natural resources from Africa), but quite possibly to complicate India's security equation in times of tension. Whatever is the case, all the evidence suggests that traffic in energy from the Persian Gulf to east Asia will continue to grow inexorably, a reality which increases the maritime stakes in great power calculi.

The Chinese have also begun to develop the PLAN in an uncharacteristically aggressive manner. Traditionally, the Chinese had little sense of sea power and in the years following the declaration of the People's Republic in 1949, they embraced Soviet naval doctrine, which relegated naval vessels to coastal and riverine activities in support of army operations ashore. Since the 1980s, however, Beijing has broken that minimalist legacy and embraced a Mahanian vision of sea power, namely, that great states have great navies and great navies make for great states. Nevertheless, it would be a mistake to conclude that China has a great navy at present. What is significant about the PLAN is not its size or its emerging modernity, but the resolute way in which the Chinese leadership has continued, year after year, to develop new ship classes, focus on greater seagoing capability, push the maritime "boundaries" of China farther and farther to sea, and advertise their presence on the world's oceans.

The PLAN is still a navy in the making. Two features of this navy are critical to any overall assessment. First, is the emphasis on submarines. China's submarine fleet is an uneven one with elderly conventional boats tied up alongside brand new Russian conventionally powered submarine (SSK), indigenously produced nuclear attack (SSN), and ballistic missile boats (SSBN). Nevertheless, the Chinese thrust appears to be unequivocal to utilize submarines to achieve sea denial in the approaches to the Chinese coast and, more particularly, in the waters around the congested island of Taiwan. Second, the Chinese have taken another page from the Russian playbook, namely, the utilization of ship-killing (and, more specifically, carrier killing) supersonic and hypersonic missiles. What Beijing wants to achieve is a powerfully offensive-defense, slowly advancing the nation's maritime margins outward to the point where the mainland is beyond the reach of U.S. land attack cruise missiles or carrier airpower.

Will China acquire a carrier? There have been tantalizing hints in the professional literatures for a decade and a half now, but the frequency of references appears to be mounting. However, carriers constitute an exquisite dilemma for the Chinese. On one hand, they realize the enormous costs involved in building and operating a carrier or carriers complete with air wings. Further, they realize that they are 85 years behind the Americans in mastering the art of carrier operations. On the other, burgeoning national pride and Mahanian impulses are locked in combat with Chinese pragmatism. The former seems destined to prevail over the next half decade or so.

A reason for carrier capability is that the Indian Navy has carrier capability in the form of the aging INS *Viraat* (ex-HMS *Hermes*) and the soon-to-be-delivered Russian carrier *Gorshkov* as well as an indigenously produced air defense ship (ah, the glories of naval euphemisms!). Long captured by the festering dispute in Jammu and Kashmir and the problematic nature of its relationship with Pakistan, India was slow to acknowledge the importance of sea power and the way in which fate had placed the sub-continent astride the supremely important SLOCs traversing the Indian Ocean. However, in the past decade India has come out unequivocally in support of sea power and India's role as the natural arbiter of seagoing affairs in the Indian Ocean. Like China, and other countries in east Asia such as Singapore and Malaysia, India has developed a robust indigenous shipbuilding capability—a capacity that will enable New Delhi to wean itself off its longstanding dependence on Russia for all but the most sophisticated naval designs and equipment.

India has begun to flex its naval muscles in an unmistakable way, dispatching a task force of five ships—headed by the destroyer INS *Mysore*—to the Pacific Ocean in March 2007 to exercise with the Japanese Maritime Defense Force and the U.S. Navy. This is history in the making. It suggests to the Japanese that they should break the mold, thereby liberating themselves from self-imposed prohibitions on collective security. The tipping point occurred on August 31, 1998, when the North Koreans launched a three-stage Taepodong missile, portions of which arced over the Japanese home islands before plunging into the North Pacific. This was Japan's 9/11. Almost overnight, Tokyo's priority switched from reviving the nation's anemic economy to reassessing Japan's national security agenda. The outlook was frankly gloomy. China's economy was on an upward trajectory and China's defense budget continued to grow at a double-digit rate every year. Beijing and Tokyo were at odds over disputed offshore oil and gas fields, whereas Seoul was little short of bellicose in its reaction to Japanese claims to the Tokdo islets in the east (Sea of Japan). Furthermore, relations between Tokyo and Pyongyang were deeply strained over the question of North Korea's abduction of Japanese nationals in the 1970s and the Russo–Japanese relationship remained problematic because of an unresolved dispute over the northern Kurile Islands.

The terrorist attacks on New York and Washington marked the next stage in the transformation of Tokyo's worldview. Prime Minister Koizumi promised support for coalition of naval forces in the north Arabian Sea despite the fact that there was no enabling legislation in place. At the speed of light, by Japanese standards, the Diet passed the requisite legislation and the Japanese dispatched warships to the Indian Ocean for the first time since 1945. At the same time, the Japanese refined their defense relationship with the United States, resolving points of ambiguity in the process, and embarked on the development of sea-based antimissile defenses with the Americans. Tokyo also decided to explore the potential of an enhanced relationship with New Delhi, something that Washington had already put in train. Although all of the players denied straightforwardly that this new security architecture had anything to do with China, their actions tended to belie their words. A further departure from Japan's customary aversion to collective security occurred in March 2007 when Australia, one of the United States' closest allies in the Pacific, penciled in a new security agreement with Japan.

Despite these developments, these have been troubling times for the United States in general and U.S. Navy in particular. Washington remains bogged down in Iraq and Afghanistan, in campaigns that are ambiguous, open-ended, costly, and increasingly unpopular. The U.S. defense budget continues to rise but the U.S. Navy is in the midst of a "sickly season." Relatively few observers probably realize that the greatest navy on earth has been cut into half in the past two decades. In the mid-1980s, the then secretary of the navy, John Lehman, fulsomely supported by President Reagan, announced the creation of a "600-ship navy." At this time, the American fleet numbered about 580 ships. Currently, 22 years later, it numbers between 276 and 281 ships, depending on the sources cited. This is budgetary disarmament on a grand scale. It is important to note that the U.S. Navy is not the only navy suffering from swinging reductions. The Royal Navy, for example, has seen its destroyer and frigate fleet fall from 52 to 27. Indeed, there is a real concern in Royal Navy circles that the two big carriers, which are on the order books will lack the number of escorts they need when they come into service.

Cost is another critical factor. In the Royal Navy's case, it is a question of one carrier or two. In the U.S. Navy's case, there is a mounting congressional criticism of the dramatic cost overruns associated with the new littoral combat ships (LCS)—rapid, versatile vessels designed to operate inshore in antisubmarine, antisurface, and antimine roles. LCS prototypes have risen in cost from around U.S.$250 million to U.S.$400 million or more. The number of big carriers in the U.S. Navy has fallen to 11 and there are many who feel that the *Arleigh Burke*–class destroyers will never be replaced, one-for-one, by the much-vaunted DDG 1000. The navy's fortunes have been further undermined by grave doubts about the capacity of the shrunken shipbuilding industry to construct enough vessels to allow the U.S. Navy to reach its mid-term goal of 313 ships. Personnel are another problem. The Canadian, American, British, and Australian navies are all wrestling with critical manning shortfalls, which (despite the prospect of reduced crew ships in the future) threaten to curtail soaring operational tempos.

The navies cited are undergoing changes of a different sort. To begin with, the post-Cold War era has placed a premium on littoral operations. The rather awkward word "amphibiosity" has made its way into naval lexicons today and more and more navies, western and otherwise, are looking to develop over-the-beach capability. The Japanese Osumi class is a case in point. Similarly, the Australians, New Zealanders, Singaporeans, Canadians, and British have joined the Americans—long exponents of amphibious operations—in acquiring ships that will permit operations in littoral waters. Littoral operations have brought to the fore, once again, power projection from the sea. This is not new in the history of navies but the range and magnitude of the power projection involved are almost entirely new. The U.S. Navy's ability to hit Al Qaeda training camps near Khost in eastern Afghanistan in 1998 and more recently Baghdad with sea-launched, land-attack cruise missiles illustrates this point. At the same time, there is a worrying counterdevelopment—power projection from the shore. This is seen in a limited way with the terrorist attacks on the USS *Cole* and MV *Limburg*. The installation of shore-to-ship missiles like the C-802, utilized by Hamas against an Israeli patrol boat, is another example of this disturbing phenomenon.

Another critical change relates to enhanced maritime domain awareness (MDA). This is largely a post-9/11 phenomenon in which there has been a fresh and powerful impetus to achieve a comprehensive understanding of what is going on in the commercial shipping realm. Traditionally navies sought to provide protection "for" shipping, whereas, they now (along with their coast guards) need to think in terms of protecting assets "from" ships. This has been the inescapable lesson of 9/11—vehicles themselves can be weapons. Ships can be used to carry dangerous cargoes (e.g., bombs in containers) or, primitively, to ram other vessels or shore installations. The international airline community has enjoyed a detailed understanding of air traffic for many decades but the commercial shipping world—conservative, secretive, and inadequately regulated—has been largely beyond the grasp of shore-based authorities. Right around the world, in the aftermath of 9/11, leading navies and coast guards joined with a variety of related maritime and security agencies to pool and fuse data in an effort to not only know what is happening at sea but also to control the movements of national and international shipping.

This is an enormous undertaking because the ships themselves are only the first line of attack. The millions and millions of containers (not to mention break bulk and other cargoes) are the second line of attack. To address the latter, the Americans (supported in a number of instances by the International Maritime Organization) have articulated an array of post-9/11 regulations designed to vet the contents of containers, exact nature of crews, and character of shipboard security regimes. Thus, in a perverse way, there has been a silver lining to 9/11. Our grasp of sea-going commerce has improved significantly. This was something that people had spoken about on many occasions before 9/11 but the attacks on the World Trade Center towers and Pentagon galvanized the maritime community as never before.

The physical manifestation of data-fusion and interagency cooperation and coordination (still very far from being perfect because of differing priorities and security cultures) are maritime domain centers. The Canadian Navy is the host of multiagency Marine Security Operation Centers (MSOCs) on Canada's east and west coasts. Similarly, Australia has achieved a far higher degree of awareness with a coastal command that brings together a variety of agencies and their assets in an integrated effort whereas Singapore has stood up its own variation on an MSOC at its huge Changi naval complex. Thus, we can see that not only are there unparalleled degrees of shipping in the early part of the twenty-first century but there is now a unique conjunction between commercial shipping, navies, coast guards (of which more and more have been stood up or redesignated, such as the Malaysian Maritime Enforcement Agency or Japanese Maritime Safety Agency—now the Japanese Coast Guard), and related security bodies.

Although some militaries are moving along the spectrum from peacekeeping to operations indistinguishable from war, navies appear, for the most part, to be moving in the opposite direction. The age of Jutland and Midway, set-piece naval encounters on the high seas, is behind us (lest one foresees some future encounter between the U.S. Navy and PLAN close up to the Asian shore). Instead, navies are beginning to spend more and more time in the diplomatic and constabulary roles outlined in Booth's famous triangle of naval power. Navies are *sans pareil* when it comes to diplomacy; no other weapon system has the flexibility, versatility, and appeal of a visiting warship. Naval diplomacy can range from benign port visits to full-blown naval exercises, such as Aman 2007, hosted by the Pakistani Navy in March 2007 off Karachi.

At the same time, there is a category of activity that tends to bridge the diplomatic and constabulary roles that Booth identified. In December 2004, in the aftermath of a catastrophic tsunami that devastated the coastal regions of northwestern Sumatra and a number of coastal communities in Sri Lanka, India, Thailand, and other parts of the Indian Ocean, an armada of ships assembled off the shores of Banda Aceh in Indonesia. They represented, among others, the Australian, American, and Singaporean navies. They brought order and relief to chaos, exploiting helicopter operations to ferry supplies and personnel ashore, utilizing the services of unique vessels such as U.S. Navy's *Mercy*, the American hospital ship, and suppressing—by their very presence—incidents of piracy in the neighboring Strait of Malacca. Other navies such as the Indian Navy, were also hard at work providing humanitarian assistance and disaster relief. The U.S. Navy also provided support during a disastrous earthquake in the mountainous areas of northern Pakistan and floods and mudslides in Indonesia subsequent to the great tsunami.

These activities galvanized regional navies and cut across institutional barriers and cultural conservatism in a highly positive manner. One could argue that multinavy cooperation during the Banda Aceh tsunami was a source of inspiration for the subsequent standing up of trilateral anti-piracy patrols in the Strait of Malacca in July 2005, involving the Indonesian, Singaporean, and Malaysian navies (with indirect support from Japan by way of the Nippon Foundation). Cooperation of this sort was also embodied in the American 1000-ship navy concept in 2006. This concept had two origins. First, it reflected a pragmatic assessment by Washington of the gulf opening up between available naval assets and the growing number of maritime challenges that need to be addressed worldwide. Quite clearly, the U.S. Navy needed help and this was likely to come from like-minded navies willing—as they had been with the coalition antiterrorist Task Force 150 in the northern Arabian Sea—to work together with the U.S. Navy. Second, it reflected a realization that the high seas were the last great oceanic commons and all the nations of the world had a responsibility to work together to safeguard this oceanic heritage. This was much more than just high-sounding rhetoric. The parlous state of global fisheries is an illustration of the need for united action at sea. Thus, the 1000-ship navy concept was a plea for greater naval or maritime cooperation in the face of unparalleled challenges on the world's oceans. Navies and coast guards have the mobility, versatility, and adaptability to rise to those challenges if the requisite levels of political will and institutional daring are present.

Time is running out. Maritime commerce is growing dramatically, even explosively. This, in turn, is changing the maritime landscape in terms of port development, traffic flows, shipbuilding patterns, and the rise of naval ambitions, buttressed by the largest submarine fleets in the world. Now, more than ever before, we must exploit the inherent companionship of the sea, galvanizing navies and maritime agencies in the Indian and Pacific oceans to work together to ensure peace and good order on the world's last great frontier—it's oceans.

18 The North Atlantic Treaty Organization's Evolving Role in Maritime Security Operations

Robert Snoddon

CONTENTS

Maritime security operations (MSO) are a complex business, requiring specialist tasking and a legal framework that allow individual vessels and those of multinational task groups to function effectively. This chapter considers these challenges; examines what North Atlantic Treaty Organization (NATO) is doing specifically with regard to MSO; and what commercial maritime companies, merchant vessels, and others in the shipping industry can expect in terms of NATO's areas of responsibility, operational activity, and its limitations, including the legal parameters under which warships must function. This chapter examines NATO's Operation Active Endeavor (OAE) in the Mediterranean—specifically the identification of maritime security concerns such as possible terrorist use of the sea for conducting offensive operations and managing appropriate operational responses. This chapter also examines NATO's expanding roles in MSO in areas outside of its nominal areas of operational coverage, such as counternarcotic operations and counterpiracy patrols in the Gulf of Guinea and Horn of Africa.

The role of naval forces has always been changing, and the twenty-first century is no different. In the past, the major navies of the world looked to their fleets to provide "power projection," to "show the flag" and protect its maritime interests and trade routes (or sea-lanes of communication) across the globe. Except the U.S. Navy, many navies are constantly reducing in size and capability; and over the past 40 years, they have also been reducing their naval bases in foreign lands. NATO warships that are currently in commission were essentially designed for conventional naval warfare against a perceived or extant maritime threat. Formerly, this threat came from the Soviet Union and Eastern Bloc countries of the Warsaw Pact. However, the collapse of communism in the former USSR and breakaway of the Eastern Bloc have resulted in the displacement of this threat by the contemporary concern of asymmetrical threats such as terrorism and the persistent concerns of criminal activity in both international and territorial waters around the world.

Although this conventional threat axis is still somewhat residual and remains the focus of doctrine and training for NATO commands, most of the Western navies of today are currently engaged in a fight against an enemy that has no visible identity or established bases. This enemy is not a fleet of enemy ships, submarines, and aircraft, for which the sophisticated combat systems were originally developed, but maritime units for which both the weapon systems and tactics used will require reorientation and even redevelopment.

The current asymmetrical threat facing modern Western navies with the greatest potential for large-scale political and lethal consequences is terrorism emanating from, or directed at, the maritime domain. Added to this is the concern of piracy in the Horn of Africa, Strait of Malacca, South China Sea, and littoral and coastal regions of the Gulf of Guinea. With these new and embryonic threats maturing (although they can wax and wane in intensity and regularity), navies are only now coming to terms with a new requirement, which will not necessitate (or in some cases favor) the array of complex weapon systems currently fitted such as larger-caliber naval guns, antishipping missiles, and advanced torpedoes. Instead, the modern navies will need to focus on the new asymmetric threat and adopt newer nuanced tactics to confront them. On a regular basis, however, it will not be the actions of terrorists who pose this threat to naval units, but those of pirates and criminals and the effects of environmental disasters such as the Aceh tsunami of December 2004.

OPERATION ACTIVE ENDEAVOR

Currently, NATO's primary contribution to MSOs is OAE,[1] which is focused predominately in the Mediterranean Sea and its approaches. OAE represents the first operation in NATO's history in which Alliance assets have been required in support of Article V operations.[2] The operation commenced on October 26, 2001, and was initiated in direct response to the attacks of September 11, 2001. Following on from the events of 9/11, the then NATO Secretary General, Lord Robertson, announced that as it had been determined that the attacks had been directed from abroad, they were regarded as an action covered under Article V of the Washington Treaty.

Initially for NATO, the focus was one of deterrence against the potential terrorist use of the sea, and as a result, OAE focused primarily on possible illicit and terrorist maritime activity in the eastern Mediterranean. The use of NATO vessels and those of the U.S. 6th Fleet was widely reported at the time of the operation's beginning, and because of this activity and the events surrounding MV *Nisha*,[3] media reports of a massive worldwide search for a supposedly sizeable fleet of Al Qaeda vessels began to emerge. In the Mediterranean, it was initially the U.S. 6th Fleet warships that were conducting boarding operations involving suspect vessels, whereas NATO assets were initially on hand to identify, track, and compile a list of high-interest vessels.[4] During the early stages of OAE, neither vessels belonging to an Al Qaeda "fleet" were identified, nor were any suspected ships seized. In fact, the only suspect activity detected or suspected was mostly criminal in nature (narcotics, contraband, and human trafficking) rather than terrorist-related. As more information was gathered and intelligence produced, the list of high interest and suspect vessels eventually decreased. What was initially thought to be a suspect was eventually identified as normal commercial maritime practices—practices that on the surface appear anomalous or that present a possible security risk partially due to the lack of sufficient oversight and operational and regulatory transparency.

What NATO was in fact revealing, although it was not completely clear at the time, was the identification of existing and potential criminal activity at sea; primarily illegal immigration as well as narcotic and contraband smuggling. NATO was, however, not in a position to act on the intelligence that they received and were developing; and this intelligence was normally passed onto maritime law enforcement agencies in countries such as Italy and Greece. It was not until April 2003, when the North Atlantic Council made a decision to allow NATO units to conduct boarding operations, that the Alliance could start to play a more complete role. Boarding operations by NATO are only conducted in accordance with the rules of international law and remain compliant with norms governing the strictures under which member states can operate in a law-enforcement capacity within their own territorial waters or those of their allies.

OAE's mission remains focused at countering terrorist threats incubated within, or directed at, the maritime realm and all other illegal activity that could possibly be associated (directly or tangentially) with maritime terrorist operations in OAE's geographical remit, such as human trafficking and the smuggling of small arms or components for weapons of mass destruction (WMD). NATO's success has been in its use of military assets to track, either overtly or covertly, merchant vessels suspected of criminal activity. By its very nature, this operation has become more intelligence-led, through the sharing of intelligence and information gathered at sea with its allies and their intelligence agencies ashore, to further enhance the security of all member states. The operation has been running for over five years and has done much to provide NATO forces with the background information on "what merchant vessels do." In no uncertain terms, OAE has been breaking new ground in the utilization of military and naval assets, supporting coast guards, police, and other non-military agencies in a coordinated fashion to enhance the security of the vessels, ports, and littoral waters of member states.

In reflection of the importance attached to this new priority, in early 2007, NATO's Military Committee stated that "The significance and priority of Maritime Situational Awareness has risen toward the top of both NATO's Strategic Commander's priorities."[5]

There are currently two joint force commanders (JFCs) within NATO—one based at Brunssum in the Netherlands and the other at Naples in Italy. Each has an air (ACC), land (LCC), and Maritime Component Commander (MCC). One MCC is located in the United Kingdom at Northwood and collocated at the Permanent Joint Force Headquarters and is under the command of JFC Brunssum. The other MCC is located at Naples and is under the command of JFC Naples. At Naples, the MCC is at the forefront of MSOs as the coordinator of OAE. Whereas in Northwood, the focus is on developing the procedures and tactics for dealing with a vast fleet of merchant vessels and their movements; and acting as the primary point of contact for shipping companies, vessel owners and operators, and other commercial actors that have interests and operations within OAE's area of activity. Two maritime groups are under the operational control of both MCCs. These groups, made up of vessels from the navies of several member states, enable the maritime policy of NATO to be implemented and operational effect to be established on the water.[6]

NATO has used its ships in MSOs on earlier occasions—during the conflict in the former Yugoslavia—where warships maintained a blockade of the Adriatic Sea and monitored the movement of all commercial and military maritime traffic within its boundaries. Primarily, this was to prevent cargoes that could support the warring factions from arriving at their destinations. This proved extremely effective, but it was an expensive method of policing a relatively small area in terms of the assets required. In contrast, OAE covers the entire Mediterranean, also extending east into the Black Sea, south into the Suez Canal and approaches the Red Sea, and west past the Strait of Gibraltar (STROG) into the Atlantic approaches to the Mediterranean. This is clearly a much larger area. To patrol a maritime space of the aforementioned scale requires significant sea-based and air assets. Therefore, maritime patrol aircraft and intelligence streams to support the ships assigned to OAE were essential if it was going to be effective. Additionally, signals intelligence gathering vessels (SIGINT)–configured ships and aircraft and other maritime assets are tasked and deployed when and where available.

Notwithstanding the large-scale geographical expanse and commensurate operational tempo noted earlier, since its inception, OAE ships have tracked and contacted thousands of merchant ships of all kinds; and of these, several hundred have been boarded. However, no arrests have been made; and more noteworthy, no specific terrorist activity has been identified yet.

IDENTIFYING MARITIME SECURITY ISSUES AND OPERATIONAL RESPONSES

Identifying maritime security issues and formulating ways to implement NATO policy rests with the MCC at Northwood in the United Kingdom. This headquarters is becoming a world leader in the coordination and reporting of all maritime-related events within its designated area of responsibility.

The headquarters is at the forefront of liaising with the commercial shipping industry, and the command group regularly meets with members from commercial policymaking organizations such as the International Maritime Organization (IMO) and British Chamber of Shipping. At the heart of all of this is the MCC Northwood Surveillance Coordination Centre. This center, along with the recently formed NATO Shipping Centre are manned 24/7 to provide NATO-deployed maritime units and individual national agencies with an easily accessible organization that can provide quick access to maritime and air assets for surveillance and interdiction tasking. The center is also available to provide advice and guidance to commercial agencies on the purpose and nature of OAE.[7] Essentially, the shipping center has been set up to support the exchange of information between the military and commercial shipping communities in addition to supporting military commanders.

The center also works closely with the MCC in Naples, Italy, in identifying suspect or high-interest vessels and analyzing intelligence on merchant vessel activity. Its mission is to:

1. Collect and process factual merchant-vessel details and associated navigational movement data and develop an accurate shipping (surface) plot of relevant merchant ships
2. Advise merchant shipping of potential security risks in their area and identify possible interferences with nominal commercial operations and trade
3. Act as the point of contact in NATO for the shipping community to exchange merchant-shipping information between NATO's military authorities and commands and with the wider international shipping community

The main tasks of the shipping center are:

1. To produce the relevant merchant-shipping picture (recognized maritime picture) for the military organization
2. To provide other ancillary shipping information to military and governmental authorities
3. To provide general information regarding relevant operations to the civilian shipping community

For merchant vessels and their owners and operators, there is a NATO publication that can be downloaded from the MCC Northwood Shipping Centre, available at http://shipping.manw.nato.int. The document is ATP 2(B) Volume II.[8] This publication provides information to ship owners, operators, masters, and ship officers regarding the interaction between NATO naval forces and commercial shipping. Specifically, the publication serves as a handbook for the worldwide application of naval cooperation and guidance for shipping (NCAGS),[9] which are the principles and procedures that exist to enhance the safety of shipping in times of elevated security risk, tension, crisis, and conflict.

COUNTERING ILLEGAL ACTIVITY AT SEA IN OTHER MARITIME AREAS

Although OAE is the focus for NATO operations in the Mediterranean, the Alliance is also moving toward establishing a more robust operation in the Atlantic, and in particular off the west coast of Africa. NATO is keen to make a footprint within the Gulf of Guinea, Cameroon, and other west African countries in a bid to stem the prospect of an energy supply crisis as a result of attacks on tankers and offshore platforms, a concern that is exacerbated by weak law enforcement and limited maritime patrolling and interdiction capabilities of countries in the region. The Gulf of Guinea is a significant and increasing source of petroleum (specifically crude and liquefied natural gas) for the United States and Europe, with oil exports providing vital revenue for producers in the region. It is the uneven distribution of this revenue, coupled with poor fiscal management, and chronic levels of corruption within some government organizations that has fueled the intensity of attacks by groups such as the Movement for the Emancipation of the Niger Delta (MEND). These attacks, mostly occurring in the Niger Delta region of southern Nigeria, include raids on oil terminals; floating production, storage, and offloading vessels (FPSOs); platforms; and tankers; often characterized by kidnapping, murder, and extortion.

Attacks such as those outlined earlier are what NATO and individual countries are keen to prevent. Lawlessness in regions of Nigeria, as well as other bordering countries, has led to a significant rise in organized criminal activities. In recognizing the commercial and strategic vitality of this littoral area, groups such as MEND have successfully exploited the maritime domain to further their operations and raise their profile. Additional concerns center on the rise in the utilization of some west African ports as transfer hubs for both South American cocaine and Southeast Asian heroin bound for Europe. Significant quantities of African-grown marijuana are also being trafficked from the continent by sea to Europe and the United States via the ports in the region.

It is precisely these phenomena that have seen the emergence of maritime domain awareness (MDA), MSO, and maritime situational awareness appearing in naval doctrine. Maritime security is vital to every sea-trading nation. Much of world's energy supplies, gas and oil are moved by sea; and over 90 percent of all trade moves by ship. The IMO estimates that cargo to the value of $3.5 trillion is transported annually by container vessels alone. As container vessels account for approximately 10 percent of the world's trade carrying merchant fleet, it becomes apparent that they move the largest proportion of goods. Container vessels use a network of specially configured high-volume hub ports that are strategically located and are supported by lower-volume regional feeder ports for maximum efficiency and throughput. This high-speed loading and unloading dynamic, almost perpetual movement, and the complex and often obscured administrative and documentation trail associated with containers render the container trade susceptible to illicit activity. Criminal organizations have identified that moving illicit cargo by container is clearly the preferred method of disguising its contents. Unless authorities suspect or have timely intelligence to identify specific shipments, illicit cargoes will remain undetected. Logically thus, any explosive device (including WMD) concealed in a container would certainly be the preferred method for any terrorist organization intent on causing damage to the Western economy.

With this concern in mind, the container security initiative (CSI) was developed. The U.S. Bureau of Customs and Border Protection, an agency of the Department of Homeland Security, launched CSI in 2002. CSI is a program that works cooperatively with foreign government agencies to target and prescreen high-risk maritime containerized cargo bound for the United States. CSI is primarily focused on the terrorist threat; attempting to identify personnel, weapons, explosives, and, in particular, potential WMD being "imported" into the target country. By using a combination of automated high-risk alerts activated by the scanning of bills of lading, manifests, points of origin, and identifying the owners and freight forwarders of particular containers, searches are focused on shipments identified as high risk or anomalous in nature. The World Customs Organization (WCO) and European Union (EU) are actively engaged in developing programs along the CSI model.

NATO and specifically the existing MSOs in the Mediterranean and putative operations to other theaters further afield are not linked to CSI or the ISPS code protocols in any codified or operational sense; nevertheless, intelligence-led surveillance and interdiction of high-interest vessels contribute to the holistic maritime security effort that is in place and evolving by sharing of intelligence, boarding, and discoveries, and so on.

COUNTERPIRACY OPERATIONS IN AFRICAN WATERS AND NORTH ATLANTIC TREATY ORGANIZATION

The deployment of Standing NATO Response Force Maritime Group 1 (SNMG1) in the circumnavigation of Africa in the summer of 2007, an unprecedented NATO maritime operation in a geographical sense, raised the prospect of more deliberate counterpiracy operations in the littoral waters around the continent; particularly in the Gulf of Guinea and off the coast of Somalia and the wider waters of the Horn of Africa. NATO's military arms are essentially intended and configured for conventional war-fighting roles; however, with the advent and success of OAE, MSO in the Mediterranean has raised the prospect of NATO warships becoming involved in coming to the aid of merchant vessels, which have become a victim of a piracy attack, or providing a clear deterrent to piracy and armed robbery at sea through a conspicuous presence in waters prone to these crimes.

In the wake of increasing piracy and armed robbery at sea off the coast of Somalia in 2005, highlighted in particular by attacks on vessels under charter by the World Food Program (WFP) conveying aid to this country, a United Nations Security Council resolution (UNSCR A.979(24)) addressing the issue and calling for mitigating action by those member states in a position to offer it was passed in November 2005. This resolution was followed by a statement by the president of the Security Council in March 2006, reaffirming the tenets of the resolution and further stressing that

> "The council encourages Member States whose naval vessels and military aircraft operate in international waters and airspace adjacent to the coast of Somalia to be vigilant to any incident of piracy therein and to take appropriate action to protect merchant shipping, in particular the transportation of humanitarian aid, against any such act, in line with relevant international law."[10]

In the summer of 2007, it became clear that attacks against shipping in this area had reduced due to the operational presence and support of NATO warships and evolving liaison between the shipping community and the NATO Shipping Centre at Northwood. However, the widely reported attacks against the 4787 deadweight tonnage (DWT) Jordanian-registered general cargo ship MV *Victoria* on May 19, 2006 and 1616 DWT Danish-flagged MV *Donica White* on June 2, 2006 highlighted the continued threat to vessels in Somali waters.[11] Against this backdrop, the continuing and solidifying relationship among the United Nations' WFP, IMO, and NATO's North Atlantic Council is important for continued efforts of NATO's MCC to help reduce the threat of piracy to shipping in these areas.

Notwithstanding the strictures governing the norms of conduct for warships covered under United Nations Convention on the Law of the Sea (UNCLOS) (see the following section), which at once confer the ability of NATO warships to react to acts of piracy in international waters and ensure the legal integrity of operations in the eyes of the international community and concerned states, the recent deployment of SNMG1 around Africa represents a vital, high-profile opportunity for NATO to demonstrate and build on its counterpiracy and MSO capabilities in elevated risk waters.

THE LEGAL ISSUE: NORTH ATLANTIC TREATY ORGANIZATION'S LEASH IN MARITIME SECURITY OPERATIONS

Maritime operations, just like any other type of military operation, must have a legal dimension. There must be a clear legal basis for the operation and it must be conducted in a lawful manner. This legal basis may derive from domestic law, international law, or from a combination of both. International law may be defined as that body of rules that nations consider binding in their relations with one another. International law derives from the practice of nations in the international arena (the "custom and practice of states") and international agreements (treaties, conventions, memoranda of understanding).

The oceans have traditionally been classified under the broad headings of internal waters, territorial seas, and high seas. In recent years, there has been the development of a number of more modern concepts, which have further divided the seas, such as economic exclusion zones. This expanding maritime jurisdiction and the clamor from coastal states to expand their territorial sea jurisdiction from 3 to 12 nm prompted a series of United Nations Conferences on the Law of the Sea. The result was the UNCLOS. UNCLOS is a treaty binding on those states, which have ratified or acceded under international law.[12]

With few exceptions, warships have limited rights to board any vessel. The right to board is a restriction on the rights of the vessels to exercise freedom of navigation on the high seas and must therefore only be used when reasonable grounds exist. If a ship is boarded under Article 110 UNCLOS and is later found to have committed no offensive act, then the vessels owners are entitled to seek compensation for any loss or damage that may have been sustained.

One of the rights for a noncompliant boarding exists when a vessel is suspected of being involved in piracy.[13] But this can be conducted only in international waters. Because most reported piracy is in fact an act of robbery, takes place within territorial waters, and thus constitutes a crime under the laws of the country in which the act was committed. Under these circumstances, a boarding by a NATO warship cannot take place. Although complex, these rules are essential to prevent warships from acting illegally, even if it was with the best of intentions. These are precisely the kinds of loophole within international maritime jurisprudence that criminals and terrorists can take advantage of.

HUMAN TRAFFICKING AND ILLEGAL MIGRATION

When it comes to human trafficking, NATO warships have no specific powers to enforce laws related to migrant smuggling or human trafficking. As discussed earlier, the provisions of UNCLOS and those state laws governing the seizure of suspected criminals inside sovereign territorial waters apply. There are no specific powers to stop, board, search, detain, or arrest ships reasonably suspected of being engaged in this activity. However, enforcement action could potentially be authorized if the trafficking is suspected to amount to slavery.[14]

Slavery is defined as "the status or condition of a person over whom any or all of the powers attaching to the right of ownership are exercised," and a slave means a person in such condition or status.[15] Persons in debt bondage[16] and illegal immigrants fall beyond the scope of the definition of slaves. Therefore, if a ship is transporting slaves, it is deemed to be engaged in the slave trade. If a ship is transporting illegal immigrants, then this would be an act in contravention of United Nations protocols.[17] The primary purpose of the protocol against the smuggling of migrants by land, sea, and air is "to prevent and combat the smuggling of migrants." The protocol obliges states to cooperate in the prevention of migrant smuggling by sea and requires states to assist other states in suppressing the use of vessels for migrant smuggling.

The prospect of encountering a vessel engaged in human trafficking is extremely problematic for commanding officers of warships. If they interdict the vessel on the high seas, then it is preferable that the vessel is allowed to proceed to its intended destination, having first informed the concerned country's authorities who can apprehend the vessel when it arrives. However, if the vessel appears unseaworthy and is in danger of sinking or the passengers appear to be in distress, then there is a duty to render assistance. This includes providing food and water or engineering support. The passengers should be transferred to the assisting warship only in extreme cases, as this could lead to claims for asylum. NATO as an organization is not in a position to authorize such action; this decision rests with the government of the specific warship concerned.

So it can be seen that despite the growing concern for maritime security, UNCLOS does not allow NATO warships to police and enforce the law on the high seas on behalf of the member states and wider international community. Even the policing of its own territorial waters by a warship requires the authority of law enforcement authorities to permit any direct action. Warships are certainly not permitted to take direct action while in territorial waters of any other state, unless the state specifically asks for assistance.

MSOs and MDA are becoming the key words in maritime doctrine principally for navies, coast guards, and marine police units and are widely advocated by politicians and senior military figures concerned with mitigating possible terrorist activity within the maritime realm and the ongoing activity intended to confront criminal activity at sea. However, when dealing with merchant shipping involved in illicit activity, whether as an instigator or victim, NATO warships have limitations imposed on them under international law and the laws of sovereign states that determine whether they can respond and act and to what extent both on the high seas and especially in territorial waters. Merchant vessels seeking the protection of warships while transiting international waters can call for protective assistance, but a vessel being attacked at anchor inside territorial waters will have to rely on the assistance of the military and maritime law enforcement authorities of that state.

CONCLUSION

Illicit activity at sea, such as piracy and trafficking has been a problem for seafarers and governments through the ages; concerns that have more recently been amplified by the spectre of high-consequence terrorist operations emanating from, and directed at, the maritime domain. Further, in the wake of 9/11, the subsequent invocation of Article V has necessitated a refocusing of NATO's maritime security posture to confront asymmetrical threats, principally terrorism. Given the extent and potential maturing confluence between criminal activity and trafficking networks at sea and the evolution of terrorist purpose and intent in the maritime domain, a compelling opportunity has emerged for NATO's maritime forces to evolve MSO both operationally and geographically. However, notwithstanding the success of the Alliance to date and the clear intent of the political organs and component commanders within NATO to evolve its MSO capabilities, thorough maritime security will only be possible with the participation of commercial seafarers and relevant industry bodies. Given the enormous expanse of the maritime realm, complexity and size of the commercial shipping industry, and scope for both asymmetric threat and criminal intent, continued and expanded cooperation is not merely desirable to fortify security, it is essential too.

NOTES

1. OAE is NATO's only Article V in response to a request from the U.S. Ambassador during a brief to the North Atlantic Council in October 2001.
2. Article V of the Washington Treaty states that an armed attack against one or more of the Allies in Europe or North America shall be considered as an attack against all.
3. MV *Nisha* was detained in the English Channel in December 2001 after intelligence reports suggested that a biological weapon was hidden in its cargo.
4. The United States, United Kingdom, and NATO maintained their own lists of suspect vessels, with the United Kingdom and United States liaising with their own intelligence agencies.
5. NATO's Military Committee in February 2007.
6. MCC Northwood manages the direction of the Standing NATO Maritime Group 1 (SNMG1) and Standing NATO Mine Counter Measures Group 1 (SNMCMG1). MCC Naples groups are SNMG2 and SNMCMG2.
7. MCC Northwood shipping center is contactable through internet and phone.
8. Allied Tactical Publication 2(B) Volume II. It can be download from http://shipping.manw.nato.int.
9. NCAGS: The provision of NATO military co-operation, guidance, advice, assistance, and supervision to merchant shipping to enhance the safety of participating merchant ships and support military operations.
10. United Nations Security Council, S/PRST/2006/11, March 15, 2006, Statement by the President of the Security Council.
11. Lloyd's Marine Intelligence Unit, Shipping Information Database.
12. All of the NATO nations, with the exception of the United States, have ratified UNCLOS.
13. Article 110(1)(a) UNCLOS.
14. 1926 Slavery Convention and adopted by the United Nations 1956 Supplementary Convention on the Abolition of Slavery.
15. The United Nations 1956 Supplementary Convention on the Abolition of Slavery.
16. The status or condition arising from a pledge by a debtor of his personal services or of those of a person under his control as security for a debt (United Nations 1956 Convention).
17. Article 3 of the United Nations Protocol against the Smuggling of Migrants by Land, Sea, and Air.

Section 5

National Responses

19 U.S. Maritime Transportation and Port Security: An Update and Analysis of Current Efforts

Ashley W. Craig and John F. Seher

CONTENTS

INTRODUCTION

This chapter provides a comprehensive overview of high-profile U.S. maritime transportation and port security measures that have been initiated since the terrorist attacks of 2001. Note that although this chapter focuses on those matters more recently considered by the U.S. Congress and the executive branch, emphasizing the role and importance of the U.S. Customs and Border Protection (CBP) in the area of global supply chain security and trade facilitation, "maritime domain awareness" stretches across many fronts and federal agencies. Although various other aspects of the U.S. approach to a comprehensive maritime security regime have been briefly discussed here, we would be remiss if we did not disclaim that there is more to the U.S. maritime security regime than found in the following pages.

Therefore, the reader must keep in mind how the private sector is, first, dealing with compliance issues resulting from the litany of new maritime security measures and second, may proactively collaborate with the U.S. government (and its trading partners who are also concerned with security) now and for the foreseeable future; for the only certainty is that "maritime transportation security" is now the new norm and will likely be a constant priority for decades to come.

This chapter aims to provide a firm understanding and awareness of recent developments affecting the American views on maritime and port security, as well as provoking a sense that the private sector can—and should—be doing more to assist government with this most important endeavor.

FOUNDATION OF THE U.S. MARITIME TRANSPORT SECURITY

THE U.S. MARITIME SECURITY FOUNDATIONAL MEASURES

Although the U.S. maritime security efforts predate the terrorist attacks of September 11, 2001, it was only after the events of that infamous day that a broad-based and concentrated effort along many government sectors was initiated. Interestingly, the U.S. Department of Homeland Security (DHS) is a product of these very attacks—thus, the initial U.S. response in the wake of September 11 was orchestrated by numerous federal agencies, including the Department of Defense, Department of Transportation, Department of State, Department of the Treasury, Department of Energy, and others. Yet, it was soon realized that the establishment of a new agency—DHS—was necessary to respond to the attacks, and help deter and prevent future incidents.

The American effort was historic, measured, and calculated counteroffensive to the new face of maritime transportation security issues—threats that literally materialized overnight. In particular, the then-U.S. Customs Service[1] (then a part of the Department of the Treasury) moved to secure global air and ocean trade, while instituting new measures designed to prevent (or substantially deter) the chances of domestic and foreign transportation from being used to advance the cause of international terrorism. The then U.S. Customs Commissioner Robert J. Bonner, quickly realized that the international trade community needed to collaborate closely with the U.S. government to effectively implement new and expanding transportation security measures across many modes—including maritime.

Additionally, Commissioner Bonner and his staff understood new security measures (some based on existing customs initiatives such as counternarcotics programs) had to be timely, agreed to by the trade community, and, finally, implemented in such a way so as to ensure effective deterrence. To that end, in a relatively short period following September 11, the U.S. Customs, under Commissioner Bonner, advanced the following security initiatives:

- *Customs-trade partnership against terrorism (C-TPAT).* This initiative essentially created a public–private and international partnership between CBP and over 6,000 business (till date over 10,000 have applied), including most of the largest U.S. importers. C-TPAT, CBP, and partner companies are working together to improve baseline security standards for supply chain and container security. Functionally, this initiative reviews the security practices of not only the company shipping the goods, but also the companies that provided them with any services.
- *Container security initiative (CSI).* Enables CBP, working in conjunction with host government customs services, to examine selected high-risk maritime containerized cargo at foreign seaports before they are loaded onboard vessels destined for the United States. In addition to the current 43 foreign ports participating in CSI, many more ports are in the planning stages. By the end of 2007, the number is expected to grow to 50 ports covering 82 percent of transpacific maritime containerized cargo shipped to the United States.
- *24-Hour rule.* A requirement that shippers, carriers, and others involved in an ocean import transaction provide CBP with manifest information at least 24 hours before the shipment being loaded aboard a vessel bound for the United States.
- *Automated targeting system (ATS).* Various enhancements to the ATS. Requiring and obtaining additional data from the trade has been identified as a priority for DHS/CBP.

Collectively, the foregoing measures form a "layered approach" to increase maritime security, as overseen by the U.S. CBP. Throughout his tenure, Commissioner Bonner articulated the need to balance free and legitimate trade with safe and secure means—something that has proven to be challenging at the very least.

According to CBP, the U.S. maritime and port security has been dramatically strengthened since 9/11.[2] Proof of this is found in federal funding for maritime and port security. For example, CBP has stated that "[f]unding has increased by more than 700 percent since September 11, 2001."[3] An examination of federal funding levels for port security illustrates the dramatic impact that Commissioner Bonner's initiatives have had

- Funding for port security was approximately $259 million in fiscal year (FY) 2001.
- DHS spent approximately $1.6 billion on port security in FY 2005.

The CBP also reports that "new technologies have been deployed with additional technologies being developed and $630 million has been provided in grants to the U.S.'s largest seaports, including $16.2 million to Baltimore; $32.7 million to Miami; $27.4 million to New Orleans, $43.7 million to New York/New Jersey; and $15.8 million to Philadelphia."[4] In other words, CBP utilizes and relies on "intelligence and a risk-based strategy to screen information on 100 percent of cargo" before loading aboard a ship bound for the United States. The CBP's stated objective is to ensure that "all cargo that is identified as high risk is inspected, either at the foreign port or upon arrival into the [United States]."[5]

Others Involved in the U.S. Maritime Security Operations

DHS/CBP has provided a very good summary of the key players in the maritime sector.

The U.S. Coast Guard. The coast guard routinely inspects and assesses the security of the U.S. ports in accordance with the Maritime Transportation and Security Act and the Ports and Waterways Security Act. Every regulated U.S. port facility is required to establish and implement a comprehensive security plan that outlines procedures for controlling access to the facility, verifying credentials of port workers, inspecting cargo for tampering, designating security responsibilities, training, and the reporting of all breaches of security or suspicious activity, among other security measures. Working closely with local port authorities and law enforcement agencies, the coast guard regularly reviews, approves, assesses, and inspects these plans and facilities to ensure compliance.

Terminal operators. Whether a person or a corporation, the terminal operator is responsible for operating its particular terminal within the port. The terminal operator is responsible for the area within the port that serves as a loading, unloading, or transfer point for the cargo. This includes storage and repair facilities and managing offices. The cranes they use may be their own, or they may lease them from the port authority.

Port authorities. An entity of a local, state, or national government that owns, manages, and maintains the physical infrastructure of a port (seaport, airport, or bus terminal) to include wharf sides, docks, piers, transit sheds, cargo-loading equipment, and warehouses. Port authorities often provide additional security for their facilities that have been leased to other operators and subcontractors. The role of the port authority is to facilitate and expand the movement of cargo through the port, provide facilities and services that are competitive, safe, and commercially viable. The port manages marine navigation and safety issues within port boundaries, and develops marine-related business on the lands that it owns or manages.

CBP's Layered Defense

The CBP reports that it "screens 100 percent of all cargo before it arrives in the U.S. using intelligence and cutting edge technologies ... [and] inspects all high-risk cargo."[6] According to recent statements, CBP is "currently utilizing large-scale X-ray and gamma ray machines and radiation detection devices to screen cargo [and] ... [p]resently ... [o]perates over 825 radiation portal monitors at [U.S.] ports (including 181 radiation portal monitors at seaports), utilizes nearly 200 large scale non-intrusive inspection devices to examine cargo, and has issued over 14,000 hand-held radiation detection devices."[7]

The importance of embracing and deploying cutting-edge technology to aid in CBP's ongoing counterterrorist activities is demonstrated in the Bush administration's FY 2007 budget request of $157 million "to secure next-generation detection equipment at [U.S.] ports of entry."[8] Additionally, the CBP has over 1200 canine detection teams, which are deployed at major U.S. ports of entry, capable of identifying narcotics, bulk currency consignments, human beings, explosives, agricultural pests, and chemical weapons.

The CSI, as noted earlier, is a key component in the overall "layered approach" to the U.S. maritime security policy. In particular, the CSI consists of four core elements, including (1) establishing security criteria to identify high-risk containers, (2) prescreening those containers identified as high risk before they arrive at the U.S. ports, (3) using technology to quickly prescreen high-risk containers, and (4) developing and using smart and secure containers. To be eligible to participate in CSI, the member state's customs administrations and the seaport authorities/owners/operators must meet the following three requirements:[9]

- The customs administration must be able to inspect cargo originating, transiting, exiting, or being transshipped through a country.
- Nonintrusive inspectional (NII) equipment (including gamma or x-ray imaging capabilities) and radiation-detection equipment must be available and utilized for conducting such inspections. This equipment is necessary to meet the objective of quickly screening containers without disrupting the flow of legitimate trade.
- The seaport must have regular, direct, and substantial container traffic to ports in the United States. As part of agreeing to participate in CSI, a member state's customs administration and the seaport must also
  - Commit to establishing an automated risk management system to identify potentially high-risk containers. This system should include a mechanism for validating threat assessments and targeting decisions, and identifying best practices.
  - Commit to sharing critical cargo and trade data, security intelligence, and risk management information with the U.S. CBP to affect collaborative targeting, and to assist in developing an automated mechanism for these exchanges.
  - Conduct a thorough port security risk assessment to ascertain vulnerable links in a port's infrastructure, and commit to resolving those vulnerabilities.
  - Commit to maintaining integrity programs to prevent lapses in employee integrity, and to identify and combat breaches in integrity.

IMPORTANCE AND EFFECT OF THE DUBAI PORTS WORLD ACQUISITION OF PENINSULAR AND ORIENTAL STEAM NAVIGATION COMPANY PORTS

In March 2006, Dubai Ports World (DPW) acquired the global port terminal, stevedoring, and related maritime operations of Peninsular and Oriental Steam Navigation Company Ports (P&O Ports), which included several U.S. terminal operations.[10] Normally, this type of transaction would not have made front-page news, except for trade and financial publications. However, what initially was deemed a "routine" business transaction quickly became a political controversy in the United States, based on perceived national security concerns—despite the Bush administration's decision to approve the deal.[11]

In a matter of weeks, the fallout associated with congressional opposition to the proposed sale resulted in rarely seen political posturing, including congressional actions to block the deal, a presidential veto threat, a counter claim to override a veto, and the introduction of numerous pieces of legislation killing the sale, as well as dealing with various aspects of the DPW–P&O Ports transaction and related maritime transportation security issues.

The following section provides a summary of the DPW–P&O Ports transaction, and the potential for often substantial legislative action in this area of interest to the international trade community.

SUMMARY OF THE PENINSULAR AND ORIENTAL STEAM NAVIGATION COMPANY PORTS SALE

In November 2005, DPW, a state-owned company located in the United Arab Emirates, announced its intention to acquire the global operations of P&O Ports, a U.K.–based company, with port terminal operations in the United States. It is important to note that P&O Ports only operated port terminals—thus, the transaction did not include the sale or transfer of actual whole ports. (In the United States, it is typical for ports to be owned by local or regional port authorities, which, in turn, contract with private companies to operate the various terminals that comprise a port.) The DPW acquisition of P&O Ports came with a $6.8 billion price tag. DPW had originally offered $5.7 billion for the sale. However, in January 2006, P&O Ports received a competing offer from Port of Singapore Authority (PSA) International. Ultimately, PSA dropped out of the bidding, and on February 10, 2006, DPW's counteroffer of $6.8 billion was formally accepted.

The initial proposal called for DPW to assume ownership and operational control of all P&O-owned ports facilities; specifically, the six U.S. terminals that were at the heart of the political controversy. Shortly after outbidding PSA, a group of Republican and Democratic House and Senate members began questioning whether a foreign government-owned entity should assume ownership and control of U.S. port terminals. Ultimately, congressional members called on the Bush administration to, first, further scrutinize the plan, and second, halt temporarily the DPW–P&O Ports deal, citing "security concerns" with a foreign government-owned operator of the U.S. terminals in question.

THE COMMITTEE ON FOREIGN INVESTMENT IN THE UNITED STATES PROCESS

To counter the rising political opposition to DPW's planned takeover of the P&O Port's U.S. terminals, Bush administration officials quickly defended its decision to approve the transaction as a sound national security policy. In particular, the administration cited the voluntary Committee on Foreign Investment in the United States (CFIUS) review and the unanimous decision by its members to approve DPW's ownership and operation of P&O Port's U.S. terminals as a testament to the integrity of its position.[12]

Generally, CFIUS operates under the authority granted by the Exon–Florio amendment (Section 721 of the Defense Production Act of 1950). The CFIUS includes 12 U.S. federal departments and agencies encompassing a wide-ranging area of regulatory responsibilities relevant to foreign investment in the United States. The secretary of the Department of the Treasury acts as CFIUS chair. The other member departments/agencies include the Council of Economic Advisors, the Department of Commerce, Department of Defense, DHS, Department of Justice, Department of State, National Economic Council, National Security Council, Office of Management and Budget, Office of Science and Technology Policy, and Office of the U.S. Trade Representative.[13]

On receiving a request from a party (or a joint filing by two or more parties) to a proposed transaction involving a U.S. person, CFIUS will conduct an initial 30-day review of the submission (sometimes requesting additional, supplemental information on the nature of the pending deal). During this timeframe, each CFIUS member department/agency examines the proposed transaction independently by focusing on potential national security concerns. Final decisions of CFIUS are made by consensus of the member departments/agencies. If any CFIUS member concludes that a pending transaction raises concerns, questions, or should be further examined, a formal 45-day investigation period will commence following the initial 30-day period.[14]

CFIUS Consideration of DPW–P&O Ports Deal

In October 2005, DPW and P&O Ports contacted CFIUS to advise on their intention to file notification for a national security review.[15] On October 31, 2005, the companies held a joint briefing for the DHS and other CFIUS members having oversight responsibilities in the areas of security, defense, or law enforcement.[16] On November 2, 2005 (before the formal filing by DPW and P&O Ports), CFIUS requested an intelligence assessment of the foreign acquirer (i.e., DPW).[17] Later in the month of November, the treasury department reported that the U.S. intelligence community provided a "threat assessment" on whether DPW had the intention or capability to "threaten the U.S. national security,"[18] if the acquisition and control of the terminals was enabled.

On December 16, 2005, DPW and P&O Ports tendered a formal joint submission to CFIUS, thus initiating the 30-day review period.[19] The treasury department reported that during the review period, the DHS (as the lead department for port and maritime security) negotiated an "assurances letter" with DPW and P&O Ports relating to the transaction, before port and maritime security commitments, and future cooperation with the U.S. government on such issues.[20] On January 17, 2006, CFIUS unanimously agreed that the sale of P&O Port's U.S. terminals to DPW should proceed, finding no national security concerns with the proposed transaction (pending compliance by the parties with other applicable [non-CFIUS] regulatory requirements).[21]

Congressional Opposition and the White House Support

Notwithstanding the decision by CFIUS to approve the deal, congressional concerns with the DPW acquisition of P&O Port's U.S. terminals continued to mount throughout February. Democrat Senator Charles Schumer from New York was one of the first members of congress to openly oppose the DPW–P&O Ports deal and criticize the White House examination of the transaction. On February 17, 2006, Democrat senators Hillary Clinton and Robert Menendez announced their intentions of introducing legislation specifically to block the P&O Ports sale.[22] One day later, Republican House Representative Frank LoBiondo remarked that he was contemplating legislation requiring the U.S. citizenship of port security officials.[23]

Despite the increasing congressional attention to the deal and clear and gathering opposition within the Congress, the administration continued to defend its decision making to approve the P&O Ports sale. In particular, DHS Secretary Michael Chertoff argued publicly on February 19, 2006, in support of CFIUS' findings and recommendations. Yet, such remarks had no affect on the Congress. Two days later, Senate Majority Leader Bill Frist (R-TN) and House Speaker Dennis Hastert (R-IL) joined a growing list of congressional members calling on President Bush to reconsider the decision approving the deal.

In what would prove to be an important moment in the controversy, on February 22, 2006, President Bush responded to questions about the DPW–P&O Ports transaction by vowing to veto any legislative attempt to block the deal from moving forward.[24] The president also further signaled his support, saying "[t]he transaction should go forward, in my judgment … [i]f there was any chance that this transaction would jeopardize the security of the United States, it would not go forward."[25] Although President Bush's strong commitment to the CFIUS recommendations was very apparent, politically, his comments reinforced congressional interest in the matter, as well as propelling the possibility of legislative action by halting the sale via a veto-proof bipartisan margin. In the end, the P&O Ports deal produced something not usually seen in Washington: Republican–Democratic unity on a homeland security issue that conflicts with a president's stated position.

It has been noted that the initial concerns with the P&O Port sale stem from Eller & Co., a small terminal operator based in Miami, Florida.[26] Eller & Co., claimed that the deal would put them in an involuntary partnership arrangement with a foreign government-owned company (DPW), something it never bargained for when entering into its business relationship with P&O Ports. In addition to pursuing lobbying activities in Washington on the issue, Eller & Co., also commenced legal proceedings in London (headquarters for P&O Ports). On March 2, 2006, Britain's High Court dismissed Eller & Co.'s claims, thereby authorizing the takeover to continue (including the U.S. terminals). Eller & Co., subsequently appealed the U.K. court's initial decision. On March 6, 2006, London High Court refused Eller & Co.'s appeal, thus bringing closure to the legal challenges initiated overseas.

In Washington, realizing the political reality of the situation, DPW and P&O Ports voluntarily submitted to a formal 45-day extended investigation by CFIUS and also announced separation of the U.S. operations from the rest of DPW under the terms of a "hold separate commitment."[27] The Bush administration welcomed this decision of DPW and P&O Ports, as it provided much-needed time to work with the Congress, as well as correct some of the initial inadvertent conclusions reached on the deal (e.g., only terminals would be acquired, not the U.S. ports).[28] The DPW and P&O Port's decision to submit to the 45-day investigation was truly unique. In reality, CFIUS had already reviewed the initial submission of the parties and found (with assurances) that the deal did not present complications. As noted earlier, CFIUS had, in fact, approved the transaction in January, 2006. Submitting to a 45-day investigation raised a host of questions: Would the outcome be any different this time? If CFIUS later concluded there were national security concerns, would the initial decision be void? Would the action serve as a cumbersome precedent for future CFIUS reviews?

The Dubai Ports World's Decision to Sell the U.S. Terminals

Despite DPW's voluntary call for a formal 45-day CFIUS review, bifurcating the U.S. operations, and a compromise offer by Representative Peter King (R-NY), an early critic of the P&O Ports sale to DPW, requiring DPW subcontract the U.S. terminals to a third party, congressional hostility continued to increase. In fact, on March 8, 2006 (only days after the sale was finalized), the House Appropriations Committee voted to block the deal by 62–2. On March 9, 2006, House Speaker Hastert and Senate Majority Leader Frist informed President Bush that legislative action blocking the P&O Ports sale was inevitable. Later the same day, Senator John Warner (R-VA), a supporter of the deal, read a statement on the Senate floor announcing that DPW had agreed to turnover operations of the U.S. terminals to a "U.S. entity."[29] Yet, questions remained as to whether DPW would sell or transfer (yet retain some form of ownership of) the U.S. terminals to another party. As a result, many in the Congress continued to call for legislative action blocking the transaction.

Owing largely to the potential for congressional intervention at any time, on March 15, 2006, DPW and P&O Ports announced further details on how it would handle the U.S. terminals. Specifically, DPW announced it would sell the U.S. business to "an unrelated U.S. buyer."[30] The statement noted that the sale process would be supervised by P&O's head office in London, and the New York office of Deutsche Bank Securities, Inc., would act as financial advisor.[31]

DPW noted that "[a]n expedited sale process is underway and with the cooperation of the port authorities and joint venture partners, it is expected that a sale can be agreed within four to six months ... [u]ntil the sale is complete, P&O Ports North America will be operated independently from DP World in accordance with the Hold Separate Commitment announced on February 26, 2006."[32]

Legislative Consequences of Dubai Ports World Controversy

During February and March 2006, as a result of the attention paid to the P&O Ports sale, numerous pieces of legislation were introduced either blocking the transaction or more broadly touching maritime transportation security issues and concerns.

In summary, key aspects of that legislation, in part, included the following:[33]

- Reject CFIUS approval of the DPW acquisition (H.J. Res. 73)
- Require a new investigation of the DPW transaction (H.R. 4807)
- Suspend all proposed mergers and acquisitions by foreign entities, pending further review (H.R. 4814)

- Prohibit foreign government-owned or controlled entities from operations at the U.S. ports (H.R. 4817)
- Upgrade security investigations; require U.S. CBP to verify on-site security measures of each customs-trade partnership against terrorism and FAST participant within first year of enactment and biannually thereafter (H.R. 4820)
- Prohibit leasing, owning, operating, or managing of the U.S. port facilities by foreign government-owned or controlled entities (H.R. 4842)
- Require DHS and defense department to identify the "U.S. critical infrastructure" and require all foreign entities to transfer to the U.S. owners and operators; require inspection of all truck cargo before the U.S. entry and all vessel cargo before the U.S. unloading (H.R. 4881)
- Require all containers entering the United States to be scanned and sealed before loading on vessels at origin port or transshipment port (H.R. 4899)
- Transfer CFIUS to DHS (from Treasury Department) and shift chair to DHS secretary (from treasury secretary), require congressional notice of all proposed and pending mergers and acquisitions by foreign entities (H.R. 4917)
- Create Office of Cargo Security Policy, joint government operation centers for information sharing, upgrade CBP's National Targeting Center and ATS (S. 2008)
- Require new investigation of DPW deal (S. 2333)
- Clarify requirements for congressional notification and investigation of acquisitions by non-U.S. entities (S. 2335)
- Create National Commission on the Infrastructure of the United States (S. 2388)
- Identify "cause of action" by the U.S. port operator if ownership shifts to non-U.S. person, allow public ports to nullify a lease on demonstrating security risk (S. 2367)
- Replace CFIUS with DHS-only committee, require reports from the White House on mergers and acquisitions of critical technology and infrastructure risks (S. 2400)

In the wake of DPW's decision to sell the U.S. terminals to a "U.S. buyer," there was no longer a political necessity for the individual bills prohibiting the P&O Ports deal. However, until the U.S. terminals were, in fact, sold to a U.S. entity, the Congress is likely to monitor closely the situation and use the pending legislation as leverage.

As initially anticipated, it was more likely that a bill (or series of bills) dealing with improved maritime transportation security (e.g., Collins–Murray's the so-called "Green Lane Act," S. 2008[34]) would make it through last year's session of Congress. As noted earlier, these types of legislative proposals affect almost all aspects of intermodal transportation and related security measures. Thus, the international trade community (e.g., shippers, importers, exporters, carriers, intermediaries, and terminal operators) should expect congressionally mandated "improvements" to the existing U.S. government transportation security measures. In particular, changes to C-TPAT, the CSI, advanced reporting of shipment information, data, content, as well as new and additional regulatory requirements should be expected.

In the end, as discussed in the following section, the U.S. Congress eventually did reach a consensus on maritime security legislation—just before adjourning for 2006.

SECURITY AND ACCOUNTABILITY FOR EVERY PORT ACT OF 2006

BACKGROUND

Owing largely to the political fallout from the DPW controversy, the U.S. Congress deliberated for months over improved maritime security legislative proposals and suggested measures. Over the course of almost six months, the Congress and the White House considered various "improvements" in maritime security—from the so-called "100 percent scanning" of import containers bound for the United States to increased deployment of overseas U.S. customs inspectors involved in supply chain security.

In the end, the Bush administration concurred with the then-Republican-controlled Congress (joined by the Democratic minority at the time) on additional maritime and port security initiatives, measures, and operational structures (largely being built on top of existing security measures implemented in the wake of the September 11, 2001 terrorist attacks). On October 13, 2006, President Bush signed into law the "Security and Accountability For Every Port Act of 2006" or the SAFE Port.

SUMMARY OF KEY LEGISLATIVE PROVISIONS

This section provides a summary and commentary of the SAFE Port Act. It should be noted that many of the dates specifically mentioned in the legislative have come and gone; however, much of DHS's work is still ongoing in these important maritime security issue areas.

The SAFE Port Act is a comprehensive piece of maritime security legislation, covering a wide range of concerns. Some of the noteworthy areas are listed as follows. The Act

- Amends the Maritime Transportation Security Act of 2002 (MTSA) to require area maritime transportation security plans to include a salvage response plan to identify equipment capable of restoring operational trade capacity and to ensure that waterways are cleared as quickly as possible after a maritime transportation security incident (defined as "a security incident resulting in significant loss of life, environmental damage, transportation system disruption, or economic disruption in a particular area").
- Requires vessel and security plans under MTSA to regulate access by persons (including drayage companies) engaged in the surface transportation of intermodal containers in or out of a facility (i.e., a structure or facility of any kind located in, on, under, or adjacent to any waters subject to the U.S. jurisdiction). Requires the submission of a new vessel and security plan after a change of ownership of a vessel or port facility.
- Requires U.S. citizenship for individuals implementing security actions for a facility, but allows a waiver of such requirement after a complete background check and review of terrorist watch lists.
- Requires the secretary of homeland security to verify, at least twice annually, the effectiveness of a vessel and facility security plan, with at least one unannounced inspection.
- Imposes additional requirements under MTSA for issuing transportation security cards, requiring the secretary to (1) establish a priority for each U.S. port based on risk, (2) implement the transportation security card program at all U.S. ports not later than January 1, 2009, and (3) process all applications for transportation security cards for individuals with current and valid merchant mariners' documents by January 1, 2009.
- Directs the secretary to (1) conduct a pilot program to test transportation security card readers at secure areas of the marine transportation system, (2) issue regulations to require the deployment of such card readers, (3) make a comprehensive report to the Congress on the pilot program, and (4) promulgate final regulations for issuing such cards by January 1, 2007.
- Directs the department secretary to establish interagency operational centers for port security at all high-risk priority ports not later than three years after the enactment of this Act. Describes the required characteristics of these security measures. Designates the coast guard captain of the port in an operational center as the incident commander in the event of a transportation security incident. Requires the secretary to submit to the Congress a budget and cost-sharing analysis for such operational centers.
- Directs the department secretary, not later than 180 days after enactment, to update and finalize the rulemaking on notice of arrival for foreign vessels on the Outer Continental Shelf.
- Establishes a deadline of one year after the enactment for the implementation of identification requirements for crewmembers on vessels calling at the U.S. ports.

- Identifies port security grants and training and exercise programs. Requires the department secretary to make available a risk-assessment tool that uses standardized risk criteria for updating area maritime security plans and for applying for port security grants.
- Requires the allocation of port security grants based on risk. Limits the use of grant funds for construction costs. Expands eligible costs under such grant program to include (1) training exercises related to terrorism prevention or recovery, (2) sharing of terrorism threat information, and (3) equipment costs for storing classified information.
- Requires the secretary to (1) develop a strategy for the deployment of radiation detection capabilities, (2) submit such strategy to the Congress within 90 days after enactment, (3) report to the Congress on the feasibility of and strategy for the development of equipment to detect and prevent shielded nuclear and radiological threat material and chemical, biological, and other weapons of mass destruction (WMD) from entering the United States, (4) publish technical capability standards and recommended standard operating procedures for the use of nonintrusive imaging and radiation detection equipment in the United States, (5) fully implement the strategy for the deployment of radiation detection capabilities within three years after the enactment, (6) expand such strategy to all other U.S. ports by December 31, 2008, and (7) establish an intermodal rail radiation detection test center.
- Requires the secretary to (1) develop a plan for the inspection of car ferries bound for a U.S. seaport, (2) develop and implement a plan for random searches of shipping containers, (3) implement a threat-assessment screening for all port truck drivers with access to secure areas of a port, and (4) establish at least one border patrol unit for the U.S. Virgin Islands and report to the Congress on the schedule for establishing such unit.
- Directs the secretary to (1) develop, implement, and update a strategic plan to enhance the security of the international supply chain (defined as the end-to-end process for shipping goods to or from the United States beginning at the point of origin through a point of distribution to the destination) and (2) submit an interim and final report to the Congress for such plan. Specifies requirements for the strategic plan.
- Requires the secretary to (1) issue regulations for collecting data elements for improved high-risk targeting of cargo imported to the United States before loading on vessels at foreign seaports and (2) take certain actions to improve the effectiveness and capabilities of the ATS.
- Requires the secretary to (1) initiate, not later than 90 days after enactment, rulemaking proceedings to establish minimum standards and procedures for securing containers in transit to the United States and (2) issue, not later than 180 days after enactment, an interim final rule for securing such containers. Requires all such containers to meet security standards and procedures not later than two years after enactment.
- Directs the secretary to establish and implement a CSI to identify and examine or search maritime containers that pose a security risk before loading in a foreign port for shipment to the United States.
- Authorizes the secretary, acting through the commissioner of the U.S. CBP (commissioner), to establish the customs-trade partnership against terrorism (C-TPAT), as a voluntary government–private sector program to strengthen and improve the overall security of the international supply chain and the U.S. border security and to facilitate the movement of secure cargo. Requires the secretary to review the minimum-security requirements of C-TPAT at least once annually.
- Requires the secretary to (1) ensure that all incoming cargo containers are screened to identify high-risk containers and that all these containers are scanned or searched and (2) report to the Congress on the status of full-scale implementation of integrated scanning systems for cargo containers.
- Amends the Homeland Security Act of 2002 to establish within DHS a Domestic Nuclear Detection Office, to be headed by a presidentially appointed director. Makes such office

responsible for the coordination of federal efforts to detect and protect against the unauthorized importation, possession, storage, transportation, development, or use of a nuclear explosive device, fissile material, or radiological material in the United States.

The foregoing is only a partial summary (based on the actually statutory language of the SAFE Port Act). Readers are encouraged to review the entire statute for a thorough understanding of many of the other provisions affecting maritime and port security as it relates to the United States.

CONCLUSION

Despite the amount of attention, funding, and effort that the U.S. maritime and port security measures have (and continue to) received in the past six years, it is obvious that more needs to be done. Although this statement is somewhat simplistic, it is also cautionary. The so-called experts all seem to claim that the use of the world's ocean-borne transport system for a future terrorist incident is inevitable—the only unknowns remain when and where such an attack will occur.

Such pessimistic forecasting should not deter either the government or the private sector from the historic partnership that has been formed in the past few years, and which continues to evolve; resulting in a safer and more secure maritime industry. The U.S. Customs' stated "twin goals" of trade facilitation and secure commerce are not only honorable, but are also guiding principles for the world's trading partners.

Although many may not have welcomed the United States leading the formulation of policy in the area of maritime domain awareness, no one should dispute that this has resulted in an unprecedented amount of focus and attention for the maritime industry (The 2006 DPW political debate in the United States illustrates this well and so does the continuing call for "100 percent inspection" of import containers). This, in the end, is a positive consequence of the 9/11 attacks, notwithstanding all that remains to be done.

We call on governments and all the stakeholders within the private sector of the international maritime trading community to closely monitor and participate in the continued deliberation and formulation of maritime security policy, law, and regulations. Like it or not, most of this debate will occur within, and be led by, the United States. Thus it is only prudent to closely follow the unfolding of events in Washington—and the likely ripple effects they will have on the global maritime industry.

NOTES

1. Following the establishment of the U.S. Department of Homeland Security in 2003, the U.S. Customs Service was transferred from the Department of the Treasury to the new agency, as well as provided with the new name of "U.S. Customs and Border Protection" (CBP). The distinction is made herein to use CBP when referring to activities or events associated with the agency following its transfer to DHS.
2. See http://www.cbp.gov/xp/cgov/newsroom/fact_sheets/port_security/securing_us_ports.xml.
3. Ibid.
4. Ibid.
5. Ibid.
6. Ibid.
7. Ibid.
8. Ibid.
9. The following requirements are extracted from CBP's published material on the CSI program and can be found at www.cbp.gov.
10. Included in the sale, DPW assumes the leases of P&O Ports's U.S. subsidiary to manage port facilities in New York, New Jersey, Philadelphia, Baltimore, New Orleans, and Miami, as well as operations in 16 other ports.
11. The DPW–P&O Ports transaction was subject to a voluntary review by the Committee on Foreign Investment in the United States under Section 5021 of the Omnibus Trade and Competitiveness Act of 1998, amended Section 721 of the Defense Production Act of 1950. See also 31 C.F.R. § 800, et seq.

12. The Treasury Department noted, "[e]ach of the CFIUS 12 members (departments and agencies) conducts its won internal analysis … [i]n this case, the Departments of Transportation and Energy were also brought in to the CFIUS review to widen the scope and to add the expertise of those agencies reviewing the transaction." See http://treas.gov/press/releases/js4071.htm.

13. The Treasury Department comments that the Departments of Energy and Transportation, the Nuclear Regulatory Agency, and other U.S. agencies are called on for particular transactions that affect certain industries under the respective agency's jurisdiction. Id.

14. The Committee on Foreign Investment in the United States (CFIUS) is an interagency committee of the U.S. Government that reviews the national security implications of foreign acquisitions of the U.S. companies or operations. Chaired by the Secretary of the Treasury, CFIUS committee members includes representatives from 12 government agencies and departments, including the defense, state and commerce departments, and the Department of Homeland Security, which was added following the latter's establishment post-9/11.

15. Ibid.

16. Ibid.

17. Ibid.

18. Ibid.

19. According to the Treasury Department, the 30-day review period officially began on December 17, 2006. Id.

20. Ibid. Additionally, the Department of Homeland Security apparently consulted with other CFIUS members before the assurances were finalized on January 6, 2006. Id.

21. Ibid.

22. See S. 2334, 109th Congress, 2nd Session (2006).

23. See H.R. 4880, 109th Congress, 2nd Session (2006).

24. See http://news.bbc.co.uk/2/hi/americas/4737940.stm.

25. See http://www.whitehouse.gov/news/releases/2006/02/20060221-2.html.

26. Neil King, Jr. and Greg Hitt, *Small Florida Firm Sowed Seed of Port Dispute, The Wall Street Journal*, at A3, February 28, 2006.

27. Terms of the Hold Separate Commitment: As announced, DPW intends to complete the $6.85 billion global transaction as scheduled, but will voluntarily separate the U.S. assets that would otherwise be part of the deal to permit the Bush administration, congressional leadership and relevant port authorities to seek additional information regarding the acquisition. The formal commitment, which is in addition to commitments made by DPW to CFIUS last month, states that:
    - DPW will guarantee the independence of all terminal operations managed by POPNA by establishing the operations as a completely separate business unit.
    - DPW will not exercise control over or influence the management of the U.S. operations, either directly or via P&O headquarters in London.
    - Final authority over the management and operations of the U.S. terminals rests exclusively with the Chief Executive Officer of P&O in London, who is a British citizen.
    - The Chief Security Officer for POPNA will remain a U.S. citizen, unless the U.S. Coast Guard agrees otherwise.
    - The current management of POPNA will be retained and DPW will not in any way influence or attempt to influence any operations, policies, procedures, or security in place in the U.S. operations (see http://portal.pohub.com/pls/pogprtl/docs/PAGE/DP_WORLD_WEBSITE/ DP_WORLD_MEDIA_CENTRE/MEDIA_CENTRE_NEWS_RELEASES/14%20DP% 20WORLD%20PRESS%20STATEMENT%2026FEB.PDF).

28. Additionally, certain state port authorities contemplated canceling/terminating leases with P&O Ports on the basis, *inter alia*, of failing to provide timely and proper notice of the change in ownership to DPW (as well as failing to permit the port authorities to examine possible security risks with the proposed deal). In particular, the Port Authority of New York/New Jersey initiated legal action seeking to terminate the P&O Ports leases. See http://www.cnn.com/2006/ POLITICS/ 02/24/port.security/index.html.

29. http://www.cnn.com/2006/POLITICS/03/09/port.security/.

30. See News Release, P&O Ports North America, March 15, 2006.

31. Ibid.

32. Ibid.

33. See also R.G. Edmonson, *A Roar from Congress, The Journal of Congress*, at 11, March 20, 2006.

34. S. 2008 was reintroduced, following technical revisions, on March 27, 2006 as S. 2459.

20 Setting, Strengthening, and Enforcing Standards for U.S. Port Security

Bruce B. Stubbs and Scott C. Truver

CONTENTS

BOUNDING THE PROBLEM

The tragedies of September 11, 2001 dramatically underscored America's vulnerability to terrorist attacks by all modes of transportation. Although airport security has perhaps received the greatest attention and funding in the United States, recently maritime port security has emerged as a significant element of the debates on the best way to assure homeland security.

More than 90 percent of U.S. exports and imports by volume transit U.S. seaports, and the efficient and safe movement of foreign, coastal, and inland-water trades are critical for America's just-in-time and just-enough globalized economy. The U.S. maritime system comprises about 360 sea and river ports and more than 3700 cargo and passenger terminals. However, a large fraction of maritime cargo is concentrated at only a few major ports. Most ships calling at U.S. ports are foreign-owned and operated by non-U.S. crews. Currently, some 8000 vessels call at U.S. ports each year—a total that could double by 2025. Non-U.S. registered container ships have been the focus of much of the attention amid seaport security because they are seen as most vulnerable to terrorist infiltration. More than 9 million marine containers enter U.S. ports each year. Indeed, a broad spectrum of threats challenge U.S. ports and waterways security, including mines and improvised explosive devices (IEDs) as well as the possibility of weapons of mass destruction (WMD) ranging from chemical weapons and "dirty bombs" to nuclear devices, which could be transported surreptitiously in commercial vessel shipping containers. Although the Bureau of Customs and Border Protection (CBP) analyzes cargo manifests and other information to target specific shipments for closer inspection, it physically inspects only a small fraction of the containers.

The U.S. Department of Homeland Security (DHS) focuses on a few key principles to develop its strategy for port security. First, DHS does not believe in security at any cost. It believes in risk management, which means analyzing and assessing threats, vulnerabilities, and consequences, weighing what risks are most likely, considering the measures to counter them in terms of benefits and costs, and then weighing those measures to support strategic and operational planning. Second, the department also believes in a layered-security approach, a recognition of the fact that there is no magic bullet for security. Any single approach, or a single layer if unsupported, can fail.

DHS, thus, believes that the right answer is to build multiple layers of security that provide concentric rings of protection. It relies on redundancy and randomness to fashion a total security network. And this approach recognizes that ports themselves are part of a large network, a network that extends across the globe and requires us to measure security at every point from the point of manufacture through to the ultimate delivery at the destination. A third element of the department's strategy is to recognize that every port is different, but each resembling an "ant farm" of feverish activity and movement with access to all but unimpeded.

A "cookie-cutter" or "one size fits all" approach to security will not work, and the department does not want its security measures to do more harm than good. For example, although the Safe Port Act of 2006 mandates that U.S. inspectors screen 100 percent of all containers entering the U.S. maritime system, this does not mean that each container be subjected to a physical search. To attempt this would undermine the economic efficiency of our ports, and ultimately might not work. In a joint testimony at a House Homeland Security Border Subcommittee hearing in April 2007, for example, DHS officials acknowledged that technology gaps prevent full compliance with the Safe Port Act:

> The department does not believe that, at the present time, the necessary technology exists for such solutions. The department is actively working with industry to test different technologies and methodologies that would provide economically and operationally viable enhancements to container security.

Instead, the department wants to use a risk-managed, layered, and cost-benefit approach to triage, and select those elements of the container supply chain deemed of greater risk for a very close look, including nonintrusive inspection and where necessary, physical searches, while letting the vast majority of our commerce go unimpeded.

Within the ports themselves, two of the department's key components—the U.S. Coast Guard and CBP—are the federal agencies with the strongest presence, with the Coast Guard serving as the lead federal agency (LFA) for domestic maritime security matters. The Coast Guard has expanded its traditional 24-hour notice of arrival (NOA) for ships to a 96-hour NOA. The NOA allows Coast Guard officials to select high-risk ships for boarding on their arrival at the entrance to a harbor. CBP has also advanced the timing of cargo information it receives from ocean carriers ensuring that manifests can be scrutinized before the vessel's arrival in U.S. waters. Through the Container Security Initiative (CSI) program, CBP inspectors prescreen U.S.-bound marine containers at foreign ports of loading. The Customs-Trade Partnership Against Terrorism (C-TPAT) offers importers expedited processing of their cargo if they comply with CBP measures for helping to ensure security to the entire supply chain from container stuffing to consignment delivery. To raise port security standards, Congress passed the Maritime Transportation Security Act (MTSA) of 2002 (P.L. 107-295) in November 2002.

THE COAST GUARD'S LEAD ROLE

DHS continues to implement a multilayered defense strategy to keep U.S. ports safe and secure. Relying on the expertise of its bureaus, the private sector, and state and local authorities, DHS has made significant improvements since 9/11 to ensure that there are protective measures in place from one end of a sea-based journey to the other.

As the LFA for domestic maritime security, the Coast Guard routinely inspects and assesses the security of the 3200 regulated facilities throughout the United States at least annually, in accordance with the MTSA and the Ports and Waterways Safety Act (PWSA). Every regulated U.S. facility, regardless of owner/operator, is required to establish and implement a comprehensive Facility Security Plan (FSP) that specifically addresses the vulnerabilities identified in the facility security assessment and outlines the measures and procedures for controlling access to the facility, for example, personnel screening, designating employees with key security responsibilities, verifying credentials of port workers, inspecting cargo for tampering, designating security responsibilities, quarterly training, no-notice drills and annual security exercises, and the reporting of all breaches of security or suspicious activity, among other security measures.

Working closely with local port authorities and law enforcement agencies, the Coast Guard regularly reviews, approves, assesses, and inspects these plans and facilities to ensure compliance. In accordance with MTSA, the Coast Guard has completed verification of security plans for U.S. port and facilities and vessels operating in U.S. waters. Specifically,

- Port threat assessments for all 55 militarily or economically critical ports have been completed. The Coast Guard has developed 44 Area Maritime Security Plans covering 361 seaports, the Great Lakes, the Inland and western rivers, and the outer continental shelf regions.
- By July 1, 2005, the Coast Guard completed initial security plan verification exams on all 6200 U.S. flag-inspected vessels.
- By December 31, 2006, the Coast Guard completed 4800 verification examinations on uninspected vessels regulated under the MTSA.
- The Coast Guard has also reviewed and approved 3200 facility security plans and 60 off-shore facility security plans.

In addition to the Coast Guard's broad authorities for ensuring the security of U.S. port facilities and operations, the United States Coast Guard (USCG) worked with the International Maritime Organization (IMO) to develop the International Ship and Port Facilities Security (ISPS code). Through the International Port Security Program, the Coast Guard has also partnered with other nations worldwide to ensure compliance with ISPS. The Coast Guard has assessed the requisite port facility security plans of the 44 countries that are responsible for 80 percent of the maritime trade bound for the United States. Of these 44 countries, 37 have been found to be in substantial compliance with the ISPS Code. The seven countries that were not in substantial compliance in mid-2007 have been or will soon be notified to take corrective actions, or risk being placed on a port security advisory, and have conditions of entry imposed on vessels arriving from their ports. The Coast Guard is on track to assess approximately 36 countries per year.

Moreover, the Coast Guard has taken multiple steps to enhance its situational awareness in the maritime domain. Publication of the 96-hour NOA regulation allows sufficient time to vet the crew, passengers, cargo, and relevant documentation of all vessels before their entering the United States from foreign ports. The USCG also has expansive authority to exercise positive control over a vessel intending to enter a port or place subject to the jurisdiction of the United States, should the need arise. Between July 2004 and mid-2007, the Coast Guard boarded 16,000 foreign-flag vessels to check for security compliance with the ISPS Code and the MTSA, and imposed 143 detentions, expulsions, or denials of entry. In addition, the Automatic Identification System (AIS) has been fielded at nine ports with vessel traffic service systems, which allows the Coast Guard to identify and track vessels in the coastal environment. Long-Range Identification and Tracking (LRIT), currently under review for implementation by the international community under the auspices of the IMO, could enable the Coast Guard to identify and track vessels in the oceanic realm, long before they reach coastal zones. In a more parochial context, the Inland River Vessel Movement Center provides critical information about the movement of hazardous cargoes along inland rivers and waterways.

The Coast Guard has also increased its operational presence through several other initiatives. For example, it has established processes to identify, target, and assess vessels for further physical inspection. Till date, USCG teams have conducted over 3400 security boardings of high interest vessels. These boardings included 1500 positive-control vessel escorts to ensure that these vessels could not become a security threat within U.S. territorial waters and port confines. The Coast Guard has currently established 12 maritime safety and security teams, and is enforcing hundreds of fixed and moving security zones to protect maritime critical infrastructure and key assets (MCI/KA), including naval vessel protection zones (NVPZ) to protect U.S. navy and maritime administration ships. Further, the Coast Guard has developed a risk-based decision-making system, which will prioritize high-capacity passenger vessels (HCPV) escort requirements. Although initially developed for high-capacity ferries, its application is being expanded to enhance current security measures for other HCPVs, including cruise ships and excursion vessels carrying 500 or more passengers.

A MULTIAGENCY STRATEGY

The USCG is also working closely with numerous other agencies to implement the September 2005 National Strategy for Maritime Security and its eight supporting plans. Together, the plans provide the road map for the integration of national efforts in supporting the four primary pillars of maritime security: awareness, prevention, protection, and response and recovery. The Coast Guard is DHS's executive agent for implementing and updating plans related to maritime domain awareness (awareness), global maritime intelligence integration (prevention), maritime transportation system security (protection), and maritime operational threat response (response/recovery), and, in cooperation with other stakeholders, is leading the efforts to increase the coordination, effectiveness, and efficiency of existing governmentwide initiatives.

In close coordination with the Coast Guard, the U.S. CBP service seeks to prevent terrorists and terrorist weapons from entering the United States by eliminating potential threats before they arrive at U.S. borders and ports. For example, through Container Security Initiative, which is administered by CBP, DHS has implemented the 24-Hour Advanced Manifest Rule, requiring all sea carriers, with the exception of bulk carriers and approved break-bulk cargo, to provide proper cargo descriptions and valid consignee addresses 24 hours before cargo is loaded "at the foreign port" for shipment to the United States. Failure to meet the 24-hour advanced manifest rule results in a "do not load" message and other penalties.

This program gives DHS greater awareness of what is being loaded onto ships bound for the United States and the advance information enables DHS to evaluate the terrorist risk from sea containers.

Similarly, the CSI and the Customs-Trade Partnership Against Terrorism initiative bolster port security. Through CSI, CBP works with host-government customs services to examine high-risk maritime containerized cargo at foreign seaports, before they are loaded onboard vessels destined for the United States. CSI is now active in more than 50 ports outside the United States, accounting for 85 percent of container traffic bound for the United States. This includes nine CSI ports in the Western Hemisphere—in Canada, Brazil, Argentina, Honduras, the Dominican Republican, Jamaica, and the Bahamas; four more CSI ports in Colombia and Panama will come online by the end of 2007.

Through C-TPAT, CBP has created a public–private and international partnership with approximately 5,800 businesses (more than 10,000 have applied), including most of the largest U.S. importers. C-TPAT, CBP, and partner companies are working together to improve baseline security standards for supply chain and container security. CBP reviews the security practices of not only the company shipping the goods, but also the companies that provided them with any supporting and logistical services.

Through December 2006, the C-TPAT program has completed validations on 27 percent (1545 validations) of the certified membership, which is up from 8 percent (403 validations completed) a year ago. Additionally, validations are in progress on another 39 percent (2262 in progress) of certified members, such that, by the end of 2007, the C-TPAT program validations will be 100 percent.

In another effort, CBP's "Secure Freight" program is increasing the data it collects on containers that are going to transit the international supply chain. It gives the department better information to select specific containers deemed of elevated potential risk to be inspected. The Secure Freight program is also another example of the indispensable need for multiagency and international cooperation to secure the supply chain.

CBP is also embracing cutting-edge technology to screen cargo. And there are many candidates for this mission, including such exotic-sounding technologies as gamma-ray imaging, advanced spectroscopic portal radiation monitoring, nuclear-resonance fluorescence imaging, high-purity germanium radiation sensing, and muon tomography—some of which promise about 100 percent effectiveness, whereas others might be frustrated by the most mundane of materials.

By mid-2007, CBP had over 680 operational radiation portal monitors at U.S. ports, including 181 radiation portal monitors at seaports. CBP was scanning more than 90 percent of the cargo for radiation sources, planed to reach 98 percent scanning at all U.S. major seaports by the end of 2007, and achieve almost 100 percent for all ports of entry, sea, and land, by the end of 2008. CBP also relies on 170 large-scale nonintrusive inspection devices to examine cargo and has issued 12,400 handheld radiation-detection devices. About 600 canine detection teams, capable of identifying narcotics, bulk currency, human beings, explosives, agricultural pests, and chemical weapons, are deployed at all ports of entry.

CBP is also testing the feasibility of overseas scanning for radiation to prevent the entry of WMD into the U.S. maritime domain. This "pressing out our borders" approach intends to move the scanning, where practicable, overseas at the earliest point at which containers enter the international freight domain. CBP is working with six foreign ports, including Puerto Cortez in Honduras, to install radiation-detection equipment to scan cargo for radiological and nuclear emissions. Construction began in Port Cortez in November 2006, and operational testing began in the summer of 2007.

CBP's National Targeting Center (NTC) is also a critical component of DHS' layered port-security efforts. The NTC provides tactical targeting and analytical research support for CBP counterterrorism efforts. Experts in passenger and cargo targeting at the NTC, using such tools as the Automated Targeting System (ATS), identify potentially high-risk cargo and personnel and support intradepartmental and interagency antiterrorist operations. The ATS serves as the primary means for transactional risk assessments and evaluating potential national security risks posed by cargo and passengers arriving by sea, air, truck, and rail. Using prearrival information and input from the intelligence community, this rules-based system identifies high-risk targets before they arrive in the United States. The Department's Science & Technology Directorate (S&T) is supporting the introduction of advanced intelligent algorithms to improve these risk-assessment capabilities.

A key responsibility of the NTC is the support that it provides to the field, including tactical targeting and research support for the CSI personnel stationed at critical foreign ports throughout the world. The NTC, combined with CSI, C-TPAT, the 24-hour rule, and ATS ensures that all containers onboard vessels destined for the United States are risk-scored using all available information, and that all cargo determined to be of high risk are examined. The NTC, working closely with the Coast Guard, also vets and risk scores all cargo and cruise-ship passengers and crew before arrival. This ensures that DHS has full port security awareness for international maritime activity.

In addition to increased screening efforts at U.S. ports of entry for radioactive and nuclear materials, DHS fully endorses the concept of increased active and passive detection at foreign ports of departure. The systems that the Domestic Nuclear Detection Office (DNDO) is acquiring and developing can also be used by foreign ports that have a CSI presence, as well as in the Department of Energy's Megaports program. The U.S. Department of Energy's National Nuclear Security Administration (NNSA) Megaports Initiative, which began in 2003, teams up with other countries to enhance their ability to screen cargo at major international seaports. The initiative provides radiation detection equipment and trains their personnel to specifically check for nuclear or other radioactive materials. In return, NNSA requires that data be shared on detections and seizures of nuclear or radiological material that resulted from the use of the equipment provided.

In cooperation with foreign governments, Megaports representatives determine the most effective placement of radiation equipment for each seaport. Installed sensors then screen cargo containers for special nuclear or other radioactive materials. If anything is detected, the sensors alert foreign port officials of the need to further examine the cargo, so that they can take appropriate action. The Megaports Initiative has three main objectives:

1. Deterring terrorists from using the world's seaports to ship illicit materials
2. Detecting nuclear or radioactive materials if it is shipped via sea cargo
3. Interdicting harmful material before it is used against the United States or one of its allies

The DHS S&T directorate is also developing technology solutions that can be applied across the entire international maritime supply chain. Part of this effort is the development of a new class of security devices that will monitor the integrity of intermodal shipping containers and enable CBP officers, CSI personnel, and the NTC to gather information on the status of a container to improve risk assessment and data collection. When coupled with the broad supply chain security architectural framework currently under development by S&T, DHS will have the capability to bridge data and information between container security devices, shippers, and the NTC.

One of the DHS' six strategic goals is to protect the United States from potentially dangerous people, who might be masquerading as legitimate employees or service personnel. To do so, DHS is developing the Transportation Worker Identification Credential (TWIC) program to ensure that people who work in U.S. seaports (as well as airports and land points of entry) are not a security risk, that they are authorized to be in the port, and that they are not using fraudulent or stolen credentials. TWIC is a tamper-resistant, biometric credential that will be issued to three-quarters of a million port workers. TWIC cards will be required for all individuals who expect unescorted access to secure areas of MTSA-regulated facilities and vessels.

The DHS Transportation Security Agency (TSA) is responsible for conducting the security threat assessment on TWIC applicants, which includes a background check of terrorist watchlists, an immigration status check, and a Federal Bureau of Investigation (FBI) fingerprint-based criminal history records check. TWIC is going to generate an immediate security benefit in terms of having a standard secure credential. DHS will issue the first set of regulations for TWIC in January 2008, and the rules will become effective in a matter of days, at which point DHS will begin enrolling port workers. DHS plans to work subsequently on the more complicated issue of access control and use of TWIC readers. TWIC is a complicated undertaking because it is used in a demanding operational environment—the "ant farms" that are America's ports. DHS has calculated that by taking its implementation in stages—background checks first, credentials next, and then access readers third—it will be able to rapidly move forward, while ensuring that it carefully evaluates technology and operational impact at every step of the process.

Finally, in addition to the work of the Coast Guard, CBP, S&T, and the DNDO, through 2006 the Port Security Grant program has awarded more than $700 million to owners and operators of ports, terminals, U.S.-inspected passenger vessels and ferries, as well as port authorities and state and local agencies to improve security for operators and passengers through physical security enhancements. The mission of the Port Security Grant program is to create a sustainable, risk-based effort for the protection of ports from terrorism, especially explosives and nonconventional threats that would cause major disruption to commerce and significant loss of life.

PROMISES ABOUND BUT SEARCHING QUESTIONS REMAIN

With the layered-security efforts already in place, and the efforts that are proposed for the future, port security will be substantially improved. But questions remain as to how much security "is" too much for the globalized U.S. economy, and at what point could unintended logistical ripple effects throughout the U.S. international maritime supply chain linger as a result of overly draconian or intrusive security protocols? As American statesman Benjamin Franklin wrote in 1759: "Those who would give up essential liberty to purchase a little temporary safety deserve neither liberty nor safety."

DEPARTMENT OF HOMELAND SECURITY SCORECARD FOR PORT SECURITY ACCOMPLISHMENTS

- *Increased the number of containers inspected before entering the United States.* Almost 7 million cargo containers arrive and are offloaded at U.S. seaports each year. CBP increased the percent of shipping containers processed through its CSI before entering U.S. ports from 48 percent in FY 2004 to 82 percent in FY 2006. This significantly decreases the risk of terrorist materials entering our country while providing processes to facilitate the flow of safe and legitimate trade and travel from more foreign ports.
- *DHS deployed over 880 radiation portal monitors (RPMs) at land and seaports.* DHS deployed 283 new radiation portal monitors throughout the nation's ports of entry, bringing the number of radiation portal monitors to 884 at the nation's land and seaports of entry. These additional RPMs allow us to inspect 90 percent of incoming cargo containers, an increase of approximately 30 percent from this time last year.
- *DNDO awarded over $1 billion for next generation nuclear detection devices.* DNDO announced the award of Advanced Spectroscopic Portal (ASP) program contracts totaling $1.15 billion to enhance the detection of radiological and nuclear materials at the nation's ports of entry. ASP models were deployed to the Nevada Test Site, where they will be tested using nuclear threat material. Portals have also been delivered to the New York Container Terminal for data collection.
- *Secure freight initiative launched to begin screening at foreign ports.* DHS and the Department of Energy announced the first phase of the secure freight initiative, an unprecedented effort to build on existing port security measures by enhancing the federal government's ability to scan containers for nuclear and radiological materials overseas and to better assess the risk of inbound containers. The initial phase involves the deployment of a combination of existing technology and proven nuclear detection devices.

21 Managing Port and Ship Security in Singapore

Joshua Ho

CONTENTS

INTRODUCTION

Singapore is the world's busiest port, situated at the crossroads of maritime traffic between the East and the West. More than 50,000 ships pass through the Straits of Malacca and Singapore every year, carrying half of the world's oil and almost one-third of the world's trade. Singapore is the focal point of approximately 200 shipping lines with key links to more than 600 ports in 120 countries. It remains the world's busiest port in terms of shipping tonnage—a laurel the Republic has carried proudly since 1986. In 2006, 128,922 vessels called at the Port of Singapore. Total vessel arrivals in terms of shipping tonnage reached another new high of 1.3 billion gross tons (GT).[1]

The Port of Singapore also handled 24.8 million twenty-foot equivalent units (TEUs) of containers in 2006, and is one of the world's busiest container ports.[2] Singapore is the third largest oil-refining centers in the world with major oil companies such as Shell, ExxonMobil, and Chevron operating. More than 18,000 vessel calls were made by oil/chemical and gas carriers. The port also received about 50,000 calls by regional ferries and cruise vessels.[3] Last year, 28.4 million tons of bunker fuel were supplied to some 27,000 ships.[4] This places Singapore again as the world's top bunkering port. With the rapid development of Jurong Island into a major petrochemical hub, there will be an increase in the number of tanker calls. At any one time, there are some 1000 seagoing vessels operating within Singapore's port waters.

To cater to all these vessels, the Port of Singapore has a host of marine service providers, which include providing tug services, supplies, launches, pilotage services, bunker tankers and barges, and repair services. There are about 1200 of these harbor craft operating in the port daily. Given the background on the high volume of marine traffic movements, the Maritime and Port Authority of Singapore (MPA) must ensure that the safety of these ships is well managed, security measures are in place, and it has the capabilities to support the security agencies in providing a prompt and effective response to a maritime security threat in the port waters.

SECURING PORT WATERS POST-9/11

Before September 11, 2001, the various security agencies in Singapore were already operating in a well-coordinated and thorough security framework. Following the September 11 attacks, Singapore intensified its port security measures. Broadly, the measures aimed to safeguard sensitive installations such as the major oil and chemical terminals and cruise and ferry terminals. These measures included maintaining surveillance of the Port of Singapore major waterways. Key areas within the Port of Singapore, such as the waters around chemical and offshore oil terminals have been declared as restricted areas, and small craft entering these areas are to seek written approval from the MPA.[5]

The MPA also closely monitors the movement of sensitive vessels including liquefied petroleum gas (LPG), liquefied natural gas (LNG), chemical tankers, passenger ships, and oil tankers. Relevant security agencies conduct sea patrols to ensure compliance with the port security restrictions. Regional ferries, Indonesian barter trade craft and pleasure craft have their routes revised to prevent such craft from passing close to sensitive areas and vessels in port. Entry checkpoints at sea were also strengthened. The security at sea entry checkpoints was tightened to prevent entry of undesirable persons and dangerous weapons. Persons entering or leaving Singapore by sea, including passengers and crew members going ashore are subjected to full face-to-face checks by the Immigration and Checkpoints Authority at designated landing points. All arriving vessels, other than those proceeding direct to Port of Singapore Authority Container (PSAC) terminals or Jurong Port, must anchor at designated immigration anchorages, where the Immigration and Checkpoints Authority (ICA) officers board and conduct face-to-face checks.

IMPLEMENTATION OF THE ISPS CODE

In December 2002, the International Maritime Organization (IMO), at its diplomatic conference, adopted amendments to the Safety of Life at Sea (SOLAS) convention to enhance the maritime security measures for ships and port facilities. This comes in the aftermath of the terrorist attacks of September 11, 2001. The amendments to SOLAS, incorporating the International Ship and Port Facility Security (ISPS) Code, came into force on July 1, 2004. Singapore also participated actively in various regional and international meetings as well as correspondence groups initiated at these meetings to discuss and develop the necessary instruments for the maritime security requirements.

Chapter XI-2 was added to SOLAS. The ISPS Code is associated with this new chapter. Part A of the code is mandatory, whereas Part B is recommendatory. Part A contains mandatory provisions covering the appointment of security officers for shipping companies, individual ships, and port facilities. It also includes security matters to be covered in security plans to be prepared in respect of ships and port facilities. Part B contains guidance and recommendations on preparing ship and port facility security plans. The ISPS Code is applicable to passenger ships, cargo ships of 500 GT and above, and mobile offshore drilling units. Port facilities that serve such ships on international voyages will need to comply with the ISPS Code.

As both the administration (for Singapore-registered ships) and designated authority (for port facilities) defined under the ISPS Code, the MPA is Singapore's focal point for the code and is responsible for coordinating its implementation in cooperation with other agencies such as the Singapore Police Force, Police Coast Guard (PCG), ICA, and the Republic of Singapore Navy (RSN). MPA appointed eight organizations to be Recognized Security Organizations (RSOs) for Singapore-registered ships and six RSOs for Singapore port facilities to assist ship and port facility owners in conducting security assessments, formulate security plans, and have these approved by the MPA.[6] Certificates of compliance have been issued to ships and port facilities on successful verification.

The MPA has also endorsed the Ship Security Officer, Company Security Officer, and Port Facility Security Officer courses conducted by several training providers, although such endorsements are not a requirement under the ISPS Code.[7] The reason is that MPA wants to guide and encourage ship and port facility owners to use good training providers to train their security staff according to IMO maritime security training guidelines. Legislation was put in place to give effect to the SOLAS amendments, incorporating the special measures to enhance maritime security and the ISPS Code requirements.

By working closely with the port facility operators, shipowners and their representatives, as well as the security agencies, the MPA was able to ensure that Singapore was one of the first countries in the world to fully comply with IMO requirements. There are 1270 Singapore-registered ships and 118 port facilities that are in compliance with the ISPS Code.[8] Of the 118 port facilities, 25 of them serve ships of less than 500 GT and hence, they need not comply with the code. However, they have chosen to do so as they felt that the ships that they interface with go outside the port waters. Under the ISPS Code, ships and port facilities are required to conduct maritime security drills every three months and an exercise at least once each calendar year. As part of these efforts, the MPA has carried out three major maritime security exercises at sea involving all the security agencies, operators of sensitive installations such as Shell and ExxonMobil, and sensitive vessels such as LPG carriers. Together with the security organizations, the MPA also conducts audits to ensure that security procedures are adhered to at port facilities and on ships.

The ISPS Code contains three security levels. The security level will be set by MPA with the aid of intelligence agencies in Singapore and the Ministry of Transport. Currently, the Port of Singapore is at Security Level 1. The three levels of security are as follows:

1. *Security Level 1.* Normal—the level at which ships and port facilities normally operate. It means the level for which minimum appropriate protective security measures shall be maintained at all times.
2. *Security Level 2.* Heightened—the level applying for as long as there is a heightened risk of a security incident. It means the level for which additional protective measures shall be maintained for a period of time as a result of a security incident.
3. *Security Level 3.* Exceptional—the level applying for the period of time when there is a probable or imminent risk of a security incident. It means the level for which further specific protective security measures shall be maintained for a limited period of time when a security incident is probable or imminent, although it may not be possible to identify the specific target.

The MPA also set up a 24-hour Maritime Security Unit to monitor and receive all ISPS ships' submission of security-related information before the entry of the ship into the port. The information known as Pre-Arrival Notification of Security (PANS) is to be submitted at least 24 hours before the ship's arrival in Singapore. The information includes the last ten ports that the ship has called and any special security measures included in the said ports.[9]

ISPS ships are to be provided with a ship security alert system (SSAS). The SSAS when activated will transmit a ship-to-shore security alert to the administration identifying the ship, its location, and indicating that the ship is under threat. The alert will not be received by any other ships nor any alarm will be raised on board. All Singapore-registered ships will send the security alerts to the MPA regardless of their locations. The MPA has a standard operating procedure (SOP) with the RSN and the PCG to handle ship security alerts. Control measures are also put in place for non-ISPS-compliant ships such as denying entry, inspection of the ship, delaying the ship, detention of the ship, restriction of operations, including movement within the port, or expulsion of the ship from port.[10]

BEYOND THE ISPS CODE: SECURING PORT WATERS

The ISPS Code largely focused on commercial facilities and the larger vessels. Therefore, small vessels[11] engaged on international voyage are not compelled to comply with the ISPS Code. These small vessels are also vulnerable to security threats and could be used as a weapon of mass destruction, just like vessels that are required to comply with the ISPS Code. In the "USS *Cole*" attack in Yemen on October 2000, a small craft manned by two suicide bombers and laden with explosives pulled up to the guided missile destroyer and rammed their boat into the vessel as it was refueling in the Port of Aden. Seventeen sailors died in the attack. In October 2002, the French tanker *Limburg* was hit by a water-borne attack off Yemen similar to the *Cole* incident. The *Limburg* attackers blew a hole about 3 m wide in the tanker, killing one crew member and spilling some 12,000 t of oil into the Gulf of Aden.

Despite tough new global security regulations that came into force on July 1, 2004, the port remains vulnerable to security threats including the arrival of non-ISPS-compliant vessels and those coming from non-ISPS-compliant ports. Hence, control measures have been put in place by the MPA to deal with such vessels coming from non-ISPS-compliant ports. However, the MPA has also gone beyond the provisions of the ISPS Code to implement additional measures to safeguard ships and port facilities to further enhance maritime security within Singapore's port waters. It is for this reason that the MPA developed the following guidelines:

1. Guidance for establishing security measures when vessels call at non-ISPS-compliant ports
2. Ship Self-Security Assessment (SSSA) checklist
3. Harbor Craft Security Code
4. Pleasure Craft Security Code (PCSC)
5. Harbor Craft Transponder System

GUIDANCE FOR ESTABLISHING SECURITY MEASURES WHEN VESSELS CALL AT NON-ISPS-COMPLIANT PORTS

As not all the port facilities in the world are ISPS compliant, the MPA has also provided guidance to ISPS-compliant ships calling at non-ISPS-compliant ports. This will be in the form of additional measures that the ship has to take while in the noncomplaint port. Examples of such measures are restricting access to the ship; deployment of security guards at gangway; restricting visitors to ship; securing accommodation, engine room, and store rooms; checking for stowaways; checking on unidentified packages; and baggage checks on departure. The U.S. Coast Guard has recently asked to post the guidance on their Web site, as a means of exchanging experiences and sharing best practices to enhance port security.[12]

SHIP SELF-SECURITY ASSESSMENT CHECKLIST

There are about 80 small seagoing vessels of less than 500 GT calling at the Port of Singapore on a daily basis. These vessels are generally coastal tankers, freighters, or tugs and barges operating within the regions. They do interface with the larger oceangoing vessels and the port facilities and hence become an important link in the security chain. MPA requires such small seagoing vessels to complete a SSSA checklist before entry into the port. This SSSA checklist is to be kept on board for verifications by the security agencies or port officials.

The "SSSA checklist" for small seagoing vessels would benefit both the port facility and the shipmaster as follows:

1. It would raise the security awareness of the master and crew members and provide information on the security measures that need to be implemented by the vessel during various security levels of the port.
2. ISPS Code requires a Declaration of Security (DOS) to be completed by the port facilities when they interface with vessels including small vessels that are not ISPS Code compliant.

As shipmasters of small vessels may not be familiar with ISPS Code, it would take time to interpret and complete the DOS. Therefore, a completed SSSA checklist would assist the port facility security officers and shipmasters of small vessels to complete the DOS. The items covered in the DOS are elaborated in the SSSA checklist.[13]

HARBOR CRAFT SECURITY CODE

There are about 1200 licensed harbor craft operating daily within Singapore port waters. These harbor craft contribute to the operational efficiency of the port as they provide essential services such as supplying bunker fuel and stores to ships, transporting passengers and crew, or serving as lightering craft. These harbor craft, which are less than 500 GT, do not operate beyond the port waters but interface with oceangoing vessels within the port and as such become another important link in the security chain.

All harbor craft registered in Singapore are to comply with the Harbor Craft Security Code (HCSC) and the security log. The HCSC encompasses simple and practical actions that should be taken by harbor craft masters to protect the crew members and the craft so as to mitigate vulnerabilities to security incidents on board. The HCSC contains the key security measures to ensure the security readiness of the harbor craft when operating in the port waters.

The HCSC focuses on four key areas, which are as follows:

1. Access control security measures
2. Activity security measures (when conducting ship-to-ship or ship-to-port facility activities)
3. Security measures while navigating in port waters
4. Communication security measures

As record and evidence of complying with the aforementioned measures, the master of the harbor craft is required to make entries in the logbook on the ship to ship or ship to port facility interface and the activities conducted. The security agencies and MPA's port inspectors on patrol would randomly check on the harbor craft to ensure that the security measures are complied.[14]

PLEASURE CRAFT SECURITY CODE

To further enhance security in the port waters and in addition to the HCSC, MPA developed a PCSC. The code is user friendly and developed in consultation with the pleasure craft community. The PCSC provides security guidance to the pleasure craft community and focuses on four key areas, namely, need for preparedness, vigilance when navigating, maintaining an observant posture, and being proactive in reporting to the appropriate authorities.[15]

HARBOR CRAFT TRANSPONDER SYSTEM

Harbor craft that are less than 300 GT and not engaged on international voyages, do not come under the SOLAS regulations and hence are not required to carry the Automatic Identification System (AIS) transponders. Recognizing this fact, the MPA and the security agencies developed a vessel tracking system known as the Harbor Craft Transponder System (HARTS) as an added defense against potential threats of attacks by small craft. Currently, all the 2800 MPA-licensed powered harbor and pleasure craft are fitted with the HARTS transponders. The system became operational from January 1, 2007.

To prevent unauthorized usage, a special coded identity of each transponder ensures that the transponder deployed can only operate on the harbor craft it is first installed on. The coded identity must match that of the mounting bracket. This security feature ensures that the transponder does not work if it is used on another craft. In the event of a security breach, an alert would be sent to the control center operator. Every transponder is also equipped with a panic button. The panic button allows the craft's owner/master to alert the MPA in the event of distress or a security threat. After activating the panic button, an alert message containing the identity, position, and time will be sent to the control center operator. This function is similar to the IMO SSAS for oceangoing vessels.[16]

ACCOMPANYING SEA SECURITY TEAMS

For the purposes of protecting the port and vessels from security threats, all vessels entering or leaving the Port of Singapore may be boarded by a team of police officers or authorized representatives of the port master. The teams will, as far as practicable, board arriving vessels with pilots at the pilot boarding grounds. For departing vessels, the teams will, as far as practicable, board with the pilots at anchorages or berths.[17]

MULTIPRONGED APPROACH TO MARITIME SECURITY

The MPA adopts a multiagency approach in ensuring maritime security, and works closely with the home teams and the RSN. Various task forces, committees, and working groups have been established to look at the different aspects of maritime security.[18] The smooth implementation of the various security measures in the port including conducting of security exercises has been possible only because of the close operation among the security agencies and the stakeholders such as the port facilities' operators and the shipowners.

As for the global approach, the MPA participates in various regional and international fora as well as correspondence groups initiated at these fora to share expertise and exchange information among the member countries. The MPA has engaged other like-minded countries to better the safety and security of the maritime world. These fora include the IMO, Asia-Pacific Economic Cooperation (APEC), and Association of South East Asian Nations (ASEAN). The MPA has and will continue to provide the necessary technical assistance to the member countries as required. For example, the MPA has provided training and expertise to various regional countries under the umbrella of these fora, such as the IMO-Singapore Third Country Training Programme, and also on a bilateral basis.[19] Singapore was also the first port in the world that participated in the U.S.'s International Port Security Programme.[20] Among other things, the program seeks to ensure that uniform standards are applied globally and that the best practices are shared and aligned.

Sea Lines of Communications (SLOCs), such as the Straits of Malacca and Singapore, are important international waterways for the transport of commerce and energy supplies. Singapore is actively cooperating with its neighbors to safeguard the Straits of Malacca and Singapore. The launching of the Trilateral Coordinated Patrols and "eye in the sky" among the navies of Indonesia, Malaysia, and Singapore are good examples.[21] The IMO, as the authority on international maritime affairs, is well positioned to bring together the many straits stakeholders to forge a common understanding with the littoral states for collaborative efforts in the straits. The MPA has been actively involved in the IMO's "Protection of Vital Shipping Lanes" initiative to secure key shipping lanes against threats such as maritime terrorism.[22]

Singapore is also host to the Information Sharing Centre (ISC) established by the Regional Co-operation Agreement on Combating Piracy and Armed Robbery against Ships in Asia (ReCAAP).[23] ReCAAP and its ISC represent the commitment of 16 regional countries in Asia to fight piracy in the region. The 16 countries include the 10 ASEAN member states, Japan, China, Republic of Korea, India, Bangladesh, and Sri Lanka.

CONCLUSION

The development and implementation of maritime security measures requires a high degree of multilevel coordination and a close working partnership among all stakeholders, be they government agencies or private organizations. To avoid any disruption to Singapore's trade and businesses, the MPA continues to work closely with the enforcement agencies, the vessel owners, and the port facility operators to review the security measures for the port waters and its ships. As maritime security is not an issue that any one country can address on its own but requires cooperation and concerted efforts from countries around the world, the MPA continues to work with its maritime counterparts to put in place a stable maritime security regime and share its best practices.

NOTES

1. Maritime and Port Authority of Singapore website. Available online at http://www.mpa.gov.sg/infocentre/pdfs/vessel-arrivals.pdf (accessed on January 25, 2007).
2. Maritime and Port Authority of Singapore website. Available online at http://www.mpa.gov.sg/infocentre/pdfs/container-throughput.pdf (accessed on January 25, 2007).
3. Maritime and Port Authority of Singapore website. Available online at http://www.mpa.gov.sg/infocentre/pdfs/vessel-arrivals.pdf (accessed on January 26, 2007).
4. Maritime and Port Authority of Singapore website. Available online at http://www.mpa.gov.sg/infocentre/pdfs/vessel-purpose.pdf (accessed on January 26, 2007).
5. Maritime and Port Authority of Singapore, "Prohibition on Movement of Vessels in Waters Surrounding: (A) Jurong Island; (B) Pulau Busing & Pulau Bukom; (C) Pulau Sebarok & Shell SBM; and (D) Sembawang Wharves and Approaches thereto," *Port Marine Circular No. 21 of 2006*, December 8, 2005. Available online at http://www.mpa.gov.sg/circulars_and_notices/pdfs/pc06-21.pdf (accessed on January 27, 2007).
6. Maritime and Port Authority of Singapore website. Available online at http://www.mpa.gov.sg/maritimeportsecurity/list_rso.htm (accessed on January 28, 2007).
7. Maritime and Port Authority of Singapore website. Available online at http://www.mpa.gov.sg/maritimeportsecurity/pdfs/trainingproviders.pdf (accessed on January 28, 2007).
8. Maritime and Port Authority of Singapore website. Available online at http://www.mpa.gov.sg/maritimeportsecurity/pdfs/ispscodecompliantlist.pdf (accessed on January 29, 2007).
9. Maritime and Port Authority of Singapore, "Revision to the Pre-Arrival Notification of Security (PANS)," *Port Marine Circular No. 25 of 2005*, December 1, 2005. Available online at http://www.mpa.gov.sg/circulars_and_notices/pdfs/pc05-25.pdf (accessed on January 29, 2007).
10. International Maritime Organization website. Available online at http://www.imo.org/home.asp (accessed on January 27, 2007).
11. Small vessels refers to all vessels calling Port of Singapore excluding the following that are covered by the ISPS Code, that is, passenger ships, including high-speed passenger craft; cargo ships, including high-speed craft of 500 GT and upward; and mobile offshore drilling units.
12. Maritime and Port Authority of Singapore, "Guidance for Establishing Security Measures when Vessels call at Non-ISPS Compliant Ports," *Port Marine Circular No. 25 of 2005*, December 1, 2005. Available online at http://www.mpa.gov.sg/circulars_and_notices/pdfs/pc05-25.pdf (accessed on January 30, 2007).
13. Maritime and Port Authority of Singapore, "Security Advisory for Small Vessels Calling Singapore that are not Required to comply with the ISPS Code," *Port Marine Circular No. 18 of 2004*, June 30, 2004. Available online at http://www.mpa.gov.sg/circulars_and_notices/pdfs/pc04-18.pdf (accessed on January 30, 2007).
14. Maritime and Port Authority of Singapore, "Harbour Security Code and Harbour Craft Security Log," *Port Marine Circular No. 18 of 2004*, June 30, 2004. Available online at http://www.mpa.gov.sg/circulars_and_notices/pdfs/pc04-18.pdf (accessed on January 31, 2007).
15. Maritime and Port Authority of Singapore, "Pleasure Craft Security Code," *Port Marine Circular No. 8 of 2006, 28 March 2006*. Available online at http://www.mpa.gov.sg/circulars_and_notices/pdfs/pc06-08.pdf (accessed on January 31, 2007).
16. Maritime and Port Authority of Singapore, "Harbour Security Code and Harbour Craft Security Log," *Port Marine Circular No. 18 of 2004*, June 30, 2004. Available online at http://www.mpa.gov.sg/circulars_and_notices/pdfs/pc04-18.pdf (accessed on February 1, 2007).
17. "ASSeT escorting vessels," *The Straits Times*, May 13, 2005.
18. National Security Coordination Secretariat, *1826 days: A Diary of Resolve — Securing Singapore Since 9/11* (Singapore: National Security Coordination Secretariat), 2006, pp. 23–28.

19. Capt Foong Yee Kuan, "Regional Training Course for Simulator Instructor—a first for ISC," *Nautilus*, October/December 2003, p. 13. Available online at http://www.mpa.gov.sg/infocentre/pdfs/oct-dec03. pdf (accessed on 2 February 2007).

20. "Singapore is First Country to Participate in the U.S. International Port Security Programme," *Nautilus*, April/June 2004, p. 6. Available online at http://www.mpa.gov.sg/infocentre/pdfs/nl04-04.pdf (accessed on February 5, 2007).

21. Graham Gerard Ong and Joshua Ho, "Maritime Air Patrols: The New Weapon Against Piracy in the Malacca Straits," *IDSS Commentaries 70/2005*, October 13, 2005.

22. Maritime Safety Committee, "Report of the Maritime Safety Committee on its Eighty-First Session," *IMO MSC 81/25*, May 24, 2006. Available online at http://www.mpa.gov.sg/circulars_and_notices/ pdfs/msc81-25.pdf (accessed on 6 February 2007).

23. T. Rajan, "Pirate Attack? Team in Singapore will Alert 14 Nations," *The Straits Times*, November 20, 2006 and T. Rajan "14-Nation network's anti-piracy coordination centre opens here; $2.2 million info-sharing centre starting next week will help joint effort to fight sea piracy," *The Straits Times*, November 23, 2006.

22 Canada and the ISPS Code

John W. Lavers

CONTENTS

Contracting governments of the International Maritime Organization (IMO) adopted the International Ship and Port Facility (ISPS) Code in December 2002. Canada, known as a world maritime leader and innovator, soon discovered that it was ill-prepared to meet the challenges of putting into place a maritime security framework, but in reality, it was not alone within the community of maritime nations.

CANADIAN MARITIME SECURITY PRE-9/11

During the time leading up to the tragic events of September 11, 2001, Canadian transportation security was primarily focused on aviation security. Canadian awareness of air security was extremely acute with the 1985 bombing of Air India flight 182 off the south coast of Ireland.[1] With the loss of 329 persons (most of whom were Canadian citizens)[2] it remains to this day, the most prominent mass murder investigation involving an act of terrorism in Canadian history. Within the maritime realm there existed no such polarizing event for Canada.

Canada has enjoyed a relatively safe and secure maritime transportation system. Given the fact that there has not been a major security incident involving a ship or port facility, the government has prided itself in promoting this aspect. Like most western developed countries, Canada remained a target for drug and human smuggling operations that were conducted off both the east and the west coasts of the nation's vastly unprotected coastline.

Specific to the maritime realm, Canada had only a very basic federal law known as the Marine Transportation Security Act (MTSA), which came into force in the early 1990s.[3] Within this broad legislative framework, there were cruise ship and cruise ship facility security measures.[4] Overall these measures were to insure that the very basic of security-screening functions were performed by (at that time) unqualified ship's crew that often doubled this task with other cruise ship chores. As well, the government security inspectors charged with enforcement, or what may be better defined as observing the screening process, were individuals that came from the government's aviation security branch and were armed with little knowledge and application of the workings of the maritime world. The government's transportation security policy, regulations, and operations were firmly grounded within the aviation mode and resources to that effect were primarily devoted to enhancing aviation security. Maritime, or marine security as it is better known in Canada, was limited to the cyclical rotation associated with cruise ship visits to Canadian waters between May and October of each year. At that time the bulk of cruise ship activities were more concentrated to the three major ports of Canada (Halifax, Montreal, and Vancouver), with some cruise ships visiting other smaller Canadian ports.

Maritime security in Canada may be compared to that of its coastline, open and unprotected for the most part. In reality, Canada was not under threat and the risk of a major unlawful act (i.e., terrorism) occurring was assessed as being very low. Although before 9/11 there had been some notable acts of maritime terrorism (and crime) that had occurred in other parts of the world, but the perception of the day was that those were events that took place in other "troubled waters" and that there was no risk of such an occurrence happening in Canada. As shall be discussed in the next section, security awareness within the maritime mode would quickly change and the impact on Canada would be profound.

CANADIAN MARITIME SECURITY POST-9/11 AND THE GROWTH OF NORTH AMERICAN SECURITY COOPERATION

Although the events of 9/11 shocked the world and western countries reevaluated transportation security, particularly within the aviation mode, it is noteworthy that it was a maritime industry leader who first called for wholesale changes to worldwide transportation security. The head of Hutchison Port Holdings of Hong Kong[5] quickly realized the significant impact of such an act of terror had on aviation transportation and rightly assumed that if the same occurred within the maritime mode, the devastation of such an attack could severely impact the global economy.

In the weeks that followed the 2001 attacks on U.S. territory, the Government of Canada began to reexamine its overall security strategy and how it could combat new developments in terrorism. Outside of various foreign policy and military engagements, the government focused on domestic security issues that were greatly in need of review. What occurred, almost at the same time but not in unison, were a number of security overtures that would affect the maritime sector. First, planning was accelerated on developing the first-ever national security policy for Canada.[6] This included enhancing North American defense arrangements between Canada and the United States, This was soon followed by the establishment, in principle, of Canada Command by the Department of National Defence[7] to deal with natural as well as man-made disasters effecting Canada. The opposite organization in the United States is Northern Command.[8] Additionally, the U.S. government created the Department of Homeland Security,[9] while in Canada the Department of Public Safety and Emergency Preparedness Canada (now called Public Safety) gathered together various agencies, policing and security services of the government having a security mandate and placed them under one organization.[10] The exception to this was the Department of Transport that retained its security role and was not included in a major government reorganization that saw many calling for all governmental security functions to be placed under one roof. Finally, and beyond the various measures to enhance aviation security, there came an international agreement for a maritime security framework known as the ISPS Code.[11]

Maritime security in Canada evolved slowly but transportation security planners soon realized a new marine security program for Canada was required and that it would be founded in the contents of the ISPS Code. Although not having the time to create a new legal act for Canada, it was decided that implementation of the code could be best accelerated by using the enabling legislation of the MTSA. The question now was how to meet Canada's requirements to this international convention and achieve this task in less than 18 months.

GOVERNMENT OF CANADA AND THE ISPS CODE

At the IMO conference that adopted the ISPS Code in December 2001, the Government of Canada greatly supported the work of the U.S. government to enhance maritime security. The impact of 9/11 had clearly affected government security planners within Canada and the working policy of the day was very much a Canada–U.S. approach on most things security. Although having adopted the ISPS Code, Canada was not in a strong position to implement it. In the late 1990s, the government, in an effort to save money, had abolished the Canadian Ports Police Service. This was seen as a major blow to port security and was heralded as giving organized crime a freer hand to conduct illegal activities within the major ports of Canada. The corporate knowledge that was lost with the disbanding of the Ports Police was not truly realized until former members of the organization were once again asked to play a leading role in national consultations on what should be included in a new national marine security policy for Canada.

The government of the day first needed to decide who would be responsible for the ISPS Code. Following a quick discussion at senior levels, it was decided that the Department of Transport should be responsible for implementation and not any other department charged with public security. This was understood by the government to be in line with what other western countries had previously done, that is, place transportation security within a ministry responsible for the safe and secure movement of people and goods. The Department of Transport then needed to wrestle with the question of which directorate within the department would be responsible for performing the details of actually implementing the ISPS Code for Canada. On this matter the debate fell between the Directorate of Marine Safety and the Directorate of Security and Emergency Preparedness (SEP). At the 2002 IMO meetings in London, it was Marine Safety that represented the department and the government on matters effecting maritime safety, and now, the growing issues concerning security were becoming part of that process. This was a natural reach for Marine Safety as the ISPS Code contained some overlapping issues pertaining to maritime safety, for example, Automatic Identification System (AIS) as a carriage requirement for Safety of Life at Sea (SOLAS) vessels. Marine Safety felt convinced that the ISPS Code was their responsibility and senior managers of the department agreed and the file was placed into the care of Marine Safety.

As these were early days (winter–spring 2003) for the government and the ISPS Code, many new and challenging questions on key issues were being asked concerning the fundamental aspects of maritime security from a regulatory and operational perspective to that of policy. It quickly became apparent that the more suitable directorate for implementation was within the Directorate of Security and Emergency Preparedness and the senior departmental officials promptly directed the file to be handled by the security professionals. Within the shuffleboard game of departmental politics, a situation developed involving a major international security convention in need of quick implementation. However, the marine knowledge associated with the ISPS Code rested within one particular directorate of the Department of Transport, that of Marine Safety, and the security knowledge aspect of the ISPS Code rested within another particular directorate of the department called Security and Emergency Preparedness. Up and until that time, neither of the two directorates had any real contact with other, which created a very unique set of circumstances and at times an awkward relationship.

FRAMEWORK FOR IMPLEMENTATION

During the early spring of 2003 and with less that 18 months before the coming into force date of July 1, 2004, the government had not properly resourced departmental requirements for effective implementation of the ISPS Code. Officials within the directorate of SEP were asked to perform double-hatted responsibilities between aviation and marine security. In retrospect some have argued that this may not have been the best solution, but at the time, it appeared to be the only solution available to an already stretched department with an ever-growing security mandate and new daily demands to keep in step with U.S. transportation security developments.

Security planners within SEP quickly got to work and began to map out a security policy for the department in support of the government's domestic security strategy. To begin a process of creating a sustainable regulatory system whether it is for security, safety or other reasons, the government normally engages in a process of national consultations with industry stakeholders and Canadians overall to seek their opinions and input in deciding what shape the security framework should be and how it should work. This first part of building a basic framework for ISPS implementation was placed upon the marine security policy group which created general broad-ranged policy working groups to manage the task of meeting key deadlines and milestones on the path to implementation. As a major project management exercise, the SEP marine security policy group was equipped with the fundamentals to achieve the task but was lacking in the resources (both financial and personnel) as well as the knowledge and experience of implementing such a convention, in and through a legislative portal of the MTSA. To that end, SEP reached out to Marine Safety and other government departments for support, as well as within its own ranks, to bring together a collection of people having both knowledge and experience in matters of security and marine.

By the beginning of the summer of 2003, the Department of Transport through the directorate of SEP had what may be defined as an assembly of individuals dedicated to the objective of implementing the ISPS Code. The assembly was broken down and meshed within the existing aviation security group of the same directorate. Lines of communication were blurred and as mentioned earlier many individuals were performing double duties of maintaining aviation security responsibilities along with their newfound marine security requirements. The fundamental point achieved was that an identifiable face could be placed next to a marine security issue and with any luck a question could be answered to move the process of implementation forward.

Over the course of the summer of 2003, events were easily overtaking the government's ability to adjust and respond to growing demands for clarification, insight, and most importantly action on the ground. There was a growing frustration with industry stakeholders as they wished to move further and faster in meeting the requirements of ISPS in order to stay competitive internationally. The maritime industry cautiously welcomed the new security measures but not the forecasted costs that would accompany the new regulations associated with implementing the ISPS Code into law. From the industry's perspective the government could not answer many key questions. One reason for this lack of response was the fact that in Canada maritime stakeholders and their issues were as long and broad as the great Canadian coastline. Each region of Canada came to the national information and stakeholder meetings with a variety of comprehensive questions and related issues.

Within transportation security in Canada, the Department of Transport has the national or headquarters office located in the nation's capital of Ottawa. Across Canada, the country is divided into five separate regions beginning with the Atlantic region, followed by Quebec, Ontario, Prairie and Northern Region and finally the Pacific Region. During the 1990s, the federal government divested much authority and autonomy to regional offices of the various federal departments. The Department of Transport was one such department that enjoyed greater autonomy for operational decision-making requirements within the region, whereas Ottawa retained a functional authority for national consistency. This meant that national marine security policy, regulatory and operational policy matters would be decided at that national level with regional input into the process. Strict operational issues would fall to the regions on matters of implementation and enforcement.

Of course not every system of government is truly effective and the current system now deployed within the federal Department of Transport for ISPS implementation soon revealed the difficulty of achieving national consistency against maritime security issues of regional diversity.[12] Given the sheer size of Canada's maritime sector, these issues of diversity ranged from the large-scale tug and barge industry in the Pacific Region to the Canada–U.S. joint management and security concerns of the St. Lawrence Seaway System in the Ontario and Quebec Regions, to the over 400 small- and medium-size ports that receive on occasion SOLAS class vessels within the other regions of Canada. Also, Canada had many shared maritime security concerns with its U.S. neighbor, which included shared navigable waterways at the St. Lawrence Seaway and the Straits of Juan de Fuca, new terms and definitions involving dangerous goods, and finally, the lowering of the already adopted international standard of applying the ISPS code to SOLAS class vessels of 500 gross ton and over to a new regulatory standard of applying the code against all vessels that were 100 gross ton and above.[13] The very impact on lowering this international benchmark captured many more vessels and created additional problems toward enforcing compliance across Canada and the whole of North America.

Many other issues did plague and challenge the department, but without the support and cooperation of industry stakeholders Canada would not have made its commitment to the IMO. This government–industry success story was founded in and through the national and regional consultation forums. By the late fall of 2003, the department's marine security policy, regulatory and operational personnel were working in tandem with industry stakeholders in building a maritime security framework for the country. It is fair to say that at the beginning of the process the industry had doubt and suspicion of the department, as real motives were often challenged against the onset of new regulatory and oversight instruments. This was clear when it came to the department consulting with the various union representatives that represented the port workers of the major ports of Canada. In this case, there were many examples of miscommunications and false rumors that surrounded the entire consultation process, so the unions threatened action against some ports in the country. Overall the unions were very concerned about how new regulations would be implemented within their immediate workspace.[14] As discussed earlier the Canadian Ports Police Service was disbanded in the 1997. Within that period of the past ten years, union influence and dominance within the ports had increased and now this was under threat against newly proposed security regulations involving issues such as defined restricted areas within the ports, background checks for certain port workers, and new types of identification cards.[15] As well, corporate maritime stakeholders were being challenged by unions as using the newly proposed security regulations to further intimidate union employees.

As these concerns were refereed through intense negotiations and compromise, all parties involved in the process were allotted their place at the table and the opportunity to exercise their right to challenge any aspect of the proposed new marine security regulations. The result of this process brought together a new understanding and respect between industry stakeholders and a government department faster than ever before. Distrust in the process gave way to mutual cooperation for all concerned and with that, the key element was cemented in place to meet Canada's international obligations.

THE JULY 1ST DRIVE

In the months leading up to the July 1st, 2004 deadline a heightened awareness griped the Department of Transport as some key milestone were met while others began to slide to the right. In accordance with the ISPS Code the required security assessments and plans were drafted, reviewed, and approved and with only some modifications required, the industry for the most part had found the acceptable standard. Awareness training and industry security courses were steaming along throughout the country all in preparation to meet the new regulations that were timed to coincide with the implementation of the ISPS Code. New monies were found to bolster the personnel ranks and support fatiguing government workers, while operational rooms were being made ready to monitor port and vessel activities throughout Canada. Industry and the government were committed and determined to meet the standard and when a shortfall was identified the issue was immediately rectified.

In the run-up to the July 1st implementation date, a unique occurrence was developing in Canada with regards to the contents of the code against the proposed new marine security regulations. Although most of the world was adopting the code as it was written, Canada and the United States were developing enhanced regulations above and beyond the requirements of the code. The Canadian government, like its partner to the south, could not wait for new regulations to be ready and to meet its international commitments by July 2004, developed an interim scheme to approve the assessment and plan requirements under the ISPS Code. The industry could not forecast and react to all potential new additions to the new security regulations that would coincide with the implementation date of the code. And as the industry had only the code as the primary guidance tool, the government realized that, from a technical standpoint, many maritime industry stakeholders would be in noncompliance with the new security regulations. In short, the government met the conditions as laid out in the code first, then revisited the process in the following months and assisted the industry with meeting the requirements of its new marine security regulations.

Some have argued that this caused an imbalance in the process and additional costs to both government and industry, although it may be suggested that this was in the end a real commitment by the government and industry to meet the standard of the code and to do one better by enhancing the standard of security across North America.

On implementation day of 2004, the Government of Canada and departmental officials were anxious to see the results of the ISPS Code. The question that everyone was asking was "had they got it right?" With less than 35 newly minted marine security inspectors across Canada, and mostly clustered in the larger population centers, assessing compliance of over 400 port facilities and the volume of vessel traffic entering, departing, and transiting through Canadian waters would be a challenge of the highest order.

To address the vastness of the problem it is worthy to note, among the many solutions found, two accomplishments that assisted the government in checking compliance standards. The view of the government was that port and port facilities were in good shape in terms of compliance, but the big concern was the vessels. Just before July 1st two critical solutions were found, one that came from within the department and the other from outside of the country.

The first solution rested with Marine Safety. As discussed earlier, Marine Safety and SEP had some initial difficulty with the concept of who was better suited to implement the ISPS Code. In the end, the result was that both were best suited to do the task. Marine Safety has over 200 marine safety inspectors across the country located in both urban and rural communities. The opportunity to have a marine safety inspector visit a vessel, anywhere in Canada, to determine compliance with the code was unprecedented. This was a critical resource that could be utilized by the department and extend the eyes and ears of the government for security reasons. To make this work marine safety inspectors were provided with ISPS Code training and awareness, and also these safety inspectors, who already performed various activities under Port State Control, were made security inspectors under the MTSA.

The second solution was with the United States Coast Guard (USCG) and managing the security of the St. Lawrence Seaway (SLS). The SLS is a waterway system and an engineering marvel that provides a vital marine link to the U.S. mid-west and central Canada. The seaway has 13 major locks in total, two of the locks are controlled by the United States and the other 11 are controlled by Canada.[16] Having a shared waterway such as the St. Lawrence Seaway posed some benefits, but also problems for Canada and the United States. One such potential problem was that if Canada allowed a vessel to enter Canadian waters belonging to the seaway system and then in the middle of the system (if) the USCG denied the entry of that vessel to U.S. waters, there would be a problem not only from a security point of view but also from a safety standpoint, as it would be extremely difficult for a vessel to maneuver and exit the seaway system. To achieve the best solution for maintaining security and safety for vessels entering the SLS, Canada and the United States entered into an agreement where USCG security inspectors would board vessels with their Canadian counterparts in the Port of Montreal at the entrance of the St. Lawrence Seaway. For reasons of maintaining Canadian sovereignty, the USCG inspectors were present only as observers, while Canadian authorities conducted security verifications and inspections on vessels intending to enter the SLS. This solution of enhanced cooperation between Canada and the United States was met with a very positive response by the international shipping community. Potential complications were avoided and security was maintained, which allowed for the continuance of commerce to flow within the SLS with little or no negative effects upon the economies of either nation.[17]

As with just-in-time transportation delivery systems in the world, Canada found just-in-time solutions to meet the security needs of the day in accordance with the ISPS Code.

MEETING THE KEY OBJECTIVES OF THE ISPS CODE

In the *foreward* section of the ISPS Code, in broad terms, are the key strategic objectives of the code:

1. To establish a framework of cooperation (between all levels of government and industry) designed to detect, assess, and take preventative measures against security threats
2. To establish respective roles and responsibilities of all parties to ensure maritime security
3. To ensure early efficient collation and exchange of security information
4. To provide for a methodology for security assessments leading to plans and procedures to react to changing security levels
5. To ensure confidence that adequate and proportionate maritime security measures are in place

From these key objectives many countries of the international maritime community followed one of the five possible paths or potential combination of same toward implementing the ISPS Code:

1. Follow the ISPS Code as stated
2. Follow the ISPS Code as stated, but add a combination of security procedures and measures thus raising the standard
3. Follow the ISPS Code in spirit, but interpret the code to meet local needs, which would mean a watering-down effect of the code
4. Develop a security framework completely different from the ISPS Code
5. Maintain the status quo, which could also mean doing or having no security framework

In meeting its international obligations as well as the key objectives of the ISPS Code, Canada may be classified as having followed the number "2" path toward implementation. Strategic security policy in Canada was geared to maintaining an effective standard that kept in step with U.S. maritime security concerns. One such concern was in the potential of SOLAS class vessels "port shopping" in North America. This may be understood as that it was essential for Canada and the United States to have consistency in their port and port facility security framework. If both the counties were not consistent, then it was assessed that vessels would choose to visit ports that were not as stringent in their security procedures. This would also mean a loss of business and revenue for some major ports, as the U.S. government was insisting that maritime port security needed to be approached and adopted as a North American issue and related security strategies needed to reflect that position. Given the fact that Canada and the United States manage two major waterway systems and that cross-border intermodal transportation systems are invariably linked, it has been argued that the U.S. security position aided in elevating Canada's security application to achieving an enhanced North American maritime security framework, which resulted in both countries adopting the number "2" path toward ISPS Code implementation.

CANADA'S FIRST NATIONAL SECURITY POLICY: MARINE SECURITY OPERATIONS CENTERS

Canada's first-ever National Security Policy (NSP) was released to Canadians in April 2004, just over two months ahead of the ISPS Code coming into force in July of that same year. The NSP was designed to address many critical security issues one of which was maritime security.[18]

One important aspect of the NSP called for the establishment of Marine Security Operations Centers (MSOCs). The main purpose of the MSOC is to bring together the main departments and agencies having a maritime security mandate, within the Government of Canada under one umbrella-type structure for achieving transportation security in general and maritime security in particular.[19] The core function of the MSOC is founded in information generation in support of the intelligence cycle. In fact, it may be suggested that the MSOC core function could have been taken directly from one of the key objectives of the ISPS Code on the need to ensure early efficient collation and exchange of security information. Although this link between the ISPS Code and Canada's NSP has not been confirmed, the relationship and the applied logic in this case is worth noting.

Because of the vastness of Canada's maritime sector, maritime domain awareness (MDA) became a key strategic and tactical requirement for the government. With that in mind MSOC facilities were established on both the Atlantic and the Pacific coasts of Canada with another holding responsibility for the Great Lakes and St. Lawrence Seaway. The Arctic Ocean area and what Canada will do there remains an open question. The MSOCs are designed to provide close support to the Government of Canada maritime security operational needs. Having the availability of traditional and nontraditional information collection abilities, maritime domain awareness has benefited from enhanced support of ongoing surveillance operations to protect the sovereignty of Canada.

Although MDA has yet to achieve and realize its full capability, the awareness of approaching vessels and their intention has become better known to Canadian security personnel. Unfortunately, there is a lack of domestic maritime domain awareness within the internal waterways, ports, and harbors of the country. This issue is not suffocated due to a lack of technology, for the technical and reporting means exist to provide for a comprehensive picture, but the entanglement of various legal and *privacy concerns* are holding back a true realization of what MDA could really achieve toward a successful and fully functional maritime security system.

Current legal restrictions notwithstanding, the MSOC project has been able to bring together various departments and agencies that existed as rivals in the past. Although true and effective integration for information sharing is still some time away from being fully realized, the fact remains that some of the information stovepipes are being broken down. Also, working cultures among the government departments and agencies with a maritime security mandate are better understood. Limitations are recognized and new ways of doing business are being explored.

The MSOC project on paper looks to be a very viable security project overall. To make the project a success, the various government departments and agencies involved will need to cross a threshold and embrace three essential points. First, the senior officials of the departments and agencies involved in the project must give way on seeing their participation as an individual departmental contribution and move to a more aggressive position of having the project operated as a collective unit. This may require a new governance structure and individuals will have to give ground to a unified command and control structure. Second, there needs to be a legal means for the MSOC to operate effectively in utilizing all information available for the detection and prevention of a security incident from occurring. Presently, there are legal barriers that prevent all of the dots from being connected. This was one of the major issues addressed within the U.S. government's 9/11 Commission on the various shortcomings of its security services.[20] Third, and final point, any government security project such as the MSOC needs to include the expertise and knowledge of the maritime industry. This would require industry professionals, provided with the proper security clearances, to share the responsibility for the security function. Industry professionals can provide that essential expertise and in-depth knowledge that most inexperienced security analysts do not have. It is suggested that if these three points are adopted by the government this would aid in the success of the MSOC project and would better enhance the concept and application of MDA overall.

From the perspective of the ISPS Code, there are a number of issues that affect both the MSOC project and MDA development. The code discusses the requirements for vessels intending to enter the waters of another contracting government. Comprehensive questions, along with vessel documentation from a control and compliance position is essential in determining if a threat exists either to or from vessels entering Canadian waters. This process is now covered under the MTSA, but the current set of questions is restricted. It is agreed that various challenging questions need to remain part of the government's arsenal in security control and threat assessment matters, but that rigidity needs to be replaced by flexibility in order to adapt to a potential security situation. In this regard industry is not opposed to a host of challenging questions, but would prefer maritime nations, when exercising their right to control the entry of vessels into its territorial waters, to do so in a more coordinated fashion. Another aspect that the code has had on maritime security is the requirement for the Ship Security Alert System (SSAS). Although Canada has seen its fair share of false alerts, the impact on how a nation would respond is very much in question. When given the various unknown elements that are generated as a result of an alert, the rush to respond may not be the best option. This position would be, as expected, taken differently in other parts of the world that endure problems of piracy and other related maritime crime issues. For Canada, the very aspect of vessels having such emergency security equipment has been seen as a good thing. But because there are those departments with overlapping responsibility for receiving the SSAS, then assessing the signal, and finally determining the course of action to the SSAS, one may consider the thought as to the state of readiness and response should a major maritime security incident be made known by an activation of the SSAS.

HAS CANADA MADE IT OR HAS IT JUST BEGUN?

Canada has matured when it comes to maritime security. The implementation of the ISPS Code has brought back the realization to concentrate time and recourses on maritime transportation security. The positive results of the code upon Canada are many. The code became a rallying point and brought together levels of government and industry. All realized that a true spirit of cooperation was needed to achieve success to meet an international standard, and this has been accomplished. The challenge now is to continue the positive energy at the grassroots level, once senior bureaucrats focus their attention on other matters.

In the immediate wake of 9/11, industry and governments alike welcomed new security measures found within the ISPS Code. Although costs were of a major concern to maritime industry stakeholders, the Government of Canada came forward with a contributions scheme to aid industry in meeting some of the issues associated with physical security infrastructure requirements. Additionally, the communications between levels of government and industry have greatly improved. Although communications have improved, the sharing of information has not. Industry continues to request that it has to be involved with the threat assessment process. Government has not effectively responded but is looking at other ways to communicate sensitive information to stakeholders. As noted within the debate, the government remains focused on attempting to communicate information to the industry, whereas the industry is really talking about being included and accepted into the intelligence process. What is stopping the industry from being accepted into the process is, oddly enough, the security culture within the government. Much has been discussed and written about the need to change from a "need to know" culture to a culture of "need to share." This has been openly tabled at government–industry meetings, but while the industry is united in its position, certain individual government departments and agencies remain very cool to the concept.

The ISPS Code for Canada has opened the doors of opportunity for a better and safer transportation system for Canada and Canadians. From bottom floor broom-sized offices, industry professionals now find themselves occupying spaces with large windows next to the chief executive officer of their company. These same industry professionals are the key individuals that provide input at security forums and committees. The government too has grown and responded by creating separate directorates within its security apparatus to accommodate the need of more personnel in the development of maritime security policy, regulations, and operations.

Across the country there is an increased awareness into the many issues that make up maritime security. Security training courses in the ISPS Code are continuing and overall, the code has become part of the maritime lexicon. Some have argued that the code is nothing more than a paperweight, but the positive impact of the code on Canada is very apparent and quite realistic.

The key element for Canada is to maintain the momentum and build upon the foundations established by the ISPS Code. There will always be the overarching concern that the ISPS Code, like many other international conventions in the past, will become only a bureaucratic process to be maintained with a loss of enthusiasm over time. For its part, Canada can continue to enhance its position domestically and within the international community. This may be achieved in a number of ways.

On the domestic front, Canada needs to get the MSOC formula right and be willing to examine new ways of integrating command and control systems as well as information systems, while respecting the Canadian Charter of Rights and Freedoms. Also, as part of its domestic maritime security agenda, the government needs to examine the relationship between potential maritime threats and illegal financing. In this regard, closer linkages need to be developed with Financial Transactions and Reports Analysis Centre (FINTRAC), as it must be realized that big money moves big ships around the world. Founded within the ISPS Code, there needs to be a better reporting of maritime security information to lawful authority on not only incoming vessels to the country, but also internal movements and functions, as well as departure security information. Also there is a need to enhance the analysis of vessel certificates and other transportation documents found within the code. Finally, the maritime industry needs to be included within the threat assessment process and not just limited to vulnerability assessments found within the code. This will add value to the intelligence process of including industry's experience and knowledge.

On the international scene, Canada needs to develop the next generation of the ISPS Code. One such step would be in making the requirements of Part B of the code mandatory. Also as fraud and fraudulent documentation remains a constant problem within the maritime industry, Canada should encourage more security measures associated with the current usage of security certificates. At present, there are stricter controls within the SOLAS convention on the usage and movement of safety certificates than there are on security certificates. Finally, Canada has always been a leader in drafting international agreements, legal formulas, and other matters. Building on that expertise, it may be suggested that Canada could once again lead in adding more definition and clarity to the ISPS Code and attempt to change the many phrases that use the word "should" to "shall." This, it is expected, would provide for the desired effect in generating more awareness of the code internationally, continue the debate on maritime security with the objective of advancing security within the maritime domain to a new level, and counter stagnation and a false sense of security from embracing the maritime establishment.

In the beginning, Canada might have been less than ready to meet the requirements and challenges of the ISPS Code, but the country has rallied well to the task and stands in a position to take the next step in the evolution of maritime security. Although having yet to be truly tested by a major maritime security incident or of the threat of one occurring … is Canada *really* ready?

NOTES

1. Available at http://www.theglobeandmail.com/backgrounder/airindia/pages/s_Suspected.html. Also see http://en.wikipedia.org/wiki/Air_India_Flight_182.
2. Ibid.
3. C. 29, May 20, 1997. Available at http://www.tc.gc.ca/acts-regulations/GENERAL/m/mtsa/act/mtsa.htm.
4. Ibid., section 4.
5. The world's largest independent port operator. See http://www.hph.com/business/ports/ports.htm.

6. Launched in April 2004 the policy covered areas such as the evaluation of foreign intelligence, secure communications and the protection of electronic information and information systems. Available at http://www.cse-cst.gc.ca/nat-sec/can-national-security-policy-e.html.
7. Formed in 2006, it is the organization responsible for all routine and emergency operations in Canada. See http://www.canadacom.forces.gc.ca/en/index_e.asp.
8. See http://www.northcom.mil/.
9. See http://www.dhs.gov/index.shtm.
10. This department covers various areas such as emergency management, national security, community safety, law enforcement, crime prevention, and corrections. See http://www.securitepublique.gc.ca/index-en.asp.
11. Available at http://www.imo.org/.
12. See http://www.tc.gc.ca/mediaroom/releases/nat/2003/03-h123e.htm.
13. Ibid., p. 5.
14. See http://www.ilwu.ca/05_Feb3_PriceArticle.html.
15. See http://www.portsecuritycanada.org/s_17.asp.
16. See http://www.greatlakes-seaway.com/en/aboutus/seawayfacts.html.
17. See http://www.greatlakes-seaway.com/en/commercial/seaway-security/ISPS_compliance/.
18. See http://www.publicsafety.gc.ca/pol/ns/secpol04-en.asp.
19. See http://www.msoc-cosm.gc.ca/index_e.asp.
20. 9/11 Commission Report, National Commission on Terrorist Attacks Upon the United States, pp. 399–428. Available at http://www.9-11commission.gov/report/911Report.pdf.

23 The ISPS Code: The Australian Experience and Perspective

Devinder Grewal

CONTENTS

INTRODUCTION

This chapter describes the Australian response to the introduction of the International Ship and Port Facility Security (ISPS) Code. Extensive new legislation was introduced to implement the code along with the establishment of a large new government agency, the Office of Transport Security (OTS) to manage transport security at the federal level in Australia, including the security of shipping and seaborne trade. This chapter identifies the problems encountered with introducing the new maritime security regime, including the impact on seafarers, the costs to industry of new measures, and a possible lack of understanding in the bureaucracy of shipping operations.

THE INTERNATIONAL SHIP AND PORT FACILITY SECURITY CODE

The ISPS Code was developed by the Maritime Security Working Group of the International Maritime Organization (IMO)'s Maritime Safety Committee. The resolution was adopted in November 2001 and the ISPS Code was adopted by the Conference of Contracting Governments to the International Convention for the Safety of Life at Sea (SOLAS) on December 12, 2002. This is the fastest ever convention to be adopted in the IMO. The urgency was probably the reason for locating the code within the SOLAS convention, of which chapter XI was amended, to become chapters XI-1 and XI-2, to accommodate the new code. The code itself is divided into two parts—Part A provides the mandatory requirements of the code and Part B provides guidance.

The stated purpose of the code (IMO, 2003) is to

- Establish an international framework for cooperation between governments "and the shipping and port industries to detect/assess security threats and take preventive measures against security incidents affecting ships or port facilities *used in international trade*" [emphasis added]
- Identify the roles and responsibilities of all parties in this cooperation
- Provide a network for the collection and exchange of security-related information
- Provide a system for assessing security plans of maritime industry participants (MIPs)
- Identify procedures that will be followed when security levels are changed
- Provide confidence that, at an international level, adequate security measures are in place in the commercial maritime network

The code requires that each MIP designate a specific person responsible for implementing their security plan, much as a designated person ashore (DPA) is required by the ISM Code.

THE MARITIME TRANSPORT AND OFFSHORE FACILITIES SECURITY ACT 2003

The Maritime Transport and Offshore Facilities Security Act (MTOFSA) is the key piece of legislation implementing the ISPS Code in Australia. Its full title is "An Act to safeguard against unlawful interference with maritime transport and offshore facilities, and for related purposes" of the Australian Federal Parliament was assented to on December 12, 2003. The Act can be downloaded from http://www.comlaw.gov.au/.

The MTOFSA allows the establishment of a regulatory framework for the development and implementation of maritime security plans in relevant sectors of the industry. The outcomes that the Act seeks to achieve are identified as

- Comply with Australia's international treaty obligations, particularly with regard to the SOLAS convention, including the rights, freedoms, and welfare of seafarers
- Reduce the vulnerability of Australian and foreign ships within Australian waters, ports, and port and offshore facilities to terrorist attack "without undue disruption to trade" (MTOFSA 2003, 3(4)(b))
- Reduce the risk of maritime transport being used for terrorist or other unlawful activities
- Establish a system of effective communications of security-related information between government agencies and MIPs

The Act clearly states, in section 3(5), that the purpose of the Act is not "to prevent lawful advocacy, protest, dissent or industrial action that does not comprise maritime security." The Act then identifies, in various parts, security levels and security measures to be implemented at each level, and provides security directions when they may be needed, security plans, International Ship Security Certificates (ISSCs), regulation of foreign ships in Australian waters, establishing maritime security zones, screening for weapons and prohibited items, powers of officials, reporting obligations in relation to maritime security incidents, the obligations of MIPs to comply with security information requirements, enforcement mechanisms, and review mechanisms for decisions.

The Act is implemented through the Maritime Transport and Offshore Facilities Security Regulations (2003), which can be downloaded from http://www.comlaw.gov.au. The regulations require that

- Specific matters are addressed in security plans.
- Enough information is provided to those preparing security plans to ensure that these plans will be compliant and be consistent in format.

- The criteria for approval is clear.
- There is adequate guidance for the issuing of control or security directions.
- Adequate guidance is provided on setting of security zones in ports, on and around ships.
- Adequate guidance is provided for screening and identifying weapons and prohibited items.

THE OFFICE OF TRANSPORT SECURITY

The OTS is an agency of the Australian Department of Transport and Regional Services (DOTARS). The purpose of the OTS is to regulate transport security and advise the federal government on transport security matters. The OTS implements audit, compliance, and security measures; handles transport security operations and intelligence; and ensures that transport security regulation, planning, and policy follow government guidelines. The basis for the functioning of the OTS is provided by the national counter-terrorism plan (http://www.nationalsecurity.gov.au).

The main focus of the OTS is on the development of effective security policy and planning. It has no mechanism or capability for responding to any security incident. This responsibility is given to police and other response agencies in each state or territory of Australia.

The OTS, at the time of implementation of the ISPS Code, was divided into four main streams—maritime, aviation, regional and freight, and analysis. Over time, in keeping with organizational efficiency requirements, these streams may change to merge or split but the focus remains to provide a national security approach across the transport spectrum. The OTS is headed by a first assistant secretary (FAS).

The approach taken to address security risks and develop security plans is that of risk management and guidance is taken from Australian Standard AS/NZS 4360. Key steps in this process are

- Establish the context
- Identify risks
- Analyze risks, determine likelihood and consequences
- Evaluate risks and set priorities
- Treat these through security plans

The risks are identified against the national maritime risk context statement (NMRCS), issued by the relevant federal government agencies (DOTARS, 2003). In the maritime context, the NRCS states that

> World trade is dependent on maritime transport and progress has been made in recent years to render this system as open and frictionless as possible in order to foster economic growth. Unfortunately, what has enabled the maritime sector to contribute so significantly to global economic growth also leaves the sector vulnerable to exploitation by terrorist groups (p. 6).

A key fear with the industry, shared by OTS, was the possible inability on the part of civil servants to understand the industry in terms of expression and commercial needs. A continuous process of capability building was started at various levels to make staff within OTS capable of understanding the requirements of the regulations and match them with the operational needs of the industry. This extended to OTS staff within the office in Canberra, offices in each state and territory, and in neighboring countries, and to industry participants who were invited to attend workshops held by OTS in each state and territory.

SECURITY PLANS

When the task of implementing maritime security was given to the OTS in December 2003 to ensure national compliance by July 1, 2004, a wide range of activities was initiated. Externally, a high level of consultation processes was set up with the industry through peak bodies and associations as well as with independent organizations. The OTS staff held workshops to advise industry about their legal requirements to comply with the regulations by July 1, 2004 as well as the requirements of security plans that the MIPs were required to submit for approval by OTS and subsequent gazettal. The main challenge, shared by OTS and the industry, was to comply with the regulation in a very tight timeframe of six months. For the industry, it meant preparing suitable security plans and lodging them with OTS for approval in the schedule developed by OTS. For OTS, the challenge was to go through the approval process, which had quite stringent quality assurance, for a very large number of security plans within those six months.

Maritime security requirements for assessments and plans apply to passenger ships, including high-speed craft, cargo ships of 500 gross ton and more, engaged on international or interstate voyages, mobile offshore drilling units (MODUs) on international voyages; and port facilities serving such vessels engaged on international voyages. In the case of ports and port facilities, the responsibility for complying with the regulation rested with the relevant security officer. Elements that formed a part of the assessments included (ISPS Code Part A, section 15.5)

- Identification and evaluation of important assets and infrastructure
- Identification of possible threats and their likelihood of occurrence
- Identification, selection, and prioritization of counter measures and procedural changes
- Identification of weaknesses, including in policies, infrastructure, human factors, and practices

For ships, security assessments were expected to include on-scene security surveys in the context of key shipboard operations. The ship's trading route is meant to be considered when assessing security risks, in view of piracy areas and several "choke points" to international trade around the world. The safety of sea-lanes of commerce was brought into focus, once again, in the long history of maritime trade.

THE OFFICE OF TRANSPORT SECURITY OPERATIONS CENTER

During the run-up to July 1, 2004, the OTS set up an operations center. The primary role of the OTS operations center is to check compliance with the regulations by security-regulated ships. The center operates 24 hours a day and has evolved to cover all the modes of transport.

The operations center is a regulatory compliance office between the maritime industry and the OTS, the designated authority responsible for implementing maritime security regulation in Australia. The center is responsible for

- Logging of events relating to security and developing incident reports
- Dissemination of these reports
- Communicating security-related information to relevant MIPs

It undertakes the following functions:

- Compliance checking and risk profiling of all ships before their entry into Australian waters
- Information and advice to the maritime industry, particularly port authorities and shipping companies
- Instructions to DOTARS regionally based security inspectors
- Security and control directions to ships and MIPs
- Coordination with other commonwealth and state/territory agencies
- Advice to other countries and the IMO on maritime security matters
- Domain awareness for Australian ships worldwide and for foreign ships wishing to enter Australian waters

- Coasting trade permits to foreign flagged ships
- Aviation cabotage approvals

Based on their risk profiles, ships may be issued with security or control directions, which may include an instruction to enter into a declaration of security (DOS) with a port or port facility. Ships may also be directed to change their level of security when they are within the limits of a security-regulated port in Australia, if circumstances so dictate. Only the secretary of DOTARS, or his delegate, can direct the change of security level for ships or any other MIP in Australia or in Australian waters.

Risk profiling includes considering any specific or general intelligence information available to the OTS about the ship, the cargo and the crew, as well as the ports that the ship has visited, through the various national and international intelligence agencies and other sources. For the ships on which there is specific or general intelligence information, a range of options, from a possible inspection with the purpose of verifying security records, to arrangements under the national counterterrorism plan, is available.

The OTS operations center is not available for contact by the general public, who must contact the police or the national security hotline for security-related communications.

There are some things the operations center does not do

- It does not provide security clearance to ships nor advise MIPs of the clearance of every ship that visits every port.
- It does not provide security information on any ship's last 10 ports of call.
- It does not respond to security threats.

Three elements that are of interest to maritime operators around Australia are

- DOS
- Control direction
- Security direction

DECLARATION OF SECURITY

The DOS is a documented agreement reached between a ship and another party that identifies the security activities or measures that each party will undertake or implement in specific circumstances (MTSA section 10). The DOS is signed by the security officer of the ship and the security officer of the other party, be it ship, port, or port facility, and a copy of it is retained for inspection, for a period of seven years.

In essence, a DOS is a security-focused ship–shore or a ship–ship agreement (similar to a safety checklist used under the ISM Code) on which each party's agreed roles and responsibilities are defined.

CONTROL DIRECTION

Typically, control directions may be issued to security-regulated foreign ships. Under MTOFSA (section 99) these may include (but are not limited to)

- Removing a ship from Australian waters
- Removing a ship from a security-regulated port
- Moving the ship within a security-regulated port
- Holding position for a specified period
- Taking particular actions on board the ship
- Allowing inspections of the ship or ship security records

A ship may be subject to control directions even if it has been granted free pratique. In such circumstances, the control direction will take precedence over pratique. Only in the case where the safety of the ship or the port/port facility is at stake can control directions be deviated from or not complied with. In such a case, the OTS should be notified immediately. It is an offense, under MTOFSA, to not follow control directions. Heavy penalties, as specified in MTSR, can be applied.

SECURITY DIRECTION

Under MTOFSA (section 33), security directions may be given to an MIP, passengers, or persons within a security-regulated port. In effect, this includes practically everybody within the boundaries of a security-regulated port, including a ship operator, a ship's agent, or the master of a ship. If a security direction is given to a ship, it may be issued to the operator of the ship, its agent, or the master.

All security directions, control directions, and change of security level directions given to ships must be acknowledged by the recipient, and must be followed.

THE FUTURE

The OTS is planning a review of the maritime security regime in 2009, five years after it came into effect. Key points, outlined by the OTS (Wallace, 2007) at the regional ports in Focus 2007 conference, for review, include

1. Develop an environmental scan that provides an economic impact of a security incident, evaluates the environment and new issues, and identifies roles and responsibilities of domestic and overseas agencies
2. Develop a maritime transport system action plan that, in its application, considers the functions of outsourced third parties and the implications for other modes; a wider strategy that covers all ships (Australian and foreign) and whole of port operations; and the practice to develop capability to respond to, and recover from, a security incident
3. Develop a domestic outreach action plan that clearly identifies the responsibilities of federal and state/territories jurisdictions and enhances inter- and intragovernment agencies communications and those with MIPs
4. Develop an international outreach action plan to support the development of appropriate international policies, allow the development of capability, and allow a "last port-of-call" approach to maritime security in a supply chain context
5. A maritime transport system recovery plan that incorporates the principles of business continuity management
6. Propose amendments and review funding arrangements

PERSPECTIVES

The maritime industry is complex in its structure and relationships, sophisticated in its global operations, and far reaching in its output. It moves over 90 percent of global trade (over 99 percent by weight, in the case of Australia), comprises over 50,000 ships of over 500 t, employs large numbers of people directly and an even larger number indirectly. The effect of the ISPS Code has been unprecedented in the history of regulation in this industry. In the sections below, a selective view of some of the effects, both positive and negative, is presented.

THE SEAFARER

The effects of the ISPS Code–related regulations on mariners are far reaching and not always acknowledged. Mariners can no longer go around the world, engaged in their work, unhindered.

Before the ISPS Code came into effect, shipping companies could apply for visas for their crew to join ship or transit through ports. Crew could get visas when ships arrived at ports, where this was necessary. In many instances, this is no longer the case. If a visa is not held, the crew member may not be allowed to leave the ship, for recreation or for returning home after a contract or swing that may have lasted six months or more.

It is ironic that the SOLAS convention, which was aimed at making the life of the seafarer safer at sea, now has a chapter that severely impacts on his freedom to go about his profession. Discussions with many seafarers indicate that they are increasingly feeling the effects of being treated like potential criminals.

Shore leave, or "liberty," provides individuals the opportunity to get away from the 24/7 work environment, unwind, socialize, and contact their families, and return to the ship feeling more like normal members of society. When they return to work, they are more likely to be attentive and safe in their workplace. In many cases, shore leave has been made difficult for seafarers to avail. The experience of seafarers might most often be to remain on board a ship in a port, which displays its compliance with the security regime through high fences, checkpoints, and security guards—not an environment very conducive to relaxing.

When a ship gets to a security-regulated port, even when seafarers cannot get ashore, the security regime requires them to maintain their ship as if it is under threat—locked down and distrustful, restricting visitors to their ships, and contact with the world outside, unable to meet any real threat if it were actually to happen. At the same time, the port in which the ship is berthed is required to provide a secure environment for the ship to conduct its operations. Both the ship and port maintain a wary watch on each other. In some countries, armed guards man the bridge before some types of ships enter the port. The value of such "marshals" being on the bridge during manoeuvring operations is not established, except perhaps to provide an assurance to voters ashore that foreign seafarers are being treated with suspicion.

Although the IMO and the International Labor Organization (ILO) have developed guidelines and protocols for the treatment of seafarers by national authorities in an attempt to prevent them from prosecution, indeed persecution, this is often not the case and seafarers may find themselves in jail in various countries, most often on their own, being subjected to very enthusiastic, extensive, and aggressive regulatory regimes. Such treatment of professional seafarers imposes a considerable burden on the shipping industry because it affects, in a direct and negative way, the future availability of maritime professionals, compounded by the increasing level of ship building, against a backdrop of increasing global trade, and related demand for skilled crew.

THE COST

The issue of cost and sustainability has often been raised. The OECD (2003) estimated that the burden imposed by implementing the regulation is approximately U.S.$1.3 billion, followed by approximately U.S.$730 million per year as running costs, internationally. Okayama (2003) estimated that the cost to Japan alone, in new infrastructure, personnel, and systems, exceeded U.S.$2 billion. Although some countries have the systems already in place and have the capability to absorb the costs, others cannot economically sustain this burden. This leads to redirected trade with added social costs for vast numbers of countries and their people.

In Australia, the Economic Analytical Unit of the Department of Foreign Affairs and Trade (DFAT) have published a paper, "Combating Terrorism in the Transport Sector: Economic Costs and Benefits" (http://www.dfat.gov.au), in which the short- and long-term impacts of a security incident on the economies of various countries are estimated. The value of security regulation to the economy, when costs of implementing it are weighed against the cost of an incident, is clear. The burden of maritime security is borne by the industry, which, in most cases, passes it on to users. As the industry is forced to install new technology, increase staff, and other control mechanisms, benefits are also noted. These include faster processing times for cargo, better asset control, better traceability, reduced theft, and insurance costs. These savings counterbalance, to some extent, the costs of implementation.

In Australia, the estimated costs of implementation of the ISPS Code–related preventative maritime security regime are estimated to be A$313 million in the first year, with A$96 million annually after that. The cost to each Australian ship is estimated to be between A$750,000 and A$900,000 (www.dfat.gov.au). The maritime security identification card (MSIC), now required by all workers in Australian maritime industry, has raised a number of issues, one of which is the cost of the card, said to be between $120 and $150.

While some processes may impose new costs and slow trade, others may lead to some benefits. What is true, however, is that the regime has the potential to change long-established practices that had become familiar to the industry.

THE EFFECTIVENESS

The wide-scale use of containers in freight movement has enabled a world economy with goods being freely moved around the globe at remarkable speed. In the case of FCL containers, the cargo as such is only handled in a few instances but the container moves through a number of locations where it is vulnerable to tampering. In theory, the box should move in closed condition from source to destination and any illicit cargo could only be placed into it at source.

In the case of an less than container load (LCL), the possibilities of interfering with the innocent transport of containers are much greater. Perhaps supply chain managers can learn from the banking industry trying to combat money laundering where the "know your customer" policy has already brought some interesting results.

The vulnerability of cargo containers to tampering has led to the development of a variety of tracking systems including electronic seals, RFID, and automated-position reporting, which not only record unscheduled changes in the internal environment but also can be used beneficially in the supply chain to monitor the progress of the container. Likewise, better monitoring of the container status in ports or terminals can achieve better information flow for the supply chain and may enable a better management of the supply chain.

OBSERVATIONS

The considered response to a security dilemma should be to address the situation in the short term as well as the long. The aim in the short term is to be able to survive into the long term, when acceptable changes can be put in place, at acceptable cost. The aim in the long term must be to return the ambience of life to a normality that is devoid of the security dilemma such that the conduct of life and commerce takes place against a backdrop of normalcy and inclusivity. The realism that identifies this aim is that no amount of insurance (through policing, checks, and controls) is sufficient to completely protect against a security incident or threat. There is no alternative to careful planning and the development of credible intention that is crucial to the well-being of the community of nations. Only this can break the cycle of fear and suspicion that threatens the social and commercial fabric of our daily lives. Although the "fence-and-gate" structures of security are necessary in the short term, the long-term remedy must focus on returning the ambience of free commercial practice without fear and systemic hindrance.

It is important that, to be effective, all regulation is subject to regular periodic scrutiny to ensure that they remain focused on the desired outcomes and that the cost does not exceed the benefits. In an era of globalization, it is essential that the overall costs of transport (including those of security regimes) are recognized as barriers to trade and governments must eliminate or change appropriately any regime where the associated costs outweigh the economic, social, or environmental benefits that accrue from it, while assuring the safety of their citizens.

REFERENCES

Department of Transport and Regional Services (DOTARS). 2003. *Maritime Risk Context Statement.* Department of Transport and Regional Services, Canberra, available at http://www.infrastructure.gov.au/transport/security/maritime/risk.aspx.

http://www.dfat.gov.au/publications/combating_terrorism/index.html (accessed on June 5, 2007).

http://www.comlaw.gov.au/ComLaw/Legislation/ActCompilation1.nsf/0/A6701ECE263902F1CA2572B2001B6D45/$file/MaritimeTransOffshoreFacilSecurity2003_WD02.pdf (accessed on June 4, 2007).

http://www.comlaw.gov.au/ComLaw/Legislation/LegislativeInstrumentCompilation1.nsf/0/B3EEB8A4F647E778CA2572AA007E7809/$file/MaritimeTranspOffshoreFacSecurity2003.pdf (accessed on June 4, 2007).

IMO. 2003. *International Ship and Port Facility Security Code.* IMO, London.

OECD. 2003. *Security in Maritime Transport: Risk Factors and Economic Impact.* Directorate for Science, Technology and Industry Division, Paris.

Okayama, H. 2003. Trade Facilitation and Security. *15th PECC General Meeting,* Focus Workshop on Trade, Brunei, September 1 (available at http://www.pecc.org/PECC2003Brunei/papers/trade-workshop/session-3/okayamappt.pdf).

Wallace, L. 2007. A Look at Maritime Security over the Horizon. *Proceedings of Regional Ports in Focus,* May 24 and 25, 2007. Informa, Australia.

24 ISPS Code: Implementation in Malaysia

Noor Apandi Osnin

CONTENTS

On July 1, 2004, the International Ship and Port Facility Security (ISPS) Code was enforced. It was introduced to enhance maritime security by outlining minimum security standards for ships and port facilities (PF) employed in maritime commerce. Furthermore, the ISPS Code aims to establish an international framework for cooperation in efficiently collecting and sharing information to detect security threats and take preventive actions. Malaysia, being a responsible member of the International Maritime Organisation (IMO), has taken action to comply with this security measure.

The institutional framework for maritime administration in Malaysia is depicted in Figure 24.1. Malaysian ports and shipping fall under the jurisdiction of the Ministry of Transport (MOT), Malaysia, which is why it became responsible for the implementation of the ISPS Code in Malaysia.

MALAYSIAN PORTS AND SHIPPING

The development of the Malaysian shipping industry has been closely linked to its national policy, which emphasizes greater self-sufficiency in shipping services. This is primarily aimed at reducing the outflow of freight payments to nonnational shipping lines. Malaysia being a trade-dependent economy, the government felt that it is necessary to promote the growth of a national merchant fleet to enable the carriage of more national cargo on national-flagged ships. The demand for ocean transportation in Malaysia's international trade is very high due to the size of its external trade sector and its high dependence on foreign trade. Of these 95 percent are seaborne and it is estimated to consist of a trade volume of more than 300 million ton valued in excess of U.S.$ 180 billion in 2006.[1]

Over the years, the Malaysian industry grew gradually as a result of various measures and initiatives specifically launched for this purpose by the government. The Malaysian shipping fleet size, which stood at just 200,000 GRT in 1968, grew to 7.9 million gross registered tonnage (GRT) in 2005, composed of a diversified fleet of 3857 ships.[2] Malaysia International Shipping Corporation, the national shipping line established in 1968, has expanded to become the largest owner/operator of liquefied natural gas (LNG) carriers. Apart from this there are more than 200 shipping companies operating in Malaysia.[3]

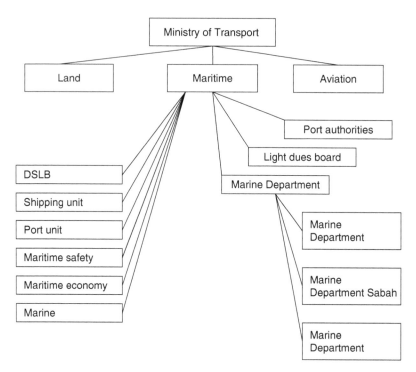

FIGURE 24.1   Maritime administration in Malaysia. (From Ministry of Transport.) DSLB - Domestic Shipping Licensing Board.

In tandem with the large external trade sector, the ports industry has also seen substantial growth. Ports in Malaysia can be classified as federal ports and state ports. Apart from these major ports, there are other minor ports and landing places that come under the purview of the Marine Department (MARDEP). The federal ports, which are under the jurisdiction of the MOT, are further divided into major and minor ports. There are at present seven major federal ports consisting of Port Klang, Penang Port, Bintulu Port, Johor Port, Pasir Gudang Port, Pelabuhan Tanjung Pelepas, Kuantan Port, and Kemaman Port. Out of seven federal ports, six of them except Kemaman Port have been privatized. These privatized ports are regulated by port authorities. Apart from the ports mentioned earlier, there are additional minor ports and jetties under the control of the MARDEP, making a total of 78 PF. Out of these 78 PF, 71 are listed as being in compliance with the ISPS Code.[4]

INSTITUTIONAL FRAMEWORK FOR INTERNATIONAL SHIP AND PORT FACILITY SECURITY IMPLEMENTATION

The secretary general of the MOT Malaysia is the focal point for all matters relating to the IMO. The MOT is responsible for planning, formulating, and implementing policies related to the maritime industry, including ports. Policy matters in this context include maritime safety, shipping, pollution, and development of merchant shipping. Merchant marine matters fall under the purview of the MOT with the MARDEP as the implementing agency responsible for that sector (Figure 24.2).

In the matter of ISPS implementation, the MOT is the lead ministry; however, as this involves security issues the National Security Council (NSC), an agency under the Prime Ministers Department came into the picture. This is because the NSC has the authority to mobilize security forces such as the Royal Malaysian Navy, Malaysian Maritime Enforcement Agencies, Royal Marine Police, and the Immigration Department if there is a need to do so. Based on this, it was also agreed that the NSC shall be responsible in determining the security level in consultation with the

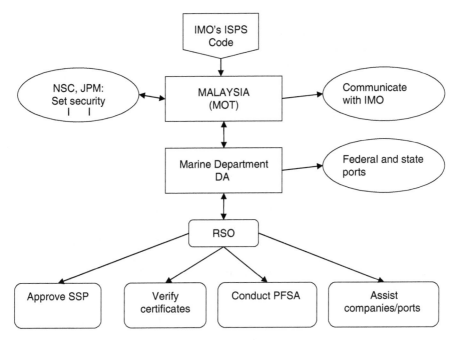

FIGURE 24.2 Institutional framework for ISPS implementation in Malaysia. (From MIMA.) JPM - Prime Minister's Department.

MARDEP, which is the designated authority (DA) responsible for the implementation of the ISPS Code in Malaysia.

The first requirement for a ship to comply with the ISPS Code is to have a ship security plan (SSP) on board. For this purpose, the company must appoint a company security officer (CSO) who, among others, is responsible for conducting the ship security assessment (SSA). From this assessment, an SSP will be drawn up which is then submitted to the administration for approval. The administration may appoint a Recognized Security Organization (RSO) to approve the SSA and SSP on its behalf. In the Malaysian context, MSC/Circ. 1074 was amended to incorporate certain Malaysian requirements, which were then used to approve RSO. There are seven approved RSOs in Malaysia. They are Ship Classification Malaysia, Det Norske Veritas, American Bureau of Shipping, Lloyds Register, Bureau Veritas, Korean Register, and Nippon Kaiji Kyokai. These are further supplemented by eight approved consultants for security assessment and preparation of security plans, whereas training is provided by five approved training centers to conduct ISPS Code courses.

An International Ship Security Certificate (ISSC) that is valid for five years is issued to the ship once the SSA and SSP have been approved by the administration or by the RSO on behalf of the administration.

The company is required to appoint a ship security officer (SSO) on board the ship who, among others, will be responsible to the master of the ship in implementing the SSP. He or she will ensure the effective implementation of the SSP as well as the efficient and effective use of any security equipments placed on board the ship, which must be tested on a regular basis. This would include the Ship Security Alert System (SSAS) installed on board the ship. The location of the SSAS would only be known to the master, CSO, SSO, and any other management officers identified by the CSO or master. The CSO and the SSO must attend approved training courses at any of the five approved training centers. Those who have successfully undergone such training will be issued a certificate by the MARDEP.

It will be the responsibility of the SSO to communicate with the port facility security officer (PFSO) for the PF that the ship will be calling at. The SSO is required to communicate certain information such as whether the ship is in possession of a valid ISSC, the last port of call, the security level the ship was at the last port of call, any additional measures that were instituted at the last port, the present security level on the ship, and the record of the last ten ports of call by the vessel. Similarly, the SSO can communicate with the CSO to obtain any pertinent information relevant to the port the ship is going to call at. Generally, the first contact of communication will be through the agent of the ship whereby the agent will inform the ship of the requirements of the PF and its security level.

On receiving the information from the ship, the PFSOs will decide on the impact of security by the incoming ship on their PF. If there are any doubts about the security of the ship that can affect the security of their PF, the PFSOs will then notify the port area security officer (PASO) of their concerns. The PASOs can at their discretion impose International Convention for the Safety of Life at Sea (SOLAS) XI-2/9—control and compliance measures where the ship, on arrival at the PF will be subjected to security inspections by a duly authorized officer (DAO) who is appointed by the DA. On noting that his ship will be subjected to a control and compliance measure by the PF personnel that his ship intends to call, the master has the option of withdrawing his intention to enter that PF. In such cases, the control and compliance measures intended by the DAO shall not apply. When a ship calls into a PF that has a higher security level than the ship, the ship is required to raise its security level as equivalent to the PF. In this instance, the ship is required to communicate with its flag state stating the requirements to raise the security level as the ship is entering into a PF that has a higher security level than the ship.

The ship can only raise its security level on the instruction of its flag state. If a ship is entering into PF whereby the ship's security level is higher than the PF, then the ship is required to complete a Declaration of Security (DOS) with the PF to identify additional security responsibilities that each will conduct. The validity of the DOS will be identified in the DOS by the PFSO. A ship is not able to raise its security level on its own accord without the direction of the administration. However, this does not prevent the ship from implementing additional security measures if the master of the ship intends to do so.

During security level 1, it is expected that a ship will have enough manpower to maintain the security of the ship on its own. However, at higher security levels, additional personnel may be required. The masters can request additional security personnel from the PFSO if they deem it necessary. This will ensure that the ship on sailing will have personnel who will be able to carry out their ship's task effectively as they have had adequate rest in accordance with Resolution A.925 (23)—amendments to the principle of safe manning. When a ship is in port, it is the only opportunity for the ship's crew to relax themselves by going ashore. The PF should ensure that there is a mechanism for allowing the ship's crew to go ashore.

Every ship that needs to comply with the ISPS Code is also required to install the SSAS and the Automatic Identification System (AIS). The SSAS when activated will identify the ship, its location, and indicate that the security of the ship is under threat or has been compromised. Once activated, the flag state of the ship will notify the coastal state or port state nearest to the ship for assistance. In Malaysia, if there is a notification that a ship that is in the Malaysian territorial waters has activated an SSAS, the flag state of the ship that has activated the SSAS will forward the message to the director of marine industrial control division of the MARDEP. The message will then be relayed to the Malaysian Maritime Coordination Center based in Lumut and to the NSC, which will then direct appropriate assistance to the ship that has activated the SSAS. As the activation of the SSAS is of covert nature, the mode of assistance provided will similarly be in covert form.

Passenger ships have the extra burden of having hundreds of stewards and stewardesses, boutique operators, and so on, apart from the thousands of passengers on board their ships at any one time. Because of this, the CSO should ensure that there is a procedure in place to prevent unauthorized access of persons on board their ships. Similarly, apart from crew members who have undergone special training to carry out security-related duties, other workers in the ship should also be provided a certain amount of security awareness, especially in the identification of the SSO. For effective implementation of the SSP on board passenger ships, the SSO should ensure that all the ship's crew is conversant with their relevant security duties. The SSO is required to conduct drills on a three-month basis or if more than 25 percent of the crew complement has been changed at any one time.

The SSO along with the CSO is also required to conduct a security exercise with other organizations on an annual basis. However, the interval between conducting exercises can be extended, but not for more than 18 months. The MARDEP also encourages ships to participate in any exercises that are conducted by a PF within the same time interval as mentioned earlier. The CSO should ensure that internal security audits are conducted by competent auditors to ensure the effective implementation of the SSP. Similarly, the ship is subjected to at least one intermediate security audit by the administration or the RSO on the administration's behalf during the validity period of its ISSC. If the ship is engaged on international voyages, calling at different PF or is engaged on voyages other than those identified during the ship's life, the CSO shall take into account the changing threat scenario and review the SSA on a regular basis to incorporate any changing threats. Once the SSA is amended, the SSP will require amendments as well, whereby these amendments will require the approval of the administration or the RSO that has issued the ISSC.

The CSO is also required to apply for a continuous synopsis record (CSR) for each ship. The CSR is issued to record the history of the ship including how often it has changed flags, ship's names, owners, and recognized organizations. This would be a good guide for the DAO to monitor whether the ship presents any security threat during port state control inspections. The CSR will be issued by the administration and any amendments to the CSR shall be approved by the administration within three months from the date of the amendment. During this transition period, the administration can authorize either the company or the master of the ship to amend the CSR as necessary.

The designated authority is required to identify the PF that is required to comply with the ISPS Code. It should further identify those PF that, although not used primarily by ships not engaged on international voyages, are required, occasionally, to serve ships arriving or departing on an international voyage. The PF is required to identify a PFSO who is required to attend an approved PF security course. This course would also be conducted by approved maritime training institutions. A certificate will be issued by the MARDEP.

Before a port facility security plan (PFSP) can be drawn up, a PF security assessment should be conducted. If the PF personnel are unable to conduct such assessment, they have the liberty of appointing any consultants that have been approved by the designated authority (DA). Once the part facility safety assessment (PFSA) and PFSP have been drawn up, it is forwarded to the DA for approval. The DA is unable to delegate this responsibility to any other organization. Once a PF has been approved, it will be identified under which port area jurisdiction it lies. The PF will be part of a port area security committee, and the PFSO is required to attend the port area security committee meetings as and when these meetings are called for. The meeting will be chaired by the port administrator. In Malaysia, for minor ports where a port administrator has not been identified, the director of the Marine Regional Office, or his or her delegate, will chair this port area security committee meeting.

The port security area consists of the waterways that are not included in the PF jurisdiction. This includes the waterways, anchorage areas, and those marine service providers such as pilot boats, bunker boats, tugboats, water barges, and mooring boats. As these are not addressed in the PFSP, the PASO is required to draw up a port area security plan (PASP) to address the security issues. The PASP will be under the jurisdiction of the port authority. In the absence of such authority, the marine department will take the responsibility. Before the PASP can be prepared, the PASO is required to conduct a port area security assessment (PASA). The security assessment and the security plan will include all PFSA and PFSP that are situated within the port area security.

If a ship calls at a PF that has a higher security level than the ship, the ship will request a DOS. The PFSO will liaise with the SSO on the security measures each party will implement for providing security assurance to the ship while the ship is in the PF. The PFSO will be the liaison person for any security concerns a ship will have while in the PF. The PFSO will be required to answer any queries raised by the ship on the authentication of any government personnel boarding the ship.

This can include the immigration, customs, port state control or any other officers. In this aspect, the PFSOs must have a close rapport with all the government agencies located in their PF. Before the implementation of the ISPS Code, the PF in Malaysia generally required to be notified 48 hours before the arrival of a ship and the ship's intentions. With the implementation of the ISPS Code, a ship is required to provide additional information relating to the security details of the ship. This will include among others the fact that the ships possess a valid ISSC, the security level at which the ship is operating, the security level at which the ship operated in the last ten PF it visited, any special or additional security measures that were taken by the ship in any of the last ten PF, that the appropriate ship security procedures were maintained during any ship-to-ship activity within the last ten ports of calls and any other security-related information. On receiving this information, the PFSOs can relay this information to the PASO if in their opinion the vessel mentioned earlier would cause a security concern to their PF.

As there are a lot of personnel entering and leaving a PF, the PFSOs should ensure that their security personnel are adequately trained to initiate the security procedures identified in the PFSP. The training that is required for their security personnel can be conducted by the PFSOs themselves or they may request the assistance of a qualified trainer. As the contents of the PFSP are confidential, the PFSO should check the background of the trainer who would be giving the training. However, the PFSO should be trained at a training institution that has been approved by the MARDEP. On successful completion of the training, the MARDEP would issue the successful candidate a certificate. The PFSO should also ensure that there is a minimum level of awareness by other port users such as how they can notify the PFSO if they encounter suspicious objects or persons loitering in or near the PF.

The PFSOs should ensure that the communication links between all the interested parties in their PF are effective and communicable at any time of the day. This would include having the contact details of the security organizations that will assist the PF in the event of a security incident. The PFSOs should also ensure that all the personnel transiting in their PF have identification tags to ensure that no unauthorized personnel can gain access into their PF. Regular rounds inspecting the perimeter of the PF should be conducted by their security personnel in accordance to the PFSP. As the ship in the PF would be taking cargo and ship stores during the ship's stay in the PF, the PFSOs should ensure that the security measures outlined in the PFSP are followed by their security personnel. The PF shall also have procedures in place in the event a ship in their PF activating the PFSO. To monitor the effective implementation of the PFSP, the PFSO is required to conduct a security drill every three months and one security exercise annually. The interval between exercises can be extended but not for more than 18 months. This exercise would be coordinated by the PASO.

In the PASP, the PASO conducts port area security committee meetings on a regular basis. The port area security committee is a framework for communication and coordination of security arrangement. Its purpose is to exchange and disseminate information concerning port security measures among the members. The committee members consist of the PFSO; government institutions such as immigration, customs, quarantine, marine department, police, fire brigade, and other government agencies; and will be chaired by the PASO. PF owners and users such as ship operators and ship's agents will also form part of the committee. The PASO will liaise with the PFSO on the security of ships calling at the port area. In the event that PFSOs notify the PASO that a ship that intends to enter their PF would cause a concern to the security of their PF, the PASO who is appointed as a DAO shall conduct control and compliance measures as stipulated under regulation XI-2/9. Any measures taken by the PASO would be relayed to the DA. At times, if there is a report of a ship that may be carrying suspicious materials such as drugs or weapons, the DAO would board the ship with trained security personnel who will assist in identifying the suspicious materials. In this aspect, the port area security committee plays an essential role as all the relevant security organizations are members of the committee who should be aware of their requirements and responsibilities.

The PASOs are responsible for ensuring that all the PF in their jurisdiction conduct security drills on a quarterly basis. The PASOs with the commitment of other stakeholders in their jurisdiction is required to conduct a security exercise annually but no later than 18 months after the last one. The security exercise, when conducted, should involve the ships that are inside the port area as far as practical. The DA in cooperation with the NSC will notify the PASO on any change of security levels in the country. The PASOs on receiving the change of security levels from the DA will notify the PFSO in their jurisdictions and will also ensure that the relevant security measures are implemented.

The effective implementation of the ISPS Code on board Malaysian ships and PF has provided confidence to the international community that adequate and appropriate security measures are in place. It needs to be stressed that the code only stipulates the functional requirements rather than the specified requirements. Functional requirements or goal-based requirements only stipulate generally what needs to be achieved, whereas the specified requirements will stipulate specific measures for specific cases. As an example, a functional requirement may stipulate that "People should be prevented from falling over the edge of the cliff." A specified requirement may stipulate that there shall "be a fence of 5 ft height erected 1 ft away from the edge of the cliff" to prevent falling over the edge of the cliff. The difference here is that in case of a functional requirement the stipulation will remain the same unless the requirement is amended. A specified requirement could be changed with regard to the availability of new equipments or gadgets employed to ensure that people are prevented from falling over the edge of the cliff. The new equipments or gadgets will depend on the advancement of new technology or the frequency of incidents where persons fall over the cliff. Part B of the code has stressed the requirements of security personnel being trained on techniques used to circumvent security measures. The CSO, SSO, PFSO, and PASO are advised to be vigilant in the various aspects of undesired parties trying to circumvent the security measures that have been incorporated in their respective security plans. The objective of the ISPS Code requires an establishment of an international framework involving cooperation among contracting governments (CG), government agencies, local administrations, and the shipping and port industries to detect security threats and take preventive measures against security incidents affecting ships or PF used in international trade.

Implementation of the provisions of the ISPS Code and ensuring security on ships and in PF will require continuous effective cooperation and understanding among all those involved with, or using, ships and PF, including ship's personnel, port personnel, passengers, cargo interests, ship and port management, and those in the national security agencies. Existing practices and procedures will have to be reviewed and changed if they do not provide an adequate level of security. In the interests of enhanced maritime security, additional responsibilities will have to be carried by the shipping and port industries and by the national security agencies.

THE COST OF IMPLEMENTATION

A survey was carried out in 2004/2005 to determine the cost implication to Malaysian port authorities/operators and shipping companies in implementing the ISPS Code. Two separate survey questionnaires were prepared. Both the questionnaires used for the survey are divided into three sections.

- Section A gathers basic details on the background of the port authorities/operators and shipping companies.
- Section B deals with questions on the compliance of the ISPS Code, training courses, and comments on implementation and effectiveness of the code in Malaysia.
- Section C is the cost of implementation involved in complying with the code.

The respondents were identified based on port information from the MARDEP and shipping directory published by Maritime Institute of Malaysia.[5] As each ship and PF is required to carry out different tasks in complying with the code, different costs also apply. The findings of this survey identifies that each major port spends an average of U.S.$269,339 in complying with the code. As for the minor ports, it has been estimated that each minor port spends an average of U.S.$15,368 to comply with the code. To determine how much the Malaysian port spends, the total average cost is multiplied with the total number of major ports and minor ports. Therefore, to comply with the ISPS Code, the 78 Malaysian PF will spend an estimated U.S.$5,770,228.

There are a total of 257 shipping companies in Malaysia according to the list supplied by the MARDEP, cross-checked with MIMA's own list. From the survey conducted, it is estimated that each shipping company spends at least U.S.$9205 for each ship that they own in complying with the code. Based on the information published on July 5, 2004 by a local paper, out of 400 Malaysian flagged ships, 341 met the requirements of the code. Therefore, in complying with the ISPS Code, Malaysian shipping companies spend an estimated U.S.$3,139,183 for 341 ships.

BIBLIOGRAPHY

Osnin, N.A. 2003. *Information Paper: The Implication of the ISPS Code, Board Paper No. 37/2003*. Kuala Lumpur: Maritime Institute of Malaysia.

Raymond, C.Z. *The Challenge of Improving Maritime Security*, http://www.idss.edu.sg (accessed on December 21, 2004).

Marine Department. 2005. *Total of Ships Registered in Malaysia by Type (New Classification) and Weight, 2001–2005*. Port Klang: Jabatan Laut Malaysia.

MIMA. 2005a. *Directory of Malaysian Ships 2005*. Kuala Lumpur: Maritime Institute of Malaysia.

MIMA. 2005b. Ibid.

MOT. 2001. *Transport Statistics Malaysia 2001*. Kuala Lumpur: Ministry of Transport.

Portsworld. 2004. *The Structure of the Malaysian Port Industry*. http://www.portsworld.com (accessed on December 20, 2004).

Portsworld. 2006. *Malaysian Maritime Yearbook 2005/2006: An Overview of the Shipping Sector in Malaysia*. Kuala Lumpur: MASA.

NOTES

1. Portsworld. 2006. Malaysian Maritime Yearbook 2005/2006: An Overview of the Shipping Sector in Malaysia. Kuala Lumpur: MASA.
2. Marine Department. 2005. Total of Ships Registered in Malaysia by Type (New Classification) and Weight, 2001–2005. Jabatan Laut Malaysia.
3. MIMA. 2005. Directory of Malaysian Ships 2005. Kuala Lumpur: Maritime Institute of Malaysia.
4. Portsworld. 2004. The Structure of the Malaysian Port Industry. http://www.portsworld.com (accessed 20 December 2004).
5. MIMA. 2005. loc. cit.

25 Do British Military Intelligence and Royal Navy Operations Have a Part to Play in the Fight against Organized Crime in the Maritime Domain?

Peter Dodd

CONTENTS

To answer this question, this chapter builds on the reality that the United Kingdom's armed forces have been involved with operations other than war, such as the fight against international drug trafficking syndicates, for many years. It explores how the military is often called on to support the civil authorities in fighting organized crime wherever it impacts the United Kingdom's interests and national security. Finally, it argues that this can only be effective if supported by military intelligence (MI), not only for its operational- and tactical-level contribution, but also because of its unique strategic-level collection and assessment capabilities, such as those provided by the Defence Intelligence Staff (DIS). Focusing on the Royal Navy, this chapter concludes with an example of how successful interaction between the civil authorities and the military can bring a unique capability in combating organized crime (see vignette for definition).

BACKGROUND

Military intelligence has helped in the fight against organized crime for centuries. In the early decades of the 1800s, following years of state-sponsored piracy against the Spanish, British naval, and merchant fleets, navies began to vilify and hunt down the buccaneers using intelligence gleaned from the pirates own journals.

Organized Crime Threats in the United Kingdom—As Defined
by the Serious Organised Crime Agency (SOCA)

Organized crime covers a very wide range of activity and individuals involved in a number of crime sectors.

The most damaging sectors to the United Kingdom are judged to be trafficking of class A drugs, organized immigration crime, and fraud.

In addition, there are a wide range of other threats including high-tech crime, counterfeiting, the use of firearms by serious criminals, serious robbery, organized vehicle crime, cultural property crime, and others.

When Britain passed the Abolition of Slave Trade Act in 1807, slavery became a crime. Those who continued to profit from the slave trade were, and continue to be, involved in a form of organized crime. Since the abolition of slavery, and arguably up to this day, the Royal Navy has been engaged in fighting this heinous form of smuggling. Without the knowledge or intelligence of the seas around them—the routes used by the slavers and the types of ships involved—the navy may not have won the fight. Today, Bosnia, Kosovo and more recently the streets of Basra have all seen the British military involved to some extent in fighting organized crime.

The modern examples mentioned earlier, however, should be seen as ancillary tasks rather than the direct tasking of the military to fight organized crime. By this, and particularly with regard to Bosnia, I mean the intervention of the military in theaters of conflict normally comes as a part of a policy decision to reestablish a stable environment. The collapse of democracy and the resultant turmoil within failed countries can often leave a lawless vacuum that is so often filled by organized crime.

All three of the U.K. military Services are trained to fight conventional warfare, rather than being tasked to engage in the fight against organized crime; however, in recent years organized crime is gradually being recognized as another form of warfare. In this context, it is useful to examine the various types of modern warfare.

Conventional warfare (symmetric warfare) is conducted by using conventional military weapons and battlefield tactics, normally between two or more States in open, set-piece confrontation. It relies on MI to gather, analyze, protect, and disseminate information about the enemy. In the United Kingdom, this information is augmented by the DIS providing timely intelligence products, assessments, and advice to the Ministry of Defence (MOD) from sources otherwise not available to MI. With approximately 60 percent of its staff being military brings the DIS both advantages and disadvantages. Having the knowledge and understanding of the "military way" of doing things is of benefit when it comes to supporting military operations. However, serving members of the armed forces are normally restricted in the time they can serve in any given post, and so the level of experience is constantly changing. The reverse is also true. Civilian analysts can remain in post for years thereby gaining a deep knowledge of a subject, but not having a full and up-to-date understanding of the military's changing role.

Organized crime does not fit under this heading of warfare, but rather under the relatively new term of "asymmetric warfare." Asymmetric warfare can be manifested in a variety of dimensions (or battle spaces) including cyberspace, outer space, land, sea, and air.[1] States can use asymmetric tactics, although guerrilla and insurgent groups have also adopted these methods. Although the majority of violent organized crime syndicates are not terrorists *per se* (they do not typically have a political agenda), a few do have tentative links to terrorist persons and organizations. The Revolutionary Armed Forces of Colombia or People's Army (FARC) in South America, for instance, uses the funds from producing cocaine to financially bolster their organization. Within the United Kingdom, the Irish Republican Army (IRA) was another example of such a group, transferring the proceeds of its illicit activities, such as trafficking, to fund its terrorist operations.

UNITED KINGDOM DOCTRINE

The MOD policy and doctrinal direction for military involvement in combating organized crime appears confused. As a consequence, there is no direct focused doctrine on the subject; thus, it tends to emerge from a combination of other military instructions such as Military Aid to the Civil Power (MACP)[2] or Peace Support Operations (PSO).[3] The MACP provision allows military support to be called on to maintain law, order, and public safety in situations where the civil power (CP) cannot cope. (The armed forces have a range of resources that can be used to assist CP including equipment, international contacts, as well as their mere presence.)

PSOs are usually undertaken as a part of a United Nations–led operation, and makes use of a number of means to restore and maintain peace in fragile states. Some of the key terms used are as follows:[4] conflict prevention, peace support force, peacemaking, peace enforcement, peacekeeping, and peace building—all of which will require a level of MI to support them if they are to be successful. Organized crime flourishes as the intensity of a conflict passes from peace enforcement to peacekeeping where the state remains in turmoil without any political, civil, or military stability of its own. The collapse in state authority, privatization of state economic assets, and demobbed soldiers with guns but no work are all postconflict features that help breed organized crime. Bosnia is a good example of this, where armed conflict occurred within the former Yugoslavia from 1992 to 1995. The ceasefire, and subsequent intervention of North Atlantic Treaty Organization (NATO) forces following the Dayton Peace Agreement signed in December 1995, did not stop the growth of organized crime. In the end, British forces were present for 15 years in the region to promote a stable and secure environment that would allow the political solution to work. However, the political system was corrupted by the influence of former ethnic militias that morphed into organized crime syndicates, which with their gangs were intent on undermining the reconstruction program and inward foreign investment into the region. (Given its role, Defence Intelligence [DI] is likely to have played an important part in providing the strategic support to the U.K. troops deployed in Bosnia.)

THE MARITIME REALM

From a maritime perspective, MACP can include anything from simple fishery protection patrols up to low-intensity counterterrorist operations in riverine and coastal areas and littoral waters further offshore. In recent years, the Royal Navy has increasingly been called upon to assist the Serious Organised Crime Agency (SOCA) (HM Customs now forms a part of the SOCA) in countering drug trafficking on the high seas. Unfortunately, due to the suppressed and "less than robust" rules of engagement and a lack of direct policy, the Royal Navy's involvement is often restricted to that of providing a platform from which law enforcement agencies (both national and international) can operate. That said, the Royal Navy is in a unique position from the perspective of understanding the environment around them, as every ship gathers data and develops intelligence within its area of operations. Radar, sonar, communications interception, Automated Identification System (AIS), visual surveillance, and ship-borne helicopters are all used to gain an appreciation of the surrounding area. Naval ships will often conduct routine communications with merchant ships obtaining general information about their voyage and enquire as to any suspicious activity they may have encountered during their passage.

Royal Navy warships maintain communications with headquarters ashore, which also provides additional supporting intelligence for their area of operation, which can also confer wider context for operations at sea. This understanding helps toward building knowledge of normality and there by determining abnormal activity when it occurs (often referred to as a Pattern of Life). One of the main challenges of operators at sea, and intelligence analysts ashore, is determining what constitutes "normal" as it pertains to the commercial maritime milieu. Trading activity, navigational routings, crew profiles, cargo documentation, and the administration and oversight that links vessels with owners, vendors, charterers, freight forwarders, agents, and cargo recipients is esoteric at best. Detecting anomalies that can point to organized criminal activity is problematic even under favorable circumstances.

NORTH ATLANTIC TREATY ORGANIZATION'S OPERATIONS

Another example of where the maritime fight against organized crime is well developed is with Operation Active Endeavor (OAE), currently being conducted in the Mediterranean Sea. The OAE mission aims to demonstrate NATO's solidarity and resolve in the fight against terrorism and to help detect and deter terrorist activity in the region. Despite having a counterterrorist focus, OAE has yet to demonstrate any tangible effect on terrorist elements. Instead, it appears that much of the success cited by OAE relates to detecting and deterring organized crime in the maritime domain—specifically, countering people smuggling and other forms of trafficking. In a part of a speech to celebrate the fifth anniversary of OAE, Admiral H.G. Ulrich III (Commander Allied Joint Force Command, Naples) said "Because of these efforts (of the mission) we are beginning to gain an advantage over those who abuse the freedom of the seas through illegal immigration, and illegal trafficking in arms, drugs, and human beings".[5] This is a direct reference to organized crime, something OAE was not initially designed to tackle, but has rather become an issue that has come to light while conducting their nominal counterterrorism (CT) operations. Units from OAE (warships and aircraft) are having a deleterious effect on organized crime in the Mediterranean as they develop and increase their intelligence gathering and sharing procedures, while conducting counterterrorist patrols and vessel boardings.

Turning from the tactical to the strategic maritime perspective, it is important for DI/MI agencies to have an interest in criminal activity within many regions of the world, a task that should not be restricted to conflict zones alone. Currently, ships from Maritime Security Coalition Forces in the Northern Arabian Gulf (NAG), for instance, are actively involved in trying to stop the illegal oil smuggling from Iraq in addition to their primary counterterrorist/counterinsurgent operations. Supported by both MI and DI, without the knowledge of the maritime environment and the nature of the criminal gangs involved, this task would be made more difficult.

Another area where MI/DI should be focusing is West Africa, specifically the Gulf of Guinea. With the exception of Sierra Leone, the United Kingdom does not have a regular presence on land or at sea in this region. There are several issues within this region that are having an effect on the United Kingdom, and could in some cases worsen sometime in the future. The trafficking of people, drugs, and oil as well as illegal fishing are all illicit activities that continue to fuel and plague the instability within West Africa. The trafficking of narcotics and persistent guerrilla activity in the littoral directed at the oil industry are of particular concern.

Trafficking in heroin and cocaine, particularly crack cocaine, poses the greatest single threat to the United Kingdom in terms of the scale of serious organized criminal involvement, the illegal proceeds secured, and the overall harm caused. The estimate for cocaine entering the United Kingdom each year is 35–45 t.[6] Colombia continues to dominate the global supply of cocaine although Peru and Bolivia also produce and export significant quantities. The bulk of cocaine deliveries to Europe arrive through the Iberian Peninsula, Spain, or The Netherlands *via* maritime means. Recently however, due to persistent insecurity off West Africa including the littoral and ports in the Gulf of Guinea, this region has developed into an important transhipment region for drugs from Latin America bound for Europe.[7]

For many years, the Royal Navy has conducted countersmuggling operations in the Caribbean in support of the U.S. Coast Guard and numerous local government operations. These counterdrug activities in the region form a significant part of the military mission for the warship assigned to the Atlantic Patrol Task (North). These patrols have resulted in a number of interdictions of large quantities of cocaine heading through the Caribbean Islands to the United States or across the North Atlantic toward Europe normally via the Iberian Peninsula. Recently, however, as just stated, West Africa has evolved into a transhipment point of increasing concern.

THE CURRENT SITUATION

For many years, drug traffickers in South America have used the most direct routes between their continent and Europe for the delivery of narcotics. The Iberian Peninsula has acted as an important entry point for bulk shipments of cocaine arriving by maritime means. Merchant ships, fishing vessels, and yachts are the favored transportation method. However, over the past few years European law enforcement agencies have been successful in disrupting large quantities of the drug arriving through this region. This success has led the traffickers to explore and exploit new routes to continue their trade.

The majority of West African countries have a very limited, or nonexistent, maritime patrol capabilities due to the high cost of maintaining this capability to a meaningful level and lack of sufficiently trained personnel. The poverty, instability, and lack of law enforcement in many countries within the region also allow illicit activity to thrive. Intelligence gathering along this coast is particularly difficult and none more so than in Guinea Bissau—one of the ten poorest nations in the world. Press reports from the region have already indicated that shipments of drugs are appearing in and around the Archipelago dos Bijagos off the Guinea Bissau coast. The archipelago is made up of a maze of uninhabited islands and inlets offering the ideal environment for the consolidation, storage, and onward transportation of drugs. Islands scattered over a wide sea area and the aggregate size of coastline render archipelagos particularly vulnerable to illicit trafficking given the problems of establishing sufficiently endemic patrolling and surveillance.

In October 2006, "acting on [British intelligence],"[8] the Royal Navy helped seize nearly 2 t of cocaine from a ship off the coast of West Africa including its crew of Senegalese and Guinea Bissau nationals. Following the operation, the commanding officer said, "It highlights the valuable role the Royal Navy plays in support of international efforts to suppress the illegal use of the high seas." Fortuitously, the Royal Navy ship was exercising in the region and was therefore able to assist in transporting the Spanish law enforcement agency to conduct the interdiction. Although referred to as "British intelligence," the successful seizure would only have been possible due to a combination of MI and DI support.

These recent seizures have cast a spotlight on the existence of multi-ton consignments arriving in Guinea Bissau from South America. Once in West Africa, the shipments can be broken down for delivery to Europe in much smaller loads aboard a multiplicity of smaller vessels. This dispersal clearly complicates efforts to interdict shipments both in terms of diffusing originally focused intelligence efforts and expanding the spread of operational assets. According to a Drug Enforcement Administration (DEA) congressional testimony, West African drug trafficking organizations ship cocaine to Europe *via* fishing vessels or sail boats.[9]

EFFORTS TO TACKLE THE WEST AFRICA PROBLEM

Currently, CT is doubtless the largest draw on the U.K. intelligence resources. With the U.K. troop deployments in Iraq and Afghanistan, MI is focused on providing adequate support to both these regions. The Royal Navy also contributes to the fight against terrorism in the form of Maritime Security Operations (MSO) by providing security and stability through surveillance, patrolling, and interdiction in the maritime environment. MSO attempts to deny the illegal use of the seas as a domain for attacks or the transportation of personnel, weapons, or other material.[10]

Of the current standing naval operations in the Middle East (Arabian Gulf), Falkland Islands, the Caribbean, and the Mediterranean, MSO is the most prevalent in the Arabian Gulf, particularly in the northern reaches. There is no permanent Royal Navy presence off the west coast of Africa. Coverage for this area is intermittent and often coincides with the turnaround of the ship dedicated to the Falkland Islands patrol or ships on exercise. As mentioned, occasionally Royal Navy ships are utilized under the MACP process for interdiction operations against smugglers in the North Atlantic with varying degrees of success. The use of the navy in this role is very much dependent on the availability of a unit in that region where already the French, Portuguese, and Spanish navies are also involved in antidrug smuggling operations.

One of the U.K. Foreign and Commonwealth Office (FCO) Drugs and International Crime Department's principal objectives is to reduce the flow of cocaine to the United Kingdom.[11] It works to coordinate the implementation of the United Kingdom's international effort against drugs and organized crime, in partnership with a number of U.K. agencies. As seen from the example earlier, this "flow" of cocaine comes across the sea. It is here that the effort should be concentrated long before the drugs land and disappear in a plethora of diverse distribution networks that are prevalent to the West African region.

CONCLUSION

The military has been actively involved in combating organized crime for many years although usually in parallel with, or following, the primary counterterrorist and other conventional missions and exercises. Policy from Whitehall does not currently exist that specifically directs the military to tackle organized crime as a specified discrete role. The Royal Navy is ideally suited for the task of providing interdiction capability as it currently does for the Caribbean theater. If properly tasked, and with the right policy and direction in place, it could also help to further stem the flow of narcotics between South America and West Africa. None of this would be achievable, however, without the support of MI and DI, both of which are currently stretched sustaining the large-scale operations in Iraq and Afghanistan. Thus, if MI were split into its constituent parts (Army, Navy, and Air Force), and provided that the Royal Navy is less involved in supporting Iraq and Afghanistan compared to the other two Services, it should be able to dedicate at least limited support to this task. The trafficking of drugs into the United Kingdom is a huge problem and one that should not be ignored as a consequence of the efforts currently directed at Iraq and Afghanistan. I believe the Royal Navy, MI, and DI, in partnership with other states and agencies, has the capacity, capability, and expertise to help further disrupt narcotic smuggling in the Caribbean and off West Africa, and aid in the wider fight to disrupt organized criminal activity in the maritime realm.

BIBLIOGRAPHY

Braun, M.A. (2006). Chief of Operations, US Drug Enforcement Administration Statement to House Judiciary Committee on Crime, Terrorism and Homeland Security, September 21, 2006, http://www.dea.gov/pubs/cngrtest/ct092106.html.
Herman, M. (1996). *Intelligence Power in Peace and War.* Cambridge, UK: Cambridge University Press.
IJDP 02 (2004), *Interim Joint Doctrine Publication 02.* Shrivenham: The Joint Doctrine & Concepts Centre, Ministry of Defence.
JWP 3-50 (2004), *The Military Contribution to Peace Support Operations,* Joint Warfare Publication, 3-50, Chapter 4.
Matai, D.K. (2005) Cyberland Security, *Organised Crime, Terrorism and the Internet.* Oxford Internet Institute Speech, www.oii.ox.ac.uk/collaboration/lectures/20050210_matai_speech_v1.0_web.pdf.
NATO AF South Press Release (2006), CC-MAR Press Release, December, http://www.afsouth.nato.int/organization/CC_MAR_Naples/PressReleases/CC-MAR/PressReleases06/PR_19_06.htm.
NATO Allied Publication (2000) AAP-6 *NATO Glossary of Terms and Definitions.*
Serious Organised Crime Agency (2006/2007) *The UK Threat Assessment of Serious Organised Crime 2006/2007.*
Wannenburg, G. 2005. *African Security Review,* 14(4).

NOTES

1. D.K. Matai (2005) p. 5.
2. IJDP (2004) p. 2-2.
3. JW 3-50, Chapter 4.
4. AAP-6.
5. NATO AF South Press Release (2006).
6. SOCA Threat Assessment (2006/2007) p. 25.
7. Wannenburg, G. (2005).
8. BBC News, http://news.bbc.co.uk/1/hi/uk/5414352.stm.
9. Braun, Michael (2006).
10. www.royalnavy.mod.uk—Maritime Security Operations.
11. www.fco.gov.uk, International Priorities—Drug Trafficking.

Index

A

Lightning Source UK Ltd.
Milton Keynes UK
UKHW050018130220
358628UK00008B/70

9 781420 054804